Macroeconomic Policy after the Crash

Richard Barwell

Macroeconomic Policy after the Crash

Issues in Monetary and Fiscal Policy

Richard Barwell
BNP Paribas Investment Partners
Dartford, UK

ISBN 978-1-137-51591-9 ISBN 978-1-137-51592-6 (eBook)
DOI 10.1057/978-1-137-51592-6

Library of Congress Control Number: 2016961205

Cover image © Pinar Gözen Ercan

Printed on acid-free paper

This Palgrave Macmillan imprint is published by Springer Nature
The registered company is Macmillan Publishers Ltd.
The registered company address is The Campus, 4 Crinan Street, London, N1 9XW, United Kingdom

Preface

This book is about economic policy. Perhaps before we go any further, I ought to establish my credentials and explain why I just might have something interesting to say about this subject. The short answer is that having worked at a central bank for the best part of a decade and then spent the next six years working in financial markets watching central banks, I ought to be qualified to comment on the practical details of what was done and why.

Finding the right career has a lot in common with finding the right partner in life: there is an element of luck involved and you might have to kiss a lot of frogs before you find a productive match. Lady Luck was certainly smiling on me when I landed a job at the Old Lady (or the Bank of England as she is better known).

If you are fascinated by macroeconomics, there is simply no better place to work. I had the opportunity to work with and for some inspirational people. Looking back, I think the Bank changed me as a person. It certainly made me a much better macroeconomist. At their best, central banks create a culture which values intellectual rigour, technical expertise, institutional memory, attention to practical detail and, above all, capacity to deliver an answer—however preliminary—to a deadline. 'Don't let the best be the enemy of the good' was a motto of an early mentor of mine at the Bank, and this book was written in that spirit. I can think of no better finishing school for macroeconomists than working at a central bank (you can be the judge of whether I left too soon). I also became more passionate about the subject and more opinionated. There is a school of thought that you can have too much of those good things, but those traits do help explain how I ended up writing books on economic policy.

A central bank may be the ideal employer if you want to immerse yourself in macroeconomics and the conduct of policy, but it is not necessarily an ideal home for those who want to express their own views on the subject. Central bank staff are there to help someone else take a difficult decision. With the best will in the world, they need answers to the questions that they think are important, presented in a form and discussed within a framework that they find useful, and they will have finite appetite for anything else that drops in their inbox (if it ever gets that far). And then of course there are the incentives (who would have thought that the economists who populate these institutions and spend their working lives thinking about incentives that drive behaviour outside the building would ever stop to contemplate whether speaking inconvenient truths to their superiors would have consequences for their careers inside the building?). This is not to imply that I disagreed with everything that was done during the time I was there. Indeed, even when I did disagree with the outcome of the process, it was still a privilege to be in the room, to be able to hear the likes of Mervyn King, Charles Bean and Paul Tucker discuss policy. Nonetheless, most people (myself included) conclude that regretfully you need to leave if you want to develop and express your own thoughts about how policy should be set, and so I did.

I followed a well-worn path out of the Bank into an investment bank (in my case, the Royal Bank of Scotland [RBS]) to join the community of central bank watchers. Although we are all being paid to do the same basic job, it turns out that there are a number of different ways to watch a central bank. Once again, I had a stroke of luck. Throughout my time at RBS, I was lucky enough to have managers who bought into my hunch that there was already a more than ample supply of 'sell side' commentary on the endless flow of data releases that are published each day and updates of central case forecasts, so it made less sense to compete in what was low value-added terrain. I was confident that there was a demand out there among the clients on 'the buy side' for something else: a rigorous discussion of fundamental questions of monetary strategy and the challenges posed by puzzles in the data (after all, that was the analysis that was driving the internal policy debate within central banks), so it made sense to specialise in producing that work. I therefore spent five years of my life devoting an increasing proportion of my time thinking about economic policy. I changed job in 2015 and crossed over to the other side of the street—joining an asset manager, BNP Paribas Investment Partners—but I still find myself thinking about the interplay between economic policy, macroeconomics and markets as much as ever, only now alongside a kindred spirit (you guessed it: a former central banker).

The random walk that is my career has also involved some unanticipated detours into interesting places. My interest in macroeconomics and policy has also led me to get involved with the Money, Macro and Finance Research Group (or MMF for short), a network of UK-based academics working in those fields. One thing led to another and I am now on the organising committee of an annual conference on UK monetary and financial policy, designed to encourage robust and constructive debate on the conduct of policy. I have also had the good fortune to be invited to participate on the expert advisory group for a *Review of UK Consumer Price Statistics* chaired by the inimitable Paul Johnson. The subject matter of that review was not directly relevant to the material in this book, but it was a hugely enjoyable experience to sit with such esteemed colleagues and discuss the fate of the data. I presume I did something right because I was subsequently asked to join Kate Barker's Advisory Panel for Consumer Prices.

This brief biography is intended as an explanation for how I reached the point where writing a book about economic policy seemed like the natural thing to do. My first effort was published in 2013 and was about Macroprudential Policy. I had spent a fair amount of time working on this particular subject in the months before I left the Bank of England, having moved over to the Financial Stability directorate in Spring 2008. Once outside the building, I was struck by the fact that so few people working in financial markets were even aware of this new regime that was slowly taking shape and was intended to serve as the first line of defence in guarding against cyclical and structural risks to financial stability. Over time, I became increasingly concerned about the lack of progress within the official sector in translating the original macroprudential vision into an operational reality. Eventually, I became convinced that I had something useful to say on this subject. After all, so little was known about this subject that I *was* an expert of sorts, at least in a relative sense.

When the sky did not fall in after the publication of that book, I started to think about writing a book for a much wider audience. It seems to me that people have always been interested in the conduct of economic policy. The post-crash period has been one of near-constant innovation in the conduct of economic policy, so a discussion of this period should be of particular interest—not least because if you studied macro before the crash it is highly unlikely that you spent much time thinking through the economics of Quantitative Easing, discussing sovereign debt crises, considering the importance of bank capital or even hearing mention of Macroprudential Policy. Moreover, I am not comfortable with the version of macroeconomic events that is presented to the public. One UK academic economist has described the version of the dismal science that features in the public debate as 'mediamacro' (although to be clear: we have different perspectives on who is propagating the simplistic treatment of macroeconomics).

To be fair, an awful lot is written about these issues every day in the press, in publications by professional economists and the institutions which employ them, in countless blogs by the great and good (and sometimes not so good—my personal bugbear is commentary about the conduct of economic policy or the solution to economic puzzles that is prefaced with a diatribe about the dismal state of economics and economists) and even in speeches by policymakers about the particular issue of the day. Much of that material is entertaining or illuminating, and sometimes both. However, the link between that particular issue and the broader debate often goes unspoken, and in any case, the conversation all too quickly moves onto another topic, leaving much of the value added lost in the electronic ether. Then there are weighty tomes which explore a specific question in great depth or provide an academic but all too often abstract treatment of a given literature. Unfortunately, these contributions will almost always focus on one aspect of the debate—it is unusual to find 'serious economists' who write about the systemic risk buffer in the Basel III capital structure and Quantitative Easing and certainly not in the same place (except perhaps the serious economists working within central banks). Even within the confines of a book dedicated to one or other branch of economic policy, the text may skirt over the 'tedious' detail of what policymakers actually did in order to model the salient stylised features and may not have a clear focus on what was done in the UK.

As far as I am aware, there is no comprehensive treatment of the post-crash policy debate that has a deliberate UK focus; there is no one-stop shop if you want to learn about these issues. To be fair, I fail that test too, since my story is spread across two volumes, although that was not the original intention. The objective of this book and the companion volume is to plug this gap: to provide a comprehensive treatment of the UK policy debate since the crash.

It was not hard to figure out where to pick up the story of UK economic policy; we begin with the outbreak of stress in financial markets in the summer of 2007 and only discuss what went before to the extent that it is essential to understand what came after. However, it was far less clear to me where the story should end as I was in the process of writing. At one point, it seemed as though the first increase in Bank Rate and the first increase in the counter cyclical capital buffer would represent a natural bookend, marking the UK's exit from the post-crash malaise. However, politics would ultimately intervene and write a very different ending. The UK voted to leave the European Union after the first drafts of these two volumes had been put to bed, and that decision precipitated a fundamental shift in the direction of UK economic policy. The economics of Brexit—the cyclical and structural implications for the UK economy and the appropriate policy response—is far too complicated a subject to be swept up in marginal additions to this text. So these books end up telling the tale of UK economic policy between two momentous events: the crash of 2007 and the Brexit referendum of 2016.

There is no original research here—no theoretical exposition which improves our understanding of some feature of the economy or empirical analysis which refines our estimates of the efficacy of some aspect of the transmission mechanism. Instead, the book aims to review the current state of knowledge on the questions of interest, and hence, there are plenty of references to research throughout the text, which should be of interest for those looking for a more detailed analysis of a particular issue. In many cases, those references are to the speeches made by policymakers and research published by official institutions. This is not to imply that academic research can shed no light on the questions in hand (rest assured there are plenty of references to journal articles too), but in some cases, academic research necessarily abstracts from the interesting institutional detail of policymaking.

There are no equations, charts or regression results breaking up the text. Ideas are presented in as simple and straightforward a fashion as the author is able to muster. Mervyn King is a past master in the art of decoding a complex argument and then revealing it to the masses with a simple turn of phrase (and more often than not, a sporting metaphor). This book does not measure up to the standards Lord King has set any more than it would satisfy his demand for brevity when he was a consumer of economic analysis, but the principle that you do not have to choose between explaining a point clearly and explaining a point properly is one that I have tried to apply. Jargon and acronyms are unavoidable in the world of economic policy—particularly because one of the key objectives of this book is to document the details of the policy innovations and the institutional arrangements during this period—but explanations and introductions are provided along the way.

Finally, a health warning: opinion will creep into the text at points—whether on the appropriate monetary–fiscal mix during the crisis or the optimal mode of communication for a central bank—but hopefully the reader will find that both sides of the debate are presented and the conclusions are backed up by solid argument. In my defence, it is hard to write about economic policy without expressing opinions, and even harder to motivate yourself to write about economic policy if you do not have an opinion. A professor I once knew used to tell his students (including yours truly) that you ought to have a preliminary opinion on the key issues of the day, but stand ready to revise those views in the light of new evidence. If the book serves its purpose, then it ought to prompt you, the reader, to do precisely that.

When you have spent a decade and a half in a never-ending conversation with friends, colleagues and clients about economics and economic policy, it is hard to be sure which ideas and opinions are truly your own and which belong to someone else. The prudent approach is to assume that all the good ideas belong to someone else if you talk to smart people and therefore thank everyone whilst retaining responsibility for any errors that have crept into the text. In crude chronological order and given the available space constraints, I would therefore like to thank: Richard, Merxe, Pablo, Mark, Mike, Guillermo, Francesco, Jens, Colin, Charlotta, Conall, Simon, Emilio, Sally, Andrew, Mark, Lea, Rob, Katie, John, Jamie, Charlie, Tony, Spencer, Ryland, Mick, Jamie, Fergal, Jack, David, James, Rohan, Konstantinos, Jens, Paul, John, Niki, Andy, Andrew, Marnoch, Paul, Gareth, Oliver, Matthias, Matt, Roland, Lewis, Geoff, Ben, Riccardo, Peter, Jacques, Nick, Alberto, Gareth, Prateek, Brian, Michelle, John, Chris, Jens, Arnaud, Jef, Jagjit, Paul, Guy, Cedric, Boriana, Colin, Sven and Steve. I am sure I have left many people off this list who deserve a mention, but thanks to each and every one of you.

I would like to pay particular thanks to Riccardo Rebonato. Riccardo is a distinguished author in his own right and has set a very high bar when it comes to what they call 'thought leadership' in my industry. He was the one who encouraged me to write my first book and made the dream a reality by matching me with a willing publisher. I would also like to express my thanks to the good folks at Palgrave Macmillan for seeing the manuscript through to publication. Most of all I want to thank Katharine for the unstinting support in the three month window of gardening leave when the lion's share of the work was done and providing impeccable proof reading in a short space of time at the last minute.

Finally, I want to thank my friends and family. I want to thank my mum and dad for their unstinting love and support; whatever success I have had in life, they ought to take the lion's share of the credit. My older brother and my friends should be thanked for inadvertently encouraging and indulging, respectively, a belief that there is no better way to refine your view of the world than through rational, relentless argument. But above all, I want to thank Katharine, Layla and David for filling my life with love, laughter and the occasional rollercoaster ride.

Richard Barwell

Contents

1

Introduction

This book is about the pillars of economic policy that you read about in an introductory macroeconomics textbook: *monetary and fiscal policy*. However, if you studied economics before the financial crisis. then the policy regimes described in the textbook may bear only a passing resemblance to the post-crash conduct of policy. A companion volume discusses the pillars of economic policy that have come to the attention of macroeconomists since the crash—but which up to that point were alien concepts to most—which can be broadly thought of as policies designed to restore or safeguard financial stability. In practice, even the post-crash treatment of these respective pillars of macroeconomic policy may only scratch the surface of what has been done.

Once upon a time the conduct of monetary policy was presented in terms of the central bank setting the quantity of money. Over time, this discussion was re-framed in terms of the central bank setting the price of money, although the precise details of how this was done might have been glossed over. The possibility that central banks might take official interest rates into negative territory, print money and purchase assets on an industrial scale or even contemplate helicopter drops of money would not have featured. Fiscal policy would likely have played a more minor role in that pre-crisis conversation about macroeconomic policy, with little more than a terse reference to taxes and non-descript 'government spending' influencing aggregate demand. That was not necessarily an oversight: arguably, discussion of fiscal policy belongs as much to the microeconomic realm as to the macroeconomic. However, with the coming of the crash, there was a renewed interest in using fiscal levers to achieve traditional macroeconomic goals (demand management).

© The Editor(s) (if applicable) and The Author(s) 2016
R. Barwell, *Macroeconomic Policy after the Crash*,
DOI 10.1057/978-1-137-51592-6_1

The purpose of this book is to bridge the gap between the rudimentary coverage of conventional macroeconomic policy in that textbook or the baseline level of knowledge that many people who work in financial markets and beyond have acquired and the key debates in the policy world.

The section on monetary policy has two key objectives: to introduce the unconventional measures that central banks have deployed during the crisis and to explain the key issues in the policy debate that guided the use of these tools during this period. The names of those unconventional measures will already be familiar to most readers of this book: Quantitative Easing (QE), Negative Interest Rates and Forward Guidance. Likewise, the debates over the Productivity Puzzle, the Secular Stagnation and Good, Bad and Ugly Deflations may not be entirely new to those who regularly read the financial press. The purpose of this book is to place these tools and themes within a common framework, to shed some light on the conduct of policy during this period and to arrive at a more informed assessment of the future direction of monetary policy.

The second chapter deals with the conventional tool of monetary policy: interest rates. We begin by introducing the particular interest rate that central banks set, the mechanics of how policy is implemented and the monetary transmission mechanism which describes how the level of that interest rate impacts behaviour in the wider economy, enabling central banks to achieve their price stability goals. We then describe the asymmetric constraint on the conduct of monetary policy, 'the lower bound', which is the reason why we have seen so much innovation in the central bank's toolkit since the crash. We review the initial dash towards that lower bound that took place in the opening act of the crisis and the reasons why different central banks stopped in different places, and then document the more recent decision to take official interest rates into negative territory. Finally, we evaluate the costs and benefits of negative interest rates as a tool and the case for resolving this problem of the lower bound once and for all.

The third chapter focuses on the key innovation in the toolbox since the crash: QE. We begin by outlining the reason why several central banks launched large-scale asset purchase programmes in the immediate aftermath of the crash before documenting the what, when, why and how of the Bank of England's (BoE) QE programme. Different central banks have purchased different assets in different ways for different reasons since the crash, so we place QE in its proper context by presenting a taxonomy of central banks' purchase programmes, identifying differences in size, scope and duration of those programmes according to the ultimate objective. We then address the fundamental concern of many commentators and discuss the theory and evidence on the transmission mechanism of QE. We then turn to the thorny issue of the distributional consequences of QE—the claim that it disproportionately benefits the wealthy—and end with a review of a controversial alternative to QE that has been proposed by a number of commentators: helicopter drops.

The fourth and fifth chapters focus on two key puzzles in the policy debate during the post-crash period: the surprising initial resilience of inflation and the puzzling weakness of productivity. It is impossible to understand the conduct of policy during this period without a proper understanding of these related issues.

Economic history and common sense suggested that the advanced economies were likely to slide into deflation in the depression that followed a systemic financial crisis, but this time it was different. This puzzle was particularly marked in the UK, where inflation was too high for much of the post-crisis period. Central bankers take it for granted that there is a reasonably stable relationship between the cyclical state of the economy and the extent of inflationary pressure, so the absence of deflation despite the collapse in demand prompted a bout of introspection about the state of the economy, the nature of this relationship between inflation and the state of the local economy and the influence of global demand conditions. In the fourth chapter, we review the various explanations for the puzzle and discuss possible consequences for the conduct of policy.

Macroeconomists spend remarkably little time thinking about the supply side of the economy given its central importance to our collective standard of living. Indeed, in the pre-crisis period, it was often implicitly assumed that productivity growth was exogenously given and constant. The financial crisis shook the profession out of that complacent attitude: the absence of deflation in the face of a collapse in demand implied that the supply side had been damaged by the crisis and the anaemic state of productivity during the recovery in the years that followed revealed that this scar to supply was proving painfully persistent. The level of activity is currently far below an extrapolation of its pre-crisis trend and shows little indication of returning to it in the near future. In the fifth chapter, we introduce a range of plausible explanations for this persistent hit to productivity and offer some thoughts on their relative role in accounting for the puzzle.

The sixth chapter focuses on the increasing importance that central banks attached to communication about the conduct of monetary policy during this period—or what is known as 'forward guidance'. We begin with a review of the tradition of central banks' communication and provide a useful framework for thinking about the nature of the information that central banks release. Next, we outline an influential academic proposal for a particular variant of forward guidance that in theory could be used to ease monetary conditions at the lower bound (i.e., as a substitute for asset purchases). We then review the BoE's iterations of forward guidance before outlining an alternative, more comprehensive, approach to communication and then ending with a discussion of the role of communication in a crisis.

The seventh chapter introduces the conjunctural development that dominated the policy debate from late 2013 onwards. Having spent most of the post-crisis period defying economic gravity and the Bank's 2 % target, UK inflation fell to earth and eventually into negative territory in early 2015. Two factors played a key role in driving the UK economy into deflation during this period: an appreciation in the value of the pound and a collapse in the price of oil. We review the transmission of these two shocks into consumer prices before turning to discuss the real issue that was raised by this brief run of near-zero and sub-zero inflation prints—the possibility that inflation expectations might be dislodged, leading to a more sustained period of low or no inflation.

In the eighth and final chapter of the section on monetary policy, we discuss the exit strategy from the lower bound. At the time of writing, Bank Rate was still at 0.5 %, more than seven years after the Monetary Policy Committee (MPC) had stopped cutting rates and despite a sustained recovery in output and employment, and seemingly at odds with the output of simple monetary policy rules. We discuss the tactical reasons why central bankers might choose to keep interest rates low for longer at (or near) the lower bound: from a traditional risk management approach; to a deliberate attempt to over-heat the economy in an attempt to heal the supply-side scars caused by the crisis; to concerns about the reputational damage in the event that the central bank has to reverse course and return to the lower bound. We then turn to more structural reasons for very low level of interest rates—often referred to as the Secular Stagnation. We distinguish between the various concepts of equilibrium interest rates, both nominal and real and short and long term, and introduce a number of explanations for the low level of rates. We conclude by noting how the Federal Reserve (Fed) and the BoE parted company at the end of 2015, with the Fed lifting off and the Old Lady hunkering down as the referendum on the UK's continued membership of the European Union loomed into view.

The objective of the section on fiscal policy is to provide a framework for thinking about the central macroeconomic issue of the day: austerity. The financial crisis dealt a savage blow to the health of the public finances across many of the advanced economies. Deficits ballooned out and the debt stock was placed on a worrying trajectory even in countries where the burden of debt was still relatively low. But with the economy still in fragile shape, finance ministers faced a dilemma over the appropriate pace of deficit reduction: move too early and they might prolong the depression in activity; move too late and the stock of debt would grow ever larger and they may even struggle to continue funding that debt. A great deal has been said by macroeconomists on this question since the crash. This book does not attempt to resolve this issue decisively but it does try to systematically review the key issues in this debate.

The ninth chapter begins with the basics of fiscal arithmetic. We start with the facts of the deterioration in the public finances as the wheels fell off the Great Stability. We then turn to discuss cyclical influences on the health of the public finances, differentiating between the well-known impact of the business cycle on tax receipts and government spending and the less well-understood relationship between the financial cycle and the public finances. Next, we introduce the basic relationship which economists use to think about the dynamics of debt and the factors which dictate the primary surplus that finance ministers need to run if they wish to stabilise the burden of debt. Then, we step back to take a more comprehensive perspective on the state of the public finances before turning to discuss the pros and cons of the conventional approach to calibrating the pace of fiscal consolidation, so-called structural balance targeting. Finally, we end with a discussion of the stance of fiscal policy from a macroeconomic perspective and the inevitable interdependence with monetary policy.

The tenth chapter steps back and evaluates the objectives of fiscal policy. We begin with the stylised case for inaction on the part of government before turning to identify the traditional sources of market failure to build the case for government intervention. Although this book is about macroeconomics, we then take a brief detour into microeconomics to discuss the scale and source of the inequality problem and the literature on the trade-off between the pursuit of equity and efficiency. Next, we discuss what economics has to say about the objectives of the fiscal authority, distinguishing between the social planner seeking to maximise welfare and a politician seeking re-election. We then introduce the other key dimension of fiscal policy: the stability agenda, offering a broader perspective than just leaning against the business cycle. Finally, we pivot towards a key theme of the post-crash policy debate: structural policies.

The eleventh chapter reviews the traditional literature on the subject on which so much ink has been spilled: the fiscal multiplier. We start with the simple arguments that economists deploy to explain the efficacy of a fiscal stimulus and the concepts of crowding out that others use to query its macroeconomic impact. We then turn to discuss the more sophisticated literature on crowding out that introduces forward-looking households and endogenous private sector saving that can potentially neuter the impact of fiscal stimulus.

We highlight the reasons why the extreme result in this literature—Ricardian Equivalence—does not hold in practice before introducing the possibility that fiscal policy can influence the supply side too. Finally, we review how the impact of fiscal stimulus might vary according to how it is implemented— that it makes a difference whether you increase spending on public sector pay, transfer payments or procurement of private sector output—before discussing the macro- and micro-econometric evidence on the impact of fiscal policy.

The twelfth chapter turns to the issue at the heart of the debate over the conduct of macro-policy since the crash: whether fiscal policy has any role to play in stabilising demand in the presence of an independent central bank using monetary levers to pursue its price stability mandate. We discuss the mechanics of monetary dominance, wherein central banks systematically neu-tralise the macroeconomic impact of fiscal stimulus, and then highlight the three situations in which this result will not hold: when there is a geographical mismatch between the focus of fiscal and monetary policy, when the central bank bows to political pressure and when monetary policy becomes ineffec-tive. We then discuss whether the final scenario applied when interest rates hit the lower bound when central banks still had access to unconventional levers. Finally, we focus on a particular moment in early 2011 when some commentators were advocating a looser fiscal stance and argue that, based on the tone of the internal policy debate at the BoE, it seems likely that monetary dominance would have applied.

The thirteenth chapter turns to another key issue: the risk that over-indebted governments can face a crisis in financial markets. Potential creditors in financial markets will start to demand a higher return for lending money to weak governments and, at some point, the public finances become so frail that a government may face difficulties rolling over its debts. We begin with a review of what constitutes debt sustainability. We then develop a framework for thinking about how the interest rate that governments are obliged to pay to raise funds can vary according to the state of the public finances and finan-cial markets. We introduce positive feedback mechanisms through which the initial impact of bad news on market conditions and the cost of debt are amplified, potentially to the point where funding markets effectively close. In particular, we highlight a critical source of amplification—the interplay between the health of the public finances and the banking sector—and the role it played in driving the sovereign crisis that unfolded in the Eurozone in the years that followed the financial crash.

The fourteenth chapter focuses on unconventional solutions to a debt problem. We begin with a claim that attracted a lot of attention as the era of austerity began: the idea that fiscal consolidation could paradoxically boost activity when the public finances are in a fragile state. We then turn to discuss the options that have been pursued in the past—inflating away debt, financial repression and restructuring debt—and highlight how none of these options are painless, in that someone ultimately pays the price of reducing the debt burden. Finally, given events on the Continent and the resolution of the Eurozone sovereign debt crisis, we review whether and how domestic and international institutions can rescue a sovereign engulfed in a fiscal crisis.

The fifteenth and final chapter focuses on the institutions of fiscal policy and the role they can play in preventing and resolving crises. We begin with the theory of political business cycles and the tendency of politicians to run deficits. We then turn to discuss the pre-crisis solution to this problem: fiscal rules. We review the literature on writing fiscal rules and evaluate how these rules have performed in practice. Then, we turn to the recent innovation in this area—the creation of fiscal councils—and end with an evaluation of the UK's fiscal council: the Office for Budget Responsibility.

Part I

Monetary Policy

2

The Lower Bound: To Zero and Beyond

The story of monetary policy during the financial crisis is one of experimentation with unconventional tools and unexpected macroeconomic developments. We begin with the conventional tool of monetary policy and the tale of official interest rates. It is often said central banks hit the zero lower bound (ZLB) on official interest rates during the crisis and were then forced to turn to those unconventional tools to continue injecting stimulus into the economy. However, the story is a little more complicated than that: in practice, some central banks stopped cutting the policy rate above zero (and started doing something else) whilst others managed to eventually push through zero into negative rate territory. This section explains what happened where and why. But before we turn to explain the unconventional conduct of monetary policy during the crisis—the experimentation with negative interest rates, asset purchases and forward guidance—we will first recap the conduct of conventional monetary policy: how central banks set interest rates, and how changes in the stance of monetary policy influence activity and inflation.

2.1   How Central Banks Set Interest Rates

Contrary to common mythology, central banks which set monetary policy do not control the amount of money circulating in the economy or the level of interest rates in the economy. Instead, central banks have control over a single interest rate in the economy on an asset that is held by a small number of financial institutions. In this sub-section, we briefly review what constitutes money and how central banks set monetary policy.

© The Editor(s) (if applicable) and The Author(s) 2016   **11**
R. Barwell, *Macroeconomic Policy after the Crash*,
DOI 10.1057/978-1-137-51592-6_2

2.1.1 What Is Money?

Money is a commodity which serves three purposes (Asmundson and Oner 2012):

- *Store of value*: The commodity retains its value through time allowing the owner to use resources acquired today to fund consumption and investment in the future;
- *Unit of account*: The commodity provides a common reference point against which the price of other items can be compared;
- *Medium of exchange*: There is a social convention that the commodity is accepted by other people as payment in transactions.

These functions are intertwined: a commodity which is a poor store of value cannot be an effective medium of exchange because people will be reluctant to accept payment in the form of a commodity if they expect that the value of the bundle of goods and services which they can purchase with that commodity will decline through time; likewise, a commodity which is not the common unit of account is a less effective medium of exchange because both buyers and sellers would need to agree on an exchange rate (between the medium of exchange and the unit of account) in every transaction (McLeay et al. 2014a).

Money's function as a medium of exchange is fundamental to a modern market economy because it solves the problem of the double coincidence of wants in a barter economy (Jevons 1875) and allows people to specialise in niche occupations (otherwise a doctor would need to find a sick farmer every time she wanted to eat). In practice (and fortunately in theory too, see Kiyotaki and Wright [1989]), commodities which have value in their own right can serve as money, although over time commodity money has been supplanted by fiat money, a commodity than has no intrinsic value other than in its role as money (Ritter 1995).

When we talk about money we tend to instinctively think of cash or currency—that is, the notes and coins in our pockets. Cash is an example of base money, which is money issued by the state's monetary authority (the central bank). However, the lion's share of the household and corporate sectors' money holdings is accounted for by a form of money created by the private sector: the electronic money created by deposit-taking institutions. Banks create money in the form of a deposit when they lend money, crediting their customer's account with a positive balance which can then be exhausted (spent) to facilitate the purpose of the original loan. So, the deposit is an asset of the customer and a liability of the bank, whilst the loan is an asset of the bank and a liability of the customer.

Banks offer a range of deposits which to varying degrees are substitutes for, and can be converted into, cash—there are 'sight deposits' which can be instantaneously converted into cash but will offer a minimal rate of return, and 'time deposits', which can only be accessed with a delay but will offer a higher rate of return. In a modern economy, the majority of transactions involve transfers of payments between deposit accounts without cash changing hands. In the UK, less than 2 % of sterling payments *by value* are made by notes and coins or cheque (Dent and Dison 2012); electronic transactions are not only increasingly common in retail transactions, but also cover the payment of salaries by employers, benefits by the government as well as large transactions in wholesale markets—all of which contribute to flows of money between deposit accounts.

The final type of money circulating in a small but important backwater of the economy is central bank reserves, which is the electronic money that the banks and building societies hold on deposit at the central bank. Central bank reserves are the other form of base money, being issued by (and therefore a liability of) a central bank. It is the price of—or equivalently the rate of interest on—central bank reserves that is the instrument of monetary policy, so in the UK, Bank Rate *is* the rate (of interest) at which central bank reserves are remunerated.

To understand how the price of this niche asset that is only held by a small set of financial institutions can influence activity in the real economy, we need a brief digression on the reasons why the banks and building societies choose to hold this asset.

2.1.2   The Demand for Central Bank Reserves

The banks and building societies that choose to hold deposit accounts with the central banks demand to do so in order to conduct their core functions on behalf of their customers. That demand for central bank reserves reflects three considerations.

Commercial banks need central bank reserves to purchase the hard currency that their customers require. Imagine for the sake of argument that households and companies had a fixed demand for the amount of cash they collectively want to hold. To a first approximation we would observe a near-constant stock of notes and coins circulating around the economy and periodically into and back out of the banking system. At any moment in time, the banks would absorb bank notes of those agents who have too many and distribute those notes to those who have too few (for much more detail on how this process works in practice see Allen and Dent 2010). In reality, the demand for cash is likely to vary through time with the trend increase in the value of spending in the economy driving an increase in the demand for cash to finance those transactions and the trend towards electronic forms of payment having the opposite effect (Janssen 1996; Grant et al. 2004; Fish and Whymark 2015). The banking system cannot create cash to meet any net increase in demand from their customers; the banks have to obtain those notes from the central bank. The banks will 'purchase' that cash for their customers by running down their deposits at the central bank (central bank reserves), and then households will 'purchase' that cash by running down their bank deposits. From a balance sheet perspective, the customer of the bank is swapping one asset for another (electronic money in a deposit account for cash); the central bank is swapping one liability for another (central bank reserves for cash); and the bank's balance sheet shrinks as both its assets (central bank reserves) and liabilities (customer deposits) fall.

Commercial banks also need central bank reserves as the ultimate means of settlement, and have done in the UK since as far back as the 1770s (see Tucker (2004) and the references therein). If there was only one bank in the economy then the cashless transactions described above would simply lead to offsetting changes in the value of different deposit accounts on that bank's balance sheet, with no change in the bank's total deposit liabilities to its customers. In reality, the two parties in the transaction (the individuals or companies) may bank with different institutions and that will require banks to make payments to one another in order to facilitate the transactions between their customers. On a typical day, there will be a huge number of these transactions flowing in both directions but aggregating across those transactions each bank is likely to owe money to some of its peers and be owed money by the others. Central bank reserves are the ultimate means of settlement on those positions, with the reserves flowing between the separate deposit accounts of the commercial banks according to the net payment flows between their customers.

Finally, banks will choose to hold central bank reserves as a form of self-insurance against liquidity shocks. There is always a risk that a bank will suffer a sudden and significant surge in withdrawals, as a result of a large imbalance in the net flow of transactions between the bank's customers and the rest of the population or a large number of customers trying to withdraw money from the bank at the same time (either in the form of cash or by transferring their deposit to another institution). Banks will tend to hold a buffer of assets which can be quickly converted into money to meet those funding shocks. As the ultimate means of settlement in the economy, central bank reserves are a natural component of that buffer of liquid assets.

Before moving on, it is worthwhile addressing a misconception about central bank reserves: that the anaemic recovery in credit and activity since the crash reflects the fact that banks have been unwilling to 'lend' central bank reserves. Banks can (and do) lend central bank reserves to each other, but they cannot lend them to their customers because households and companies do not have accounts with the central bank. As noted above, when banks originate a loan they may create a deposit which sets in train a chain of transactions which will ultimately lead to a transfer of central bank reserves between the banks in the settlement process, but that is not the same thing as lending out reserves. What people presumably mean when they talk about banks failing to lend out central bank reserves to households and companies is that the banking sector's holdings of central bank reserves are excessive relative to the size of its balance sheet and the banks could safely create more deposits to lend more money to households and companies without having to increase that stock of central bank reserves. To the extent this observation carries any weight, it does so in systems in which banks are required to hold a minimum stock of reserves given the configuration of their balance sheet, rather than setting their own voluntary targets (McLeay et al. 2014b).

2.1.3 Setting Interest Rates

Central banks have a monopoly over the supply of central bank reserves and can therefore set the price, or equivalently the interest rate. One of the two core purposes of the central bank's market operations is to ensure that the interest rate which is chosen by the monetary policymaker is reflected in the interest rate at which financial institutions lend reserves to each other over short horizons, because that rate should then filter out into other interest rates in financial markets and ultimately influence activity in the real economy.

In the UK, the BoE remunerates central bank reserves at a rate selected by the MPC: Bank Rate. The size of the stock of central bank reserves is then *normally* demand determined. The banks are asked to set their own targets for the amount of reserves that they wish to hold on average over the course of a maintenance period between one meeting of the MPC and the next. The BoE then makes sure that the banking system *as a whole* is square (has sufficient liquidity) via so-called open market operations (OMOs), which inject or withdraw liquidity as appropriate. The default approach to OMOs is for the central bank to inject liquidity (central bank reserves) through short-term loans secured against high-quality collateral, although in theory central banks can purchase assets outright; and where necessary central banks can drain liquidity by issuing short-term (debt) liabilities or by selling assets. The key point to note is that the BoE is *not* using the OMOs to set interest rates by varying quantities along some known demand curve (Tucker 2004; Disyatat 2008).

The BoE prefers to use an interest rate corridor to anchor market rates on the rate selected by the MPC. Central bank reserves are remunerated at Bank Rate so long as the stock of reserves for a particular bank is sufficiently close to the target. However, if reserves balances stray too far from that target in either direction, then banks are obliged to pay a penalty: reserves balances are remunerated at Bank Rate but any excess reserves above the top or shortfall of reserves below the bottom of the specified range are charged at Bank Rate and deducted from the interest paid. Banks are therefore incentivised to make use of the Operational Standing Facilities (OSFs) which allow surplus banks to deposit excess reserves at a rate below Bank Rate, and deficit banks to borrow reserves (secured against collateral) at a rate above Bank Rate. The deposit and lending rates in the OSFs create a corridor within which market rates should settle, since surplus banks have little incentive to lend money in the market when rates fall below that deposit rate, and deficit banks have little incentive to borrow when rates exceed the lending rate. More generally, the flexibility which the reserve averaging system provides should further stabilise market rates: for example, banks have the capacity to lend reserves in the market if interest rates drift up, and that increase in supply should help drag rates back down.

The precise details of how central banks implement monetary policy vary from place to place, but the basic mechanics are the same. Some central banks require their banks to hold a minimum level of 'required reserves' rather than set voluntary targets; other central banks employ a floor system rather than a corridor, in which the central bank injects excess liquidity into the system and remunerates all reserves at the policy rate (see Clews et al. 2010). However, the basic principle is the same: the central bank is trying to anchor the rate at which banks lend each other central bank reserves in the market on the policy rate.

Finally, in the explanation above we noted that the stock of central bank reserves is usually demand driven. As we shall go on to discuss, once central banks turned to unconventional monetary policy the stock of central bank money became an instrument of policy, determined on the supply side. In the UK, the BoE would rapidly inflate the stock of central bank money in order to conduct the MPC's asset purchase programme (a.k.a. QE). The standard demand-driven arrangements were therefore put into hibernation.

2.1.4 An Aside on Crushing the Corridor

In passing, since the purpose of this element of the market operations is to anchor market rates on the policy rate chosen by the MPC, it is not entirely clear why the BoE does not design its market operations to do precisely that (Wiseman 2007; Buiter 2008). The Bank could instead operate a near-zero corridor regime, with a minimal bid ask spread, to crush the volatility in the overnight rate:

- *Active regime*: The central bank could stand ready to lend against eligible collateral at a rate marginally above the policy rate and borrow (remunerate reserves) at a rate marginally below.
- *Passive regime*: Banks which end the day with a deficit are automatically charged a rate marginally above the policy rate on the shortfall and those which end each day with a positive balance (up to some limit) are remunerated at a rate marginally below the rate.

Just because the central bank stands ready to lend in size at the policy rate rather than requiring that banks access the Standing Facilities, it does not follow that the near-zero regime is more lax. In any secured refinancing operation, the fundamental constraint lies with the banks' stock of high-quality collateral and the terms on which the central bank will convert a given piece of collateral into cash. Indeed, to the extent that there is a stigma attached to using the Standing Facilities (which discourages usage) the near-zero corridor regime is a clear improvement on the existing model.

The BoE has raised a number of concerns about the near-zero corridor regime (Clews et al. 2010; Fisher 2011); we briefly review some of the key objections and responses (Wiseman 2011) below:

- *The central bank would lose control over the size of its balance sheet*: The central bank has already 'lost control' over the size of its balance sheet in any demand-driven scheme. Under the Bank's scheme, the commercial banks set their own reserves targets.
- *The near-zero regime would mean the end of the overnight money market*: It is true that activity would decline in the overnight market but it is unclear that volatility around the rate selected by policymakers serves any socially useful purpose; as Wiseman (2007) puts it, what point is there in price discovery in a 'pretend market' when the policymaker has already set the socially optimal price?

- *The central bank would lose valuable information from usage of the Standing Facilities*: In theory, it is possible that the central bank could learn something about the fragility of the banks' funding position from their usage of the Standing Facilities, although it is not clear how much market intelligence has been gathered through this route in practice (Wiseman 2011), and in any case, now that the BoE has regained responsibility for microprudential supervision, Bank staff surely have access to superior information on the health of the banks.

2.2   The Transmission Mechanism of Monetary Policy

Changes in the price of, or equivalently the interest rate on, central bank reserves will ultimately influence the decisions of millions of households and companies in the real economy and hence the level of aggregate activity and the rate of consumer price inflation. The process through which changes in monetary policy affect output and inflation is known as the monetary transmission mechanism. In this sub-section, we briefly review the key links in the transmission mechanism of changes in Bank Rate, drawing heavily on the official account of the MPC's assessment of the transmission mechanism in the UK (BoE 1999).

2.2.1 Financial Markets

The first link in the transmission mechanism is the impact of changes in Bank Rate on other interest rates of a similar horizon to the one over which Bank Rate is set (i.e., the interval between the scheduled meetings of the MPC), or to interest rates that are contractually linked to Bank Rate (such as 'tracker mortgages') or market rates which tend to move with Bank Rate. In these markets, pass-through is typically rapid and near complete: that is, the *change* in Bank Rate will soon lead to a near-equivalent *change* in these market rates, although the *level* of these rates varies according to the nature of the investment. Monetary policymakers are trying to influence the decisions of households and companies so as far as they are concerned, *changes* in Bank Rate should ideally be reflected in *changes* in retail lending and deposit rates as far as possible. The presence of 'menu costs' (Caplin and Spulber 1987) in adjusting retail lending rates could certainly distort pass-through. For example, pass-through could depend on whether the actual rate is becoming more or less out of line with fundamentals (i.e., the optimal price/rate), which implies that whether the gap between the retail rate and Bank Rate is widening or narrowing matters for pass through (Hofmann and Mizen 2004).

As soon as we move beyond the transmission to ultra-short-term interest rates and those interest rates that are contractually linked to Bank Rate we need to clarify whether the change in Bank Rate was expected or not. The rate of return that the market demands from a long-term investment should reflect the opportunity cost of that decision to invest money in a physical or financial asset for an extended period—namely, making a sequence of short-term investments that together match the duration of the long-term investment. On that basis, long-term interest rates should reflect the expected future path of short-term interest rates, and therefore the expectations of the decisions that the MPC might take in the future.

It follows that longer-term interest rates—and, by extension, the broad constellation of asset prices—will not respond to a change in Bank Rate that was fully anticipated. This is not to say that an anticipated change in Bank Rates serves no purpose. When the expectation of that decision originally arose, asset prices responded and that *would* have had a macroeconomic impact. If the policymaker wants that impact to persist then it is important that she validates that expectation: long rates would shift back in response to an unexpected decision not to change the stance of monetary policy in the direction that had originally been expected.

More generally, it is the nature of the news (or the surprise) in a policy announcement that determines the move in long rates (Haldane and Read 1999). For example:

- *News on timing*: A change in Bank Rate that was expected to occur at some point in the future implies a modest change in asset prices that simply reflects news on the future path of short rates between today and the date at which the change in Bank Rate was originally expected.
- *News on the path*: The impact of a change in Bank Rate that was unexpected may be compounded by a change in view about the likelihood of further changes in the future (potentially in either direction) which potentially implies a more significant correction in asset prices. For example, a surprise rate cut might lead the market to infer that the economy is weaker than previously thought and that further rate cuts may be required.
- *News on the framework*: If the surprise reveals information about the monetary policy framework itself—about the speed with which the Committee will try to bring inflation back to target in response to shocks or even about

the inflation target itself—then the announcement could imply a correction in yields even at very long horizons. For example, the surprise decision to cede operational independence over the conduct of monetary policy to the BoE led to a significant correction in long-term interest rates consistent with market participants revising their expectations of the determination with which monetary policymakers would lean against volatility in inflation (Chadha et al. 2007).

Changes in the expected future path of short rates will pass through into the price of financial and physical assets. There is a straightforward relationship between the price of a fixed income asset like a bond and the expected future path of rates: for example, as market interest rates rise, the price of a bond must fall in order that the coupon and principal repayments on that bond deliver the new higher interest rate. Changes in market rates will also have a pervasive impact on the price of other assets via the rate at which the future returns on those assets are discounted back to the present day in order to calculate a presented discounted value. For example, when interest rates rise a smaller sum of money needs to be invested today in order to match the flow of dividend payments that an investment in the stock market is likely to deliver (Vila Wetherilt and Weeken 2002) or the flow of housing services that an investment in the property market is likely to deliver (Weeken 2004), so other things equal, an increase in market rates will depress the value of equities and housing.

The prices of these financial and physical assets are not pinned down by just the flow of returns that they are expected to deliver. Asset prices will typically incorporate a risk premium, reflecting the excess compensation that investors demand for holding that asset, which from the perspective of the consumption capital asset pricing model (C-CAPM) should depend on whether the asset delivers strong returns when investors need them most (consumption is low, and the marginal utility of consumption is high) or when they need them least (Breeden 1979). In theory, changes in the stance of monetary policy could influence those risk premia, because the perceived quantity of risk is endogenous with respect to the policy stance. As we shall go on to discuss, one of the key contributions of monetary policy during the post-crash period was the capacity to convince investors that central bankers can and will do 'whatever it takes' to avoid catastrophic outcomes, which helped to provide a floor under the price of risk assets (i.e., compressed risk premia).

Changes in market interest rates in the UK that are not replicated overseas should influence the exchange rate—a critical asset price channel of the transmission mechanism in an open economy like the UK. A bilateral exchange rate defines the relative price of one currency compared to another; a trade-weighted effective exchange rate index reflects the movement in a narrow or broad set of these bilateral exchange rates for a given country, weighted by their relative importance in that country's trade in goods and services. We shall return to discuss the determinants of the exchange rate in more detail later in this book, but one important driver is the relative returns on assets in different currencies. If the rate of return on sterling-denominated assets falls relative to the rest of the world then those assets will become less attractive, and we should expect international investors to rebalance their portfolios away from sterling accordingly. That shift in demand away from sterling should lead to a depreciation until the expected appreciation in the value of the pound in the future (from the new lower level) is sufficient to compensate the interest rate differential, so that investors face the same expected returns across jurisdictions when those returns are converted back into a common currency at the end of the investment horizon.

2.2.2 Demand

Policy-induced changes in interest rates and asset prices described above will gradually feed through into the spending decisions of households and companies and hence the level of aggregate demand.

In most of what follows, we will focus on the partial equilibrium effects of changes in interest rates on the decisions of individual households and companies to spend or save, taking the aggregate level of activity, employment and prices as given. In general equilibrium, those changes in spending will have macroeconomic consequences, which will then feed back into the decisions of those households and companies.

Before moving on, it is worth noting that households and companies might take decisions to spend or save *in anticipation* of these changes in the state of the aggregate economy driven by these coordinated responses to the change in official interest rates (and the shock to which the central bank responded). Indeed, a change in the stance of monetary policy—particularly a significant change in the stance—could also impact domestic demand by influencing the beliefs of households and companies about the future, both in terms of the most likely path of the economy and the probability of bad outcomes. These confidence and uncertainty channels could have a significant impact on spending, magnifying the direct effects described below: for example, influencing households' precautionary motive to save or the hurdle rate on irreversible investments by companies.

2.2.2.1   Households

For the household sector we can identify a number of offsetting channels through which changes in market rates can influence consumption using the standard permanent income model of consumption (Friedman 1957): an income and substitution effect driven by changes in real interest rates; a revaluation of human wealth via changes in the discount rate on future income; a wealth and net worth effect driven by changes in the price of financial and physical assets; and a cash flow effect that operates through disposable income.

Changes in *real* interest rates can influence aggregate consumption by encouraging households to bring forward or push back the timing of their consumption plans. Central banks set the short-term *nominal* rate; it is the stickiness in prices (or nominal rigidity) that creates the inertia of inflation expectations that gives policymakers traction over real rates. Indeed, without the distortions created by nominal rigidity policymakers would be unable to influence real interest rates: prices would instantaneously adjust to clear markets and real interest rates would be pinned down by the balance between demand and supply for loanable funds. Indeed, in simple models optimal policy involves adjusting nominal interest to replicate the path for real interest rates that would otherwise emerge in a world of flexible prices (Goodfriend and King 1997; King and Wolman 1999). Real interest rates define the relative price of consumption today versus tomorrow when borrowing or lending funds, and by changing that relative price the policymaker encourages households to change the timing of their consumption plans.

Alongside the standard substitution effect, there is also an income effect on consumption from a change in real interest rates (for a graphical exposition of the inter-play between these two effects see Cromb and Fernandez-Corugedo [2004]). The income effect captures the fact that the present discounted value of the future flow of consumption that can be supported by a given stock of assets hinges on the discount rate; so when interest rates rise, a given path of consumption is more easily affordable for a household with a stock of assets.

In just the same way that changes in interest rates influence the present discounted value of future consumption, they can also impact on permanent income: the present discounted value of future income (Elmendorf 1996). In theory, the discount rate is moving both discounted expenditure and income in the same direction, so these two effects could cancel if the profiles of consumption and income are similar (Cromb and Fernandez-Corugedo 2004).

Changes in the prices of physical and financial assets will have an impact on the net worth of the household sector through its direct and indirect holdings of financial and housing assets. If households have significant holdings of financial assets denominated in foreign currency then any policy-induced change in the exchange rate will lead to a further revision to net financial wealth. Those changes in net worth could have an immediate impact on consumption via a wealth effect (Case et al. 2001); for example, households might withdraw some of the increased equity in their home to fund consumption. Moreover, changes in asset prices could have an indirect effect via a 'credit channel': change in the value of the collateral that households own and their net worth will influence the terms on which they can borrow money, or the external finance premium they pay (Bernanke and Gertler 1995), and in the limit their access to credit.

Finally, changes in market interest rates will have a direct effect on the disposable income of those households with interest-bearing assets or liabilities. When Bank Rate rises, debtors lose and creditors gain, and vice versa when Bank Rate falls. In each case, one group has the option to increase spending, whilst the other will be under pressure to cut back spending. If the individuals on the wrong end of the cash flow effects are not currently saving a significant share of income, do not have a buffer of savings to fall back on or do not have easy access to credit, then the redistributive effect of changes in interest rates could have an immediate impact on spending. Miles (2015) argues that these cash flow effects are likely to be powerful in an economy like the UK where the stock of household debt is large relative to income and the interest rate on a significant proportion of that debt is variable or soon will be (as households fall off fixed rate deals).

2.2.2.2   Companies

Companies raise funds through a number of channels: by borrowing money from banks; by borrowing funds secured against assets ('asset based lending'); by borrowing money from other companies ('trade credit'), where larger companies are concerned by issuing short- and long-term debt in capital markets (commercial paper and bonds); and by issuing fresh equity. Changes in Bank Rate will pass through, to a greater or lesser extent, into the cost of these different forms of finance, and that will influence investment spending via the hurdle rate on potential investment opportunities. The same basic principle applies to an investment in a new job opening, which will offer a flow of profits to the firm over the lifetime of the job (Yashiv 2000).

Changes in interest rates will also influence the corporate sector's demand for inventories: the stock of raw materials, semi-finished and final output which companies hold in order to be able to quickly service customer demand given lags in the production process and potential disruptions in the supply chain (Elder and Tsoukalas 2006). An increase in interest rates will raise the cost of holding inventories, potentially prompting companies to 'de-stock'— that is, to temporarily scale back production and meet customer demand by running down inventories to achieve a lower ratio of stocks (inventories) to output. Gertler and Gilchrist (1994) and Kashyap, Stein and Lamont (1994) both find evidence of this dynamic, with a significant response of inventories where financing constraints bite.

As with households, changes in interest rates will give rise to cash flow effects in the corporate sector: companies which owe debts will have to devote more resources to servicing debts when interest rates rise which may constrain investment spending, particularly given the importance of cash flow in financing investment (Fazzari et al. 1988). Likewise, companies will also be influenced by changes in asset prices via the 'credit channel' in just the same way that households are. Companies will tend to be offered credit on less attractive terms if the collateral on which loans can be secured declines in value, and that will weigh on their investments in capital, jobs and inventories.

2.2.2.3   Demand Overseas

Finally, the change in the exchange rate will have an impact on the demand for domestic output relative to overseas competitors by changing the relative price of domestic output. In theory an exchange rate depreciation will make domestic output more competitive in overseas markets, and overseas output less competitive in domestic markets, and that will tend to lead to an increase in the volume of goods and services the UK exports and a decrease in the volume of goods and services we import, which implies a favourable shift in the net trade contribution to gross domestic product (GDP). In practice, this story is a little more complex (see Buisán et al. 2006; Mac Coille et al. 2009; Kamath and Paul 2011):

- *Pricing to market*: Changes in the exchange rate may not pass through (immediately) into the price of UK exports in overseas markets or overseas imports in UK markets, with the change in the exchange rate being partially or completely offset by shifts in profit margins for one of a number of reasons: the companies concerned believe that the exchange rate move will reverse; strategic considerations (e.g., to maintain market share); or because of contractual constraints.

- *Price inelastic demand*: The demand for traded goods and services might be largely insensitive to price; for example, if there is no domestically produced competitor it is much harder for consumers to substitute away from more expensive imports.
- *Exporters consume a lot of imports*: Rather than the simple textbook treatment of domestic consumers substituting away from more expensive imports and overseas consumers substituting towards less expensive domestic exports, it turns out that the consumption of imports at home and exports abroad may be linked via the production function: companies which are large exporters often consume large quantities of imports in the production of final output (Amiti et al. 2014).

2.2.3 Inflation

The primary channel through which monetary policy influences the ultimate variable of interest (inflation) is via its impact on demand, given the trade-off that exists between output and inflation in the short run.

At any moment in time, there is a level of output and employment in the economy which if achieved is consistent with price stability—that is, with a stable rate of inflation consistent with the target of monetary policy. That level of output, referred to as the sustainable level of output or potential supply, will depend on the size of the capital stock and the adult population and the level of technical progress (which determines the efficiency with which companies can combine inputs to produce output) as well as the structural features of the economy which collectively determine how far the economy operates from the perfectly competitive benchmark.

The level of aggregate demand relative to that (unobservable) level of potential supply—known as the output gap—will influence the trajectory of costs and prices in the economy. The pattern of relative prices will remain largely unaltered: the prices of certain commodities will continue to diverge from others, reflecting the microeconomic determinants of individual prices (the relative rate of technical progress for that particular good, changes in the degree of competition in the product market for that good, etc.). However, the imbalance between demand and supply at the aggregate level will gradually influence the rate of change of all costs and prices as they are reset.

The output gap and its impact on inflationary pressure can be decomposed into two component parts:

- *Labour market slack*: defined as the imbalance between the actual employment of labour and the sustainable level of employment that is consistent with no inflationary pressure coming out of the labour market. If employment exceeds its potential level, the cost of employing labour will tend to rise faster than the value of output that labour produces, putting upwards pressure on costs and ultimately prices, and vice versa (Barwell et al. 2007). A comprehensive definition of labour market slack would reflect not only the number of people who are employed but also the number of hours they work and even the type of role in which they are employed (e.g., whether they are on a temporary contract).
- *Capacity utilisation*: defined as the imbalance between the actual level of output and the level of output that companies can sustainably produce given their current inputs. When companies work their inputs at above normal levels of utilisation (e.g., asking their workforce to work harder, producing more per hour) in order to meet demand there will be further pressure on costs and prices (Ellis and Turnbull 2007). Moreover, in those circumstances in which demand is strong and capacity utilisation is above normal levels companies may try to increase profit margins, putting further upwards pressure on costs relative to prices.

The key point to note here is that so long as an output gap persists, there will be inflationary pressure, so if a central bank wishes to anchor inflation on the target, it must eliminate that output gap. Failure to do so will sooner or later disturb medium-term expectations of inflation, causing inflation to spiral further from the target. Put another way, there is no long-run trade-off between output and inflation: the central bank can deliver price stability at any rate of inflation with inflation outturns in line with expectations *if and only if the output gap is closed*.

Alongside this indirect link between changes in interest rates and inflationary pressure via the level of demand and the output gap, there is an offsetting direct link that operates through the supply side that is referred to as the cost channel of monetary policy. Interest rates may feature directly in the costs of production, for example, via the cost of financing a company's stock of inventories, or if a company has to borrow money to pay its workforce when payment for output is received with a lag (Christiano and Eichenbaum 1992). An increase in interest rates could therefore lead to a counter-intuitive *increase* in inflationary pressure via this cost channel (Barth and Ramey 2002). In theory, this supply-side transmission channel could even dominate the conventional demand side channel, although opinions differ on how significant the cost channel is in practice (Ravenna and Walsh 2006; Rabanal 2007).

For an open economy like the UK, there is another critical channel in the transmission mechanism which does not operate via the output gap: imported inflation. As we noted earlier, changes in the stance of monetary policy will influence the level of the exchange rate and to the extent that the depreciation or appreciation is passed through into the sterling price of imported goods and services there is a powerful link between changes in interest rates and inflation. Some of these imported goods may feature in the consumption basket, whilst others may be consumed as inputs in the domestic production process, and the change in import prices will then gradually pass along the supply chain into the price of final consumption.

2.2.4 The Long and Variable Lags of Monetary Policy

Changes in Bank Rate do not have an immediate impact on inflation. The asset price response to a surprise change in the policy rate is fairly rapid: the price of financial assets like bonds and equities will respond almost instantaneously to the surprise decision (although it may take rather long for market participants to identify the news in the decision, and therefore the appropriate asset price response), and retail lending and deposit rates will typically be re-priced within a matter of weeks. However, the demand response builds over a much longer time horizon, as households and companies gradually respond to these price signals, and then the cumulative impact of the change in spending on activity, employment and prices at the aggregate level then triggers a further adjustment in spending at the individual level. The implied adjustment in the output gap then gradually influences price-setting behaviour, such that the peak impact on inflation tends to lag the peak impact on demand. According to the empirical estimates published in the Committee's description of the transmission mechanism (BoE 1999), the peak impact of an unexpected change in interest rates occurs five quarters after the change, whilst the peak impact on inflation arrives after nine quarters—that is, more than two years after the change in interest rates.

The lags in the transmission mechanism are a resilient feature of the economy. Milton Friedman's work in this area is more than half a century old (Friedman 1961, 1972), but Batini and Nelson (2001) note that the lags in the transmission mechanism in the UK and the USA have remained stubbornly persistent down the decades, despite numerous changes in the conduct of monetary policy in both countries, advances in information processing and the sophistication of financial markets. Indeed, Havranek and Rusnak (2013) argue that the transmission mechanism of monetary policy is more gradual in more financially developed economies, perhaps reflecting the fact that in less developed economies financial institutions lack the means to hedge unexpected moves in interest rates and are therefore obliged to respond faster to actual changes in official interest rates.

As Milton Friedman famously observed, the impact of monetary policy is subject to long and variable lags—indeed, so long and variable that in his view well-meaning attempts to use monetary policy to stabilise the economy could prove counterproductive. Setting monetary policy is rather like trying to drive down the *other* Lombard Street (the one in San Francisco, with a series of hairpin bends) in a car in which there is a large and unpredictable delay between turning the steering wheel and the wheels responding. As a result, there is no alternative but for central bankers to look ahead when setting interest rates, or in the jargon, monetary policy must be forward looking (King 1997).

2.3   The Near-Zero Lower Bound and How to Avoid Hitting It

There is an asymmetric constraint on the conduct of monetary policy: nominal interest rates can be raised without limit but can only be cut so far. We now turn to discuss the location of this constraint, its consequences for policy and the pre-crisis consensus on the appropriate way to manage the problem.

2.3.1   The Location of the Lower Bound Near Zero

The root cause of the ZLB is that there are two forms of base money but central banks only affect the price of one of them. As described above, central banks vary the remuneration of central bank reserves to ensure that the interest rate on reserves in the inter-bank market reflects the rate chosen by the policymaker. However, the interest rate on the other form of base money (cash) is fixed at zero.

Now imagine that the central bank was able to impose a negative interest rate on central bank reserves and that this interest rate then filtered out into the private economy. Any individual who lends at a negative interest rate receives back less money in the future than she lent today. If she has the option to instead invest her funds in cash (hard currency), she can avoid the loss of purchasing power. It appears then that at the point at which market interest go negative investors will run to cash. This is the ZLB on nominal interest rates.

In theory, the ZLB could pinch in one of two places. First, when the central bank imposes a negative interest rate on central bank reserves the banks could substitute out of reserves into cash, slashing their reserves targets to very low levels and carrying out the business of settlement away from the BoE's balance sheet, perhaps via transfers of high denomination notes between vaults located at a secure facility. Second, if the banks pass through the negative rate into the interest rates they offer on retail deposits, then households and companies could liquidate their deposits and instead hold a much larger fraction of their financial wealth in the form of cash.

This discussion should hopefully reveal the reason why the lower bound is not in fact at zero. Neither of the scenarios described sound like an attractive proposition for the agent running to cash. Cash is not a convenient medium of exchange or store of value where large sums are concerned, which is precisely why its role in the modern economy has dwindled: currency can be stolen or damaged (and therefore demands expensive storage facilities) and has to be recounted every time it is involved in a transaction (McAndrews 2015).

The true lower bound therefore lies somewhere below zero reflecting the 'convenience yield' of the substitute for cash: electronic money. In other words, financial institutions, companies and households will tolerate a small negative return on bank deposits but at some point the interest rate differential between bank deposits and cash will become too large to resist. At some point, there is an incentive to invest in a secure storage facility and then borrow as much money as possible at a negative interest rate and invest it in cash and earn profit without taking risk (Cœuré 2015a).

Another problem thrown up by the transition to negative interest rates is the need to unpick the zero interest rate conventions that exist in a modern economy which evolved in a world of positive nominal interest rates but are ripe for exploitation in a negative interest rate environment (McAndrews 2015). In normal circumstances, it is in your interest to cash a cheque as soon as you receive it in order that you start to earn interest on the sum as soon as possible and to rule out the possibility that the counterparty defaults on the payment. In a negative interest rate environment, you might be tempted to delay cashing the cheque as long as possible, extending the period of time that the counterparty pays the negative interest rate on the sum. Jensen and Spange (2015) note that the pass-through of a negative policy rate into corporate deposit rates in Denmark prompted some companies to place liquidity with the Danish tax authorities, leading the government to draft legislation which would adjust the interest rate on the settlement of corporation tax receipts and place a cap on the amount that could be placed in corporate tax accounts.

The more negative interest rates become and/or the longer they remain negative, the greater the incentive to seek out such ways of managing your affairs so as to minimise your exposure to the negative rate on deposits or to exploit these arbitrage opportunities.

2.3.2   The Policy Problem

In theory, the near-ZLB poses an existential threat to price stability. Once the central bank has reached the lower bound, it becomes impotent unless it has access to other means of stimulating the economy, and at this point the system can become unstable.

If the economy is hit by a negative shock when the central bank is marooned at the lower bound then there will be no countervailing force leaning against the deterioration in economic activity as the shock works its way through the system. Demand will fall, the output gap will widen, disinflationary pressure will build and expectations of inflation will fall. But with nominal interest rates at the lower bound any fall in inflation expectations translates into a rise in real interest rates. Rising real interest rates are contractionary, raising the relative price of consumption today versus tomorrow, which will lead to a further fall in demand, widening of the output gap and a further fall in inflation expectations. The end result could be a deflationary spiral.

If this situation sounds bad enough, it can be made a good deal worse by the redistributive effect of a surprise fall in inflation or the emergence of outright deflation. The real value of debt increases relative to expectations—that is, an indebted household or company will have to devote more resources to repaying the loan than she had originally anticipated. Creditors gain and debtors lose from surprise disinflation, and if (as seems likely) debtors have a higher marginal propensity to consume out of wealth than creditors then aggregate demand will likely fall further as a result of this redistributive effect (Bean 2002).

In the limit, a full-blown debt deflation can emerge. As the real debt burden is revised higher over-indebted agents are forced to liquidate assets to reduce that burden but in the process they may depress asset prices and aggravate the depression in demand that leads to a further fall in the general price level, which only leads to a further erosion of net worth and increase in the real debt burden. As Fisher (1933) observed, the more debtors pay, the more they owe, so the system becomes inherently unstable.

2.3.3 Learning to Live with the Problem

The implications of the so-called ZLB for the conduct of monetary policy were appreciated before the crash of 2007/08. Monetary policy was unconstrained in the UK for the first decade of the MPC's lifetime—Bank Rate averaged around 5 % over that period and was never lower than 3.5 %. However, other central banks were not quite so fortunate. Those that had to deal with episodes of financial instability got up close and personal with the lower bound. The Fed cut the Fed Funds Rate to 1 % in the aftermath of the collapse of the DotCom bubble, and the Bank of Japan (BoJ) reached zero in the wake of a full-blown financial crisis.

The implications of the ZLB problem for the conduct of monetary policy was a key topic of discussion within the global central banking community in the decade before the financial crash of 2007/08. Yates (2003) provides an excellent review of the potential solutions which we shall briefly summarise here:

- *Quick off the blocks in response to large shocks*: Central banks might be able to avoid running up against the lower bound if they respond disproportionately (i.e., more pre-emptively and more aggressively) to very large downside shocks, which in turn could help to moderate the decline in inflation expectations following the realisation of the shock, producing a lower (and more expansionary) real interest rate.
- *A more muted response the rest of the time*: The central bank may be able to gain traction over longer-term interest rates (expectations of the policy rate further into the future) by changing the policy rate in a more gradual fashion in response to news. The central bank tolerates higher volatility of output and inflation most of the time in order to achieve a more powerful transmission mechanism in a crisis (changes in the policy rate have a bigger effect) which reduce the risk of hitting the lower bound.
- *Forward guidance*: The central bank would cut rates aggressively in response to the shock but once rates reach a low level (above the bound) the central bank would inject additional stimulus by trying to lower long rates through communication that rates will remain low(er) for longer than would be usually by the case, which if effective would lower expectations of the future path of the policy rate (that are implicit in long rates).

Ben Bernanke famously discussed these issues in a speech given early in his stint as a member of the Board of Governors of the Fed (Bernanke 2002) titled 'Deflation: Making sure "it" doesn't happen here'. Bernanke concluded that central banks were not out of ammunition if they reached the lower bound: they would still have access to unconventional tools should the need arise, but those tools are unfamiliar and would not be easy to use. Instead, he argued that prevention was preferable to cure: if the central bank moved 'decisively and early' it might be able to avoid the slide into deflation.

2.4   The Race to the Bottom

As the financial crisis gathered to a crescendo it became increasingly clear that there would be significant collateral damage in the real economy, and by the end of 2008 it was clear that the global economy was facing a major economic crisis. Central bankers were confronted with a collapse in demand, the very real prospect of a slide into deflation and potentially a repeat of the Great Depression could not be ruled out. They responded by cutting interest rates to the floor.

- *BoE*: Bank Rate was 5.5 % at the start of 2008, and by early April had been reduced to 5 %. Between early October and early December Bank Rate was cut to 2 %, and by early March 2009, Bank Rate had fallen to 0.5 %.
- *European Central Bank (ECB)*: The main refinancing rate (or 'refi rate') was 4 % at the start of 2008 and was raised in July to 4.25 %. Between October and May 2009, the refi rate was reduced to 1 %.
- *Fed*: The Fed Funds Rate was 4.25 % at the start of 2008, but by the end of April, the Fed Funds Rate had already more than halved, standing at 2 %, and by December was effectively at the floor, with a target range for the rate of 0 to 0.25 %.

One interesting feature of this period is the coordinated nature of the easing in monetary policy. On 8 October 2008, six central banks (the Bank of Canada, the BoE, the ECB, the Fed, Sveriges Riksbank and the Swiss National Bank [SNB]) simultaneously reduced their policy rate, and a seventh (the BoJ) expressed its strong support. The fact that they all decided to loosen monetary policy is not so surprising given that all those central banks were dealing with more or less the same shock. The timing was a little more of a surprise: the MPC convened a special meeting (a little ahead of the normal schedule) to agree the cut in Bank Rate. At first glance, the direct impact on output and jobs of following the timetable and waiting a day before cutting Bank Rate by 50 basis points appears insignificant. However, it seems clear the world's central bankers bought into the principle that the stimulus of a coordinated response is greater than the sum of its parts—that there is some additional benefit to be had from acting together to re-inject confidence in the outlook and the power of central bankers to avert disaster.

Another interesting feature of this race to the bottom is the speed with which official interest rates are taken to the floor. In particular, in just one meeting (November 2008), the MPC reduced Bank Rate by 150 basis points, with the Minutes of that meeting revealing that an even larger cut ('possibly in excess of 200 basis points') might be required (BoE 2008).

Central bankers are thought to follow a gradualist strategy based on the observed pattern of interest rate changes, which tend to follow cycles with a series of typically small changes in the same direction and very few reversals (changes of direction), although there is a dispute about whether this persistence in interest rates is intrinsic or extrinsic to the central bank. The serial correlation of interest rates may simply reflect the serial correlation in the information flow that the policymaker receives (Rudebusch 2006), with periods when the policymaker receives increasingly good news about the state of the economy leading to a series of interest rate rises, and then periods when the reverse is true. Alternatively, under intrinsic persistence the policymaker is only partially adjusting to the news at any given policy meeting, which implies further adjustments in the policy stance in the future in the absence of further news.

There are a number of reasons why central bankers might behave in this slow and predictable fashion: given uncertainty over the impact of interest rate changes and an aversion to injecting unnecessary volatility into the economy, it may make sense to do less than appears necessary to begin with, and then top up in light of the observed impact of the initial decision (Brainard 1967; Blinder 1998); by making future policy moves predictable, the central bank can gain traction over long-term interest rates (Woodford 2003); or financial stability concerns that stem from the large capital gains and losses on asset prices that can follow from surprise moves in interest rates (Bernanke 2004). If we return to the November 2008 meeting where the MPC unanimously decided to cut rates by 150 basis points despite the internal projections suggesting a larger cut was warranted, we find the Committee citing a number of reasons for its decision, several of which have a flavour of intrinsic persistence (BoE 2008):

- *Waiting for a fiscal response*: The Bank's projections were predicated on the existing fiscal stance but the Committee expected the Chancellor to announce new measures in the Pre-Budget Report which might reduce the need for further monetary stimulus;
- *Uncertainty over the global impact of crisis measures*: The Committee noted that the crisis response had restored 'a degree of stability' to the banking system but more time was required to assess their impact on credit and the real economy, and therefore the degree of stimulus that was required.
- *Do not scare market participants*: The Committee was concerned that too large a surprise move in interest rates (market participants were only anticipating a 50 to 100 basis point cut) could be misinterpreted as a change in the Committee's fundamental strategy (its 'reaction function'), which might damage the credibility of the inflation targeting framework.
- *Keep your powder dry*: Some members of the Committee argued in favour of doing less (easing) at the meeting in order to be able to do more in the future which might support confidence as the economy weakens.

Another interesting feature of the monetary policy in Europe but not the USA is that at least with the benefit of hindsight, the BoE and the ECB appeared to slash interest rates late in the day. Both the UK and Eurozone economies were in recession before the central banks took action to aggressively cut interest rates—that is, output had contracted in both 2008 Q2 and Q3. To use Bernanke's watchwords, the European policy response might have been decisive but it certainly was not early.

The final feature of the race to the bottom that is worth noting is that different central banks stopped in different places: the Fed near zero, the BoE at 0.5 % and the ECB at 1 %. We shall now turn to explain why.

2.5   The BoE Stops at 0.5 %: The Endowment Effect and the Back-Book Effect

In the UK, it appeared as though the lower bound was located above zero during the crisis: the MPC chose to stop cutting official interest rates once Bank Rate reached 0.5 % and started injecting stimulus by other means (asset purchases). The reason why the MPC stopped short of zero has to do with the parlous state of the banking system at that moment in time.

Banks will habitually pay a lower interest rate on their deposits than they charge on the funds they lend out. The spread between the interest rate on loans and deposits is a key source of a retail bank's income and is therefore a critical ingredient in the process of rebuilding bank capital in a crisis—if banks earn a healthy margin between gross interest payments and receipts the flow of net interest income can absorb losses and can be used to organically regenerate lost capital. The sharp fall in Bank Rate threatened to disrupt that process via the interaction of the so-called endowment effect and the back-book effect (Button et al. 2010).

- *Endowment effect*: Deposit rates typically settle below Bank Rate, so even though Bank Rate did not technically hit the zero bound, some retail deposit rates did, and once retail deposit rates hit the floor, further falls in Bank Rate would mechanically reduce net interest margin if the cut is passed through into retail lending rates. This problem was exacerbated by an increase in the banks' overall funding costs, with higher funding costs in wholesale markets reflecting their fragile balance sheets and higher funding costs in retail markets reflecting a preference shift among the banks towards funding a higher share of the balance sheet with retail deposits (for which banks had to pay).
- *Back-book effect*: The interest rates on some loans (such as tracker mortgages) were contractually tied to Bank Rate, so the banks could not immediately readjust the interest rate on those loans to reflect the fact that their funding costs had not fallen one for one with Bank Rate, squeezing net interest income.

Given that banks could not re-price existing mortgages there was obvious pressure to increase the price of new loans to restore the spread between interest payments and receipts in order to provide much needed earnings to help rebuild capital (indeed, stickiness in retail deposit rates may have further exacerbated the problem). Rather than cuts in Bank Rate being passed through into lower interest rates in retail lending markets there was the very real prospect that the opposite might occur, with banks widening the spread on new lending relative to Bank Rate. As Button, Pezzini and Rossiter (2010) note, in general the interest rates charged on new lending to households did not fall by as much and indeed some interest rates rose.

As the Minutes of the policy meetings of the MPC in early 2009 reveal there were differences of opinion over exactly how important this channel was and how far the Committee could reduce Bank Rate without the cuts becoming counterproductive; for example, in the February policy meeting we discover that (BoE 2009a):

a majority of members concluded that a cut of 50 basis points was appropriate this month. There were also arguments for cutting Bank Rate by 100 basis points this month. There were parts of the monetary transmission mechanism that still worked and did not rely on the banking sector. The larger the cut, the larger the stimulus that would be achieved through these channels. It was possible that banks could find other means for raising revenue to replace the money lost from any reduction in the spread. In any event, other policies were more appropriate for addressing the problem of the adequacy of banks' capital, not the level of Bank Rate. For one member, it was especially appropriate at this time to reach the lower bound for Bank Rate without delay. Historically, policy errors had been made by cutting too late rather than too soon.

The same discussion resurfaced the following month, with arguments being made for both leaving Bank Rate at 1 % and making further cuts (BoE 2009b). In the event, the Committee unanimously agreed to cut Bank Rate by 50 basis points to 0.5 %, where it would stay for years to come. From this point, on stimulus would come via asset purchases, and arguably via forward guidance.

The Minutes of the November 2012 MPC meeting reveal that Bank staff had consulted with the Financial Services Authority (FSA) and the Building Societies Association on the possible consequences of a cut in Bank Rate, prompting a discussion within the Committee of the case for cutting below 0.5 %. The view remained that a cut in Bank Rate would hit profitability and weaken balance sheets and potentially have a counterproductive impact on credit supply, and hence the Committee judged that 'it was unlikely to wish to reduce Bank Rate in the foreseeable future' (BoE 2012). This was still the position in May 2013 as the Deputy Governor responsible for Monetary Policy commented that cuts in Bank Rate could have 'adverse consequences on bank profitability and the supply of credit' and that asset purchases and targeted measures designed to repair the monetary transmission mechanism were more 'reliable tools for stimulating aggregate demand' in a note submitted to the Treasury Select Committee (Bean 2013).

However, this is not quite the end of the story. In his letter to the Chancellor in early 2015 to explain why CPI (Consumer Price Index) inflation had fallen more than a percentage point below the target, the Governor announced that the Committee no longer felt constrained by the potentially counterproductive transmission of Bank Rate cuts via the banking system (BoE 2015):

> The Committee could also decide to expand the Asset Purchase Facility or to cut Bank Rate further towards zero from its current level of 0.5%. The scope for prospective downward adjustments in Bank Rate reflects, in part, the fact that

the UK's banking sector is operating with substantially more capital now than it did in the immediate aftermath of the crisis. Reductions in Bank Rate are therefore less likely to have undesirable effects on the supply of credit to the UK economy than previously judged by the MPC.

As we will go on to discuss later in this book, this statement had important ramifications for the conduct of monetary policy. Bank Rate was no longer deemed to be at the lower bound: the Committee had the option to cut interest rates in the future if it needed to. It follows that the risk-management argument for keeping rates lower for longer that might otherwise be deemed appropriate because the central bank had little scope to stimulate the economy in a future downturn was now less valid for the UK.

2.6 The ECB Stops at 1 %: Excess Reserves and the Deposit Rate

The ECB stopped cutting interest in early 2009 even further above zero than the BoE. The main refinancing rate (or refi rate) was cut to 1 % in May 2009 and remained at that level until April 2011 when the Governing Council raised interest rates. However, the level of the main refinancing rate gave a misleading impression of the *effective* monetary stance in the Eurozone during this period.

The Governing Council sets three key interest rates at its policy meetings:

- *The main refinancing rate*: the reference rate on the Eurosystem's main refinancing operations, either in the form of a minimum bid rate in variable rate tenders or the chosen rate in fixed rate tenders.
- *The marginal lending rate*: the interest rate on the marginal lending facility, the standing facility through which banks can borrow reserves overnight from the Eurosystem.
- *The deposit rate*: the interest rate on the deposit facility, the standing facility through which banks can deposit excess reserves (i.e., over and above required reserves).

In normal times, the purpose of the ECB's market operations is to keep short-term money market rates, and in particular the overnight rate (known as EONIA, or Euro OverNight Index Average (EONIA)) in line with the minimum bid rate in the main refinancing operations set by the Governing Council (ECB 2010). However, the overnight rate drifted away from the main refinancing rate towards the end of 2008 and settled close to (but a little above) the deposit rate, as a result of the changes to those market operations that were introduced by the Governing Council and the banks' demand for liquidity.

Our story begins with the series of measures that the Governing Council announced during October 2008:

- *Switch to fixed rate full allotment*: On 8 October, the Governing Council decided to switch from variable rate to fixed rate tenders for the main refinancing operations, with banks able to obtain as much liquidity as they wanted (subject to having sufficient collateral). On 15 October, this decision was extended to the set of longer-term refinancing operations that the Eurosystem was conducting.
- *Widening the collateral pool*: On 15 October, the Council expanded the set of collateral that banks could use to obtain cash in the refinancing operations (ECB 2008). In particular, the Council added the following instruments: marketable debt denominated in other major currencies; euro-denominated syndicated credit claims; debt instruments issued by banks (such as certificates of deposits) traded in unregulated markets; and subordinated debt protected by a guarantee, which together amounted to assets worth €870 billion, or about 7 % of the total amount of eligible marketable assets (ECB 2009). Moreover, the Council lowered the ratings threshold for marketable and non-marketable assets from A- to BBB-, with the exception of asset-backed securities.
- *Narrowing the corridor*: On 8 October, the Council decided to narrow the corridor between the interest rates on the standing facilities from 200 to 100 basis points, so despite a 50 basis point cut in the main refinancing rate to 3.75 % the deposit rate was left unchanged and the marginal lending rate was cut by 100 basis points.

As a result of the first measure, the stock of central bank reserves became entirely demand-determined subject to the collateral constraint, and as a result of the second measure the banks were able to demand more cash if they wanted to. As anticipated, demand for reserves increased significantly: total provision of liquidity stood at €463 billion on 7 October but averaged around €800 billion through November and December.

The system had a surplus of reserves: the total stock of reserves was far in excess of the total reserves that the banks were required to hold. Of course, those excess reserves were not evenly distributed across the system, with chronic imbalances in the payment flows between banks leading to surpluses piling up in predictable places. As a result of the third measure the incentive to lend those excess reserves in the interbank market has diminished, because the return on the 'inside option'—depositing excess reserves at the Eurosystem and being paid the deposit rate—had not fallen in line with the main refinancing rate. The average daily volume in the overnight market dropped from €52 billion to €34 billion after the corridor was narrowed, and usage of the deposit facility ballooned (ECB 2009). But what activity did take place in the market was at a lower rate: for those banks who could still raise funds in the money market the cost of funding fell below the main refinancing rate.

With a narrow corridor, the Eurosystem balance sheet was crowding out activity in the money markets to some extent: surplus banks redeposited those reserves with the Eurosystem rather than lend them out in the market. With tensions easing in the money markets, the Council decided on 18 December that, as of the maintenance period that would start in late January 2009, the corridor would be widened back out again to 200 basis points to encourage a resumption of normal activity in the money market. Turnover did recover as the 'inside option' on excess liquidity fell: the deposit rate was now 1 % (relative to a main refinancing rate of 2 %), and unsurprisingly the cost of funding in the interbank market fell too: between 9 October 2008 and 20 January 2009, the spread between EONIA and the main refinancing rate stood at 27 basis points, but the spread rose to 62 basis points in the period from 21 January to 12 May 2009.

In short, the introduction of fixed rate full allotment tenders and the widening of the collateral pool led to a chronic surplus of reserves within the system, which drove overnight rates below the main refinancing rate and towards the 'inside option' for banks with excess reserves (the deposit rate). As the ECB staff noted, this represented something of a break with the normal practice of ensuring that overnight rates settle on the main policy rate selected by the policymaker (ECB 2010):

> Market participants' strong demand for liquidity, which has been fully accommodated by the Eurosystem, has caused overnight money market rates to fall significantly below the main refinancing rate and relatively close to the deposit rate. In this respect, the non-standard measures have temporarily led to a different relationship between monetary policy decisions and monetary policy operations.

In other words, the level of the main refinancing rate was no longer an accurate gauge of the monetary stance as reflected in the level of official interest rates as ECB Executive Board member Benoît Cœuré would later observe at a moment when the main refinancing rate was 0.05 % (Cœuré 2014):

[I]n an environment of excess liquidity and persistent frictions in financial markets, as we see today, it is no longer possible to define our stance by a unique "main" policy rate. If one were willing to proxy such a rate with the EONIA, one would conclude that our policy rates stand at around minus 10 basis points.

2.7   Continental Europe Goes Sub-Zero: Negative Interest Rates

After the initial race to the bottom, the interest in official interest rates as a tool of monetary policy waned in the world's major central banks and attention turned to the impact of outright purchases. However, the case for cutting rates further came back on the agenda in 2014 and would ultimately lead to several central banks introducing a negative policy rate.

For central banks that are operating a corridor system the decision to go 'sub-zero' initially concerns the deposit rate (i.e., the interest rate at which reserves can be deposited via the Standing Facilities, at the lower end of the corridor). The central bank has a choice. Either you continue to lower the main policy rate and leave the deposit rate at zero and therefore narrow at least the bottom half of the corridor, or you take the plunge and take the deposit rate into negative territory. Initially, the Governing Council of the ECB chose the former option: the main refinancing rate was cut twice in 2013, in May (from 0.75 % to 0.5 %) and November (from 0.5 % to 0.25 %), whilst the deposit rate was left unchanged at zero. There were two key concerns around the asymmetric rate cuts which left the deposit rate unchanged and narrowed the corridor that would help tip the balance in favour of taking the deposit rate into negative territory (Cœuré 2014):

- *Financial stability*: Compressing the corridor, and in particular the spread between the deposit rate and the main refinancing rate in a fixed rate full allotment regime, crowds out activity in the money market, potentially causing lasting damage to that core market, which central bankers are keen to avoid (Bini Smaghi 2008; Cœuré 2012).
- *Monetary stability*: An interest rate cut that includes a deposit rate cut is likely to be more powerful in an environment of excess reserves, because the deposit rate is the anchor for overnight rates, which ultimately feeds into the broad constellation of asset prices. Allied to that, the decision to lower the deposit rate was also seen as enhancing the credibility of the Council's strategy and its commitment to restore price stability.

The next time the ECB cut rates the main refinancing rate was left unchanged and the deposit rate was taken into negative territory (although the main refinancing rate would later be taken down to 0 % in March 2016 when the deposit rate hit −0.40 %). In the end, a number of European central banks would decide to take at least one of their key interest rates into negative territory, and in some cases quite far into negative territory (for more details see Bech and Malkhozov (2016)):

- *Denmark*: The Danmarks Nationalbank cut the interest rate on certificates of deposits (seven-day deposits at the central bank) to −0.20 % in July 2012. The rate was later raised and was briefly back into positive territory in 2014, but was subsequently taken back below zero and reached −0.75 % in February 2015, before being raised by 10 basis points in January 2016.
- *Euro area*: The ECB took the deposit rate into negative territory in June 2014 (reducing the rate from zero to −0.10 %) and then cut the rate a further 10 basis points in September 2014, by a further 10 basis points in December 2015 and then again by a further 10 basis points in the March 2016 meeting
- *Sweden*: The Riksbank took the deposit rate into negative territory in July 2014 (reducing the rate from zero to −0.50 %) and then took the repo rate into negative territory in February 2015 (reducing the rate from zero to −0.10 %). By July 2015, the repo rate had reached −0.35 % and the deposit rate −1.10 %, and by February 2016 those rates were cut further to −0.50 % and −1.25 % respectively.
- *Switzerland*: The SNB imposed a negative rate (−0.25 %) on reserve balances and relocated its target range for the three-month interbank lending rate to the interval from −0.75 to 0.25 % in December 2014. In January 2015, the SNB lowered the rate on reserve balances to −0.75 %, and relocated the target range by a further 50 basis points to between −0.25 % and −1.25 %.

As we will go on to discuss, the debate over the transmission mechanism of negative policy rates has primarily focused on the impact via the banking sector (remember that the reason that BoE decided to stop cutting Bank Rate at 0.5 % in 2009 and more recently reached the conclusion that further cuts were possible was a direct result of an assessment of the impact of monetary policy on the banking sector). However, it would be a mistake to think that the transmission of negative rates operates exclusively through the banking system. There are the traditional channels which operate via wholesale financial markets, with a lower expected path of the policy rate in, say, the Eurozone, priced into the yield curve and then on into the broad constellation of euro-denominated asset prices. Indeed, there might be an additional impact on the yield curve as the cut in the policy rate today shifts investors' expectations of how low central banks can take the policy rate at any point in the future, and a less truncated distribution of possible outcomes for the policy rate in the future ought to lower the average expected rate. Given that asset price response, a negative policy rate can therefore be expected to boost aggregate demand in the standard fashion through the transmission channels that operate via wholesale financial markets: via net trade, thanks to a cheaper currency (given news on interest rate differentials); via investment, thanks to a cheaper cost of capital for companies looking to issue debt or equity in capital markets; and via consumption thanks to the wealth effects from higher asset valuations.

In practice, the transmission of negative official interest rates through wholesale markets has been relatively straightforward: through money markets and out into the broader constellation of asset prices, including the exchange rate. Jensen and Spange (2015) note that the pass-through of the policy stance into Danish money market rates was unaffected by the move into negative territory, and Cœuré (2014) notes that volumes actually *rose* when EONIA started trading in negative territory following the first ECB rate cut in June. Pass-through in retail markets is more complicated on account of the endowment effect discussed earlier: if banks cannot or will not charge negative rates (or impose charges for access to sight deposits) to retail customers then it is unlikely that the negative rate will be fully passed into retail lending rates too. Jensen and Spange (2015) note that whilst pass-through of the policy rate into retail rates is usually high and rapid in Denmark, it has reduced since the advent of negative rates. In particular, banks have not introduced negative rates on household deposits; in contrast, the average effective rate for insurance and pension companies in spring 2015 was broadly in line with the negative policy rate (on certificates of deposit).

One interesting challenge presented by the decision to take the policy rate into negative territory is how to communicate how low rates can ultimately go in a world where there are concerns about whether negative rates are potentially counterproductive (for an excellent exposition see Cœuré (2016)). The problem is there are three distinct issues here: whether the central bank sees any need to cut rates further at a particular juncture (i.e., the likely floor on rates); the point at which the cost benefit analysis of taking the policy rate more negative becomes more counterproductive (i.e., the effective lower bound); and the point at which a negative policy rate starts to lose traction because private sector agents—whether banks or the customers of banks—start running to cash (i.e., the technical lower bound). In practice, the ECB signalled that it had likely reached the lower bound as it cut into negative territory only to cut further at a later date. At the time of writing, the door was left open to testing new lows in the Council's forward guidance that rates would remain 'at present or lower levels for an extended period of time' (ECB 2016).

2.8   Negative Rates and Bank Profitability

As negative policy rates started to become a more familiar feature of the policy landscape, commentators started to question whether they might have unintended side effects—in particular, squeezing bank profitability, which might then lead to a counterproductive tightening in the terms on which banks are willing to lend, blunting the impact of the original monetary stimulus. By the time the Bank of Japan took the decision to go negative, the 'sub-zero' issue had become a central concern of market participants, leading to a decline in bank stocks.

In theory, the BoJ's rate cut package was designed to insulate the banks from the impact of negative policy rates. The BoJ introduced a multi-tiered system, in which the total stock of central bank reserves is allocated to separate tiers so that the central bank can apply the negative rate to a small fraction of the total stock (in the case of the BoJ, the third of three tiers—the 'policy-rate balances'—attracted a negative rate of -0.1 %). In this way, the direct hit on interest receipts from paying a negative rate on central banks reserves is significantly reduced, but so long as the negative rate applies to a sufficiently large stock of reserves it can still act as an anchor on short-term market rates, and then out to the wider spectrum of asset prices including the exchange rate. However, tiering is not quite the panacea it is made out to be.

The fundamental problem is that the impact of negative policy rates on bank profitability is far more complex than purely the mechanical effect of the remuneration of central bank reserves.

First, the threat to bank profitability from the remuneration of central bank reserves is over-stated. Where the stock of reserves is concerned, the impact of a negative policy rate on net interest margin—the gap between the interest receipts from the bank's assets and interest payments on its liabilities— will depend on the interest rate that the commercial banks are paying on their liabilities relative to the rate received on the reserves. When the central bank is conducting a large-scale asset purchase programme, we should expect to see the deposits of non-bank financial institutions increase alongside the stock of central bank reserves (as those institutions sell assets to the central bank). But this is the one customer where the commercial banks are able to charge a negative rate on deposit liabilities, because the outside option for non-bank financial institutions wishing to hold a liquid asset is a whole-sale market rate which should reflect the new (negative) policy rate. Indeed, Jensen and Spange (2015) note that in Denmark, the negative policy rate has been passed through into negative rates on deposits for large companies and financial institutions, for whom those deposits are a substitute for investing funds short-term in the money market. If a commercial bank is paying a nega-tive rate on its central bank reserves but is also paying a negative rate on an equivalent stock of deposits then there is no hit on net interest income.

Second, the threat to bank profitability is not confined to the current remu-neration of central bank reserves. The rate at which market participants expect reserves to be remunerated in the future—which is reflected in the slope of the yield curve—also influences bank profitability given the structural maturity mismatch across banks' balance sheets. Commercial banks borrow short and lend long so if you flatten the curve then you squeeze the in-built return from intermediation, other things equal. Indeed, Borio, Gambacorta and Hofmann (2015) argue that this impact of monetary policy on bank profitability via the yield curve is non-linear—that is, the effect is particularly pronounced when the yield curve is unusually flat (they find a similar non-linearity for short rates: the hit to profitability is particularly pronounced when the short rate is unusually low). If the interest rate on the banks' long-term assets re-price as long-term yields fall then net interest margin will be squeezed so long as banks are unwilling or unable to lower the interest rate they pay on their household and corporate deposits—which remember may already be at the zero bound. The fundamental concern around negative rates is that banks will not feel able to pass through the lower policy rate into the terms on which it offers new loans unless or until it can lower the rate it offers on deposits, and as a result, there is limited pass-through of monetary policy via the banking sector. Of course, where the interest rate on loans is contractually tied to wholesale mar-ket rates, the banks do not get a say in the matter: the squeeze on net inter-est margin is immediate and persists until the banks can re-price the loans. Fortunately, banks can at least get some relief to the extent that the cost of wholesale market debt should fall in sympathy with lower wholesale rates too.

Third, the impact of negative rates on bank profitability is not a one-way street. Given their large leveraged investments in the real economy, banks will benefit from improvement in the macroeconomic backdrop that uncon-ventional monetary stimulus provides (Genay and Podjasek 2014). Default rates will fall and recovery rates on loans will rise as collateral values rise. It is hard to defend the proposition that banks' balance sheets would be in better shape if monetary policy was left on hold, and the economy was allowed to slide into debt deflation. Moreover, it is a mistake to assume that banks' asset portfolios are purely composed of loans to households and companies. Banks also hold financial securities in their available-for-sale or trading portfolios (i.e., not held to maturity), and they should earn capital gains when the lower policy rate inflates asset values.

Fourth, we should expect the banks to adjust their business model in response to the shock of negative rates. Indeed, it is reasonable to assume that banks will have taken out some insurance against this shock in advance—that is, banks ought to be at least partially hedged against movements in the yield curve (Alessandri and Nelson 2015). After the event, we might expect banks to: impose or increase the fees that they charge their customers to have access to current accounts to proxy a negative rate; raise the spread they charge their customers over wholesale rates when they re-price loans; and where possible, encourage their retail customers to switch to term deposits where there is still the capacity to cut rates (although the yield pick up the customer receives for illiquidity is shrinking).

If we assume for a second that negative policy rates *do* squeeze bank profitability what does that imply about the location of the lower bound on the policy rate? The answer likely depends on two factors: the role that banks play in the real economy, and the health of the banking sector.

In an economy where the transmission mechanism of monetary policy around the banking sector is significant then there might still be a lot of stimulus to be had from negative rates even if the banking sector does not pass through the negative policy rate. Of course, one key transmission channel that does not operate via the banking sector is the exchange rate channel. In theory, a central bank in bank-centric economy might still take the policy deep into negative territory even if it expects little transmission through the domestic economy so long as that economy is open (i.e., imports and exports account for a significant share of GDP) and the central bank expects the shift in interest rate differentials to trigger a large movement in the exchange rate. The problem with this policy is that it starts to look a lot like the central bank has adopted an intermediate exchange rate target or, in market parlance, is engaging in currency wars, and if all central banks resort to the same strategy, then relatively little is achieved (Cœuré 2015b; Carney 2016).

If the banks are in relatively good health then a squeeze on net interest margin is probably no big deal from a macro policy perspective. The hit to net interest income can be accommodated through a tweak in dividends and variable compensation of staff. The squeeze on net interest margin matters when banks are reliant on income to absorb expected future losses or to organically regenerate capital that has been depleted by past losses. In this scenario, the implied news on future income can leave banks stranded closer to the resolution boundary for longer, which is clearly a cause for concern for the shareholders of banks and the supervisory community. From a macroeconomic perspective (our focus in this book), the risk that a banking sector might remain in a fragile state for longer is a concern because it suggests that the impediment to the supply of credit is likely to persist for longer.

2.9   Dealing with the Lower Bound

Before the crisis, the consensus in the academic literature was that the probability that policy rates would reach the lower bound was pretty small (with a 2 % inflation target, an economy would be at the lower bound 0 to 5 % of the time) and the probability of falling into a deflationary spiral whilst at the lower bound was very small indeed (Yates 2003). Experiences during the crisis have given fresh impetus to the debate about how to deal with the lower bound. As Cœuré (2015a) observes there are essentially two ways to deal with the problem: reduce the likelihood of hitting the lower bound or remove the lower bound altogether.

2.9.1 Reducing the Likelihood of Hitting the Lower Bound

The probability of hitting the near-ZLB hinges on two key factors:

- *How much room do you have to cut?* The higher the level of the policy rate on average, the more room for manoeuvre the policymaker enjoys—that is, the more scope she has to cut the policy rate before hitting zero.
- *How bad can things get?* The more often that an economy is hit by very large downside shocks, the more likely it is that the central bank will be required to make large cuts in official interest rates that could run up against the lower bound.

It follows that there are several things that policymakers could try in order to reduce the probability of hitting the lower bound in the future:

- *Raise the inflation target.* A higher inflation target will translate into a higher average policy rate (or neutral rate—see later) via the Fisher condition and is therefore the easiest way to significantly reduce the probability of hitting the lower bound (Hunt and Laxton 2001; Ball 2014). However, that higher inflation comes with potentially significant social costs (see Briault [1995] for a discussion).

- *Structural reforms*: In theory, finance ministers could engage in structural reforms to try and raise the potential growth rate of the economy and thereby raise the equilibrium real interest consistent with that average policy rate (Cœuré 2015a). However, it is debatable whether reforms will raise *the growth rate* of potential supply on a scale sufficient to have a meaningful impact on the equilibrium real interest in the medium term.

- *Tighter micro- and macro-prudential regulation*: It is noteworthy that the extreme shocks that drive interest rates policy rates down to very low levels have tended to come in the form of financial crises. Indeed, as we shall go on to discuss, the conventional wisdom before the crisis was that the appropriate monetary policy response to mounting financial imbalances was to wait for any bubble to burst and then 'mop up' afterwards by aggressively cutting interest rates. It follows that prudential interventions which can reduce the frequency and severity of systemic financial crises should reduce the need for large cuts in interest rates in the future.

Another way to reduce the probability of hitting the lower bound is to use other policy instruments to support the economy when it is hit by a large shock, reducing the burden on monetary policy. The obvious candidate here is fiscal policy: for the fiscal authority to cut taxes or raise spending to support aggregate demand. Indeed, the design of the tax and benefit system ensures that fiscal policy serves this role *without finance ministers having to lift a finger*. The so-called automatic stabilisers (see later) ensure that tax receipts fall and spending increases when the economy slows, although finance ministers can and do top-up the automatic stabilisers with discretionary fiscal stimulus, although their contribution to demand management may be tempered by long implementation lags (the need for ministers to agree a policy, to introduce legislation and for the change to take effect). It follows that the more significant the automatic stabilisers are, the smaller the required monetary stimulus in response to any given shock to demand. However, there are costs associated with using fiscal policy in this way: the volatility in tax rates and spending over the cycle can complicate and distort the plans of households and companies (Yates 2003); and the moment where central bankers need a fiscal stimulus the most (in a crisis when there is a significant risk of hitting the lower bound) is also likely to be the moment when finance ministers are least able to provide that stimulus (the public finances are likely to be in a relatively weak state in such a crisis).

2.9.2   Removing the Lower Bound

The more radical solution to the constraint imposed by the lower bound is to eliminate the root cause of the problem: the fact that the nominal return on the other constituent of base money (cash) is zero. Buiter (2009) proposes three ways in which this can be done:

- *Abolish cash*: One radical solution to the asymmetric constraint on the conduct of monetary policy is to remove the lower bound altogether by addressing the root cause of the problem: the fact that the return on the other form of base money (that the private non-bank sector can hold) is bound at zero. If the monetary authority withdraws hard currency from circulation altogether then she can eliminate the source of the lower bound. By happy coincidence this solution doubles as an effective crime-fighting measure, since cash lubricates the underground economy: 'those engaged in tax evasion, money laundering and the financing of terrorism, and those wishing to store the proceeds from crime and the means to commit further crime' (Buiter (2009)). Even if the authorities do not abolish cash altogether they can at least ban high denomination notes (which will increase the cost of storing large amounts of wealth in the form of paper money) and can apply moral pressure on insurance companies not to insure significant holdings of physical cash (which makes storing large amounts of wealth in the form of paper money a far more risky proposition).
- *Tax currency*: Alternatively, the monetary authority 'pays' the same positive and negative interest rate on cash as is applied to central bank reserves—a century-old idea that originally belongs to Silvio Gesell (see Buiter and Panigirtzoglou 2003). This solution requires that the state can identify whether the interest (positive or negative) has been paid on individual notes. One option is to impose expiry dates on cash; if the interest rate is not paid or received by the owner of the cash by the expiry date the note ceases to become legal tender.
- *Break the link between medium of exchange and unit of account*: Finally, the monetary authority removes the existing currency and replaces it with a new medium of exchange (let us call it the groat), but pound sterling is retained as the unit of account (Buiter suggests a number of ways in which the authorities might encourage this outcome from requiring all contracts involving the state to be denominated in sterling to outlawing bank deposits denominated in groats or even declaring all contracts denominated in groats null and void). The BoE sets the interest rate on central bank reserves

(still denominated in pound sterling) and the sequence of spot exchange rates between sterling and groats. The interest rate on sterling-denominated assets can go negative without limit, but the lower bound still applies to groats; however by calibrating the sterling: groat exchange rate that will prevail in the future (relative to the current spot rate) the central bank can remove the incentive to run to groats when the return on sterling assets turns negative (groats offer a higher return than sterling today but will purchase less sterling tomorrow).

Finally, it is worth noting that there are potential drawbacks to these radical proposals, aside from the non-trivial issues of implementation. First, if the reforms led to a reduced demand for base money then governments may lose one (unconventional) source of revenue: seigniorage—that is, the difference between the interest that the monetary authority earns on the assets in which it invests the proceeds of issuing cash and the (negligible) costs of issuing those notes. Second, these reforms might prove deeply unpopular: Cœuré (2015a, b) argues that the guaranteed zero nominal return on cash is deeply ingrained in the psyche of the general public and introducing negative returns on cash would be seen as an unfair wealth tax that would impact on those at the bottom of the wealth distribution.

References

Alessandri, P., & Nelson, B. (2015). Simple banking: Profitability and the yield curve. *Journal of Money, Credit and Banking, 47*(1), 143–175.

Allen, H., & Dent, A. (2010). Managing the circulation of banknotes. *Bank of England Quarterly Bulletin, Q4*, 302–310.

Amiti, M., Itskhoki, O., & Konings, J. (2014). Importers, exporters, and exchange rate disconnect. *American Economic Review, 104*(7), 1942–1978.

Asmundson, I., & Oner, C. (2012). What is money? *IMF Finance and Development, 49*(3).

Ball, L. (2014). *The case for a long-run inflation target of four percent.* IMF Working Paper 14/92.

Barth, M., & Ramey, V. (2002). The cost channel of monetary transmission. In B. Bernanke & K. Rogoff (Eds.), *NBER Macroeconomics Annual.* Cambridge, MA: MIT Press.

Barwell, R., Bell, V., Bunn, P., & Gutiérrez-Domènech, M. (2007). Potential employment in the UK economy. *Bank of England Quarterly Bulletin, Q1*, 60–69.

Batini, N., & Nelson, E. (2001). The lag from monetary policy actions to inflation: Friedman revisited. *International Finance, 4*(3), 381–400.

Bean, C. (2002, November 25). *The MPC and the UK economy: Should we fear the D-words?* Speech.

Bean, C. (2013, May 16). Note on negative interest rates for Treasury Committee.

Bech, M., & Malkhozov, A. (2016). How have central banks implemented negative policy rates. *BIS Quarterly Review, March*, 31–44.

Bernanke, B. (2002, November 21). Deflation: Making sure "it" doesn't happen here. *Speech*.

Bernanke, B. (2004, May 20). *Gradualism*. Speech.

Bernanke, B., & Gertler, M. (1995). Inside the black box. *Journal of Economic Perspectives, 9*(4), 27–48.

Bini Smaghi, L. (2008, December 1). *Restarting a market: The case of the interbank market*. Speech.

Blinder, A. (1998). *Central banking in theory and practice*. Cambridge, MA: MIT Press.

BoE. (1999). *The monetary transmission mechanism*. Report prepared by Bank of England staff under the guidance of the Monetary Policy Committee and published in the *Bank of England Quarterly Bulletin*, May, 161–170.

BoE. (2008). Minutes of the November 2008 meeting of the Monetary Policy Committee.

BoE. (2009a). Minutes of February 2009 meeting of the Monetary Policy Committee.

BoE. (2009b). Minutes of March 2009 meeting of the Monetary Policy Committee.

BoE. (2012, November 21). Minutes of the November 2012 Monetary Policy Committee meeting.

BoE. (2015, February 12). Governor's letter to the Chancellor.

Borio, C., Gambacorta, L., & Hofmann, B. (2015). *The influence of monetary policy on bank profitability*. BIS Working Paper 514.

Brainard, W. (1967). Uncertainty and the effectiveness of policy. *American Economic Review, 57*(2), 411–425.

Breeden, D. (1979). An intertemporal asset pricing model with stochastic consumption and investment opportunities. *Journal of Financial Economics, 7*, 265–296.

Briault, C. (1995). The costs of inflation. *Bank of England Quarterly Bulletin, February*, 33–45.

Buisán, A., Learmonth, D., & Sebastiá-Barriel, M. (2006). UK export performance by industry. *Bank of England Quarterly Bulletin, Q3*, 308–316.

Buiter, W. (2008, March 25). How do the Bank of England and the monetary policy committee manage liquidity? *Blog*.

Buiter, W. (2009). *Negative nominal interest rates*. NBER Working Paper 15118.

Buiter, W., & Panigirtzoglou, N. (2003). Overcoming the zero bound on nominal interest rates with negative interest on currency: Gesell's solution. *The Economic Journal, 113*, 723–746.

Button, R., Pezzini, S., & Rossiter, N. (2010). Understanding the price of new lending to households. *Bank of England Quarterly Bulletin, Q3*, 172–182.

Caplin, A., & Spulber, D. (1987). Menu costs and the neutrality of money. *Quarterly Journal of Economics, 102*(4), 703–725.

Carney, M. (2016, February 26). *Redeeming an unforgiving world*. Speech.

Case, K., Shiller, R., & Quigley, J. (2001). *Comparing wealth effects: The stock market versus the housing market*. NBER Working Paper 8606.

Chadha, J., Macmillan, P., & Nolan, C. (2007). Independence day for the 'Old Lady': A natural experiment on the implications of central bank independence. *Manchester School, 75*(3), 311–327.

Christiano, L., & Eichenbaum, M. (1992). Liquidity effects and the monetary transmission mechanism. *American Economic Review, 82*(2), 346–353.

Clews, R., Salmon, C., & Weeken, O. (2010). The Bank's money market framework. *Bank of England Quarterly Bulletin, Q4*, 292–301.

Cœuré, B. (2012, February 19). *Central banks and the challenges of the zero lower bound*. Speech.

Cœuré, B. (2014, September 9). *Life below zero*. Speech.

Cœuré, B. (2015a, May 18). *How binding is the zero lower bound?* Speech.

Cœuré, B. (2015b, November 21). *Paradigm lost*. Speech.

Cœuré, B. (2016, July 28). Assessing the implications of negative interest rates, *Speech*.

Cromb, R., & Fernandez-Corugedo, E. (2004). *Long-term interest rates, wealth and consumption*. Bank of England Working Paper 243.

Dent, A., & Dison, W. (2012). The Bank of England's Real-Time Gross Settlement infrastructure. *Bank of England Quarterly Bulletin, Q3*, 234–243.

Disyatat, P. (2008). *Monetary policy implementation: Misconceptions and their consequences*. BIS Working Papers 269.

ECB. (2008, October 15). *Measures to further expand the collateral framework and enhance the provision of liquidity*. Press release.

ECB. (2009). The implementation of monetary policy since August 2007. *ECB Monthly Bulletin, July*, 75–89.

ECB. (2010). The ECB's monetary stance during the financial crisis. *ECB Monthly Bulletin, January*, 63–71.

ECB. (2016). Introductory statement to the March 10 press conference.

Elder, R., & Tsoukalas, J. (2006). Investing in inventories. *Bank of England Quarterly Bulletin, Summer*, 155–160.

Ellis, C., & Turnbull, K. (2007). Gauging capacity pressures within businesses. *Bank of England Quarterly Bulletin, Q1*, 79–85.

Elmendorf, D. (1996). *The effect of interest-rate changes on household saving and consumption: A survey*. Board of Governors of the Federal Reserve System Finance and Economics Discussion Series, 96–27.7.

Fazzari, S., Hubbard, R., & Petersen, B. (1988). Financing constraints and corporate investment. *Brookings Papers on Economic Activity*, 141–195.

Fish, T., & Whymark, R. (2015). How has cash usage evolved in recent decades? What might drive demand in the future? *Bank of England Quarterly Bulletin, Q3*, 1–12.

Fisher, I. (1933). The debt-deflation theory of great depressions. *Econometrica, 1*(4), 37–357.

Fisher, P. (2011, March 30). *Recent developments in the sterling monetary framework.* Speech.

Friedman, M. (1957). *A theory of the consumption function.* Princeton: Princeton University Press.

Friedman, M. (1961). The lag in effect of monetary policy. *Journal of Political Economy, 69*(5), 447–466.

Friedman, M. (1972). Have monetary policies failed? *American Economic Review, 62*(2), 11–18.

Genay, H., & Podjasek, R. (2014). *What is the impact of a low interest rate environment on bank profitability?* Chicago Fed Letter, Essays on Issues, 324.

Gertler, M., & Gilchrist, S. (1994). Monetary policy, business cycles, and the behavior of small manufacturing firms. *Quarterly Journal of Economics, 109*(2), 309–340.

Goodfriend, M., & King, R. (1997). The new neoclassical synthesis and the role of monetary policy. In B. Bernanke & J. Rotemberg (Eds.). *NBER Macroeconomics Annual, 12,* 231–296.

Grant, K., Vlieghe, G., & Brigden, A. (2004). Assessing the stability of narrow money demand in the United Kingdom. *Bank of England Quarterly Bulletin, Summer,* 131–141.

Haldane, A., & Read, V. (1999). Monetary policy and the yield curve. *Bank of England Quarterly Bulletin, May,* 171–176.

Havranek, T., & Rusnak, M. (2013). Transmission lags of monetary policy: A meta-analysis. *International Journal of Central Banking, 9*(4), 39–75.

Hofmann, B., & Mizen, P. (2004). Rate pass-through and monetary transmission: Evidence from individual financial institutions' retail rates. *Economica, 71,* 99–123.

Hunt, B., & Laxton, D. (2001). *The zero interest rate floor (ZIF) and its implications for monetary policy in Japan.* IMF Working Papers 01/186.

Janssen, N. (1996). Can we explain the shift in M0 velocity? Some time-series and cross-section evidence. *Bank of England Quarterly Bulletin, February,* 39–48.

Jensen, C., & Spange, M. (2015). Interest rate pass-through and the demand for cash at negative interest rates. *Danmarks Nationalbank Monetary Review, Q2,* 1–12.

Jevons, W. (1875). *Money and the mechanism of exchange.* New York: D. Appleton.

Kamath, K., & Paul, V. (2011). Understanding recent developments in UK external trade. *Bank of England Quarterly Bulletin, Q4,* 294–304.

Kashyap, A., Stein, J., & Lamont, O. (1994). Credit conditions and the cyclical behavior of inventories. *Quarterly Journal of Economics, 109,* 565–592.

King, M. (1997, October 29). The inflation target five years on, *Speech.*

King, R., & Wolman, A. (1999). What should the monetary authority do when prices are sticky? In J. Taylor (Ed.), *Monetary policy rules.* Chicago: University of Chicago.

Kiyotaki, N., & Wright, R. (1989). On money as a medium of exchange. *Journal of Political Economy, 97*(4), 927–954.

Mac Coille, C., Mayhew, K., & Turnbull, K. (2009). Accounting for the stability of the UK terms of trade. *Bank of England Quarterly Bulletin, Q4*, 286–292.

McAndrews, J. (2015, May 8). *Negative nominal central bank policy rates: Where is the lower bound?* Speech.

McLeay, M., Radia, A., & Thomas, R. (2014a). Money in the modern economy: An introduction. *Bank of England Quarterly Bulletin, Q1*, 4–13.

McLeay, M., Radia, A., & Thomas, R. (2014b). Money creation in the modern economy. *Bank of England Quarterly Bulletin, Q1*, 14–27.

Miles, D. (2015, January 22). *What can monetary policy do?* Speech.

Rabanal, P. (2007). Does inflation increase after a monetary policy tightening? *Journal of Economic Dynamics and Control, 31*, 906–937.

Ravenna, F., & Walsh, C. (2006). Optimal monetary policy with the cost channel. *Journal of Monetary Economics, 53*, 199–216.

Ritter, J. (1995). The transition from barter to fiat money. *American Economic Review, 85*(1), 134–149.

Rudebusch, G. (2006). Monetary policy inertia: Fact or fiction? *International Journal of Central Banking, 2*(4), 85–135.

Tucker, P. (2004, July 28). *Managing the Central Bank's balance sheet: Where monetary policy meets financial stability.* Speech.

Vila Wetherilt, A., & Weeken, O. (2002). Equity valuation measures: What can they tell us? *Bank of England Quarterly Bulletin, Winter*, 391–403.

Weeken, O. (2004). Asset pricing and the housing market. *Bank of England Quarterly Bulletin*, Spring, 32–41.

Wiseman, J. (2007). The pretend market for money. *Central Banking, 18*(1), 27–36.

Wiseman, J. (2011, May 18). *The Old Lady's defence.* Blog.

Woodford, M. (2003). Optimal monetary policy inertia. *Review of Economic Studies, 70*, 861–886.

Yashiv, E. (2000). Hiring as investment behavior. *Review of Economic Dynamics, 3*(3), 486–522.

Yates, A. (2003). Monetary policy and the zero bound to nominal interest rates. *Bank of England Quarterly Bulletin, Spring*, 27–37.

3

Quantitative Easing: Bond Buying to the Rescue

From a monetary policy perspective, the key event during the post-crash period was the emergence of asset purchases as the primary tool of policy. However, it would be a mistake to think that this was a revolution in the conduct of monetary policy. The BoJ had resorted to so-called QE in an attempt to reflate the economy as the policy rate approached the lower bound (Spiegel 2006). Indeed, Paul Tucker made the following observations about how the MPC might go about implementing QE in the UK during the so-called Great Stability when most thought it most unlikely that the Bank would ever hit the lower bound (Tucker 2004):

> We would, for example, need to form a view – or individual views – on whether the injection of base money was expected to work through affecting the risk-free rate, or risk and liquidity premia on other financial assets, or both. But that lies beyond my scope today. Rather, I want to make two points about the implementation framework. First, as I have described, the Bank's new framework will make provision for the acquisition of longer-term assets (eg government securities) as part and parcel of managing our overall balance sheet in a sensible way, while making sure that the banking system is square. Faced with a liquidity trap, the Bank could in principle make purchases of securities to inject base money, which would be within our vires and technically would be 'excess reserves'. We would need to do so in a way that preserved the integrity of our balance sheet.

Nor is it even valid to argue that the Japanese 'invented' QE. Chabot and Herman (2013) note that in the era before the creation of the Fed, the US Department of the Treasury regularly engaged in interventions which had a

© The Editor(s) (if applicable) and The Author(s) 2016
R. Barwell, *Macroeconomic Policy after the Crash*,
DOI 10.1057/978-1-137-51592-6_3

distinctly QE flavour: changing the volumes of bonds and duration risk in the private sector's portfolio. All that having been said, we now turn to discuss the design and implementation of QE in the UK.

3.1   The Bank Rate Shortfall

We have already described the race to the bottom that occurred in late 2008 and early 2009: official interest rates were cut close to the floor. However, for several central banks those interest rate cuts would prove insufficient. The MPC reached the same conclusion as the Federal Open Market Committee (FOMC) in the USA: something more would need to be done.

Rudebusch (2009) offers a neat illustration of the scale of the problem facing the Fed. Based on simple policy rules (rules of thumb which are intended to capture the optimal monetary policy response to a given set of circumstances—see later), Rudebusch estimated that the FOMC would have to reduce the Fed Funds Rate to −5 % by the end of 2009—that is, well beyond most reasonable estimates of where the true lower bound lies if it wanted to impart the optimal stimulus. That gap between that optimal policy setting and the actual policy rate—which Rudebusch dubbed the 'monetary policy funds rate shortfall'—was not only sizeable but was also expected to persist: Rudebusch estimated that it would take several years of strong growth before the policy rules would point to an interest rate above zero. Rudebusch observed that the FOMC's decision to expand its balance sheet through a programme of asset purchases was one way to respond to that funds rate shortfall and the constraint imposed by the lower bound; looking ahead, he also made what would turn out to be a prescient remark about the potential expansion of the Fed's balance sheet (Rudebusch 2009):

> Some outside forecasters have warned of a deeper and more protracted recession, in which case, the monetary policy funds rate shortfall and the balance sheet expansion would be even larger and more persistent.

The MPC was confronted by a 'Bank Rate shortfall' of its own in March 2009 when Bank Rate reached an effective floor of 0.5 %. The previous month the Committee had already reached the conclusion that it might need to rely on asset purchases in order to achieve its remit and had agreed that the Governor should write to the Chancellor to seek approval for the Bank to conduct asset purchases of government bonds and other securities funded by the creation of central bank reserves (BoE 2009a). The Minutes of the March meeting reveal that the Committee believed that the deteriorating outlook for nominal demand implied 'a substantial risk that inflation would undershoot the target in the medium term', and the Committee concluded that asset purchases funded through the creation of central bank reserves would be 'necessary in order to increase nominal spending growth to a rate consistent with meeting the inflation target in the medium term' (BoE 2009b). BoE-QE had begun.

3.2   The Modalities of BoE-QE: What the Bank Bought, When and Why

The Committee launched BoE-QE in March 2009 and in the months and years that followed both the scale and the design of the scheme would change. The details of the asset purchase programme that was agreed at the March 2009 meeting were as follows:

- *Scale of purchases*: The Committee ultimately agreed that an increase of between £50 and £100 billion of central bank reserves was required in order to achieve the Committee's remit. Brainard-type arguments were made for a modest initial announcement, given the uncertainty around the impact of asset purchases, whilst the fact that the risks to the inflation outlook were skewed to the downside and the need to convince people of the efficacy of this new instrument were cited as reasons for a more aggressive first response. Ultimately, the Committee agreed a £75 billion package of asset purchases to be conducted over a three-month period.
- *Assets*: The Bank had already begun purchases of private sector assets (discussed elsewhere in this book) as an agent of the government, funded by issuance of Treasury bills. The Committee decided to begin financing those purchases via the creation of central bank reserves. However, the Committee concluded that this market lacked the sufficient depth to conduct purchases on the required scale, and noted that the original purpose of the private sector asset purchases scheme was 'to reduce spreads and to improve the flow of credit' rather than to enable the injection of a given quantity of money into the system. The Committee therefore chose to focus on purchases of government debt.
- *Restrictions*: The Committee believed that purchases would be more effective if assets were purchased from non-bank financial (NBF) institutions and therefore chose to exclude bonds with residual maturity of less than five years (because the short end of the curve was the preferred habitat of banks and overseas central banks) and the Bank was also conscious of

minimising the disruption to institutional investors and therefore chose to exclude conventional bonds with residual maturity in excess of 25 years and index-linked gilts altogether. Gilts that had recently been issued by the Debt Management Office (DMO) were also excluded.

- *How*: The purchase were conducted via reverse auctions, in which counter-parties were invited to sell assets to the Bank. Each auction would include both a competitive and non-competitive offer element (i.e., with and without an offer price), with the amount allocated to the latter announced before the competitive auction. The Bank's original plan was to conduct two auctions each week: one for bonds with a residual maturity of between five and ten years, and the other for bonds between 10 and 25 years,

- *By whom*: The purchases were conducted by the BOE Asset Purchase Facility Fund Limited (the Fund or APF), a wholly owned subsidiary of the Bank, which had been originally established on 30 January to conduct the Bank's T(reasury)-bill-financed purchases of private sector assets. The APF's QE purchases are funded by a loan from the Bank on which it pays Bank Rate, and the Bank funds that loan through the creation of central bank reserves.

- *Risk management*: The APF's operations were fully indemnified for loss by the Treasury. Likewise, any residual surplus that remained at the end of the purchase programme (net of any fees, operating costs and any tax payable) was also due to the Treasury. In effect, the Bank has no economic interest in the Fund. Whilst Bank Rate remained at 0.5 %, the coupon income that the Fund would receive was set to far exceed the interest rate on its loan from the Bank, leading to an accumulation of cash.

- *Excess Reserves*: The asset purchase programme would inevitably lead to a significant increase in the stock of central bank reserves in the system, likely far in excess of the cumulative targets of the banks. The Bank therefore suspended the system of reserve targets and penalties; instead, the Bank announced that it would remunerate all reserves at Bank Rate.

By May, the programme was upscaled by £50 billion to £125 billion and then in August the scheme was expanded again by another £50 billion to £175 billion. Those expansions in the scale of purchases required modifications to the design of the programme:

- *Issue limits*: The Bank announced that it would not buy individual gilts where its holdings exceeded 70 % of the 'free float' (i.e., the total amount in issue minus government holdings).

- *Buy longer maturities*: At its August meeting, the Committee agreed to remove the self-imposed constraint not to buy at the long end: from this point on, conventional gilts with a minimum residual maturity of greater than three years were eligible.
- *More auctions*: The Bank moved over to running three reverse auctions a week, split by maturity: for bonds with maturity of three to ten years on one day, 10–25 on another and greater than 25 years on the third day.
- *Gilt lending*: The Bank decided to make purchased gilts available to the DMO, which could then be loaned back to market participants in exchange for other gilts to ease shortages of particular bonds; to have loaned the bonds out for cash would have undermined the whole premise of QE.

In November 2010, the Committee agreed a further £25 billion expansion in the asset purchase programme, taking the stock of purchases assets to £200 billion. This would mark the end of the first of what would turn out to be three instalments of QE in the UK (this is one example where the narrative in this book has been over-taken by events: the Bank would relaunch QE in the aftermath of the EU referendum)..

In October 2011, the Committee agreed to re-commence asset purchases, increasing the stock of purchased assets by £75 billion over a four-month period, with purchases spread evenly over the eligible maturity spectrum. Almost as soon as that programme was completed, the MPC agreed a further £50 billion expansion in the stock of purchased assets at the February 2012 meeting over a three-month period. At this point, the Bank made a minor tweak to the 'maturity buckets' used in the auction process—with auctions in the 3- to 7-year sector, the 7- to 15-year sector and the over-15 year sector—to bring the Bank's operations in line with those of the DMO.

The final instalment of BoE-QE came in July 2012 when the Committee decided to expand the stock of purchased assets by a further £50 billion over a four-month period, taking the grand total to £375 billion.

Upon completion of that set of purchases, the Chancellor and Governor agreed that the APF would transfer the net interest income that had been accumulating on its balance sheet (the difference between the coupon income on bonds and the interest rate on the loan) to the Treasury, with the Chancellor arguing that the APF hoarding that cash was inefficient, since the government was required to borrow in the market to fund those coupon payments (Osborne 2012).

Each quarter the net interest income less any income or expenses incurred in that quarter and any known expenses of the APF in the following quarter would be transferred (and if the latter is greater than the former then a transfer is made in the opposite direction), with the outstanding stock of net interest income disbursed over the course of nine months (McLaren and Smith 2013). The flip side of this decision is that it increases the expected scale of future payments *to the APF*, by removing the buffer of cash that could otherwise have absorbed losses. The gilts were purchased in an era of ultra-low interest rates (and hence elevated prices) so the APF will likely receive less for the bonds that it paid for the bonds if the bonds are sold back into the market and it will almost always lose money if it holds the bonds to maturity; and of course, in the meantime, the APF's net interest income will sooner or later be squeezed by increases in Bank Rate (see McLaren and Smith [2013] for a detailed discussion of the likely path of payments between the Treasury and the APF). In short, the government was trading off borrowing less in the present day when the costs of servicing debt were low but the fiscal rules were constraining the Chancellor's room for manoeuvre, for borrowing more in the future.

Another interesting implication of this decision is its impact on the effective monetary stance (Giles 2012). As the Committee observed in its November policy meeting, this decision was broadly equivalent to the Committee expanding the stock of purchased assets since the government planned to use these funds to pay down debt, which would involve a reduction in the stock of government debt in private hands, and a corresponding increase in the amount of cash. The Committee therefore concluded that the Chancellor's proposal amounted to a 'small easing in monetary conditions' (BoE 2012).

The final issue to deal with here is reinvestment. Given that the Bank began its QE programme in spring 2009 it was simply a matter of time before QE gilts started to mature. That moment arrived in February 2013 when the Committee duly voted to reinvest the £6.6 billion proceeds of the March 2013 gilt which was set to mature at the time of the March policy meeting. These rules of engagement on reinvestment would later be set within the parameters of the Bank's forward guidance (to which we shall turn in due course).

3.3   A Taxonomy of Asset Purchase Programmes

Central banks have launched a number of asset purchase programmes since the crash but not all of them correspond to the gilt purchase programme described above (see Fawley and Neely [2013] for an extensive review). For example, the ECB alone has created:

- *CBPP1-3*: three separate covered bond purchase programmes
- *ABSPP*: an asset-backed security purchase programme

- *SMP and OMT*: two sovereign bond purchase programmes for countries in distress (of which only one was activated)
- *PSPP*: a public sector purchase programme (which includes conventional and index-linked sovereign debt, agency debt and supranational debt, and later extended to include paper issued by regional and local governments)
- *CSPP*: a corporate bond purchase programme, covering investment-grade euro-denominated bonds issued by non-bank corporations established in the euro area

These schemes varied in terms of the asset class that was the focus of the programme and the size and duration of purchases, reflecting a more fundamental difference in terms of the objective of the programme—in particular, whether the scheme is designed to achieve *monetary (or price) stability* or whether the objective of the scheme fits under the broad umbrella *financial stability*. Our focus in this section is on the former scheme (with the latter discussed in the companion volume). However, given the confused nature of the debate over these different types of programme (see Klyuev et al. 2009) we shall now briefly review the key differences between these programmes.

At first glance, it would seem that there is little ambiguity around the objective of purchase programmes motivated by monetary stability concerns. However, even here we can differentiate between a conventional and an unconventional use of the balance sheet to achieve monetary objectives that reflect the nature of the nominal anchor in a particular regime:

- *QE*: a scheme designed to achieve the central bank's inflation target
- *FX interventions*: a scheme designed to manage or maintain the value of the currency with the ultimate objective of achieving price stability

Both of these asset purchase programmes are designed to aid the pursuit of price stability, although the latter is clearly expressed in terms of an intermediate objective: stabilising the currency. In practice, the former—QE—has dominated the academic and policy debates during this period and we will focus on this form of purchase programme in what follows. Nonetheless, it is worth noting that the latter—large-scale asset purchases to stabilise the currency—was attempted during this period. The SNB had to make significant purchases of foreign currency between 6 September 2011 and 15 January 2015 in order to enforce its 'minimum exchange rate policy'—the central bank stated that it would not tolerate a bilateral exchange rate of the Swiss franc to the euro below CHF1.20—before the policy was ultimately discontinued (Zurbrugg 2015).

Indeed, although these two forms of intervention may feel very different, it is worth noting that the transmission mechanism of these currency interventions has a lot in common with that of the more conventional QE programmes, with the literature emphasising the same portfolio balance and signalling channels that we will go on to discuss in the context of QE (Sarno and Taylor 2001). To give one example, the Japanese FX interventions in 2003–04 are thought to have lowered bond yields around the globe via the portfolio rebalancing channel as the Japanese Ministry of Finance invested their newly acquired dollars in US government bonds (Gerlach-Kristen et al. 2012).

When it comes to interventions for financial stability purposes, we can identify a number of distinct objectives for asset purchase programmes (which will be discussed in more detail elsewhere):

- *Market maker of last resort (MMLR)*: a scheme designed to restore liquidity in capital markets—typically for debt securities issued by companies—thereby limiting the compensation that investors may demand for liquidity risk
- *Risk taker of last resort (RTLR)*: a scheme designed to put a floor under the price of a risk asset—that is, including the compensation for credit risk as well as liquidity risk
- *Flow credit easing (Flow-CE)*: a scheme designed to ease the flow of bank credit to the real economy when the constraint is perceived to be that the costs of originating and either holding or distributing the marginal loan are excessive (i.e., out of line with fundamentals)
- *Stock credit easing (Stock-CE)*: a scheme designed to ease the flow of bank credit to the real economy when the constraint is perceived to be the banks' collective desire to shrink balance

The size and duration of these different programmes will be driven by their objective respect. Asset purchases designed to achieve monetary policy objectives have tended to be large in absolute size, reflecting central bankers' beliefs about the scale of the disinflation problem they were facing and the transmission mechanism of asset purchases (the impact of $100 billion/£100 billion/€100 billion of asset purchases on inflation). There are two stylised variants of QE, although the ECB programme was actually a blend of the two (with a calendar year reference point for the monthly flow of purchases but with a clear signal that purchases will continue beyond that point if circumstances dictate):

- *Fixed amount over a fixed period*: The policymaker announces a given flow of purchases within a specific period of time, but retains the option to

extend the programme or even curtail the announced programme of purchases as circumstances dictate. This is the model used by the BOE.

- *Open-ended*: The policymaker announces that purchases will continue,
typically at some specified pace (amount per period) until some objective
has been achieved. This is the approach taken by the Fed in its QE3 programme and the ECB in its public sector purchase programme.

The size, flow and duration of purchase programmes driven by financial
stability objectives can and do vary significantly. For example, the BOE's
MMLR interventions had relatively modest ambitions and were therefore
conducted on a modest scale (Fisher 2010). Similarly, a Flow-CE scheme is
likely to involve a more modest rate of purchases spread over a much longer
period of time than a Stock-CE scheme. Indeed, the Flow-CE scheme may
require a commitment to conduct a steady flow of asset purchases over an
extended period of time in order to convince banks that at some point in the
future they will be able to distribute the loans that they originate today and
to convince investors that at some point in the future they will be able to sell
securitised bundles of loans that they purchase today.

The focus of the purchase programme will reflect the objective. It is often
the case that monetary stability programmes focus on public sector assets
(debt issued by government) and financial stability programmes focus on private sector assets (securities issued by private sector institutions) but this need
not be the case. The focus of schemes motivated by financial sector objectives
will be driven by the location of the problem: an MMLR operation might be
focused on the market for corporate bonds (such as the BOE's scheme) whilst
an RTLR might be focused on sovereign bonds (such as the ECB's Securities
Market Programme [SMP]). The set of eligible assets in a scheme driven by
monetary stability objectives is largely determined by the scale of purchases
in those schemes: central banks will focus on markets that are large enough to
withstand the anticipated cumulative flow of purchases without eviscerating
market liquidity, which explains the preference for government bonds given
the relative size of public versus private debt markets. However, the key point
to note here is that one cannot classify a purchase programme purely on the
basis of what assets were purchased: a monetary policy scheme could involve
purchases of private sector assets and a financial stability scheme could involve
purchases of public sector assets (e.g., the ECB's SMP).

The extent to which these purchase programmes will have macroeconomic
consequences, and in particular influence monetary conditions (and the pursuit
of price stability), will depend on the design of the programme. If a central
bank is purchasing assets for the two different purposes (monetary and financial

stability) at the same time, then it may be simpler to fund the purchases for financial stability purposes by issuing central bank reserves and not sterilise the purchases (issue short-term liabilities to drain the reserves out of the system), so at the point of purchase these two schemes may look observationally equivalent (note: the central bank may purchase different assets and be more likely to sell assets acquired in the financial stability programme). If the financial stability scheme does lead to an injection of base money then the central bank may scale back purchases under the monetary stability scheme: this is essentially what was done when the BOE launched its gilt purchase programme.

Even if the purchases do not involve the creation of central bank reserves they can still have a macroeconomic impact by addressing a market failure which is suppressing an efficient allocation of resources. Indeed, these schemes are often described as repairing some element of the transmission mechanism, in the sense that they increase the effectiveness of a given accommodative monetary stance—for example, by ensuring the low level of official interest rates is better reflected in the terms on which households and companies can borrow. When the need to inject more stimulus emerges in circumstances where the transmission mechanism starts to degrade, central banks therefore face a choice over how much to repair the transmission mechanism (to increase the potency of the existing stimulatory stance) and how much to inject more stimulus to compensate for the impaired transmission.

3.4 Do Believe the Hype: The Transmission Mechanism of Asset Purchases

Having discussed the modalities of the BOE's gilt purchase programme and placed it within the broader set of asset purchases programmes which central banks conducted during the crisis, we now turn to discuss the theory and evidence on whether and why central bank purchases of assets influence the economy. The debate in the academic literature centres upon the first leg of the transmission mechanism: that is, whether asset purchases can have a lasting impact on asset prices. If QE does have a lasting impact on asset prices then QE almost surely works: QE can mimic the initial impact of a Bank Rate cut (influencing asset prices) and the QE stimulus will then pass into demand and ultimately inflation through the rest of the transmission mechanism. To be clear, some elements of the standard transmission mechanism may not operate under QE—for example, there may be little pass-through into tracker mortgages where the interest rate is contractually linked to Bank Rate—but so long as there is a meaningful pass-through into asset prices then QE is a crude substitute for rate cuts near the lower bound.

3.4.1   Irrelevance Propositions for Asset Purchases

It may surprise the reader to learn that there is a good deal of controversy in the academic world about whether QE works. However, as we shall go on to discover with fiscal policy (Ricardian Equivalence) and micro- and macro-prudential policy (Modigliani–Miller propositions), it is not uncommon to find that within an abstract theoretical setting traditional instruments of policy can prove ineffective.

This is not to say that economic theory is at odds with the conduct of economic policy; rather that these extreme results highlight the assumptions we need to relax in order to explain the transmission mechanism of policy. There are two versions of the irrelevance proposition for asset purchases in circulation.

- *The Ricardian private sector hedges public sector purchases*: If rational forward-looking households realise that they are the ultimate beneficiaries of any asset purchase programme (since they stand behind the sovereign that back-stops the central bank) and have unfettered access to financial markets, then they will systematically hedge the risk that purchases pose to their future consumption plans (via higher taxes to recapitalise the central bank or transfers from capital gains on the programme), nullifying the impact of the purchase programme (Wallace 1981; Woodford 2012).
- *More money now without more money later means nothing*: If forward-looking agents believe that the central bank will reverse the purchase programme (sell assets back to the private sector and drain liquidity) then the scheme will fail to stimulate the economy: only an increase in the money supply today that is expected to persist into the future will raise prices, which in turn suggests that the central bank must credibly promise to deliver a higher price in the future via its purchases (Krugman 1998; Eggertsson and Woodford 2003).

3.4.2   Signalling Effects and the Most Expensive Communication Exercise in History

We begin with an explanation of the transmission mechanism of asset purchases that sits comfortably within mainstream finance—the signalling channel through which purchases provide information about the future path of policy rates. To be clear from the outset, there is some dispute within the literature about how powerful this channel has been in practice: for a positive assessment, see Krishnamurthy and Vissing-Jorgensen (2011) and Bauer and Rudebusch (2014); for a more modest assessment, see Gagnon, Raskin, Remache and Sack (2011).

3.4.2.1   Signalling as a Form of Stimulus

Expectations about the future conduct of policy play a critical role in the transmission mechanism of monetary policy. Those expectations about the future will be reflected in the current constellation of asset prices and therefore the behaviour of households and companies. Policy actions which validate those expectations will therefore appear to have no effect. However, when policymakers take the market by surprise—whether through communication that challenges the market's understanding of the policymaker's assessment of the outlook or the appropriate response, or by taking a decision that was unexpected or not taking a decision that was expected—that will lead to a correction in those expectations, and hence asset prices and ultimately behaviour. As we discussed earlier, the impact of the surprise is largely determined by the way that the market interprets the news—in other words, it is the signal in the surprise that matters. To fix ideas, note that the macroeconomic impact of a surprise rate hike is **not** driven by the fact that the remuneration of reserves and hence the price of money in the overnight market has increased between now and the next policy meeting (which is what the policymaker announces), rather it is determined by the revision to expectations of the likely path of the policy rate *beyond the next policy meeting* in light of the fact that the policymaker raised the policy rate today.

The decision to launch an asset purchase programme and the scale of purchases will send a signal to market participants about the future stance of monetary policy, and in particular how long the central bank expects to remain at the lower bound. The announcement of the asset purchase programme can potentially shift the risk-free forward curve (expectations of the policy rate at any given horizon) that underpins the broad constellation of asset prices. In theory, this channel should have its greatest impact at intermediate maturities since the implicit signal on the path of the policy rate extends only so far: it seems unlikely that agents would infer something about the level of Bank Rate several decades in the future from an announcement about asset purchases today.

The signalling channel described here focuses on the potential for asset purchases to shift the *modal* expectations of the future path of the policy rate that is priced into the broad constellation of asset prices—in other words, the single most likely path given the current state of the economy. However, there is a second, perhaps more important, signal which QE announcements can send: about how the central bank and the policy rate will respond to unexpected events. If the central bank can signal a willingness to 'do whatever it takes'—to keep the policy rate low for as long as possible it could influence risk premia across a broad range of assets. We shall return to these issues in more detail later in this section.

In passing, this signalling channel raises interesting questions about the design of QE (Krishnamurthy and Vissing-Jorgensen 2011). If this is the only channel through which QE influences asset prices, activity and inflation then we are left to conclude that central banks have invested billions of dollars, pounds and euros in financial assets, massively expanding their balance sheets in the process, simply in order to convince market participants to lower their expectations of the future path of the policy rate. Under the pure signalling hypothesis, QE is the most expensive communication exercise in history.

You might think that central bankers would baulk at the idea that QE was first and foremost a crude signalling exercise, calibrated to convince investors that interest rates were likely to remain low for a very long period of time. For one thing, if they really wanted to send a strong signal on the future path of interest rates it would have been a lot cheaper to communicate that path directly (see the discussion on complete forward guidance later). For another, this portrayal of QE as a signalling device implies that further doses of asset purchases would have a modest impact if interest rate expectations were already aligned with the implicit signal that the central bank wanted to send, leaving us to conclude that central banks are closer to being out of monetary ammunition than we might otherwise have thought at the lower bound. However, at least one member of the MPC appears to hold this view: Vlieghe (2016) argues that 'most of the fall in long-term interest rates was… due to expectations of the future path of policy rates' and that 'there is nothing anomalous about the low level of long-term interest rates, nor is there any evidence that government bond yields are "distorted" by central banks' asset purchases'.

3.4.2.2   The Counterproductive Signal

If we relax the benchmark assumption of well-informed agents with access to the same information about the state of the economy as the central bank then the transmission of stimulus via this signalling channel becomes more complex, and potentially counterproductive. It is possible, if not probable, that relatively uninformed agents will infer something about the state of the economy from how the central bank reacts: in other words, policy decisions are likely to be interpreted as news on the state of the economy. For example, agents would infer from a rate cut or increase in asset purchases that was larger than expected, earlier than expected or in the limit totally unexpected that the central bank has a more pessimistic assessment of the state of the economy than they had previously thought, and since the central bank is believed to have an absolute advantage in assessment of the economy that prompts agents to revise down their economic forecasts, potentially including their forecast for inflation. In theory, it is possible in this scenario that the negative impact of the downwards revisions to agents' economic forecasts dominates the positive impact of the stimulus through the monetary transmission mechanism—indeed, if households revise down their forecasts for inflation by more than the move in nominal interest rates, then real interest rates will rise—so the surprise announcement *appears* to depress demand (if the central bank's assessment is valid, then the revision to agents' expectations is inevitable, so there is little to be gained from failing to respond pre-emptively).

This perverse response to policy stimulus is most likely to arise in circumstances where the information asymmetry between the central bank and individual agents about the state of the economy is material—typically in states of nature which are unfamiliar, where agents have little experience to guide their forecasts and the range of possible outcomes is seen to increase because extreme tail risks which are normally seen as being so unlikely that they are effectively ignored (the so-called 'threshold heuristic') must now be considered. In other words, it is not unreasonable to assume that surprise asset purchase announcements during a financial crisis could have a larger impact on agents' beliefs about the state of the economy. For example, Cochrane (2011b) offers one straightforward explanation of the fall in long-term bond following the Fed's August 2010 announcement that it would reinvest the principal repayments on maturing assets in its portfolio:

> More deeply, maybe the August event does not represent cause and effect, but rather markets inferred 'wow, the Fed is desperate. They think things are really terrible. If they're doing something this big, even if it's totally useless, it means

they're going to keep short term rates low for years to come. Time to buy long term bonds.' In this interpretation, the announcement has nothing to do with segmentation, illiquidity, risk bearing, or anything else, it simply is a signal of the likely path of short rates many years ahead.

3.4.3 Imperfect Substitutability, Preferred Habitats and Bang for Your Buck, Pound, Yen and Euro

The central bank narrative of the transmission mechanism of QE does not rely on the signalling effect alone. But in order to rationalise the more powerful transmission mechanism of asset purchases that central banks have outlined, we have to swim against the tide of academic finance and re-discover an argument that *quantities* determine asset *prices* (Bauer and Rudebusch 2014), in order that a central bank purchase programme which reduces the quantity of assets in private sector hands might drive up the price.

The starting point is an idea that belongs to James Tobin: that financial assets are imperfect substitutes for one another (Tobin 1969) and therefore changes in the supply of different assets available to the private sector—including those induced by policymakers—may influence the price of those assets, because the demand for assets is price inelastic. This assumption is the key that unlocks a more muscular impact of asset purchases, giving central banks traction over a whole spectrum of yields so that monetary policy is only truly constrained when the entire yield curve is flat at the effective lower bound on the policy rate (Cœuré 2015a). Interestingly, Bernanke (2012) notes that Tobin proposed that the Fed should purchase longer-term securities when short rates were close to the floor during the Great Depression.

The standard justification for these quantity effects in a deep and liquid market like the gilt market is the presence of institutional investors who occupy 'preferred habitats' within segments of the yield curve, in that their particular business model leads them to have a strong preference for holding assets with a certain maturity (Culbertson 1957; Modigliani and Sutch 1966). For example, pension funds may prefer to hold—or may even be legally obliged to hold—long-dated bonds as assets to match their long-term liabilities even if other securities offer a higher risk-adjusted return (Williams 2013).

The presence of these preferred habitats can distort the shape of the yield curve (relative to the curve implied by expectations of the policy rate). Shocks to supply can lead bond prices to move out of line given price inelastic demand for particular bonds within a particular segment. In contrast, over maturities where the demand is relatively price elastic forward rates should be broadly consistent with expected future policy rates, after adjusting for risk premia in the curve (principally on account of interest rate risk).

There is evidence that policymakers can gain traction on long-term yields via these preferred habitat effects. In retrospect, an attempt in the 1960s to flatten the yield curve—known as Operation Twist—which sought to simultaneously encourage investment (through lower long-term yields) and boost the balance of payments (through higher short-term yields), appears to have delivered statistically significant but economically modest effects, lowering long-term yields by around 15 basis points (Swanson 2011). In their review of Japanese interventions during the 'Lost Decade', Bernanke, Reinhart and Sack (2004) conclude that the authorities were able to lower long-term yields. Finally, Greenwood and Vayanos (2010) identify two episodes in which the authorities disturbed the demand–supply balance at the long end of the curve—pension reforms in the UK which encouraged funds to purchase long-term index-linked government bonds and a US Treasury scheme to buy back long-dated securities—and in both cases, the intervention depressed long-term yields.

The key question is whether those investors who do not have a preferred habitat are ready, willing and able to arbitrage away the kinks in the yield curve that other investors have created: that is, the fact that the certain bonds can become 'rich' (over-valued) relative to bonds elsewhere on the curve if there is a shortage of bonds in that particular segment. In theory, arbitrageurs could short (sell) the market where there is insufficient supply and go long (buy) where there is excess supply. In practice, the arbitrageurs are exposed to risk—in particular, that the curve twists against them—and that may limit their capacity to smooth out kinks in the curve that preferred habitat demand creates (Vayanos and Vila 2009). Moreover, we might expect that in an environment where the capacity of arbitrageurs to bear risk was constrained—for example, in the dysfunctional markets in which QE was first launched—that large preferred habitat effects might be more likely to persist (Doh 2010).

One thing is clear: in a world in which imperfect substitutability drives the transmission mechanism, the central bank cannot buy assets which look like cash if it wants to have an out-sized impact on asset prices. With official interest rates at the floor and not expected to budge in the near future (that, remember, is the whole point of the signalling channel) then short-term government debt becomes a near perfect substitute for cash: both are highly liquid safe assets with no interest rate risk. The private sector should be broadly indifferent about the relative shares of these two assets in its portfolio, so there will be no quantity effect here as Cochrane (2010) observes:

The Fed knows that its usual open-market operations – buying short-term debt from banks, and giving the banks more reserves in exchange – have no effect whatsoever. This is like taking your red M&Ms, giving you back green M&Ms. It has no effect on your diet.

One takeaway here is that if the central bank wants to maximise the multiplier from its asset purchase programme—that is, if it wants a given flow of purchases to have the largest possible impact on demand and inflation—then it would not necessarily choose to purchase government debt, and certainly not short-term government debt (to be fair, 30-year government debt should not be considered a close substitute for cash!).

3.4.4 Portfolio Rebalancing and Liquidity Risk Premia: An Aside on the Mechanics of QE

The preferred habitat channel described is often referred to in the literature as a portfolio rebalancing channel (to capture the idea of preferred habitat investors being forced to rebalance their portfolios). However, that terminology seems unfortunate. Whether you believe in the preferred habitat effect or not, QE leads to portfolio rebalancing: the investors who sold gilts for cash will almost without exception have purchased another financial asset with that cash. The question is simply whether this process leads to a larger move in asset prices than conventional finance theory suggests via the pure signalling channel.

Whilst we are on the topic of portfolio rebalancing it makes sense to briefly review the mechanics of the process. The initial transaction disturbs the private sector's portfolio, which for simplicity we assume was in equilibrium prior to the intervention—that is, prior to the launch of QE, quantities and relative prices are in equilibrium. The initial transaction leaves the private sector holding more cash and fewer assets, although the precise details depend on who sold the asset to the central bank:

* *If the seller was a bank*: there is a straightforward exchange of assets with the bank's account at the central bank credited with an increase in central bank reserves.
* *If the seller was a non-bank financial (NBF) institution*: the NBF gains a liquid deposit with a commercial bank in exchange for the asset it sold, whilst the bank gains an increase in its reserve holdings at the central bank.

This initial transaction will then set off a chain of additional transactions, as a sequence of investors exchange an asset in their portfolio for cash, and then reinvest the proceeds. At each stage in the chain, we might expect an individual to reinvest cash in a close substitute for the asset that they sold (where possible) and perhaps modestly increase the share of money in the portfolio. The process will have run its course when the private sector portfolio is back in equilibrium—that is, the private sector is now comfortable holding more money, given the new level of asset prices and distribution of asset holdings. This story should sound familiar, because it is an old-fashioned 'hot potato' explanation for how money leads to inflation, through a series of transactions. The only difference is that the story is now being told in financial markets, and to begin with, at least, the inflation created by 'too much money' is in asset prices.

In theory, an asset purchase programme could influence asset prices simply by virtue of the fact that it inevitably triggers this sequence of transactions. Investors should demand compensation (in the form of a higher return or liquidity risk premium) from assets that may be hard to sell in certain states of the world, particularly if in those states of the world access to credit is likely to be restricted. An asset purchase programme will inflate the number of trades taking place in financial markets and that could inflate asset prices by squeezing the liquidity risk premium that investors demand because they perceive it will be easier to sell assets should the need arise (at least for as long as the programme lasts). Likewise, market makers should be willing to hold a larger inventory of bonds and charge a smaller bid ask spread (the difference between the prices at which they stand ready to buy and sell) if they expect more active trading in their market, and that should further improve liquidity. This is the basic motivation of the MMLR operation. However, it is unclear how significant this channel is in the context of the Bank's QE programme: remember the Bank chose to conduct purchases in the gilt market precisely because it was a deep and liquid market.

Given the global nature of capital markets, it is reasonable to suppose that some of the investors rebalancing their portfolios as a result of the sequence of transactions triggered by QE may choose to invest in assets denominated in other currencies, and that in turn requires a transaction in foreign exchange markets. Of course, that does not mean that sterling deposits are destroyed; they simply change hands, to the investor on the other side of the FX transaction. In any case, one might reasonably expect that a series of such transactions will weigh on the value of the currency.

One plausible outcome of the central bank injecting cash into the economy is that private sector agents may choose to pay down debt rather than reinvest the cash into another asset. This statement appears to run counter to the basic economist's rule of thumb: if agents wanted to shrink the balance sheet, then they would do so anyway with or without an asset purchase programme. This point should not be glossed over but there is something to be said about agents having the resources at their disposal to pay down debt. It might take a bid for the assets on the agent's balance sheet to facilitate deleveraging. A reasonable position here might be that this 'portfolio shrinkage' channel is most likely to arise if and when the asset purchase programme reaches those illiquid assets for which there may not be a bid in febrile financial markets—or more precisely a bid which the owner of the asset can afford to accept without an unacceptable hit to net worth.

3.4.5 Transmission via the Banking Sector

Another key area of controversy is the extent to which the standard transmission channels through the banking sector operate when central banks purchase assets rather than cut interest rates. The BOE was relatively downbeat on the scope for QE to stimulate demand through this channel; for example, in his review of the impact of QE on its first anniversary the then Chief Economist observed (Dale 2010):

> An important issue when thinking about the likely channels of monetary transmission is the state of the banking system. In normal times, a key channel through which asset purchases might be expected to operate is by increasing banks' stocks of liquid assets, which may encourage them to extend new loans. But we are not in normal times. Banks are pulling back on their lending as they seek to strengthen their balance sheets and reduce their leverage. For this reason, when making an assessment of the likely impact of asset purchases, the Committee did not factor in a material expansion of bank lending

This conclusion seems too pessimistic in all but one respect. The first thing to note is that the channel through which the Bank expects asset purchases to influence bank lending is via the 'money multiplier' (the same argument features in the Bank's formal exposition of the design, operation and impact of QE (Joyce et al. [2011b]). The money multiplier is an old-fashioned mechanism through which the amount of loans that a bank can originate and therefore deposits it can create is constrained by the stock of central bank reserves it holds. However, nobody believes this mechanism (constraint) operates in practice; indeed, the Bank's own research on the subject (McLeay et al. 2014) notes:

While the money multiplier theory can be a useful way of introducing money and banking in economic textbooks, it is not an accurate description of how money is created in reality

Instead, it is more useful to think of the terms on which banks are willing and able to supply credit to the real economy and how an asset purchase programme might influence that supply schedule. Essentially, we can think of the price of bank credit in retail markets as reflecting the sum of three factors: the risk-free rate; a risk premium or spread which banks pay (over and above the risk-free rate) in funding markets, compensating investors for the risk of default, the potentially illiquidity of the investment, and so on; and finally a risk premium or spread that the bank charges its customers over and above that marginal cost of funding to compensate the bank for the illiquidity of the loan and the risk of default as well as to cover costs and generate a return on intermediation. There are a number of channels through which QE could influence the terms on which banks supply credit through one of these three factors:

- *Signalling effects, the risk-free rate and the cost of term funding*: Asset purchases may convey a signal to the market about the future path of Bank Rate and in particular the timing of the lift-off from the lower bound so QE can depress the risk-free rate at longer maturities which is implicit in the interest rate that banks will pay on new debt that they issue.
- *Preferred habitat effects, mark to market gains and bank default risk*: Asset purchases can inflate asset prices in the presence of a price inelastic private sector demand for assets, and where banks hold those assets in their portfolios they will enjoy mark to market gains. Where risk has not been hedged elsewhere in the portfolio, banks can regenerate capital which should reduce the compensation that the bank has to pay investors for the risk that the bank will default.
- *Preferred habitat effects and spread compression in bank-funding markets*: If the money displaced out of the government bond market is driven into the markets in which banks issue debt and encounters price inelastic demand there, then the price of those securities will rise too, reducing the cost of funding.
- *Real economy effects, bank default risk and spread compression in funding markets*: If asset purchases can boost income, reduce unemployment and raise property prices in the real economy through other (non-bank) channels then the probability of default and loss given default on the banks' existing credit exposures will fall, driving the bank further away from the default threshold and therefore reduce the cost of issuing new debt for the bank.

- *Real economy effects, customer default risk and spread compression in lending markets*: If asset purchases reduce the probability of default and loss given default on loans to the real economy, then banks need to charge a lower spread over their funding costs to compensate for the default risk of their customers when they price loans.
- *Cyclical risk aversion and spread compression*: If risk appetite is cyclical—in particular falling sharply in a crisis (this shift in sentiment is sometimes referred to as a switch in investment strategy from 'return *on* capital' to 'return *of* capital')—then any policy intervention which can lift the economy out of a crisis may deliver a cross-asset compression in risk premia because investors will not demand such a high price to bear risk, and that can lower spreads on both sides of banks' balance sheets.
- *Flatter yield curves, net interest margin and spreads*: Finally, if asset purchases end up flattening the yield curve then that will tend to squeeze the net interest income that banks earn from borrowing short and lending long and that might lead banks to widen the spread over funding costs in retail lending markets in response to protect margin.

In short, there are a number of channels through which one might expect asset purchases to influence the terms on which banks lend to households and companies, most of which are positive. To repeat a familiar message, it does not follow that a programme of asset purchases will necessarily shift the supply schedule out or deliver an increase in net lending; simply that an asset purchase programme should lead to a more generous supply of credit than would otherwise have arisen.

There is one important exception to this argument that asset purchases work through the banking channels of the transmission mechanism. Some retail lending rates are contractually linked to Bank Rate—for example, so-called tracker mortgages. Asset purchases will not pass through into the cost of servicing those mortgages for households who took out the loan before the programme was activated (strictly anticipated). However, it is possible that banks might start to offer new loans on more attractive terms—for example, a lower spread over Bank Rate—if QE can reduce the marginal cost of funding through the channels described above.

3.4.6   Fear and Uncertainty and the Discrete QE Multiplier

There is a final channel of the transmission mechanism through which asset purchases could influence the outlook for demand and inflation that is typically glossed over as little more than an aside in a conventional treatment of monetary policy—that is, via the beliefs of households and companies. The level of demand can be sensitive to beliefs about what *might* happen in the future, over and above the single most likely outcome. If households and companies become more uncertain about the future, and in particular, if they become increasingly concerned about the economy taking a sharp turn for the worse, they will tend to spend less.

Where companies are concerned, many if not most investment opportunities have four key features: the returns to the investment opportunity are uncertain; as time passes the company can learn more about the likely returns from the project; the decision to invest can be delayed; and the investment is at least partially irreversible, in that there are sunk costs which cannot be recouped if the project turns out to be unprofitable. These features give rise to a real option—there is a value in waiting and not investing today in order to learn more about the project, and hence making a better decision tomorrow. The value of that option should be reflected in the hurdle rate on investment: projects may need to offer a bumper expected return in order to convince investors to invest today in a project offering uncertain returns (Dixit 1992). The size of that option should reflect in part the degree of uncertainty about future returns so an increase in 'macro uncertainty' can lead to a delay in irreversible investments, and in particular, an increased fear of very bad returns in a dire economic scenario is likely to have a pronounced impact on spending (Bernanke 1983).

For households, we would expect to see an increase in uncertainty and in particular increased fear of economic catastrophe leading to an increase in precautionary savings and a corresponding drop in consumption as they try to build up a buffer of assets which can be used to fund consumption in the future if there is a shock to income (Leland 1968). Research suggests that this precautionary savings channel is significant both at a micro and macro level; for example:

- Carroll and Samwick (1998) estimate that if the uncertainty facing each household was reduced to the level faced by the least uncertain household that would virtually halve the net worth of households below the age of 50, and would reduce the stock of very liquid assets by around a third.
- Slemrod (1988) showed how variation in the perceived risks of a nuclear war in the 1980s could explain variation in savings behaviour: with a 10 % increase in the fraction of the population which believes a nuclear world war was likely associated with a decline of 4.1 percentage points in the net private savings rate.

- Romer (1990) argues that precautionary savings played a material role in turning a stock market crash into a Great Depression, with the increase in income uncertainty precipitating a collapse in spending on durable goods.
- Finally, Mody, Ohnsorge and Sandri (2012) argue that more than 40 % of the increase in savings across countries during the current crisis can be explained by rising unemployment risk and the volatility of output.

In short, fear and uncertainty about the future can have a material impact on domestic demand. What is less clear is how companies and households form these beliefs about the future, and how and why they update them, because it seems unlikely that many of these agents will be involved in the constant process of constructing forecasts using the true model of the economy (model-consistent rational expectations) and then making the optimal spending plans that conventional macroeconomics pre-supposes. Agents may be inattentive, either in the sense that they make plans on an infrequent basis, and then not adjust their behaviour in response to the news flow in the interim (Reis 2006), or in the sense that they are unable to process complex information (Sims 2003).

In this environment, it is possible that a major policy announcement could shift these beliefs about the path that the economy might take—reducing fear and uncertainty—and that might then have a material impact on demand. It is a bit of a stretch to believe that the marginal change in the stock of purchased assets would have a material impact through this channel but the decision to launch QE—as opposed to doing nothing and hibernating at the lower bound—might have had a meaningful impact on beliefs and therefore demand.

In essence, central banks communicated that it was business as usual at the lower bound: that they would be able to approximate the optimal policy response that would emerge in a world in which there were no constraints on official interest rates and supply stimulus through unconventional means. The Lucas critique suggests that in the counterfactual where central bankers had not delivered that message we might have seen a detrimental shift in beliefs and behaviour as agents learned that there had been a break in the policy rule and that no further monetary easing would be forthcoming to support the economy in this recession (Lucas 1976). As a result, alongside the continuous QE multiplier which describes the *marginal* impact of an increase in the stock of purchased assets on demand and inflation there is a discrete QE multiplier, which captures this one-off boost to the economy from launching the programme (relative to doing nothing).

3.5   Evidence on the Impact of QE

As noted above, there is a good deal of debate within the economics community about whether QE is an effective substitute for conventional rate cuts at (near) the lower bound. As we shall go on to discuss later in this book, much of the debate about the conduct of fiscal policy hinges on whether central banks can provide stimulus via asset purchases: if (and arguably *only if*) asset purchases have little impact on aggregate demand and inflation then there is a compelling case for using fiscal stimulus to support aggregate demand at the lower bound. We now turn to discuss the attempts that have been made to gauge the impact of asset purchases in the UK.

3.5.1   The Macroeconomic Impact of QE and the Counterfactual Problem

The acid test of QE as a monetary policy tool is whether asset purchases can influence aggregate demand and inflation. However, it is very hard to convincingly identify the quantitative impact of a given change in the stock of purchased assets on those variables of interest.

The fundamental problem is a familiar one: the counterfactual problem. An effective monetary stimulus will raise the level of demand and rate of inflation relative to *what it would otherwise have been*, so the appropriate benchmark to evaluate the impact of that stimulus is to compare observed outcomes with a counterfactual or hypothetical scenario in which there was no change in the monetary stance. In particular, an assessment of whether the rate of inflation rose back to the target two years after a change in the monetary stance does **not** tell us whether monetary policy works or not, although it might tell us with the benefit of hindsight whether policymakers loosened the stance *enough*.

Managing this counterfactual problem is much more complicated when it comes to the evaluation of QE because of the circumstances in which asset purchases were conducted:

- *Unusual instrument*: The size and speed of the propagation of the stimulus through the conventional channels of the transmission mechanism are inherently more uncertain for asset purchases (compared to a change in official interest rates), making it harder to search for signature of QE in the data we observe (we are less confident about what we are looking *for*).

- *Unusual circumstances*: Economic agents may not respond in the usual fashion to news in the midst of a financial crisis: for example, spending may be less sensitive to changes in real interest rates when balance sheets are stretched and credit is tight, and investors may not be able to lean against the price responses that asset purchases generate.
- *Unusual shocks*: A series of large and atypical shocks were working their way through both the domestic and global economy, and their cumulative impact on the state of the UK economy is uncertain, making it harder to identify what caused what.
- *Unusual policy mix*: The MPC was not the only policymaker taking decisions during this period, and changes in fiscal policy and micro- and macro-prudential at home and abroad, and changes in monetary policy by the major central banks abroad could all have had a material impact on the UK economy but the cumulative impact of those policy responses is uncertain.

In short, we can observe what happened to demand and inflation in the UK but we have a large number of factors which will have contributed to that outcome of which BoE-QE is only one, and the quantitative importance of the other factors is inherently uncertain.

This is not to say that it is impossible to search for the macroeconomic impact of asset purchases. We have to impose some structure on the data in order to identify the QE needle in the haystack. Kapetanios, Mumtaz, Stevens and Theodoridis (2012) use several macroeconometric models to estimate the impact of asset purchases on activity and inflation *via the transmission through long-term bond yields*. Based on the Bank's estimate that the first phase of QE (the first £200 billion of purchases) depressed long-term yields by around 100 basis points (see below), Kapetanios, Mumtaz, Stevens and Theodoridis estimate that QE1 may have had a peak effect on the level of output of around 1½ % and a peak effect on the rate of inflation of about 1¼ percentage points.

3.5.2 The Impact of Asset Purchases on Bond Yields

An alternative and potentially more profitable approach to examining whether QE is an effective tool is to focus on the impact of news on asset purchases on asset prices. If changes in the stock of purchased assets are found to have a significant and long-lasting impact on asset prices then it is at least reasonable to assume that QE will ultimately feed through into demand and inflation as those changes in asset prices gradually influence behaviour. Indeed, since the contentious elements of the transmission mechanism of QE are the scale and persistence of link from asset purchases into asset prices, it seems appropriate to focus on this link in the mechanism.

3.5.2.1   The Initial Announcements

The standard approach to measuring the impact of surprise policy interventions on asset prices is to use event studies (Bernanke et al. 2004). The transmission mechanism of monetary policy into output and inflation may exhibit long and variable lags but the pass-through into asset prices is thought to be far more rapid. We can take advantage of that rapid reaction to better isolate the impact of QE on financial markets by focusing on the change in asset prices during the short interval immediately after a policy announcement regarding the future path of asset purchases during which it is unlikely that there will have been other significant news for the level of asset prices.

Results from event studies were front and centre in the evidence base that the central banking community used to justify the efficacy of QE. In the USA, Gagnon, Raskin, Remache and Sack (2011) show that longer-term interest rates declined by up to 150 basis points around key announcements concerning the Fed's asset purchase programme. Interestingly, Neely (2010) uses the same approach to illustrate how announcements about the Fed's large-scale asset purchases had an immediate impact on bond yields in other countries, including those in the UK.

Joyce, Lasaosa, Stevens and Tong (2011a) summarise the BOE's research into the impact of the first round of gilt purchases (QE1) on asset prices. In their event study they focus on six key announcements regarding the scale of purchases and they report that aggregating across the market reaction over a two-day window following each announcement yields fell by an average of just under 100 basis points, with declines ranging between 55 and 120 basis points across different maturities. They note that government bond yields in other major economies were relatively stable during the event windows, which suggests that the yield moves were local effects. The lion's share of this 100-basis point impact is driven by the market reaction to the March 2009 announcement of asset purchases. To illustrate the sensitivity of this methodology to the calibration of the window note that when Joyce, Lasaosa, Stevens and Tong reduce the size of their window from two days to one the estimated impact of QE1 is approximately cut in half.

The Bank study uses the relative response of gilt yields and the fixed rates in overnight index swap (OIS) contracts to attempt to isolate the channel through which the announcements are influencing asset prices. In theory, the response of OIS rates should capture just the signalling effect, whilst gilt yields could capture both the preferred habitat and signalling channels. In the event, the fall in OIS rates was relatively modest (around 10 basis points) which appears to suggest that the preferred habitat channel is the key driver of gilt yields. However, this result hinges on the reliability of OIS rates as a proxy for expectations of Bank Rate which is at least open to dispute given the lack of liquidity in these contracts at longer maturities.

Finally, it is worth noting that gilt prices are not the only asset that reacted in the two-day windows to these QE announcements. Joyce, Lasaosa, Stevens and Tong report that corporate bond yields also fell markedly around announcements, there were modest falls in the exchange rate too but the impact on equity prices is harder to pin down.

3.5.2.2   News on the Location of Bond Buying

The more familiar that market participants became with MPC's use of asset purchases as a tool of monetary policy, the better able they were to predict future increases in the stock of purchased assets. In just the same way that an anticipated change in Bank Rate will not have a material impact on asset prices, an anticipated change in the stock of purchased assets will appear to have little effect on asset prices. However, in neither case can we conclude that the change in the stance of policy is ineffectual: it is simply that the macro-economic impact of the change in Bank Rate or the stock of purchased assets builds in the hours, days, weeks and even months before the decision as investors become more confident that the decision will be taken. Unfortunately, the fact that the later QE announcements had less shock value might have contributed to the sense that QE was becoming less effective. We therefore need to search for 'surprise QE' announcements if we want to refine our estimate the macroeconomic impact of QE using subsequent changes in the design of the programme.

Banerjee, Latto, McLaren and Daros (2012) argue that some of the changes in the design of the Bank's QE programme provide us with these surprises. As discussed earlier, the Bank changed the number of auctions it conducted each week and the set of bonds (the range of residual maturities) that it was willing to buy on several occasions—in particular extending the range of maturities (in August 2009) and then realigning the 'maturity buckets' of the three weekly auctions to conform with the DMO's approach (in February 2012). These announcements were not expected by the market and implied a shift in the relative pattern of bond buying along the yield curve which in turn might imply news about the shape of the yield curve. News that bonds with a residual maturity in excess of 25 years would now be included in the scheme might be expected to lead to an increase in the price of bonds in that sector relative to other gilts. Likewise, news that one reverse auction would now be confined to bonds with residual maturities between three and seven years (rather than three and ten) might imply an increase in the relative price of those bonds, given the same amount of purchases would be concentrated on a smaller number of bonds.

Banerjee, Latto, McLaren and Daros use the same basic event study methodology described above to assess the impact of these surprises. They begin by estimating the news on the likely purchases of each bond, aggregate within a given segment of the curve, and then express the news as a percentage of the eligible outstanding stock within that segment. They then regress the change in gilt yields in different parts of the curve *over the two-day window after each announcement* on a constant, the duration of bonds in that part of the curve and the variable of interest (the news on purchases). They find that for all three announcements (the initial announcement of eligible maturities in March 2009, the extension in August 2009 and the realignment in February 2012), the coefficient on the news variable is negative and statistically significant: in other words, an announcement that shifts expectations of the likely weight of bond buying *towards a given segment* is associated with a decline in yields (increase in price) in that segment.

Miles (2014) claims that the impact on monetary conditions of a change in the central bank's stock of purchased assets is highly state contingent: if purchases (or sales) are conducted when markets are dysfunctional then QE can have a material impact on asset prices; however, those changes will likely have little impact if conducted in a period when financial markets are working well. It would be a bit of a stretch to describe the state of markets at *any* of these three points in time as 'working well'. However, it would be hard to claim that markets were in a similar state at each of these moments in time. It is therefore interesting to note that the authors cannot reject the hypothesis that the coefficients on the news in each announcement are identical. In other words, Banerjee, Latto, McLaren and Daros (2012) find that 'the strength of (what they call) the "local supply channel of QE" does not appear to have changed significantly since gilt purchases were introduced in early 2009'.

3.5.2.3 The Problem with Event Studies

The premise of the event study is that if we choose a sufficiently small window of time around a surprise announcement we can attribute the change in asset prices during that window to the announcement. The longer the window, the more courageous that assumption becomes, and we therefore want to select the shortest window possible and still capture the full effect of the announcement. The question is how long is long enough to capture that full effect?

It is unreasonable to think that markets would process the news in a significant monetary policy announcement—such as the launch of QE—*instantaneously*. Instead, market participants will gradually assimilate the news and estimate the implications for asset prices. Indeed, Daines, Joyce and Tong (2012) argue that the first announcements took 'days rather than hours to be fully priced in', and therefore using too short a window to estimate the impact of QE would underestimate its impact.

However, it may not be safe to assume that the window which shows the largest asset price response is the right one. In theory, market participants could over-react to the news, in which case prices would overshoot and then gradually track back over a longer time frame. Indeed, Duffie (2010) argues that 'a sharp reaction to the shock and a subsequent and more extended reversal' is the characteristic financial markets' response to a surprise about the balance between demand and supply in the market. The more one thinks about financial markets as populated by a large number of inattentive agents with limited private information about the fair value of assets who take time to observe, reflect on and then respond to news *and the way other investors and therefore prices react*, the less one would expect to see an orderly and rapid processing of the news into prices. Moreover, if some investors use positive feedback strategies (buy an asset when the price rises, and sell when it falls) there is an inherent tendency for prices to overshoot in response to news.

It follows that event studies which are calibrated to capture the peak asset price response to QE are likely to give a misleading impression of the true impact of the change in the stock of purchased assets, because they focus on the initial overshoot and ignore the subsequent correction. In practice, this is exactly what happened: after tumbling in the immediate aftermath of the announcement, gilt yields rose in the weeks that followed (Martin and Milas 2012). If we take the example of the ECB's announcement of large-scale purchases of government bonds it appears that the overshoot in bond yields extended *for several months*.

3.5.3 Following the Money

Bridges and Thomas (2012) provide an alternative approach to gauge the macroeconomic impact of the Bank's asset purchases based on what they refer to as 'monetarist arithmetic'. Their approach is based on two steps: first, estimate the implied stimulus to 'broad money' (the UK non-bank private sector's holding of cash and deposits) from assets purchases; and then second, to estimate the macroeconomic consequences of that stimulus based on historical relationships between money, asset prices and nominal spending.

A sensible starting point for an estimate of the impact on broad money of an asset purchase programme financed by the creation of £200 billion of central bank reserves is that the stock of deposit money would also increase by £200 billion—that is, for every asset that the Bank purchased from the private sector a deposit was created (a liability of the banking sector that matches the asset that the banks acquired: central bank reserves). However, there are at least three ways in which that assumption is likely to prove unreliable:

- *Not all gilts were purchased from members of the UK non-bank private sector:* If and when the Bank purchased gilts from the UK banks or non-residents, then the transaction would not lead to an increase in the headline measure of broad money. Bridges and Thomas dismiss this channel on account of the fact that the banking sector and the non-resident sector actually increased their holdings of gilts during the period over which asset purchases took place.
- *Balance sheet repair in the banking sector:* If banks issue long-term debt or equity, then that will lead to a decline in the stock of broad money as investors purchase those securities (another way to think about this is the banking sector changing the composition of its liabilities) and QE may have facilitated that process. Bridges, Rossiter and Thomas (2011) estimate that the net issuance of equity, long-term debt and the retention of profits by the banks reduced the stock of broad money by around £240 billion between 2008 Q2 and 2010 Q4, and Bridges and Thomas note that £62 billion of that drag could plausibly be attributed to the impact of QE.
- *Impact on bank lending:* Companies might have taken advantage of the low level of corporate bond yields brought about by QE to issue bonds and pay back bank loans, leading to a shrinkage in banks' balance sheets. Indeed, Bridges and Thomas note that capital market issuance was about 40 % stronger during the QE period than in the 1990s recession and estimate that QE-induced disintermediation likely reduce the stimulus to broad money by around £16 billion.

Bridges and Thomas thus arrive at a central estimate of the stimulus to broad money of £122 billion (£200 billion—£62 billion—£16 billion). They then use a suite of models to estimate the macroeconomic impact of that stimulus. These models estimate the demand for money in the long run, from which a 'money gap' can be inferred (the current stock of money relative to the equilibrium stock implied by the long-run demand function), which can then be entered into a system alongside other measures of disequilibria (such as the output gap) to explain the dynamics of money, asset prices and nominal spending. Bridges and Thomas experiment with a range of models—both aggregate and sectoral—but based on their central estimate of the impulse to broad money and their preferred specifications they find that QE boosted asset prices by just over 20 % by 2010 Q1, which raised the level of output by around 2 % and the level of inflation by around one percentage point.

3.6   The Distributional Consequences of QE

As time passed the distributional consequences of QE became increasingly controversial: for example, Altmann (2013) argued that the BOE's QE programme had 'acted like a tax cut for certain privileged groups, while imposing a tax increase on the majority of UK households'. Indeed, the Bank's own analysis of the distributional impact of QE appeared to corroborate that claim, noting that wealthier households will have gained the most from the Bank's purchase programme via their direct holdings of financial assets (Bell et al. 2012):

> [B]y pushing up a range of asset prices, asset purchases have boosted the value of households' financial wealth held outside pension funds, but holdings are heavily skewed with the top 5% of households holding 40% of these assets

However, the criticism that asset purchases increased inequality is flawed on a number of levels. This is not to say that inequality does not matter; just that this criticism of asset purchases is misplaced.

The first thing to note about this critique is that it is predicated on the assumption that QE works. The debate around whether QE is an effective substitute for cuts in the policy rate rests on whether asset purchases can have a significant and persistent impact on asset prices: if they can then the standard transmission mechanism should ensure that this stimulus is passed to the real economy. A criticism that QE has increased wealth inequality by driving up the price of financial assets which are disproportionately owned by a small number of households is an implicit endorsement of the power of QE to support the economy.

The second point to note is that if QE is effective as a form of monetary stimulus then it follows that the Bank's asset purchase programme has helped to boost aggregate demand and reduce unemployment. Those gains in income will be felt right throughout the income distribution; indeed, the income gains from increases in employment might be felt more at the bottom of the distribution than the top. Moreover, to the extent that monetary stimulus reduced the long-term damage to the supply side of the economy via hysteresis effects by supporting aggregate demand (see later) then asset purchases could have protected permanent income prospects throughout the distribution. By averting another Great Depression, central bankers might have prevented a significant increase in poverty (Cœuré 2012). Ignoring these positive effects of asset purchases through the income distribution—another instance of a failure to consider the counterfactual—gives a misleading impression of the impact of QE on inequality.

Third, if we consider the simplest monetary alternative to asset purchases—lowering Bank Rate further today, potentially into negative territory—then these measures will also have what the critics perceive to be a detrimental impact on inequality. Were household deposit rates to go into negative territory there is no doubt that the central bank would be accused of imposing a tax on savers (see, e.g., Heath (2015)).

Fourth, it is inevitable that any effective stimulus package—whether monetary, fiscal, macro-prudential or whatever—would appear to raise inequality given the initial conditions. Any effective stimulus package would close the output gap and limit any further damage to the supply side, delivering a higher level of income today and into the future. However, given the current structure of the economy that income gain is not distributed equally. In particular, a small number of households hold a disproportionately large residual claim on the profits of UK companies, so they will disproportionately benefit from the increase in the profits of those companies in the form of higher dividends and an increase in the value of their residual claim (share prices). In short, if the wealth distribution in an economy is highly skewed such that a small number of people own most of the assets in that economy then any successful attempt to resuscitate that economy will benefit the wealthy.

Fifth, and perhaps most fundamentally of all, it does not fall to central bankers to address inequality in the distribution of income or wealth. Inequality falls under the umbrella of fiscal policy (see later) so that task falls to the elected politicians and finance ministers in particular. Having said that, the MPC is instructed to be mindful of the government's wider economic objectives, and as the latest remit notes: 'The Government's economic policy objective is to achieve strong, sustainable and balanced growth that is more evenly shared across the country and between industries' (HMT 2015). The logical separation of responsibilities in a depression is that central bankers deliver price stability by any monetary means necessary and finance ministers use fiscal levers to address collateral damage on inequality. In any case, the *change* in wealth inequality on account of the particular selection that the MPC made from the set of available policy instrument is likely second order relative to the first-order problem of the *absolute* degree of inequality in 2006, 2011 or 2016.

3.7 Helicopter Drops

The decision to resort to QE was, and remains, controversial in some quarters. QE sceptics argue that there is a more efficient way to revive the economy via the printing press, urging the authorities to reconsider Milton Friedman's famous thought experiment (Friedman 1969):

> Let us suppose now that one day a helicopter flies over this community and drops an additional $1,000 in bills from the sky, which is, of course, hastily collected by members of the community. Let us suppose further that everyone is convinced that this is a unique event which will never be repeated.

In fact, there are a variety of proposals which sit within the umbrella of the 'helicopter drop' and it is useful to differentiate between them according to three key criteria:

- *Who calls the shots*: Does the central bank choose whether to conduct the operation and how much to expand the stock of base money, or is the government calling the shots?
- *Central bank solvency*: Can a central bank continue to perform its basic function and in particular maintain control of inflation expectations if it becomes technically insolvent as a result of the drop?
- *The end game for monetary expansion*: Do the authorities commit today that the expansion in the money supply is permanent?

Let us begin with the least controversial form of helicopter drop where the MPC is still in charge of the process and does not give a commitment about the future path of the money supply other than to pledge to deliver price stability and simply wants to stimulate the economy by distributing cash direct to households in the belief that the seeming boost to their net financial wealth will be spent and that will provide a more significant boost to aggregate demand than could be achieved through more conventional QE. The fundamental mechanism is the same: we get the same process of portfolio rebalancing, but in this case the private sector receives a gift of cash and that leads to a sequence of transactions which this time are more likely to take place in goods markets. In passing, the first round boost to demand is likely to be most effective if the helicopter only drops cash on credit-constrained households (Bean 2012) but that observation only goes to illustrate that we have now strayed deep into fiscal territory.

Indeed, the distribution of cash to households is clearly a task in which the fiscal authority should take the lead: it has the mandate, the expertise and the infrastructure (via the tax and benefit system) to execute the task effectively. Central banks have experience at distributing cash to commercial banks not millions of households. It therefore seems more probable that in the real world—if not the textbook –the original stimulus would come from the government. The central bank now finances the drop, but does not distribute it. In the traditional parlance, this is permanent monetary financing of government deficits.

The first problem we encounter is that the BOE's liabilities have increased whether the drop was intermediated via the fiscal authority or delivered directly, but there has been no corresponding increase in its assets: there is no loan to the APF, and no purchased gilt. If we treat the central bank as a standalone entity then simple balance sheet accounting suggests that the central bank's capital is reduced by this gift of cash to the fiscal authority or the household sector. If the helicopter drop is conducted on a sufficient scale the central bank could be driven into technical insolvency.

Some economists believe it is of no great importance if the central bank is insolvent: it can continue to perform its core function, including the pursuit of price stability which involves maintaining control of inflation expectations, whilst insolvent. It is true that a central bank can rely on the net present value of seigniorage income that it derives from its privileged position as the monopoly producer of domestic currency (at next to zero cost) and its right to insist that certain financial institutions must hold its liabilities to recapitalise itself (Stella 1997). However, this is not the pain-free solution that it is sometimes presented as being, and may end up compromising the central bank's capacity to deliver its monetary and financial stability mandates. It is worth keeping in mind that just because we can observe central banks with negative capital positions it does not follow that these concerns are not of practical importance. The question we need to ask in each case is how the finance minister and the market expect that negative capital position to be resolved.

One option is for the central bank to retain more of the seigniorage income it currently earns rather than distributing those funds to the shareholder (the fiscal authority). This is exactly what the Chief Economist of the ECB had in mind when discussing how a drop might work in theory (Praet 2016):

> [A]ll central banks can do it. You can issue currency and you distribute it to people. That's helicopter money. Helicopter money is giving to the people part of the net present value of your future seigniorage, the profit you make on the future banknotes.

However, the helicopter drop now leads to a drain on the resources of the fiscal authority, and could therefore lead to a compensating increase in taxes. In that situation, all the drop may end up achieving is distributing cash to households with which they can then pay the new taxes.

If instead, the central bank is recapitalised by raising additional seigniorage income, then that will likely lead to a significant increase in the central bank's balance sheet and the rate of inflation. Seigniorage income is the net interest margin that banks earn between their assets and liabilities. If that margin is relatively small then the central bank will need to significantly increase the size of its balance sheet if it wants to significantly increase the present discounted value of that flow. The scale of the required increase in the balance sheet will be hard to predict in advance, as is the link between money growth and inflation, but it is reasonable to conclude that this outcome could easily lead to high and uncertain inflation. In short, the central bank may have to print a lot of money and tolerate a lot of inflation to raise sufficient resources through the inflation tax to recapitalise itself (Buiter 2008).

If instead we assume that the authorities will not contemplate an insolvent central bank—which is entirely consistent with the fact that the APF is fully indemnified by the Treasury against any potential losses on the QE programme—and will not countenance the level of money creation and inflation required to recapitalise the central bank via seigniorage then an alternative solution must be found to the 'missing asset' problem when the central bank makes a gift of cash.

One solution is for the government to give the central bank an asset—either a marketable security (a bond) or a non-marketable security (a promissory note—essentially an IOU). The central bank now has an asset to go with its new liabilities. However, the nature of the policy intervention is fundamentally changed: the helicopter drop is not a gift anymore. These assets derive their value via a claim on future tax receipts which *at least in theory* (see below) will be paid by the household sector. The intervention now looks a lot like the combination of two different policies:

- *Unconventional fiscal stimulus*: with the central bank issuing cash today that is ultimately financed by higher taxes tomorrow.
- *Recapitalisation through the gift of an asset:* with the central bank acquiring a government bond or IOU.

This curious package looks somewhat similar to what took place during the crisis, when governments engaged in fiscal stimulus and central banks temporarily engaged in monetary financing by purchasing the bonds that the fiscal authority had to issue in order to finance stimulus – namely:

- *Conventional fiscal stimulus*: with transfer payments today financed by higher taxes tomorrow.
- *Conventional QE*: with the central bank issuing central bank reserves to purchase government bonds.

The difference comes down to what happens when the asset on the central bank's balance sheet matures. With our unconventional thought experiment, the government could simply issue a new promissory note (paying one IOU with another), or the central bank could purchase a new bond to fund the principal repayment on the bond that matures. This is the variant of helicopter drop that is closer to the intervention that is discussed in the academic literature. Fiscal stimulus—whether it is the monetary or fiscal authority distributing the cash; that is, whether the drop is direct or intermediated—is never paid for through higher taxes. There are now no conventional 'Ricardian offsets': with a conventional fiscal stimulus household saving *might* rise in anticipation of the taxes that households might have to pay in the future (see later) and the announcement of the drop may therefore have a more powerful impact on aggregate demand. As so often in economics, *might* is the operative word here, for two reasons.

- *Inflation taxes matter too*: Although the quasi-fiscal stimulus is not financed through conventional taxes, households may still end up paying for the stimulus via an inflation tax (on any security, contract or benefit entitlement that provides nominal returns which are not indexed to inflation) and anticipation of paying that inflation tax could also lead to higher savings.

- *Households may have got the joke already*: If households have already reached the conclusion that the bonds will remain on the central banks' balance sheet for the indefinite future—that monetary financing has already taken place—then they may have already revised their spending plans accordingly. From this perspective, it is only when the decision to permanently monetise debt is a genuine surprise given the state of the economy (which seems unlikely) that the drop is a game changer.

The balance sheet of the central bank may look to be in perfect working order if it has additional liabilities on one side and a government bond on the other but if the central bank credibly commits to permanently reinvest the proceeds from that asset back into the market to acquire new bonds and to never sell its asset holdings then the treatment of the bond as an asset is arguably an illusion. In effect, the central bank has acquired a zero coupon perpetual: a bond that never pays any interest and never matures, so never repays the principal. Under the terms of the commitment, the asset is worthless (to the central bank). That in turn implies that there has been a hit to the capital of the central bank, which again may need to be solved via seigniorage. However, so long as the central bank retains some wriggle room, that is, if it inserts a material adverse change (MAC) clause, where it retains the right to sell the assets or to stop reinvesting at some point in the event of a first-order threat to monetary or financial stability then this issue can (arguably) be sidestepped. One could reasonably argue that the insertion of this MAC clause would simply recognise the reality of the situation: no central bank governor or prime minister can bind the hands of his or her successor, and a promise to carry on regardless if the policy proves counterproductive is not credible.

In practice, we arrive at a continuum between the plain vanilla QE where there is a clear expectation that the bonds will eventually be sold back into the market on one end of the spectrum and permanent (and permanently credible) QE on the other, where there is an iron-clad commitment to permanently increase the stock of money (to qualify as an academic drop) with, say, the BOE pledging to reinvest the proceeds in the gilt markets as and when bonds mature into the infinite future. Somewhere in the middle there are 'stealth drops', where the fiscal authority announces fresh stimulus and the central bank restarts or upscales its asset purchase programme and agents begin to suspect (or are invited to conclude) that the bonds may remain on the balance sheet for the foreseeable future. This brings us neatly back to the discussion on the QE irrelevance propositions: that is, from one perspective it is only by committing to more money later as well as more money now that the central bank is more likely to have a macroeconomic impact. This brings us to a familiar problem with the helicopter drop—time inconsistency.

We will go on to discuss these issues in more detail later in this book but for now simply note that when the authorities announce a helicopter drop they are making promises to private sector agents about the future conduct of policy: they are promising that the injection of money or the purchase of government debt is permanent. The problem is that private sector agents may not believe them. Scrambling the helicopters represents a fundamental shift in monetary strategy—away from what is normally considered to be the optimal policy—and investors may worry that the authorities will renege on the promise of permanence, reverse the drop (e.g., by selling the bonds) and revert back to 'business as usual' inflation targeting once the economy has been sprung from a deflation trap. If investors do not believe the promise of permanence, then the policy will prove ineffective; so policymakers need to find some form of commitment device to anchor expectations around the conduct of the drop.

One solution to this problem is to adjust the mandate of the central bank. For example, the central bank could adopt a price level path target which would oblige them to temporarily exceed their inflation target in order to drive the price level back towards the path prices would have followed if the central bank had achieved its mandate in the present and recent past. Now a permanent injection of money and purchases of assets are *required* in order to achieve this more ambitious goal of monetary policy.

Thus far, we have focused on a helicopter drop launched at the behest of the central bank. However, the default assumption when it comes to helicopter drops is that the finance ministers are in the driving seat—for example, Ball (2008):

> To implement a helicopter drop, the government makes a fiscal transfer to the public, financed by issuing bonds, and the central bank purchases the bonds. That is, the government creates debt to finance a fiscal expansion, but the debt is monetized.

Now the tension between monetary policy and debt management is out in the open. In effect what is happening is that we have the combination of conventional monetary and fiscal policy, but the difference is that the scale of asset purchases is being driven by the finance minister rather that what is required in order to achieve the inflation target. The effective subordination of monetary policy to other objectives may damage the credibility of the regime and the stability of inflation expectations. There may also be legal constraints on the drop: there is a prohibition on 'monetary financing' of deficits in Article 123 of the Treaty on the Functioning of the European Union (TFEU) and it seems likely that many of the proposed interventions in this area could fall foul of this prohibition. In theory, the central bank could dutifully follow orders by purchasing all the debt that the government wants but use the other lever of monetary policy to still achieve the inflation target—raising rates earlier than it otherwise would have done. However, this outcome, with the central bank enjoying operational independence over some aspects of monetary policy but not others, seems unlikely: if the finance minister has gone to the effort of wrestling back control of one lever of monetary policy from the central bank then it is unlikely that she will be content for the central bank to crowd out her stimulus using other levers.

Finally, we should address a challenge to the framework presented above raised by Buiter (2003, 2014), which says that fiat money is an asset of the private sector agent who holds it but not a liability of the issuer, because it is irredeemable. Each agent confidently assumes that she can exchange fiat money with other agents for goods and services at the prevailing price level. Nobody takes into account the fact that the private sector as a whole can only exchange those notes with the monetary authority for newly minted replacements. Buiter thus argues that there is a fundamental asymmetry in the intertemporal budget constraints of the private and public sectors: money appears as an asset in the former but not a liability in the latter (it is not quite clear where this line of argument leaves conventional government bonds, which are nothing more than claims on a stream of payments in the form of an irredeemable currency). In this setting the helicopter drop can have a 'pure fiscal effect', boosting demand through net wealth. However, one could reasonably argue along Lucas Critique lines that we cannot guarantee that private sector agents will continue to treat money in this way when the monetary authority attempts to systematically exploit their collective failure to internalise the irredeemability of money (see Yates [2014] for an excellent exposition of this argument). Wren-Lewis (2014) rejects this critique as 'real angels and pins stuff that can come from taking microfoundations too seriously'; however, a word of caution here—like it or not—modern macroeconomics is all about taking microfoundations deadly seriously.

References

Altmann, R. (2013, June 3). *Ultra-easy Bank of England policy is worsening economic inequality*. City AM.

Ball, L. (2008). Helicopter drops and Japan's liquidity trap. *Bank of Japan Monetary and Economic Studies, 26*, 87–106.

Banerjee, R., Latto, D., McLaren, N., & Daros, S. (2012). Using changes in auction maturity sectors to help identify the impact of QE on gilt yields. *Bank of England Quarterly Bulletin, Q2*, 129–137.

Bauer, M., & Rudebusch, G. (2014). The signaling channel for federal reserve bond purchases. *International Journal of Central Banking, 10*(3), 233–289.

Bean, C. (2012, October 31). Central banking in boom and slump. *Speech.*

Bell, V., Joyce, M., Liu, Z., & Young, C. (2012). The distributional effects of asset purchases – A Bank of England report submitted to the Treasury Select Committee. *Bank of England Quarterly Bulletin, Q3*, 254–266.

Bernanke, B. (1983). Irreversibility, uncertainty, and cyclical investment. *Quarterly Journal of Economics, 98*(1), 85–106.

Bernanke, B. (2012, August 31). *Monetary policy since the onset of the crisis.* Speech.

Bernanke, B., Reinhart, V., & Sack, B. (2004). Monetary policy alternatives at the zero bound: An empirical assessment. *Brookings Papers on Economic Activity, 35*(2), 1–100.

BoE. (2009a). Minutes of February 2009 meeting of the Monetary Policy Committee.

BoE. (2009b). Minutes of March 2009 meeting of the Monetary Policy Committee.

BoE. (2012, November 21). Minutes of the November 2012 Monetary Policy Committee meeting.

Bridges, J., & Thomas, R. (2012). *The impact of QE on the UK economy—Some supportive monetarist arithmetic.* Bank of England Working Paper 442.

Bridges, J., Rossiter, N., & Thomas, R. (2011). Understanding the recent weakness in broad money growth. *Bank of England Quarterly Bulletin, Q1*, 22–35.

Buiter, W. (2003). *Helicopter money.* NBER Working Paper 10163.

Buiter, W. (2008). Can central banks go broke? *CEPR Policy Insight, 24.*

Buiter, W. (2014). The simple analytics of helicopter money: Why it works – always. *Economics, 8*, 1–51.

Carroll, C., & Samwick, A. (1998). How important is precautionary saving? *Review of Economics and Statistics, 80*(3), 410–419.

Chabot, B., & Herman, G. (2013). A history of large-scale asset purchases before the Federal Reserve. *Federal Reserve Bank of Chicago Economic Perspectives, Q4*, 140–152.

Cochrane, J. (2010, December 7). *Sense and nonsense in the quantitative easing debate.* VoxEU.

Cochrane, J. (2011b). *Inside the Black Box.* Comments on Hamilton and Wu's paper 'The Effectiveness of Alternative Monetary Policy Tools in a Zero Lower Bound Environment' at the spring NBER Monetary Economics meeting.

Cœuré, B. (2012, October 17). *What can monetary policy do about inequality?* Speech.

Cœuré, B. (2015a, May 18). *How binding is the zero lower bound?* Speech.

Culbertson, J. (1957). The term structure of interest rates. *Quarterly Journal of Economics, 71*(4), 485–517.

Daines, M., Joyce, M., & Tong, M. (2012). *QE and the gilt market: A disaggregated analysis.* Bank of England Working Paper 466.

Dale, S. (2010, March 12). *QE – One year on.* Speech.

Dixit, A. (1992). Investment and hysteresis. *Journal of Economic Perspectives, 6*, 107–132.

Doh, T. (2010). The efficacy of large-scale asset purchases at the zero lower bound. *Federal Reserve Bank of Kansas City Economic Review, Q2*, 5–34.

Duffie, D. (2010). Asset price dynamics with slow-moving capital. *Journal of Finance, 65*(4), 1237–1267.

Eggertsson, G., & Woodford, M. (2003). The zero bound on interest rates and optimal monetary policy. *Brookings Papers on Economic Activity, 1*, 139–233.

Fawley, B., & Neely, C. (2013). Four stories of quantitative easing. *Federal Reserve Bank of St. Louis Review, January/February*, 51–88.

Fisher, P. (2010, February 18). The corporate sector and the Bank of England's asset purchases. *Speech*.

Friedman, M. (1969). *The optimum quantity of money and other essays*. Chicago: Adline.

Gagnon, J., Raskin, M., Remache, J., & Sack, B. (2011). The financial market effects of the federal reserve's large-scale asset purchases. *International Journal of Central Banking, 7*(1), 45–52.

Gerlach-Kristen, P., McCauley R., & Ueda, K. (2012). *Currency intervention and the global portfolio balance effect: Japanese lessons*. BIS Working Papers 389.

Giles, C. (2012, November 14). Policy ploys risk UK economic credibility. *Blog*.

Greenwood, R., & Vayanos, D. (2010). Price pressure in the government bond market. *American Economic Review, 100*(2), 585–590.

Heath, A. (2015, September 18). We musn't ban cash or inflate the pound. *Telegraph*.

HMT. (2015, March 18). Remit for the Monetary Policy Committee.

Joyce, M., Lasaosa, A., Stevens, I., & Tong, M. (2011a). The financial impact of quantitative easing. *International Journal of Central Banking, 7*(3), 113–161.

Joyce, M., Tong, M., & Wood, R. (2011b). The United Kingdom's quantitative easing policy: Design, operation and impact. *Bank of England Quarterly Bulletin, Q3*, 200–212.

Kapetanios, G., Mumtaz, H., Stevens, I., & Theodoridis, K. (2012). Assessing the economy-wide effects of quantitative easing. *Economic Journal, 122*, F316–F347.

Klyuev, V., de Imus, P., & Srinivasan, K. (2009). *Unconventional choices for unconventional times*. IMF Staff Position Note 09/27.

Krishnamurthy, A., & Vissing-Jorgensen, A. (2011). The effects of quantitative easing on interest rates: Channels and implications for policy. *Brookings Papers on Economic Activity, Fall*, 215–265.

Krugman, P. (1998). It's baaack: Japan's slump and the return of the liquidity trap. *Brookings Paper on Economic Activity, 29*, 137–206.

Leland, H. (1968). Saving and uncertainty: The precautionary demand for saving. *Quarterly Journal of Economics, 82*(3), 465–473.

Lucas, R. (1976). Econometric policy evaluation: A critique. *Carnegie-Rochester Conference Series on Public Policy, 1*, 19–46.

Martin, C., & Milas, C. (2012). Quantitative easing: A sceptical survey. *Oxford Review of Economic Policy, 28*, 750–764.

McLaren, N., & Smith, T. (2013). The profile of cash transfers between the Asset Purchase Facility and Her Majesty's Treasury. *Bank of England Quarterly Bulletin, Q1*, 29–37.

McLeay, M., Radia, A., & Thomas, R. (2014). Money creation in the modern economy. *Bank of England Quarterly Bulletin, Q1*, 14–27.

Miles, D. (2014, February 27). *The transition to a new normal for monetary policy.* Speech.

Modigliani, F., & Sutch, R. (1966). Innovations in interest rate policy. *American Economic Review, 56*(1/2), 178–197.

Mody, A., Ohnsorge, F., & Sandri, D. (2012). *Precautionary savings in the Great Recession.* IMF Working Paper 12/42.

Neely, C. (2010). *The large-scale asset purchases had large international effects.* Federal Reserve Bank of St. Louis Working Paper 2010-018G.

Osborne, G. (2012, November 9). Letter to Governor of the Bank of England regarding transfer of excess cash from the Asset Purchase Facility to HM Treasury.

Praet, P. (2016, March 18). Interview with La Repubblica.

Reis, R. (2006). Inattentive consumers. *Journal of Monetary Economics, 53*(8), 1761–1800.

Romer, C. (1990). The great crash and the onset of the Great Depression. *Quarterly Journal of Economics, 105*, 97–624.

Rudebusch, G. (2009). *The Fed's monetary policy response to the current crisis.* Federal Reserve Bank of San Francisco Economic Letter 2009–17.

Sarno, L., & Taylor, M. (2001). Official intervention in the foreign exchange market. *Journal of Economic Literature, 39*, 839–868.

Sims, C. (2003). Implications of rational inattention. *Journal of Monetary Economics, 50*(3), 665–690.

Slemrod, J. (1988). *Fear of nuclear war and intercountry differences in the rate of saving.* NBER Working Paper 2801.

Spiegel, M. (2006). *Did quantitative easing by the Bank of Japan "work"?* Federal Reserve Bank of San Francisco, Economic Letter, 2006–28.

Stella, P. (1997). *Do central banks need capital?* IMF Working Paper 97/83.

Swanson, E. (2011). Let's twist again. *Brookings Paper on Economic Activity, 42*(1), 151–207.

Tobin, J. (1969). A general equilibrium approach to monetary theory. *Journal of Money, Credit and Banking, 1*, 15–29.

Tucker, P. (2004, July 28). *Managing the Central Bank's balance sheet: Where monetary policy meets financial stability.* Speech.

Vayanos, D., & Vila, J.-L. (2009). *A preferred habitat model of the term structure of interest rates.* NBER Working Paper 15487.

Vlieghe, J. (2016, May 19). *Monetary policy expectations and long term interest rates.* Speech.

Wallace, N. (1981). A Modigliani-Miller theorem for open-market operations. *American Economic Review, 71*(3), 267–274.

Williams, J. (2013). *Will unconventional policy be the new normal?* Federal Reserve Bank of San Francisco, Economic Letter 2013–29.

Woodford, M. (2012). *Methods of policy accommodation at the interest-rate lower bound.* Proceedings – Economic Policy Symposium – Jackson Hole, Federal Reserve Bank of Kansas City, 185–288.

Wren-Lewis, S. (2014, October 22). *Helicopter money.* Blog.

Yates, A. (2014, October 8). *Don't call the helicopters yet!* Blog.

Zurbrugg, F. (2015, March 26). *After the minimum exchange rate.* Speech.

4

Deflation: The Dog That Didn't Bark

Having discussed the BOE's monetary policy response during the opening years of the post-crisis period, we now turn to discuss some of the key puzzles which shaped the monetary policy debate during this period. We begin with the behaviour of inflation.

4.1 The Curious Incident of Consistently Above Target Inflation in a Post-crisis Depression

In the Sir Arthur Conan Doyle story *Silver Blaze* about the disappearance of a race horse from its stable, Sherlock Holmes draws the attention of a detective (and the reader) to 'the curious incident of the dog in the night-time', namely the fact that a dog who was in the stable at the time the horse disappeared did nothing. From this curious incident, Holmes deduces that the working hypothesis of the police that the race horse was stolen by a stranger must be wrong: the dog must have known the person who took the horse otherwise it would have barked.

For those wondering what all this has to do with post-crash monetary policy, the working assumption of many, if not most, macroeconomists when the level of activity collapsed in many developed economies in late 2008 and early 2009 was that significant disinflationary pressures would emerge and there was a genuine threat of outright deflation—but that is not what happened (IMF 2013a):

© The Editor(s) (if applicable) and The Author(s) 2016
R. Barwell, *Macroeconomic Policy after the Crash*,
DOI 10.1057/978-1-137-51592-6_4

While previous recessions were usually associated with marked declines in inflation, the Great Recession barely made a dent.

Deflation was the dog that did not bark during this crisis—or at least during the opening act of the crisis. The behaviour of inflation in the UK was even more surprising: in the four-year period between 2010 and 2013, the annual rate of consumer price inflation was never once below the 2 % target and averaged 3.3 %. For central banks charged with delivering price stability the behaviour of inflation represented a profound puzzle. In this section we discuss why.

4.2   Cautionary Tales of Deflation: The Lost Decade and the Great Depression

In theory, it made perfect sense that inflation rates should tumble around the world in the aftermath of the financial crash. The idea that an output gap—an imbalance between the level of aggregate demand and the sustainable capacity of the economy to produce output (potential supply)—puts pressure on inflation to rise or fall is central to narrative of monetary policy and the transmission mechanism. In late 2008 and early 2009, the level of aggregate demand collapsed and it seemed clear that a large negative output gap must have opened up that would drag down on costs and drag down on prices *given costs*.

Central bankers had more than just theory to go on: they could reflect on Japan's ongoing travails during the Lost Decade. Japan experienced a persistent bout of modest deflation that lasted for over a decade, with a cumulative fall in consumer prices of just 4 % between 1998 and 2012, following the financial crisis of the early 1990s and the banking crisis of the late 1990s (Borio et al. 2014). What is less often said about this period is that the slide into deflation came as something of a surprise *at the time*: it was not expected by the Japanese policymakers, nor by financial markets, nor by Japanese companies and not by overseas observers either (Ahearne et al. 2002).

Interestingly, the consensus outside Japan prior to our own financial crisis was that the economic malaise in Japan was partly self-inflicted, that the Japanese authorities had made mistakes in their handling of the crisis, as Krugman (2014b) observes:

> In the 1990s, we assumed that if the United States or Western Europe found themselves facing anything like Japan's problems, we would respond much more effectively than the Japanese had.

Indeed, as discussed earlier, the implications of Japanese deflation for Fed's strategy was the key theme of his famous 'Making Sure "It" Doesn't Happen Here' speech, in which he concluded (Bernanke 2002):

> Japan's deflation problem is real and serious; but, in my view, political constraints, rather than a lack of policy instruments, explain why its deflation has persisted for as long as it has. Thus, I do not view the Japanese experience as evidence against the general conclusion that U.S. policymakers have the tools they need to prevent, and, if necessary, to cure a deflationary recession in the United States.

Looking further back into economic history, the Great Depression provided another cautionary tale of chronic deflation. In the USA, the GDP deflator—an index which reflects the price of a representative basket of the goods and services which an economy produces—fell by around a quarter over the four-year period from 1930 to 1933 (Meltzer 1976). The sustained fall in prices leaked into inflation expectations: people started to expect prices to keep falling, which implied a higher real interest rate which then exacerbated the decline in output (Cecchetti 1992; Eggertsson 2008).

In both of the instances above, the deflationary episode coincided with a period of weak economic activity that followed a financial crisis: in the case of the Lost Decade, Japan suffered a period of meagre growth punctuated by periods of recession; in the case of the Great Depression, the US economy experienced a sharp contraction in output. However, before we move on it is worth highlighting that not every period of falling prices has been associated with those outcomes. Bordo and Filardo (2004) identify three types of deflationary episode according to the source of the deflationary pressure:

- *The Good*: A positive supply shock causes a significant output gap to open up as the level of aggregate demand fails to keep pace with the increase in potential supply, and that in turn creates the downward pressure on costs and prices which in a low inflation environment could lead to deflation.
- *The Bad*: A demand shock causes a significant output gap to open up relative to an unchanged level of supply, and that in turn creates the downward pressure on costs and prices which in a low inflation environment could lead to deflation.
- *The Ugly*: an extreme variant of bad deflation in which feedback effects emerge from falling prices amplifying the initial decline in demand and prices, typically via financial channels (e.g., debt deflation)

4.3   Monetary Policy in the Era of PLOGs

With the level of activity collapsing in the immediate aftermath of the financial crash monetary policymakers, including those in the UK, were confronted with the prospect of very large negative output gaps that were likely to persist for some time in the absence of a robust and sustained bounce-back in demand. Disinflation—a fall in the rate of inflation—seemed near certain. Moreover, thanks to the Herculean labours of the previous generations of policymakers that had tamed the rampant inflation of previous decades, inflation entered this crisis at already low levels so there was little margin for error before disinflation tipped the economy into outright deflation.

Meier (2010) looked back at the historical record to search for evidence of the disinflationary forces that emerge in practice during episodes of persistent large output gaps (PLOGs), identifying 25 episodes in 14 countries from the last 40 years in which an economy is estimated to have endured eight consecutive quarters of negative output gaps that exceed 1.5 % of potential output. Meier finds that output gaps matter: episodes of PLOGs do indeed almost always lead to significant disinflations, emanating in large part from the labour market, with high and/or rising unemployment exerting downward pressure on wages, a key element of costs. However, Meier also uncovers a surprising feature of PLOG inflation dynamics: the disinflationary pressures within these episodes appear to taper off at very low inflation rates. In part, he attributes this result to the impact of cost shocks, such as movements in the exchange rate or oil prices which have a persistent impact on the price level but only a transitory impact on inflation.

With these surprising empirical regularities in mind, we now turn to a more in-depth discussion of the reasons why inflation proved so resilient in the early years of the crisis. We shall begin with global stories, which apply to a greater or lesser extent to any economy during this period, before turning to explain the curious developments in the UK. Given our framework, it is not too hard to come up with possible explanations as to why the deflation dog might not have barked—the output gap was smaller than we thought, the impact of a negative output gap was (is?) smaller than we thought, or something else was masking the disinflationary impact of a negative output gap—although identifying the culprit from the list of usual suspects is another matter.

4.4   Output Gap Stories

Estimates from a number of different techniques—statistical filters, production functions, survey data and even model-based estimates (see the discussion in Benito et al. (2010))—all suggest that a large negative output gap opened up at the start of the crisis that should have put significant downward pressure on costs and prices. However, we cannot observe the output gap and those estimates are inevitably imprecise. It is possible that those estimates may be flawed and could be giving a misleading impression of the degree of disinflationary slack in the economy. Indeed, real-time estimates of the output gap have often turned out to provide a misleading impression of slack (Orphanides and van Norden 2002) and have contributed to significant policy errors in the past (Nelson and Nikolov 2003).

4.4.1   The Data on Demand Are Wrong

According to IMF data, output in the advanced economies expanded at an average rate of 2.8 % between 1997 and 2006 but managed a meagre 0.2 % in 2008, and contracted by 3.4 % in 2009. It was the cumulative news on the level of activity, relative to an extrapolation of the pre-crisis trend (of 2.8 %), that led policymakers to infer that the output gap must have ended 2009 far into negative territory—on the basis that a swing in aggregate demand on this scale must be reflected in the output gap. We will go on to discuss more sophisticated reasons why this inference might have been wrong but perhaps the simplest explanation is the demand data are wrong, and activity may not have fallen by as much as the data suggest.

The national statisticians publish their first official estimate of the level of activity in a given quarter within a matter of weeks of the end of that quarter. In the months and years that follow more information will become available to the statisticians which they can use to refine and revise their estimates. In the past those revisions have been significant—in the sense that the initial estimates are found to have given a misleading impression of the true state of the economy and therefore policy decisions taken on the basis of those early estimates turn out to be flawed with the benefit of hindsight (Lomax 2004). Policymakers cannot wait until the mature data are available before taking a decision (a decision not to act until more information is available is a decision to stick with the current monetary stance) and therefore often turn to alternative sources of evidence on the state of the economy as a cross-check on the official data (Cunningham and Jeffery 2007). For example, one potential source of information is the business surveys which aggregate together qualitative information on the change in activity among a sample of companies in a diffusion index; for example, an output index describes the net balance of companies which reported an increase in output a month earlier. However, even if the survey responses on the direction in which output has changed on the month are accurate, all information on the size of the change is lost, so the diffusion index can only ever offer a crude gauge of the true path of output.

It is true that the initial estimates on the path of activity in the immediate post-crash period have been revised through time. However, those revisions are second order relative to the measured decline in demand relative to its pre-crisis trend on *any vintage of data* so we therefore dismiss this argument and move on to the next.

4.4.2   The Output Gap Was More Positive than We Thought Before the Crisis

A given change in the level of demand relative to its pre-crisis trend will feed through into a corresponding *change* in the size of the output gap for any particular assumption about the evolution of potential supply. If we infer that the output gap cannot have been very large and negative in say end 2009 given the resilience of inflation in 2010 and 2011 but we are willing to take the data on demand at face value then one way to square the circle is to assume that the output gap must have been more positive than we thought it was before the crash. Implicitly here we are revising our view of the pre-crash level of potential supply down: for a given level of demand in 2007, we are assuming that the level of potential supply was lower than previously thought, so demand has to fall further in order to end up meaningfully below that level of supply by end-2009 to create the large negative output gap that is hard to reconcile with the post-crash path of inflation. As a matter of record, estimates of the output gap in the pre-crisis period have changed in this direction. For example, real-time estimates of the output gap in the euro area in 2007 had been revised up by between one and three percentage points by the end of 2010 (ECB 2011).

However, there is a limit to how much of the puzzling post-crash resilience of inflation can be explained away through these revisions to the pre-crash output gap—at some point we solve one puzzle at the cost of creating another. Our original estimates of the output gap in 2007 should have been calibrated to best match the observed path of demand and inflation. Raising our estimate of the output gap in 2007 might make the path of inflation in 2010 and 2011 easier to explain but only at the cost of making inflation in 2007 and 2008 harder to explain. If there was a positive PLOG in the pre-crash era—given the relatively smooth profile of growth before the crash a very large positive output gap cannot easily emerge over-night in 2007—then it ought to have caused inflation to drift up away from the target.

Some commentators point to the fact that *asset* price inflation was rampant in this period as evidence of a large positive output gap, but it is hard to explain why imbalances in the real economy—companies in the real economy working their labour and capital above normal levels of utilisation and too many companies chasing too few job seekers in the labour market—would show up in the price of structured credit products in financial markets.

4.4.3   The Collapse in Supply

Leaving to one side the issue of measurement error around the published data on demand, the fundamental reason why we cannot observe the output gap is that we cannot observe the level of potential supply against which we compare those published data on demand. If we apply Occam's razor to our puzzle of the surprising resilience of inflation in the years that followed the crash—that is, the principle that among the set of possible explanations for a puzzle we should *favour* the one that involves the least assumptions (of course, the simplest explanation is not always the right one)—then we conclude that the most likely explanation is that there must have been a significant decline in the level of potential supply around the same time as the observed fall in the level of demand.

Macroeconomists often assume for the sake of convenience that total factor productivity (TFP), which is the fundamental driver of increases in potential supply capturing improvements in the efficiency with which companies can combine inputs to produce output, expands at a constant rate, which in turn delivers a relatively smooth upward trend in potential supply. It is the juxtaposition of that sudden collapse in the level of demand and the assumption of that smooth upward trend in supply that is suggestive of a large change in the output gap during this period. However, there is no reason to believe that potential supply actually follows such a smooth trend in practice. Indeed, model-based estimates of the so-called flex-price level of output—that path of output we would observe if prices could adjust to clear markets—tend to be quite volatile (Neiss and Nelson 2005; Vetlov et al. 2011). Moreover, as we shall go on to discuss in the next section, there are good reasons to suppose that the level of potential supply may have fallen during this period. Clearly, if the level of supply is falling at the same time as the level of demand then the news on the gap between them and hence on inflationary pressure is correspondingly smaller.

Once again, there is a limit to the extent to which we can reverse engineer the profile for potential supply that reconciles the observed path of demand and inflation without creating a new puzzle. The level of demand is endogenous with respect to the level of supply. In particular, a large and persistent fall in the level of potential supply means that households' permanent income is lower—they will earn less in the future—and that should lead them to revise down consumption. In other words, too large a revision to our estimate of potential supply simply creates a new puzzle: why did the level of demand not fall further during the crisis?

4.5   Slope Stories

It might be that the intuitive estimates of the output gap—that is, the collapse in demand in 2008–09 must deliver a large negative output gap in end 2009—are in the right ballpark and there was a large margin of spare capacity in many advanced economies at that point in time but the impact of that output gap on inflation is much weaker than we thought—or in the technical jargon, the slope of the short-run Phillips curve is extremely flat.

4.5.1   Structural Change and the Slope

The claim that the sensitivity of inflationary pressure to the output gap has declined over time such that by the time of the crisis a large output gap will exert only a modest impact on inflation might strike the reader as a convenient way to explain away the facts after the fact. However, numerous studies had pointed to an apparent flattening of the Phillips curve across countries (e.g., Atkeson and Ohanian 2001; Roberts 2006; Benati 2007), leading policymakers to speculate about the lack of inflationary consequences of large real imbalances *before the crisis*—for example, Mishkin (2007) argues:

> In traditional Phillips-curve equations, inflation depends on past values of inflation, an unemployment gap (the difference between the unemployment rate and an estimate of its natural rate), and variables such as the relative price of energy and import prices. When researchers estimate these equations, they typically find that the coefficient on the unemployment gap has declined (in absolute

value) since the 1980s, often by a marked amount. In other words, the evidence suggests that the Phillips curve has flattened. The finding that inflation is less responsive to the unemployment gap, if taken at face value, suggests that fluctuations in resource utilization will have smaller implications for inflation than used to be the case.

There are essentially two classes of explanation for the apparent flattening of the Phillips curve: those that have to do with changes in the monetary policy regime; and those that reflect other structural changes in the economy.

The transition to a transparent and credible framework for the delivery of price stability could have influenced inflation dynamics in two key respects—changing the way companies adjust prices and how often they adjust prices:

- *Expectations (of good policy) stabilise prices*: When they come to resetting prices, companies will base their decisions on how they expect the future to evolve over the period that prices are fixed. If there is an output gap today and companies expect it to persist indefinitely, then they will adjust prices accordingly—for example, raising prices by more in a boom. The more confident that companies are that the monetary authority is willing and able to lean against an output gap today, the smaller the weight that companies will place on the *current* output gap when setting prices in a boom or bust (Laxton and N'Diaye 2002). To be clear, this mechanism hinges on companies believing that the output gap will be small(er) in the future, thanks to monetary policy.
- *Companies set prices less often*: If changing prices is a costly business—in terms of collecting and processing information to calculate the new optimal price, the 'menu cost' of physically changing prices and the costs of upsetting customers—then one might expect the transition to low and stable inflation to lead to companies economising on the frequency with which they change prices. That increase in price stickiness will reduce the sensitivity of inflation to the imbalance between demand and supply at any moment in time (Ball et al. 1988).

There are a host of other structural factors which might have influenced the slope of the Phillips curve, and not all in the same direction:

- *Migration of labour*: As the costs (and barriers) to international migration decline then the supply of labour to domestic companies should become more elastic. Whereas a boom might once have led to a tight labour market in which large number of companies are chasing a small number of job-seekers leading wages to rise faster than marginal revenue product, now companies can source additional workers from abroad. In the limit, the concept of a domestic output gap starts to lose any meaning if potential supply endogenously responds to cyclical swings in demand via flows of labour into and out of the country (Barwell 2007).

- *Competition from abroad*: A reduction in tariffs, quotas and other trade barriers or transportation costs will place local companies selling output in domestic markets under greater competition from companies overseas. Those local companies will enjoy less pricing power, reducing their capacity to absorb shifts in costs—including cyclical shifts in costs—in profit margins rather than adjusting prices, and will tend to adjust prices more frequently for fear of their price moving out of line with competitors (Rogoff 2003, 2006). In other words, increased competition from abroad should lead to a steeper trade-off.
- *Internet*: The Internet should reduce the search costs of customers and lower barriers to entry, eroding the pricing power of companies and reducing the menu cost of changing prices and therefore other things equal the frequency of price changes (Wadhwani 2000). These changes should in theory also lead to a steeper trade-off.

4.5.2 The Cost Channel of Monetary Policy and the Credit Crunch

In our earlier treatment of the transmission mechanism of monetary policy, we discussed a set of mechanisms—known as the cost channel of monetary policy—through which tighter monetary policy can perversely lead to rising inflation because interest rates enter the costs of production. In the opening phase of the crisis a variant of this mechanism turned out to have a significant impact on the supply schedule—effectively the amount of goods and services that companies could supply to the market at a given price. The slope of the Phillips curve would therefore appear to flatten because the disinflationary drag from spare capacity would have been masked by the inflationary impulse coming through the cost channel.

The reason that the cost channel flared up is because the interest rate that enters that cost function of a standard company is not the official policy rate, which as we have already seen was falling fast. The terms on which companies can get access to credit in various forms—not just conventional loans from a bank—include a spread or risk premium that was moving fast in the opposite direction, given the increase in the price and quantity of risk.

Even the small- and medium-sized companies that are typically thought to be reliant on banks for credit have access to alternative sources of finance: companies habitually borrow and lend money to each other up and down the supply chain through a process referred to as trade credit. The receipt of goods may not be perfectly synchronised with payment, so the supplier is effectively making a short-term loan: if you supply output to a customer today and he promises to pay you in a month's time then in the interim you have lent him money.

Trade credit has historically been a critical source of finance: thirty years ago the outstanding stock of trade credit far exceeded the business lending of the entire banking system (Lee and Stowe 1993) and the survey data suggested that in excess of 80 % of small businesses in the USA had taken trade credit from suppliers (Elliehausen and Wolken 1993). Trade credit is typically expensive, reflecting the compensation that the provider demands for the provision of liquidity insurance (delays in payment are common) and the risk of default (Cuñat 2007). Trade credit will naturally arise along the supply chain and therefore creates a network of interdependence—companies may simultaneously lend money to their customers and borrow from their suppliers— and that creates fertile ground for the propagation of funding shocks through the real economy (Delli Gatti et al. 2009). Banks and other financial companies have evolved to help companies manage the strain on cash flow that the provision of trade credit can engineer via a variety of forms of invoice financing—essentially allowing companies to borrow against the promise of future payment—or trade credit insurance. However, the capacity of the financial sector to provide those services dried up at precisely the moment that the capacity of companies to service their debts within the trade credit network was being stretched to the limit. The cost of short-term trade credit facilities rose to 300 to 600 basis points above LIBOR (London Interbank Offered Rate), relative to a normal spread of 10 to 20 basis points (Auboin 2009). In truth this was a global phenomenon, and the sudden scarcity of trade finance helps to explain the magnitude of the collapse in world trade during the acute phase of the global economic crisis (Wynne 2009).

The crisis has revived interest in the link between credit conditions and price setting (see, for example, Gilchrist and Zakrajsek [2015]), but there is an established literature which pre-dates the crash by a decade or more that investigates this mechanism. That literature builds on the insight in Phelps and Winter's (1970) 'customer markets' model, in which customers are sticky, in the sense that they do not immediately switch to a competitor when a company raises the price of its output. That inertia creates an incentive for a company to invest in future market share: cutting prices today in order to attract more customers, from whom the company can earn higher profits in the future. Gottfries (1991) argues that credit market imperfections can help explain why prices are relatively insensitive to demand. In Gottfries' model those imperfections constrain the ability of a company to make these investments in market share. An increase in demand eases that constraint: profits and cash flow are strong so companies can cut prices without having to borrow money. Chevalier and Scharfstein (1996) obtain a similar result, showing how companies facing liquidity constraints will scale back investments in market share in a recession (i.e., cutting prices) in order to boost cash flow. There is little point investing in market share if you will not survive until the boom to reap the rewards. Moreover, unconstrained companies will follow suit, leading to a counter-cyclical mark-up. This mechanism could explain why prices did not fall when demand slowed and access to credit tightened.

The result that credit constraints moderate the decline in profit margins and prices in a sharp downturn is not uncontroversial. One way companies can respond to a sudden and sharp contraction in access to finance is to liquidate their stock of finished and semi-finished output. Hendel (1996) captures this reallocation within working capital in a model in which inventories serve as a buffer of output when times are good, and as a buffer of liquidity when times are bad. Hendel illustrates how inventory management and price setting depend on whether companies are financially fragile. Fragile companies hold more of their working capital in cash and less in stocks so that they have the resources to survive economic downturns. And when demand does slow, and their survival is at stake, these companies try to raise cash by cutting prices and running-down inventories to meet the additional demand. Hendel also considers the strategic response of cash-rich companies in an environment where their fragile competitors are under threat. Companies that are not in peril may still cut prices in a slowdown, trading off lost profits today for the higher profits they could potentially earn in the future if they can force their competitors out of the market today.

4.5.3 Nominal Wage Rigidities and the Slope of the Long-Run Trade-Off

We argued earlier that there is no long-run trade-off between output and inflation: if a central bank wants to deliver price stability then it must eliminate any gap between the level of aggregate demand and potential supply and conversely any rate of inflation is feasible as a stable equilibrium if aggregate demand is in line with potential supply. Akerlof et al. (1996) challenged that basic proposition of macroeconomics: they argued that at low inflation rates the long-run Phillips curve is downward sloping: there is a permanent sacrifice ratio with permanently higher unemployment the price of permanently lower trend inflation.

The mechanism that generates Akerlof, Dickens and Perry's long-run trade-off is the interaction of imperfect competition in product markets, downward nominal wage rigidity (DNWR) in the labour market and meaningful shocks to demand and supply at the micro level. Given imperfect competition in product markets, companies will employ labour up to the point where wages are a mark-down on marginal revenue product. Wages and prices would fall in the absence of downward rigidities that prevent wages falling when a company is hit by a negative shock. However, when companies cannot cut wages they are driven off the labour demand curve by negative shocks: constrained wages move out of line with the ideal mark-down on marginal revenue product. Companies respond by both raising prices and scaling back on employment (which raises marginal physical product) in order to raise marginal revenue product relative to wages.

The extent to which this constraint binds, leading to an inefficient increase in unemployment, hinges on two key trends: the rate of inflation and the rate of productivity growth—which together pin down the trend in marginal revenue product—which provides companies with a buffer which can be used to absorb shocks without having to cut wages. Furthermore, we might expect companies to supplement that buffer by raising wages by less in good years than they otherwise might have done in the absence of the downward rigidity in anticipation of the risk that they might not be able to cut wages enough in the bad years (Altonji and Devereux 2000).

Akerlof, Dickens and Perry presented simulations which illustrate the long-run Phillips curve starts to bend away from the vertical when trend inflation drops below 3 %; beyond that point, more and more companies will run up against the constraint and equilibrium unemployment increases at an increasing rate as the long-run Phillips curve becomes surprisingly horizontal. Moving from a 3 % inflation target to a price level target is found to increase the equilibrium unemployment rate by between one to two percentage points. In a deflationary environment like the Great Depression, the downward nominal rigidity may buckle under the pressure of economic reality, but it does not disappear entirely and the cost in terms of unemployment could be severe.

The Akerlof, Dickens and Perry thesis refers to the long-run trade-off between unemployment and inflation. Daly and Hobijn (2014) transplant these arguments into the short-run Phillips curve, illustrating how downward nominal wage rigidities bend the short-run trade-off in two key respects, with the effects more pronounced in an era of low inflation:

- *Less weak wages on the way down*: When aggregate demand slows, the rigidities bind and more of the business cycle adjustment operates through higher unemployment and less through weaker wages.
- *Weaker wages on the way back up*: The distortions created by the rigidities lead to 'pent-up wage deflation' such that when the economy recovers, wage growth is surprisingly weak.

In short, DNWR offers one explanation for the curious behaviour of inflation during the crisis; indeed, those who maintain that there has been a lot of slack in the post-crash economy tend to attribute a lot of weight to DNWR as the explanation (Krugman 2014a). The key question is how important downward wage rigidity is as an empirical phenomenon.

The incidence of downward wage rigidity is difficult to estimate. The micro-data on individual wages are often polluted by measurement error, which introduces large wage changes in the data (imagine what happens to measured pay growth in consecutive years if you misreport your pay in any given year—particularly in the case of a decimal point error). Payroll data collected from companies ought to be more reliable than survey data collected from households, but even when we focus on payroll data on base pay (that is, stripping out the more volatile elements of pay, like bonus payments) we still find that the distribution of wage changes from one year to the next is disperse, with significant numbers of extreme observations (large pay rises and pay cuts).

Barwell and Schweitzer (2007) document that nominal and real wage rigidities are persistent features of British wage change distributions—that is, a disproportionately large number of individuals with wages that are unchanged on the year before and a clustering of individuals with wage increases close to a reasonable expectation of inflation over that year. The fraction of the workforce protected from real wage cuts was found to have declined over the 1980s and 1990s, although that increase in flexibility did not appear to be driven by changes in the characteristics of the workforce (such as the decline in unionisation). Finally, Barwell and Schweitzer find evidence that rigidities in wage setting are associated with economically significant variation in job destruction rates at the micro level: those more likely to be protected from wage cuts are also more likely to lose their job.

Babecký et al. (2009) present evidence on the extent of nominal and real wage rigidity across Continental Europe using surveys of companies from 14 countries. Whilst around one in ten companies report that they have frozen wages and close to one in five report an automatic link between wages and inflation (which can give rise to real wage rigidity), less than one in a hundred report cutting wages in the five-year period leading up to the survey.

4.5.4 Speed Limit Effects

Our final explanation for an apparent flattening of the Phillips curve has to do with the specification of the relationship between slack in the economy and the amount of inflationary pressure—in particular, the idea that the change in the output gap matters as well as the absolute level.

This is not the first time that a large number of advanced economies have simultaneously endured large negative output gaps. During the 1980s, many European countries suffered very high levels of unemployment—the most visible manifestation of slack in the economy. However, when the European economy started to recover inflationary pressures started to re-emerge long before the unemployment rate had been brought back down to its level of earlier decades. One explanation for that puzzling phenomenon was the presence of 'speed limit' effects where inflationary pressure is sensitive to the change in the output gap as well as its level (Layard et al. 1991).

Speed limit effects are typically rationalised in terms of the emergence of bottlenecks: even though there may be productive resources lying idle somewhere in the economy companies may not be able to source them and integrate them into the production process quickly (Dwyer et al. 2010). Inflationary pressure could therefore emerge in key sectors and regions of the economy even when across the economy as a whole there is a surplus of resources. However, the evidence on whether speed limit effects are economically significant is inconclusive (Turner 1995; Meier 2010; ECB 2014).

In principle these speed limit effects could explain why inflation was relatively resilient in those countries where the recovery in demand from the trough was reasonably robust: the output gap was still large and negative but the change in the output gap was large and positive. However, for those countries where the post-crash recovery in demand was more anaemic than in previous recessions, the discussion of speed-limit effects is moot.

4.6 Global Gaps

Thus far, we have tried to explain away the surprising absence of disinflation in the post-crash era in two ways: that the imbalance in the domestic economy (the output gap) was smaller than at first thought, and that the link between the domestic output gap and domestically generated inflation was smaller than at first thought. We now turn to an alternative explanation for our puzzle: that this local channel which operates through the product of a 'domestic gap' and 'domestic slope' is less important than first thought, and was offset by developments elsewhere in the global economy. It is possible that in an increasingly interconnected global economy, where many goods and services are traded across borders, that it is the pressure of demand on supply at the global level—the global output gap—that drives inflationary pressure in all countries.

In the context of our puzzle, the fact that growth had been robust in the years before the crisis and output did not collapse to anywhere near the same degree in the emerging economies (particularly in Asia) might therefore help explain the behaviour of inflation in the advanced economies. One particular channel through which the level of demand in the emerging economies might have been particularly important is via the prices of commodities (Pain et al. 2006), but we shall delay discussion of this particular channel until we turn to the particularly puzzling behaviour of UK inflation over this period.

Once again, the claim that local inflation was increasingly being driven by capacity pressures in the global economy was being made before the crisis and our particular puzzle emerged. However, there is no consensus in the literature, and the economic significance of this global output gap channel remains controversial.

Borio and Filardo (2007) argued that the conventional models of inflation were too 'country-centric' and that a 'globe centric' approach was appropriate, which reflected the reality of 'globalisation': the fact that product markets were becoming increasingly integrated across countries. They report that including proxies for global economic slack allows them to better explain domestic inflation, even controlling for the traditional channels of transmission, such as oil prices. Moreover, they find the role of such global factors has increased over time and in some instances has supplanted the domestic measures of slack. Consistent with that, Ciccarelli and Mojon (2005) report evidence that inflation has become a global phenomenon: a simple average of inflation across 22 OECD countries accounts for 70 % of the variance of inflation in these countries between 1960 and 2003.

In contrast, Ihrig et al. (2010) find that the estimated effect of foreign output gaps on domestic consumer price inflation across a number of industrial countries is generally insignificant and often of the wrong sign, and no evidence that inflation has become more sensitive to import prices. Likewise, Calza (2008) finds very limited evidence that measures of global spare capacity can explain or predict developments in domestic consumer prices in the euro area.

In theory, it is possible that some countries might be more affected by the global gap channel than others. The companies in large industries in relatively closed economies may be less beholden to the prices set by competitors overseas, with more scope to set prices according to domestic costs. In contrast, small companies in a relatively small domestic industry based in an open economy—the situation for many companies in the UK—may enjoy far less pricing power so prices may be far more sensitive to global prices (Busain et al. 2006).

Central bankers had acknowledged to varying degrees the potential importance of the global output gap in driving local inflation dynamics before the crisis—for a range of views see Bean (2006), Papademos (2006), Yellen (2006) and Bernanke (2007). However, acknowledging the importance of globalisation should not be confused as a counsel of despair: that local monetary policy had become impotent in the face of global pressures on domestic prices. Central banks retain the power to control the domestic price level. Indeed, the sterling effective exchange rate should appreciate to offset the impact of a positive global output gap on the sterling price of foreign output (Tanaka and Young 2008).

Ironically, this global output gap story might have worked in the opposite direction in the decade or two leading up to the crash, during which time the global economy experienced a huge positive supply shock. The entry of China, India and Eastern Europe effectively doubled the global supply of labour to the market economy: from around 1.5 billion to 3 billion people (Bean 2006). The rapid expansion of production of industrial goods in those so-called 'low-cost economies' had a material impact on prices in the advanced economies. Mac Coille (2008) estimates that the increase in the import share of those economies may have reduced the rate of inflation of manufactured goods by 0.7 percentage points between 2000 and 2006, but that this disinflationary drag appears to have dissipated as the price of these cheap imports rose.

4.7   The Puzzling Strength of UK Inflation

We have discussed reasons why inflation in the advanced economies did not slow as much as might have been expected in the aftermath of the financial crisis, given the collapse in demand. We now turn to discuss a puzzle closer to home.

In the months immediately after the crash, the rate of inflation in the UK did what you would expect under the circumstances: it slowed at a pretty rapid rate. As a matter of fact, CPI inflation peaked at 5.2 % in September 2008—a rate far in excess of the target, which goes a long way to explain why Bank Rate was still so high on the eve of the crash—and then declined to a low of 1.1 % a year later in September 2009. However, inflation then reversed course climbing to 2.9 % by December 2009 and was never lower than 3.0 % throughout the whole of 2010 and 2011, reaching a peak of 5.2 % in September 2011. Inflation would not fall below 2 % until January 2014.

The arguments presented earlier in this section to do with the gaps and slopes surely apply to the UK too. However, we need to look elsewhere to explain why inflation was so much stronger in the UK than in many other advanced economies during this period. It turns out that there is no one silver bullet explanation which can account for the surprising strength of UK inflation throughout this period; instead we need to take the story in stages.

The other interesting feature of the strength of UK inflation is that it came as a surprise to the BOE: in the August 2010 Inflation Report, the MPC expected inflation to gradually drift lower. Indeed, inflation turned out on average 1½ percentage points higher than expected despite the fact that the level of GDP was almost 7 % lower than expected (Hackworth et al. 2013).

Before we get to our puzzles, we need to extend our description of how prices are determined. The output gap channel which crops up repeatedly in this book, that links the amount of slack in the economy to the evolution of costs and prices, refers to the price of the value added that companies produce. The price we pay in the shops will reflect that price of value added, but it will also reflect the price of raw materials that are consumed in the production process and the cumulative impact of taxes and subsidies on products and production that are levied along the supply chain.

4.7.1 Indirect Taxes: One Step Down, Two Steps Up

There is one obvious factor which can explain both why UK inflation fell at a rapid rate through the first year of the post-crash period and then rose sharply thereafter: changes in the rate of value-added tax (VAT).

One of the discretionary measures that the Chancellor announced in late 2008 was an immediate cut in the headline rate of VAT from 17½ % to 15 % which came into effect in December 2008 and was scheduled to last until the end of December 2009, when the headline rate would revert to its former level. In June 2010, one of the austerity measures that the new Chancellor announced was a permanent increase in the headline rate of VAT from 17½ % to 20 % that would come into effect in January 2011.

At face value these changes in the headline rate of VAT implied an immediate drop in the level of consumer prices in late 2008, which would then reverse at the beginning of 2010 to be followed by another step higher in prices at the beginning of 2011. Those step changes are consistent with a temporary drag on inflation (as prices at the 15 % rate are compared to prices the year earlier at the 17½ % rate) followed by a more sustained lift (as prices at the 17½ % and 20 % rates are compared to prices the year earlier at the 15 % and 17½ % rates).

In reality, the impact of these changes in the rate of VAT on the rate of inflation is not so clear cut because changes in indirect taxes will not tend to be passed through in full into consumer prices in the month in which they come into effect (Blundell 2009). Even permanent changes in indirect taxes may not be fully passed through (Benedek et al. 2015), but in particular where temporary changes are concerned, given non-trivial costs of changing prices (the menu cost of changing the price, the opportunity cost of the resources used to calculate the new optimal price and the reputational damage of upsetting customers by changing prices), companies may decide to pass through only a fraction of the change. Second, whether pass-through is complete or not, the timing of any change in prices is unlikely to be concentrated just in the month in which the change takes effect: the process of adjustment will be driven by the calendar of when a company usually changes its prices as well as what its competitors are doing. Where changes in indirect taxes are announced far in advance this can further complicate the dynamics of pass-through, with prices adjusting before the change takes effect. Taking these two points together it is interesting to note that the increase in prices due to the reversal of the temporary cut in the headline rate in January 2010 (which was pre-announced over a year earlier) was estimated by the national statistician to be roughly half the size of the increase in January 2011 (which was known about for about half the time) which was also permanent (ONS 2011).

The final point to note here is that these changes in the rate of VAT cannot shed any light on the reasons why inflation did not behave as the MPC expected over the post-crash period. The puzzling behaviour described earlier (Hackworth et al. 2013) was benchmarked against the August 2010 Inflation Report projections—a point in time at which all these changes in rates were known.

4.7.2 Exchange Rate

Perhaps the single most important factor in driving the puzzling strength of UK inflation over this period—certainly relative to outcomes in other advanced economies—was the significant depreciation in the sterling effective exchange rate. Between the middle of 2007 and the end of 2008 the pound depreciated by in excess of 25 % against the dollar and the euro and approaching 50 % against the yen. The exchange rate moves over the course of the last quarter of 2008 were particularly striking: the pound depreciated by approaching 20 % against the euro and the dollar and around 30 % against the yen in the space of three months.

We shall delay discussing the fundamental drivers of the exchange rate until later in this book; for now we will focus on the reasons why the value of the pound might have fallen so far as the crisis unfolded where, as is so often the case in macroeconomics, there is a plethora of plausible explanations (Astley et al. 2009):

- *Bad news about the depth of the recession in the UK:* If market participants expected the crisis to trigger a deeper and/or more protracted recession in the UK relative to the other advanced economies, they should also have expected the MPC to ease monetary policy more aggressively than other central banks, depressing the relative return on sterling-denominated assets, and for the pound to depreciate accordingly in order to boost the contribution of net trade to growth (the difference between the lift from exports and the drag from imports) to help close that wider margin of spare capacity in the UK.

- *Chronically higher UK inflation:* As we have already noted, inflation was particularly strong in the UK in the post-crash period. If that inflation differential relative to other advanced economies was expected to persist into the medium-term then we should expect the pound to depreciate in order to ensure that the UK prices of goods and services that can be traded in international markets do not move out of line with prices in other markets when measured in common currency.

- *The UK economy is believed to be a riskier place to invest money:* If investors believed that there was a greater risk of very bad returns on investments in sterling-denominated assets and, in particular, very poor returns in moments where the rest of their portfolio was performing badly, then that would lead to a reduced demand for sterling and a depreciation in the currency until the currency is cheap enough to be sufficiently attractive to encourage investors to hold sterling-denominated assets. It is not too hard to imagine why investors might have become concerned about the fragility of the UK relative to other economies during a banking crisis: the UK banking sector is large relative to the size of the economy and that raised questions about the capacity of the UK sovereign to support the banks and the likelihood that the UK economy might suffer a more protracted slow-down in the aftermath of the economy.

- *End of the carry trade*: In the run-up to the crisis, investors had borrowed money in currencies where interest rates were already low (the dollar and the yen) to invest in currencies where interest rates were still high (like the pound). Once the race to the bottom began the return on that carry trade collapsed, and as investors unwound the positions we would have expected to see the pound depreciate and the yen and the dollar appreciate.
- *Rebalancing and the equilibrium exchange rate*: Finally, market participants might have looked further ahead and concluded that the pound would have to depreciate in the long run in order for the economy to achieve external balance which would weigh on the value of the currency. Market participants may have reached that conclusion in light of the crisis for a number of reasons: that the demand for one of UK's key exports (financial services) had diminished post-crisis or that fiscal consolidation would lead to a shift in aggregate demand towards more import-intensive expenditure.

We noted above that inflation turned out much stronger than the forecast that the MPC published in mid-2010. However, the sharp depreciation in the pound was over and done with by the end of 2008: the pound actually recovered some lost ground after its nadir in the immediate aftermath of the collapse of Lehman Brothers. The fact that the value of the pound collapsed in late 2008 does not help us explain the surprising resilience of UK inflation relative to forecasts made in mid-2010. What can explain those forecast errors and our inflation puzzle is a failure to forecast the inflationary consequences of that known depreciation—a mistake made by a number of forecasters, not just the MPC (Broadbent 2013).

When thinking about the macroeconomic implications of these alternate explanations for the depreciation of the currency we ought to have in mind a number of potential transmission channels from the source of the shock to the outlook for UK output and inflation. However, for the purposes of this discussion we are interested purely in the transmission through sterling import prices into UK consumer prices.

It is natural to assume that a lower exchange rate will lead to an increase in the sterling price of imported goods and services. However, in practice it mat-ters a great deal which currency importers set their prices in. One option is to set prices in the currency in which their costs are denominated (a.k.a. pro-ducer currency pricing). An alternative is to set prices in the currency of the market in which they are selling output (a.k.a. local currency pricing). In the case of the former then sterling import prices will indeed rise when sterling depreciates in order that the importer receives the same price in foreign currency. However, in the case of the latter sterling import prices will not move when the currency depreciates, but the margin between the price that the importer receives and her costs—when measured in common (foreign) currency—will shrink, and if the currency move turns out to be persistent then at some stage (perhaps when currency hedges roll off) we might expect to see a gradual adjustment in sterling import prices. Even once sterling import prices adjust it might take time before the full impact of the exchange rate fall on consumer prices is felt. At each stage in the domestic supply chain between an imported commodity and a good or service which features in the consumption basket there is scope for profit margins to absorb and temporarily delay the pass-through of costs into prices.

As Dale (2010) explains, the MPC believed that the pass-through from the depreciation of the currency into consumer prices would be very gradual, in line with the consensus in the literature at that time that pass-through into consumer prices was glacially slow (Campa and Goldberg 2006). As Mishkin (2008) concludes:

> Now let me summarize the lessons from the empirical evidence on exchange rate pass-through. Sizeable depreciations of the nominal exchange rate exert fairly small effects on consumer prices across a wide set of industrial countries, and these effects have declined over the past two decades. Exchange rate depreciations are thus likely to have less adverse effects on inflation than they have had in the past.

This time would be different: pass-through was more rapid than the MPC had forecast, compressing the period over which the adjustment in the level of consumer prices consistent with higher sterling import prices took place, which implies a short period of surprisingly strong inflation (Dale 2010). It is hard to know why this time was different: but it might be that in a period where credit conditions were tight and cash flow was precious companies felt less able to absorb rising costs in prices at any point along the supply chain.

4.7.3 Commodity Prices

Earlier on we noted that one factor which might explain the increasingly weak link between imbalances in the real economy and inflationary pressure is the growing importance of the imbalances in the global economy—that is, it is the global and not the domestic output gap that matters.

One obvious channel through which that global output gap could influence prices in the UK is via the price of commodities traded in international markets. However, the global output gap will likely only drive the cyclical dynamic in commodity price inflation. The driver of the trend in commodity prices is likely to reflect the race between two factors: the rate of increase in global potential supply (which pins down aggregate demand at the global level) and developments in the supply of these commodities (Tanaka and Young 2008). For example, rapid growth in the sustainable level of global demand will put upward pressure on the price of commodities in relatively fixed supply. Likewise, structural and transitory shifts in the supply of these commodities can also influence prices—for example, El Niño and La Niña can influence food prices by disrupting yields (Brunner 2002).

Global commodity prices rose sharply in late 2010 and into early 2011. Strong growth in the emerging economies which account for a disproportionate share of global demand for commodities (relative to their share of global GDP) was clearly instrumental in driving the sharp increase in prices from palladium to frozen pork bellies. However, over and above that common demand shock there were also important supply shocks (IMF 2011):

- *Food prices*: Bad weather had a material impact on supply across a range of items (regions), from wheat (Russia, Ukraine), to rice, rubber, cotton, and local vegetables (south and southeast Asia), to corn (USA), to sugar (India) thanks in part to La Niña.
- *Oil prices*: the surprisingly modest production response of the Organisation of Petroleum Exporting Countries (OPEC) to rising oil prices and unrest in the Middle East and North Africa (IMF 2011)

These increases in commodity prices were not easy to predict even in summer 2010—especially those driven by supply shocks and they inevitably took their toll on UK inflation. For example, if the price of crude oil and natural gas increase at the global level then the price of petrol at the pump and household utility bills in the UK will almost surely follow. Indeed, Hackworth et al. (2013) note that on average just over a third of the 1½ percentage points of news on annual inflation (relative to the Committee's August 2011 forecast) can be accounted for by the direct effect of unexpected rises in energy costs alone.

Of course, unlike the impact of sterling, this commodity shock was common to all countries and therefore helps to explain the surprising resilience of inflation across the board and not why the UK stood out from the crowd. Indeed, price level shocks from commodity prices have been an important driver of movements in global inflation in recent years: energy and food prices contributed around three percentage points to the global inflation spike at the onset of the crisis and detracted half a point in mid-2015 (Carney 2015).

4.7.4 Tuition Fees

The final element of the puzzle turns out to be the changes in student tuition fees. The university tuition fees paid by UK and EU students account for close to 1 % of the consumption basket (accounting for close to half of the expenditure in the education sub-aggregate of the consumption basket, which itself accounts for a little under 2 % of the entire basket in 2012). The sizeable increase in tuition fees therefore had a non-trivial impact on consumer price inflation even though the consumers concerned (the students) would not actually pay the costs of higher tuition for years to come, once they had graduated from university (King 2013).

The actual increase in tuition fees was phased in over several years (ONS 2014):

- In the 2012/13 academic year, the maximum fee that undergraduates could be charged for the first year of their course was raised to £9000 from the previous maximum of £3375 in 2011–12. For students already enrolled on courses the maximum fee for the second and higher years was increased from £3375 to £3465.
- In the 2013/14 academic year, the maximum fee for the second year of a course was increased to the new higher fee, whilst the maximum fee for third and fourth year courses was left at the lower level.
- In the 2014/15 academic year, the maximum fee for the third year of a course was increased to bring it in line with the new higher structure.

As a result of the gradual introduction of the higher maximum, the impact of the introduction of tuition fees on the price of university education was spread over a number of years (n.b., consumer prices were calculated on the basis of actual fees, not the theoretical maximum). In the first year, the step change in the average fee paid by students led to an increase in the inflation rate for this item in the basket. The average fee kept rising in subsequent years but the percentage rate of change falls with a smaller increase compared to a higher starting level of fees and as a result the inflation rate for this item falls back. Hackworth et al. (2013) note that in the 2013 Q2 (during the first academic year when the impact on inflation was at its highest), the introduction of tuition fees could account for around a quarter of a percentage point of the surprise in inflation at that horizon, relative to the Committee's August forecast.

4.8   Endnote: Conclusions and Consequences

We have discussed a number of plausible explanations for the surprising resilience of inflation in the face of the persistent weakness of aggregate demand following the financial crisis. This is more than an exercise in recent economic history. The solution to the puzzle of why the disinflationary dog did not bark matters because it has implications for the conduct of economic policy going forward.

- *Implications for monetary policy in the short run*: The more our puzzle can be explained by a flat slope, the more scope (need) there is for policy to remain accommodative in the recovery in the face of above trend growth (because there is a larger output gap to be closed).
- *Implications for monetary policy in the long run*: The more our puzzle can be explained by a flat slope, the less influence policymakers will have on inflation via the standard transmission channels through the output gap, which implies that policymakers might have to tolerate more volatility in inflation and the policy instrument, and a higher probability of hitting the lower bound.
- *Implications for fiscal policy*: The more our puzzle can be explained by a smaller output gap, the smaller the fraction of the deficit we can attribute to cyclical weakness, and therefore the larger fraction that reflects a structural deficit (that would remain when the output gap is closed) that must be corrected through consolidation (changes in spending and tax).
- *Implications for prudential policy*: The more our puzzle can be explained by a smaller output gap thanks to a post-crash contraction in the level of supply the stronger the case for a tougher micro- and macro-prudential regulatory regime that makes the financial system more resilient and therefore reduces the frequency and severity of damage to the supply side in future financial crises.

The solution of this puzzle remains controversial. As we will go on to discuss it seems likely that the supply side was damaged by the crisis: the questions here are simply by how much, and how long the scar will last? However, it is still hard not to conclude that a significant margin of spare capacity opened up in the economy and therefore costs and prices were less sensitive to the output gap than one might have expected, thanks in no small part to the anchoring effect of stable long-run inflation expectations (IMF 2013a). In other words, even though there was considerable slack in the economy, costs and prices did not adjust by as much as they once might have done because agents expected policymakers to close that output gap.

It logically follows from the claim that the stability of long-term inflation expectations dampened the disinflationary pressure that might otherwise have emerged given a large and persistent margin of spare capacity in the economy that preserving that anchor is of paramount importance to the successful conduct of monetary policy. If the anchor starts to slip then large output gaps are much more likely to drive inflation far from the target. We shall return to discuss this issue later in this book in the context of the collapse in oil prices that began in late 2014.

References

Ahearne, A., Gagnon, J., Haltmaier, J., Kamin, S., Erceg, C., Faust, J., Guerrieri, L., Hemphill, C., Kole, L., Roush, J., Rogers, J., Sheets, N., & Wright, J. (2002). *Preventing deflation: Lessons from Japan's experience in the* 1990s. International Finance Discussion Papers, Board of Governors of the Federal Reserve System.

Akerlof, G., Dickens, W., & Perry, G. (1996). The macroeconomics of low inflation. *Brookings Papers on Economic Activity, 1*, 1–75.

Altonji, J., & Devereux, P. (2000). Is there nominal wage rigidity? Evidence from panel data. *Research in Labor Economics, 19*, 383–431.

Astley, M., Smith, J., & Pain, D. (2009). Interpreting recent movements in sterling. *Bank of England Quarterly Bulletin, Q3*, 202–214.

Atkeson, A., & Ohanian, L. (2001). Are Phillips curves useful for forecasting inflation? *Federal Reserve Bank of Minneapolis Quarterly Review, 25*(1), 2–11.

Auboin, M. (2009, January 28). *The challenges of trade financing*. VoxEU.

Babecký, J., Du Caju, P., Kosma, T., Lawless, M., Messina, J., & Rõõm, T. (2009). *Downward nominal and real wage rigidity*. ECB Working Paper 1105.

Ball, L., Mankiw, N., & Romer, D. (1988). The new Keynesian economics and the output-inflation trade-off. *Brookings Paper on Economic Activity, 1*, 1–82.

Barwell, R. (2007). The macroeconomic impact of international migration. *Bank of England Quarterly Bulletin, Q1*, 48–59.

Barwell, R., & Schweitzer, M. (2007). The incidence of nominal and real wage rigidities in Great Britain: 1978–98. *Economic Journal, 117*, 553–569.

Bean, C. (2006, October 24). *Globalisation and inflation*. Speech.

Benati, L. (2007). The time-varying Phillips correlation. *Journal of Money, Credit and Banking, 39*(5), 1275–1283.

Benedek, D., De Mooij, R., Keen, M., & Wingender, P. (2015). *Estimating VAT pass through*. IMF Working Paper 15/214.

Benito, A., Neiss, K., Price, S., & Rachel, Ł. (2010). The impact of the financial crisis on supply. *Bank of England Quarterly Bulletin, Q2*, 104–114.

Bernanke, B. (2002, November 21). Deflation: Making sure "it" doesn't happen here. *Speech*.

Bernanke, B. (2007, March 2). Globalization and monetary policy. *Speech*.

Blundell, R. (2009). Assessing the temporary VAT cut policy in the UK. *Fiscal Studies, 30*(1), 31–38.

Bordo, M., & Filardo, A. (2004). *Deflation and monetary policy in historical perspective*. NBER Working Paper 10833.

Borio, C., & Filardo, A. (2007). *Globalisation and inflation*. BIS Working Paper 227.

Borio, C., Erdem, M., Filardo, A., & Hofmann, B. (2014). The costs of deflations: A historical perspective. *BIS Quarterly Review, March*, 31–54.

Broadbent, B. (2013, May 1). *Forecast errors*. Speech.

Brunner, A. (2002). El Niño and world primary commodity prices: Warm water or hot air? *The Review of Economics and Statistics, 84*(1), 176–183.

Busain, A., Learmonth, D., & Sebastia-Barriel, M. (2006). UK export performance by industry. *Bank of England Quarterly Bulletin, Q3*, 308–316.

Calza, A. (2008). *Globalisation, domestic inflation and global output gaps*. ECB Working Paper 890.

Campa, J., & Goldberg, L. (2006). Exchange rate pass-through into import prices. *Review of Economics and Statistics, 87*(4), 679–690.

Carney, M. (2015, August 29). *Inflation in a globalised world*. Speech.

Cecchetti, S. (1992). Prices during the Great Depression: Was the deflation of 1930–1932 really unanticipated? *American Economic Review, 82*(1), 141–156.

Chevalier, J., & Scharfstein, D. (1996). Capital-market imperfections and counter-cyclical markups: Theory and evidence. *American Economic Review, 86*(4), 703–725.

Ciccarelli, M., & Mojon, B. (2005). *Global inflation*. ECB Working Paper 537.

Cuñat, V. (2007). Trade credit: Suppliers as debt collectors and insurance providers. *The Review of Financial Studies, 20*(2), 491–527.

Cunningham, A., & Jeffery, C. (2007). Extracting a better signal from uncertain data. *Bank of England Quarterly Bulletin, Q3*, 364–375.

Dale, S. (2010, September 22). *Inflation, inflation, inflation*. Speech.

Daly, M., & Hobijn, B. (2014). *Downward nominal wage rigidities bend the Phillips curve*. Federal Reserve Bank of San Francisco Working Paper 2013–08.

Delli Gatti, D., Gallegati, A., Greenwald, B., Russo, A., & Stiglitz, J. (2009). Business fluctuations and bankruptcy avalanches in an evolving network. *Journal of Economic Interaction and Coordination, 4*(2), 195–212.

Dwyer, A., Lam, K., & Gurney, A. (2010). *Inflation and the output gap in the UK.* Treasury Economic Working Paper 6.

ECB. (2011). Recent evidence on the uncertainty surrounding real-time evidence on the uncertainty surrounding real-time estimates of the euro area output gap. *ECB Monthly Bulletin, November*, 51–55.

ECB. (2014). The Phillips curve relationship in the euro area. *ECB Monthly Bulletin, July*, 99–114.

Eggertsson, G. (2008). Great expectations and the end of the Depression. *American Economic Review, 90*(4), 1476–1516.

Elliehausen, G., & Wolken, J. (1993). *The demand for trade credit.* Board of Governors of the Federal Reserve System Staff Study 165.

Gilchrist, S., & Zakrajsek, E. (2015). *Customer markets and financial frictions.* Paper presented at the Federal Reserve Bank of Kansas City Symposium.

Gottfries, N. (1991). Customer markets, credit market imperfections and real price rigidity. *Economica, 58*, 317–323.

Hackworth, C., Radia, A., & Roberts, N. (2013). Understanding the MPC's forecast performance since mid-2010. *Bank of England Quarterly Bulletin, Q4*, 336–350.

Hendel, I. (1996). Competition under financial distress. *Journal of Industrial Economics, 44*(3), 309–324.

Ihrig, J., Kamin, S., Lindner, D., & Marquez, J. (2010). Some simple tests of the globalization and inflation hypothesis. *International Finance, 13*(3), 343–375.

IMF. (2011, April). *Tensions from the two-speed recovery.* World Economic Outlook.

IMF. (2013a). *The dog that didn't bark.* World Economic Outlook, Chapter 3.

IMF. (2013b). *Greece: Ex post evaluation of exceptional access under the 2010 stand-By arrangement.* IMF Country Report 13/156.

IMF. (2013c). *The functions and impact of fiscal councils.* Policy Paper.

King, M. (2013, February 13). Comments in the February Inflation Report press conference.

Krugman, P. (2014a, August 25). Yellen, wages, and intellectual honesty. *New York Times.*

Krugman, P. (2014b, October 20). Apologizing to Japan. *New York Times.*

Laxton, D., & N'Diaye, P. (2002). *Monetary policy credibility and the unemployment-inflation trade-off.* IMF Working Paper 02/220.

Layard, R., Nickell, S., & Jackman, R. (1991). *Unemployment – Macroeconomic performance and the labour market.* Oxford: Oxford University Press.

Lee, Y., & Stowe, J. (1993). Product risk, asymmetric information, and trade credit. *Journal of Financial and Quantitative Analysis, 28*(2), 285–300.

Lomax, R. (2004, November 23). *Stability and statistics.* Speech.

Mac Coille, C. (2008). The impact of low-cost economies on UK import prices. *Bank of England Quarterly Bulletin, Q1*, 58–65.

Meier, A. (2010). *Still minding the gap.* IMF Working Paper 10/89.

Meltzer, A. (1976). Monetary and other explanations of the start of the Great Depression. *Journal of Monetary Economics, 2*, 455–471.

Mishkin, F. (2007, March 23). *Inflation dynamics*. Speech.

Mishkin, F. (2008, March 7). *Exchange rate pass-through and monetary policy*. Speech

Neiss, K., & Nelson, E. (2005). Inflation dynamics, marginal cost, and the output gap: Evidence from three countries. *Journal of Money, Credit and Banking, 37*(6), 1019–1045.

Nelson, E., & Nikolov, K. (2003). UK inflation in the 1970s and 1980s: The role of output gap mismeasurement. *Journal of Economics and Business, 55*(4), 353–370.

ONS. (2011, April 12). *VAT rise added an estimated 0.76 percentage points to the January CPI*. News release.

ONS. (2014). *University tuition fees in the CPI*. Briefing note.

Orphanides, A., & van Norden, S. (2002). The unreliability of output gap estimates in real-time. *Review of Economics and Statistics, 84*(4), 569–583.

Pain, N., Koske, I., & Sollie, M. (2006). *Globalisation and inflation in the OECD economies*. OECD Economics Department Working Paper 524.

Papademos, L. (2006, December 1). *Monetary policy in a changing world – Commitment, strategy and credibility*. Speech.

Phelps, E., & Winter, S. (1970). Optimal price policy under atomistic competition. In E. Phelps et al. (Eds.), *Microeconomic foundations of employment and inflation theory*. New York: Norton.

Roberts, J. (2006). Monetary policy and inflation dynamics. *International Journal of Central Banking, 2*(3), 193–230.

Rogoff, K. (2003). *Globalization and global disinflation*. Federal Reserve Bank of Kansas City Symposium at Jackson Hole.

Rogoff, K. (2006). *The impact of globalisation on monetary policy*. Federal Reserve Bank of Kansas City Symposium at Jackson Hole.

Tanaka, M., & Young, C. (2008). The economics of global output gap measures. *Bank of England Quarterly Bulletin, Q3*, 299–305.

Turner, D. (1995). Speed limit and asymmetric inflation effects from the output gap in the major seven economies. *OECD Economic Studies, 24*, 57.

Vetlov, I., Hlédik, T., Jonsson, M., Kucsera, H., & Pisan, M. (2011). *Potential output in a DSGE model*. ECB Working Paper 1351.

Wadhwani, S. (2000, February 23). *The impact of the Internet on UK inflation*. Speech.

Wynne, M. (2009). *The financial crisis, trade finance and the collapse of world trade*. Federal Reserve Bank of Dallas Globalization and Monetary Policy Institute Annual Report, 4–15.

Yellen, J. (2006, May 26). *Monetary policy in a global environment*. Speech.

5

The Productivity Puzzle

We now turn to the other great macroeconomic puzzle of the post-crash era: why the supply side of the economy appears to have been so badly damaged by the financial crisis. This issue is typically referred to as the productivity puzzle because the anomalous behaviour of supply is easiest to observe in the data on labour productivity.

For policymakers understanding the productivity puzzle was in part an exercise in economic history: as discussed above, the hit to the supply side can help explain why inflation proved so resilient to the collapse in demand. However, solving the productivity puzzle was much more important than that: understanding the reasons why the level of potential supply had fallen could help policymakers forecast how the supply side might evolve in the future and what if anything could be done to repair the damage done.

5.1 Terminology: What Is Labour Productivity

The term productivity is often used by economists as if it were a well-understood term which unambiguously refers to a specific well-defined concept. Unfortunately, that is not the case: indeed, the published data on labour productivity do not capture the concepts we are interested in. We therefore need a quick digression on different measures of productivity before we can make any progress (see Hulten (2001) for more detail).

The only sensible starting point is the production function: the economist's toolkit for explaining how companies transform a particular combination of

© The Editor(s) (if applicable) and The Author(s) 2016
R. Barwell, *Macroeconomic Policy after the Crash*,
DOI 10.1057/978-1-137-51592-6_5

inputs to produce output. We can use the production function to predict how the level of output will vary through time given data on the quality and quantity of inputs that are employed. However, that estimate will only capture a fraction of the dynamics of output both within and across the cycle: there is a residual variation in the level of output that is left unexplained by variation in the arguments of the production function. That Solow residual is effectively a 'measure of ignorance' (Abramovitz 1956), since it reflects both the contribution of relevant factors that were excluded from the analysis and the limitations of the framework—such as an imperfect specification of the production function at the level of the individual company, the errors introduced through aggregation from the micro to the macro and so on.

One factor which can help explain some of the unexplained cyclical variation in output is capacity utilisation. As discussed earlier, the intensity with which inputs are used to generate output might vary through the cycle. In a recession, companies might choose to hoard labour rather than lay-off surplus workers when the demand for their output falls if there are significant costs of firing and then re-hiring labour across the business cycle. If companies do hoard labour in recessions then the amount that companies produce will fall by more than the number of workers they employ, which means that the workforce will either reduce average working hours and maintain the same level of effort per hour, or maintain the same level of average hours but reduce effort per hour. In the case of the former, output per head (i.e., per worker employed) falls but output per hour worked falls by less, whereas in the latter output per head and per hour both fall.

The evidence suggests that these cyclical swings in productivity are significant. Fay and Medoff's (1985) survey of the US manufacturing sector provides direct evidence of labour hoarding in action. They found that the typical plant paid for 8 % more blue-collar labour than was strictly necessary on production grounds in the trough of the recession, and paid for 4 % more labour than was necessary even allowing for the other worthwhile activities these individuals performed. And from a macro perspective, Burnside, Eichenbaum and Rebelo (1993) argue that a significant proportion of the variation in the Solow Residual is driven by labour hoarding behaviour, and correspondingly less by 'pure' technology shocks.

If we strip out the impact of variation in the utilisation of factors of production over the cycle from our residual and we abstract away from the potential impact of specification bias then we are left with a through the cycle measure of underlying productivity, often referred to as TFP. TFP captures the efficiency with which companies can combine inputs to produce output at normal levels of utilisation.

We are now in a position to provide a more formal definition of two related concepts of aggregate supply:

- *Capacity output:* the output of the 'true' production function given the inputs that companies are currently employing, the current level of TFP and utilisation at normal levels;
- *Potential supply:* the output of the 'true' production function given the 'equilibrium inputs' that companies can sustainably employ without triggering pressure for inflation to deviate from expectations (to rise or fall relative to the target), the current level of TFP and utilisation at normal levels.

Growth in potential supply is therefore driven by two sets of factors: changes in equilibrium inputs, such as increase in the size of the population or a change in the fraction of the population that can sustainably be employed, and changes in TFP, which are driven by any one of three factors:

- *Innovation:* new ideas about the production process (how to better combine inputs to produce existing products), or products (how to combine inputs to produce new outputs);
- *Trimming the fat:* where companies can structurally increase the efficiency with which they can combine inputs to produce output (reducing so-called X-inefficiency); and
- *Reallocation to a better purpose:* if resources are reallocated both within and across companies towards tasks with a higher level of TFP.

Our interest here is on news about potential supply—that is, factors which could reduce equilibrium inputs or the level of TFP. The data on labour productivity will reflect those factors but as noted above those data will also incorporate changes in capacity utilisation and are therefore imperfect proxies of the developments we are interested in.

5.2   Creative Destruction

The topic of this section is how the financial crisis might have caused significant damage to the supply side of the advanced economies, giving rise to the so-called productivity puzzle. However, we begin by putting the opposite case—by discussing the claim that the deep recession brought about by the financial crisis ought to have had a positive impact on productivity.

5.2.1 Liquidationism and the Great Depression

In the years leading up to the Great Depression, there was a school of thought that the economy needed to periodically go through a period of liquidation, in which unproductive investments fail releasing resources for more productive uses, as a precondition for a period of sustained growth. Those liquidationists pointed to the long expansion of the 1920s that followed the short sharp recession of 1921 as an argument not to intervene as the economy entered the Great Depression (De Long 1990).

Thanks to the recollections of President Hoover, this view is often associated with Andrew Mellon, the American Treasury Secretary during the opening phase of the Great Depression (Hoover 1952):

> The 'leave-it-alone liquidationists' headed by Secretary of the Treasury Mellon felt that government must keep its hands off and let the slump liquidate itself. Mr. Mellon had only one formula: 'Liquidate labor, liquidate stocks, liquidate the farmers, liquidate real estate.' He held that even panic was not altogether a bad thing. He said: 'It will purge the rottenness out of the system. High costs of living and high living will come down. People will work harder, live a more moral life. Values will be adjusted, and enterprising people will pick up the wrecks from less competent people.'

Hoover differentiated the views which he attributed to Mellon from his own and the other members of his Administration who instead felt:

> [W]e should use the powers of government to cushion the situation. To our minds, the prime needs were to prevent bank panics such as had marked the earlier slumps, to mitigate the privation among the unemployed and the farmers which would certainly ensue. Panic had always left a trail of unnecessary bankruptcies which injured the productive forces of the country. But, even more important, the damage from a panic would include huge losses by innocent people, in their honestly invested savings, their businesses, their homes, and their farms.

Whether Hoover's characterisation of the internal debate within his administration and Mellon's advocacy of liquidationism is fair or not is unclear. There is less room for doubt where certain esteemed economists are concerned. For example, Schumpeter (1934) notoriously claimed that recessions

> are the means to reconstruct each time the economic system on a more efficient plan. But they inflict losses whilst they last, drive firms into the bankruptcy

court, throw people out of employment, before the ground is clear and the way paved for new achievement of the kind which has created modern civilization and made the greatness of this country.

Moreover, it appears that the sheer number of people who were thrown out of work during the Great Depression did not temper Schumpeter's belief in the cleansing capacity of recessions (Stiglitz 1993):

> The students who attended his classes in the late 1930s were regularly shocked to hear this expositor of capitalist growth declare, with obvious enjoyment, that depressions, far from being unmitigated social evils, were actually in the nature of 'a good cold douche' for the economic system!

5.2.2 The Two Faces of Recession: Exposure and Insulation

The idea that relatively unproductive companies might be driven to the wall in a recession, releasing resources to more productive uses seems eminently plausible. However, Caballero and Hammour (1994) illustrate that the process of creative destruction is a little more nuanced than this. There are in fact two opposing forces at work:

- *More net destruction*: In a recession, the decline in demand leads to the standard mechanism in which unproductive and unprofitable units are more likely to be scrapped in a recession, helping to raise underlying productivity.
- *Less gross creation*: The arrival rate of new companies (that should adopt the most efficient production process) will also tend to slow during a recession alleviating pressure on gross destruction of unproductive incumbents.

Whether recessions actually cleanse will therefore depend on the relative strength of these two forces, which in turn will hinge on the costs of starting up a new business from scratch.

If those costs are very small—which in effect means that a company can almost instantaneously go from nothing to a significant production process—then it makes sense for potential new entrants to wait until demand recovers before deciding to enter a market because those new entrants can rapidly achieve scale and service a significant share of an expanding market. In this scenario, unproductive incumbents are insulated somewhat in a recession because the adjustment in production comes about largely from a reduction in new entry.

If on the other hand it is very difficult to quickly achieve scale in production then companies cannot afford to wait until the recovery is mature before deciding to start investing in their productive capacity. Entry is now smoothed out across the cycle and recessions cleanse with more of the adjustment in production coming through the destruction of unproductive units.

5.2.3 Hoarding Today Is Investing for Tomorrow

In theory, a recession could depress measured productivity in the short run but ultimately raise underlying and measured productivity in the long run by helping to squeeze X-inefficiency out of the system. The 'pit stop' hypothesis captures the idea that companies need to periodically invest resources in re-optimising their production processes—the particular 'recipe' that each company uses to combine inputs to produce a particular good, or set of goods—if they want to continue to squeeze as much output as possible out of the inputs they employ.

Indeed, in exactly the same way that companies make investments in physical capital, we can think about companies making investments in their organisation capital (Prescott and Visscher 1980). Indeed, that recipe—the organisation capital—is what differentiates a company from its peers, what makes it unique and what allows the leading companies in any given industry to earn significant 'organisation rents' (Atkeson and Kehoe 2005; Lev and Radhakrishnan 2005). Moreover, just like investments in physical capital, there may be a time lag between the initial expenditure and the ultimate pay-off in terms of higher productivity (Brynjolfsson et al. 2002), so there are good and bad times to make those investments in organisation capital, and like a racing car, it is probably best to carry out running repairs when the economy is stationary (Scott 2009):

> A recession needs to be used to reorganize, refocus and place bets on future strategy. A successful pit stop will lay the seeds for future success.

In a recession, the opportunity cost of diverting resources towards investments in organisation capital is likely low precisely because companies are hoarding labour (Bean 1990; Hall 1991). In contrast, when demand is strong, labour utilisation rates are high: labour is working flat out to produce output to service current demand. From this perspective, the conventional explanation for the variation of labour utilisation over the cycle is incomplete. Rather than a simple story of labour hoarding, companies may be reallocating labour between production today and investments in productive capacity tomorrow. Hall (1991) provides a practical example of how this process works:

> The way many professionals run their own offices provides an analogy that may be useful. During periods of intense effort, one's office becomes more and more disorganized. Piles of unsorted materials develop first on desks and tables and later on the floor. As disorganization cumulates and the office's level of organizational capital deteriorates further and further, the professional's productivity begins to suffer. Finally, at the first letup in the need to produce output, the professional turns to reorganizing the office. Measured output may be low during that period, but the time spent reorganizing pays off in its contribution to future productivity. That time represents a type of capital accumulation.

Whether recessions actually do trigger an increase in investment in organisation capital is a matter of debate. Survey evidence from both the early 1990s recession (Geroski and Gregg's 1997) and the post-crash period (van Wanrooy et al. 2013) cast doubt on this claim: UK companies do invest in reallocating resources to improve efficiency, but it is not clear that this activity is more pronounced among those companies who are more affected by the collapse in demand.

5.3   Working Capital Constraints

We noted earlier that the sharp tightening in the terms on which companies could get access to short-term financing at the state of the crisis, from both formal (banks) and informal (other companies in their supply chain) sources, could have contributed to the surprising resilience of inflation through the cost channel of monetary policy. It is also possible that the tightening in credit conditions—and in particular the rationing of access to credit—could have had a more dramatic impact on the supply side.

- *Constraints on inputs*: Hard constraints on the quantity of short-term funding that companies can borrow will cap the amount that some companies can produce if they have to pay for the labour and intermediate inputs that are employed in production in advance of receiving payment for output. In effect, the amount that you can borrow determines the value of inputs you can employ and, given the input prices and the production function, that determines the amount that can be produced.

- *Supply chain compression*: The reduction of barriers to trade and transportation costs which underpin the increased globalisation of product markets coupled with easy credit conditions could have encouraged the proliferation of supply chains which cross borders, with decisions over the location of production at each stage in the chain being driven by comparative advantage. A sharp and persistent tightening in credit conditions might throw that process into reverse, with cross-border supply chains being replaced by less efficient but more resilient chains: for example, with cash-rich companies only willing to extend credit to companies which they can easily monitor in the local economy.
- *Consuming management time*: The credit crunch might have impacted on the supply side by diverting precious resources away from investing in the future of the company towards ensuring its survival today (Dale 2011). The management of countless companies up and down the land will have had to devote considerable time to evaluating how the contraction in the supply of bank and trade credit has affected their business model and then how best to re-optimise in response: time which could otherwise have been spent on identifying X inefficiencies within the production process or evaluating investments and innovations which might increase productivity.

5.4   Hysteresis

Hysteresis is a concept that most people will have encountered in school in science experiments designed to introduce students to Hooke's law. If you attach a load to a spring it will stretch and a linear relationship emerges between the extension of the spring and the load that was attached to it and once the load is removed the spring returns to its original shape. However, if too heavy a load is attached to the spring then it is deformed, and when the excessive load is removed the spring will not return to its original shape: it has been permanently stretched. This property is known as hysteresis.

There is a concern that large shocks could deform an economy in a similar fashion: the modest load of a normal recession has no lasting impact on an economy once it has passed, but an excessive load of a deep recession could cause persistent damage. Hysteresis involves permanent damage to the capacity of the economy to produce goods and services. From a top-down perspective the supply side of the economy reflects the quality and quantity of inputs that companies employ and the efficiency with which companies use those inputs. In this sub-section, we shall discuss a number of hysteresis mechanisms through which a protracted recession could impact the supply side via one of these channels.

5.4.1 Capital Scrapping

One obvious mechanism through which a deep recession could damage the supply side of the economy is through the destruction of capital that is used to produce output—or what is commonly referred to as capital scrapping.

Whenever a company fails, there is a risk that some of its plant and machinery may be destroyed. Indeed, the idea that a deep recession can leave behind a legacy of vacant plants and idle machinery has been immortalised in the name for the former industrial heartland of the American Midwest: the Rust Belt. The standard information problems constrain the demand for physical capital in the second-hand market: potential buyers will not be able to ascertain the quality of the capital until it has been installed in their own production process and there may be an adverse selection problem too (potential buyers may be sceptical about the unobservable quality of capital goods that were owned by companies that have failed). In any case, the costs of moving certain types of physical capital may be prohibitively high making re-sale uneconomic.

Estimates of the quantitative importance of capital scrapping vary. Research by the BoE on the volume of capital services employed by UK companies in production suggests that allowing for scrapping does not have a material impact on the supply side (Oulton and Srinivasan 2003), although that result is based on a sample period during which there were no year-on-year falls in output outside the manufacturing sector. Analysis on UK plant level data for the manufacturing sector over the more volatile period 1970–1993 reveals that failure to take account of scrapping due to plant closures over that period (predominantly during the 1980s recession) produces an estimate of the capital stock 44 % larger than the adjusted series at the end of the period (Harris and Drinkwater 2000).

Capital scrapping is not restricted to companies that go bust. Companies may invest in a capital stock that is strictly larger than is required to service normal levels of demand in order that they have the capacity to meet infrequent periods of strong demand (Hartman 1972). Once companies have invested in that capital, there is still a flow cost of maintaining that insurance policy (the capacity to service strong demand) in terms of the cost of replacing depreciating capital. Companies may choose to scale back the size of that insurance policy in response to a significant and protracted demand shock as the possibility of receiving a surge in demand that could not be serviced by a more modest capital stock is seen to fall. In this scenario, we might expect to see investment fall as companies allow that excess capital to depreciate away.

Physical capital—plants, machinery, equipment, computers and so on—is not the only capital that may be scrapped in a recession. Some elements of intangible capital—the stock of knowledge embedded within a company, its particular recipe for how to produce output—will also be scrapped when a company fails, unless another company in the same industry is able to acquire that information by employing members of the workforce.

Human capital will also be scrapped when jobs and companies are destroyed. The search and matching literature formalises the idea that when agents want to trade in a decentralised market, finding a suitable counterparty with whom to transact is a time-consuming and costly process. Rationing is a standard feature of these markets with constraints on the number of transactions that can be completed, which no amount of price flexibility can address. In the context of the labour market, we have large numbers of employers and job seekers simultaneously looking to find a productive match—that is, a vacancy in which they will be particularly productive—and it may take time and a number of failed experiments before they achieve success (Rogerson et al. 2005). A recession can disrupt that process by destroying some of those productive matches, forcing workers to start again searching for a high-quality match. Moreover, any firm specific human capital that the displaced workers had acquired will also be destroyed. Data on the subsequent earnings of those workers who lose their jobs suggest that the loss of human capital could be substantial. Wages in future jobs tend to be lower, and may take a long time to recover. These wage scars are a particular concern for workers with significant tenure, because there is likely to have been a more significant accumulation of job-specific human capital and the fact that the match has survived a long time indicates its quality. Five years after losing such a job, wage losses still amount to 25 % earnings prior to the destruction of the match (Jacobson et al. 1993).

5.4.2 Reduced Investment in Capital

Over and above the destruction of existing capital through scrapping, a recession could also depress investment in the accumulation of capital elsewhere in the economy, further depressing the supply side. The typical recession is short-lived, so unless the rate at which capital depreciates is very high, transitory weakness in the level of investment is unlikely to have a material impact on the stock. Indeed, even if the depression in investment lasts for an extended period, the hit to the capital stock is relatively contained; for example, Dale (2011) argues:

> The annual flow of business investment prior to the recession averaged around 7% of the UK capital stock. A 20% reduction in business investment for 5 years would result in the capital stock being only around 2% lower (assuming plausible assumptions for the rate of depreciation).

However, it is not just investment in physical capital that may slow as a result of a protracted period of weak aggregate demand. Spending on research and development (R&D) appears to be pro-cyclical (Fatas 2000): companies appear to cut back on investing in the future—innovating new products and processes that could deliver high profits—when their survival today is under threat. Macroeconomists struggle to explain what drives improvements in TFP but spending on R&D should be linked to improvements in the implied efficiency with which companies in aggregate combine inputs to produce output. It is plausible—if not probable—that a reduction in the resources devoted to R&D would lead to a slowdown in underlying productivity growth. Interestingly, spending on R&D held up during the post-crash periods—perhaps as a result of policy interventions (R&D tax credits)—but the effectiveness of that spending does appear to have tapered off: the proportion of companies introducing product or process innovations has fallen (Barnett et al. 2014).

Investments in human capital could also slow during a prolonged recession leading to a reduction in 'labour quality' (Bell et al. 2005). Graduates who enter the labour market during a recession tend to earn less over their lifetime than other cohorts which may reflect the fact that these individuals accumulate less human capital during their first few years in the job market (Kahn 2009). It might be that companies are investing less money on training these new entrants, or it may be that more of these individuals are forced to accept job offers for which they are poorly matched so they fail to accumulate relevant skills on the job. Finally, the combination of tighter credit conditions and lower lifetime expected earnings will likely have weighed on investments in academic and vocational qualifications that are not provided by an employer.

5.4.3 Reduction in Equilibrium Labour Supply

The conventional explanation of hysteresis operates through the quantity of labour that companies employ (Blanchard and Summers 1986). A key determinant of the level of potential supply is the level of potential employment—the amount of labour that can be employed at any given moment in time, without pressure for the compensation of labour to rise or fall relative to the value of output that labour produces, putting pressure on inflation to rise or fall. Potential employment can be broken down into a number of factors (Barwell et al. 2007):

- *Population*: The ultimate constraint on the amount of labour that can be employed is the size of the (adult) population. Clearly, the demographics of the population matter too (Barwell 2000); for example, prime-age men are more likely to be *able* to work than those in old age.
- *Equilibrium participation rate*: the fraction of the population who are willing and able to supply labour—to work or to look for work—when the labour market is in balance (real wages are in equilibrium);
- *Equilibrium unemployment rate*: the fraction of the labour force that can sustainably be employed without putting pressure on inflation to rise or fall via the evolution of wages relative to productivity;
- *Equilibrium average hours*: the number of hours (and the number of jobs) that individuals are willing to work when the labour market is in balance.

Hysteresis effects could operate through each of these components. For example, although it is conventionally treated as exogenous, the size of the population could be endogenous with respect to the cycle through net migrant flows (Barwell 2007) and in particular a sharp reversal in the economic fortunes of a country which has enjoyed large migrant inflows in the past might trigger large outflows leading to a reduction in potential employment (Izquierdo et al. 2015).

The equilibrium employment rate—which encapsulates the equilibrium unemployment and participation rates—could fall if a sustained period of slack in the labour market leads to a reduction in the search intensity of those who are either recurrent or long-term unemployed, whilst others may leave the labour force for good, with the result that there is less downward pressure on wages for any given employment rate because those out of work are less effective substitutes for the insiders that are currently employed. In passing, although this mechanism is widely discussed by policymakers its quantitative importance is controversial (van den Berg and van Ours 1996; Machin and Manning 1999). We know for example that the long-term unemployed are less likely to find work than the short-term unemployed but it is hard to convincingly prove that this does not reflect differences in the characteristics of the two groups (a.k.a. unobserved heterogeneity) rather than the prospects of finding a job declining with the duration of unemployment for a given individual (a.k.a. genuine state dependence).

Equilibrium working hours may also fall in a recession. It seems clear that actual working hours fall, both not only as a result of labour hoarding but also as a result of job seekers accepting part-time jobs, which they would reject in a healthy labour market, to continue searching for a full-time job (see the discussion on sullying). That decline in working hours may facilitate an ultimate decline in desired working hours. There has been a clear downward trend in working hours over the past century: as people get richer they want to consume more leisure (Goldin 1998; Barwell et al. 2007). However, that trend is not smooth: in particular, hours worked appear to fall in recessions and then not fully recover, perhaps because workers become accustomed to their new hours, so that when demand recovers hours worked do not.

5.5   Recessions Retard Resource Reallocation

The Schumpeterian view is that recessions cleanse, leading to a productivity-enhancing reallocation of factors of production. However, there is a modern literature which argues the exact opposite—that recessions can sully as well as cleanse, depressing productivity by impeding the reallocation of resources. The relative strength of these two mechanisms is a matter of debate, but what seems clear is that resource reallocation matters: the reallocation of resources between employers is a major driver of productivity growth at the industry level, as opposed to productivity growth at the unit level (Baily et al. 1992; Foster et al. 2006). We now turn to discuss the mechanisms through which these sullying effects can arise.

5.5.1   Job to Job Flows

The labour market is often described as if it is populated by three groups of people—those in work (the employed); those out of work but looking for a job and available to start work (the unemployed); and those out of work who do not fulfil one or both of those criteria—that is, not looking or not available (the economically inactive)—with people flowing between these labour market states at any moment in time. However, this simple characterisation misses an important element of labour market activity: that within the stock of employed people, there are large flows of people between different jobs that are a key ingredient of the productivity-enhancing reallocation of resources discussed above.

Barlevy (2002) illustrates how the introduction of on the job search—the mechanism through which people already in employment look for a better job—can give rise to the sullying effect of recessions, because vacancies for high productivity jobs are less likely to be created in a recession. Without this feature a collapse in job creation in a recession would not have long-term consequences for the allocation of resources: high productivity matches survive, some low productivity don't, the unemployed remain out of work for slightly longer (thanks to weak job creation) but the shelf-life of low productivity jobs is not artificially extended. However, if workers who are currently employed in poor (unproductive) matches search for work, as well as the unemployed, then a decline in job creation will lead to those workers remaining in those jobs for longer.

In Barlevy's model, the return from opening a vacancy depends on the relative proportion of people searching for jobs and companies searching for potential employees—which we can think of as a proxy of how loose the labour market is (how many people are chasing each job)—for three reasons: the looser the labour market, the easier it is to fill a vacancy; the looser the labour market is, the harder it will be for a worker to find a better job, and therefore the longer the match will survive (generating profits for the employer); and the looser the labour market is, the larger the number of workers stuck in low productivity matches and hence the easier it will be for a company to recruit an on-the-job searcher. Companies will adjust the number of open vacancies in response to demand shocks to drive that expected return back towards the flow cost of keeping the vacancy open—hence when demand collapses the ratio of vacancies to job seekers falls. The recession may lead to the destruction of jobs below some threshold level of productivity ('cleansing'), but it will also lead to workers becoming trapped in those matches just above that threshold ('sullying').

5.5.2   Scrambling and the Role of Credit

A key feature of the post-crisis period has been the anaemic supply of bank credit to the real economy, and it turns out that credit frictions play an important role in the theoretical literature in generating poor productivity outcomes in a recession through a number of channels.

In a simple economy without credit frictions, the least productive units are destroyed in a recession when demand slows, contributing to a productivity-enhancing reallocation of resources. Cabellaro and Hammour (1999) show that credit frictions attenuate that cleansing effect by exacerbating sclerosis and introducing scrambling. Sclerosis arises in their model as a consequence of two frictions: between the entrepreneur and the worker and between the entrepreneur and her creditor, where in both cases, the former cannot credibly commit not to 'misbehave' (to withhold labour or to default) and therefore must be rewarded with a share of the surplus from production. Those frictions lead to sub-optimally low level of restructuring in a recession, with low job creation going hand in hand with low destruction. Scrambling occurs when job matches are not destroyed purely on the basis of their position in the distribution of productivity, and instead a company's survival prospects are based in part on its financial arrangements. Indeed, not only can credit constraints hamper job creation in a downturn, they can continue to bite during the recovery phase, which in turn implies less destruction, and hence the cumulative reallocation across the recession and the recovery is significantly lower.

Barlevy (2003) argues that credit constraints are both more likely to bind in recessions and more likely to bind on the most productive employers. Barlevy argues that those investment projects which involve large set-up costs must generate a larger surplus in equilibrium if potential entrepreneurs are to be indifferent between investing in those projects and low-cost projects although the workers employed in higher-return projects will be able to demand higher wages. The standard moral hazard problem arises in this model when projects are financed through debt: the creditor will be concerned that once the entrepreneur has the funds he may take actions which are not in her interest (in this case, spend the loan on consumption rather than investment and then default) and will limit access to credit accordingly. The high cost–high return projects require greater financing and therefore the moral hazard constraint bites here first: as returns to all projects drop across all projects in a recession, the entrepreneurs in the high cost–high return projects are the first to face the private incentive to default. Therefore in a recession, financing will be available only for low cost–low return projects.

Kiyotaki and Moore (1997) present a similar credit-driven reallocation mechanism in a model in which an asset (in their model, land) serves as both a factor of production and the collateral on which finance is secured. Asset valuations are therefore hard-wired into credit constraints, and if asset prices fall, credit-constrained companies that have leveraged up to invest in the productive asset are forced to cut back on their investment (in land). The marginal productivity of the constrained companies is higher than that of their unconstrained peers (consistent with the observation that they are constrained from borrowing to invest as much as they would ideally choose to do) and therefore the reallocation of resources when these constraints bite leads to a hit to aggregate productivity. Ownership of the asset has passed to a less productive employer.

A final mechanism through which credit constraints are thought to distort the allocation of resources is via ever-greening of loans. Caballero et al. (2006) argue that Japanese banks that lacked the resources to write off bad loans during the Lost Decade were forced to keep companies on life support that would otherwise have been driven into insolvency. These so-called zombie companies created congestion in product and labour markets: by artificially suppressing the rate of job destruction, the banks pushed the burden of adjustment onto job creation. Cabellero, Hoshi and Kashyap argue that the impact on the reallocation of resources was significant: at the industry level, investments in jobs and physical capital decline as the fraction of these so-called zombie companies rises as does the productivity differential between healthy companies and the zombies. To take an extreme example, their results suggest that had the incidence of zombie companies in the wholesale sector remained at its average level between 1981 and 1992 (as opposed to rising) then a cumulative loss of 43 % in investment in physical capital by healthy companies could have been avoided between 1993 and 2002.

5.5.3   Learning on the Job About the Job

Another mechanism through which a recession could distort the allocation of resources and depress aggregate productivity growth is by interrupting the learning process within the company.

In most cases, jobs are experience goods (Nelson 1970): that is, the employer and potential employee will not know how productive the match will turn out to be until the applicant fills the vacancy. As a result, workers have to engage in a process of 'job shopping' as they sample a number of matches until they find one that fits (Jovanovic 1979); likewise, employers might have to 'sample' a number of potential applicants for a vacancy before they find a good match. That process of learning on the job is not instantaneous: the employer and employee will take time to figure out if the match is productive (Farber 1994).

The rate at which the employer and employee learn about the quality of the match could vary over the cycle. A bust could provide a much more exacting test of evolutionary fitness of a particular match than a boom (Dellas 2003) if, for example, mistakes are more likely to be punished in hard times. Under those circumstances, recessions could compress the process of job shopping, increasing churn and boost productivity at the aggregate level. If on the other hand, employers and employee learn faster in a boom, when labour utilisation rates are high and the employer demands more of the employee in a given space of time, then the reverse could be true.

Ouyang (2009) proposes a complementary learning-based mechanism which is consistent with recessions depressing aggregate productivity. In Ouyang's model, the entrepreneur does not know how successful a start-up will be at the outset: she will gradually learn based on the demand for the company's output and the returns it generates. New entrants are presumed to use the latest vintage of technology and are therefore at an advantage relative to previous generations of start-ups. However, the less productive members of previous generations have been weeded out. Recessions in the model have two offsetting effects on average productivity: first, the rate of destruction of existing companies rises in a recession and that leads to a productivity-enhancing reallocation of resources to new generations who work with a superior vintage of technology; second, the recession truncates the learning process, in that young companies are destroyed before enough time has passed to reveal their true productivity. Ouyang argues that the second effect likely dominates the first, based on analysis on a calibrated model, which in turn implies that recessions sully rather than cleanse.

5.5.4 The Quiet Life and Competitive Cleansing

John Hicks once observed: 'the best of all monopoly profits is the quiet life.' This insight has been formalised in what is referred to as the 'quiet life hypothesis' (Berger and Hannan 1998; Koetter et al. 2012)—the idea that the security of monopoly power breeds inefficiencies in the production process. If competitive pressure varies over the cycle then it is possible that the extent of X-inefficiency could also vary over the cycle, as those companies which enjoy significant pricing power are temporarily shaken out of the quiet life, and required to bear down on costs.

Kehrig (2011) provides an example of this competitive cleansing mechanism by introducing a quasi-fixed factor of production. In a boom, robust product demand drives up the price of that quasi-fixed factor, squeezing profitability. As a result, only those plants with sufficiently high productivity can enter or survive when product demand is robust, and that leads to a compression of the cross-sectional distribution of productivity across plants through destruction of the lower tail. In other words, booms rather than busts cleanse the economy of unproductive companies, and therefore by extension the sustained weakness of demand during the post-crash era might have led to an elongation of the quiet life and an increase in X-inefficiency within companies.

A similar competitive cleansing mechanism is at work in Melitz and Ottaviano's (2008) model of trade in which entrepreneurs must make an irreversible investment in the capacity to produce a particular variety of good, in the face of uncertainty about their likely productivity in that task. In their model, market size and trade determine the degree of competition in the market, which then influences market structure. Trade liberalisation—lowering the cost of trading across borders—increases competition and then raises average productivity by driving the least productive companies from the market, with their market share swallowed up by exporters.

Ever-greening of loans by weak banks may also have contributed to the quiet life in the post-crash era, depressing productivity. The decision to continue supporting ailing companies removed the pressure that might otherwise have arisen on those companies to squeeze inefficiencies out of the production process in order to ensure continued access to funding and ultimately the survival of the firm (Sekine et al. 2003). Moreover, moral hazard may exacerbate the problem: inefficiencies may start to arise in anticipation that a weak creditor will be forced to ever-green loans (Berglöf and Roland 1997).

5.5.5   Evidence

We have discussed a number of sullying mechanisms through which a deep and protracted recession could in theory depress underlying productivity, consistent with the persistent weakness we observe in productivity in the data. Finally, we review the evidence—such as it is—on these sullying mechanisms.

Direct evidence on the sullying mechanism can be found in Foster et al. (2014). They show that in previous recessions the pace of resource reallocation increases which in turn boosts productivity—in other words, the Schumpeterian result. However, in the post-crash recession, the reverse is true: the intensity of reallocation falls and what reallocation did take place made a smaller than normal contribution to productivity growth.

There is also a large body of indirect evidence on the potential for reallocation within the recessions to raise productivity:

- *Job to job flows*: The flow of workers between jobs appears to be highly pro-cyclical (Fallick and Fleischman 2004). Although job-to-job flows have been on a downward trend in the USA for over a decade, the decline in churn appears to have been driven by a sharp decline during consecutive recessions with a failure to recover thereafter (Hyatt and Spletzer 2013). Lazear and Spletzer (2012) estimate that four-fifths of the reduction in hiring during the post-crash recession reflected a reduction in churn: replacing workers who have left the company.

- *Wages of jobs created in recessions*: If we are willing to treat wages as a proxy of the productivity of a match, we find the quality of new jobs tends to fall in recessions. Bowlus (1993, 1995) finds evidence of significant variation in the quality of new matches across the business cycle. Carneiro et al. (2009) find that starting salaries tend to fall further during a recession than those of incumbents in the Portuguese labour market: a one percentage point increase in the unemployment rate lowers the wages of newly hired male workers by 2.8 %, roughly double the decline in wages of those already in employment.

- *Job duration*: Another proxy for the quality of a job is its duration, on the basis that employees (and employers) will be more likely to destroy a match that they learn to be of low quality (Jovanovic 1979). Mustre-del-Rio (2014) finds that jobs which are created in recessions do indeed tend to have a shorter shelf-life: surviving for almost a year less than those created in a boom.

- *Frustrated workers*: Another metric of the increase in the number of mismatched workers during a recession is the number of workers who report that they are unhappy with their job (either because they are on a temporary contract and would like a permanent job, or because they have a part-time job and would like a full-time job). Blanchflower and Levin (2015) argue that these frustrated workers should be thought of as underemployed, and the significant increase in their number has contributed to disinflationary slack in the labour market.

- *Trapped in bad jobs and in bad companies*: Employment growth appears to be less sensitive to the cycle in lower-quality employers (defined according to the wages they offer, the duration of their jobs, and size), largely because they find it easier to hold onto workers in a downturn (higher-quality employers are less likely to poach workers) and therefore progress up the job ladder slows by around 20 % in a large bust relative to a boom (Kahn and McEntarfer 2015).

Finally, studies from the emerging economies provide an alternative and somewhat unconventional cross-check on the potential for the post-crash recession to have damaged productivity through this mechanism:

- *Sullying in a sudden stop*: A collapse in output that can be accounted for primarily by a sharp fall in measured TFP is actually a standard feature of a crisis in an emerging market economy (Calvo et al. 2006), and the crisis in Chile in 1982 was no exception. Oberfield (2013) uses establishment data from the Chilean manufacturing census to search for evidence of a misallocation of resources at the micro level that could explain the fall in TFP at the macro level and finds that if anything within-industry allocational efficiency improved in 1982, whilst there was a marked decline in between-industry allocational efficiency that could account for about one-third of the reduction in TFP.
- *The consequences of being behind the frontier*: No economy measures up to the ideal benchmark in which the marginal product of resources is equal across all plants so that it is not possible to increase potential supply by reallocating resources. However, some economies are further away from the benchmark than others. Hseih and Klenow (2007) quantify the extent of the misallocation of resources at the micro level within the Chinese and Indian economies, by comparing outcomes to the US economy. Using plant level data, they find that Chinese productivity would rise 30–45 % and Indian productivity by 40–50 % if the cross-sectional variation in productivity within a given sub-sector was reduced to US levels.

5.6 Uncertainty and Supply

Another key feature of the post-crisis period—alongside the contraction in the supply of credit—has been a significant and sustained increase in, for want of a better word, uncertainty. That increase in uncertainty may also have contributed to the productivity puzzle.

5.6.1 Terminology

Before we discuss the consequences of an increase in uncertainty, it is important to clarify what exactly is meant by this terminology in the literature. In particular, we need to clarify two issues:

- *The shape of the distribution*: As the probabilities attached to different outcomes change, the moments of the implied distribution function will shift. Technically speaking, the literature focuses on an increase in the spread of the distribution that does not influence the mean (expected value), but often when we speak about an increase in uncertainty we have in mind situations in which the shift in probabilities may affect the mean and the skew of the distribution as well as the spread.

- *The difference between risk and uncertainty*: Following Knight (1921), we can differentiate between circumstances where the outcome is unclear but agents can attach probabilities to the different possible outcomes (e.g., tossing a coin) and those circumstances where they cannot. Technically speaking, only the latter is referred to as genuine uncertainty.

Following the crash, the world likely became both a riskier place—with agents attaching a higher probability to extreme outcomes (tail events) —and a more uncertain place, with agents unable to forecast where financial markets and the real economy were headed. However, those developments will have been accompanied by a more conventional shift in beliefs: agents marking down their central expectation of the future. In other words, there will have been a simultaneous shift in the location and shape of the distribution, and it is difficult to disentangle that part of any resulting change in behaviour which was driven by the shift in the first moment of the distribution (the location) and that which is driven by higher moments of the distribution that we are interested in (the shape).

5.6.2 Measuring Uncertainty

If we want to quantify the impact of this 'uncertainty' channel on productivity, we need to be able to measure risk and uncertainty. The literature suggests a number of imperfect proxies, which vary according to whose uncertainty is being measured and what they are uncertain about:

- *Asset price volatility*: Bloom (2009) identifies episodes of increased uncertainty based on the volatility of US stock prices, pin-pointing 17 events between 1962 and 2008 in which there was a spike in volatility which was coincident with an economic or geo-political event.
- *Unpredictability of macroeconomic data*: Jurado et al. (2015) construct estimates of macroeconomic uncertainty based on the common component of forecast errors across a rich set of macroeconomic indicators.
- *Disagreement among professional forecasters*: Bachmann et al. (2010) proxy uncertainty via the dispersion of forecasts produced by professional forecasters, which unsurprisingly they find is positively correlated with the variance of forecast errors.

- *Discussion in the media*: Baker et al. (2013) identify episodes of uncertainty based on the frequency with which key phrases appear in stories in a sample of newspapers.

Haddow et al. (2013) construct a measure of uncertainty from these diverse sources of information using a statistical technique which extracts a 'principal component' that captures as much of the common variation in these different series as possible. Interestingly, the principal component is found to be most correlated with the measures of uncertainty drawn from financial markets data. Unsurprisingly, uncertainty is found to rise during the post-crash recession, but the principal component also picks up other events such as the failure of the US hedge fund Long-Term Capital Management and the second Iraq War.

In contrast to the search for uncertainty in macro indicators, Bloom et al. (2012) use an establishment-level panel dataset for the US manufacturing sector to identify uncertainty at the micro level. They use the production function to pin down the level of TFP, using the level of value added and three factors of production (structures, equipment and hours worked), and back out the shocks at the establishment-level from a first-order auto-regression of TFP on itself and a set of plant-level fixed effects and year dummies. The residuals from that regression will capture a mixture of true productivity shocks and demand shocks. The cross-sectional dispersion of those shocks is taken as a proxy of uncertainty at the micro level, which is found to be clearly counter-cyclical and is at its highest level across the near four-decade sample period during the Great Recession of 2007–09. Indeed, comparing the distribution of plant-level shocks for a balanced panel of manufacturing plants in the period immediately before the recession struck (2005–06) and the two recession years (2008–09) the variance of the shocks increases by three quarters.

Bloom et al. (2012) also provide evidence on the extent to which the increase in 'uncertainty' is being driven by the state of aggregate demand. They focus on China's accession to the World Trade Organization, and the resulting abolition of quotas on imports of Chinese clothing and textiles in 2005 which had a predictable impact on domestic producers. They find that the second-moment (uncertainty) shocks are not primarily driven by first-moment shocks and more broadly that our narrative of the cause of recessions should encompass both negative first-moment shocks and separately positive second-moment shocks.

Although there is a negative relationship between growth at the industry level and the uncertainty proxy within the affected sectors of the economy, once they instrument growth at the industry level using the abolition of the quotas the effect disappears. In other words, their second-moment shocks are not purely driven by the more familiar first-moment shocks.

5.6.3 Theory

The main focus of the emerging literature on uncertainty is to investigate whether shifts in beliefs are a quantitatively important source of fluctuations in demand over the business cycle—and hence whether an increase in uncertainty can account for a significant proportion of the weakness of demand in the post-crash period. However, our interest is in a different aspect of the impact of an increase in uncertainty: the effect on supply.

Bloom (2009) develops a structural model of investment behaviour at the micro level which he simulates to illustrate the impact of uncertainty on business cycle dynamics. In the model, each production unit (plant) within a given company is assumed to be an independent decision-taking unit and therefore 'uncertainty' has three distinct dimensions in the model, with volatility at the level of the economy, the level of the company and at the level of the decision-making unit. The simulations reveal that a zone of inaction exists thanks to the presence of factors adjustments costs: the outlook has to be sufficiently good in order to elicit investment in additional capital and labour, or sufficiently bad to lead to shedding of factors of production. Bloom demonstrates that this zone of inaction expands as uncertainty increases, so that investment becomes less sensitive to current conditions. An interesting corollary of this result is that monetary and fiscal stimulus becomes less effective in periods of high uncertainty (Bloom et al. 2007).

A large transitory increase in uncertainty—to be precise an increase in the volatility of demand—leads to a sharp drop in investment in jobs and physical capital. Indeed, the majority of companies stop hiring and employment falls, thanks to the continuous flow of exogenous job separations. However, once that uncertainty dissipates, pent-up demand leads to a surge in recruitment. In fact, the simulations reveal a 'volatility overshoot' in investment, whereby the more uncertain environment (demand is more volatile) drives units towards the perimeter of the zone of inaction and a burst of investment in jobs and physical capital.

A critical feature of these simulations is that the reallocation of factors of production from inefficient to efficient units slows down—remember fewer units are expanding their stock of capital and labour, and fewer are contracting—and that in turn leads to a slowdown in measured productivity at the macro level. Given a temporary shock to uncertainty the impact on productivity is correspondingly short-lived: once investment recovers then the implied reallocation of labour and capital will drive a recovery in productivity. In fact, with a more volatile economy there is greater scope for reallocation of resources, so productivity also overshoots in the simulations.

Finally, it is worth noting that there is a long-standing result that a permanent increase in uncertainty could actually have a positive impact on productivity (Oi 1961; Hartman 1972; Abel 1983), separate to the reallocation channel discussed above. As noted earlier companies confronted by a more volatile environment—very low and very high levels of demand are now more likely—may invest in a larger capital stock in order that they have the capacity to service demand in periods when demand is very high.

5.7   Monetary Policy: Part of the Problem Not Part of the Solution?

Over the course of this chapter, we have discussed how the competitive pressures that normally prompt the efficient reallocation of resources within and across companies and sectors in a well-functioning economy might have abated in the post-crash era, whether as a direct result of the depressed state of aggregate demand, the elevated level of uncertainty about the future or the atrophied state of credit supply. In the final section of this chapter, we briefly highlight one final candidate explanation: monetary policy.

In theory, it is possible that central banks might have unwittingly been the custodians of 'the quiet life' since the crash. By keeping interest rates at rock-bottom levels, central banks have allowed highly indebted companies to survive if not exactly thrive whilst demand has been weak because it has been relatively easy to service even large debt burdens. In effect, central banks might have had the same impact on resource reallocation as zombie banks: allowing highly indebted companies to congest product markets and hoard factors of production that might otherwise have been released.

Micro-level analysis by the BoE provides some circumstantial evidence in support of this mechanism (Arrowsmith et al. 2013). A survey of the relationship managers working in commercial banks who cover the small- and medium-sized enterprises (SME) sector reveals that those individuals put more weight on the low interest rate environment as the driver of low levels of corporate insolvency as opposed to loan forbearance. The survey reveals an acute perceived sensitivity to official interest rates: 0.6 % of companies were thought to be more likely than not to default but that forecast rose to 4.7 % in the event of a 400 basis point rise in interest rates.

In that parallel universe in which central banks had returned policy rates to more normal levels many highly indebted companies would have come under pressure and it seems likely that more companies would have failed. Of course, the outlook for demand and inflation would have been different too with less loose monetary policy. So if the loose monetary stance is to blame for a non-trivial part of the productivity puzzle then that would be an argument for a different monetary–fiscal mix.

5.8   Conclusion: Accounting for the UK Productivity Puzzle

We have discussed a number of plausible mechanisms through which an extended period of weak aggregate demand could depress aggregate productivity. To conclude this section, we will now briefly review analysis by BoE staff which attempted to take these stories to the data, to quantify the respective contribution of these various factors in explaining the UK's puzzle. The key conclusions of that study were as follows (Barnett et al. 2014):

Sizing the puzzle: At the time the study was published, Bank staff calculated that there was a shortfall in the level of labour productivity relative to its pre-crisis trend of 16 percentage points in 2013 Q4.

The contribution of mis-measurement: It is possible that the data on output and labour input under- and overestimate respectively the true picture (e.g., many individuals who report themselves as being self-employed may not be making a meaningful contribution to output) which could collectively explain up to two percentage points of the puzzle.

The declining contribution of the off-shore economy: The trend in productivity may have slowed for reasons that have nothing to do with the cyclical state of the economy—for example, the extraction of oil and gas from fields in the North Sea had been in decline for a number of years before the crash, and that could potentially explain a percentage point of the puzzling weakness of productivity relative to a long-run trend.

The declining contribution of the financial sector: Structural changes in the financial sector since the financial crisis have contributed to the sector accounting for a disproportionately large share of the UK's productivity puzzle, which can account for a further percentage point of the puzzle.

Re-sizing the puzzle: Once we control for potential measurement issues and structural changes which are largely independent of the state of aggregate demand since the crisis, we are left with a productivity shortfall of around 12 percentage points, which is left to be explained.

Labour hoarding: Some fraction of the observed weakness of labour productivity could reflect a low level of labour utilisation. Bank staff argue that so-called labour hoarding should explain very little of the productivity puzzle at the end of 2013 because there is a limit to how long companies can hoard labour for.

Accounting for increases in labour supply: The crisis could have induced an increase in labour supply among those individuals who were reliant on financial assets to support consumption, via the hit to asset values and the decline in nominal interest rates. A similar mechanism could work through the reduction in human wealth (lower expected future labour income). In theory that positive labour supply shock could account for an increase in employment and a decline in labour productivity (the Bank analysis does not quantify the contribution of this channel).

Weak investment: The cumulative impact of a protracted period of weak gross investment in the physical capital and intangible capital (i.e., intellectual capital, embodied in patents and trademarks and more generally 'know how') had a significant impact on the capital labour ratio (broadly defined), which could potentially explain three to four percentage points of the puzzle.

Sullying: Finally, the Bank analysis attributes a further three to five percentage points to the impaired reallocation of resources in the economy noting the unusually low level of corporate failures and elevated level of loss-making companies during this period.

The Bank study leaves in the region of three to six percentage points of a 12-percentage-point puzzle unexplained. In other words, the productivity puzzle remains something of a puzzle - a some what dismal conclusion that reflects the limits of our knowledge about the structural and cyclical determinants of TFP.

References

Abel, A. (1983). Optimal investment under uncertainty. *American Economic Review, 73*, 228–233.

Abramovitz, M. (1956). Resource and output trends in the United States since 1870. *American Economic Review, 46*, 5–23.

Arrowsmith, M., Griffiths, M., Franklin, J., Wohlmann, E., Young, G., & Gregory, D. (2013). SME forbearance and its implications for monetary and financial stability. *Bank of England Quarterly Bulletin, Q4*, 296–303.

Atkeson, A., & Kehoe, P. (2005). Modeling and measuring organization capital. *Journal of Political Economy, 113*(5), 1026–1053.

Bachmann, R., Elstner, S., & Sims, E. (2010). *Uncertainty and economic activity: Evidence from business survey data*. NBER Working Paper 16143.

Baily, M., Hulten, C., & Campbell, D. (1992). Productivity dynamics in manufacturing plants. In C. Winston & M. Baily (eds.) *Brookings Papers on Economic Activity*.

Baker, S., Bloom, N., & Davis, S. (2013). *Measuring economic policy uncertainty*. Chicago Booth Working Paper 13–02.

Barlevy, G. (2002). The sullying effect of recessions. *Review of Economic Studies, 69*(1), 65–96.

Barlevy, G. (2003). Credit market frictions and the allocation of resources over the business cycle. *Journal of Monetary Economics, 50*(8), 1795–1818.

Barnett, A., Batten, S., Chiu, A., Franklin, J., & Sebastiá-Barriel, M. (2014). The UK productivity puzzle. *Bank of England Quarterly Bulletin, Q2*, 114–128.

Barwell, R. (2000). *Age structure and the unemployment rate*. Bank of England Working Paper 124.

Barwell, R. (2007). The macroeconomic impact of international migration. *Bank of England Quarterly Bulletin, Q1*, 48–59.

Barwell, R., Bell, V., Bunn, P., & Gutiérrez-Domènech, M. (2007). Potential employment in the UK economy. *Bank of England Quarterly Bulletin, Q1*, 60–69.

Bean, C. (1990). Endogenous growth and the procyclical behaviour of productivity. *European Economic Review, 34*, 355–363.

Bell, V., Burriel-Llombart, P., & Jones, J. (2005). *A quality-adjusted labour input series for the United Kingdom*. Bank of England Working Paper 280.

Berger, A., & Hannan, T. (1998). The efficiency cost of market power in the banking industry. *Review of Economics and Statistics, 80*(3), 454–465.

Berglöf, E., & Roland, G. (1997). Soft budget constraints and credit crunch in financial transition. *European Economic Review, 41*, 807–817.

Blanchard, O., & Summers, L. (1986). Hysteresis and the European unemployment problem. *NBER Macroeconomics Annual*, 15–90.

Blanchflower, D., & Levin, A. (2015). *Labour market slack and monetary policy*. NBER Working Paper 21094.

Bloom, N. (2009). The impact of uncertainty shocks. *Econometrica, 77*(3), 623–685.

Bloom, N., Bond, S., & van Reenen, J. (2007). Uncertainty and investment dynamics. *Review of Economic Studies, 74*, 391–415.

Bloom, N., Floetotto, M., Jaimovich, N., Saporta-Eksten, I., & Terry, S. (2012). *Really uncertain business cycles*. NBER Working Paper 18245.

Bowlus, A. (1993). Job match quality over the business cycle. In H. Bunzel, P. Jensen, & N. C. Westergard-Neilsen (Eds.), *Panel data and labour market dynamics*. Amsterdam: North Holland.

Bowlus, A. (1995). Matching workers and jobs: Cyclical fluctuations in match quality. *Journal of Labor Economics, 13*(2), 335–350.

Brynjolfsson, E., Hitt, L., & Yang, S. (2002). Intangible assets: Computers and organizational capital. *Brookings Papers on Economic Activity: Macroeconomics*, 137–199.

Burnside, C., Eichenbaum, M., & Rebelo, S. (1993). Labour hoarding and the business cycle. *Journal of Political Economy, 101*(2), 245–273.

Caballero, R., & Hammour, M. (1994). The cleansing effect of recessions. *American Economic Review, 84*(5), 1350–1368.

Caballero, R., & Hammour, M. (1999). *The cost of recessions revisited: A reverse-liquidationist view*. NBER Working Paper 7355.

Caballero, R., Hoshi, T., & Kashyap, A. (2006). *Zombie lending and depressed restructuring in Japan*. NBER Working Paper 12129.

Calvo, G., Izquierdo, A., & Talvi, E. (2006). *Phoenix miracles in emerging markets*. NBER Working Paper 12101.

Carneiro, A., Guimaraes, P., & Portugal, P. (2009). *Real wages and the business cycle*. Banco de Portugal Working Paper 10.

Dale, S. (2011, September 21). *Productivity and monetary policy*. Speech.

Dellas, H. (2003). *The informational role of the business cycle*. CEPR Discussion Paper 4076.

De Long, B. (1990). "Liquidation" cycles. NBER Working Paper 3546.

Fallick, B., & Fleischman, C. (2004). *Employer-to-employer flows in the U.S. labor market: The complete picture of gross worker flows*. Board of Governors of the Federal Reserve Finance and Economics Discussion Series 2004–34.

Farber, H. (1994). The analysis of inter-firm worker mobility. *Journal of Labour Economics, 12*(4), 554–593.

Fatas, A. (2000). Do business cycles cast long shadows? *Journal of Economic Growth, 5*, 147–162.

Fay, J., & Medoff, J. (1985). Labor and output over the business cycle: Some direct evidence. *American Economic Review, 75*(4), 638–655.

Foster, L., Haltiwanger, J., & Krizan, C. (2006). Market selection, reallocation and restructuring in the U.S. retail trade sector in the 1990s. *Review of Economics and Statistics, 88*, 748–758.

Foster, L., Grim, C., & Haltiwanger, J. (2014). *Reallocation in the great recession: Cleansing or not?* NBER Working Paper 20427.

Geroski, P., & Gregg, P. (1997). Coping with recession.

Goldin, C. (1998). Labor markets in the Twentieth Century. In S. Engerman & R. Gallman (Eds.), *The Cambridge economic history of the United States*. Cambridge: Cambridge University Press.

Haddow, A., Hare, C., Hooley, J., & Shakir, T. (2013). Macroeconomic uncertainty: What is it, how can we measure it and why does it matter? *Bank of England Quarterly Bulletin, Q2*, 100–109.

Hall, R. (1991). Labor demand, labor supply and employment volatility. *NBER Macroeconomics Annual*.

Harris, R., & Drinkwater, S. (2000). UK plant and machinery capital stocks and plant closures. *Oxford Bulletin of Economics and Statistics, 62*, 243–265.

Hartman, R. (1972). The effect of price and cost uncertainty on investment. *Journal of Economic Theory, 5*, 258–266.

Hoover, H. (1952). *The memoirs of Herbert Hoover*. New York: Macmillan.

Hseih, C.-T., & Klenow, P. (2007). *Misallocation and manufacturing TFP in China and India*. NBER Working Paper 13290.

Hulten, C. (2001). Total factor productivity – A short biography. In C. Hulten, E. Dean, & M. Harper (Eds.), *New developments in productivity analysis*. NBER.

Hyatt, H., & Spletzer, J. (2013). *The recent decline in employment dynamics*. IZA Discussion Paper 7231.

Izquierdo, M., Jimeno, J., & Lacuesta, A. (2015). *Spain: From immigration to emigration?* Bank of Spain Working Paper 1503.

Jacobson, L., LaLonde, R., & Sullivan, D. (1993). Earnings losses of displaced workers. *American Economic Review, September*, 685–709.

Jovanovic, B. (1979). Job matching and the theory of turnover. *Journal of Political Economy, 87*(5), 972–990.

Jurado, K., Ludvigson, S., & Ng, S. (2015). Measuring uncertainty. *American Economic Review, 105*(3), 1177–1216.

Kahn, L. (2009). The long-term labor market consequences of graduating from college in a bad economy. *Labour Economics, 17*(2), 303–316.

Kahn, L., & McEntarfer, E. (2015). *Employer cyclicality and firm quality*. NBER Working Paper 20698.

Kehrig, M. (2011). *The cyclicality of productivity dispersion*. CES Working Paper 11–15.

Kiyotaki, N., & Moore, J. (1997). Credit market cycles. *Journal of Political Economy, 105*(2), 211–248.

Koetter, M., Kolari, J., & Spierdijk, L. (2012). Enjoying the quiet life under deregulation? *Review of Economics and Statistics, 94*(2), 462–480.

Lazear, E., & Spletzer, J. (2012). Hiring, churn, and the business cycle. *American Economic Review, 102*(3), 575–579.

Lev, B., & Radhakrishnan, S. (2005). The valuation of organization capital. In C. Corrado, J. Haltiwanger, & D. Sichel (Eds.), *Measuring capital in the new economy*. Chicago: NBER, University of Chicago Press.

Machin, S., & Manning, A. (1999). The causes and consequences of long-term unemployment in Europe. In *Handbook of labor economics* (Vol. 3C, pp. 3085–3319). Amsterdam: Elsevier.

Melitz, M., & Ottaviano, G. (2008). Market size, trade and productivity. *Review of Economic Studies, 75*, 295–316.

Mustre-del-Rio, J. (2014). *Job duration and the cleansing and sullying effects of recessions*. Federal Reserve Bank of Kansas City Working Paper 12–08.

Nelson, P. (1970). Information and consumer behaviour. *Journal of Political Economy, 78*(2), 311–329.

Oberfield, E. (2013). Productivity and misallocation during a crisis. *Review of Economic Dynamics, 16*(1), 100–119.

Oi, W. (1961). The desirability of price instability under perfect competition. *Econometrica, 29*(1), 58–64.

Oulton, N., & Srinivasan, S. (2003). *Capital stocks, capital services and depreciation: An integrated framework*. Bank of England Working Paper 192.

Ouyang, M. (2009). The scarring effect of recessions. *Journal of Monetary Economics, 56*(2), 184–199.

Prescott, E., & Visscher, M. (1980). Organization capital. *Journal of Political Economy, 88*(3), 446–461.

Rogerson, R., Shimer, R., & Wright, R. (2005). Search-theoretic models of the labor market. *Journal of Economic Literature, 43*, 959–988.

Schumpeter, J. (1934). Depressions. In D. Brown, E. Chamberlin, & S. Harris (Eds.), *The economics of the recovery program*. New York: McGraw-Hill.

Scott, A. (2009). Notes from a recession. *Business Strategy Review, Autumn*, 5–10.

Sekine, T., Kobayashi, K., & Saita, Y. (2003). Forbearance lending: A case for Japanese firms. *Monetary and Economic Studies, 21*, 69–92.

Stiglitz, J. (1993). *Endogenous growth and cycles*. NBER Working Paper 4286.

van den Berg, G., & van Ours, J. (1996). Unemployment dynamics and duration dependence. *Journal of Labor Economics, 14*(1), 100–125.

van Wanrooy, B., Bewley, H., Bryson, A., Forth, J., Stokes, L., & Wood, S. (2013). *Employment relations in the shadow of recession: Findings from the 2011 workplace employment relations study*. Palgrave MacMillan.

6

Loose Talk: Guiding Interest Rate Expectations Lower

In addition to deciding to keep the target for the federal funds rate at 1 % at its August 2003 meeting, the FOMC chose to provide guidance about the future path of interest rates to market participants and households and companies in the wider real economy: that rates were likely to remain low for a 'considerable period' (FOMC 2003):

> While the Committee could not commit itself to a particular policy course over time, many of the members referred to the likelihood that the Committee would want to keep policy accommodative for a longer period than had been the practice in past periods of accelerating economic activity. Reasons for such an approach to policy stemmed from the need to encourage progress toward closing the economy's currently wide output gap and, with inflation already near the low end of what some members regarded as an acceptable range, to resist significant further disinflation. In the view of these members, appreciable added disinflation would potentially blunt the effectiveness of further policy easing in the event of strong adverse shocks to the economy. At the same time, maintaining an accommodative policy stance was seen as involving little risk of inducing rising inflation so long as high levels of excess capacity and very competitive markets continued to characterize economic conditions.

This is a classic example of forward guidance: a central bank talking about the decisions it might take in the future in order to influence expectations and hence behaviour today. As time passed in the post-crash era, forward guidance came to the fore as a tool of monetary policy. In this section, we explain why

© The Editor(s) (if applicable) and The Author(s) 2016
R. Barwell, *Macroeconomic Policy after the Crash*,
DOI 10.1057/978-1-137-51592-6_6

and how central banks talk about the actions they plan to take in the future and whether and why their words have any impact.

6.1   Why Talk at All?

These days central bankers like to talk. They release an account of the discussions within policy meetings, they hold press conferences to discuss their latest set of forecasts, they give speeches in which they describe their personal assessment of the outlook and/or the appropriate policy response and they give interviews to the press on a regular basis. Then there are the publications of the staff of the central banks who support the policymakers: the economists who publish articles and more formal research papers which provide additional colour on the institution's thinking. For the world's major central banks like the Fed and the ECB it seems like barely a day goes by without some form of new communication hitting the news wires. It may therefore come as a surprise to the reader to learn that in the workhorse model, which is the industry standard in modern macroeconomics, central bankers are wasting their breath when they talk.

The assumption that agents have rational expectations is so pervasive in modern macroeconomics that it is all too easy to forget that it is an assumption. Under the strong variant of rational expectations it is assumed that the agents in an economy (for which read an economic model) understand the structure of the economy (for which read the precise calibration of the economic model, hence the label model-consistent expectations) and use that structure to forecast the future. Of course, the conduct of monetary policy is part of the structure of that economy, so the agents in the model are assumed to understand how central bankers set interest rates too (strictly speaking the rule which central bankers are assumed to slavishly follow). In other words, the agents in the model see the same data that the central bankers see, share the same assessment of how the economy behaves as the central bankers, and understand how the central bankers will respond in any given situation. When central bankers speak in this economy (model) about the actions that they will take in the future they have zero impact: their words are statements of the obvious. Notions of transparency and accountability are similarly redundant because it is assumed that agents see everything and understand everything.

Central bankers are economists and are familiar with the rational expectations assumption and what it implies. If they believed that the considerable resources that they devoted to communication served no useful purpose they would stop. Revealed preference suggests that central bankers do not believe that they are stating the obvious. The revealed preference of the audience suggests the same: when they speak, we listen, and since our time is precious it follows that we must think that there is some value in what central bankers say. Indeed, some financial institutions employ so-called 'central bank watchers' (including yours truly) whose job is to closely follow what central banks say in order to better predict what they will do. The question we should be asking is not whether there is information in central bank communication but what precisely that information is.

The answer is clear. We listen to the central bank because we do not necessarily see what they see; for example, the central bank may have access to information that the private sector does not. We listen because we do not know what they know: we do not necessarily share their assessment of the current state or structure of the economy (the shocks that are currently working their way through the economy and how the economy responds to those shocks). And we listen because we do not perfectly understand how central banks respond to a given assessment of the economy. It should therefore come as no surprise that we cannot predict how central banks behave, and when monetary policy is more a black box than an open box, the case for communication on accountability and transparency grounds also becomes compelling.

6.2   Myth and Mystique

Once upon a time central bankers said very little. There was a lot of 'myth and mystique' about central banking in general, and communication in particular (Goodfriend 1986). That mindset was captured in Brunner's (1981) famous critique:

> The mystique thrives on a pervasive impression that Central Banking is an esoteric art. Access to this art and its proper execution is confined to the initiated elite. The esoteric nature of the art is moreover revealed by an inherent impossibility to articulate its insights in explicit and intelligible words and sentences.

and in Alan Greenspan's (1987) possibly ironic aside:

> Since I've become a central banker, I've learned to mumble with great incoherence. If I seem unduly clear to you, you must have misunderstood what I said.

In the words of a famous advertising slogan, previous generations of central bankers *just did it*, without preparing the ground first by signalling their intentions. They were content to take policy decisions that on occasion might shock and surprise investors in financial markets and households and companies in the real economy. There was no regular update on the central bank's assessment of the outlook for the economy let alone the likely path of interest rates. Blinder (2002) recounts how during his induction as Vice Chairman of the Fed in 1994 a senior press officer informed him that when it came to the Fed's communication strategy, 'we don't talk about the economy'. However, attitudes gradually changed. Central bankers came to the conclusion that it was better to communicate their thinking, to steer expectations, for reasons of both monetary and financial stability.

The monetary stability case for clearer communication follows immediately from an appreciation that expectations matter. The current level of Bank Rate—the rate at which central bank reserves are remunerated in the interval until the next policy meeting—is not a sufficient summary statistic of the stance of monetary policy. The path that Bank Rate is expected to take in the future matters a great deal: a cut in Bank Rate that is certain to be reversed the following meeting will have a negligible impact on the economy; if instead, that cut is set to persist for the years to come then the impact on output and inflation could be material. Likewise, expectations of the likelihood and extent of central bank asset purchases or sales matter too, since they will be reflected in current market prices. Critically, it is investors' expectations of the decisions that central bankers will take in the future that is reflected in asset prices today, whether the value of the pound or the interest rate on a new fix-rate mortgage. If the central bank perceives that the expectations of the future path of policy that is reflected in asset prices is faulty then in some sense the stance of monetary policy is faulty too, because those asset prices will influence the variables that the central bank ultimately cares about: demand and inflation.

The financial stability case for clearer communication follows immediately from an appreciation that faulty expectations can lead to bad decisions. If agents' expectations of the future path of rates are out of kilter with reality then when reality dawns those agents could wind up in financial distress, so it makes sense for the central bank to issue a wake-up call. For example, if households are convinced that interest rates will remain on hold for the indefinite future then they may be comfortable taking on more debt. If the central bank believes rates must rise then it is makes sense for the central bank to warn households to lean against the build-up of a potentially unsustainable debt burden. These financial stability concerns around interest rate surprises also arise in markets. Shock changes in interest rates can trigger a sharp move in asset prices which can lead to mark to market losses, which may be particularly problematic among leveraged investors (where the implications for the bottom of line of a given move in asset prices are magnified by financing an investment through debt).

6.3   The Pre-crisis Conversation: One Game at a Time

Central bankers certainly cranked up the volume in their communication strategies in the years leading up to the crisis, engaging in a far more sophisticated conversation with financial markets and the general public than previous generations had done. However, most central banks did not go as far as explicitly discussing the future path of policy. The focal point of the communication strategy was the current state of the economy and the path it might take in the future.

The BoE's principal tool for communicating the Committee's thinking on the state of the economy was the Inflation Report that was published each quarter. The Report described the latest macroeconomic data releases in considerable detail, placing them in proper context using the monetary transmission mechanism as an organising framework and drawing out the key developments for policy. Indeed, the Bank's Inflation Report once won the dubious honour of the 'fill the bathtub' award, given the tendency to 'report as many facts about the data as possible, regardless of their relevance or importance', with the risk that the reader can drown in that 'bathtub of economic statistics' given little guidance on how each statistic mapped into the Bank's outlook (Leeper 2003).

The Bank also published the Committee's latest set of projections for economic growth and inflation in the Inflation Report in the form of fan charts which illustrated the uncertainty around the future path of the economy. The Report offered two different perspectives on those projections, which reflected different assumptions on the future path of interest rates: one set was produced under the assumption that Bank Rate remained unchanged at its current level; the other under the assumption that interest rates followed the path implied by market prices (essentially the path expected by market participants, although market prices include a risk premium). There is no reason to believe that either of those interest rate 'conditioning assumptions' delivered the best possible outcome for growth and inflation.

The Committee did not vote on, and therefore did not publish what it considered to be the optimal interest path that would deliver that best possible outcome for growth and inflation. The Bank was concerned that any formal discussion of the future path of policy would be misinterpreted no matter how hard the Bank might try to emphasise the probabilistic nature of the statement—that is, that whilst a central projection for interest rates might be the single most likely path for rates, it was still highly unlikely to emerge given the uncertainty over the outlook, and was certainly not a commitment, as former Governor King argued (Giles and Daneshkhu 2007):

> There is a real danger that the personal finance correspondents on the papers would encourage people to draw the conclusion that we'd announced what the interest rate would be, and that people would make decisions on how much to borrow and lend on the assumption that that's what interest rates would be instead of a probability that there might be this path, but it could be quite a lot higher or quite a lot lower. So I'm not sure if there's a real value in publishing that path. I was quite struck that when the Riksbank, for example, published their first fan chart for their own policy rate, that even very sophisticated investment banks published a commentary on it without a single reference to the fan chart nature – only about the central projection.

However, it was possible to infer something about what the Committee might consider to be that optimal path from the projections that the Bank published. Imagine for the sake of the argument that market participants expected a sharp rise in interest rates and that the fan chart for inflation conditioned on that path showed inflation undershooting the target two years from now but the fan chart conditioned on a constant, unchanged path for Bank Rate showed inflation overshooting two years from now. Based on those projections, one might reasonably conclude that the Committee believed that the optimal path for Bank Rate over the future likely lay somewhere in the interval between those two paths (the constant rate and the market path).

In theory, the Bank also provided a signal about the near-term path for rates by publishing evidence of divergent views within the Committee, via the speeches and the votes of individual Committee members. Information on the existence, extent and nature of dissent within the Committee provided clues about where interest rates might be heading next (Gerlach-Kristen 2004). In theory, members of the Committee were supposed to vote their view, and not search for a 'false consensus'. Much used to be made of the incidence of dissent in the Committee's vote during its first decade as evidence that there was a healthy debate within the MPC (King 2007). However, it is worth noting that the magnitude of dissent within the Committee was almost always economically insignificant (Barwell 2016b). With one exception, all dissenting votes between November 1998 and the outbreak of the financial crisis were a mere 25 basis points from the consensus. Given a conventional estimate of the impact of a change in Bank Rate, that level of dissent translates into an ultra-marginal impact on the variables the Committee ultimately cares about. For example, the Bank's own estimates of the transmission mechanism suggest that a 100-basis point increase in the policy rate that is maintained for a whole year reduces inflation by around 30 basis points after two years (BoE 1999). In short, whilst the words of the Committee suggest significant dissent over monetary strategy, their votes suggest an enduring consensus over strategy, and since votes are ultimately what matters then it not clear what signal can reliably be extracted from the evidence of dissent within the Committee.

6.4   It's All Greek to Me: De-coding Central Bank Communication

The President of the Federal Reserve Bank of Chicago, Charles Evans, wrote a paper in 2012 with colleagues from the Chicago Fed which neatly identified the key criterion we should use to classify central bank communication. The Chicago team argue that the acid test for central bank communication is whether it signals a change in the central bank's strategy, or to be precise commits the central bank to a change in strategy or not.

Most central bank communication is what Campbell et al. (2012) describe as Delphic: the central bank is describing its current assessment of the economy, its forecasts of how the economy will evolve in the future and the actions it is considering. Remember, these would all constitute statements of the obvious in a model-consistent rational expectations world, where the agent has access to the same information set as the central bank, shares the same forecasting model (the true structure of the economy) and understands the optimal rule which the central bank uses to set interest rates. Back in the real world, those statements will contain useful information and therefore can have an impact on behaviour and therefore the prospects of the central bank achieving its objectives. Unfortunately, once we step outside the orthodox paradigm of model-consistent rational expectations it is hard to be sure how agents will respond to central bank communication.

If the representative agent is inattentive and boundedly rational, if she does not constantly track and forecast the state of the economy and re-optimise in response to news, but instead takes decisions infrequently on the basis of a limited information set and rules of thumb that have worked well in the past then we need to understand how central bank communication influences that limited information set or those rules of thumb—if at all—if we want to be able to forecast how central bank communication impacts the economy.

One possibility is that most people do not construct their own forecasts of how the economy will behave in the future; they simply free ride on the consensus view that is discussed in the media, which itself may reflect to some extent the assessment of the central bank (Carroll 2003). In this environment, central bankers should think twice before responding to bad news by either describing the downgrade in their forecasts as an implicit signal that policy may be eased in the future or by explicitly signalling the monetary stance may be eased to cushion the blow. That well-intentioned attempt to reassure investors, companies and households could trigger panic since those agents may not have noticed the news which prompted the central bank to talk but they know enough to understand that if the central bank is worried, then they should be scared, and therefore save more and spend less. As Bullard (2013) argues:

> [A]ny attempt to provide additional policy accommodation today by promising easy policy in the future can be viewed as suggesting the future will be characterized by poor macroeconomic performance. This can be extremely counterproductive, as firms and households may prepare for a prolonged stagnation.

The alternative form of communication is what Campbell et al. (2012) describe as Odyssean. Now the central bank is communicating a change in its strategy—that it will respond in a different way to a given outlook in the present and future than it has done in the past. This form of communication is effective even in the model-consistent rational expectations benchmark because the agents learn that part of the structure of that economy has changed—the monetary policy rule. Indeed, a change in the rule could have significant consequences in that framework—the most extreme example of which would be a change in the inflation target which in the orthodox framework would rapidly lead to an adjustment in the path of nominal variables. There is a small caveat here: agents have to believe the communication if it is to impact behaviour. In other words, the change of strategy has to be credible.

Macroeconomists have been brought up to fear the bogeyman of time inconsistency—an insight that earned Kydland and Prescott the Nobel Prize (Kydland and Prescott 1977). Policymakers often talk today about actions that they plan to take in the future. Whenever there is a tension between the incentives for those policymakers to talk about those future policies today and the likely incentives for those policymakers to take those decisions when the time comes, there is a credibility problem. Rational agents will not believe 'cheap talk': if you do not believe that the policymaker will deliver on the announcement tomorrow, then the announcement will not influence your behaviour today. The problem with guidance that the central bank's strategy has changed is that it appears to signal a desire to stray from what has long been perceived to be optimal, and is therefore likely to be received with scepticism: agents may reasonably conclude that the policymaker will soon shift back to the optimal strategy.

The logical conclusion of the time consistency problem is that—at least within the model-consistent rational expectations benchmark—the central bank needs to provide a credible commitment device that will convince agents today that the policymaker will follow through on her promise tomorrow, hence the Odyssean label attached to this form of guidance. Odysseus solved the problem of how to safely navigate the danger posed by the Sirens but still be able to listen to their song by having himself tied to the mast of his ship and stuffing his sailors' ears with bees wax so they would not be swayed by his orders to change course once he had fallen under the spell of the Sirens. Central bankers need to provide the equivalent of the bees wax and rope to make their Odyssean guidance credible—to convince the market that they will not stray back to the timeless strategy—if they want their words to have maximum effect. Of course, if we step outside the model-consistent rational expectations benchmark it is much harder to say how the central banks' words will be received: will agents understand that the reaction function has changed and will they have any reason to doubt the central bankers' words?

In the final analysis, central bankers may enjoy operational independence but they are ultimately answerable to the elected representatives of the public. Those elected representatives themselves cannot bind the hands of their successors in future parliaments (a problem with fiscal rules, as we shall later discuss) and therefore it is very hard to see how central banks can provide a watertight commitment to do anything. However, central bankers can provide a practical commitment device by using their reputation for truth-telling to inspire confidence that they will follow through on their communication, or as Woodford (2012) puts it:

> [T]he most logical way to make such commitment achievable and credible is by publicly stating the commitment, in a way that is sufficiently unambiguous to make it embarrassing for policymakers to simply ignore the existence of the commitment when making decisions at a later time.

6.5   Forward Guidance and Looking Back

Although forward guidance has come to be understood as a device to gently steer expectations of the path of interest rates in a particular direction, several high profile academics have advocated using Odyssean forward guidance for more radical ends. Indeed, those economists believe that forward guidance is a far more effective tool to ease monetary policy and support the economy at the lower bound than the tactic that central banks actually employed: QE.

The catalyst for this debate about the role of forward guidance in the central bank's toolkit at the lower bound was the unfolding deflationary episode in Japan in the Lost Decades of the nineties and noughties. As interest rates hit the lower bound, economists grappled with the question of what more could be done to resuscitate the economy and inflation expectations. Krugman (1998) and then later Eggertsson and Woodford (2003) advocated a radical solution, rooted in forward guidance. The policy rate might be constrained today but expectations of the policy rate in the future are not, and those expectations are part of the monetary stance. Central banks can therefore ease the stance if they can lower those expectations of the future path of rates by convincing investors that the reaction function has changed—in particular, if they can convince investors that they will keep rates lower in the recovery that is yet to come than past experience would suggest.

Krugman's proposal was simple and to the point: the BoJ should commit to a positive inflation target and in particular 'an inflation rate of not less than x percent over y years'. The new target can lend valuable credibility to the central bank's forecasts that it will deliver inflation because the central bank is now obliged to do so; or put another way, the target alleviates concerns that the BoJ would start to tighten the stance as soon as the green shoots of inflation start to emerge. If raising the target succeeds in raising inflation expectations in this way then it will help to deliver the much-needed reduction in real interest rates that helps to deliver the recovery in demand that makes expectations of a future increase in inflation internally consistent. Although strictly speaking beyond the scope of the book (if only by a matter of months), the Bank of Japan *did* eventually follow Krugman's advice. At the September 2016 policy meeting the   committed to over-shoot its inflation target by pledging to expand the monetary base 'until the year-on-year rate of increase in the observed consumer price index (CPI) exceeds the price stability target of 2 percent and stays above the target in a stable manner' (Bank of Japan (2016)).

Eggertsson and Woodford's variant of forward guidance was slightly more subtle: they advocated that the central bank should adopt a backward-looking reaction function. Central banks at the lower bound would now set policy taking account of the macroeconomic consequences of the policy rate having been stuck at the lower bound, with a sub-optimally low price level given a bout of deflation. In short, the more deflation you get today, the more reflation you are required to deliver tomorrow, or to use the familiar shorthand: bygones are not bygones. These considerations do not feature in conventional monetary strategy, which focuses on where the output gap is today (not where it has been) and the inflation outlook today and tomorrow, and therefore the Eggertsson and Woodford proposal is indeed consistent with the policy rate remaining at the lower bound for longer than the conventional approach as the economy recovers. As with the Krugman proposal, the guidance should raise inflation expectations but the objective is in some sense more limited: the central bank is trying to reflate the price level but it is not obliged to deliver a higher 'trend' inflation rate post-recovery.

Of course, this history-dependent strategy only works to the extent that private sector agents trust the central bank not to switch back to the forward-looking strategy once it has room to manoeuvre. Eggertson and Woodford reflect on the bees wax and rope that the central bank could use whilst at the lower bound in order to make the communication more credible, by providing the central bank with private financial incentives to honour the guidance, including:

- *Purchasing assets denominated in foreign currency:* If the central bank is able to achieve the recovery in inflation that is not currently anticipated by market participants, then it will stand to make a capital gain on those assets when the domestic currency depreciates.
- *Purchasing long-dated securities*: If the central bank purchases long-dated bonds at prices consistent with the central bank's pledge to keep rates low for long, then it will stand to suffer a capital loss on those bonds if it reneges on that pledge.
- *Selling options on the policy rate:* The most direct way for the central bank to stand behind its guidance is to write options where it stands to lose money if it does not deliver on that guidance.

Interesting though these financial incentives are, it seems highly unlikely that central bankers would ever be comfortable entering into such contracts. In any case, these are decisions that rightly belong to finance ministers, not central bank governors.

If we cannot rely on these financial penalties to incentivise time consistency then we need to fall back on the identification of visible, credible and quantitative yardsticks which the private sector can use to independently assess whether the central bank has reneged on the history-dependent strategy.

Eggertson and Woodford's favoured measure is an 'output-gap adjusted price level'—which in log form is defined as the log of the price level plus a term which reflects the size of the output gap and the weight of the output gap in the central bank's loss function (which captures how much output gap stabilisation matters, relative to stabilising inflation). In this context, a history-dependent strategy would require that rates remain at the lower bound so long as that gap-adjusted measures is below target path, that for the sake of simplicity should rise through time according to the inflation target (the key is not to readjust that path down in response to the current weakness of prices).

In his restatement of the wisdom of forward guidance at the lower bound, Woodford (2012) proposes an alternative benchmark, which is easier to explain, communicate and verify: a nominal GDP level projection. This idea was also discussed by the then Governor of the Bank of Canada and the soon to be Governor of the BoE Mark Carney in a speech on forward guidance in late 2012, in which he framed the idea as a kind of 'break glass in case of emergency' idea—beyond the conventional inflation targeting framework and one which was likely to deliver modest gains in normal circumstances, but of potential use in exceptional circumstances (Carney 2012).

In passing, discussion of a nominal GDP levels target as the anchor of a history-dependent strategy gave rise to a wider debate about the merits of using a nominal GDP growth target as the nominal anchor for monetary policy rather than an inflation target. However, there remain long-standing concerns about making that switch on both theoretical and practical grounds. From a theoretical perspective, a target for nominal GDP growth does not provide a stable anchor for the rate of change of prices unless one is willing to assume that trend growth in real GDP is stable through time; otherwise, changes in the rate of trend growth mechanically feed through into an equal and offsetting change in the implicit target rate of change in the GDP deflator. From a practical perspective, early vintages of data on nominal GDP are routinely revised which will greatly complicate the conduct of policy in real time. Imagine trying to drive a car at a constant speed when you cannot trust what the speedometer is currently saying and you only gradually learn how fast you were travelling some time ago.

A more practical way to implement Odyssean guidance may therefore lie in price level path targeting (PLPT). The central bank is now obliged to drive the price level back towards the path it would otherwise have taken if the central bank had achieved its mandate, and that in turn implies that prices must rise at a faster rate than the inflation target in order to 'catch up'. This objective is easier to communicate, easier to justify (in terms of the observed shortfall in prices through failure to achieve the target in the recent past and present), easier to verify in real-time (given the absence of revisions) and therefore can provide a credible form of bees wax and rope to guide monetary strategy (Barwell 2016a).

Interestingly, a loose version of PLTP started to creep into the policy debate in the Eurozone as this book was about to go to press (and as we highlighted above, the Bank of Japan embraced the idea of inflation over-shoots). The Accounts of the January 2016 Governing Council meeting reveal that (ECB 2016):

> A view was put forward in this regard that, in order to counter misperceptions of an asymmetric interpretation and to underline the symmetry of the ECB's mandate, it appeared logical from a medium-term perspective for the Governing Council, after a prolonged period of undershooting of its inflation aim, to consider a limited period of overshooting in future.

Indeed, one member of the Governing Council—the Governor of the Italian Central Bank, Ignazio Visco—argued that it was 'almost simple arithmetic' that as inflation had been below 2 percent for so long 'it's comprehensible that we should exceed that objective for a certain period of time' (Jones (2016)). However, President Draghi remained resolute, arguing against a change in the definition of price stability in *either* direction (Draghi (2016)):

'Why don't you revise the inflation target?" Now, there are two schools of thought. Some people say we should revise it downward and simply accept the fact that we'll never reach 2%, and we should take 1% or 0%. And some say, "Oh, you should revise it upward and go to 3% or 4%, because in this way you will elicit expectations that you will go up with your policies." Now, the ECB position has been basically contrary to revising the inflation objective either way, and the reasons are different in different cases. The revision upward, frankly, would test seriously our credibility, because people would actually say, "How come you want to go to 3% when you're not even able to reach 1.5%?" And by the way, each revision on both sides undermines the credibility of the central bank—for different reasons, but it undermines the credibility of the central bank.'

6.6 FGUK: The UK's Experiment with Forward Guidance

We now turn to discuss the introduction and evolution of forward guidance in the UK: the calibration of the guidance and the implicit message about the MPC's strategy.

6.6.1 The Chancellor Sets the Committee Some Homework

Credit for the UK's experiment with forward guidance as a tool of monetary policy lies with the HM Treasury not the Bank of England. The Chancellor announced in his 2013 Budget statement that the MPC's remit would allow it to provide forward guidance if it wished to influence expectations of the future path of policy, including the use of intermediate thresholds, and he set the Bank a deadline to consider and report back on the merits of forward guidance that rates might stay 'lower for longer' by the time of the publication of the August 2013 Inflation Report (Osborne 2013).

It just so happened that the deadline for the Bank to hand in its assignment on forward guidance was set for a little over a month after Mervyn King's successor as Governor, Mark Carney, was set to take control at Threadneedle Street. As we have already noted, Carney had very clear views on the topic of forward guidance. Indeed, Carney had been an early pioneer of guidance during his term of office as Governor of the Bank of Canada. In April 2009, the Bank of Canada has issued an explicit commitment that, conditional on the outlook for inflation, the policy rate (the target for the overnight rate) would remain at 0.25 % until the end of the 2010 Q2 (He 2010). More recently, and more to the point after his appointment as BoE Governor had been announced, Carney had given a speech in which he discussed the limits of what could be achieved with forward guidance which is worth quoting at length (Carney 2012):

> Today, to achieve a better path for the economy over time, a central bank may need to commit credibly to maintaining highly accommodative policy even after the economy and, potentially, inflation picks up. Market participants may doubt the willingness of an inflation-targeting central bank to respect this commitment if inflation goes temporarily above target. These doubts reduce the effective stimulus of the commitment and delay the recovery. To 'tie its hands,' a central bank could publicly announce precise numerical thresholds for inflation and unemployment that must be met before reducing stimulus. This could reinforce the central bank's commitment to stimulative policy in the future and thus enhance the stimulative impact of its policies in the present, helping the economy escape from the liquidity trap.

It is interesting to note Carney's use of the Odyssean metaphor of 'tying hands' in his description of the role of thresholds in state-contingent forward guidance. If the new Governor was to have his way the Old Lady would soon be tying her own hands to the mast.

6.6.2 The Bank Delivers

It came as no surprise that when the Old Lady handed in her forward guidance homework she reached the conclusion that it would be appropriate for the MPC to adopt state-contingent forward guidance linked to the unemployment rate. To be precise, the MPC declared its intention not to begin raising Bank Rate at least until the unemployment rate (as measured by the Labour Force Survey) had fallen to a 'threshold' of 7 %. Where the stock of purchased assets was concerned, the Committee signalled that it would add to the stock if necessary and otherwise would reinvest the proceeds from maturing bonds in the portfolio for so long as the unemployment rate remained above the threshold.

The guidance simplified the complexity of the monetary policy debate into a threshold condition on one variable and therefore unsurprisingly had MAC clauses attached to it. The guidance would not apply if one of three 'knock-outs' were breached:

- *Inflation too far above the target*: if inflation was expected to be on average half a percentage point or more above the 2 % target 18–24 months in the future
- *Expectations slipping their anchor:* if medium-term expectations were no longer considered to be sufficiently close to the target
- *Financial instability:* if the Financial Policy Committee (FPC) reached the conclusion that the conduct of monetary policy posed a risk to financial stability that could not be managed through appropriate action by the relevant authorities (the FPC, the Prudential Regulation Authority [PRA] and the Financial Conduct Authority [FCA])

So much for the technical details, what was the purpose of the Bank's forward guidance? The Governor argued in the Inflation Report press conference in which the guidance framework was unveiled that the guidance did not reveal a change in strategy (Carney 2013a):

> That's one of the advantages of guidance in this context. It's giving a better sense, to use the technical term, of the MPC's reaction function. It's not a change in the reaction function, but it gives a better sense of the MPC's reaction function to financial market participants.

Indeed, the Bank argued that its forward guidance would 'enhance the effectiveness of monetary stimulus' in three ways (BoE 2013b):

- *Greater clarity over the loss function*: The Bank believed that the guidance revealed information to the market about the relative importance that the Committee attached to bringing inflation back to the target (from above, at that point in time) and reducing the slack that remained in the economy:

in particular that the Committee would be willing to take a flexible approach to slowing inflation so long as it did not jeopardise the nominal anchor.

- *Temper expectations of an imminent increase in Bank Rate*: The Bank believed that the guidance would reduce uncertainty about the future path of policy by reassuring investors, companies and households that a continuation of growth would not rapidly lead to a withdrawal of monetary stimulus because the Committee cared about the level of demand relative to supply rather than the growth of demand.

- *Creating a safe environment for the Committee to learn*: The Bank argued that the optimal monetary strategy was particularly unclear at that juncture, given uncertainty around the slope of the trade-off between activity and inflation and the extent of any trade-off between monetary and financial stability. The Bank argued that the guidance created the space for the Committee to develop its strategy over time as it learned, rather than having to commit to a particular course of action.

6.6.3   Why Unemployment?

One obvious question about the calibration of the state-contingent forward guidance is why unemployment?—that is, why was the unemployment rate used to define the threshold condition on the first rate hike? The importance of the variable used to define the threshold should certainly not be downplayed—in effect, the policy process switches to rule-like behaviour under forward guidance, so the unemployment rate is effectively acting as a summary statistic of the entire macro-outlook (with the knockouts there as a fail-safe in case the 'rule' goes too far astray).

In some sense, the unemployment rate was an obvious choice: central bankers needed a variable which could be combined with a threshold to produce a transparent and easily understood proxy of the output gap that was not prone to revision. The unemployment rate fits the bill. Unfortunately, there was one other key criterion: that unemployment gap had to be a credible proxy of the output gap, and from the outset that was debatable.

As we will go on to discuss, practical central bankers instinctively resist a rules-based approach to monetary policy because they believe that *all rules* are too simplistic. Consequently, we might expect those practical central bankers to be uncomfortable with state-contingent forward guidance, irrespective of which variable was used to define the threshold. Beyond that generic concern there was also a specific concern about the extent to which the unemployment rate is a reliable measure of labour market slack. A more comprehensive quantity-based measure of labour market slack might also consider:

- the duration structure of unemployment and relatedly the intensity with which the unemployed search for work;
- the contribution to labour supply of those who report that they are not available to start work or are not looking for work (a.k.a., the economically inactive) but who nonetheless find jobs;
- the change as well as the level of these unemployment and non-employment measures;
- the incidence of underemployment, with people who are in employment but not in the type of job they want (e.g., those on temporary contracts who want a permanent job) and in particular where people would like to work longer hours (to increase their pay);
- the intensity and extent to which employees search for a better and/or an additional job;
- the extent to which self-reported self-employment is a form of hidden unemployment and the intensity with which those individuals search for work; and
- the contribution of migrants to labour supply and labour market tightness.

Indeed, the BoE's own research on labour market tightness had identified problems with the unemployment rate as a summary statistic of slack (Brigden and Thomas 2003). To sum up, the Bank opted for a familiar measure of slack that features in an introductory business cycle treatment of the labour market to anchor the guidance on rates, but one which years of accumulated experience suggested was liable to give an imperfect impression of the amount of slack in the economy. Unfortunately, this weakness was all too quickly exposed.

6.7 An Appraisal of the Old Lady's Forward Guidance

One could argue that there is little point in discussing the Bank's forward guidance in any detail because the whole framework was rendered redundant within months by the rapid fall in the unemployment rate. However, the design of the framework does reveal information about the strategy of the Committee which does matter, so we shall now briefly review what can be learned from the design of FGUK.

6.7.1   Following the Fed

When the BoE embraced forward guidance it essentially adopted the template that had recently been established by the Fed. The Fed has experimented with a number of different forms of forward guidance (Mester 2014), but in December 2012 it switched to a state-contingent model, in which the FOMC signalled that it anticipated keeping the target range for the federal funds rate between 0 % and ¼ % for at least as long as:

- the unemployment rate remains above 6½ %;
- inflation between one and two years ahead is expected to be no more than a half percentage point above the Committee's 2 % target; and
- longer-term inflation expectations remain well anchored.

The observation that the Bank's guidance was clearly modelled on the Fed template is not intended as a criticism: if the objective of the exercise was to provide a clear signal to agents about the conduct of monetary policy then it makes sense to use a device that at the very least investors should have been familiar with. However, although the Bank's guidance is very similar in form to the Fed model, there were important differences.

One obvious difference between the Bank's variant and the Fed's template is the addition of a financial stability 'knockout', although given how that knockout was framed—the MPC's guidance would only be considered null and void if there was a threat to financial stability *and* if the proper authorities (FPC, FCA and PRA) were unable to deal with that threat using the tools at their disposal—it is not clear that the inclusion of this knockout materially affected the expected shelf-life of the guidance.

The other major difference is the calibration of the threshold for unemployment itself. However, it would be a mistake to focus on the absolute size of the threshold. What matters is the location of the threshold relative to the central banker's estimate of the equilibrium unemployment rate because that tells you how much slack will remain in the labour market at the point at which rate hikes might be considered appropriate. In the case of the Fed, we know that the median view on the FOMC at that time was in the interval 5.2–5.8 % (Bernanke 2013b) and a natural rate of 5.5 % was assumed in an influential paper written by senior Fed staff during this period (English et al. 2013), so on that basis an unemployment threshold of 6.5 % is consistent with a threshold on labour market slack of about a percentage point. In contrast, the Bank staff's estimate of the equilibrium rate was around 6.5 % which with an unemployment threshold of 7 % suggests a threshold on labour market slack roughly half the size (50 basis points).

In short, the calibration of the unemployment threshold implies that the MPC was comfortable continuing to provide guidance that rates would remain low beyond the point at which the reduction in labour market slack would cause the FOMC's low for longer guidance to expire. To return once again to the familiar monetary analogy of driving a car: deciding when and how to raise interest rates from the floor during a recovery has a lot in common with deciding when and how to apply the brake as a bend in the road approaches, and the thresholds demarcate the distance from the bend at which the driver is willing to contemplate applying the brake (remember, the guidance has thresholds not triggers). The MPC placed its unemployment threshold at half the distance (in basis points) from the bend (the equilibrium rate) than the Fed chose. Given that the Fed has a dual mandate, with a statutory obligation to achieve maximum employment as well as stable prices, and the BoE does not, it is interesting that the BoE's guidance demonstrated a greater commitment to reducing unemployment before interest rate hikes which might slow the pace of labour market normalisation were considered.

6.7.2 Bees Wax and Rope: Was the Bank's Forward Guidance Odyssean?

In terms of the bottom line of the macroeconomic impact of forward guidance, the Committee argued that its new communication strategy made the monetary stance 'more effective'. However, when pressed on whether the guidance was basically a 'clarification of communication' or a 'loosening of policy' in the August press conference, the Governor gave a somewhat equivocal answer (Carney 2013a):

> First and foremost it is a clarification. What this does is make stimulus more effective.

Likewise, when asked whether the forward guidance signalled a change in the reaction function or not, the Governor responded that it did not, but that it might nonetheless move expectations (Carney 2013a):

> That's one of the advantages of guidance in this context. It's giving a better sense, to use the technical term, of the MPC's reaction function. It's not a change in the reaction function, but it gives a better sense of the MPC's reaction function to financial market participants.

In other words, Carney's answer implies that he believed that market participants' understanding of the Committee's reaction function had somehow become detached from reality and the guidance could therefore play a positive role in re-educating the market, which is hard not to interpret as a criticism of the communication strategy of the previous regime, including the other eight members of the MPC. However, as we discussed above, the calibration of the Bank's forward guidance—and in particular the positioning of the unemployment threshold relative to the equilibrium rate—*did* appear to embody a change in the reaction function, with the Committee comfortable with maintaining a loose monetary stance (interest rates at very low levels and the lingering impact of the stock of purchased assets) until very little of the output gap remained. That shift is also apparent in commentary by individual Committee members. For example, compare and contrast the following statements about the optimal degree of slack at the moment of lift-off that were made before and after the launch of forward guidance, and in passing, the change of Governor (Fisher 2011; Bean 2014):

> [O]nce the spare capacity in the economy has been eliminated, monetary policy is to be consistent with the 2% target. And because of the lengthy lags involved, Bank Rate will need to start the long journey back to more normal settings *well before the degree of spare capacity is eliminated.* [emphasis added]

> I think it's reasonable to expect that you would want to start tightening policy before slack is *completely eliminated*, simply because of the lags between changing monetary policy and its impact on activity. If you leave it until slack has closed, that's a recipe for going too far, if you like. [emphasis added]

Another illustration of the same point can be found in the then Vice Chair of the Fed's argument that the calibration of the Fed's guidance (which remember was less aggressive in the calibration of the unemployment thresholds than the Bank's) reflected the Woodfordian argument for holding rates 'lower for longer' than a conventional policy rule implies (Yellen 2013). However, whilst the Bank's guidance does indeed appear to signify a shift in strategy in the direction of lower for longer it was still two steps removed from a wholesale adoption of Woodford's history-dependent strategy because the knockouts were not loose enough (did not allow a sufficiently large inflation overshoot) and the unemployment rate is not a backward-looking variable.

To see this point more clearly, consider the proposal of the President of the Federal Reserve Bank of Chicago (Charles Evans) who argued that his own preferred calibration of forward guidance featured a higher 'inflation-safeguard threshold' of 3 % (alongside a higher unemployment threshold of 7 %) than the 2½ % threshold the FOMC adopted. Evans' (2012) proposal takes us one step towards Woodfordian guidance: he justifies the higher threshold on the basis that central banks should be willing to tolerate an inflation overshoot in the exit strategy, to compensate for the undershoot that occurs whilst at the lower bound. However, Evans' (2012) calibration is still based on the unemployment rate—as the Bank's calibration was—and therefore does not capture the essential essence that of Woodfordian guidance that bygones are *not* bygones. Neither calibration includes an explicit commitment to compensate for the extent of the disinflation that might have occurred whilst policy was constrained at the lower bound (Woodford 2012):

> In the context of the simple macroeconomic model considered by Eggertsson and Woodford (where inflation and output determination are also purely forward-looking), such a rule will not imply any reason to delay immediately returning to the low-inflation steady state as soon as this is consistent with the zero lower bound on interest rates (i.e., as soon as the natural rate of interest returns to positive territory); it would not imply any commitment to keep the policy rate low for longer than would a strict inflation target or a purely contemporaneous Taylor rule.

6.7.3   Misunderstood?

The final aspect of the guidance package that is worth commenting on is the extent to which the message in the Bank's forward guidance was understood by the intended audience. The Governor argued in late 2013 that it was (Carney 2013b):

> My experience, having met more than 300 businesses around the country, is that business people understand forward guidance well.

The Bank's February 2014 Inflation Report presented a variety of survey evidence on the extent to which the guidance had been understood. The key results for the two key audiences in the real economy were as follows (BoE 2014):

- *Companies*: Depending on the survey between 75 % and 90 % of companies knew what guidance the Bank had given when asked to choose from a list of options. Around half of the sample interpreted the message as meaning that rates would now stay lower for longer, and the majority felt more confident about the prospects for the UK economy. In terms of the impact of the guidance on behaviour, the net balance of companies reported that they planned to bring forward investment in capital and jobs.

- *Households*: Only around a fifth of households were able to correctly identify the Bank's guidance from a list of options; indeed, only around half
understood it referred to Bank Rate. Less than a quarter of households had
lowered their expectations of the future path of interest rates as a result of
the guidance. The large majority of households reported that the guidance
would have no impact on their behaviour.

These results clearly indicate that awareness of the Bank's communication
was far higher in the corporate sector and underscore the need to think about
the impact of central bank communication (and indeed behaviour more generally) within a framework that treats households as inattentive rather than
the rational automatons that populate much of macroeconomic analysis.
However, just because most companies are aware of the Bank's guidance and
it appears to have prompted a shift in behaviour it does not necessarily follow
that those companies understood the message.

Drawing calendar inferences from state-contingent guidance as these companies appear to have done is not straightforward. In order to draw firm conclusions about the future path of rates and the prospects for the UK economy from
the Bank's forward guidance requires a detailed macroeconomic forecast—and
in particular a reliable forecast for the unemployment rate (something it turns
out that the BoE did not have). Immediately prior to the launch of the guidance, professional forecasters appear to have expected the first rate rise to arrive
in mid-2015 (BoE 2013a). If that view was in any way representative of the
expectations of the companies in this survey then only those companies that
were reasonably confident that unemployment would take the best part of two
years to fall to the threshold (rather than say six months!) should have reported
being reasonably confident that the guidance implied rates would now stay lower
for longer (technically speaking these companies would have also had to have
reassured themselves that none of the knockouts would have been triggered).

In conclusion, it seems a bit of a stretch to argue that companies updated
sophisticated forecasts of the future in light of the Bank's forward guidance.
Instead, it feels far more likely that companies understood a much simpler
message: that the Committee wanted to keep rates lower for longer. That may
indeed have been the message that the Committee wanted to send. The key
point to note of course is that this simpler message is not state contingent.

6.8   FG 2.0: The Forward Guidance Reboot

At the time that the Bank's forward guidance framework was launched the
MPC did not expect the unemployment rate to fall to the 7.0 % threshold
for several years. The Bank published a formal forecast for the unemployment

rate in the August Inflation Report which suggested that the unemployment rate would fall gradually at a pace determined by the relative recovery in aggregate demand versus labour force participation and productivity. The MPC concluded that it was as likely that the unemployment rate would reach the threshold before the three-year forecast horizon as after it. However, reality turned out somewhat differently.

Unemployment fell rapidly towards the threshold in the six months following the launch of the state-contingent forward guidance framework, in part reflecting the strength of demand, but in part reflecting the apparent weakness in labour productivity. The Committee was not ready to raise rates and wanted to continue to provide guidance to that effect so the imminent prospect of the unemployment rate breaching the threshold prompted a reboot of the communication strategy in February 2014. The Committee could have chosen to simply move the goalposts: lower the unemployment threshold and push back expectations of the first hike. Instead, the Committee revised the way in which it provided guidance to the market, in part driven by an assessment that the increase in employment and decline in unemployment was giving a misleading steer of the extent of spare capacity in the economy (Carney 2014):

> [T]here is greater slack in the labour market than we would have expected, given the strong jobs growth. In part that is because a substantial share of the fall in unemployment has been driven by a fall in the number of long-term unemployed. That means a lower level of unemployment is consistent with stable inflation. In addition, the share of people working part-time because they can't find a full-time job remains close to a record high, and almost half of the recent increase in employment has been driven by self-employment, which is now at a record level.

The new guidance was focused on the variable that ultimately matters—the output gap—rather than one less than perfect proxy of it (the unemployment rate), and the Committee's strategy both before and after the moment of lift-off. Unfortunately, the output gap cannot be measured, so the Bank disclosed that the Committee would be monitoring a number of indicators to estimate the gap in real-time. Of course, what matters is the gap between these indicators (unemployment, participation, average hours and so on) and their corresponding equilibrium values. Alongside the launch of this new approach, the BoE staff marginally lowered the in-house estimate of the equilibrium unemployment rate from 6½ % to an interval between 6 % and 6½ %, signalling a correspondingly modest reassessment of the extent of slack in the UK economy.

The second phase of guidance had a number of elements (Carney 2014):

- *Calibrating slack*: The Committee published a forecast of the current size of the output gap—of around 1–1½ % of GDP, concentrated in the labour market (and in particular, in unemployment and average hours worked) rather than within companies.
- *Guidance on slack reduction*: The Committee provided guidance that it intended to eliminate the output gap entirely within two to three years.
- *Guidance on the link between slack and lift-off*: The Committee signalled that it saw scope to further reduce the output gap before the first hike was warranted.
- *Gradual rate hikes*: The Committee communicated that when the moment of lift-off arrived the pace of rate hikes would be gradual in order to preserve a sustained and balanced recovery.
- *Limited rate hikes*: The Committee signalled that given the persistence of the headwinds buffeting the UK economy the scope for rate hikes was limited, so that even in the medium-term the level of interest rates would be materially lower than the pre-crisis average.

In some respects, the guidance reboot brought the Bank closer to home: the MPC was signalling that it was once again monitoring a broad set of indicators to estimate the output gap in real-time, rather than relying on a single proxy (the unemployment rate). However, the response to that broad set of indicators remained unorthodox: the Committee was comfortable leaving rates unchanged whilst slack diminished further.

The February reboot and the mantra of 'limited and gradual' would provide the basis of the Bank's communication strategy in the period that followed. To be fair, the Bank would make clear that this was an expectation not a promise—a signal that attentive agents might be expected to heed. Whether households, companies or even investors read the small print is unclear.

6.9 Lifting Off and Winding Down

Although the timing of the first hike and the pace of tightening post lift-off were the focal points of the discussion as the economy recovered there was a 375 billion elephant in the room when it came to the stance of monetary policy: the fate of the stock of purchased assets. We now turn to discuss guidance on this feature of the exit strategy.

6.9.1   Guidance on Asset Sales in Theory

Even though the BoE and the Fed were no longer actively expanding those stocks, they were both still reinvesting the proceeds as assets within those portfolios matured in order to keep the stock from shrinking. Both central banks subscribed to the stock theory of QE—that is, they believed that so long as they continued to reinvest to hold the stock constant, they would continue to preserve the stimulus that they had originally injected by holding down long rates (Bernanke 2013a):

> [I]f the stock theory of the portfolio is correct, which we believe it is, holding all of those securities off of the market and reinvesting and still keeping the, you know, rolling-over maturing securities, will still continue to put downward pressure on interest rates. And so, between our commitments to a low federal funds rate and the large portfolio, we will still be producing a very large amount of stimulus—in our view, enough to bring the economy smoothly towards full employment without incurring unnecessary costs or risks.

Before moving on, it is worth noting that there is an argument that the macroeconomic impact of asset purchases depends on the circumstances under which those purchases take place: a state-contingent stock theory of QE if you will. It is claimed that investors will be willing and able to arbitrage away 'distortions' (deviations from fair value) in a well-functioning market, so the kinks in the yield curve that shocks to net supply would otherwise create in segments where preferred habitat demand is significant are systematically ironed out. If this view of the world is correct—that QE only inflated asset prices because (too many) investors were capital constrained and hence markets were dysfunctional during the period that purchases were conducted—then it follows that unwinding those purchases would not have a significant impact on prices, so long as the asset sales were conducted in normal market conditions (Miles and Schanz 2014).

Central banks that have accumulated large portfolios of assets have two options when it comes to tightening policy: they can act on the price of central bank money by raising the policy rate; or they can act on the quantity of central bank money and shrink their asset portfolios. These two levers are imperfect substitutes for one another. They both tighten monetary conditions, and bear down on demand and ultimately inflation but through slightly different transmission mechanisms: in particular, the impact of raising the short-term policy rate on the slope of the yield curve will not mirror the impact of sales of long-dated assets. Nonetheless, there is a basic truism: the more you do of one, the less you have to do with the other. One potential appeal of asset sales featuring as part of the mix of a tightening strategy is therefore to reduce the burden of adjustment on rates hikes, and in the process increase the credibility of the guidance that rate hikes will be limited and gradual during the recovery ex ante, and to increase the likelihood that this expectation is validated ex post.

The chief argument against using asset sales to tighten policy is that it prolongs the period over which rates stay low and therefore there remains a significant risk that the conduct of policy could be constrained by the lower bound. If one believes that asset purchases are no longer an effective substitute for rate cuts at the lower bound then there is a compelling risk management argument for exclusively relying on rate hikes to tighten policy when the circumstances permit in order to get the policy rate as far away as possible from the lower bound as fast as possible. On that basis, not only should central banks not sell assets when they raise rates from the floor, but they should continue to reinvest all the proceeds from maturing assets until the policy rate is far above the lower bound. However, this argument is less compelling than it first appears. After all, if you believe that further asset purchases would not prove effective as a means of easing the monetary stance then you should not be overly concerned that selling assets would materially tighten the stance. For central bankers who believe that QE is ineffective, asset sales should be a near-irrelevance which would not lead them to delay raising rates.

An alternative explanation for the reluctance of central bankers to embrace asset sales as a key instrument in the tightening cycle is fear of policy reversals. It seems likely that any decision to sell assets would at least mirror the duration of the programme of purchases during QE, with a near-commitment to sell bonds over a 3-, 6- or even 12-month period (although most likely at a more modest monthly pace). At this point the central bank has hard-wired an incremental modest tightening into monetary conditions over the duration of that programme. If bad news arrives in the months that followed, the central bank would ideally want to respond via the marginal instrument (the policy rate) and the required adjustment in the stance might necessitate a rate cut, reversing the trend of limited and gradual hikes on the exit trajectory. To the extent that policymakers are reverse averse as discussed earlier (cuts rarely follow soon after hikes and vice versa) then that fear of potentially needing to cut rates over the lifetime of a programme of sales would explain a reluctance to put asset sales on autopilot in the first place.

In much of what follows, for the sake of convenience we will treat these two decisions—around reinvestments and outright sales—as if they were one in the same. Indeed, the November 2015 Inflation Report states that the Committee views sales and reinvestment decisions as equivalent from a monetary policy perspective (BoE 2015). However, in practical terms there will be an upper bound on what can be done to the stock of purchased assets through failure to reinvest alone (given the bonds in the portfolio) and there is greater scope to have an immediate impact on net supply in the long end of the curve, where there is likely a preferred habitat demand from institutional investors, via outright sales. There may also be an important signal (in terms of the degree of confidence around the improving outlook) associated with selling assets in the portfolio as opposed to just letting the portfolio go into run-off.

It is not too hard to understand why central bankers saw the need to provide guidance about the considerations which will influence the design of the tightening cycle—the mix of rate hikes and asset sales—as well as the overall pace of tightening, presuming they believed that asset purchases and sales matter. Policymakers dislike injecting volatility into markets through unanticipated changes in the stance of policy and unexpected changes in the policy mix in the tightening cycle fall into that category. Imagine for the sake of argument that a central bank initially tightened policy exclusively through rate hikes but in response to a revised assessment of the inflation outlook that central bank felt compelled to use asset sales in addition to rate hikes to tighten more aggressively (perhaps because to have done otherwise might have required an increase in rates that would be considered inconsistent with the limited and gradual mantra). It seems likely that this decision could trigger a discontinuous shift in market expectations about the net supply of assets for the following two reasons:

- *The initial news is significant*: It seems unlikely that the central bank would implement such a change in strategy to implement a marginal top-up—a modest programme of assets sales that would deliver a marginal impact on the outlook over and above the impact of rising interest rates. In other words, the implied change in the stock of purchased assets would likely be large
- *The implications for future sales magnify the initial impact*: In the light of this abrupt change in strategy, market participants would most likely attach a higher probability to asset sales playing a more central role in the exit strategy in the future.

Central banks were therefore tempted to provide guidance about the fate of their asset portfolios in order to avoid the sharp correction that might occur after the event given a shock to net supply in preferred habitat segments of the yield curve and perhaps a term premium being priced into yields before the event (compensation for the risk that the central bank might suddenly announce it was selling a lot of the asset that you currently own).

6.9.2   Guidance on Asset Sales in Practice

We have already seen how the Bank's first version of forward guidance involved a commitment to continue reinvesting the proceeds of maturing assets in the APF portfolio until the unemployment threshold is reached. That commitment to reinvest was extended to at least the moment of lift-off under the guidance reboot in February 2014. However, a lot was still left unsaid: the circumstances under which reinvestment would cease, and the circumstances under which outright sales would begin. Within three months, the Committee set out its thinking on the how it planned to manage the stock of purchased assets post lift-off in the May Inflation Report (BoE 2014a):

- *Asset sales are not the primary lever*: The Committee confirmed that Bank Rate will be the 'active marginal instrument' for achieving the objectives of monetary policy post lift-off, and not outright sales of assets in the APF portfolio.
- *Room to reverse*: The Committee explained that it planned on deferring asset sales until such time as Bank Rate had reached a level from which it could be cut materially, should it prove necessary to inject more stimulus. In other words, the Committee wanted to get as far as possible away from the lower bound as soon as possible in order that the conduct of monetary policy would be constrained in most future states of nature and selling assets would only delay that process by slowing the pace of rate hikes.
- *Modest shrinkage on autopilot*: The Committee noted that a modest reduction in the stock of assets could be achieved on autopilot—that is, by not reinvesting the proceeds as assets in the portfolio mature.
- *Orderly and gradual wind-down*: The Committee signalled that any asset sales would be conducted as part of an orderly programme rather than a short, sharp shock in order to minimise the disruption to the government bond market and prevent an unwarranted monetary tightening.

The guidance clearly speaks to the concerns within the Committee about the need for risk management near the lower bound that it would be counterproductive to unnecessarily prolong the period that Bank Rate remained low by tightening policy by some other means when the circumstances dictate a change in the stance. The key question was therefore what exactly constituted a level from which Bank Rate could be cut materially—or put another way, how far above the lower bound the Committee felt it would be safe to start tightening by other means. Back in late 2013, one external MPC member had argued that in his opinion (Weale 2013) we should wait until interest rates have returned to much more normal levels – so that we have plenty of room to support the economy, should the need arise, without carrying out any more quantitative easing.

Viewed in the context of the Committee's 2014 guidance that Bank Rate would rise gradually to a lower level than was seen in previous cycles, Weale's criteria of near-normality set a relatively high hurdle on gilt sales. However, the Committee would ultimately agree a somewhat lower hurdle. In the November 2015 Inflation Report, noting that whilst the definition of sufficient room to cut materially might vary through time (not least on account of the perceived risks to the outlook), the Committee judged that at that moment in time around 2 % was a reasonable estimate. Until that point had been reached, the Committee would continue to reinvest as assets in the portfolio matured. Interestingly, at the point in time at which the Committee made this announcement, the yield curve was so flat that the moment at which gilt sales could theoretically come into play did not occur until far beyond the forecast horizon.

6.10 Complete Forward Guidance

Central banks have chosen to provide forward guidance about the most likely path of official interest rates in the exit from (near) the lower bound. As the BoE has been keen to remind investors and the general public that guidance on the future path of interest rates is 'an expectation, not a promise': it is based on an underlying forecast of how the future will unfold being approximately right.

Central bankers are fond of reminding us that the probability that the most likely point forecast (the mode) is almost certain not to materialise, and even a forecast expressed in the form of a sizeable interval around that mode is far from certain to occur. If the world turns out very differently to the MPC's forecasts for output and inflation then the Committee's expectation that interest rate rises are likely to be limited and gradual may also go astray. However, the Committee has refused to spell out what the alternative path for interest rates might look like in these off-central case scenarios.

There is another way: complete the forward guidance and provide a much richer description of the outlook for the stance of policy. In this sub-section, we will describe how central banks could provide a comprehensive description of the outlook for policy (for more detail, see Barwell and Chadha (2013)). But in order to build the case for complete forward guidance, we need to start from first principles.

6.10.1 Setting Policy According to What Might Happen

As discussed earlier, monetary policy influences the economy with long and variable lags. Policymakers therefore have to think about the future state of the economy when they set policy today: otherwise they could end up amplifying the cycles in the economy. For this reason, policymakers have to devote significant resources into forecasting the future; indeed, the regime commonly known as inflation targeting should be really thought of as inflation *forecast* targeting (Svensson 1997).

Most economic forecasts are modal point forecasts—that is, they describe a particular scenario that the producer considers more likely than any other, often with a fair amount of precision (e.g., with the rate of growth described to the first decimal place). However, as noted above, the probability of any particular precise scenario materialising is surely very low given our limited understanding of how the economy behaves, so calibrating the stance of monetary policy purely on the basis of the policymaker's modal forecast of the economy is probably not prudent.

Imagine for the sake of argument that the economy is in balance (the output gap is zero and inflation is at target) and the single most likely outcome is for that situation to persist with the economy continuing to expand at around its trend rate, but the policymaker believes that the probability of a rapid expansion in activity over the policy horizon (with growth significantly above trend consistent with an inflationary output gap opening up) is considered far more likely than a contraction on the same scale. It would make sense in that scenario to incorporate the balance of risks into the calibration of the policy stance with a higher level of official interest rates than the one which would be considered appropriate according to the modal forecast in order to temper the rapid expansion in demand that *might* emerge.

The mean forecast—the probability-weighted average of all possible outcomes—is a more appropriate basis for setting policy. Indeed, the mean forecast is a sufficient statistic for setting policy under certain strong assumptions: the policymaker can ignore her uncertainty about the future and act if she is certain that the economy will evolve as described by the mean forecast (Tinbergen 1952; Theil 1958). Nevertheless, to calculate that mean and calibrate the stance accordingly the policymaker needs to estimate the entire distribution of possible outcomes, including tail risks: the unlikely but extreme scenarios. Of course, if the distribution is symmetric then the mode and the mean will coincide and in those fortuitous circumstances the so-called certainty equivalence result allows that policy can be safely set according to the modal forecast because the symmetric uncertainty around that mode (and mean) is not policy relevant.

Producing forecasts of the entire distribution in order to calculate the mean is clearly more complex than just producing a single modal forecast. Policymakers need to: interrogate simulations from a large suite of theoretical models which capture different features of the economy; draw upon the output of statistical models which can be used to generate forecasts of distributions; distil whatever useful information can be extracted from options markets about market participants' beliefs about the range of possible future outcomes; and then apply a good dose of judgement. That may be a difficult task but it is what the academic literature on monetary policy implies central bankers do: a robust approach to the conduct of policy requires policymakers to inspect distributions and not just fixate on point forecasts when setting interest rates.

If that distribution of possible outcomes is seen to shift—for example, if the economy is found to be evolving along a path that was previously thought to be an extreme and highly unlikely scenario—then the stance of policy will change accordingly. Indeed, if shifts in the distribution are largely driven by the shifts in the location of the modal forecast, with the shape of the distribution around that mode perceived to be broadly symmetric and stable through time, then we can think of a policy stance consistent with each forecast scenario in the distribution and the optimal policy stance at any point in time shifting between them according to the scenario that the policymaker selects as a modal forecast at any point in time.

6.10.2 Communicating What Could Happen to Interest Rates

Central banks habitually describe how uncertain the future is, illustrating the range of possible outcomes for the macroeconomy (Fracasso et al. 2003). For example, the BoE has long published fan charts which describe almost all of the distribution of possible outcomes for growth and inflation at each moment in time over the forecast horizon.

What the Bank does not do—like most, but not all, central banks—is publish fan charts for the stance of policy itself: illustrating the modal path of interest rates and the stock of purchased assets and the uncertainty around it. This is not because the task of calibrating that fan chart is overly complex. The BoE publishes fan charts for growth and inflation conditioned on a fixed policy setting—for example, an unchanged path for interest rates or the expectations of the future path of interest rate implicit in the current constellation of market prices (Britton et al. 1998; Elder et al. 2005). This is not a particularly natural thought experiment: along those scenarios in which growth and/or inflation prove surprisingly strong or weak there is no policy response, which is not what would happen in reality and therefore it is hard to use theory or evidence to calibrate the width of these conditional fan charts.

It is far more natural to think in terms of an internally consistent set of fan charts for growth, inflation and the stance of policy in which the stance of policy responds to surprising economic developments as they unfold. The mode of the policy fan chart would describe the single most likely path for official interest rates and asset purchases: the policymaker's estimate of how the optimal stance of policy should evolve. To repeat the message from before, the mode of that fan chart would encompass information from *the entire distribution for growth and inflation.*

These internally consistent fan charts could provide the centrepiece of a more sophisticated communication strategy. The BoE has already made great strides in its efforts to describe the Committee's forecast and the judgements that underpin it (McKeown and Paterson 2014). However, the Bank could usefully go further, articulating scenarios that flesh out the nature of the uncertainty around the central case view and discuss the policy response in those scenarios to teach the market about the policymaker's reaction function. For example, as the moment of lift-off from the lower bound approaches the mode and width of the fan chart for the policy rate at the end of the forecast horizon would have communicated useful information about the precise nature of the Committee's expectation that rate hikes would be limited and gradual.

It is sometimes claimed that it would not be possible for a committee of policymakers to agree on the fan chart for the stance of monetary policy. However, it is not clear why this might be so if those self-same committees can reach an agreement about the fan charts that they do publish (for growth and inflation) which are said to reflect the balance of views on that committee. Indeed, where significant differences of opinion do exist within a policy committee there is a convincing argument for individual members to publish their own set of probabilistic projections including for the policy rate. Once again, as the moment of lift-off approaches, central banks could usefully communicate the nature of the debate within a policy committee—between those who favour an early and gradual exit and those who favour a late but more rapid exit—by communicating the paths for the policy rate and inflation (including the extent and duration of any period of above-target inflation) that each group prefers, rather than simply describing differences of opinion over the current level of interest rates.

6.10.3 The Defence of the Status Quo and Revealed Preference

Policymakers typically cite three reasons for not publishing information about the future path of policy, even when it is nested with a statement about the uncertainty around any given modal forecast, which are all variants of the generic concern that this information will be misunderstood or misused:

- *Financial instability*: Households, companies and market participants might misunderstand the policymaker's modal forecast of the future path of policy as a promise or commitment and take imprudent decisions on that basis which could ultimately lead to instances of financial distress at the micro and perhaps macro level.
- *Reputational damage*: Inevitable revisions to the forecast for the future path of interest rates and the policymaker's assessment of the outlook changes could damage the central bank's reputation for competence, which could then impair its capacity to serve its core function.
- *Herding*: In a world where higher-order beliefs matter (where other agents actions influence my pay-off so I care what you believe about what everyone else believes and so on), a public signal about the future path of policy gets magnified through those beliefs because it provides an all too tempting focal point for herds.

These are valid concerns and led many pre-crisis central bankers to avoid talking about how interest rates might change in the future and instead focus on describing why interest rates were at the current level and outlining how the economy might evolve in the future and leave agents to figure out the rest. That is a perfectly defensible position (though in the view of the author, suboptimal). However, by revealed preference, many of the current generation of central bankers no longer find these arguments convincing because they have begun providing forward guidance on the future path of interest rates, including statements about the terminal point for rates over the current cycle relative to past cycles. It is harder to explain why the current crop of central bankers do not want to provide complete forward guidance—after all nesting the forward guidance that they are willing to provide about the future path of policy within a rigorous description of the uncertainty around that path should reduce the risk that the message is misunderstood or misused. Emphasising the uncertainty and illustrating the range of possible paths that could emerge should discourage agents from treating the modal optimal path as a promise.

6.10.4 The Benefit of Complete Forward Guidance

The virtue of complete forward guidance is that it provides the private sector with a much richer description of the state of the current policy debate and in particular the strategy beyond the current policy decision. Unnecessary uncertainty about the future path of policy is eliminated. The central bank places all relevant information in the public domain and it is then down to individuals—from market participants considering a financial investment to a household planning to take out a mortgage to buy property—to make a judgement about how the future will evolve because that will determine the actual path of rates.

If central bankers want to dispel the myth and mystique about the conduct of policy and teach the market about their reaction function—how the central bank will adjust interest rates in response to the events—then they could do a lot worse than publish information about how policy would respond in off-central case scenarios within the fan charts for growth and inflation that are published. These considerations are almost certainly more compelling when interest rates are at the floor and there is particular uncertainty about the exit strategy.

Complete forward guidance is sometimes misunderstood and criticised as policymakers giving 'the answer' to an informed set of market participants who have the resources to monitor central bank communication. That is not what is happening. As already discussed, if the central bank publishes an estimate of the optimal path for interest rates it is not promising to deliver that path come what may. Indeed, if anything publishing forecasts of the policy rate helps to level the playing field because otherwise this information is left implicit in the projections for growth and inflation that central banks do publish and central bank watchers employed by financial institutions may be better placed to distil that information than the average retail investor.

6.11 Endnote: Whatever It Takes...

We have concentrated here on the role of communication about the decisions that policymakers are likely to take in the future. However, there is another form of communication which was used to great effect in the post-crash era: namely communication about how policymakers would respond in a crisis. It is not too much of a stretch to say President Draghi's emphatic verbal intervention in July 2012 was the pivotal moment in the history of the Euro crisis Eurozone sovereign debt crisis and arguably the Euro itself. Draghi managed to use the bully pulpit of the Presidency of the ECB to arrest the self-fulfilling panic that threatened to tear the currency union apart and sow the seeds for the recovery that would ultimately follow, to the benefit of millions of households and companies across the Eurozone (Draghi 2012):

> But there is another message I want to tell you. Within our mandate, the ECB is ready to do whatever it takes to preserve the euro. And believe me, it will be enough.

Of course, in the months that followed, the Governing Council of the ECB made good on Draghi's promise with the creation of the Outright Monetary Transactions (OMT) programme. However, the 'whatever it takes' statement is arguably more important than the technical details of the conditional safety net which the ECB constructed underneath the Eurozone sovereign bond market and which may never be tested. Draghi's remarks revealed information to a sceptical market about the underlying objectives of the ECB and that mattered far more than the precise details of the OMT—so long as they conformed to Draghi's 'within our mandate' caveat—just as the precise calibration of the thresholds in state-contingent forward guidance is important only to the extent that it reveals information about the underlying reaction function of the central bank. Draghi testified to the depth of the ECB's commitment to preserving the single currency, and implicitly its willingness to keep innovating further policy responses beyond OMT if necessary to preserve the euro.

Elsewhere in this book, we have discussed the corrosive impact of increased uncertainty and in particular increased fear of very bad outcomes on the health of the economy. Clear and decisive communication by central banks which addresses those fears and convinces the audience that policymakers have the tools at their disposal and are ready, willing and able to use them can prove a potential antidote. Households and companies may then attach a lower probability to these tail risks than they might otherwise have done and thereby a collapse in consumption and investment that might otherwise have occurred is prevented.

References

Bank of Japan. (2016, September 21). New Framework for Strengthening Monetary Easing. *Press Release*.

Barwell, R. (2016a). *Those who do not learn the monetary lessons of history are doomed to repeat them*. BNP Paribas Investment Partners Central Bank Watch, Issue 1.

Barwell, R. (2016b). Nine votes, one view and the never-ending consensus on the MPC during the great stability. In J. Chadha, A. Crystal, J. Pearlman, P. Smith, & S. Wright (Eds.), *The UK economy in the long expansion and its aftermath*. Cambridge: Cambridge University Press.

Barwell, R., & Chadha, J. (2013). Complete forward guidance. In W. den Haan (Ed.), *Forward guidance*. VoxEU.

Bean, C. (2014, February 12). Comments in the February Inflation Report press conference.

Bernanke, B. (2013a, June 19). Chairman's press conference.

Bernanke, B. (2013b, November 19). Communication and monetary policy.

Blinder, A. (2002). *Through the looking glass*. CEPS Working Paper 86.

BoE. (1999, May). The monetary transmission mechanism. *Report prepared by Bank of England staff under the guidance of the Monetary Policy Committee and published in the Bank of England Quarterly Bulletin*, 161–170.

BoE. (2013a). August Inflation Report.

BoE. (2013b, August). Monetary policy trade-offs and forward guidance.

BoE. (2014). May Inflation Report.

BoE. (2015). November Inflation Report.

Brigden, A., & Thomas, J. (2003). *What does economic theory tell us about labour market tightness?* Bank of England Working Paper 185.

Britton, E., Fisher, P., & Whitley, J. (1998). The inflation report projections: Understanding the fan chart. *Bank of England Quarterly Bulletin, February*, 30–37.

Brunner, K. (1981). *The art of central banking*. Centre for Research in Government Policy and Business Working Paper GPB 81–6.

Bullard, J. (2013, May 23). *Monetary policy in a low policy rate environment*. Speech.

Campbell, J., Evans, C., Fisher, J., & Justiniano, A. (2012). *Macroeconomic effects of Federal Reserve Forward Guidance*. Federal Reserve Bank of Chicago Working Paper 2012–03

Carney, M. (2012, December 11). *Guidance*. Speech.

Carney, M. (2013a, August 7). Comments in the August Inflation Report press conference.

Carney, M. (2013b, December 17). Evidence to the Treasury Select Committee.

Carney, M. (2014, February 12). Introductory statement in the February Inflation Report press conference.

Carroll, C. (2003). Macroeconomic expectations of households and professional forecasters. *Quarterly Journal of Economics, 118*(1), 269–298.

Draghi, M. (2012, July 26). Remarks at the Global Investment Conference in London.

Draghi, M. (2016, June 2). Comments in the ECB press conference.

ECB. (2016, February 18). Account of the 20–21 January Governing Council meeting.

Eggertsson, G., & Woodford, M. (2003). The zero bound on interest rates and optimal monetary policy. *Brookings Papers on Economic Activity, 1*, 139–233.

Elder, R., Kapetanios, G., Taylor, T., & Yates, T. (2005). Assessing the MPC's fan charts. *Bank of England Quarterly Bulletin, Autumn*, 326–348.

English, W., López-Salido, J., & Tetlow, R. (2013, November 7–8). *The Federal Reserve's framework for monetary policy*. Paper presented at 14th Jacques Polak annual research conference.

Evans, C. (2012, March 16). *Monetary policy communications and forward guidance*. Speech.

Federal Reserve Board. (2003, August 12). Minutes of the Federal Open Market Committee.

Fisher, P. (2011, May 23). *The economic outlook*. Speech.

Fracasso, A., Genberg, H., & Wyplosz, C. (2003). *How do central banks write*. Geneva Reports on the World Economy Special Report.

Gerlach-Kristen, P. (2004). Is the MPC's voting record informative about future UK monetary policy? *Scandinavian Journal of Economics, 106*(2), 299–313.

Giles, C., & Daneshkhu, S. (2007, May 11). Transcript of interview with Mervyn King. *Financial Times*.

Goodfriend, M. (1986). Monetary mystique: Secrecy and central banking. *Journal of Monetary Economics, 17*(1), 63–92.

Greenspan, A. (1987, September 22). Quoted in Wall Street Journal.

He, Z. (2010). *Evaluating the effect of the Bank of Canada's conditional commitment policy*. Bank of Canada Discussion Paper 2010–11.

Jones, G. (2016, September 30). ECB's Visco says would be reasonable to see HICP above two percent for a while. *Reuters Business News*.

King, M. (2007, May 2). *The MPC ten years on*. Speech.

Krugman, P. (1998). It's baaack: Japan's slump and the return of the liquidity trap. *Brookings Paper on Economic Activity, 29*, 137–206.

Kydland, F., & Prescott, E. (1977). Rules rather than discretion: The inconsistency of optimal plans. *Journal of Political Economy, 85*(3), 473–491.

Leeper, E. (2003). *An Inflation Reports report*. NBER Working Paper 10089.

McKeown, J., & L Paterson. (2014). *Enhancing the transparency of the Bank of England's Inflation Report*. VoxEU.

Mester, L. (2014, November 20). *Forward guidance and communications in U.S. monetary policy*. Speech.

Miles, D., & Schanz, J. (2014). The relevance or otherwise of the central bank's balance sheet. *Journal of International Economics, 92*, S103–S116.

Osborne, G. (2013, March 20). Budget speech.

Svensson, L. (1997). Inflation forecast targeting: Implementing and monitoring inflation targets. *European Economic Review, 41*, 1111–1146.

Theil, H. (1958). *Economic forecasts and policy*. Amsterdam: North Holland.

Tinbergen, J. (1952). *On the theory of economic policy*. Amsterdam: North Holland.

Weale, M. (2013, November 15). *Monetary policy-making and forward guidance*. Speech.

Woodford, M. (2012). *Methods of policy accommodation at the interest-rate lower bound*. Proceedings – Economic Policy Symposium – Jackson Hole, Federal Reserve Bank of Kansas City, 185–288.

Yellen, J. (2013, April 16). Remarks in a panel discussion on 'Monetary policy: Many targets, many instruments.

7

Importing Disinflation

When the Bank set sail on its forward guidance adventure in summer 2013 it might reasonably have expected that by the time the unemployment rate had reached 5½ % the Committee would have begun raising interest rates. However, any plans for lift-off were derailed by a marked deteriorated in the inflation outlook during the two years that followed. Oil prices and the currency did what a major financial crisis could not: tip the UK economy into deflation.

7.1   No Central Bank Is an Island

No central bank is an island, especially those responsible for price stability in an open economy—that is, when product, factor and financial markets are highly interconnected with other economies. Shocks elsewhere in the world can have a material impact on the macroeconomic outlook, complicating the pursuit of price stability. The crisis in the euro area is a case in point, with the UK influenced through a number of channels: lower demand for UK exports via the trade channel; wealth effects on consumption and the costs of capital effects on investment thanks to a fall in the price of certain sterling risk assets but safe haven flows into other sterling assets; tighter credit conditions in retail banking markets thanks to contagion given fears about the exposure of UK banks; and finally, lower domestic demand on account of increased fear and uncertainty.

© The Editor(s) (if applicable) and The Author(s) 2016   **197**
R. Barwell, *Macroeconomic Policy after the Crash*,
DOI 10.1057/978-1-137-51592-6_7

In terms of the importance of these overseas influences, Chowla et al. (2014) argue that global shocks can account for around two-thirds of the weakness in activity in the UK since the start of the crisis (relative to the pre-crisis trend) although only a fifth of that effect flows through the traditional trade channel, with transmission through financial channels and beliefs (on fear and uncertainty) playing a more important role. Our focus here is on the impact of the rest of the world on UK inflation.

As discussed earlier, UK inflation remained stubbornly above the target for much of the post-crisis period, only falling back to 2 % in December 2013. However, the nature of the UK's inflation 'problem' would soon change. Inflation fell sharply in the second half of 2014, reaching zero in January 2015 and then flirted with deflation over the course of the year that followed, with a couple of months in which the level of consumer prices was estimated to have fallen on a year on year basis. That deflation was largely imported from abroad, being driven by weaker sterling import prices, thanks to an appreciating currency and lower energy prices given a collapse in the price of oil.

As we will go on to discuss, most central bankers are not overly concerned about a month or two of falling prices. However, a sustained period of deflation is a totally different story. We now take a step back and review these two sources of disinflation—oil prices and import prices. Rather than provide a blow by blow account of the developments in these disinflationary drivers and their impact on headline inflation we instead focus on the timeless aspects of this phenomenon—the transmission mechanism from oil prices and import prices to consumer prices—before turning to discuss the implications of an outbreak of deflation for inflation expectations and hence the conduct of policy.

7.2 Sterling: Back from the Dead

As discussed earlier, the value of the pound depreciated sharply at the start of the financial crisis. However, after a period of treading water from 2009 to the middle of 2013, sterling started to appreciate on a trade-weighted basis. In particular, the pound appreciated in value against the yen and the euro; the appreciation against the dollar was short-lived and unwound from mid-2014. Just as the sharp depreciation helps to explain the resilience of UK inflation during the immediate post-crash period so the more recent appreciation helps to explain the weakness of inflation that followed. We will now turn to discuss the timeless drivers of movements in the exchange rate and the potential consequences for inflation.

7.2.1   Currencies and International Trade

An increasing number of goods and services are traded across borders and that ought to constrain how far apart the price of those items can drift when measured in common currency. At some point companies would buy the good where it is (too) cheap and transport it to sell in markets where it is (too) expensive. This idea is formalised in the so-called law of one price (LOOP) which states that identical goods sold in the same market should trade for the same price.

In the extreme—if we are willing to assume that all goods and services are traded in one global market, that there are no transportation costs and that consumption (tastes) and technology (production functions) are identical too across countries—then LOOP suggests that consumer prices measured in common currency would be identical too. This means that the ratio of the consumer price levels in two countries converted into common currency—the real exchange rate—is equal to one, or equivalently the nominal exchange rate is pinned down by the ratio of the level of consumer prices measured in local currency. It follows that a change in consumer prices in one country will trigger an equal (and offsetting) move in the nominal exchange rate—a condition referred to as absolute purchasing power parity (PPP).

In reality, none of these assumptions hold: there are non-trivial costs of transporting some goods; not all goods are traded and even those which are have countless varieties; preferences and technology differ across countries. A slightly weaker (*relative*) variant of PPP requires that consumer prices do not drift too far apart when measured in common currency—that is, for real exchange rates (the ratio of consumer prices measured in common currency) to be stable even if they are not equal to one (as per *absolute* PPP). That in turn implies that the nominal exchange rate would move to offset changes in the rate of consumer price inflation in any given pair of countries—a condition referred to as relative PPP.

Although our default assumption is that in a globalised economy many goods markets are now highly integrated across countries, we can still find evidence of significant departures from the LOOP at the micro level. Haskel and Wolf (2001) compare 100 identical goods sold in a particular chain store in a number of countries and find evidence of significant variation in prices when measured in common currency—often of the order of 20–50 %. Engel and Rogers (1996) famously demonstrated that prices of similar goods differ even between cities within the same country with dispersion increasing with their physical separation. Parsley and Wei (2001) argue that the placing an international border between those cities magnifies the volatility in relative prices—in the case of trade between the USA and Japan, it is the equivalent of adding as much as 43,000 trillion miles of separation. Parsley and Wei account for part of the increased dispersion in terms of transportation costs and the volatility of exchange rates and argue that the residual dispersion has declined through time. However, Rogoff et al. (2001) remind us that the volatility and persistence of deviations from the LOOP have proved remarkably persistent for all the talk of globalisation using data based on seven centuries of Dutch and British agricultural commodity prices. Goods markets remain more segmented than one would like to believe.

If we allow for the fact that production possibilities differ across countries then we might expect to see countries specialise in the production and export of certain goods and services. The global demand for those particular commodities will then shape the *volume* of goods and services that a country exports. On the other side of the market, the basket of goods and services that a country imports will reflect differences between consumers' tastes for particular varieties of goods and services and producers' comparative advantage at supplying those items and the strength of domestic demand. The terms of trade, which describes the relative price of the goods and services that a country exports and imports when both are measured in common currency, should then help explain the *value* of exports and imports *for any given level of domestic and global demand*. The terms of trade will respond to movements in the nominal exchange rate—especially in the short run when the sticky prices of exports and imports may not have had time to adjust—but they will also respond to structural shocks. For example, the terms of trade will likely rise in response to a shift in global demand towards the particular goods that a country specialises in the production and export of, or an increase in productivity overseas (lowering costs and therefore prices) in the sectors which produce the goods that a country imports (Dury et al. 2003).

The value of the goods and services that a country imports and exports will not necessarily balance. Indeed, large discrepancies between the value of imports and exports may persist for an extended period but as we will go on to discuss the exchange rate will typically adjust to close that gap. For example, where the demand for exports far outstrips consumption of imports the exchange rate will come under pressure to appreciate given the imbalance in the demand for and supply of the currency, and as exports become more expensive and imports become more cheap, overseas and domestic consumers should substitute away and towards them respectively. If the so-called Marshall Lerner conditions hold—that is, if demand at home and abroad is sufficiently responsive to news on relative prices—then changes in the exchange rate should eventually move the trade balance in the opposite direction helping to shrink any external imbalance, although whether that result holds in practice is a matter of debate (Rose 1991).

7.2.2   Currencies and Financial Investments

Although investors typically have a bias towards investing at home (French and Poterba 1991), large sums of money are invested overseas and that requires investors to transact in currency markets, creating a distinct demand for currencies over and above facilitating the trade in goods and services. When market participants invest money abroad they are exposed to movements in the value of the currency. If you invest in dollar-denominated assets like US Treasury bonds and the dollar depreciates significantly against the pound between the point at which you made the investment and the moment when the bonds mature and you ultimately want to repatriate the proceeds you could end up losing money on the investment even though the investment delivered a positive return in dollars. Financial markets offer investors a way to insulate returns from these exchange rate moves by locking in today the rate at which you can exchange one currency for another at a known date in the future. For any given bilateral exchange rate, the rate at which you can guarantee a transaction at any fixed point in the future (relative to the current rate) should exactly reflect the rates of return that can be earned in the two currencies over that horizon. Otherwise, investors can lock in 'excess returns' by investing in one currency or the other safe in the knowledge that they can repatriate those funds at a guaranteed rate—an observation known as covered interest parity (CIP).

Imagine instead that our investor is happy to bear the exchange rate risk. She will look to invest in currencies where the combination of local currency returns and anticipated future movements in the value of the currency are likely to deliver the highest returns. Imagine for the sake of argument that you believe that currencies will be stable through time: you might borrow money in currencies where interest rates are low and invest them in currencies where rates are high—or what is referred to as a carry trade. However, as a rule the demand for high yielding currencies relative to low yielding currencies should lead to an adjustment in exchange rates until expected returns are equalised across countries when measured in common currency. Otherwise investors can expect to make 'excess returns' by investing in a particular country given the anticipated path of the exchange rate—an observation known as uncovered interest parity (UIP).

The UIP condition suggests that interest rate differentials should explain future movements in exchange rates: if local currency returns are higher in the USA than the UK then it ought to be the case that the dollar is expected to depreciate against the pound in order to equalise returns in common currency. Moreover, the CIP condition suggests that the forward exchange rate that investors can lock in today should be a good forecast of exactly where the spot exchange rate is heading. However, that is not what we observe in practice: not only are forward rates not good predictors of the future path of the exchange rate, it turns out that when local currency returns are unusually high the currency often appreciates (as opposed to the depreciation implied by UIP)—the so-called 'forward discount' or 'forward bias' puzzle (Engel 1996; Cochrane 1999).

One standard explanation for the puzzle is the role of time-varying risk premia driving investment decisions and hence the exchange rate, over and above interest differentials. Market participants may demand compensation for the risks involved in investing uncovered in particular currency zones: that is the covariance of the returns from investments in that zone with returns on the rest of the portfolio when measured in common currency (strictly speaking, from the perspective of the representative agent, what matters is whether the asset delivers high or low returns when the marginal utility of consumption is high or low—that is, when you need good returns most or least). For example, market participants may tolerate a low average return from investments in a particular currency if those assets act as a hedge—that is, if they offer returns which tend to perform well when measured in common currency when the rest of their portfolio performs badly because the particular currency tends to appreciate in those circumstances. If perceptions of how currencies will behave in the future change then that would be reflected in a corresponding adjustment in the exchange rate to deliver the required 'excess return' or foreign exchange risk premium.

The cleanest way to incorporate these concerns about returns into our framework for explaining exchange rate moves via yield differentials is to focus on risk-free returns in each jurisdiction measured in local currency and therefore let the foreign exchange risk premium soak up all the cross-country variation in the risk attached to those investments in different jurisdictions (rather than say including yield differentials which also include risk premia). With that in mind, we can decompose unexpected movement in the exchange rate, relative to the rate that market participants had been able to lock-in in advance in terms of:

- news on risk-free yields out to some specific maturity;
- news on the currency risk premium; and
- news on the expected value of the currency at that terminal point.

If we want to understand what might drive changes in the expected value of the currency in the future—the long-run equilibrium—then we need to integrate the demand for currency for investment purposes alongside the demand for currency to facilitate international trade.

7.2.3 The Balance of Payments and FEERs of Currency Realignment

The balance of payments records the flow of transactions between households, companies and public sector institutions within one country and their counterparts in the rest of the world including those which are the counterpart to trade in goods across borders. At a headline level those payments must balance: money in must equal money out, but the same is not true for the constituent parts of the balance of payments and in particular the fact that money in equals money out does not tell us what we need to know: the level of the nominal exchange rate and accumulation of assets and liabilities that clears foreign exchange markets to deliver that identity.

Starting with the most familiar element of the balance of payments, the current account records the following transactions:

- *The trade balance*: the difference between the value of exports and imports of goods and services.
- *Primary income*: the net flow of: compensation of employees; profits, interest and dividend payments on the respective stocks of external assets and liabilities; and rent and taxes and subsidies on production and on the import of goods.
- *Secondary income*: the net flow of 'something for nothing' income flows across borders (such as the remittances which migrants send back home) for which no service or asset changes hands in return.

The other key account of the balance of payments records the other key constituent of cross-border transactions described above: financial investments. The financial account records the flow accumulation of external assets and liabilities that reflect those investment decisions, with the stock position recorded on the international investment position. Finally, there is the capital account which captures capital transfers and the acquisition or disposal of non-produced, non-financial assets (such as a copyright).

There is a clear link between the current and financial accounts of the balance of payments. If the current account as a whole is in deficit then a country is effectively borrowing to fund current spending on imports: overseas investors are acquiring domestic liabilities. Likewise if the current account is in surplus then a country is lending money to others to fund their consumption of its exports. The current account is therefore a proxy of the difference between national savings and investment. Countries may lend for as long as domestic agents are willing to delay consumption and lend money to other countries (acquire overseas assets). In contrast, deficit countries are not the masters of their own destiny.

Common sense suggests that there is limit on the stock of external debt that can be accumulated: at some point the terms on which international creditors are willing to provide funding will tighten, potentially quite sharply. That limit—and the corresponding constraint on the capacity of a country to run current account deficits—is likely to reflect the prospects for future growth in national income (to service that debt) and the health of the international investment position. At some point overseas investors may become uncomfortable with the accumulation of overseas liabilities and the sudden stop in financing may result in a sharp slowdown in domestic demand and ultimately a depreciation in the real exchange rate that delivers internal and external balance: that is, the level of the real exchange rate consistent with no output gap and a current account position that is sustainable given financial flows. That level of the real exchange rate is usually referred to as the FEER: the fundamental equilibrium exchange rate (Clark and MacDonald 1998).

7.2.4   Currency Wars

At least directionally the news on interest rate differentials helps to explain the resurrection of sterling since mid-2013. On the one hand, the BoJ and the ECB were required to significantly ease the stance of monetary policy in response to a deteriorating outlook, reducing the return on yen- and euro-denominated assets. On the other hand, the UK data showed a marked improvement in the economic outlook consistent with the point of lift-off from the lower bound drawing close(r). The behaviour of 'cable'—the sterling dollar bilateral exchange rate (named after the transatlantic cable that was used to transmit currency prices between London and New York in the nineteenth century)—over this period was more nuanced. Both economies were on the mend so the interest rate differential driven movements in the bilateral exchange rate will have reflected perceptions of the relative pace of improvement in the UK and US economies and the market's understanding of the reaction functions of the two central banks which together determine rate expectations.

In truth, sterling's movements during this period were just one illustration of a wider phenomenon of exchange rate volatility. As time passed and the much anticipated robust recovery in demand failed to materialise almost everywhere the behaviour of exchange rates became a much more sensitive topic of conversation. There was a perception that it would be difficult for monetary policy to stimulate domestic demand no matter how low central banks could drive real interest rates given the highly indebted state of household and corporate balance sheets—that at least to some extent, economies were trapped in a 'balance sheet recession' (Koo 2003). If domestic households and companies could not be enticed to spend money on domestic output then it followed that the only way that central banks could be confident of supporting aggregate demand was via the one unimpaired transmission channel: to cheapen the exchange rate and encourage households and companies in the rest of the world to substitute towards domestic output (and to encourage domestic agents to substitute away from imports). Of course, from the perspective of the rest of the world, monetary stimulus to cheapen the currency looks like an attempt to steal a large share of world trade at someone else's expense. Indeed, very early on the Brazilian finance minister Guido Mantega declared (Wheatley and Garnham 2010).

> We're in the midst of an international currency war, a general weakening of currency. This threatens us because it takes away our competitiveness.

The critical question is what differentiates an act of monetary aggression in a currency war from conventional monetary easing that just so happens to cheapen the currency. The appropriate yardstick here is the remit for monetary policy:

- *peace*: If the exchange rate depreciates as a consequence of a central bank pursuing its mandate, that should be no cause for concern.
- *war*: If the central bank elevates the exchange rate to the status of a distinct intermediate target, then that implies a clear departure from the conventional conduct of policy.
- *phoney war*: There is a middle ground in which the central bank does not introduce a formal exchange rate target but increasingly references the exchange rate in its communication strategy, talking about the need for a weaker currency.

To take a topical example, the monetary arrow of Abenomics almost certainly contributed to the significant depreciation of the yen (Hausman and Wieland 2014). However, it does not seem reasonable to charge the Japanese with engaging in currency wars since their objective was simply to achieve the same rate of inflation as other central banks take for granted. Indeed, a significant depreciation of the yen had long been understood as the signature of a successful escape from deflation (Svensson 2001).

Whether it was an innocent victim caught in the cross-fire of the currency wars or not, the MPC had to deal with significant appreciation of the pound and its implications for inflation. The already elevated level of sterling and the risk of a further interest rate differential induced appreciation was clearly one factor which helped explain how long the MPC was willing to remain at the lower bound (Carney 2015).

7.2.5 The Pass-Through Puzzle

In the years leading up to the crisis, the consensus among academic economists was that pass-through from movements in the nominal exchange rate into consumer prices had declined. Marazzi and Sheets (2007) argue that the extent of pass-through into core US import prices had halved in recent decades and Campa and Goldberg (2006b) provide evidence of a corresponding decline in pass-through across a range of OECD countries. That consensus helps explain why the MPC expected inflation to fall in the immediate aftermath of the crash, despite the sharp depreciation in the value of sterling.

A key ingredient in any discussion of pass-through is pricing power. If companies have the ability to deviate from LOOP and set different prices in different countries then they will do so when it is in their interests to do so. Likewise, pricing power along the supply chain has the capacity to further elongate pass-through from import prices into consumer prices. In both cases, profit margins adjust to prevent prices having to adjust (Goldberg and Knetter 1997). From a practical perspective, companies get to choose ex ante whether pass-through will be high given their choice of the currency in which they invoice customers—for example, if they set prices in advance and invoice in their own currency (a.k.a. producer currency pricing) then they are hardwiring rapid exchange rate pass-through into import prices (Engel 2006).

The standard explanation for incomplete pass-through is based on the idea that markets are segmented. Companies with pricing power will vary prices across segments (a.k.a. 'pricing to market') whenever structural or strategic considerations favour doing so. A key consideration for companies selling output across borders (segments) turns out to be the response of their local competitors—domestic companies producing a close substitute—which will influence the sensitivity of demand for their output to a change in price, which in turn pins down the optimal mark-up over costs (Dornbusch 1987).

Within the supply chain, developments in the distribution sector play a key role in damping pass-through into consumer prices since costs in this sector account for such a large share of the final prices (Campa and Goldberg 2006a; Burstein et al. 2003). For example, Nakamura and Zeron (2010) illustrate for the case of coffee that delayed pass-through occurs in the wholesale sector (a subset of distribution), with infrequent adjustments in prices that nonetheless pick up when commodity prices are more volatile.

Expectations of the persistence of any exchange rate move could matter for pass-through. In an environment in which customers are sticky and do not easily change brand (Klemperer 1995), current market share is a precious commodity since it is a key driver of future profitability, and that consideration will shape how companies respond to exchange rate movements. An exchange rate move that is not expected to persist is therefore likely to lead to an offsetting transitory move in margins (profits) with relatively modest pass-through into prices (Froot and Klemperer 1989). To the extent that a transition to a more stable nominal anchor might have led companies to treat exchange rate moves as more likely to be transitory, this argument is consistent with lower pass-through: central banks are expected to respond to inflationary pressures in the pipeline and that implies a more muted response by private sector agents (Gagnon and Ihrig 2004).

Size and speed matter too. Large and sudden moves in the exchange rate are more likely to trigger otherwise inattentive companies into revising their prices—particularly in the presence of significant costs of adjusting prices (Forbes 2014). From a theoretical perspective, large moves may be more likely to elicit more rapid pass-through, since large moves provide the necessary inducement to encourage companies to make the irreversible investment to export to a particular destination (pay the fixed cost of entry into a market) which then delivers higher pass-through as those companies establish a 'beach-head' (Baldwin 1988).

The state of credit markets at the moment of the exchange rate move may also influence the pace of pass-through by limiting the willingness or capacity of companies to absorb costs in margins. Strasser (2012) finds that financially constrained firms pass through exchange rate changes into prices at almost twice the pace of their unconstrained peers, and this channel may have proved particularly powerful in the wake of the 2008 crash: tight credit conditions may have prompted rapid pass-through.

One somewhat surprising feature of the data is that pass-through does not appear to be systematically higher in sectors where imports account for a higher share of costs: Forbes (2015) reports that if anything sensitivity to sterling is negatively correlated with import intensity. However, this might reflect the fact that companies in those sectors have a much stronger incentive to hedge their exchange rate exposure and therefore the pricing implications of actual movements in the exchange rate are stretched out over a longer time horizon. Indeed, the intelligence that the BoE receives from companies through its network of regional agents points to the expiry of currency hedges as a trigger for increased pass-through of the appreciation of sterling into materials costs (BoE 2014).

In passing, there are concerns that the sluggish pass-through we observe in the data may be a mirage. As with a number of other puzzles in macroeconomics, sluggish pass-through may be a spurious artefact of aggregation—that is, the more aggregated the data used to investigate this question, the more sluggish pass-through appears (Chen and Juvenal 2014). Moreover, until relatively recently, much of the UK data on trade prices were estimated based on an equivalent domestic price adjusted for the change in the exchange rate (MacCoille et al. 2009). That approach likely exaggerated the pace of pass-through into import prices and therefore helps to explain why pass-through into import prices decreased significantly between 1995 and 2004 (Mumtaz et al. 2006).

7.3   Trough Oil

Oil prices were on a rollercoaster ride in the period that spans the financial crisis and the immediate aftermath: in January 2007, the price of Brent crude was around $50 a barrel; by summer 2008, the price was closing in on $150 a barrel; by the end of 2008, prices were back down to around $40 a barrel; by the end of 2009, prices had recovered to around $80 a barrel, and by early 2011, prices had reached $120 a barrel. There then followed a three-year period of relative tranquillity until mid-2014 when the price of crude oil collapsed, with a peak to trough fall in excess of 50 %, and then a further fall to new lows in early 2016.

7.3.1 Why Did Oil Prices Fall

In the end, most puzzles in economics boil down to supply and demand and the explanation for the collapse in oil prices is no different.

On the demand side of the equation, oil is an input in the production process so the demand for oil like other inputs is derived—in the sense that it depends on the level of final demand for the goods and services whose production relies on energy as a direct and indirect input. For given final demand that derived demand will shift in response to a shift in preferences between goods which vary according to the amount of energy that is consumed in the production process, or changes in technology which shift the amount of energy that is consumed in the production of a given good. Globalisation and the relocation of the global production of goods towards the emerging economies where the energy intensity of production is relatively high could therefore explain an increase in the derived demand for oil in the decade before the crisis. In terms of our puzzle, it seems likely that a reassessment of the global growth outlook played some role in the fall in oil prices from mid-14 onwards, and in particular downwards revisions to growth in regions where the oil intensity of demand is high. In passing, it also seems likely that an appreciation of the dollar (as occurred in the second half of 2014) will mechanically inflate the dollar price of oil (oil is priced in dollars) in countries with depreciating currencies, putting downward pressure on dollar prices (De Schryder and Peersman (2015)).

Positive news on supply also clearly played a role in driving prices lower: after all, oil prices fell further than metals prices over this period, despite the fact that metals prices are typically more attuned to the state of global demand (Azreki and Blanchard 2014). In fact, there are a number of candidate explanations for a supply-driven decline in oil prices (World Bank 2015):

- *Positive news on supply at a given market price*: The global supply of oil—or more precisely the known reserves of oil that can be extracted at low cost—increased significantly with the arrival of shale oil in the USA.
- *Positive news on man-made disruptions to supply*: Production proved more resilient to internal tensions and conflict in several oil-exporting countries in the Middle East (Libya and Iraq), and there was the prospect of the lifting of sanctions on Iran releasing more oil to the market, which would further reduce the man-made restrictions on the supply of oil to the market.
- *Change in OPEC strategy*: In the past, OPEC (and in particular Saudi Arabia) has scaled back production in the face of falling demand in order to stabilise prices, but in November 2014, no reduction in quotas was agreed. On the contrary, there was a perception that some nations were happy to increase production to drive prices lower in order to drive high cost producers elsewhere in the world out of business.

Definitively identifying the respective roles of demand and supply in driving oil prices lower is not straightforward. From a theoretical perspective, economists at the Federal Reserve Bank of New York (Groen et al. 2013; Groen and Russo 2015) use information from financial markets to decompose movements in the oil price, arguing that a negative supply shock (which drives prices higher) tends to be associated with a decline in the currencies and stock markets of oil importers alongside an underperformance of cyclical stocks and outperformance of defensive stocks relative to the overall equity market, whereas a positive demand shock (which also drives prices higher) tends to have the opposite effect. Given the observed behaviour of asset prices over the period that oil prices fell, they conclude that increased supply was the driving factor, with some weakness in demand. Fortunately this result accords with what we can observe—the obvious positive news on supply.

7.3.2 Will Oil Prices Recover?

The collapse in oil prices was a fact of life that policymakers had to deal with. One key question for forward-looking policymakers was where oil prices would go in the future. Clearly positive news on demand—both at the global level and in particular in countries where activity is oil intensive—would put upward pressure on prices. However, given that the news on supply appears to have been a key factor in driving prices lower we now turn to discuss the potential for developments on the supply side to drive a future rally.

7.3.2.1   What Does Mr. Market Say?

Most forecasters—including central banks—base their forecasts for oil prices on the oil futures curve (Nixon and Smith 2012). The futures curve sketches out the set of prices at which agents can enter into contracts today to buy (or sell) oil at a specific point in the future. There is a basic arbitrage relationship linking the price of oil today (the spot price) and this set of futures prices. An agent who wants to own oil in the future can enter into the relevant futures contract today and pay later, or she can pay the spot price today, pay the costs of storing oil between today and that point in the future and forgo the interest that could be earned on that money over that period. It follows that the spot price should be lower than futures price at any given horizon to compensate for the costs of storage and foregone interest, in which case the oil futures curve would slope up—a configuration referred to as the curve being in contango.

However, these two strategies are not identical: if you buy oil forward, you get access to oil in the future; but if you buy oil today (and store it), you have guaranteed access to oil (for a known price) at any point between now and the given date of the futures contract, and that option has some innate value, referred to as the convenience yield. When there are concerns about the supply of oil to the market—for example, in moments of geo-political tension in oil-exporting countries—the convenience yield might be large enough to dominate the costs of storage and foregone interest so that the futures curve will slope down: a configuration referred to as backwardation, with investors paying a premium in the spot market to guarantee access.

What should hopefully be clear is that the futures curve does not describe the market's forecast of oil prices. The slope of the futures curve reflects the interest rate, the cost of storing oil and the convenience yield. Instead, the market's forecast about the future is reflected in the current spot price: if agents believe oil prices will rise in the future then the price will rise today. At best, the futures curve might tell us something about the volatility of oil prices. When the curve slopes down the convenience yield is high which suggests that the market is worried about supply: if that situation resolves itself agents would stop paying a premium in the spot market (i.e., the price would drop); however, if demand rises in an environment of limited supply prices could rise sharply.

7.3.2.2 The Crude Oil Cobweb

Most economists are introduced to the dynamic adjustment of markets to shocks via a stylised version of the Cobweb model (Ezekiel 1938). Imagine a market in which there are long 'time to build' lags between the decision to produce and the output arriving at the marketplace (think about the lag between a farmer planting seeds, harvesting the crop and delivering it to market) and in which naïve producers base their decisions on how much to produce today based on the level of prices today. In this market a transitory increase in demand will lead to an increase in the price because supply is fixed in the short run and that sets in train an adjustment in future supply. By the time that additional output arrives in the market demand may have normalised and the excess supply depresses prices below the initial equilibrium setting in train a sharp contraction in supply which with a lag will cause a subsequent bounce in the price. Price and quantities cycle around the 'true' equilibrium.

We should not pretend that supply dynamics are so simplistic in the oil market, but there are reasons to suspect that the supply of oil to the market will gradually adjust to the drop in prices helping to stop the rot (McCafferty 2015). There is a finite supply of oil in the ground that can be extracted. However, the costs of extracting that oil vary dramatically according to the location and the current state of technology. At any given market price, there are reserves which are not commercially viable to extract but over time as the reserves that are easy to extract are exhausted prices will rise to the point where it makes sense to open these fields.

When oil prices fall and are not expected to bounce back investment in new fields will be scaled back (Kochhar et al. 2005). Moreover, some of the existing fields may no longer break-even: the costs of extraction will exceed the new lower spot price. The result is a gradual stagnation in supply: for example, IMF estimates suggest that a 1 % reduction in investment is associated with a 0.4 % reduction in production relative to its trend after five years (IMF 2015). However, this process takes time as higher prices prompt increased investment in exploration and extraction—although the dynamic adjustment in the shale sector may be far more rapid than the rule of thumb based on past oil cycles.

7.3.2.3   Asset Allocation Above and Below Ground

The agent that owns an oil field faces a perennial portfolio allocation decision: should she leave the oil where it is (below ground) and extract it later at which point she will receive the future spot price net of extraction costs, or should she extract it today and invest the proceeds (the current spot less extraction costs) in financial markets. That insight suggests a simple rule of thumb about the likely path of oil prices: it should be pinned down by the real interest rate (Hotelling 1931). If real interest rates fall then it makes sense to invest wealth below ground and earn the return implied by the expected appreciation in oil prices. However, the reduction in extraction creates a shortage of supply in the spot market, causing the price to rise until the expected appreciation of oil prices falls back in line with the (lower) real interest rates.

Technically speaking, this argument should be augmented to allow for uncertainty about the future path of oil prices net of extraction costs (or for that matter uncertainty of access given potential geo-political risks) and the potential covariance of returns on oil extracted in the future with returns on other assets and the consumption of the representative investor. In other words, we should allow for a risk premium in the price. For example, if oil is a good consumption hedge in the sense that oil prices are high in states of nature when the return on most assets or consumption are low, then investors may be willing to leave wealth below ground—which means lower supply and higher prices today and a negative risk premium bridging the gap between the risk-free rate and the expected rate of appreciation of oil prices.

Finally, unlike the hypothetical agriculture market of the cobweb model in which the level of supply reflects the decisions taken by countless atomistic producers, there is scope for some element of coordination among the producers to reduce supply. OPEC provides a mechanism through which some of the key producers could discuss coordinated changes in production, and in particular cuts in production in response to falling oil prices since it seems reasonable to assume that OPEC members have an asymmetric loss function: very low prices are worse for social welfare in the countries concerned than very high prices. However, it is unclear how effective OPEC production quotas are in influencing supply and prices, since non-OPEC producers could offset any change in the quote and OPEC members may not abide by the quotas.

7.3.3 The Disinflationary Consequences of Lower Oil Prices

Lower oil prices mean lower consumer prices, with a lag. Policymakers typically distinguish between three distinct channels through which the shocks which lower oil prices influence inflation: the first round effects as the initial shock to wholesale energy prices feeds through the supply chain into consumer prices; the second round effects through which lower consumer prices influence the supply side; and finally the transmission channels through demand.

7.3.3.1 First Round Effects

Crude oil is not in the consumption basket. However, crude oil is used to produce goods and services that do feature in the consumption basket so changes in the price of crude oil can directly influence consumer prices. Using the input–output (I-O) tables, we can estimate the share of the total costs of production of each item in the consumption basket that is accounted for by direct and indirect consumption of energy along the supply chain. If we are willing to assume that there are no fixed costs of production and that the energy intensities of imported and domestically produced goods are identical, then we can calculate the impact of a given change in oil prices on the level of consumer prices by scaling that percentage increase in oil prices by the energy intensity of the CPI basket (for more details, see ECB (2010)).

These assumptions are heroic: for example, it is likely that some of the consumption of energy is a fixed cost (the costs of heating and lighting an office may be largely independent of the output of the employees) and it seems likely that imports of goods may be more energy intensive than domestically produced substitutes, given differences in the production process and environmental standards across countries. However, these I-O estimates should give an approximate estimate of the levels impact of an oil price shock on consumer prices. Of course, the impact on inflation will depend on the speed of pass-through, which will vary from item to item for much the same reasons that exchange rate pass-through varies: according to the length of the supply chain between the consumption of oil and final output; the degree of pricing power along the supply chain; the share of energy in total costs; the state of credit conditions which allow producers to absorb costs in margins; and the degree to which producers can hedge their exposure to energy prices.

The basic principle is that we can map both the direct and indirect consumption of energy—which we define in terms of the Office for National Statistics (ONS) product 'extraction of oil and gas'—through the supply chain. Given information on the composition of final consumption by item and by product we can estimate the energy intensity of the CPI basket as the total amount of energy that is used up in delivering a unit of consumption. We can then estimate the impact of a given percentage increase in energy prices on CPI inflation by multiplying that percentage increase by the energy intensity of the CPI basket. Finally, one key difference worth noting between pass-through from 'shocks' to oil prices and 'shocks' to the exchange rate is that direct and indirect (i.e., via the supply chain) consumption of energy is highly skewed towards a small number of goods (BoE 2005).

7.3.3.2   Second Round Effects

Second round effects arise where the initial shock to consumer prices triggers an endogenous supply response which then has a more broad-based impact on prices via the output gap. We shall focus here on three distinct channels— the scale effect on factor demand; 'putty clay' effects on the capital stock; and real wage resistance—and leave the fourth (the propagation via inflation expectations) to later.

A sensible starting point is with the production function. Companies combine energy with other factors of production like labour and capital to produce output. Generically speaking, we should expect to find two competing effects which will determine how the demand for those other factors depends on a change in the price of energy: a substitution effect: if one input becomes cheaper demand for other inputs will fall as companies increase their relative consumption of the cheaper input; and a scale effect: if one input becomes cheaper then final output is somewhat cheaper to produce and when output prices fall the increase in final demand raises the derived demand for all inputs. In this particular case, it seems implausible that companies can substitute away from labour and capital towards energy to any great extent so the scale effect dominates, boosting the demand for labour.

There is a school of thought that when oil prices rise there could be a material impact on the supply side via reduced utilisation of capital. Imagine that companies can choose between different types of capital good which vary according to their energy intensity, but once installed that flexibility vanishes and there is then very little scope to adjust the mix of inputs that the companies use in production (hence 'putty clay'). Rising energy prices render the most energy-intensive varieties of capital goods virtually obsolete, and therefore lower the average utilisation of the capital stock and labour productivity in the process (Baily 1981; Atkeson and Kehoe 1995). By the same token, if there were under-utilised energy-intensive capital goods in the workplace that had been moth-balled during the era of triple digit oil prices then when oil prices fell the effective capital stock might have increased, boosting effective supply.

The final supply channel is the most well known and hinges on the fact that the real cost of employing a worker for a company is not identical to the real return received by that worker. The nominal wage is clearly common to both. However, on top of the wages that companies pay their workers they also pay taxes and non-wage labour costs (and workers likely place no value on the former and do not treat the latter as equivalent to an extra pound in their pay packet) and companies compare that overall cost to the price of value added. Workers pay income taxes on their pay and they compare that post-tax wage to the price of consumption. So lower oil prices should reduce the wedge between the real cost to employers and the real return to employees by lowering the price of consumption without influencing the price of value added. If these changes in the wedge temporarily or even permanently influence labour supply then falling oil prices could boost aggregate supply. Unfortunately, there is little consensus in the literature around the scale of these 'wedge' effects: clearly in countries where wage indexation is more prevalent, these real wage resistance effects will tend to be more significant (Álvarez et al. 2009); Gruber's (1997) analysis of a very large tax-driven change in the wedge suggests little impact on supply; in contrast, Prescott (2004) argues that differences in marginal tax rates can help explain trends in labour supply over time and across countries; and Nickell and Layard (1999) conclude that the wedge likely has a small impact on supply. It is also worth noting that most of the research in this area focuses on the impact of tax-driven changes in the wedge—but the results from those studies should be broadly illustrative of the labour supply response to deflator-driven changes in the wedge.

7.3.3.3   Demand, the Output Gap and Inflation

Movements in oil prices will have a profound impact on the outlook for inflation in the UK via the demand side of the economy, which will then influence inflation via the output gap (Barwell et al. 2007):

- *Consumption:* When energy prices fall, real disposable income for most households rises because the cost of the consumption basket falls without any change in nominal labour income and that will tend to support consumer spending. The distributed profits of companies in the oil extraction sector which some households receive in the form of non-labour income may fall but it seems plausible that a visible increase in disposable income in the middle and the bottom end of the income distribution (where the marginal propensity to consume is high) will dominate a less visible decrease in dividends and gross financial wealth at the top where consumption is concerned.

- *Investment:* A decline in oil prices will almost surely weigh on investment in the extraction sector, but beyond that it is possible that a persistent fall in energy prices could influence the decision of companies to invest in particular types of energy-intensive machinery that were not commercially viable at higher oil prices.

- *Exports:* The UK economy used to be a net exporter of oil so falling oil prices would have reduced net exports; now the situation is reversed. Falling oil prices have an additional impact on the demand for UK exports in that they transfer purchasing power at the global level from oil-exporting countries to oil-importing countries, and to the extent that the UK economy tends to export more goods and services to the latter (e.g., the Eurozone) than the former (e.g., the Middle East) then transfer of global purchasing power would lead to a boost for UK exports for a given level of global demand.

- *Government spending:* Falling oil prices affect the public finances in a number of ways (OBR 2010): directly via tax receipts with reduced revenue collected from the oil extraction sector partially offset by an increase in fuel duty, thanks to increased consumption at lower prices; and indirectly via indexation effects as lower consumer prices affect the tax thresholds on earnings and the level of benefit payments.

This is not quite the end of the story where the impact of falling oil prices on demand is concerned. We need to think about the source and the nature of the shock. Forecasters may treat the collapse in oil prices as exogenously given, but in reality, falling oil prices will reflect some combination of news on supply or demand, and the overall impact of the primitive shock on the UK economy will vary accordingly. If oil prices fall because global demand is weak then we might expect to see a more broad-based deterioration in the inflation outlook, reflecting weaker trade prices via a global output channel and weaker domestic prices, thanks to a local output channel given lower demand for UK exports. On the other hand, if the source of the shock is supply driven then these other channels should not materialise. It is also likely that shocks to oil prices that are perceived to be permanent are more likely to lead to pronounced movements in demand—for example, with households more likely to adjust spending in response to news on permanent income via the positive shock to disposable income now and in the future.

Finally, central bankers will not be indifferent to the macroeconomic impact of the shock. Hamilton (1983) famously observed that seven out of the eight post-war US recessions to that point were preceded by a significant increase in the price of oil, although in later work he would document that this empirical regularity breaks down after 1986 (Hamilton 1996). Bernanke et al. (1997) argue that adequately controlling for the nature of the shocks helps refine our estimates of its consequences: the impact on output is often not significantly different from zero. The problem that bedevils all this analysis is how to control for the actual and anticipated monetary policy response to the oil shock, which will have a pervasive impact on demand.

7.4   Expecting Deflation

The fall in oil prices and the appreciation of the pound helped to drive the economy into deflation territory. On a couple of occasions during 2015, consumer prices were estimated to have been lower than a year earlier. A temporary period of deflation is not necessarily a grave cause for concern for central bankers. In any case, there is very little that central bankers can do to prevent deflation brought about by a sudden drop in oil prices or spike in the currency given the speed with which the direct first round effects materialise in consumer prices and the lags in the transmission mechanism. What matters is that the central bank avoids a persistent period of deflation.

Standard textbook theory suggests that lower oil prices and a more expensive currency do not pose a threat on this front: they both involve price level adjustments which imply a transitory period of low inflation. However, central bankers became concerned during this period that a transitory period of low headline inflation could dislodge inflation expectations and then a price level adjustment could ultimately lead to a more persistent period of low inflation.

There is an irony here. At the start of the crisis, inflation expectations had been the central banker's friend, almost certainly helping to moderate the decline in inflation given the large margin of spare capacity that opened up. Now expectations threatened to turn from friend to foe—particularly in the Eurozone and Japan. We now turn to discuss the key question during this period of low global inflation: what determines long-run inflation expectations and the risks to price stability from a temporary period of low inflation.

7.4.1 Expectations in Theory

Expectations play a central role in modern macroeconomics. We know that they matter: after all, our simple macro framework suggests that inflation will tend to be stable and in line with expectations when the output gap is closed at any rate of inflation and not necessarily just when expected and actual inflation are consistent with the target. The problem is that we know very little about how expectations are formed in practice.

7.4.1.1 The Benchmark: Model-Consistent Rational Expectations

As noted earlier, the default approach in macro theory is to assume that the agents who inhabit economic models are highly sophisticated and take decisions on the basis of forecasts of the future, and those rational expectations are derived using the true structure of economy. This has powerful implications for business cycle dynamics within these models: when the economy is hit by a shock these agents anticipate a rule-based monetary policy response that helps to stabilise the economy by eliciting an appropriate shift in behaviour. If demand is strong today and expected to remain strong tomorrow then companies may respond by hiring workers to meet that demand and/or raising prices. If on the other hand they expect demand to return to normal levels tomorrow, thanks to tighter monetary policy then it is unlikely that companies will pay the costs involved in adjusting the workforce or prices. Moreover, confidence that monetary policy can stabilise the economy may lead to a structural increase in inertia within the system—for example, if companies expect low and stable inflation they may be more willing to enter into long-term contracts which make prices more sticky (Ball et al. 1988). In short, model-consistent expectations appear to be a source of stability.

There is an important caveat to this result. Central banks cannot rely on expectations to do all the work: they cannot leave rates on hold and rely on the implicit tightening or loosening in monetary conditions that follows from an expected change in policy to stabilise the economy. If the policy response that the sophisticated agents anticipate does not materialise then those agents may revise their assessment of the policy rule. That in turn would deliver a much more persistent deviation of inflation from target in response to shocks:

for example, in the limit, if agents no longer expected central bankers to adjust nominal interest rates in response to inflation then those central bankers would end up losing control of real interest rates and in short order the economic outlook too (Goodhart 2009) and inflation could drift arbitrarily far from the target.

7.4.1.2   The Passive Deflation Equilibrium and the Risks of Low for Long

Students of macroeconomics are taught that so long as central bankers abide by John Taylor's principle—adjusting nominal interest rates by more than any deviation of inflation, so that real interest rates move in the right direction (rising to choke off an inflationary impulse, and vice versa)—then all is well with the world: monetary policy can provide a stable nominal anchor for the economy. However, it transpires that the anchor is less steadfast than it first appears: there is a risk of a self-fulfilling slide into deflation.

Benhabib, Schmitt-Grohé and Uribe (2001a, b) argue that there are two equilibria—not one—if we allow for a lower bound on nominal interest rates. Benhabib, Schmitt-Grohé and Uribe argue that an equilibrium exists where the policy reaction function (which describes how central banks adjust nominal interest rates in response to news) and the Fisher condition (which simply expresses the nominal interest rate in terms of a real rate of interest and an expected inflation rate) intersect. There is an activist equilibrium at the neutral rate of interest consistent with the inflation target and the equilibrium real interest rate along the Fisher condition around which central banks can aggressively adjust nominal interest rates in response to news. However, there is a second passive equilibrium at the lower bound where the Fisher condition is also satisfied through an expectation of deflation that compensates for the still positive equilibrium real interest rate. As Benhabib, Schmitt-Grohé and Uribe observe, all that is required for the economy to slide into this trap is that people expect it to happen.

Bullard (2010) argues that well-meaning commitment to keep rates lower for longer during a deflationary episode could prove counter-productive in these circumstances. The passive equilibrium is one where nominal interest rates are low and expected to remain so, and this 'lower for longer' forward guidance could therefore end up confirming expectations that the economy is headed towards that equilibrium. Instead, Bullard argues that central bankers would be better off engaging in asset purchases to inject additional stimulus into the economy rather than relying on communicating about the point at which interest rates will no longer be constrained.

7.4.1.3   Learning to Expect Deflation

Perhaps the key message from Benhabib, Schmitt-Grohé and Uribe's work is that expectations can destabilise as well as stabilise: if people expect interest rates will remain at the lower bound forever and prices will fall forever, then that is precisely what might happen and central bankers can fall into a trap of encouraging those expectations. This raises the important question: when would expectations shift in the direction of this passive equilibrium?

One approach to answering that question is provided by the literature on learning, which imagines sophisticated agents who are learning about the true structure of the economy and adjusting their forecasts (and hence their behaviour) in response to news (Evans and Honkapohja 2010). So if the economy is operating close to the 'zero output gap/inflation at target' steady state then agents can draw upon past experience to guide their expectations and hence their behaviour. However, when monetary policy runs up against the lower bound the dynamic response of the economy could change and that in turn sparks a process of learning among these boundedly rational agents (Williams 2010), as they try to figure out the new rules of the game.

The clear risk in this environment is the possibility of positive feedback, with an initial shock being amplified through the learning process (remember positive feedback is not necessarily a good thing: it covers both virtuous and vicious circles). In particular, a downwards revision to inflation expectations will, other things being equal, raise real interest rates, which in turn will depress demand and inflation which will sooner or later lead to another round of disinflationary learning that through iteration ultimately drives the economy into a 'deflation trap' (Evans and Honkapohja 2010).

7.4.2   Market-Based Measures of Inflation Expectations

If we know that we need to worry about inflation expectations when headline inflation falls too far below the target then it raises the obvious question: how do we measure inflation expectations and at what horizon matters most?

7.4.2.1   Introducing Break-evens and the Totemic 5y5yf

The default option is to look at what is available and that leads us to focus on the proxies for inflation expectations that can be derived from market prices, or so-called break-even inflation rates. We can derive those proxies from two distinct markets, although basic arbitrage should ensure that both give a broadly similar message:

- *The bond market:* One can impute the expected rate of inflation that would equalise the return on conventional and index-linked bonds of a given maturity, since the former provide a guaranteed nominal return if held to maturity and the latter a guaranteed real return.
- *The inflation swaps market:* The payment(s) that a counterparty in the swap is willing to make in order to receive payments linked to the future path of inflation should reflect their expectations of the future path of inflation over the lifetime of the swap.

Unfortunately, these break-even rates cannot be interpreted as pure expectations of inflation. The compensation that investors demand for bearing inflation risk should include a risk premium (Garcia and Werner 2010), that is the compensation for the impact of uncertainty over inflation on their portfolio and ultimately their well-being in future states of the world. Moreover, price inelastic demand for inflation protection of large institutional investors could distort the compensation that the 'marginal investor' demands for inflation risk—another example of the preferred habitat theory that we discussed to motivate an out-sized asset price response to QE. Finally, where bond-based break-evens are concerned the spread could also reflect liquidity risk premia.

We can back out break-even inflation rates at different time horizons with varying degrees of success from both sources: where the bond market is concerned, a lack of bonds at different maturities means that some judgement is required to sketch out the term structure of inflation expectations, but the swaps curve provides a more complete picture although lack of market depth can still complicate interpretation of observed rates in both cases. Critically, we can break up break-evens at any horizon into a sequence of forward rates which isolate expectations for inflation in the future, as opposed to an average rate of inflation between the present day and a point in the future.

A lot of attention is attached to the five year five year forward (5y5yf), which measures the implied rate of inflation that is expected to prevail over a five-year period that begins five years from now. That horizon would usually be considered beyond the duration of the standard business cycle and the interval over which prices are sticky. Inflation expectations over that interval should therefore broadly capture whether markets expect central banks to achieve their mandates in the medium-term once the current shocks have dissipated. The economy may be hit by positive or negative shocks today and that would raise or lower the output gap and expectations of inflation over the next couple of years, but if the central bank is doing its job then interest rates should rise or fall to ensure that five years from now the output gap is closed and inflation is back at the target.

7.4.2.2   The Smoking Gun: The Synchronised Fall in Oil Prices and the 5y5yf

It is not unreasonable to think that when oil prices halved in the space of six months and drove consumer prices into deflation territory that break-even inflation rates at short horizons of two or even three years might fall, especially after a period in which inflation in many advanced economies had been weak for an extended period of time. However, what is more surprising is that as oil prices fell pushing headline inflation down towards zero, longer-term break-evens fell too (Neely 2015). In the USA and the Eurozone, the 5y5yf break-evens fell almost in lock-step with oil prices and in the case of the latter to a level clearly below the target of the ECB.

The question for central bankers was whether the decline in the 5y5yf break-even reflected a genuine fall in market expectations of inflation expectations, and if so, why expectations had responded in this way (because that might suggest something about what it would take to re-anchor expectations in line with the mandate). Two stylised explanations spring to mind for the synchronised decline in oil prices and the 5y5yf:

- *Adaptive expectations of a continuation of low inflation in the past, present and near future:* After several years of inflation failing to rise back towards targets in many advanced economies market participants may have begun to mark down their expectations of the future path of inflation. In this version of events there is no formal (forward-looking) economic mechanism underpinning this revision in expectations, simply an awareness that inflation has disappointed in the recent past and present and given falling oil prices is almost certain to continue to do so in the near future and that triggers a revision to what is essentially a rule of thumb expectation for inflation at long horizons (i.e., away from the 'inflation will match the target' rule towards 'inflation will remain low' rule).
- *Rational expectations of a disinflationary crisis in the future:* In this scenario, two forward-looking asset prices—the price of oil which as noted earlier reflects expectations about future demand and supply imbalances in the oil market and the 5y5yf—both reflect a third factor: fear of a global recession, driven by weakness in the emerging economies. In that scenario, the derived demand for oil would collapse sending the spot price lower and with relatively little

easy fiscal and monetary ammunition left to fire one might expect a protracted period of very low inflation given large and persistent output gaps which policymakers will struggle to close.

An alternative explanation for the decline in the 5y5f is that it reflects a shift in the inflation risk premium—albeit a pretty significant one—rather than a change in the expected value. There are two variants of this argument: first, that a positive risk premium got a lot smaller (implicitly the risk premium must have been substantial before the summer of 2014 and therefore long-term inflation expectations have always been below the target in the Eurozone); or second, that the risk premium turned from positive to negative and may even have got larger in absolute size. Traditionally, the default assumption is that the inflation risk premium is positive, so the 5y5yf overstates true expectations (Bernanke 2004), but the Governing Council of the ECB was certainly entertaining the possibility of a negative risk premium by early 2015 (ECB 2015). From a pure macro finance perspective, where the sign of the risk premium is pinned down by beliefs about the covariance between possible news on inflation and the returns on the rest of the portfolio (strictly the benefit from an additional unit of consumption) in that state of nature, the shift towards a negative risk premium might reflect investors reaching the conclusion that in a very bad macroeconomic outcomes the inflation outlook would be similarly dire (under these circumstances, paying realised inflation in a swap is a good strategy because when that downside risk crystallises you can enter into a second swap and this time receive inflation and in return pay smaller fixed amounts—consistent with the now lower anticipated path of inflation—than you currently make on the original swap, generating profits that will fund consumption when the returns on the rest of your portfolio are poor). In practical terms, the emergence of a negative inflation risk premium over this period in Europe might have reflected investors starting to become more concerned about the risk that the Eurozone economy could slide into a deflation trap, in which case the returns on most of the rest of their portfolio would probably be poor at best.

Interestingly, it is hard to detect a comparable decline in the 5y5yf in the UK which may speak to the importance of the preferred habitat channel—and the more dominant role of institutional investors in the UK market—than necessarily any greater credibility of the UK monetary regime.

7.4.3 Expectations in the Real Economy

The inflation expectations of investors—if that is what break-evens really show—may be easy to measure. But it is the expectations of households and companies that we really care about: after all it is their decisions to spend or save in light of the real interest rates they perceive (given the nominal interest rates that confront them and their expectations of inflation) that drive activity in the economy. We now turn to a more pragmatic assessment of how those agents form expectations.

7.4.3.1   Fast and Frugal Expectations

The learning literature discussed earlier casts the representative agent as a keen econometrician, perpetually processing news in the data to learn about the economy and finesse her forecasts. This might be an appropriate assumption for large blue-chip companies that might employ people to work full time on forecasting on behalf of the CEO and the shareholders. However, it seems highly unlikely that this is a realistic description of behaviour for most households and companies in the real economy. With the best will in the world, households may be inattentive, in the sense of only infrequently responding to news (Reis 2006). Moreover, even when the time comes to periodically update their plans, the approach taken to forecasting the future may be far less sophisticated than the benchmark macro-model presumes.

Economics is about the allocation of scarce resources to their most efficient use and forecasting the future is just another use of scarce resources. Imagine that there are diminishing returns from time spent investing resources in forecasting: it takes little time or effort to arrive at an educated guess of what inflation will be next year, but the increasing amounts of resources allocated to forecasting are likely to deliver ever smaller incremental improvements in the accuracy of that forecast (i.e., diminishing returns will soon set in). In any case, the marginal benefit of that incremental improvement in forecast performance may also diminish quite rapidly: for most households whether inflation will be 2 % or 3 % might have relatively limited impact on most decisions they take. In any case, at some point the disutility of time devoted to forecasting will likely limit the resources devoted to forecasting (for those who do not enjoy econometrics) and households may run up against constraints in their capacity to process information (Sims 2003).

Given this more pragmatic assessment of the likely allocation of the resources to forecasting, we can identify a number of plausible models of household expectation formation:

* *Rules of thumb:* Households use simple rules of thumb to forecast—referred to in the literature as 'fast and frugal' heuristics (Goldstein and Gigerenzer 1996)—which avoid the costs involved in complex calculations.

- *Copy someone else:* Households might avoid forecasting altogether and instead imitate the behaviour of other agents (Conlisk 1980). After all, you only need to forecast in order to calculate the appropriate course of action given your circumstances and you may be better off copying the behaviour of other agents who you believe have invested the time and effort in forecasting and optimising if you believe that their behaviour is a reasonable guide to what you would have chosen to do had you done likewise.
- *Contract out:* Households could employ the services of a professional forecaster to guide their decisions. Although that may sound implausible in practice, we can think of trade unions and financial advisers serving this role in collective wage bargains and investment decisions respectively.
- *Free ride:* Finally, households could simply free ride on forecasts in the public domain produced by professional forecasters (Carroll 2001, 2003). In this case, the views of professional forecasters, and more generally the media, take on added importance: if the 'talking heads' are all discussing deflation then households who might otherwise have been blissfully unaware start expecting deflation too.

7.4.3.2 What If Households (Act as If They) Just Don't Care About Inflation?

This question may feel like heresy to macroeconomists but it is worth taking seriously the proposition that many households are largely indifferent to the rate of inflation.

Kahneman and Tversky (1979) offer an alternative way to think about how individuals take decisions, as opposed to the default approach of maximising expected utility: prospect theory. The first stage of that process is 'editing'—people frame a problem to simplify the process of choosing between options, and that could involve discarding extreme outcomes and largely extraneous information from the decision-making process. Inflation may fall into that category where many decisions are concerned: for example, whether to supply labour or not.

Indeed, rather than deciding that modest changes in the rate of inflation are irrelevant, households may even notice those small changes. Psychologists talk of 'just noticeable differences' below which changes in the background environment go undetected (Batchelor 1986). It follows that you will not forecast what you do not even notice.

Finally, there is the possibility that households are 'unaware' that inflation matters: that changes in the rate of inflation have an impact on their welfare

(Heifetz et al. 2007). It would be irrational to expect those individuals to have a considered expectation of the future rate of inflation. This seems incongruous to economists but as Mankiw (1997) observes: 'Economists aren't people. To be more precise, economists view inflation very differently than laymen do.'

Of course, the extent to which households care about inflation is likely endogenous with respect to the macroeconomic backdrop. Those who are unlucky enough to live through hyperinflation are unlikely to be unaware of the impact of inflation on their welfare. In contrast, Akerlof et al. (2000) argue that agents are 'near rational' in the sense that they respond less to inflation when it is low and stable.

7.4.3.3   Evidence

One feature that does stand out from surveys of households is that expectations of inflation are positively correlated with perceptions: if you believe that inflation is low today, then you will typically expect inflation to be low tomorrow. Interestingly, a significant fraction (around 30 %) of individuals who report that they have 'no idea' about the rate of inflation over the past are nonetheless willing to forecast what inflation might be in the future (Ellis 2006).

If perceptions drive expectations then the accuracy of households' perceptions of inflation matters. The evidence suggests that the visibility of price changes influences households' perceptions (and hence expectations) of the rate of change of the price of the basket of consumer goods and services (Georganas et al. 2014). That is, households' perceptions of inflation appear to be disproportionately influenced by changes in the price of goods and services that they purchase on a regular basis like food or petrol, and in contrast the marked decline in the price of durable goods (which by definition are purchased on an infrequent basis by each household but account for a non-trivial share of overall consumption given their relative price) is under-weighted in perceptions.

The observations that inflation expectations are driven by perceptions of inflation and perceptions of inflation are disproportionately driven by the rate of change of visible prices were hardly reassuring for the MPC when highly visible prices—energy and food—helped to propel headline inflation into deflation territory. Domit et al. (2015) report that measures of households' expectations of inflation one and two years ahead did indeed fall over this period. Indeed, they report that two years ahead expectations appeared to be particularly low relative to the Committee's own forecast for the path of inflation, suggesting that the nominal anchor was more fragile than it first appeared. Fortunately, expectations at longer horizons (five to ten years ahead) proved more resilient to the slowdown in headline inflation. Nonetheless, this episode illustrated the latent threat to price stability from shocks which in more tranquil times might have been written off as mere irritations.

References

Akerlof, G., Dickens, W., & Perry, G. (2000). Near-rational wage and price-setting and the optimal rates of inflation and unemployment. *Brookings Paper on Economics Activity, 31*, 1–60.

Álvarez, L., Hurtado, S., Sánchez, I., & Thomas, C. (2009). *The impact of oil price changes on Spanish and euro area consumer price inflation.* Banco de Espana Occasional Paper 904.

Atkeson, A., & Kehoe, P. (1995). *Putty-clay capital and energy.* Federal Reserve Bank of Minneapolis Working Paper 548.

Azreki, R., & Blanchard, O. (2014). Seven questions about the recent oil price slump. *IMF blog post.*

Baily, M. (1981). Productivity and the services of capital and labor. *Brookings Papers on Economic Activity, 1*, 1–65.

Baldwin, R. (1988). Hysteresis in import prices? The beachhead effect. *American Economic Review, 78*(4), 773–785.

Ball, L., Mankiw, N., & Romer, D. (1988). The new Keynesian economics and the output-inflation trade-off. *Brookings Paper on Economic Activity, 1*, 1–82.

Barwell, R., Thomas, R., & Turnbull, K. (2007). The macroeconomic impact of higher energy prices on the UK economy. *Bank of England Quarterly Bulletin, Q4*, 522–532.

Batchelor, R. (1986). The psychophysics of inflation. *Journal of Economic Psychology, 7*, 269–290.

Benhabib, J., Schmitt-Grohé, S., & Uribe, M. (2001a). Monetary policy and multiple equilibria. *American Economic Review, 91*(1), 167–186.

Benhabib, J., Schmitt-Grohé, S., & Uribe, M. (2001b). The perils of Taylor rules. *Journal of Economic Theory, 96*, 40–69.

Bernanke, B. (2004, April 15). *What policymakers can learn from asset prices.* Speech.

Bernanke, B., Gertler, M., & Watson, M. (1997). Systematic monetary policy and the effects of oil price shocks. *Brookings Papers on Economic Activity, 1*, 91–157.

BoE. (2005). August Inflation Report.

BoE. (2014, October). Agents' summary of business conditions.

Bullard, J. (2010). Seven faces of "The Peril". *Federal Reserve Bank of St. Louis Review, September/October*, 339–352.

Burstein, A., Neves, J., & Rebelo, S. (2003). Distribution costs and real exchange rate dynamics during exchange-rate-based stabilizations. *Journal of Monetary Economics, 50*, 1189–1214.

Campa, J., & Goldberg, L. (2006a). *Distribution margins, imported inputs, and the sensitivity of the CPI to exchange rates.* NBER Working Paper 12121.

Campa, J., & Goldberg, L. (2006b). Exchange rate pass-through into import prices. *Review of Economics and Statistics, 87*(4), 679–690.

Carney, M. (2015, August 29). *Inflation in a globalised world*. Speech.

Carroll, C. (2001). *The epidemiology of macroeconomic expectations*. NBER Working Paper 8695.

Carroll, C. (2003). Macroeconomic expectations of households and professional forecasters. *Quarterly Journal of Economics, 118*(1), 269–298.

Chen, N., & Juvenal, L. (2014). *Quality, trade and exchange rate pass-through*. IMF Working Paper 11/42.

Chowla, S., Quaglietti, L., & Rachel, Ł. (2014). How have world shocks affected the UK economy? *Bank of England Quarterly Bulletin, Q2*, 1–13.

Clark, P., & MacDonald, R. (1998). *Exchange rates and economic fundamentals*. IMF Working Paper 98/67.

Cochrane, J. (1999). New facts in finance. *Federal Reserve Bank of Chicago Economic Perspectives, 3*, 36–58.

Conlisk, J. (1980). Costly optimisers and cheap imitators. *Journal of Economic Behaviour and Organisation, 1*, 275–293.

De Schryder, S., & Peersman, G. (2015). The U.S. dollar exchange rate and the demand for oil. *Energy Journal, 36*(3), 91–113.

Domit, S., Jackson, C., & Roberts-Sklar, M. (2015). Do inflation expectations currently pose a risk to inflation. *Bank of England Quarterly Bulletin, Q2*, 165–180.

Dornbusch, R. (1987). Exchange rates and prices. *American Economic Review, 77*(1), 93–106.

Dury, K., Piscitelli, L., Sebastia-Barriel, M., & Yates, T. (2003). What caused the rise in the UK terms of trade? *Bank of England Quarterly Bulletin, Summer*, 164–176.

ECB. (2010). *Energy markets and the euro area macroeconomy*. Occasional Paper 113.

ECB. (2015). Account of the 21–22 January monetary policy meeting of the Governing Council of the European Central Bank.

Ellis, C. (2006). Public attitudes to inflation. *Bank of England Quarterly Bulletin, Summer*, 181–189.

Engel, C. (1996). The forward discount anomaly and the risk premium: A survey of recent evidence. *Journal of Empirical Finance, 3*(2), 123–192.

Engel, C. (2006). Equivalent results for optimal pass-through, optimal indexing to exchange rates, and optimal choice of currency for export pricing. *Journal of European Economic Association, 4*(6), 1249–1260.

Engel, C., & Rogers, J. (1996). How wide is the border? *American Economic Review, 86*(5), 1112–1125.

Evans, G., & Honkapohja, S. (2010). Expectations, deflation traps and macroeconomic policy. In D. Cobham, O. Eitrheim, S. Gerlach, & J. Qvigstad (Eds.), *Twenty years of inflation targeting*. Cambridge: Cambridge University Press.

Ezekiel, M. (1938). The cobweb theorem. *Quarterly Journal of Economics, 52*, 255–280.

Forbes, K. (2014, October 1). *The economic impact of sterling's recent moves*. Speech.

Forbes, K. (2015, September 11). *Much ado about something important*. Speech.

French, K., & Poterba, J. (1991). Investor diversification and international equity markets. *American Economic Review, 81*, 222–226.

Froot, K., & Klemperer, P. (1989). Exchange rate pass-through when market share matters. *American Economic Review, 79*(4), 637–654.

Gagnon, J., & Ihrig, J. (2004). Monetary policy and exchange rate pass-through. *International Journal of Finance and Economics, 9*(4), 315–338.

Garcia, J., & Werner, T. (2010). *Inflation risks and inflation risk premia.* ECB Working Paper 1162.

Georganas, S., Healy, P., & Li, N. (2014). Frequency bias in consumers' perceptions of inflation. *European Economic Review, 67*, 144–158.

Goldberg, P., & Knetter, M. (1997). Goods prices and exchange rates. *Journal of Economic Literature, 35*(3), 1243–1272.

Goldstein, D., & Gigerenzer, G. (1996). Reasoning the fast and frugal way: Models of bounded rationality. *Psychological Review, 103*(4), 650–669.

Goodhart, C. (2009). The interest rate conditioning assumption. *International Journal of Central Banking, 2*, 85–108.

Groen, J., & Russo, P. (2015, June 8). *Is cheaper oil good news or bad news for U.S. economy?* Federal Reserve Bank of New York Liberty Street Economics Blog.

Groen, J., McNeil, K., & Middeldorp, M. (2013, March 25). *A new approach for identifying demand and supply shocks in the oil market.* Federal Reserve Bank of New York Liberty Street Economics Blog.

Gruber, J. (1997). The incidence of payroll taxation: Evidence from Chile. *Journal of Labor Economics, 15*(3), S72–S101.

Hamilton, J. (1983). Oil and the macroeconomy since World War II. *Journal of Political Economy, April*, 228–248.

Hamilton, J. (1996). This is what happened to the oil price-macroeconomy relationship. *Journal of Monetary Economics, 38*, 215–220.

Haskel, J., & Wolf, H. (2001). *The law of one price – A case study.* NBER Working Paper 8112.

Hausman, J., & Wieland, J. (2014). Abenomics: Preliminary analysis and outlook. *Brookings Paper on Economic Activity, Spring*, 1–76.

Heifetz, A., Shannon, C., & Spiegel, Y. (2007). What to maximise if you must. *Journal of Economic Theory, 133*(1), 31–57.

Hotelling, H. (1931). The economics of exhaustible resources. *Journal of Political Economy, April*, 137–175.

IMF. (2015, April). *Uneven growth.* World Economic Outlook.

Kahneman, D., & Tversky, A. (1979). Prospect theory: An analysis of decision under risk. *Econometrica, 47*(2), 263–291.

Klemperer, P. (1995). Competition when consumers have switching costs. *Review of Economic Studies, 62*, 515–539.

Kochhar, K., Ouliaris, S., & Samiei, H. (2005). *What hinders investment in the oil sector?* IMF Research Department Paper.

Koo, R. (2003). *Balance sheet recession: Japan's struggle with uncharted economics and its global implications.* Singapore: Wiley.

MacCoille, C., Mayhew, K., & Turnbull, K. (2009). Accounting for the stability of the UK terms of trade. *Bank of England Quarterly Bulletin, Q4*, 286–292.

Mankiw, N. (1997). Comments. In C. Romer & D. Romer (Eds.), *Reducing inflation*. Chicago: University of Chicago.

Marazzi, M., & Sheets, N. (2007). Declining exchange rate pass-through to U.S. import prices. *Journal of International Money and Finance, 26*(6), 924–947.

McCafferty, I. (2015, March 10). *Oil price falls*. Speech.

Mumtaz, H., Oomen, O., & Wang, J. (2006). *Exchange rate pass-through into UK import prices*. Bank of England Working Paper 312.

Nakamura, E., & Zeron, D. (2010). Accounting for incomplete pass-through. *Review of Economic Studies, 77*(3), 1192–1230.

Neely, C. (2015). *How much do oil prices affect inflation*. Federal Reserve Bank of St. Louis, Economic Synopses, 10.

Nickell, S., & Layard, R. (1999). Labor market institutions and economic performance. In O. Ashenfelter & D. Card (Eds.), *Handbook of labor economics* (Vol. 3C, pp. 3029–3084).

Nixon, D., & Smith, T. (2012). What can the oil futures curve tell us about the outlook for oil prices? *Bank of England Quarterly Bulletin, Q1*, 39–47.

OBR. (2010, September). *Assessment of the effect of oil price fluctuations on the public finances*. Office for Budget Responsibility.

Parsley, D., & Wei, S.-J. (2001). Explaining the border effect: The role of exchange rate variability, shipping costs, and geography. *Journal of International Economics, 55*, 87–105.

Prescott, E. (2004). Why do Americans work so much more than Europeans. *Federal Reserve Bank of Minneapolis Quarterly Review, 28*(1), 2–13.

Reis, R. (2006). Inattentive consumers. *Journal of Monetary Economics, 53*(8), 1761–1800.

Rogoff, K., Froot, K., & Kim, M. (2001). *The law of one price over 700 years*. IMF Working Paper 01/174.

Rose, A. (1991). The role of exchange rates in a popular model of international trade: Does the 'Marshall-Lerner' condition hold? *Journal of International Economics, 30*, 301–316.

Sims, C. (2013). Implications of Rational Inattention. *Journal of Monetary Economics, 50*(3), 665–690.

Strasser, G. (2012). Exchange rate pass-through and credit constraints. *Journal of Monetary Economics, 60*(1), 25–38.

Svensson, L. (2001, September 25). How Japan can recover. *Financial Times*.

Wheatley, J., & Garnham, P. (2010, September 27). Brazil in 'currency war' alert. *Financial Times*.

Williams, J. (2010). Monetary policy in a low inflation economy with learning. *Federal Reserve Bank of San Francisco Economic Review*, 1–12.

World Bank. (2015). Understanding the Plunge in Oil Prices: Sources and Implications. Global Economic Prospects, January.

8

Low for Much, Much Longer: Postponing Lift-Off from the Lower Bound

The MPC stopped cutting interest rates and started purchasing assets in Spring 2009. At that time, market participants anticipated that that the Committee's stay at the effective lower bound would be relatively short-lived. By May 2009, market prices implied rates would start to rise in 2010. However, Bank Rate would remain rooted to the lower bound for years to come.

The Committee was intermittently injecting additional stimulus into the economy via asset purchases during the first few years at the lower bound so an exit from the lower bound was out of the question during those periods of 'doing more'. However, as we have discussed already, there was a moment, nestled between the first and second wave of bond purchases, when the Committee came close to raising Bank Rate.

The more surprising feature of this period of inactivity at the effective lower bound is that the Committee continued to deem it necessary to keep Bank Rate unchanged months and finally years after the Committee had reached the conclusion that further stimulus via asset purchases was no longer necessary. Remember: the impact of a single 25 basis point increase in Bank Rate on output and inflation is relatively modest. It is therefore a little surprising that as the economy recovered during this period, and the Bank's estimate of the output gap continued to close, so few members of the Committee were willing to vote for an increase in Bank Rate on this ultra-modest scale through 2013, 2014 and 2015. A similar argument could have been made about the Fed, with the lift-off in interest rates in the USA seemingly postponed despite a clear improvement in the state of the US economy for much (but not all)

© The Editor(s) (if applicable) and The Author(s) 2016
R. Barwell, *Macroeconomic Policy after the Crash*,
DOI 10.1057/978-1-137-51592-6_8

of this period. In this final section, we shall discuss the reasons why rates remained low for so much longer.

8.1   Rules-Based Monetary Policy

To assess whether there was something unusual about the conduct of monetary policy during this period that Bank Rate remained at the lower bound, we need some form of reliable benchmark against which the Committee's decisions given the conjuncture can be compared. In theory, monetary policy rules should provide the perfect yardstick. A rule describes the appropriate setting for a policy instrument given a particular set of arguments (the variables which are used as summary statistics of the macroeconomic outlook) and a particular functional form.

8.1.1   Taylor's Rule

Research into the design of monetary policy rules will forever be associated with John Taylor and in particular his paper 'Discretion versus policy rules in practice' (Taylor 1993). Taylor presented the following simple rule which summarised the appropriate conduct of monetary policy, as opposed to the actual conduct of policy (which for much of the post-war period did not necessarily measure up to the profession's understanding of optimal):

$$i = \pi + \tfrac{1}{2}\,xy + \tfrac{1}{2}\,x\left(\pi - \pi\,^*\right) + r\,^*$$

where i is the policy rate, π is the inflation rate, y is the output gap, π^* is the inflation target and r^* is the real equilibrium interest rate. In particular, if the inflation target is 2 % and the real equilibrium interest rate is assumed to be 2 %, we arrive at the following calibration:

$$i = \pi + \tfrac{1}{2}\,xy + \tfrac{1}{2}\,x\left(\pi - 2\right) + 2$$
$$= 1\tfrac{1}{2}x\pi + \tfrac{1}{2}\,xy + 1$$

Or in other words, set the policy rate equal to 1.5 times the current rate of inflation plus 0.5 times the output gap plus 1. The Taylor rule has a couple of key features which are worth highlighting:

- *Simplicity:* The rule only contains two arguments (the inflation rate and the output gap) which appear to imply that all other considerations—such as the state of the labour market or the constellation of asset prices—are irrelevant in that they have no direct bearing on the setting of the rule. However, these factors are captured indirectly via the arguments that are included: for example, the unemployment rate should be reflected in the output gap.
- *Stability:* The Taylor rule has the stabilising property that the policy rate responds more than one for one with deviations in inflation. Known as the Taylor Principle, this property ensures that real interest rates move in the right direction in response to shocks. For example, nominal interest rates are raised enough to dominate any adaptive rise in inflation expectations when a positive shock raises the current rate of inflation, and the increase in real interest rates should help to suppress demand and the initial impetus to inflation.

Taylor's research sparked an entire literature on the appropriate calibration of monetary policy rules. There is a debate about the specific selection of arguments—for example, whether to use a measure of core rather than headline inflation in the rule, so that policy does not respond to the first round effect of commodity price shocks (such as the change in oil prices discussed earlier), or whether instead to use a forecast for inflation, to make the rule forward-looking (Orphanides and Wieland 2008) in line with best practice for policy (Svensson 1997). There is also a debate about the parameters of the rule—for example, whether Taylor's Rule puts too low a weight on the output gap (Bernanke 2010, 2015b). However, the key question for our purposes is the calibration of r^*—the real equilibrium rate. Together with the inflation target, the real equilibrium rate pins down the intercept of the policy rule: it tells you the neutral level of the policy rate when the economy is in (internal) balance and the output gap is zero and inflation (or expected inflation) is in line with target. However, there is no reason to suppose that this real equilibrium rate is constant through time, which means that the intercept and hence the output of the rule for any given set of arguments should vary through time too. As we shall go on to discuss, failure to capture the implications of any change in the real equilibrium rate for the stance of policy could lead the rule to give (potentially seriously) misleading advice about the appropriate level of the policy rate.

8.1.2   Taylor's Legacy

Taylor's rule was warmly received by the academic and policy community. Variants of the rule have been used to describe the conduct of monetary policy in countless theoretical models. However, the rule has not been used to set policy in practice; rather, it has been used in the sense that it was originally intended as a quantitative rule of thumb to guide but not determine the conduct of policy. Policymakers used the rule to give themselves a 'rough sense' of whether the policy rate was at a 'reasonable level' (Asso et al. 2010). Interestingly, Taylor concluded his 1993 paper as follows:

> This paper has endeavoured to study the role of policy rules in a world where simple, algebraic formulations of such rules cannot and should not be mechanically followed by policymakers.

Central bankers noted that the rule performed well in simulations and provided the necessary anchor of stability to deliver their mandates; for example, Yellen (1996) observed that: 'A central bank that adhered to the Taylor rule would certainly deserve credibility in the public's mind for its anti-inflationary resolve'. However, central bankers were not comfortable with the idea of ceding control to such a simple rule. As former Bank Governor Mervyn King explained, the behaviour of the economy and hence the appropriate policy response was too complex to be able to put your trust in any rule (King 1997):

> Unfortunately, no such simple – or for that matter complicated – rule exists. Our understanding of the economy is inadequate. Any proposed rule would soon be made redundant by the results of new research. No sooner would the authorities have adopted a rule than improvements to the rule would appear. Knowledge increases over time, and it would be intellectual pig-headedness to stay with a sub-optimal rule. For any rule to be feasible, there would have to be a rule for updating the rule itself. And I suppose that one could go further and argue that we would need a rule to update the rule that was used to update the rule itself, and so on.

Rules can be useful for telling you what not to do as well as what to do. Central bankers instinctively understood that unfettered discretion in the conduct of policy could prove problematic. In theory (Barro and Gordon 1983), although perhaps not in practice (Blinder 1998), central bankers might be tempted to use that discretion in the conduct of policy to exploit expectations and overstimulate the economy in order to boost activity and employment.

Central bankers thought that they could have the best of both worlds—the upside of the constraint on time-inconsistent behaviour without the downside of the slavish adherence to a simplistic rule—through so-called 'constrained discretion' (Bernanke and Mishkin 1997). A transparent and credible monetary policy framework ensures the former without having to accept the latter: producing rule-like behaviour, where policymakers can deviate from the rule when the output is considered suboptimal. A couple of decades ago, Yellen (1996) described an example of those circumstances in which policymakers would value the option to deviate from the rule, which resonates with the current debate:

> It is also probably not terribly surprising that there have been times during the past decade when the Fed has departed quite markedly from the path that would have resulted from a mechanical reading of the rule. By far the most pronounced such departure occurred during the early phases of the current expansion, in 1992 and 1993, when the Fed responded to the so-called 'financial headwinds' buffeting the economy by holding short rates well below the levels that would have been prescribed by Taylor's rule.

8.1.3 Taylor's Verdict

John Taylor is in little doubt about the recent conduct of monetary policy. He has dubbed the conduct of policy before, during and after the financial crisis as 'the Great Deviation'. Taylor argues that policymakers have systematically deviated from a rules-based approach (Taylor 2011):

> You may not have heard much about the Great Deviation. I define it as the recent period during which macroeconomic policy became more interventionist, less rules based, and less predictable. It is a period during which policy deviated from the practice of at least the previous two decades and from the recommendations of most macroeconomic theory and models. My general theme is that the Great Deviation killed the Great Moderation, gave birth to the Great Recession, and left a troublesome legacy for the future.

Taylor (2013) argues that the Great Deviation is a global phenomenon, with a number of central banks following an unconventional strategy, although the reasons for that change of behaviour may differ from place to place. Echoing our earlier discussion about currency wars, fears of the financial imbalances that might otherwise develop if large interest rate differentials opened up across jurisdictions may have forced the hands of policymakers to follow the lead of the major central banks and deviate from a rules-based approach.

As time passed, the economy recovered and yet rates remained on hold. Increasingly it was clear that policymakers had deviated from the prescriptions of the pre-crisis calibration of the Taylor rule, and they were only too happy to say so (Broadbent 2015):

Can I say one thing about this Taylor rule? The Taylor rule is, when it was first written down, was not a prescriptive rule, it was not meant to suggest here's how you
should set monetary policy. It was simply a description of the way the Fed behaved
over a certain period of time…Our objective is the inflation target, and we take an
assessment each month what level of interest rate is necessary to hit that and we do
not tie ourselves to some particular feedback rule, and certainly not that one.

Such is the level of concern around the supposed deviation from rule-like
behaviour in the USA that the US Congress has initiated legislative reforms
to rein in the Fed's room for manoeuvre (Posen 2015). In the opinion of the
author at least that would be a grave mistake: incentivising slavish devotion
to a simple rule will only lead to sub-optimal outcomes. We now turn to
discuss the strategic considerations for deviating from this benchmark as the
economy recovers from a financial crisis with rates still at the lower bound.

8.2   Risk Management at the Lower Bound: Policy Rate Shortfalls and Surpluses

The design of simple policy rules like the Taylor rule makes no allowance for
the existence of the lower bound on interest rates: if the inputs of the rule fall
far enough then the output of the rule can fall potentially far below zero to a
level that real-world policymakers feel unable to deliver. As discussed earlier
in this book, this is precisely what happened in the acute phase of the crisis.
A policy rate shortfall emerged: policy rules pointed to negative policy rates
given the collapse in the output gap and expectations of inflation but central
bankers were unwilling or felt unable to follow the prescription of the rules.
Instead, they turned to unconventional tools to manage that policy rate shortfall, printing money to buy assets to proxy the stimulus that might otherwise
have been engineered via a significantly negative policy rate.

At some point both the Fed and the BoE chose to cease and desist asset
purchases from which we can infer by revealed preference that policymakers
in both jurisdictions felt that the policy rate shortfall had narrowed significantly, and what remained could be managed via forward guidance about the
circumstances under which the policy rate would be increased.

In theory, if the outlook deteriorated and the rules once again suggested
that policy rates should be taken further into negative territory then those asset
purchase programmes could be resurrected to manage the policy rate shortfall.
However, the appetite for resuming asset purchases in those circumstances
appeared to wane in both jurisdictions. It might be that policymakers were
less convinced about the benefits of further asset purchases in terms of stimu-

lating the economy (Cúrdia and Ferrero 2013; Miles 2014) or they were more concerned about the costs in terms of aggravating potential risks to financial stability (e.g., through search for yield effects) or even the political response to further balance sheet expansion.

If policymakers believed that they were less well equipped to manage another policy rate shortfall, then they would rationally take steps to reduce the probability that this situation might arise in the future. It is difficult to influence the distribution of shocks that might hit the economy although not impossible; this is one aspect of the macro-prudential policy agenda (see, e.g., the FPC's intervention on high loan to income ratios). However, central bankers can influence the state of the economy when those shocks crystallise and in particular the level of the output gap and the prospects for inflation. A prudent central bank might choose to keep interest rates at the lower bound after the point that the Taylor rule suggests lift-off, creating a policy rate surplus. If a negative shock arrives then the implied cut in the output of the policy rule can be partially or even completely absorbed by the elimination of that policy rate surplus as the output of the policy rule falls back to the unchanged policy rate. In effect the central bank tries to minimise the probability of being constrained in the future by calibrating the policy response to engineer a more robust central case (modal) projection for activity and inflation than it might otherwise have selected in the absence of the lower bound (Yellen 2015b).

This strategy is referred to as *risk management at the lower bound* (Evans et al. 2015)—an idea that is typically associated with former Fed Chairman Alan Greenspan who argued that central bankers should grapple with the sources of risk and uncertainty that confront them, and as far as possible devise a strategy that best achieves the policymaker's objectives given those risks. In this case, the central bank is modifying the strategy to ensure a not so bad outcome in the event that large downside risks materialise. In fact, Greenspan had argued that risk management strategies might indeed lead central banks to deviate from the output of the rules (Greenspan 2004):

A rule does provide a benchmark against which to assess emerging developments. However, any rule capable of encompassing every possible contingency would lose a key aspect of its attractiveness: simplicity. On the other hand, no simple rule could possibly describe the policy action to be taken in every contingency and thus provide a satisfactory substitute for an approach based on the principles of risk management.

Given the mantra of limited and gradual increases in interest rates that forms the cornerstone of many central bank's forward guidance about the future path of rates, it is worth thinking through the consequences of risk management for the exit strategy from the lower bound. At some point, the recovery in activity and inflation will be sufficiently mature—and the policy rate surplus will be sufficiently large to cushion the blow if downside risks crystallise—and the central bank must start raising rates. At that point, the actual policy rate should rise faster than the output of the policy rule to start reducing the policy rate surplus—otherwise the central bank will engineer a large, positive output gap and inflation overshoot.

As time passed, the risk management argument became a less compelling description of the behaviour of the BoE, relative to say the Fed. As noted earlier, the MPC concluded that there was scope to cut Bank Rate further if necessary. That room to cut was not unlimited so the Bank still remained close to the lower bound. The Committee might become constrained given a sufficiently large shock which provided a risk management justification for keeping rates low for longer than the Taylor rule might suggest. However, the fact that the Committee was no longer at the lower bound weakened this argument as the Governor himself noted (Carney 2015a):

> I'll make one other point on this though which is the fact that we're not at the zero lower bound any more, or the effective lower bound, loosens somewhat the sort of risk management arguments that one sometimes hears around the optimal stance of policy and the prospective start of any tightening cycle.

8.3   Anti-Hysteresis Strategies

In conventional macroeconomics, it is assumed that there is no long-run trade-off between the level of output and inflation—that is, the long-run Phillips curve is vertical. If that assumption is valid then central bankers have no business trying to systematically run the economy above normal levels of capacity. Consistent with that assumption, the loss function of monetary policy is expressed in terms of symmetric deviations of demand from supply and inflation from the target. The conventional wisdom allows for the fact that the location of that vertical long-run Phillips curve will move through time given technical progress and population growth. The key point is that it is assumed that the location of that long-run vertical trade-off does not depend on the past or present state of the business cycle, and therefore the past or present conduct of monetary policy.

The crisis has reignited interest in the economics of hysteresis—a mechanism which challenges this assumption. As discussed earlier, hysteresis occurs when the supply capacity of an economy is damaged by a long and deep recession, such that the level of potential supply is persistently and perhaps permanently reduced. A more alarming variant of this mechanism is super hysteresis where a long and deep recession lowers the future growth rate, as opposed to the level of potential supply (Blanchard, Cerutti and Summers (2015)).

The potential for hysteresis and super hysteresis has significant implications for the conduct of monetary policy (Reifschneider et al. 2013). The supply side of the economy determines our collective standard of living: the amount of goods and services we can produce as a country in the long run determines how much we can consume. If a long and deep recession can do lasting damage to the supply side of the economy then the argument for an aggressive easing strategy to support aggregate demand in response to a downside shock is far more powerful. Given the lags in the transmission mechanism, this argument primarily applies in the early phase of a crisis: that is, central banks should act decisively to minimise the depth and duration of the trough in activity and the peak in unemployment rather than fret about eliminating the last few tenths of a percentage point of any output gap that may exist. Having said that, there is still scope for activist monetary policy to limit these scarring effects months or even years after the initial collapse in demand. For example, if these scarring effects operate through a reduction in the search intensity and effectiveness when people enter long-term unemployment then an aggressive policy response could still prove effective by increasing the pace at which aggregate unemployment declines during the recovery and thereby increasing the outflow rate from unemployment for those who have been out of work for some time.

Thus far, hysteresis has been described as a phenomenon which emerges in a protracted and persistent period of weak demand, in which case the best monetary policy can do is to try and limit the incidence and severity of those periods. However, there is at least the possibility that if periods of insufficient demand can damage supply then periods of excess demand might do the opposite. For example, those long-term unemployed individuals who effectively become disenfranchised during a period of a long and deep recession might be re-integrated into the workforce, and the damage done to their search intensity and effectiveness reversed, if the central bank deliberately engineers a tight labour market for an extended period of time—that is, a period in which labour is scarce and therefore employers may be more likely to turn to long-term unemployed individuals to fill vacancies. The world's leading monetary policymaker has tentatively made this argument (Yellen 2015b):

> Finally albeit more speculatively, such an environment might help reverse some of the significant supply-side damage that appears to have occurred in recent years, thereby improving Americans' standard of living.

This argument—keeping monetary policy looser than one otherwise might choose to do in order to repair the damage done by hysteresis during the crisis—is more likely to explain a significant deviation from the Taylor rule with the central bank choosing to remain at the lower bound when the output gap and the inflation outlook improve to the point where standard rules suggest lift-off. Indeed, in this scenario the path of policy rates may deviate from the policy rule *for an extended period* precisely because the central bank is trying to engineer a positive output gap (and corresponding inflation overshoot). However, at some point, the central bank would have to reduce that output gap and—like any boom—that would require raising rates above the neutral setting.

8.4   Reputational Concerns: Trust Arrives on Foot, but Leaves in a Ferrari

Much earlier, we discussed how interest rates do not tend to follow the random walk that one might expect if policymakers fully adjusted the stance of monetary policy in response to all the news, and that news was genuinely unpredictable, as policymakers imply (King 2006):

> The MPC reaches a new judgment each month, made afresh in the light of all the new information about the prospects for inflation. We don't decide in advance. So trying to give direct hints on the path of interest rates over the next few months risks deceiving financial markets into believing there are definite plans for the next few months when no such plans exist.

In practice, policy rates tend to be persistent, following relatively smooth cycles, with a sequence of changes in the same direction and very few reversals—that is, a hike following soon after a cut, and vice versa—or what economists refer to as gradualism in the conduct of monetary policy. Indeed, economists typically insert a lagged dependent variable in the policy rule in order to compensate for the inertia we see in the data, diluting the impact of current conditions on the output of the rule; for example, Sack and Wieland (2000) find a coefficient of the order of 0.8 on the lagged dependent variable, which implies a very gradual speed of adjustment to those current conditions.

The claim that there is genuine inertia in the policy rule is controversial. Rudebusch (2006) argues that sophisticated market participants should be able to exploit inertia in the conduct of policy because changes in the policy rate should be largely predictable since decisions today should reflect news that arrived in the past and is therefore known. In particular, the expected changes in policy rates implicit in market yields should do a good job of explaining actual changes in policy. Rudebusch (2006) argues that they do not.

One familiar explanation for the inertia we observe and in particular the surprisingly small number of reversals we see in the data is reputational concerns—that is, commentators and market participants have a habit of questioning the competence of central banks who U-turn, despite the fact we should expect to see U-turns in a world where policymakers respond to news as it arrives. Central bankers might then choose to draw out the process of reversing course to minimise the reputational damage; for example, in a discussion of whether the ECB would cut interest rates in September 2011 having raised rates in April and July, one respected analyst commented as follows (Randow and Black 2011):

> The language will probably shift to neutral on inflation and downside risks to growth, which is enough to flag that the ECB is on hold…That is the intermediate step before they would even consider any easing. It is very unlikely that the ECB would do a massive U-turn so soon. That is just not how it operates.

It is reasonable for central bankers to worry about their reputations; in the words of the Governor of the BoE: 'Trust arrives on foot, but leaves in a Ferrari.' Central banks depend on their reputations for competence to execute their core functions of monetary and financial stability: to guide market expectations about the future path of the economy and to quell panic in a crisis. The market may be wrong to question the competence of central bankers who reverse course in response to news, but a prudent policymaker would want to take that irrational reaction into account.

It seems likely that these reputational concerns are more powerful at the lower bound—that is, central bankers might expect that they would be heavily criticised if they were rapidly forced to return to the effective lower bound in the aftermath of an exit, and as a result, that might lead central bankers to delay leaving until they are sure that exit is a wise course of action. As with risk management, the policymaker is creating a policy rate surplus—a gap between the actual policy rate and the optimal rate—which would allow the policymaker to leave rates on hold in response to bad news after having left the lower bound, as opposed to having cut rates if the policymaker had left the lower bound when the policy rule suggested it was appropriate to exit. Once again, as with risk management, at some point after the eventual exit rates have to rise faster than the policy rule suggests as the policymaker closes off the policy rate surplus.

8.5   The Taylor Rule Meets the Secular Stagnation

The Taylor rule tells a central bank how to adjust the policy rate around a neutral setting in response to news on a handful of macroeconomic variables which serve as summary statistics of the wider information set that central bankers traditionally use to set policy. The output of the rule depends on which particular variables are chosen as the arguments of the rule or the calibrated or estimated sensitivity of the rule to those arguments. Change any of these elements and you change the dynamic response of interest rates to shocks around that neutral level suggested by the rule. For example, Bernanke (2015b) advocates using a modified Taylor rule, which places a higher weight on the output gap and uses a 'core' measure of inflation which strips out the impact of erratic factors (food and energy prices), which he notes tracks the actual policy rate reasonably well in the pre-crisis period and was consistent with the decision to remain at the lower bound during the recovery.

However, what became increasingly clear in the years following the crisis was that the problem with the Taylor rule was not with the particular choice of arguments or coefficients but with the intercept of the rule—the pre-crisis calibration of the neutral setting of interest rates in the rule to which the policy rate is presumed to converge as the arguments tend towards normal settings. The intercept of the policy rule reflects two factors: the inflation target (π^*) and an equilibrium real interest rate (r^*). The former should be known with certainty by the central bank; the latter is not. If you get the level of that rate wrong, then the intercept of the rule and hence the output of the rule for any given state of the economy will also be wrong.

The crux of the debate over the Taylor rule in the post-crisis period was over whether that equilibrium real rate had fallen, and if so, how far, and therefore why rates needed to be lower (and therefore stay at the lower bound for longer) for a given rate of inflation and output gap. This debate has come to be dominated by a phrase that originally belongs to Hansen (1939), but was resurrected by Larry Summers: secular stagnation (Summers 2013).

Although everyone agrees that a secular stagnation is consistent with persistently low real interest rates, there is no clear consensus about what the root cause of that phenomenon is. Some economists believe that the secular stagnation is a demand-side phenomenon; others that it is a supply-side phenomenon. With some justification, Eichengreen (2014) framed the secular stagnation as the economist's Rorschach test—everyone seems to see something different in the term. Teulings and Baldwin (2014) argue that there is fairly strong consensus that a 'workable definition' of secular stagnation is that a negative real interest rate is required to clear markets. However, that outcome is perfectly feasible with nominal interest rates above the lower bound so long as inflation expectations remain anchored on the inflation target.

Summers (2015) has a more extreme disequilibrium concept in mind: namely a 'chronic excess of savings over investment', with the market for loanable funds failing to clear at a full employment level of demand, because the real interest rate cannot fall far enough to encourage a sufficient level of demand to absorb supply, thanks to the lower bound on the nominal policy rate. The claim that markets fail to clear is important because it implies a first-order welfare loss.

It might be the case that the current and expected future path of the risk-free short-term real interest rate is constrained but that is not the rate which clears the actual markets for loanable funds. Even when governments borrow long term in financial markets, they will not pay a pure risk-free rate on their debt: the yield will also reflect compensation for the liquidity of the security the government issues, uncertainty over the future path of interest rates and even modest compensation for sovereign credit risk. When small- and medium-sized companies borrow money from banks, the risk premia in the cost of debt will be substantial. Whether these markets clear will depend on how these risk premia respond to a demand–supply imbalance.

Some economists believe that risk premia are immutable where such forces are concerned, being instead pinned down by 'pure' fundamentals and therefore the constraint on the risk-free short-term real interest rate carries over into the interest rates into all other markets for loanable funds (Summers 2014b). Others believe that risk premia will compress given an excess supply of savings as investors chase yield, and therefore interest rates may fall to clear these markets, albeit with investors no longer obtaining adequate compensation for risk (Summers 2015).

In passing, the reader may be forgiven for being confused by this sudden insistence on a chronic excess supply of savings and that yields have not fallen far enough to clear the markets for loanable fund. After all, a consistent theme in the post-crisis policy debate has been the extent to which credit has been rationed: a situation of chronic excess demand where yields have not risen far enough to clear markets, because in a world of asymmetric information potential creditors believe that raising rates beyond a certain point is counterproductive, in that it encourages high-risk behaviour and high-risk customers (Stiglitz and Weiss 1981).

The bottom line is that a shift in the balance between demand and supply in the market for loanable funds has led to a material decline in the real equilibrium interest rate which will have to ultimately be reflected in the stance of monetary policy (nominal interest rates) if markets are to clear, justifying a longer staycation at the lower bound. For example, Bernanke (2015b) plays down the significance of the fact that the output of his modified Taylor rule crept into positive territory in early 2015 whilst the policy rate remained unchanged, arguing that the modified rule:

> like the original Taylor rule, assumes that the long-run real funds rate is 2 percent. If the equilibrium real funds rate is lower than that, as both financial markets and FOMC participants appear to believe, then the modified Taylor rule...may currently be predicting a funds rate that is too high.

Whilst the perceived low level of equilibrium real interest rates appeared to justify the Fed and BoE remaining at the lower bound for longer than an unmodified Taylor rule would imply, policymakers did not believe that rates needed to stay at the lower bound forever. The equilibrium real interest rate was expected to gradually rise—for reasons that we shall go on to discuss later in this section—and that implied a corresponding rise in the policy rate, albeit a limited and gradual one. For example, Yellen (2015a) argued:

> [T]he economy's underlying strength has been gradually improving, and the equilibrium real federal funds rate has been gradually rising. Although the recent appreciation of the dollar is likely to weigh on U.S. exports over time, I nonetheless anticipate further diminution of the headwinds just noted over the next couple of years, and as the equilibrium real funds rate continues to rise, it will accordingly be appropriate to raise the actual level of the real federal funds rate in tandem, all else being equal.

8.6   Natural Rates for Unnatural Times

Before turning to discuss three stories of secular stagnation and chronically low real interest rates, we shall first provide a brief taxonomy of distinct but related concepts of equilibrium real interest rates which crop up in this debate (Archibald and Hunter 2001).

8.6.1 The Natural (Short) Rate

In a fully flexible economy, prices instantaneously jump up or down in response to shocks in order that the expected future path of prices (inflation expectations) can help deliver the 'natural' real interest rate that immediately clears markets. In the real world, sticky prices and sticky behaviour mean that markets won't clear so central bankers must use monetary levers to influence nominal rates in order to approximately engineer the real interest rate that delivers this efficient outcome, closing any gap between the level of aggregate demand and supply which would otherwise lead to pressure on inflation to deviate from the target.

This 'natural' real interest rate that instantaneously clears markets in the most extreme theoretical benchmark of a fully flexible economy can, and almost certainly does, move through time, both across and within the business cycle. The real interest rate that central bankers engineer will have to respect those shifts in the natural rate if monetary policy is to help stabilise demand in the face of shocks. The fact that real interest rates looked low by historical standards in the recovery that followed the crisis was therefore no guarantee that the monetary stance was actually 'loose': the natural rate could have fallen so far that what looks like a low real interest rate is not low enough to prevent a contraction in demand given the range of factors weighing on spending. Put another way, real rates might have had to be this low just to stop the recovery losing momentum and the output gap widening.

Many of the reasons why the natural rate may have been so low during this period are discussed elsewhere in this book or the companion volume: fiscal consolidation with governments spending less and taxing more; balance sheet repair in the banking sector and regulatory reform leading to tighter credit conditions in retail markets; high debt burdens in parts of the corporate and household sector and increased fear and uncertainty attenuating the interest rate sensitivity of domestic demand; and weak demand overseas (for the same reasons). Collectively these factors are often referred to as the 'headwinds'.

In passing, a lower natural rate helps to explain away a concern about the effectiveness of monetary policy raised by the former Governor of the BoE. King (2013) correctly notes that monetary policy works by stealing spending from the future to bolster demand today, as lower real interest rates reduce the relative price of spending today versus tomorrow. However, King worries that policymakers cannot persistently pull off the same trick: 'when tomorrow arrives, an even larger stimulus is required to bring forward yet more spending from the future. As time passes, larger and larger doses of stimulus are required.' Under this thesis, the attempts by central banks to consistently support demand in the post-crash era through ever looser monetary policy are doomed to fail because at some point households will no longer be willing to bring forward spending. The secular stagnation hypothesis turns this argument upon its head: central banks may have tried to encourage people to bring forward spending but they did not take real interest rates low enough given the lower natural rate to have the desired effect, and that explains why there was no robust recovery in demand or closure in the output gap.

We have argued that one way to assess the monetary stance is to compare actual real interest rates to the theoretical benchmark of the natural rate. Alternatively, we can use the expected and the actual change in the output gap respectively as *ex ante* and *ex post* diagnostics on the monetary stance. For example, one could argue that the monetary stance is loose *ex ante* if the real interest rate is sufficiently low such that it is expected to provide sufficient stimulus to aggregate demand given the anticipated 'headwinds' to ensure that the output gap is set to narrow (become less negative, or more positive), and loose *ex post* if it ultimately engineers that narrowing given the actual headwinds. Note that these two rule of thumb diagnostics on the stance are subtly different: failure to calibrate the headwinds or tailwinds correctly can lead the actual degree of stimulus delivered (and resulting change in the output gap) to differ from what was intended. Also, to be clear, whether the stance was optimal in any of these jurisdictions—whether, for example, the output gap narrowed at a sufficiently rapid pace—is a different question.

8.6.2   The Neutral Rate and the Term Structure of Natural

The 'headwinds' narrative explains why today's natural rate of interest might be low by historical standards. However, those headwinds should abate at some point, so we might expect to see a gradual increase in the equilibrium real interest rate as time passes. For example, in remarks shortly before he left his post, former BoE Deputy Governor Charles Bean argued that Bank Rate might eventually return to pre-crisis levels (James 2014):

> I wouldn't want to say it will be back there in 10 years, but I think it's plausible over the very long run…that these headwinds will abate.

One can envisage a term structure of the natural rate: the equilibrium short real rates that are expected to prevail at different time horizons in the future. Those forward rates are generically referred to as *the* neutral rate, although the term is used to refer to slightly different concepts:

- *Yellen's* (2005) *intermediate rate concept*: 'Conceptually, policy can be deemed "neutral" when the federal funds rate reaches a level that is consistent with full employment of labor and capital resources over the intermediate run.'

- *Blinder's* (1998) *steady state concept*: 'I propose to define the neutral real interest rate as the interest rate that equates GDP along this steady-state IS curve to potential output.'
- *ECB staff's* (2014) *distant concept*: 'To identify longer-term determinants, a neutral stance concept is advisable that abstracts from business cycle dynamics. In line with this view, the equilibrium real interest rate is imagined to be given by the real interest rate that is expected to prevail in the distant future, when the effects of all shocks hitting the economy have faded away.'

One way to differentiate between these concepts of neutrality is to distinguish between stock and flow concepts. Economists typically think in terms of flow concepts of equilibrium—for example, a working definition of internal balance is the inflation rate in line with the target and an output gap of zero. However, the logical conclusion of the ECB's definition that 'the effects of all shocks hitting the economy have only truly faded away' is that all stock imbalances that were created whilst the economy was in disequilibrium have also unwound, and that would require that the capital stock, the net foreign asset position and so on, would all have to be back in equilibrium too.

For an open economy, there is always an important international dimension to the calibration of neutrality. In the past, present and no doubt the future too, the MPC has had to adjust the stance of monetary policy to compensate for flow imbalances in our major trading partners. For example, one reason why the stance of monetary policy in the UK was kept at historically low levels whilst the domestic economy recovered was the depressed state of demand in the Eurozone. So long as there are global headwinds, the domestic stance of policy will have to adjust, so one can think of an intermediate equilibrium rate oscillating around a truly long-run measure which will only emerge when (if) the global economy is in equilibrium.

8.6.3 The Natural Long Rate (the long run long rate)

When it comes to evaluating the monetary stance, the focus in the academic literature has traditionally been on the front end of the curve, which makes sense in a world where the central bank influences monetary conditions through its control of the overnight rate. However, in a QE world, where central banks have eased monetary conditions via purchases of long-dated assets we may need to broaden our horizons, depending on our model of the transmission mechanism of asset purchases.

Asset purchases can have a persistent impact on the yield curve in the presence of preferred habitat demand for those assets. By reducing the net supply of assets for which there is a price inelastic demand, the central bank can shock the relative price of long- versus short-term bonds. This is a real phenomenon that should persist so long as the central bank influences quantities—that is, so long as the central bank continues to influence the net supply of assets by reinvesting the proceeds as assets in its portfolio mature (this is sometimes referred to as the 'stock theory of QE'). That real effect should endure over and above any transitory impact on nominal yields via the stimulus imparted through asset prices which should be reflected in the expected future path of activity, inflation and the policy rate. If that relative price shift persists—if it is not arbitraged away—then it follows that long spot real rates can no longer be reliably decomposed into a sequence of short real rates that the rational 'asset-class agnostic' investor (i.e., the investor that does not exhibit preferred habitat demand) expects to emerge in the future and a real term premium reflecting the compensation that this investor demands for the uncertainty around the future path of real rates. Instead, the price of long-dated assets has been inflated above fair value by a battle of wills between a central bank determined to achieve its inflation mandate and preferred habitat investors who are determined to fulfil their own mandates. In these circumstances, we should take great care in looking at forward rates derived from the yield curve and inferring something about the expected future path of short rates.

If long rates matter—that is, if long rates influence activity—and central banks can have a lasting impact on them, then an assessment of the current stance based on a comparison of the short real rate to a natural analogue is incomplete. We should be thinking in terms of a set of real natural rates at different horizons which collectively clear markets or a natural rate curve which has been structurally flattened at the long end by asset purchases. In particular, if central banks have depressed long real yields below the levels that would otherwise emerge in equilibrium in the absence of central bank purchases then the monetary stance is structurally loose at the long end so long as the stock of purchased assets remains non-trivial in size. It follows that an assessment of the stance which focuses purely on the short real rate in this world would understate the quantum of stimulus in the system. Put another way, so long as the stock of purchased assets continues to depress long real yields, the short real rate must be somewhat higher to compensate in order to clear markets (stabilise demand).

Before moving on, it is worth briefly flagging two caveats around this argument of incorporating the long natural rate in an assessment of the monetary stance: the state-contingent stock theory of QE and the fact that the monetary stance is not determined at home.

There is a school of thought that the size of the preferred habitat portfolio rebalancing effects will depend on the circumstances under which central banks conduct asset purchases (Miles and Schanz 2014). As noted earlier, some economists think that in a well-functioning market the asset-class agnostic investors will be able to arbitrage away the 'distortions' that QE generated, ironing out the kinks that shocks to net supply would otherwise create in the yield curve. Even in a perfect world, these distortions may not completely wash out if arbitrageurs are risk averse and the shape of the yield curve can move in mysterious ways. However, in the dysfunctional markets in which the first round of assets purchases were conducted, shocks to net supply can have much more powerful effects because the risk-averse arbitrageurs may be capital constrained and lack the capacity to lean against the distortions that QE creates even if they wanted to. The state-contingent stock theory of QE suggests that if assets purchases had been conducted in current market conditions then the impact on long rates would have been far more modest. By extension, even if the central bank holds the stock of purchased assets constant, the impact of that stock on relative prices and therefore the monetary stance will fade through time.

The financial markets for long-dated sovereign debt are reasonably integrated, with a significant fraction of the investor base willing and able to buy and sell assets in multiple jurisdictions. In a preferred habitat world, it follows that shocks to net supply in one market can easily be transferred into others: that is, QE here will influence yields everywhere. Indeed, Neely (2010) documents exactly this global transmission of Fed QE. It follows that this element of the monetary stance is partially determined at the global level. For example, the launch of the ECB's QE programme likely contributed to lower long-term yields in the UK and the USA.

8.7 Explanation (i): Safety Traps

A decline in the equilibrium real interest rate to very low levels suggests an imbalance between high levels of desired savings and little appetite to invest. That is not such a surprise, given what we know about the cyclical drivers of savings and investment in a highly uncertain environment. We should expect to see a transitory surge in precautionary savings until households feel comfortable with the stock of liquid assets that they hold. We should expect to see a lull in investment, as companies delay paying the sunk costs of capital expenditure in the hope of learning more about the returns on the project. Of course, we do not really know how uncertain, and in particular how afraid of tail risks, households and companies are. So one way to rationalise the post-crash path of the equilibrium real interest rate is that households and companies have been, and remain, very scared about the future. This is a familiar 'headwinds' argument. However, there is a more extreme variant of this fear and uncertainty mechanism which should be described in its own right: the safety trap (Caballero and Farhi 2015).

Imagine a world in which there are safe and risky assets and there is a subset of investors who only feel comfortable holding the former. In this environment, changes in the demand for and supply of safe assets would naturally lead to a change in relative prices: the risk-free rate and the risk premium embedded in the return on risky assets. However, there is a limit to how far prices can accommodate a shift in demand given the lower bound on the policy rate. At some point, a flight to safety during a crisis can run up against that constraint—with conservative agents only willing to hold safe assets—and the excess demand for safe assets can only be choked off by a fall in output (and income), at which point the economy is said to be in a safety trap.

When it comes to the relative supply of safe and risky assets, there are several factors at play in the short run.

- *Crises expose fakes*: Perceptions of whether the financial assets that public and private sector institutions issue qualify as safe or not can change from boom to bust, often discontinuously, shifting the relative supply of risky and safe assets. The change in sentiment over structured credit and Eurozone sovereign debt during the current crisis are cases in point.
- *Credit ratings*: The preferred habitat demand discussed elsewhere in this book is often a function of the implicit or explicit mandates under which institutional investors operate—that is, they can only invest in, say, AAA-rated or investment grade assets, or do not feel comfortable investing outside that asset class. Changes in credit ratings—and in particular, changes implemented by all the agencies—will therefore mechanically adjust the stock of safe assets for this important subclass of investor.
- *The immediate policy response*: The appropriate policy response to a safety trap is to lean against the sudden collapse in the supply of safe assets, often via the central bank's balance sheet. The ECB's very long-term refinancing operations (vLTROs), in which the ECB injected cash into the system in return for collateral through three-year refinancing operations, is a case in point.

Looking further ahead, the shortage in the supply of safe assets may ease for several reasons:

- *Recovery breeds security*: If policymakers are able to deliver a sustainable recovery in demand that might reduce both the perceived quantity and price of risk—that is, the marginal investor may perceive that a given claim is less 'risky' and may be less risk averse. The impact of a robust recovery in nominal GDP growth on debt sustainability and therefore the riskiness of, say, sovereign debt in the periphery is a case in point.
- *Implementing the prudential agenda*: A key lesson learned from the crash is that prevention is better than cure when it comes to financial crises. Toughening up the micro-prudential standards and implementing a rigorous macro-prudential regime on top should have a lasting impact on the likelihood and severity of tail risks, and hence the perceived riskiness of different asset classes.
- *Alchemy*: Economic agents can engineer new safe assets, which represent a claim on existing or future assets, which could meet the demand for those assets. The post-crisis drive to create a new model of vanilla asset-backed securities that do not suffer from the flaws of the pre-crisis vintage and could therefore provide a sustainable model for the distribution of credit risk is a case in point.

On the demand side of the market, there are several instances where the conduct of policy at home and abroad may have contributed to the flight to quality:

- *Liquidity regulation*: The post-crisis reforms which require banks to increase the stock of high-quality liquid assets on their balance sheets to manage liquidity risk will have mechanically increased the demand for safe assets.
- *Margin requirements*: The need to post higher margin in derivative transactions, whether central cleared or conducted on a bilateral basis, will have also increased the demand for high-quality collateral. Moreover, institutions may also hold a precautionary buffer of safe assets to manage margin calls (Houben and Slingenberg 2013).
- *QE*: Where central banks purchased government bonds and other safe assets in order to achieve their price stability remits, they can have a significant impact on the net supply of safe assets to private investors—indeed, the debate around the ECB's QE programme often touches on the concern that the central bank is generating a scarcity of high-quality assets.

- *Reserves management*: Official institutions in a number of countries have accumulated a significant stock of high-quality assets—typically government debt issued by a select number of sovereign issuers, chief among them US Treasuries—in the pursuit of macroeconomic objectives, in particular with respect to exchange rate targets.

The safety trap thesis is related to the pre-crisis idea that fear of catastrophe—an unlikely event in which individuals suffer a very large fall in consumption and welfare—can explain why safe assets can offer very low returns in equilibrium with a correspondingly chunky risk premium in the return on risk assets (Rietz 1988; Barro 2006). This argument has been used to explain the low rate of return on gilts (UK conventional government bonds) in the post-crisis period (Broadbent 2012; Miles 2014). However, in order for the mechanism to apply to gilts it would have to be the case that investors were confident that this asset *would* pay-out in a catastrophe. Given that the events of the sovereign debt crisis in the European periphery should have been uppermost in the minds of investors during this period and the oft-stated claim that the reason why the UK government would not suffer the same fate was that it had retained control over the printing press and could therefore inflate its way out of a debt problem, it is not clear why investors would believe that an asset issued by a sovereign which pays a fixed nominal return necessarily qualifies as a good asset to hold in the event of a catastrophe which would likely involve a fiscal crisis.

8.8   Explanation (ii): A Dearth of Investment Opportunities

One natural perspective on secular stagnation is that the low level of real interest rates and the anaemic demand for loanable funds reflects a chronic lack of profitable investment opportunities. In short, the advanced economies have an underlying productivity problem. The chief advocate of this view is Robert Gordon, who argues that (Gordon 2012):

> Since Solow's seminal work in the 1950s, economic growth has been regarded as a continuous process that will persist forever. But there was virtually no economic growth before 1750, suggesting that the rapid progress made over the past 250 years could well be a unique episode in human history rather than a guarantee of endless future advance at the same rate. The frontier established by the US for output per capita, and the UK before it, gradually began to grow more rapidly after 1750, reached its fastest growth rate in the middle of the 20th century, and has slowed down since. It is in the process of slowing down further.

According to Gordon, there have been three pivotal moments in economy history: three industrial revolutions since the eighteenth century that involved a burst of innovative activity which were then followed by an extended process of incremental improvement in which the full potential of the original innovation is exhausted (for completeness, he identifies the first ["steam, railroads"] as occurring between 1750 and 1830; the second ["electricity, internal combustion engine, running water, indoor toilets, communications, entertainment, chemicals, petroleum"] as occurring between 1870 and 1900; and the third from 1960 to the present day [computers, the web, mobile phones]). Gordon (2015) argues that the beneficial impact of the third revolution on productivity has largely run its course—most of the economy has already benefited from the third of those revolutions; and that the capital stock used in the workplace and the productivity of the workforce has changed very little from a decade ago. Before moving on, it is worth noting that this claim is controversial. Indeed, other economists argue precisely the opposite: that we stand on the cusp of another industrial revolution (Brynjolfsson and McAfee 2014; Mokyr 2014). These 'techno-optimists' believe that the current rate of progress in the fields of artificial intelligence, materials science and genetic engineering will ultimately translate into healthy rates of productivity growth—for example, Hamermesh (2014) argues that the rise of 3D printing will spur a burst of productivity in a wide range of industries from the manufacture of airplanes to electrical equipment where companies produce numerous replications of the same part for later assembly into the final product.

An alternative—and arguably contradictory—explanation for the apparent anaemic demand for loanable funds is that the price of investment—the cost of new capital goods—has fallen through time (Summers 2014a). Cheaper capital goods might make for a lower spend on capital goods but the impact on potential supply is more complex, and depends on the ease with which companies can substitute towards cheaper inputs in the production process. Once you move beyond the Leontief production function you should expect to see a downward trend in the relative price of capital goods driving an upward trend in the constant price ratio of investment to GDP (Ellis and Groth 2003). In plain English, the price effect (as capital goods become cheaper, you spend less on investment projects) ought to be at least partially offset by a substitution effect (as capital goods become cheaper, you buy more of them), and the easier it is to substitute towards capital the stronger that substitution effect is. A related thesis is that in an increasingly digital age, companies don't need as much capital to produce output—so the demand for loanable funds has been hit by a double whammy of a decline in the price of capital goods and a reduced need for capital goods. However, that reduced demand for finance to fund investments in physical capital may be partially or even entirely offset by an increased demand for investments in training and R&D (Rajan 2006).

Gordon's and Summers' theses have nothing to do with the crisis: the productivity dividend from the Third Industrial Revolution was already petering out or perversely the surge in productivity in the capital goods-producing sector (that drove the decline in the relative price of capital goods) was picking up pace before 2007. However, there is another school of thought that says that the sudden dearth in investable opportunities and the corresponding fall in real interest rates might reflect an(other) aftershock of the crisis. We have already discussed the concept of hysteresis—the idea that a deep and protracted recession can leave a lasting scar on the supply side of the economy, reducing the level of potential supply. There is a more extreme concept of super hysteresis in which a depression can leave a lasting scar on the *rate of growth* of potential supply, which implies a much larger hit on the level of potential supply over time (Ball 2014; Blanchard et al. 2015). In theory, super hysteresis would require that a deep and protracted recession that follows a financial crisis damages the underlying drivers of economic growth through the innovation of new products and processes and the reallocation of resources—for example, by somehow lowering spending on R&D or more broadly investments in human capital, or via regulatory reforms which restrict the activity of financial intermediaries (Blanchard et al. 2015).

Although the post-crisis productivity puzzle might give us pause for thought, this sounds like a speculative hypothesis. It is notoriously difficult to estimate whether the 'trend' rate of growth has slowed in real time because we lack reliable data on what is happening now (and, by definition, in the near future). Likewise, from a theoretical perspective it is only when the economy recovers that we can convincingly differentiate between a significant levels adjustment in supply that occurs over the period when demand remains depressed (hysteresis) and a permanent hit on the growth rate (super hysteresis). Finally, we also need to be careful about interpreting the apparent robust trend in growth in the pre-crisis period—as we discussed earlier, growth in demand might have outstripped supply over this period, with an increasingly large positive output gap suppressed by a flat Phillips curve.

8.9   Explanation (iii): The Global Savings Glut

The last of our three stories of secular stagnation predates the renewed interest in the terminology. Almost a decade before Larry Summers started talking about secular stagnation, Ben Bernanke was talking about a global savings glut depressing long-term real interest rates. In 2005, Fed Chairman Greenspan famously referred to the puzzling behaviour of long-term interest rates in the USA as a puzzle: long-term interest rates had trended lower despite the fact that the Fed had raised the policy rate by 150 basis points (Greenspan 2005). Bernanke (2005) argued that whilst this yield conundrum of low long-term real interest rates might be a puzzle from a national perspective, it was more explicable from a global perspective.

Bernanke argued that a number of factors had disturbed the balance between desired savings and investment at the global level in the preceding decade that had contributed to a decline in the rate that clears that market. In part, the explanation lay in the advanced economies with the ageing baby boom cohort looking to save in anticipation of retirement in the decades to come. It is only natural that capital-rich ageing economies would look to invest part of those excess savings abroad in search of profitable investment opportunities. However, the more interesting aspect of the savings glut story relates to the emerging economies.

Following the East Asian crisis of the late 1990s, there was a conscious decision among many emerging economies to build up a significant stock of precautionary reserves of foreign exchange reserves that could act as a buffer in a future crisis, and which would coincidentally help deliver a favourable exchange rate that might support exports. This strategy of accumulating foreign exchange (FX) reserves often involved the official sector in the emerging markets purchasing US government debt, given the special status of the US dollar as the world's reserve currency, helping to inflate the price and depress the yield—in much the same way that a QE programme does; for example, Warnock and Warnock (2009) estimate that in the absence of foreign inflows, 10-year US Treasuries would have been 80 basis points higher. National savings in the emerging economies may have been aggravated by the absence of an effective social safety net, with households forced to self-insure against future risks through precautionary savings (Mendoza et al. 2009). Finally, the rise in oil prices towards the tail-end of the Great Stability may have added to the savings glut as higher oil prices transferred purchasing power at the global level towards the oil exporting nations, and where some of the proceeds were saved and not spent, those funds would have been recycled back into global financial markets.

The nature of the conundrum may have changed but the fundamental thrust of Bernanke's argument remains: that long-term real interest rates should be heavily influenced, if not uniquely determined, by global forces. Indeed, Bernanke has critiqued the parochial tone of the much of the debate about the sources of and solution to the secular stagnation (Bernanke 2015a):

My greatest concern about Larry's formulation, however, is the lack of attention to the international dimension. He focuses on factors affecting domestic capital investment and household spending. All else equal, however, the availability of profitable capital investments anywhere in the world should help defeat secular stagnation at home…In short, in an open economy, secular stagnation requires that the returns to capital investment be permanently low everywhere, not just in the home economy.

On that basis, if we want to argue that the low level of real interest rates will persist indefinitely then we need to believe that the drivers of the global savings glut will also persist indefinitely (Buiter et al. 2015). However, that is by no means a certain outcome:

- *The oil glut*: For so long as oil prices remain at their new low level—which may be some time given that the decline in oil prices appears to have been driven by news on supply—the contribution of oil exporters to the savings glut is likely to be significantly diminished, if not reversed, with some nations running down stocks of financial assets to fund government spending at home.
- *The world got old*: Demography may have depressed real interest rates in the past with a disproportionately large share of the population of prime working age saving for retirement, but this trend will soon reverse. As more and more people retire the household savings rate should naturally fall, and that should lead interest rates to rise. Indeed, Goodhart and Erfuth (2014) argue that the current low level of real interest rates are not the new normal, but rather an 'extreme artefact' of an ephemeral constellation of factors (demography chief among them) that will soon fade, and that real interest rates could have risen back to their historical average of around 2.5–3 % within a decade.
- *Emerging economies come of age*: Some emerging economies may have exported secular stagnation through their contribution to the global savings glut, but 'micro' institutional reforms in the emerging economies—such as improvements in the social safety net and financial deepening—might reduce the incentive for households to self-insure, reducing gross savings in these economies. Moroever, a shift in 'macro' strategy—to rebalance the economy away from exports towards consumption—could lead to a further decline in savings flowing out of the emerging economies.

8.10 The Federal Reserve Lifts-Off, but the Old Lady Is Not for Turning

16 December 2015 was a big day in financial markets. The world's most important central bank decided to raise rates from the floor. The FOMC agreed to raise the target range for the federal funds rate from 0 to 0.25 to a new range of 0.25 to 0.5 %. In order to implement the change in policy in an environment of excess reserves the Fed used two tools: raising the rate on required and excess reserves to the top of the range (0.50 %) and using reverse repurchase operations at a rate consistent with the bottom of the range (0.25 %), with the former geared towards creating a floor for the banking sector, and the latter for the shadow banking sector. However, when it came to the Fed's asset portfolio, there was no change. The FOMC decided to continue reinvesting principal payments until such time as 'the normalization of the level of the federal funds rate is well under way'—a form of words consistent with the MPC's guidance of needing to create room to cut if the economy turned down.

The decision was hardly a shock: the FOMC had telegraphed in advance that a change in rates was almost certainly coming. However, whilst the market might have been prepared for Fed lift-off, there remained a clear difference of view between market participants and the Fed over the likely path of the policy rate. The so-called FOMC dots—the pictographic representation of the individual views of FOMC members on the appropriate path of the policy—remained some way above the expectations priced into market securities. The median view within the FOMC was that 100 basis points of tightening would be required in both 2016 and 2017, and almost as much again in 2018, at which point rates would be close to neutral, with a longer-run policy rate of 3.5 %. Market prices suggested a far more gradual pace of tightening with only 50 basis points of hikes in 2016.

There might have been a view that where the Fed leads the BoE soon follows. For example, the Economist had published an article in August 2015 that concluded based on over 40 years of data that 'it is obvious that the British central bank follows the lead of its younger American cousin'. However, the MPC was keen to dissuade investors from expecting that the BoE was in any hurry to follow the Fed. The Minutes of the December policy meeting emphasised that there was no mechanical link between the policy stance on either side of the pond (BoE 2015):

Turning to the monetary policy stance, the Committee noted that while the ECB had recently announced further stimulatory measures, the probability attached by financial market participants to a tightening in US monetary policy at the FOMC's December meeting had risen to a high level. Meanwhile, market expectations for UK monetary policy were for a further period of unchanged interest rates. There was no mechanical link between UK policy and those of other central banks, and the UK policy stance would be determined ultimately by the inflation outlook here.

Indeed, the Bank was in the process of pushing back on expectations of an imminent rate hike. In a speech in July, the Governor had observed: '[T]he decision as to when to start such a process of adjustment will likely come into sharper relief around the turn of this year' (Carney 2015b). But when the moment arrived the Committee was in no mood to hike. The Governor used an interview to mark the halfway point in his term of office that happened to fall in the week of the Fed rate hike to give a clear signal that the conditions required for the Bank to raise rates had *not* been met (Giles 2015). He would soon go on to double down on that message in his first speech of 2016 (Carney 2016):

> [W]hat are the prospects for a rate rise in the UK? Last summer I said that the decision as to when to start raising Bank Rate would likely come into sharper relief around the turn of this year. Well the year has turned, and, in my view, the decision proved straightforward: now is not yet the time to raise interest rates.

The Fed might have raised rates but the Old Lady was not (yet) for turning. Even in late 2015, market prices suggested that investors were not anticipating an imminent rise in Bank Rate. But in the wake of Carney's intervention, those expectations were pushed back still further. As the date of the referendum on the UK's continued membership of the European Union drew ever closer expectations of the first hike started to disappear over the horizon, although that mean expectation likely reflected an average across a bimodal distribution, with policy likely to follow very different paths depending on the outcome of the vote. Indeed, by the time of the April meeting the Committee was going out of its way to signal that it was minded to sit on its hands until the result was clear (BoE 2016):

> [R]eferendum effects are likely to make macroeconomic and financial market indicators harder to interpret over the next few months, and the Committee is likely to react more cautiously to data news over this period than would normally be the case.

In the event, the referendum result would unleash a fresh round of monetary easing, with the Bank restarting purchases of government debt, launching a corporate bond buying programme, cutting Bank Rate and unveiling a Term Funding Scheme to encourage the commercial banks to pass through the rate cut. But that is a story for another day.

References

Archibald, J., & Hunter, L. (2001). What is the neutral interest rate, and how can we use it? *Reserve Bank of New Zealand Bulletin, 64*(3), 15–28.

Asso, P., Kahn, G., & Leeson, R. (2010). The Taylor rule and the practice of central banking. Federal Reserve Bank of Kansas City Working Paper, 10–05.

Ball, L. (2014). *Long-term damage from the Great Recession in OECD countries.* NBER Working Paper 20185.

Barro, R. (2006). Rare disasters and assets markets in the twentieth century. *Quarterly Journal of Economics, 121*(3), 823–866.

Barro, R., & Gordon, D. (1983). Rules, discretion and repuation in a model of monetary policy. *Journal of Monetary Economics, 12*, 101–121.

Bernanke, B. (2005, March 10). *The global saving glut and the U.S. current account deficit.* Speech.

Bernanke, B. (2010, January 3). Monetary policy and the housing bubble. *Speech.*

Bernanke, B. (2015a). *Why are interest rates so low, part 2: Secular stagnation.* Blog.

Bernanke, B. (2015b). *The Taylor rule: A benchmark for monetary policy?* Blog, Brookings.

Bernanke, B., & Mishkin, F. (1997). Inflation targeting. NBER Working 5893.

Blanchard, O., Cerutti, E., & Summers, L. (2015). *Inflation and activity.* IMF Working Paper 15/230.

Blinder, A. (1998). *Central banking in theory and practice.* Cambridge, MA: MIT Press.

BoE. (2015c, December 10). Minutes of the December 2015 Monetary Policy Committee meeting.

BoE. (2016, April 14). Minutes of the April 2016 Monetary Policy Committee meeting.

Broadbent, B. (2012, May 28). *Costly capital and the risk of rare disasters.* Speech.

Broadbent, B. (2015, November 5). Comments in Inflation Report press conference.

Brynjolfsson, E., & McAfee, A. (2014). *The second machine age: Work, progress, and prosperity in a time of brilliant technologies.* New York: WW Norton & Company.

Buiter, W., Rahbari, E., & Seydl, J. (2015, June 5). *Secular stagnation: The time for one-armed policy is over.* VoxEU.

Caballero, R., & Farhi, E. (2015). *The safety trap.* mimeo.

Carney, M. (2015a, May 13). Comments in May Inflation Report press conference.

Carney, M. (2015b, July 16). *From Lincoln to Lothbury.* Speech.

Carney, M. (2016, January 16). *The turn of the year*. Speech.

Cúrdia, V., & Ferrero, A. (2013, August). How stimulatory are large-scale asset purchases? *Federal Reserve Bank of San Francisco Economic Letter*.

ECB. (2014c). The Phillips curve relationship in the euro area. *ECB Monthly Bulletin, July*, 99–114.

Eichengreen, B. (2014). Secular stagnation: A review of the issues. In C. Teulings & R. Baldwin (Eds.), *Secular stagnation: Facts, causes and cures*. VoxEU.

Ellis, C., & Groth, C. (2003). Long-run equilibrium ratios of business investment to output in the United Kingdom. *Bank of England Quarterly Bulletin*, Summer, 177–187.

Evans, C., Fisher, J., Gourio, F., & Krane, S. (2015). Risk management for monetary policy near the zero lower bound. *Brookings Paper on Economic Activity*. Spring, 141–219.

Giles, C. (2015, December 15). Carney defends forward guidance. *Financial Times*.

Goodhart, C., & Erfuth, P. (2014, November 4). *Demography and economics*. VoxEU.

Gordon, R. (2012). Is US economic growth over? Faltering innovation confronts the six headwinds. *CEPR Policy Insights, 63*, 1–13.

Gordon, R. (2015). Secular stagnation: A supply-side view. *American Economic Review, 105*(5), 54–59.

Greenspan, A. (2004, January 3). Risk and uncertainty in monetary policy. *Speech*.

Greenspan, A. (2005, February 16). Testimony to the U.S. Senate Committee on Banking, Housing, and Urban Affairs.

Hamermesh, D. (2014, August 12). 3-D printing will be a manufacturing engine for the economy. *New York Times*.

Hansen, A. (1939). Economic progress and declining population growth. *American Economic Review, 29*(1), 1–15.

Houben, A., & Slingenberg, J. (2013). Collateral scarcity and asset encumbrance. *Banque de France Financial Stability Review, 17*, 197–206.

James, W. (2014, June 30). *Bank of England's Bean says expectations for interest rate rises "reasonable"*. Reuters.

King, M. (1997, October 29). The inflation target five years on. *Speech*.

King, M. (2006, June 21). Speech at the Mansion House.

King, M. (2013, January 22). Speech.

Mendoza, E., Quadrini, V., & Rios-Rull, J. (2009). Financial integration, financial deepness and global imbalances. *Journal of Political Economy, 117*(3), 371–416.

Miles, D. (2014, February 27). *The transition to a new normal for monetary policy*. Speech.

Miles, D., & Schanz, J. (2014). The relevance or otherwise of the central bank's balance sheet. *Journal of International Economics, 92*, S103–S116.

Mokyr, J. (2014). *Secular stagnation? Not in your life*. In C. Teulings & R. Baldwin (Eds.), *Secular stagnation: Facts, causes and cures*. VoxEU.

Neely, C. (2010). *The large-scale asset purchases had large international effects*. Federal Reserve Bank of St. Louis Working Paper 2010–018G.

Orphanides, A., & Wieland, V. (2008, July/August). Economic projections and rules of thumb for monetary policy. *Federal Reserve Bank of St. Louis Review*, 307–324.

Posen, A. (2015). *A more inflexible Fed would cause more crises*. Peterson Institute for International Economics Real Time Economic Issues Watch.

Rajan, R. (2006, November 16). Investment restraint, the liquidity glut, and global imbalances. *Speech*.

Randow, J., & Black, J. (2011, September 8). Trichet may choose liquidity over rate cut as crisis worsens. *Bloomberg News*.

Reifschneider, D., Wascher, W., & Wilcox, D. (2013). Aggregate Supply in the United States: Recent developments and implications for the conduct of monetary policy. *Finance and Economics Discussion Series*, 2013–77.

Rietz, T. (1988). The equity risk premium: A solution. *Journal of Monetary Economics, 22*(1), 117–131.

Rudebusch, G. (2006). Monetary policy inertia: Fact or fiction? *International Journal of Central Banking, 2*(4), 85–135.

Sack, B., & Wieland, V. (2000). Interest-rate smoothing and optimal monetary policy: A review of recent empirical evidence. *Journal of Economics and Business, 52*(1–2), 205–228.

Stiglitz, J., & Weiss, A. (1981). Credit rationing in markets with imperfect information. *American Economic Review, 71*(3), 393–410.

Summers, L. (2013, November 8). Remarks at IMF Fourteenth Annual Research Conference in Honor of Stanley Fischer.

Summers, L. (2014a). US economic prospects. *Business Economics, 49*(2), 65–73.

Summers, L. (2014b). Reflections on the new secular stagnation hypothesis. In C. Teulings & R. Baldwin (Eds.), *Secular stagnation: Facts, causes and cures*. VoxEU.

Summers, L. (2015). *On secular stagnation: A response to Bernanke*. Blog.

Svensson, L. (1997). Inflation forecast targeting: Implementing and monitoring inflation targets. *European Economic Review, 41*, 1111–1146.

Taylor, J. (1993). Discretion versus policy rules in practice. *Carnegie-Rochester Conference Series on Public Policy, 39*, 195–214.

Taylor, J. (2011). Macroeconomic lessons from the great deviation. In D. Acemoglu & M. Woodford (Eds.), *NBER macroeconomics annual* (Vol. 25, pp. 387–395). Chicago: University of Chicago Press.

Taylor, J. (2013). International monetary coordination and the great deviation. *Journal of Policy Modeling, 35*(3), 463–472.

Teulings, C., & Baldwin, R. (2014). Introduction. In C. Teulings & R. Baldwin (Eds.) *Secular stagnation: Facts, causes and cures*. VoxEU.

Warnock, F., & Warnock, V. (2009). International capital flows and US interest rates. *Journal of International Money and Finance, 28*, 903–919.

Yellen, J. (1996, March 13). Remarks before the National Association of Business Economists.

Yellen, J. (2005). *Update on the US economy*. Speech, October 18.

Yellen, J. (2015a). *Normalizing monetary policy: Prospects and perspectives*. Speech, March 27.

Yellen, J. (2015b, September 24). Inflation dynamics and monetary policy. *Speech*.

Part II

Fiscal Policy

9

Fiscal Arithmetic

We begin our discussion of fiscal policy in the post-crash period with some preliminaries—a review of the headline data on deficits and debt, a more comprehensive treatment of the state of the public sector balance sheet and a discussion of how the state of the business cycle and financial cycle can distort the underlying state of the public finances—before turning to discuss the evolution of policy over this period.

9.1   The Facts

The only place to start is with the data and the marked deterioration in the state of the public finances in the wake of the financial crisis, which is described in painstaking detail in Riley and Chote (2014). In what follows we shall briefly review the extent of the deterioration and the key driving factors based on their work. A sensible baseline against which that deterioration can be compared is the set of forecasts published alongside the 2008 Budget. At that time, public sector net borrowing (PSNB) for the fiscal year 2007/08 was estimated to be 2.6 % (of GDP) and was expected to increase a little to 2.9 % in 2008/09 before gradually narrowing to 1.3 % in 2012/13, supported both by an increase in receipts as a share of GDP and a decline in expenditure. Those projections for the flows were consistent with a brief upward trend in public sector net debt (PSND), which was expected to peak the right side of 40 % of GDP in 2010/11 before starting to fall back.

Reality turned out differently. In terms of borrowing, PSNB hit 11 % in 2009/10 a staggering 8½ percentage points of GDP greater than forecast,

© The Editor(s) (if applicable) and The Author(s) 2016
R. Barwell, *Macroeconomic Policy after the Crash*,
DOI 10.1057/978-1-137-51592-6_9

falling back to 7.3 % in 2012/13, still more than 6 percentage points higher than forecast in the 2008 Budget. In terms of debt, PSND hit 74.2 % in 2012/13—a slippage equivalent to around one third of GDP. From an accounting perspective, receipts were almost £100 billion lower than expected in 2009/10, or when expressed as a share of GDP, around 3.2 percentage points lower, whilst expenditure was £15 billion higher than expected at the time of the 2008 budget, or 5.3 percentage points higher when expressed as a share of GDP. There is no inconsistency here: as we shall go on to discuss, tax receipts tend to fall with GDP in a recession whilst expenditure does the opposite, thanks in no small part to welfare payments (e.g., spending on social security and tax credits can explain a 1.8 percentage point increase in the ratio of expenditure to GDP).

Clearly, the sizeable contraction in demand at the start of the crisis and the absence of a meaningful recovery in the years that followed—both of which came as a shock to most macroeconomists—were the main reasons why the 2008 Budget projections went so badly awry. The more persistent the hit to activity and income from a financial and economic crisis—the more pronounced the hysteretic effects—the greater the cumuative damage to the public finances. As we will go on to discuss, the impact of cyclical swings in activity on deficits (if not debt) will ultimately fade. The impact of structural shifts will not: if the levels of income and activity are permanently lower than they would otherwise have been, then so too is the level of tax receipts. However, that is not the end of the story.

The combination of a sizeable depreciation in the currency and significant increases in commodity prices conspired to drive a meaningful wedge between the price of final output (and in particular the price of consumption) and the price of domestic output (or in the jargon between the consumption deflator and the GDP deflator). The labour market response to the demand shock was also something of a surprise, with employment proving more resilient than might have been expected and wages and productivity correspondingly weaker. Three observations flow from those observations: first, reverse fiscal drag occurred with a tendency for income tax thresholds to rise faster than wages, consistent with lower income tax receipts; second, higher than expected employment meant lower than expected spending on unemployment-related benefits; and third, partially offsetting that, rapid increases in consumer prices put upward pressure on government spending (e.g., via the triple lock).

The crisis also had a marked impact on revenue raised from the financial and housing sector. Revenue raised from those sectors had accounted for a rising share of total receipts in the years before the crisis, rising from 3 % in 2002/03 to 4.1 % in 2007/08 on the cusp of the crisis, only to fall back to 2.9 % in 2009/10—a decline in receipts that can explain two thirds of the fall in the share of receipts to GDP over that period. Only thanks to new fiscal measures (the bank levy) would the share of receipts from this source recover to 3.2 % in 2012/13.

Another key development was the fall in interest rates over this period, which clearly helped to reduce pressure on the cost of servicing that rapidly expanding stock of debt. To give one illustration of the impact of rock-bottom interest rates on the public finances Riley and Chote (2014) report that the fact that the government was able to issue debt with a market value in excess of its nominal value helped to reduce the level of net debt by £34 billion. However, the impact of low interest rates on the public finances is not universally positive: the flow of tax receipts on the income of savers would have been correspondingly lower too.

The final element of the story is the impact of the interventions to rescue and resuscitate the financial sector at the start of the crisis on the public finances. Quantifying the impact of these financial interventions on the public finances at a given point in time is far from straightforward, and those estimates will inevitably vary through time—not least as the value of the government's equity stake in the financial institutions it rescued varies.

The single most important entry here is the impact of the reclassification of the financial corporations that were rescued by the government—most obviously Lloyds Banking Group and the Royal Bank of Scotland—on PSND, which official estimates (ONS 2009) place in the ballpark of 1½ trillion. The same study estimated the net cost of financing these interventions for central government at 4.7 billion in 2008 alone.

In the December 2014 *Economic and Fiscal Outlook* the Office for Budget Responsibility (OBR) provided updated estimates of the fiscal impact of these interventions (OBR 2014b). A total of 134 billion has been disbursed by the Treasury against which should be set the 35 billion recouped from repayment of principal, sale of shares and redemption of preference shares and a further 17 billion raised primarily through fees which together imply a shortfall of 82 billion. The Treasury is still owed 41 billion, largely in the form of loans, and holds stakes in financial institutions which were valued at that point to the tune of 48 billion, and as a result if those loans were paid in full and all shares were sold at their current market value then the government would realise an overall cash surplus of 8 billion. However, that surplus should be set against the Treasury's estimate that if all these interventions were financed through debt, then it would have incurred in excess of 20 billion in additional debt servicing costs.

The government also accumulated considerable 'contingent liabilities' by providing guarantees on debt issued by financial institutions and to the Bank of England Asset Purchase Facility: by the end of 2008, those liabilities were estimated to have reached 300 billion. Of course, a fair accounting of the impact of these financial interventions must also recognise the financial assets that the government acquired in the process of rescuing the financial system: loans to financial institutions, an equity stake in rescued banks and 'accounts receivable' (amounts owed on the capital tax levied on institutions in default, to be recouped from the residual value of those institutions).

Unfortunately, a brief aside on the data is required at this point. Thanks to the indefatigable logic of the accounting standards, those interventions had a profound impact on the headline public finances which led the official statisticians to publish estimates of the public finances which provide a cleaner read on the underlying position. The sceptical reader might question whether a statistical sleight of hand is taking place, designed to conceal the true extent of the government's debt problem. But to appreciate the misleading nature of the unadjusted data, consider that as a result of the government's decision to sell additional shares in LBG in March 2014 the statisticians determined that the government's residual holding was sufficiently small such that it no longer had the capacity to determine the commercial strategy of the bank, and at that point LBG was reclassified as a private institution knocking around £½ trillion off government debt at a stroke of the accountant's pen.

For completeness, we should note that this sharp and sustained deterioration in the public finances was anything but unique to the UK; the same fiscal pain was visited upon our major trading partners. According to the data from the October 2014 edition of the IMF's Fiscal Monitor, the headline fiscal deficit for the advanced economies ballooned from 3.6 % of GDP in 2008 to 9 % in 2009 and has gradually narrowed since then, reaching 4.3 % in 2013. Consistent with that, the ratio of general government gross debt to GDP rose from just under 80 % in 2008 to over 106 % in 2013. However, there has been significant variation across countries around that common trend. Within the euro area, Germany's budget balance never slipped too far into deficit, and by 2013 the overall budget was in surplus whilst several of the so-called peripheral economies experienced double digit deficits (as the UK did) with the debt burden rising from 40.2 % and 42.6 % in Spain and Ireland in 2008 to 93.9 % and 116.1 % respectively. It is worth keeping the scale of the problem in the periphery in mind—and the pressure on those governments to raise large sums of money in financial markets—when we return to the question of the optimal conduct of fiscal policy in the circumstances which confronted the finance ministers of this era.

By any reasonable metric, the public finances were in a pretty sorry state after the crash in most advanced economies, thanks to the damage done to the supply capacity of the economy (and therefore its capacity to generate tax receipts that fund expenditure) coupled with the cost of measures to rescue the financial sector and more conventional forms of fiscal stimulus. It was clear that at some point, finance ministers would have to balance the books—the only debate was how fast. There is not space here to do full justice to the countless measures that were announced during the consolidation period, which includes the tail end of the Labour governments reign (for an exhaustive review see Riley and Chote (2014)). However, it is worth keeping in mind that for all the talk of austerity during this period the government was consistently borrowing large sums of money by historical standards in order to plug the gap between tax receipts and spending. In the rest of this subsection, we shall discuss the yardsticks suggested by the theory with which we can evaluate the fiscal stance during this period.

9.2 The Business Cycle and the Public Finances

In the next few sections of this chapter we will introduce some key concepts in the debate over the health of the public finances before turning to discuss questions of policy at the end of the chapter. The state of the public finances will tend to vary systematically according to the state of the business cycle without policymakers having to lift a finger, thanks to the so-called automatic stabilisers, but there is also a tendency for finance ministers to make discretionary adjustments to the stance of fiscal policy in response to the state of the economy which will complicate and potentially amplify the natural correlation of the health of the public finances and the state of the cycle.

The design of the tax and benefit system ensures that the amount of money that the government spends in certain areas and receives in tax will vary according to the state of the business cycle without finance ministers lifting a finger. For example, income tax receipts will tend to rise in a boom: more people will be in employment and rising wages will tend to lead to more workers falling into higher tax brackets unless the nominal income thresholds are adjusted to keep pace with rising wages. Likewise, welfare spending on unemployment-related benefits will tend to fall in a boom. As a result, the public finances will automatically improve in a boom and deteriorate in a bust when the levers of fiscal policy are put on autopilot. The scale of these automatic stabilisers varies across countries and typically in proportion to the size of government relative to the economy (Fatas and Mihov 2001). On the one hand, there is temptation to view the presence of pronounced automatic stabilisers as a boon, since they should help to stabilise the economy in the face of transitory shocks. But by the same token, large automatic stabilisers can also pose a risk to the public finances because they are blind to the nature of the shock hitting the economy. The budgetary implications of a generous welfare system which supports household disposable income when the unemployment rate rises are largely benign when the shock to unemployment is transitory (cyclical), less so when it is persistent (structural).

Finance ministers may consciously tweak the generosity of the tax and benefit system and the overall fiscal stance in response to perceived changes in the state of the business cycle but how they choose to do so in practice is ambiguous. Typically, we would expect the fiscal authority to loosen the fiscal stance in a recession (we shall go on to discuss what we mean by the phrase 'fiscal stance' in this context later in this section), with the government cutting taxes or increasing spending on a discretionary basis in order to support demand. But the reverse may not be true in a boom: governments may not raise taxes or cut spending to drive output and employment down towards their sustainable levels. Indeed, governments may respond to the healthy state of the public finances in a boom by loosening policy—by lowering unpopular taxes or increasing popular spending —particularly if the strong state of the public finances is misinterpreted as a structural rather than a cyclical phenomenon. Finally, as recent events have demonstrated (most notably in the periphery of Europe) governments may feel compelled to tighten fiscal policy in a deep and prolonged recession if concerns about the accumulation of debt lead to concerns about debt sustainability.

Economists therefore tend to focus on a cyclically adjusted measure of the public finances—often referred to as the structural position—when assessing the health of the public finances, decomposing movements in headline borrowing into that which can be explained by the state of the business cycle given unchanged policy settings thanks to the automatic stabilisers, and that which reflects the cumulative impact of policy decisions. Conceptually, the structural position describes what the public finances would look like in the absence of any imbalance between aggregate demand and supply (i.e., if employment and output are at their sustainable levels). The structural position should therefore act as a long-run attractor in a hypothetical world of an unchanged fiscal stance in the sense that the headline balance should converge towards it in the long run if the central bank is to consistently achieve its mandate (the stance of monetary policy must be set in order to achieve an output gap that is close to zero and expected to remain so). If we further exclude the impact of debt servicing costs on the public finances—that is, if we focus on the structural primary budget position—then we have a measure of the public finances that strips out the impact of current *and* past fiscal policy interventions (which might otherwise have an effect via the consequences of the cumulative history of past deficits and surpluses).

As we will go on to discuss later in this chapter, the structural (cyclically adjusted) position plays a pivotal role in the conduct of fiscal policy, because from a conceptual point of view it is a sensible diagnostic of the underlying state of the public finances. To repeat from before: finance ministers should be able to rely upon central banks to close the output gap over a relatively short time horizon over which time the primary budget balance will converge on the corresponding structural position. However, it is not good enough for economic policy to work in theory, it must work in practice too, and in this case, that requires that the concept of the structural budget position be implementable and that is the issue we will focus on here.

There are two fundamental problems with estimating the structural budget position: first, we need an accurate estimate of the current state of the business cycle (level of the output gap); second, we need a reliable guide of the sensitivity of the budget to the business cycle (level of the output gap). Both are fraught with difficulty and, as we shall go on to discuss, errors on either score—estimating the true state of the business cycle or its impact on the headline public finances—will likely lead to policy errors.

The output gap is notoriously difficult to measure in real time. The economist seeking to estimate the output gap faces two problems. First, she has to work with data which are released with a lag and prone to revision: there is always a risk that the picture painted of the economy will change either because our description of the past changes or because new information sheds a different light on our interpretation of the past (Lomax 2004). Second, she has to call on techniques which are known to give imprecise outputs even when given accurate inputs. The literature offers a number of complementary approaches for estimating the output gap or its component parts (slack within companies and slack within the labour market) which vary according to the extent to which theory is used to pin down the estimate of the output gap. At one extreme are the atheoretic estimates based purely on information collected from the business surveys on slack and recruitment difficulties. There are then a range of estimates which appeal to economic theory, whether that be the production function (to identify the cyclical variation in factor utilisation which can explain the level of output given observed inputs) or the short-run Phillips curve (to identify the demand imbalance which can explain the behaviour of costs and prices). Finally, there are estimates that are derived from fully fledged macroeconomic models (see Vetlov et al. 2011). Murray (2014) reviews these various approaches and demonstrates the sizeable uncertainty around the implied estimates of the output gap in the UK, highlighting in particular the capacity for the arrival of new information to change our interpretation of the past: revisions from this source are on average the same order of magnitude as the output gap itself.

Estimating the impact of the output gap on the state of the public finances is not straightforward either, even given reliable historical data on the output gap. An obvious stumbling block here is the need to purge the data of discretionary changes in taxes and spending which remember are unlikely to be exogenous with respect to the business cycle to recover the exogenous response of spending. In their analysis of UK data, Helgadottir et al. (2012) find that a contemporaneous response of headline borrowing (as a share of GDP) to the output gap of 0.5 and a lagged response (to the output gap in the previous year) of 0.2—estimates which appear robust to different estimation strategies and which equate to a meaningful impact of the business cycle on the public finances. In a sense, the real concern for policymakers is to explain what is left behind, since that will determine the impact on the structural budget and hence whether a policy response is in order. For example, the fiscal authority will need to take a judgement on whether movements in, say, the welfare budget or corporation tax receipts which do not reflect the state of the business cycle are transitory or persistent phenomena.

9.3   The Financial Cycle and the Public Finances

Although economists tend to focus on the impact of the business cycle on the state of the public finances, the period leading up to the financial crash reminds us that the public finances are also sensitive to the state of the financial cycle—that is, synchronised movements in prices and transactions across a broad range of retail and wholesale markets. That financial cycle will be reflected in the level of tax receipts for a given level of nominal GDP, on account of stamp duty, capital gains tax and even inheritance tax (Pope and Roantree 2014) and it appears that the public finances are particularly sensitive to the state of the financial cycle in the UK, compared to many other OECD countries (Eschenbach and Schuknecht 2002).

Of course, we should expect some variation in prices and transactions in these markets as a natural by-product of a plain vanilla business cycle, as asset prices and market participants respond to developments in the real economy, and the corresponding ebb and flow in the proceeds from stamp duty or capital gains tax should rightly be considered part of the standard cyclical response of tax receipts. However, the financial cycle and its impact on the public finances is a somewhat distinct concept, relating to developments in those markets which are not synchronised with the standard business cycle and are more pronounced in amplitude. Indeed, one can draw a sharp contrast between the tranquillity of activity and consumer prices during the so-called Great Stability in the lead-up to the financial crash, and the behaviour of asset prices, credit flows and debt stocks during that period (Barwell and Burrows 2011).

In the limit, one could even incorporate some element of the volatility in tax receipts from more conventional sources into this alternative cyclical dimension of the public finances. For example, the financial cycle may be evident in the path of income tax receipts in those countries which are home to a large financial centre. The financial institutions that are active in those financial centres will tend to account for a disproportionately large number of those at the top end of the income distribution relative to their share of overall employment (that imbalance would rise still further if we included those companies that provide services to those financial institutions, such as consultants or lawyers). Bell and Van Reenen (2014) argue that the 'bankers' bonuses' (broadly defined) can explain two thirds of the increase in the share of income accounted for by the top 1 % in the decade before the crash (for evidence on whether flawed remuneration contracts can explain the crisis see Fahlenbrach and Stulz (2011)). The state of the financial cycle can therefore have a non-trivial impact on the shape of the income distribution in those countries: income inequality may increase in a boom, but so too should the income tax take, because income growth is tax rich.

A similar point could be made with respect to corporation tax receipts from financial institutions. Devereux et al. (2004) consider the puzzling strength of the UK corporation tax receipts in the 1980s and 1990s—revenues had been high by both historic and international standards despite the fact that the statutory rate had been low—and pinpoint the role of increased profitability in the financial sector in explaining that puzzle. In 1982, the financial sector accounted for 12 % of total corporation tax revenues; in 2000 that share peaked at 36 %, only to fall back to 27 % the following year as boom turned to bust in the stock market (which will have had a material impact on the life assurance sector, where companies are taxed on unrealised capital gains). Devereux, Griffith and Klemm conclude their research with an ominous warning:

> As long as there is only limited understanding about the reasons for the growth of the corporate sector, it is hard to make predictions for future revenue developments. We know however that revenues will depend too a much larger degree than previously on the performance of the financial sector. If the performance of that sector suffers, or if financial services manage to avoid more tax, then the puzzle treated in this article might disappear rather quickly.

True to form, corporation tax proceeds disappointed in the early noughties, which can be explained in no small part by the failure of the profitability of financial companies to match lofty expectations (Riley and Chote 2014).

Ireland represents a cautionary tale of how the financial cycle can destabilise the public finances. One striking feature of the Irish recession at the start of the crash was the extent of the collapse in tax receipts. It is not unreasonable to assume that tax receipts might decline at roughly the same rate as nominal GDP in a slump, leaving the effective tax rate broadly constant. In Ireland, tax receipts fell at almost twice the rate that nominal GDP declined: tax revenues fell by 8½ % in 2008, whilst nominal GDP fell by 4½ % (Kanda 2010). In part, that decline can be explained by the fact that turnaround in the business cycle (as measured by the decline in nominal GDP) understated the ferocity of the move from boom to bust in the financial cycle, and the corresponding impact of the collapse in prices and activity in asset markets on revenues. However, there was a second more pernicious impact of the financial cycle on the state of the public finances: the surge in receipts that the government enjoyed from 'fair weather' taxes during the boom encouraged governments to wean themselves off the more reliable (and likely politically unpopular) sources of income (i.e., tax revenue), with the government narrowing the base and lowering the rates of personal income tax (Honohan 2009). The public finances became more reliant on corporation tax, stamp duty and capital gains tax, whose collective share of total tax revenues rose from 8 % in 1987 to 30 % in 2006, before falling back to 20 % in 2008.

The logical conclusion then is that structural measures of borrowing, which adjust for the impact of the *business* cycle on the public finances, are not as comprehensive as first thought, since the output gap is not a sufficient statistic of all cyclical influences on tax receipts. In particular, governments cannot rely on the primary deficit or surplus converging towards current estimates of its structural counterpart in the presence of a significant financial cycle. A seemingly healthy structural surplus is not a sound basis for implementing sustained cuts in tax rates or the tax base or increases in expenditure if that surplus is being inflated by buoyant receipts from stamp duty and capital gains tax.

This is not quite the end of the story where the financial cycle and its impact on the public finances are concerned. As we will go on to discuss in the companion volume to this book, there is new arm of macroeconomic policy which *may* lean against the financial cycle: macroprudential policy. If that macroprudential regime is successful and the amplitude of the financial cycle is significantly reduced in the future then governments should not expect to periodically enjoy a bumper harvest of strong receipts from sources as stamp duty or capital gains tax, and if they do there is a case for saving that money (i.e., paying down debt) in the expectation that when the financial cycle turns, the feast could turn into famine where tax receipts are concerned. On the other hand, if macroprudential policy is successful in taming the financial cycle then the probability and severity of future systemic crises will have been significantly reduced and that in turn implies something about the optimal stock of debt today. One insurance motive for maintaining low levels of debt today is to allow future governments the fiscal space to support the economy in future crises. Effective macroprudential policy reduces the need to take out that insurance.

9.4 Stabilising the Debt Burden

Large cyclical and in some cases structural deficits have been the order of the day since the financial crisis, and that has inevitably led to an increase in the level of government debt, which in turn has focused attention on what governments need to do in order to stabilise the debt burden.

The usual entry point into this discussion is to focus on the surplus or deficit that a government would have to run in order to stabilise the level of government debt as a share of nominal GDP given the particular circumstances that confront the government. To fix ideas, we shall focus on the simplest variant of this thought experiment here and abstract from complications such as seigniorage income and privatisation proceeds which do not radically change the big picture except under extreme circumstances in the case of the former and only temporarily in the case of the latter (because to paraphrase a former British Prime Minister, you can only sell the family silver once).

We begin with the most basic relationship of all for any debtor, whether they are an individual, a company or a government: the level of debt today equals the level of debt yesterday, plus any interest that you owe on the debt that has to be paid today, plus any additional borrowing you make today, less any debt that you manage to repay today. Where governments are concerned we refer to the sum of the final two terms as the primary budget balance—that is, the net lending (or borrowing) position of the government, excluding the interest payments on debt.

If the objective is to stabilise the ratio of debt relative to nominal GDP—rather than reduce it—then it follows that the government must add just enough to the debt stock each period in order to keep pace with the growth in nominal GDP. That accumulation of debt can come about either through borrowing to meet the cost of servicing the existing debt—which depends on the current size of the debt stock and the interest rate that the government pays—or on account of the government's net lending position.

A delicate balance therefore exists between these key variables that must be satisfied if the ratio of debt to GDP is to remain constant. For obvious reasons that balance is typically expressed in terms of the variable that finance ministers control: the primary budget balance (expressed as a share of GDP). We end up with a battle of two rates—the rate of nominal GDP growth and the interest rate paid on debt—determining the appropriate fiscal stance. In particular, we arrive at the budget curious result that governments can permanently run (primary) deficits and still maintain a stable debt to GDP ratio so long as the economy is expanding at a faster rate than the interest rate it pays servicing that debt.

In reality, these variables will tend not to align in the correct constellations that happen to deliver a stable debt burden. In theory, we can use this basic relationship between debt today, debt yesterday, the cost of servicing debt and the primary budget balance to forecast how debt will evolve in these circumstances. However, this is a more complex process than it first appears. The mistake is to treat the key inputs in this analysis—the rate of nominal GDP growth and the rate of interest paid on debt—as exogenously given. That approach might be valid in an environment where the debt burden is believed to be stable, and therefore for modest simulations around that stable path. However, as we will go on to discuss, once questions of sustainability arise, these assumptions are no longer valid—and that of course is precisely the circumstances we are interested in.

9.5   A More Comprehensive Perspective

The headline data on deficits and debt presented earlier give a sense of the deterioration in the public finances in the advanced economies following the onset of the financial crisis. The simple expression we just encountered for the primary surplus in terms of the interest rate *versus* the growth rate differential gives a crude sense of the policy stance required to stabilise debt. However, if we want a more accurate, comprehensive account of the state of the public finances and what needs to be done in order to keep the debt burden manageable, then we need to look beyond these headline data for measures which are not so vulnerable to the vagaries of accounting treatments and which reflect the possible and probable future consequences of past and present spending commitments.

The OBR's Fiscal Sustainability Report (see, e.g., OBR (2014a)) provides a useful framework for constructing that truer reflection of the state of the public finances. The right place to start is with the traditional National Accounts measures of the government's balance sheet. Starting with Central

Government gross debt we can add the debt of local government and subtract cross holdings of debt held by those two sectors to arrive at the so-called Maastricht definition of General Government Gross Debt. If we then add the debt of public corporations, subtract the liquid assets of the public sector and add the net debt of the BoE then we arrive at the headline measure of PSND excluding the banking groups. We can then take this PSND measure and adjust for the government's holdings of illiquid financial assets and physical assets too, to produce a more rounded estimate of public sector net worth.

The next step is to account for actual and contingent liabilities that the government has accumulated which might entail future expenditure. That net liabilities concept can be found in the Whole of Government Accounts (WGA), which reflects the International Financial Reporting Standards—the system of accounts used in the commercial sector; see HMT (2014).

However, even that measure does not speak to the future activity of the government: the spending that it is likely to have to make, and the revenue it is likely to receive as well as the future assets (such as ownership of the electromagnetic spectrum) and liabilities it might acquire in the future. In order to account for the implications of a sustained imbalance between expenditure and receipts in the future we need to augment the WGA measure with long-term projections.

To put numbers on these concepts, consider the following OBR net present value estimates of the actual and contingent liabilities that feature in the WGA measure of net liabilities:

- *Future public sector pensions* (incurred as a result of employment decisions in the past): estimated at £1.172 trillion;
- *Capital payments to Private Finance Initiative providers*: estimated at £37 billion (of which only £5 billion feature in the National Accounts measures described above);
- *Provisions against expected future losses* (such as the cost of nuclear decommissioning): estimated at £131 billion; and
- *Contingent liabilities* (a varied laundry list including financial stability interventions and taxes subject to challenge): estimated at £88 billion.

As far as the long-term projections are concerned, the key driving factor is demographic change. According to the latest official forecasts, the UK population is set to age over the next half century, such that by 2063–64 there will be more elderly people and less people of working-age to support them (with a roughly similar number of children). Population ageing puts inevitable pressure on government expenditure through predictable channels such that between 2018–19 and 2063–64: health spending is estimated to rise from

6.4 % to 8.5 %; the cost of the state pension is estimated to rise from 5.5 % to 7.9 %; and the costs of long-term social care are set to rise from 1.2 % to 2.3 %. On the revenue side of the ledger the key concern is the decline in the tax dividend from North Sea Oil.

The net result of these judgements was estimated to deliver (at that time) a primary budget which moves from a 3 % surplus in 2018–19 to being broadly balanced in the late 2030s and finally a deficit of 1.7 % in 2063–64—in other words, a cumulative deterioration of 4.7 percentage points of GDP. The implications for the stock of debt are not too hard to compute: PSND is projected to fall as a share of GDP 79 % in 2015–16 to around 53 % in the mid-2030s before rising to 84 % in 2063–64. Beyond that point, the debt burden continues to rise and absent any change in policy is on an unsustainable path. That is not a reasonable assumption—at some point taxes must rise, or spending fall—and that leads naturally to a discussion of the distributional consequences of the current stance of policy on future generations. Auerbach et al.'s (1987, 1991) framework of 'generational accounting' is the default toolkit which economists use to answer this question. Generational accounts describe in present value terms what each generation should expect to pay in taxes and receive in the form of welfare benefits and government services over the course of their lifetime. Those two sums may not be equal but the government's intertemporal budget constraint must hold, so the accounts reveal the transfers that are taking place between generations in order for that constraint to hold—and in this case the tax bill that current generations are bequeathing to future generations (keep that in mind when we come to discuss Ricardian Equivalence and when you come to discuss your inheritance from your parents or with your children). As McCarthy et al. (2011) conclude for the UK:

> the framework does show that if people currently alive enjoy the existing structure of taxes and benefits, then future generations will have to face a much less favourable framework in order to deliver public sector balance.

9.6   Does Structural Balance Targeting Make Sense In Practice?

The key debate over the conduct of fiscal policy during the post-crash period (at least among macroeconomists) was around the optimal pace of consolidation—that is, how fast finance ministers should try to 'balance the books'. In order to implement that policy, finance ministers need a reliable yardstick which faithfully describes the current state of the public finances and the impact of policy decisions.

The conventional wisdom among most academics and finance ministers is that the cyclically adjusted or structural estimate of the public finances is the appropriate yardstick, and that the management of the public finances should therefore be guided by what Tereanu et al. (2014) label 'structural balance targeting'. Under this approach, finance ministers should look through the cyclical variation in tax receipts and spending and instead focus on what borrowing would have been in the absence of the business cycle. The cyclically adjusted measure of borrowing should provide a more accurate gauge of the underlying state state of the public finances so a perfectly reasonable goal for policy might be to move the structural balance to a level consistent with the long-run goals of stabilising if not reducing the ratio of debt to GDP, factoring in the debt sustainability issues—discussed earlier—that may lurk over the horizon.

From a conceptual point of view, focusing on measures of the public finances which strip out cyclical factors makes sense if the objective is a long-run goal of safeguarding debt sustainability and if the impact of the cycle on the public finances can be accurately measured. Indeed, as discussed earlier, one might reasonably argue that the impact of the financial cycle on tax receipts and spending should also be expunged from the headline data to give a cleaner read on the true state of the public finances. The alternative—basing policy on headline data, and implicitly acting as if movements in the headline data are driven by corresponding movements in the structural position—can complicate the task of monetary policy.

Imagine that the economy is hit by a significant negative shock that has a substantial impact on government borrowing: tax receipts fall and welfare payments rise. We know that the cyclical drag on borrowing will not persist into the long run. Business cycles and output gaps cannot last indefinitely. Even if we cannot rely on central banks to adjust the stance of monetary policy to close the gap, we can surely rely on prices and hence quantities to eventually adjust to any given shock, so that the level of aggregate activity is once again determined by fundamentals on the supply side. On that basis the headline data on borrowing will eventually converge back upon the unobservable cyclically adjusted measure of borrowing because in the absence of additional shocks, the cyclical component of borrowing will converge on zero. However, the additional debt that is accumulated over that interval will persist and hence so too will the increase in the cost of servicing that debt.

If the impact of the business cycle (output gap) on the public finances was modest and short-lived—presumably because the amplitude and duration of the business cycle is sufficiently small, and/or that taxes and spending are not that sensitive to cyclical shifts in aggregate demand—then one might therefore be tempted to argue that not too much is lost by anchoring fiscal policy on the headline (unadjusted) measure. However, there is no reason to believe this assumption will always hold. If instead there is a large cyclical component within government borrowing then acting as if the deterioration in borrowing is purely structural would lead to a perverse pro-cyclical variation in the stance of fiscal policy.

For example, finance ministers might find themselves seeking a cyclically adjusted surplus to compensate for a substantial cyclical deterioration in borrowing in the depths of a recession, and in theory the implied tightening in fiscal policy could then exacerbate the weakness in aggregate demand. A central bank that might be operating close to the lower bound would then have to find a way to inject yet further monetary stimulus to compensate for additional drag on demand. In practice, the opposite problem is more likely to be the case. Bumper tax receipts and low welfare spending in a boom might lull finance ministers into a false sense of security (or weaken their hand in spending reviews with other colleagues in government), leading to a structural easing in the stance—for example, cutting tax rates or a permanent increase in departmental spending—that could prove misguided in the long run when the cyclical strength in the public finances fades.

From a practical point of view the problem with the 'structural balance targeting' is clear: the structural balance is unobservable. As discussed earlier, the true level of the output gap is unknown, as is the sensitivity of tax receipts and expenditure to the state of the business cycle.

The measurement problem can lead to policy errors. Real-time estimates of the structural position are inevitably flawed and subject to revision, which may then reveal that the stance of policy calibrated on earlier vintages of data was flawed. In the case of the UK, Budget 2006 suggested that the structural deficit was a manageable 1.9 % in fiscal year 2006/07. However, by Budget 2014 that deficit was estimated to be a far more worrisome—3.2 %. There is nothing particularly special about the UK experience of structural balance targeting: significant errors in measuring the output gap and hence the underlying state of the public finances is the norm not the exception (Ley and Misch 2013). Using data for 19 OECD countries, Hughes Hallett et al. (2009) argue that real time estimates of the cyclically adjusted position are very imprecise and cannot be relied upon to identify fiscal slippages, producing too many type I and type II errors for comfort. Simply put, it is very hard to estimate the underlying strength of the public finances in real time and therefore how much needs to be done to repair the position, if anything at all.

This problem of how to set policy on the basis of uncertain and potentially flawed estimates of the output gap is clearly not unique to the conduct of fiscal policy: central bankers face a very similar task in the conduct of monetary policy. This problem is widely understood (Orphanides and van Norden 2002) although it is not considered insurmountable in that arena. However, there is one key difference here: central banks do not tend to commit to a particular path of policy over a multi-year time horizon conditional upon a particular estimate of the output gap, and even if they did, that path would almost surely be couched in a probabilistic statement which emphasised the uncertainty around that path (Barwell and Chadha 2014). Fiscal policy is therefore more vulnerable to these inevitable errors in estimating the underlying state of the economy than monetary policy.

The measurement problem also leads to potential problems on the communication front (IFS 2016). Policy calibrated on the basis of headline data is more transparent, which in turn makes policymakers more accountable (it is much easier to observe whether they have achieved their objectives or not). Contracting out ownership of the macroeconomic projections to an independent body should address concerns that policymakers are 'cooking the books' (tweaking the estimate of the output gap or the sensitivity of the public finances to that estimate in order to hit a given target), but there is still ample grounds for debate and dispute over these 'unobservables' and hence whether the government has actually achieved its mandate.

These practical problems have led some commentators to question the wisdom of building a policy regime on such shaky foundations. For example, Giles (2012) argues:

> At the centre of economic policy we therefore have a concept that cannot be measured, one whose estimates are subject to massive revisions and one that has an extremely tenuous relationship to concurrent proxies. It is useless.

9.7 A Brief History of Structural Balance Targeting in the UK

The UK signed up to the structural balance targeting orthodoxy for much of the post-crisis period: the cornerstone of the UK's initial fiscal consolidation strategy was an intention to improve the structural budget position over a specified time frame, in order that the upward trend in the ratio of debt to GDP would be arrested and ultimately reversed. However, in summer of 2015 the government introduced a new fiscal mandate which shifted the focus of policy away from a cyclically adjusted measure and back towards the headline data on borrowing. There is a cyclical knock-out clause in the new mandate such that the government is not obliged to deliver a surplus if the economy is hit by a negative shock but even then, the assessment of whether the UK economy is in normal times or not is based on the outlook for GDP growth rather than an assessment of the output gap. In this subsection, we review how structural balance targeting panned out in the UK in the post crisis period.

The timetable for eliminating the structural deficit has been subject to change. In what follows, we shall briefly review how progress on structural balance targeting evolved since the election of the Coalition government in spring 2010, using the cyclically adjusted current budget (CACB) as our yardstick:

- *Baseline (pre-budget) forecast June 2010:* The CACB was estimated to have been −3.1 % in 2008–09 and was projected to remain in deficit to the tune of −1.6 % in 2014–15.
- *June 2010:* The CACB was still estimated to have been −3.1 % in 2008–09 and was projected to move into surplus of 0.3 % in 2014–15 and 0.8 % in 2015–16.
- *November 2010:* The CACB was estimated to have been −5.3 % in 2009–10 and was projected to move into surplus of 0.5 % in 2014–15 and 0.9 % in 2015–16.
- *March 2011:* The CACB was estimated to have been −5.3 % in 2009–10 and was projected to move into surplus of 0.4 % in 2014–15 and 0.8 % in 2015–16.
- *November 2011:* The CACB was estimated to have been −4.5 % in 2010–11 and was projected to remain in deficit at −0.6 % in 2015–16 and a surplus of 0.5 % in 2016–17.
- *March 2012:* The CACB was estimated to have been −4.4 % in 2010–11 and was projected to remain in deficit at −0.7 % in 2015–16 and a surplus of 0.5 % in 2016–17.
- *December 2012:* The CACB was estimated to have been −4.3 % in 2011–12 and was projected to remain in deficit at −0.8 % in 2015–16 and a surplus of 0.4 % and 0.9 % in 2016–17 and 2017–18, respectively.
- *March 2013:* The CACB was estimated to have been −4.2 % in 2011–12 and was projected to move into surplus of 0.1 % in 2016–17 and 0.8 % in 2017–18.
- *December 2013:* The CACB was estimated to have been −3.6 % in 2012–13 and was projected to remain in deficit at −0.2 % in 2016–17 and then move into surplus of 0.7 % and 1.6 % in 2017–18 and 2018–19, respectively.

- *March 2014:* The CACB was estimated to have been −3.5 % in 2012–13 and was projected to remain in deficit at −0.2 % in 2016–17 and then move into surplus of 0.7 % in 2017–18 and 1.5 % in 2017–18 and 2018–19, respectively.
- *December 2014:* The CACB was estimated to have been −2.6 % in 2013–14 and was projected to move into surplus of 0.7 % in 2017–18 and 2.3 % by 2019–20.
- *March 2015:* The CACB was estimated to have been −2.6 % in 2013–14 and was projected to move into surplus of 0.8 % in 2017–18 and 1.7 % by 2019–20.
- *July 2015:* The CACB was estimated to have been −2.4 % in 2014–15 and was projected to move into surplus of 0.3 % in 2017–18 and then 1.8 % and 1.9 % by 2019–20 and 2020–21, respectively.
- *November 2015:* The CACB was estimated to have been −2.4 % in 2014–15 and was projected to move into surplus of 0.5 % in 2017–18 and 2.4 % in 2020–21.
- *March 2016:* The CACB was estimated to have been −2.4 % in 2014–15 and was projected to move into surplus of 0.5 % in 2018–19 and then 2.0 % and 2.4 % in 2019–20 and 2020–21, respectively.

As that brief history illustrates, there is a sense of 'running to stand still' about these projections of the CACB with the current position at the time of each forecast turning out weaker than expected and the date at which the books were expected to balance pushed back. For example, as of the November 2015, the CACB was estimated to have been in deficit to the tune of 2.4 % GDP and yet at the outset of the accelerated austerity drive (in June 2010) the OBR had anticipated that the CACB would be in surplus of 0.3 % by that point.

This observation should not necessarily be taken as a criticism. Indeed, to have attempted to stick to the original timeline despite incoming news would have required the Chancellor to 'run faster to move forward'—to compress the fiscal consolidation programme into an ever shorter window, which (as we will go on to discuss) would have put even more pressure on the conduct of monetary policy. Of course, in the aftermath of the referendum, a further 'fiscal reset' would be required, with a material slippage in the anticipated path of debt to GDP (but that is another story).

In practice, three generic factors conspired to confound the Chancellor's original timetable for 'balancing the books' at different points during this process:

- *News on supply:* Bad news on the assumed path of potential supply—the current level and expected future pace of growth—maps directly into estimates of the structural deficit (essentially less of the headline deficit can be written off as cyclical weakness) and therefore the amount of fiscal consolidation that would be required to 'balance the books'.
- *News on effective tax rates:* Bad news on the assumed 'tax take'—that is, reducing the projected level of tax receipts that the Chancellor is likely to receive for a given forecast of income and activity, and constellation of tax rates—can also feed directly into the structural budget balance.
- *News on demand:* Bad news on the level of demand relative to supply will not have a direct effect on *cyclically adjusted* measures of the public finances. However, the additional (cyclical) accumulation of debt will impact on the underlying public finances via the cost of servicing that larger debt burden. Moreover, the bad news on demand could encourage finance ministers to adjust their strategy (the desired pace of consolidation) and might even contribute to the erosion in potential supply via hysteresis effects.

At the risk of stating the obvious, even if there had been *no* slippage in the government's timetable, the strategy of gradually bringing the structural budget into balance is still consistent with the *ratio* of the stock of debt to GDP continuing to rise for a number of years. Changes in the plan—pushing back the point at which the headline budget moved into surplus and tolerating higher deficits in the meantime—simply had the effect of adding to the stock of debt, both now and, other things equal, in the future too in much the same way that the speed with which central banks seek to stabilise inflation in response to shocks in an inflation targeting regime has permanent implications for the price level.

9.8   A 'Follow the Money' Proxy for the Fiscal Stance

Stabilising demand over the business cycle may not be the primary objective for finance ministers but the impact of austerity on jobs and output and the optimal pace of fiscal consolidation has undoubtedly been *the* key theme in the debate over the conduct of fiscal policy—and arguably the key theme in the entire economic policy debate—since the crash. However, despite all the attention that has been lavished on the macroeconomic consequences of *changes* in fiscal policy—whether that be influencing the decisions of countless households and companies in the real economy to spend or save, or the appetite of investors to hold government debt or even the deliberations of central banks to provide more or less monetary stimulus—relatively little has been said about the *absolute* fiscal position. Indeed, a working definition of the actual fiscal stance from a macroeconomic perspective is hard to come by, and providing one is the purpose of this subsection; to identify whether fiscal policy has been *tight* or *loose* since the crash.

In theory, counter-cyclical monetary and fiscal policy are not so different; in a recession, the former encourages private sector agents to borrow more or save less to support demand, whilst the latter involves the government taking that decision on their behalf. In practice, we do not typically think of demand management as being the primary goal of fiscal policy (for reasons we will go on to discuss) and therefore we do not tend to think about there being an appropriate fiscal stance which would deliver the socially optimal level of output or employment. That in itself should give the academic advocates of counter-cyclical fiscal policy pause for thought. Instead, this question of whether policy is too tight or too loose is normally posed in the monetary policy arena.

Given the potentially surprising conclusion from this train of thought about the fiscal stance a quick aside on calibrating the monetary stance is probably in order. We could compare the stance of policy to the output of the preferred policy rule but that simply tells us whether policy is optimal or not. A more practical approach might be to focus on the expected impact of the monetary stance on the output gap (we could equally focus on the expected change in inflation). If the output gap is becoming more positive (or less negative) then one could say that monetary policy is loose—central bankers are pushing up on demand relative to the level of supply. To repeat whether that stance is too loose or not loose enough is a different question which takes us back to the optimal policy rule as the yardstick.

Returning to the question in hand—the fiscal stance, from a macro-stabilisation perspective—the simplest approach is to focus on the direct impact of the government on aggregate demand, namely the contribution of the volume of government consumption and investment to the level of GDP. However, the direct contribution of the government to GDP is clearly incomplete as a measure of the impact of fiscal policy on demand, for at least three reasons.

First, many of the public services that are reflected in the level of government consumption are provided free of charge and despite considerable efforts by the statisticians, the volume of services that is consumed in any given period, such as the provision of national defence, is notoriously difficult to measure. Those services may be highly valued by the general public but as far as macroeconomists are concerned, the government's demand for resources may provide a more accurate gauge of the macroeconomic impact of government spending than what is recorded in the national accounts, particularly if we are interested in the imbalance between demand and supply in the market economy and the consequences for inflation (Hills et al. 2005). By employing factors of production the government inevitably reduces the inputs available to the private sector and therefore the capacity of the market economy to supply output and by procuring goods and services the government contributes to the demand for marketable output too.

Second, even that superior measure of the government's direct contribution to the balance between demand and supply in the market economy—the government's demand for resources—fails to capture the broader impact of the public sector on aggregate demand. The obvious omissions are the instances where there is a transfer of resources between different agents in the economy that the government engineers (intermediates) which could impact spending—through the payment of benefits and debt interest, and through the collection of taxes. Then there are then a broader set of policy measures where government policy seeks to encourage a change in behaviour, such as limiting the duration of welfare benefits to encourage those out of work on benefit to intensify job search which could bolster labour supply and ultimately consumption (Katz and Meyer 1990), or even through changing the legal status of certain activities.

Third, there is the Ricardian elephant in the room: the indirect impact of the decisions that the government takes today (in terms of taxing less or spending more in a recession) on private sector spending on account of the higher taxes that individuals expect to pay in the future to finance that fiscal stimulus. The point is not to say that this effect neuters the positive impact of fiscal stimulus, but that to ignore it altogether renders any measure of the fiscal stance based on what is happening to the government's balance sheet incomplete. For all its complexity, the government's demand for resources is therefore still an imperfect measure of the net impact of numerous fiscal policy levers on the 'fiscal stance'.

An alternative and more productive approach is therefore to simply ask whether the government is a net saver or a net spender—in other words, whether the government is running a budget surplus or deficit. If the budget is in surplus (deficit) then fiscal policy is tight (loose) from a macro-stabilisation perspective, and by extension, the size of that surplus or deficit as a share of nominal GDP gives a sense of how tight or loose policy is. The advantage of this approach is that government borrowing will reflect its demand for resources as well as money spent on benefits net of cash recouped on taxes. In theory, one could make the case for focusing instead on the government's net acquisition of financial liabilities as a measure of the fiscal stance—a measure which augments the net lending position of the government for any net acquisition or disposal of financial assets by the government.

Of course, we do not pretend that a pound injected into the economy via tax cuts has the same impact on aggregate demand as a pound injected via increased government investment or welfare payments, whereas of course a measure of the fiscal stance which is based on the budget constraint implicitly assumes that they are. Indeed, if we take forward-looking behaviour on the part of taxpayers seriously it is hard to say what impact *if any* discretionary fiscal policy (tax cuts or government spending today financed by the opposite tomorrow) has on aggregate demand today. However, we are in search here for an approximate gauge of the macroeconomic impact of fiscal policy, and a 'follow the money' approach based on the budgetary position seems more appropriate than any other and has some academic pedigree (Eisner and Pieper 1984; Clark and Dilnot 2002).

The other conceptual problem with this simple definition is that the fiscal stance is not directly under the control of the fiscal authority. The sign and size of the government budget will vary according to the state of the business cycle thanks to the automatic stabilisers as noted earlier. The structural budget position—which in theory strips out the impact of the business cycle on the public finances—is arguably a superior measure of the fiscal stance. The structural position gives a sense of whether the fiscal authority is choosing to support aggregate demand, through discretionary measures.

Using the structural position as a proxy for the fiscal stance leads to a somewhat surprising conclusion; fiscal policy has been loose in the UK, and most other advanced economies, during the post-crash period because the UK government has been running a structural deficit. That is, even if you control for the impact of the business cycle, governments have been borrowing money to keep spending above the level provided for by tax recepts. It follows that finance ministers have been consciously choosing to provide additional support to aggregate demand (over and above the automatic stabilisers) by borrowing money to finance tax cuts and discretionary spending and in the process have been accumulating additional debt. Of course, fiscal consolidation has been the norm during most of that period—governments have been attempting to reduce the size of those structural deficits over time—so policy has been increasingly less loose as time has passed.

For those still struggling with the somewhat counterintuitive conclusion that fiscal policy has been loose throughout the period that the austerity debate has raged in the UK, it is worth repeating that just because policy has been loose it does not mean that fiscal policy has been *loose enough* from a macro-stabilisation perspective. But to say anything more concrete than that, we need a model and we certainly need to allow for the fact that the stance of monetary policy is not invariant to the state of the economy or for that matter the stance of fiscal policy.

9.9   It Takes Two to Make a Thing Go Right: Coordination with Monetary Policy

Of all the debates over the conduct of economic policy since the crash the one that remains the most controversial among economists and the general public alike is around the optimal pace of fiscal consolidation. It seems highly likely that cutting spending and raising taxes will depress demand, *other things equal*, so fiscal consolidation can look counterproductive whilst the economy is still mired in a depression, because it appears as though these measures will depress demand, further setting back the recovery. However, as we will go on to discuss at length, other things are not equal: the stance of monetary policy should respond to announced changes in the fiscal stance by moving in the opposite direction.

It is important to be clear about what is going on here. The Chancellor no doubt assumed that when he announced an increase in the pace of fiscal consolidation the MPC would factor the consequences for demand and inflation into its forecasts, and therefore plot a different monetary course. However, there was no need for formal coordination over this strategy of fiscal consolidation coupled with monetary activism. Operational independent central bankers are obliged to deliver on their remits, conditional on the announced plans of elected officials. The debate is whether the fiscal–monetary mix that emerged during this period was optimal, and that is the central question that runs through this entire section of the book.

Over and above this timeless aspect of coordination—that central banks instinctively respond to the macroeconomic consequences of the fiscal stance—there are two other issues relating to coordination that are worth highlighting here: the scope for disagreement over the state of the economy, and the scope for reverse causality (the impact of changes in the stance of monetary policy on fiscal policy).

Monetary and fiscal policy are both set according to an assessment of the current state of the economy and a forecast of how the economy is likely to evolve in the future. However, policymakers do not coordinate in this area: the BoE and the OBR independently construct their own assessments and forecasts of the economy and set policy accordingly, and there is nothing which guarantees that they will agree on the state of the economy. In the long run, any disagreement should eventually be resolved as incoming data allow both policymakers to learn about the economy and refine their assessment of the current state and likely future path: for example, if the Bank and the OBR disagree about the size or even sign of the output gap then data on costs and prices should ultimately reveal who is right and who is wrong. However, in the short run, it is perfectly possible that the MPC and the Chancellor could select a suboptimal monetary–fiscal policy mix given a disagreement over the true state of the economy.

To take a practical example from this period, in early vintages of OBR forecasts it was assumed that inflation would soon return to the target but that the output gap would remain large and negative for an extended period of time (and larger and for longer than the BoE expected), consistent with the projection for the UK deficit being only partially structural in nature. All forecasters reserve the right to be wrong, but it is debatable whether that forecast was internally consistent: this combination of events seemed highly unlikely to arise (Anderson and Barwell 2011). One of three assumptions was likely flawed

- *Monetary policy would turn out looser:* If the OBR's output gap forecast was right, then it seemed likely that the MPC would ease the stance of monetary policy in order to close the output gap faster, which would deliver more robust growth and healthier headline public finances (and lower government debt going forward) than was assumed in the OBR's forecast.
- *Inflation would turn out weaker:* If the OBR's output gap forecast was right but the MPC did not respond then it seemed likely that inflation would likely fall below the target, which would imply weaker nominal demand and weaker headline public finances (and higher debt going forward) than was assumed in the OBR's forecast.
- *Output gap is smaller than assumed:* Alternatively, it might be that the OBR's inflation projection was reasonable but the output gap estimate was not. However, a less negative output gap would imply a larger structural deficit and that might require an acceleration in the pace of consolidation, which might then be expected to feed back into the conduct of monetary policy via the impact on demand.

We have focused here on the impact of changes in the stance of fiscal policy on the conduct of monetary policy. However, there are occasions when the causality can appear to run in the opposite direction. As discussed elsewhere in this book, the BoE conducted large-scale asset purchases to achieve its price stability remit during the crisis. At some point, during the recovery the Bank will stop reinvesting the proceeds as those assets mature and then the Bank might sell assets back into the market. Those decisions would have consequences for the fiscal forecasts: the asset purchase programme was fully indemnified by the Treasury, but the war-chest of cash that had gradually accumulated in the APF (as the coupon payments on the bonds exceeded the cost of financing the portfolio whilst Bank Rate remained at 0.5 %) which might have absorbed future losses when interest rates rose and assets were sold back into the market for less than the Bank had paid for them had been passed to the Exchequer, to allow the Chancellor to reduce debt issuance in the short run. Changes in the anticipated timing of the wind-down of the APF portfolio therefore has the potential to materially influence the likely path of spending. This is precisely what happened in the 2015 Autumn Statement, when the OBR brought its forecast for the likely timing of the APF portfolio going into wind-down into line with MPC's guidance on the subject.

The OBR had assumed in its March 2015 forecast that the stock of purchased assets would start to shrink through redemptions once Bank Rate started to rise. However, as we have already discussed, the Committee had signalled that tightening via a reduction in the stock of purchased assets would only come into play once the MPC considered that it had established room to cut interest rates materially. In the November Inflation Report, the Committee indicated that wind-down via redemptions or outright sales would not occur until Bank Rate had reached 2 %. The combined impact of the change in the OBR's assumption about the level of Bank Rate at which wind-down might begin and the change in investors' expectations of when that Bank Rate threshold would be achieved had the effect of pushing back the expected timing of wind-down beyond the OBR's forecast horizon. That change implied a significant reduction in the cost of servicing the debt burden over that forecast horizon, with the annual savings exceeding £2 billion in 2020–21 (OBR 2015).

References

Anderson, G., & Barwell, R. (2011, December 1). *OBR did not spot the silver lining in the cloud.* Letter to the Financial Times.

Auerbach, A., Gokhale, J., & Kotlikoff, L. (1987). Generational accounting: A meaningful way to evaluate fiscal policy. *Journal of Economic Perspectives, 8*(1), 73–94.

Auerbach, A., Gokhale, J., & Kotlikoff, L. (1991). Generational accounts: A meaningful alternative to deficit accounting. In D. Bradford (Ed.), *Tax policy and the economy* (pp. 55–110). Cambridge: MIT Press.

Barwell, R., &Burrows, O. (2011) *Growing fragilities? Balance sheets in the Great Moderation.* Bank of England Financial Stability Paper 10.

Barwell, R., & Chadha, J. (2014, August 31). *Publish or be damned – Or why central banks need to say more about the path of their policy rates.* Vox.

Bell, B., & Van Reenen, J. (2014). Bankers and their bonuses. *Economic Journal, 124,* F1–F21.

Clark, T., & Dilnot, A. (2002). *Measuring the UK fiscal stance.* IFS Briefing Note 26.

Devereux, M., Griffith, R., & Klemm, A. (2004). *Why has the UK corporation tax raised so much revenue?* IFS WP 04/04.

Eisner, R., & Pieper, P. (1984). A new view of the federal debt and budget deficits. *American Economic Review, 74*(1), 11–29.

Eschenbach, F., & Schuknecht, L. (2002). *Asset prices and fiscal balances.* ECB Working Paper 141.

Fahlenbrach, R., & Stulz, R. (2011). Bank CEO incentives and the credit crisis. *Journal of Financial Economics, 99*(1), 11–26.

Fatas, A., & Mihov, I. (2001). Government size and automatic stabilizers: International and intranational evidence. *Journal of International Economics, 55,* 3–28.

Giles, C. (2012, June 13). Ditch this daft concept. *Financial Times.*

Helgadottir, T., Chamberlin, G., Dhami, P., Farrington, S., & Robins, J. (2012). *Cyclically adjusting the public finances.* Office for Budget Responsibility Working Paper 3.

Hills, B., Thomas, R., & Yates, A. (2005). The impact of government spending on demand pressure. *Bank of England Quarterly Bulletin, Summer,* 140–152.

HMT. (2014). Whole of Government Accounts: Year ended 31 March 2013.

Honohan, P. (2009). *What went wrong in Ireland?* Paper prepared for the World Bank.

Hughes Hallett, A., Kattai, R., & Lewis, J. (2009). *Can we rely on real time figures for cyclically adjusted budget balances.* Bank of Estonia Working Paper Series 2/2009.

IFS. (2016). The IFS Green Budget.

Kanda, D. (2010). *Asset booms and structural fiscal positions.* IMF Working Paper 10/57.

Katz, L., & Meyer, B. (1990). The impact of the potential duration of unemployment benefits on the duration of unemployment. *Journal of Public Economics, 41*(1), 45–72.

Ley, E., & Misch, F. (2013). *Real-time macro monitoring and fiscal policy.* World Bank Policy Research Working Paper 6303.

Lomax, R. (2004, November 23). *Stability and statistics.* Speech.

McCarthy, D., Sefton, J., & Weale, M. (2011). *Generational accounts for the United Kingdom.* NIESR Discussion Paper 377.

Murray, J. (2014). *Output gap mismeasurement: Judgement and uncertainty.* Office for Budget Responsibility Working Paper 5.

OBR. (2014a). *Fiscal sustainability report.* HMSO.

OBR. (2014b, December). *Economic and fiscal outlook.* HMSO.

OBR. (2015, November). *Economic and fiscal outlook.* HMSO.

ONS (2009). Public Sector Interventions in the Financial Crisis.

Orphanides, A., & van Norden, S. (2002). The unreliability of output gap estimates in real-time. *Review of Economics and Statistics, 84*(4), 569–583.

Pope, T., & Roantree, B. (2014). *A survey of the UK tax system.* IFS Briefing Note BN09.

Riley, J., & Chote, R. (2014). *Crisis and consolidation in the public finances.* OBR Working Paper 7.

Tereanu, E., Tuladhar, A., & Simone, A. (2014). *Structural balance targeting and output gap uncertainty.* IMF Working Paper 14/107.

Vetlov, I., Hlédik, T., Jonsson, M., Kucsera, H., & Pisan, M. (2011). *Potential output in a DSGE model.* ECB Working Paper 1351.

10

Objectives

If you have followed the discussion of austerity economics in the popular press you could be excused for thinking that the primary goal of fiscal policy was to stabilise the economy—to lean against the volatility in output and employment over the business cycle. But of course that is not the primary goal of fiscal policy; for example, the Charter for Budget Responsibility makes clear, the Treasury's objectives for fiscal policy are to:

- ensure sustainable public finances that support confidence in the economy, promote intergenerational fairness, and ensure the effectiveness of wider Government policy; and
- support and improve the effectiveness of monetary policy in stabilising economic fluctuations

At a high level, we can differentiate between three objectives: efficiency, equity and stability, which are often explained via a familiar fiscal analogy of dividing up 'the cake': efficiency is about making sure the cake is as large as possible so that everyone can enjoy more; equity is about making sure that the division of the cake is as fair as possible; and stability is about making sure that the population is not forced to shift between feast and famine, that there is always a sufficient amount of cake to go around. In this section we discuss these objectives in more detail.

© The Editor(s) (if applicable) and The Author(s) 2016
R. Barwell, *Macroeconomic Policy after the Crash*,
DOI 10.1057/978-1-137-51592-6_10

10.1 The Case for Inaction

It may seem a strange place to start, but we shall begin with the traditional reasons for finance ministers not to intervene. Our motivation here is not to construct a case for inaction, but instead simply to clarify the case for action and to highlight some of the potential risks involved in the conduct of an activist economic policy. An exhaustive treatment of these issues is far beyond the scope of this book; indeed, much of the subject matter below is *microeconomics* not *macroeconomics*. We shall briefly sketch the case for inaction around four theorems—the two fundamental theorems of welfare economics, Coase's theorem and the theory of the second best—and a health warning on the scope for policy errors.

The fundamental theorems of welfare economics formalise Adam Smith's concept of the Invisible Hand—the idea that market forces, or the cumulative consequence of the individual pursuit of self-interest in a decentralised market place, can deliver the right outcome for society. To repeat the message above, there is no dispute about the status of these theorems—Stiglitz (1991) refers to the welfare theorems as 'one of the triumphs of modern mathematical economics'—only to their empirical relevance. The first welfare theorem states that under certain conditions a competitive market economy is Pareto efficient, in that it is impossible to make any one individual better off without making another worse off. The theorem holds in a stylised economy of price takers not makers in markets which clear (i.e., zero excess demand) and which has none of the paraphernalia of externalities and public goods and information problems we shall encounter below. Essentially, the first theorem knocks down the case for intervention on efficiency grounds in the market economy under extreme circumstances: the only justification for action is on equity grounds. The second fundamental theorem of welfare economics limits the scope for action on equity grounds, under even more demanding circumstances (concave utility function and convex production functions). The second theorem says that every Pareto-efficient outcome can be delivered by the market given minimal government intervention. Finance ministers should implement a set of lump sum transfers and then leave the market well alone to achieve equilibrium.

Even those 'free market' economists who instinctively oppose government intervention recognise that the economy does not measure up to the exacting standards of the fundamental theorems of welfare economics, and there are circumstances in which markets fail. However, the *free marketeers* are likely to favour market-based solutions to those market failures and in doing so appeal to Coase's theorem. The reader will be familiar with the idea that governments tax companies which release pollution into the atmosphere. The Coasian solution to this problem is to solve the underlying source of the problem: that nobody owns the atmosphere which the companies pollute (Coase 1960). If those property rights were well established and enforceable then the companies concerned would have to pay the owner for the use of that resource. Once again the importance of evaluating policy solutions on both of the primary objectives of fiscal policy—equity and efficiency—cannot be overstated: establishing property rights addresses the efficiency problem; from an equity perspective it matters a great deal who is given property rights over this common resource.

Perhaps the most compelling theoretical challenge to the orthodoxy of government intervention lies in the theory of the second best. Simply put, the theory suggests that if there are multiple market failures then the social planner cannot be sure that even a perfectly executed policy response which is designed to address any single imperfection will not do more harm than good—or as Lipsey and Lancaster (1956) put it, the theory shows the 'futility of "piecemeal welfare economics"'. A classic example here is a company which enjoys monopoly power but which pollutes the environment: one can readily imagine that an industrial economist would want the government to intervene to *increase* production (monopolists produce too little and charge too much from a welfare perspective) and an environmental economist would want the government to intervene to *reduce* production (to reduce the production of pollutants). To be clear, the theory does not suggest that left to its own devices the market will deliver the right outcome or that all interventions are counter-productive, but it does warn the social planner of the dangers of policy prescriptions based on partial economic analysis.

The final argument for inaction is a practical one: the free marketeers accept that markets fail but they counter that policymakers can fail too and therefore the case for government intervention should factor in the possibility that the policymakers will misdiagnose the problem, will fumble the design of the policy response or the execution of the response might have an unintended and undesirable impact. Practical policymakers are forever conscious of the risk of policy errors and like medical practitioners will seek to abide by a Hippocratic Oath of economic policy: first, do no harm. In passing, the reader might spot a tension between this concern about the fallibility of policymakers and the case for limited government intervention embedded in the second theorem of welfare economics: the social planner would need a good deal of information to be able to correctly calibrate the appropriate lump sum transfers which will allow the free market to achieve the optimal allocation.

10.2 The Case for Action

Two high level objectives motivate government intervention: the pursuit of efficiency and equality: that is, governments will try to ensure that the economy operates as close to the production possibility frontier as possible, and that the division of resources is as fair as possible. The purpose of the discussion above—and in particular the brief review of the fundamental theorems of welfare economics—was to remind the reader that the economist's first instinct is that under certain circumstances the market should deliver the first of these objectives without any intervention by the government and the second objective can be engineered too with minimal involvement. The case for government action on an *efficiency* front is therefore based on identifying the reasons *why* the market fails; we shall delay discussion of the *equity* agenda until the next subsection.

The classic source of inefficiency in a market economy is the existence of non-pecuniary externalities. An externality arises when the actions of one individual have a direct impact on the utility or productive potential of another. In many cases, those externalities operate through the price mechanism: when one group in the population increases their demand for a particular good then they will typically drive up the price and that means that other individuals will have to give up more resources to consume that good. This is the mechanism through which the market ensures an efficient allocation of resources. Non-pecuniary externalities operate outside the price mechanism: the behaviour of one set of agents affects the consumption or production possibilities of other agents, but that social cost or benefit experienced by the latter will not be reflected in the private cost or benefit perceived by the former. The standard example here is when a company releases pollutants into the atmosphere as a by-product of producing output that is sold in the market: the damage done to the environment and the utility of the population will not be reflected in the price of output. Generically we can imagine these non-pecuniary externalities leading to a divergence of social marginal cost and/or social marginal benefit from the private analogues which determine allocation in the market. The example of non-pecuniary externalities is useful because it illustrates how there are multiple policy solutions to a perceived market failure: from regulations to allocating property rights to taxes and subsidies (see Helfand et al. 2003).

Another familiar flaw with the free market—which is typically traced back to Samuelson (1954)—is its failure to provide (pure) 'public goods'—that is, those goods which exhibit two key features: they are both non-rivalrous and non-excludable. A good is non-rivalrous if my consumption of that good does not reduce the amount of the good which you can consume. A good is non-excludable if the producer cannot prevent an individual consuming that good without paying for it. Pure public goods, such as street lighting or national defence, are therefore provided by the government, or not at all. In passing, some public goods may be too big even for national governments: Nordhaus (1994) extends the Samuelson concept to *global public goods*, where consumption of that good does not respect national borders, with ideas such as the cure for communicable diseases being a case in point.

Beyond the totemic issue of pure public goods there are a range of goods and services where the social planner cannot rely on the market to provide the socially efficient outcome thanks to further departures from the perfectly competitive benchmark. A particular case in point is the provision of insurance for some of the key risks that confront individuals thanks to familiar problems of asymmetric information: adverse selection and moral hazard. Those individuals who know that they are most likely to make a claim (given private information) are more likely to demand insurance, so the private sector provider will face problems pooling risks across high and low risk consumers. Moreover, once in receipt of insurance individuals' behaviour may change—they are less likely to take privately costly decisions to avoid the risk crystallising and are therefore more likely to make a claim. Those problems can make adequate private provision improbable or even impossible. There are a range of public sector quasi-insurance solutions to this problem (Barr 1992). On the one hand, there are universal benefits, where people can make claims in the event of the risk crystallising irrespective of their income and without having had to contribute to the system. Alternatively, there is social assistance where an income test is applied such that only those on low incomes can claim in the event of the risk crystallising. Finally, there is social insurance (Feldstein 2005). Social insurance has two key features: membership is compulsory, and individuals can make claims based on the occurrence of a specific risk and irrespective of their income. Contributions to social insurance might be quasi-actuarial (in order to mimic the premium that the typical member of the population would pay) or income-related (in order to mimic a tax-based system).

Another concern on the efficiency front is the risk of self-harm: that well-intentioned fiscal policy may be the cause of inefficiency. Governments need to raise money through taxation to fund expenditure. In a perfect world, governments would raise that money through 'lump sum' taxes, which do not distort behaviour because they do not influence market prices—the return or cost from any given economic activity—which guide the allocation of resources. For example, imagine that governments could replace income tax with a tax on an each individual's innate ability and talents which will determine their earnings potential. That tax liability would remain the same irrespective of how much or how little each individual earns and therefore should not distort their choices between consumption and leisure. In practice, taxes on labour income will drive a wedge between the value they provide to their employer and their take home pay and that could influence labour supply decisions. We shall return to discuss this question of the optimal design of tax policy later in this book.

One final aspect of the efficiency agenda that is worthy of discussion is a novel solution to an old problem. Policymakers have always understood that the decisions which individuals take do not always measure up to the exacting benchmark of the *Homo economicus*, who is forever optimising on the basis of rational (and therefore inevitably highly complex) forecasts of the future (see the discussion in Barwell (2013) and the references therein). The behavioural economics literature, which stretches back at least half a century to Simon (1957), suggests that people may not respond to policy interventions in the way that conventional classical economics suggests. Evidence that people make mistakes presents policymakers with a dilemma: should they intervene to prevent people making bad decisions or should they respect individual free will.

Policymakers are traditionally divided into two camps over this question: the Paternalists were willing to intervene—outlawing consumption of certain goods, making consumption of others compulsory—and the Libertarians were not. In recent years, a third school of thought has emerged: Libertarian Paternalists who seek to nudge boundedly rational agents in the right direction by framing choices in a way that encourages those agents to make 'good' decisions; see Chetty (2015) for a wider discussion of the role which behavioural economics can play in the conduct of economic policy. So popular has this third way become that the Coalition government established a Behaviour Insights Team (which became known as the 'nudge unit') with the purpose of implementing this insight to achieve outcomes. There is evidence that nudges can influence outcomes (Thaler and Sunstein 2008); the question we need to ask is whether we can safely assume that agents will always be nudged in the right direction.

Nudges look like a free lunch for policymakers but no so fast: Rebonato's (2012) critique of the nudge agenda raises awkward questions for Libertarian Paternalism. If boundedly rational agents can be 'tricked' into taking the decisions that the social planner believes that they should take simply by framing the choices that confront them, then we should think hard about the identity of the choice architect—their private incentives and the information set and cognitive capacity which somehow allows them to deduce the choices that agents should take.

10.3 The Scale and Source of the Inequality Problem

Inequality is easier to describe than to define (Cowell 1995). The fundamental concept is clear: there is the basic principle of 'equal treatment of equals' (a.k.a. horizontal equity) and 'unequal treatment of unequals' (a.k.a. vertical equity). However, there are a whole host of measurement questions: how to compress information on the distribution of experiences across the population into a single summary statistic (Gini coefficients, ratio of the percentiles of the distribution, etc.); about which outcome we should focus upon (wages, total pre-tax income, post-tax income, consumption, wealth etc.); about the time-frame over which that outcome should be measured (one year, lifetime); about which social unit we should focus on (the individual or the household) and so on. There is ample scope here for reasonable people to reach quite different conclusions about the absolute extent and even at points the direction of change of inequality in society based on the reasonable choices they make from the above list. However, the broad trend in income inequality over recent decades is beyond doubt and dispute: inequality has increased *significantly*. The Gini coefficient—which measures how far the income distribution diverges from the perfect equality benchmark (with zero implying complete equality and one complete inequality)—rose from around 0.25 in 1979 to around 0.35 at the turn of the millennium (Brewer et al. 2008).

Belfield et al. (2014) provide an excellent snapshot of income inequality (and much else besides) in the UK in 2012–13 based on a comprehensive measure of net household income (i.e., after adjusting for taxes and benefits) which is 'equivalised' to take account of differences in the size and composition of households. They find that the median individual (50th percentile) has just under twice the household income of those at the 10th percentile, and those at the 90th percentile have just over twice the household income of those at the median, and those at the 98th percentile have twice the income of those at the 90th percentile. They go on to document how the financial crisis has led to a reduction in income inequality: between 2007 and 2008 and 2012–13, real incomes measured before housing costs fell by 6.2 % at the top of the distribution (90th percentile) versus 4.5 % at the median and rose by 0.9 % at the bottom (10th percentile), and the Gini coefficient fell to its lowest level since the 1990s. The key driver was the fall in earnings relative to prices and benefit entitlements during the early years of the crisis —median income for non-working households rose from 60 % of that of working households in 2007–08 to 67 % in 2012–13—although this trend looks to be reversing as real earnings recover. This picture looks a little different if we focus on a post housing costs measure of incomes because those in the top half of the distribution will have disproportionately benefited from the decline in mortgage interest rates. Pensioners have seen a relative improvement in their position: median income after housing costs across pensioner households was 20 % below that of working-age households in 1992 and 5 % below in 2007–08 but by 2012–13 was 5 % above.

Brewer and O'Dea (2012) take an alternative perspective on inequality based on patterns of consumption rather than income. The theoretical case for focusing on consumption is strong: there could be significant and systematic differences between income and consumption for a given individual (depending on their age, employment status, access to credit, and so on) and if people prefer to smooth consumption over their lifetime then consumption should provide the more accurate gauge of well-being over their lifetime. Brewer and O'Dea illustrate the practical importance of focusing on consumption data: income may be systematically under-reported for households with few resources, giving a potentially misleading impression of the extent of inequality. In particular, inequality is now found to have increased less rapidly because consumption outperformed income at the bottom of the distribution during the 1980s and underperformed at the top during the 1990s and the 2000s.

The other key point to note here is the importance of the time period over which inequality is measured. Roantree and Shaw (2014) illustrate how our understanding of inequality changes when we compare outcomes over an extended period (in the limit, lifetimes) relative to a snapshot at a moment in time. Individuals are either in work or not at any given moment in time, but the identity of who is in work will change through time, so that the distribution of employment may be more evenly spread when measured over a long interval. Roantree and Shaw find that the Gini coefficient falls by a fifth when we measure inequality over an 18-year window rather a single year. Likewise, the tax and benefit system looks less progressive too, because we are much more likely to observe intra-personal redistribution—people paying money in at some points, and taking money out in others—over a multi-year window.

In the remainder of this section, we shall focus primarily on the research done by labour economists on inequality, who tend to focus on inequality in the wage distribution for two reasons: for most members of the population, and certainly the working age population, their wage is their primary source of income, and because they look to developments in the labour market to explain those developments in the distribution of earnings across the workforce they observe.

Wage inequality rose sharply in the UK as the twentieth century drew to a close (Machin 2011). The increase in wage inequality was particularly marked in the 1980s, where rising inequality was a pervasive phenomenon, with wage gaps rising both within and between different socio-economic groups in the workforce. The trend of rising inequality continued into the 1990s albeit at a more modest pace, and where the upper tail of the distribution was concerned the wage gap continued to rise into the 2000s. However, inequality at the bottom of the distribution stopped increasing in the years leading up to the financial crisis.

Rising wage inequality in the 1980s was an international phenomenon which suggests a common (global) force at work. However, it is important not to gloss over significant cross-country differences, which suggest that differences in labour market institutional might have an important role to play: the rise in inequality was far more marked in the UK and the USA than in Japan, and in France inequality actually declined in the first half of the 1980s (Katz et al. 1995). There are four stylised explanations for both the common trend increase in wage inequality in recent decades and the deviations around it (Katz and Autor 1999) that more or less boil down to a race between shifts in the demand for and supply of skills and the capacity of labour market institutions to influence the returns for different skills set by the market:

- *Skill-based technological change (SBTC)*: an increase in the relative demand for more highly skilled workers, thanks to the spread of technology in the workplace;
- *Increased supply of low skilled labour*: supply of high skill workers has failed to keep pace with demand thanks to a combination of demography and immigration;
- *Globalisation*: a combination of increased trade and increased outsourcing (the goods coming here or the jobs going there) has depressed the wages of those lower skilled workers who worked particularly in the traded goods sector; and
- *Labour market institutions*: changes in the incidence and influence of trade unions, wage bargaining and norms and minimum wage legislation have influenced the evolution of wages.

The first factor—SBTC—is probably the favoured candidate explanation of the academics, and one which weighs on the minds of policymakers who are concerned about what a future of further technological advances might have in store for those in the lower tail of the wage distribution. However, there are still puzzles which the simple SBTC hypothesis cannot explain: further advances in technology in the 1990s did not go hand in hand with the same significant increase in wage inequality that was experienced in the 1980s and SBTC cannot explain other dimensions of the wage inequality story—by gender, race and age (Card and DiNardo 2002).

Autor et al. (2003) suggest a more nuanced narrative of how technological changes might be influencing distributional outcomes in the labour market. Rather than the simplistic story of the rise of computers benefiting the skilled at the expense of the unskilled, Autor, Levy and Murnane argue that technological change has had the biggest impact in the middle of the distribution, where technology can substitute human labour that was previously performing 'routine' tasks in both blue- and white-collar occupations. Goos and Manning (2007) find evidence of this polarising impact of technology in the UK with the emergence of a dual labour market of lousy and lovely jobs, which can explain a third and a half of the rise in wage inequality in the bottom and top tails of the wage distribution respectively.

One strand of the wage inequality debate which has attracted increasing attention in recent years is the behaviour of incomes at the very top of the distribution *relative to everyone else*. Alvaredo et al. (2013) report that the share of income accounted for by the top 1 % more than doubled over the past three decades in the USA, and once again, whilst the increase in the upper tail in income inequality is common to many countries, the extent of the increase varies considerably. In the UK, Brewer et al. (2008) report how the incomes of the top percentile in the income distribution rose at an average rate of 3.1 % since 1997, a faster pace than any other percentile in the distribution and significantly faster than the average rate (2.3 %). Perhaps unsurprisingly, they find that the income growth of the very high income individuals (who tend to be disproportionately male, middle-aged and living in London and the South East) tends to be highly correlated with the state of financial markets—another illustration of the potential impact of the financial cycle on the state of the public finances discussed earlier.

The standard explanation for the explosion in earnings at the very top of the distribution is the superstar phenomenon. Under certain circumstances—in markets where individuals provide services to the market, which can be reproduced at relatively low costs, and where the customers perceive a clear ranking in terms of the talent or quality of the producers—then a superstar can dominate the market, and therefore earn very high returns (see Rosen (1981) for the original exposition of this idea and Adler (2006) for a review). Where the services that the most talented individual in a given sector can provide to customers are non-rivalrous but excludable then they may be able to reap huge rewards. For *free marketeers,* the superstar argument is attractive because it suggests that the income inequality is not a product of market failure. However, it is far from clear that all those being paid large salaries in the financial markets can claim to be 'superstars'. Gordon and Dew-Becker (2008) argue that policymakers (and for that matter the shareholders of large institutions) should be more concerned about one particular group who feature in the very high income bracket—chief executives—because it is less clear that the compensation of CEOs is determined exclusively in the marketplace (see Murphy 1999).

From a public policy perspective, the key question is the extent to which policy interventions can contain or even compress the rise in inequality. We shall suppress the implications of those interventions motivated by concerns over equity for the pursuit of efficiency for a second here, and briefly review the policy options. As noted earlier, labour market institutions do appear to have a role to play in explaining differences in wage inequality across countries and through time. For example, the introduction of the National Minimum Wage in 1999, and its subsequent uprating, likely played some part in preventing a further increase in wage inequality in the lower tail of the distribution over that period (Dickens and Manning 2004; Stewart 2012).

Although institutional reform can surely play its part, the principle policy lever of redistribution is always likely to be the tax and benefit system, and differences in the extent to which governments are willing to use that tool will have consequences for measured inequality. For example, Guvenen et al. (2009) argue that a more progressive tax schedule in continental Europe has contributed to a more equal distribution through two channels—by reducing the incentive to supply labour at the margin and reducing the return from that marginal hour for high earners—with the effect that the significant flattening of the US tax schedule can help explain the rise in inequality there relative to Germany.

Of course, when we think about policy interventions in this area we tend to think about changes to the tax and benefit system which impact on those in the lower tail of the distribution. Roantree and Shaw (2014) identify an example of a policy intervention at the bottom which scores highly based on both the snapshot approach to measuring inequality and the long exposure photograph approach which captures inequality in outcomes over lifetimes: the changes in the tax and benefit system enacted by the Labour Government which favoured households with children (see Blundell et al. 2005 for more details). Roantree and Shaw find that the reforms were well targeted in the sense that they were particularly effective at benefiting those at the bottom end of the distribution both at a moment in time and over a lifetime, because the individuals in receipt of support tend to remain near the bottom of the income distribution throughout their working lives.

10.4 The Tension Between Equity and Efficiency

The fact that a policymaker might have multiple objectives is not necessarily problematic, even if the pursuit of one objective happens to set back progress towards another. So long as the policymaker satisfies Tinbergen's Law—that is, the observation attributed to Nobel prize winner Jan Tinbergen that so long as she has access to a distinct and effective policy instrument for each of her objectives—then she should be able to achieve the best possible outcome through a judicious combination of those instruments. However, this rule of thumb may not apply where the pursuit of efficiency and equity are concerned, as another Nobel prize winner, Arthur Okun, argued back in the 1970s. Okun (1975) believed that the conflict between equality and efficiency was inescapable; that some measure of inequality is a necessary evil in order to achieve the efficient outcome. Four decades on, Okun's belief in an inescapable trade-off remains controversial.

Those who believe in the existence of a trade-off between efficiency and equality point to the fundamental importance of prices as signals to guide the efficient allocation of resources in a market economy, and the implied shifts in relative prices necessarily produce winners and losers and an unequal income distribution. In particular, wages are supposed to signal relative scarcity and abundance of labour encouraging a supply response (Welch 1999), whether that be workers deciding to change their occupation or migrating to a different local labour market or investing in additional human capital. For example, policymakers repeatedly state that they would like to rebalance demand—that is, they would prefer exports and investment accounted for a larger share of GDP than we observe in the data, and consumption a correspondingly smaller share. That rebalancing of product demand implies a corresponding rebalancing of labour demand too. Companies who produce capital goods or exports will need to increase the size of their workforce and for that to happen likely requires an increase in the wages that those companies offer when they post new vacancies.

Ostry et al. (2014) review a range of arguments, for and against the notion of a trade-off between efficiency and equality. In the 'for' camp they note the standard 'incentives' argument—that without the potential prize of financial rewards for those who succeed, individuals would be less likely to work hard, become entrepreneurs and so on—and that with an equal distribution of wealth too few people will have the necessary capital to fund business start-ups, which are widely thought to be an engine of productivity growth. On the other hand, they argue that a more equal society goes hand in hand with a healthier (and therefore more productive) workforce in the lower tail of the income distribution, greater scope for those individuals to invest in their own human capital (again raising productivity) One could even make the case that a more equal society makes for a more stable society, including the political direction of the country, which in turn could leave households and companies more willing to make long-term investments, whether in human or physical capital. *Macro*economists have become willing to think about these wider implications of inequality given the outcome of the referendum on EU membership and the US Presidential election.

In terms of the macro evidence, Alesina and Rodrik (1994) argue that greater inequality today tends to be associated with lower growth in the future. Forbes (2000) reaches a different conclusion: she argues that once we account for country-specific fixed effects, higher inequality tends to go hand in hand with faster growth. Berg and Ostry (2011) refocus the debate, arguing that it is the duration of growth spurts that matter, not the precise pace of growth in any particular year, because it is how long that spurt lasts which will have the greater influence on the level of activity, and they find that more equal countries tend to enjoy significantly longer growth spurts.

One key problem in the empirical literature is differentiating between the symptom and the cure when examining the impact of 'inequality' on the rate of economic growth. In other words, it might not be the unequal outcome of market forces which influences the rate of growth, but the policy response. For example, one might expect to see greater redistribution via taxes and transfer payments in societies where the pre-tax distribution of income is more unequal and those measures could weigh on economic growth. Ostry and Berg (2014) differentiate between 'market inequality' and 'net inequality' with the scope of redistribution explaining the difference between them, and thankfully find that redistributive efforts appear to have little adverse impact on economic growth.

Finally, it is important to stress that there may also be a link between inequality and the secondary fiscal objective of stability. Kumhof et al. (2015) argue that there was a potential link between the inequality of the years leading up to the financial crisis and the crash that followed: those at the top were saving and accumulating financial assets which were ultimately backed by loans to those lower down the income distribution who were relying on debt to partially support their standard of living in the face of stagnant real incomes. Inequality was therefore feeding the inflation of fragile balance sheet positions during this period.

10.5 Social Choice and Public Choice

Where monetary policy is concerned there is a consensus about the loss function that guides decision-making. In the fiscal realm we need to think hard
about how decisions are taken. There are two contrasting approaches to tack-
ling this problem: either to think about the preferences of an idealised social
planner, which should reflect the cumulative preferences of the population,
or to think in more practical terms about how the people who take decisions
(politicians) are elected, and the incentives they face.

The usual starting point in social choice is the Pareto criterion, which states
that a social planner should implement any policy measure which makes at
least one person better off whilst making nobody worse off. The problem with
the Pareto Criterion is that it does not get you very far: the social planner
will very quickly find that she exhausts all possible policy options which do
not make at least one person worse off. Projects like the construction of high
speed rail links or a new runway at an airport would not get off the drawing
board because those who live in immediate vicinity are made worse off even if
the project makes most of the population better off.

Kaldor and Hicks offered a solution to the deadlock created by Pareto: the
compensation criterion. Consider those policy measures which make a large
number of people much better off and a small number of people worse off.
Hicks and Kaldor invite the social planner to consider these 'potentially pareto
improving' policies, since with the appropriately designed set of transfers from
the former to the latter, the Pareto criterion can be satisfied. It is interesting to
note that Kaldor and Hicks did not insist that these transfers should be made
as a condition for the implementation of these measures that benefit some
and hurt others.

In order to take decisions we therefore need to find some way to combine
the preferences of the population, or what economists refer to as the social
welfare function. We can assert some basic properties of that social welfare
function: that it should be non-decreasing in the welfare of individual members of the population (if at least one person is better off, and nobody is made
worse off, then social welfare should not fall), and that social welfare should
be blind to the welfare of particular individuals in the population. But those
of a practical persuasion will immediately start to see problems for a finance
minister who wishes to implement the social welfare function agenda. Should
she include the utility of future generations who may all too often turn out to
be the ones on the losing end of fiscal stimulus today? How should she handle
the imperfections of a population that 'doesn't know what's good for them':
is a paternalistic approach where the social planner imputes the 'correct' util-

ity function for the population acceptable? It turns out that there are some formidable theoretical challenges to overcome too.

The default assumption when it comes to the social welfare function is the utilitarian specification which can be traced back to Jeremy Bentham and John Stuart Mill. The basic premise of utilitarianism is that the social planner should treat every individual the same and simply aim to maximise the public good across that population by aggregating together the welfare of each member, or what is often referred to as the pursuit of 'the greatest good of the greatest number'. Although maximising the utility of the population may sound appealing, it should be clear that the concept of inequality, whether relative or absolute, does not feature in the utilitarian construct. Indeed, there is nothing which necessarily guarantees that practices which modern society considers abhorrent, such as slavery or euthanasia, would not be the outcome of a pure utilitarian approach.

At the other end of the spectrum is the Rawlsian approach to social welfare. Rawls (1999) argues that social welfare should be measured exclusively by the standard of living of the least well-off member of society; the well-being of all other members of the population is irrelevant. This seemingly extreme position is justified by the so-called 'veil of ignorance': that is, if we did not know our own position in the income distribution we would adopt a Rawlsian standpoint for fear that we might be that person at the bottom. This Rawlsian approach is the original example of the application of the *maximin* criterion: ranking different outcomes according to the worst possible outcome (in this case, the welfare of the individual at the bottom) and then choose accordingly.

Arrow (1951) famously concluded that the quest for the right social welfare function was doomed: his so-called impossibility theorem states that there is no social choice mechanism—a way of aggregating together the preferences of individuals—which satisfies the following key axioms (Sen 2014):

- *Unrestricted domain*: For any feasible set of individual preferences, there is a social ordering that is reflexive, transitive and complete (which in plain English means that there is an internally consistent and complete ranking across all possible outcomes).
- *Independence of irrelevant alternatives*: The social ranking of any pair {x,y} will depend only on the individual rankings of x and y.
- *Pareto principle*: If everyone prefers any x to any y, then x is socially preferred to y.
- *Non-dictatorship*: There does not exist a person in the population such that when that person prefers any x to any y, then socially x is preferred to y, irrespective of the preferences of others.

Of course, there is no benevolent social planner taking decisions in an ivory tower in representative democracies; the preferences that individuals reveal via the ballot box are the fundamental driver of decision-making. Economists interested in economic policy therefore turned their attention to how voting rules perform in terms of the outcomes they select given a heterogeneous electorate.

There are a number of plausible voting mechanisms for electing politicians (Dasgupta and Maskin 2008):

- *Simple majority*: A politician is elected if she is preferred in pairwise comparisons with all other candidates.
- *First past the post*: A politician is elected if more people select her as their first choice than any other candidate (even though in a head to head contest she may lose against other candidates in a pair-wise comparison)
- *Rank ordering*: A politician is selected on the basis of the cumulative preferences of the electorate across all candidates.

The discussion of the impossibility theorem above should have warned the reader to expect that these voting mechanisms will not (*cannot*) deliver ideal outcomes in all circumstances. Indeed, an aristocratic French philosopher and a British mathematician and novelist (Lewis Carroll no less) both identified many years ago the paradoxes that can arise when individuals are asked to vote in an election with multiple candidates: for example, the simple majority rule may not be able to deliver an outcome under certain circumstances. The destructive power of Arrow's theorem is sometimes overplayed: if we restrict attention to a more plausible subset of preferences then we might be able to make progress (Dasgupta and Maskin 2004). In particular, if preferences are single peaked over the issue at hand—then voting rules perform better (Black 1948). Given unimodal preferences and a single issue being debated at the ballot box we arrive at the well-known median voter theorem (Downs 1957), where politicians will gravitate towards the views of the median person in the electorate, since by definition any position to the left or right of them will be opposed by a majority of the electorate.

Once economists started thinking about voting mechanisms they immediately started to identify problems: if there are costs to becoming informed and voting then given that the private benefit of voting depends on the probability of your vote making a difference to the outcome of the election (which is inevitably very small indeed) then the rational member of the population would not vote. More generally, it became clear that we need to worry about the design of the political process itself.

There is plenty of evidence that the institutional and legal constraints which govern how elections are conducted can influence outcomes. Besley and Preston (2007) argue that how political boundaries are drawn matters: the more politicians can gerrymander the electoral map to produce unrepresentative constituencies, the less constrained they are to espouse views consistent with the median voter. Besley and Case (1995) find that term limits matter: those politicians who cannot seek reelection are less constrained in their behaviour with ambiguous consequences (lame-duck politicians might not feel obliged to pander to lobby groups). Chattopadhyay and Duflo (2004) show that rules which restrict who can stand for election—in particular, to ensure that women are elected to office—does influence outcomes where men and women have different preferences over the nature of government spending.

The other generic concern is just another manifestation of the asymmetric information problem: the principal (the voter) has very little information on the actions that the agent she elects (the politician) is taking, and once elected their incentives do not necessarily coincide. A classic concern here is the risk of *rent seeking*: that politicians *might* systematically succumb to 'lobbying' by private individuals and institutions to take decisions which confer large benefits on a select few, but are not necessarily in the public interest (Tullock 1967; Krueger 1974). The social planner should sweep away the market failures which allow monopolies to thrive. However, the monopolist should be willing to spend large sums of money persuading the politician to do otherwise—to preserve the status quo (and the monopoly rent that goes with it). Murphy et al. (1991) highlight an interesting proxy of the scope of rent-seeking in a modern economy—pointing to the correlation between the relative size of different professions in the workforce and the rate of economic growth—for example, lawyers are bad for growth, engineers are good for growth—with the former representing a diversion of talented resources (labour) towards socially unproductive (though privately productive) rent-seeking activities rather than socially productive rent producing activities of the latter.

Another concern is that the political system *might* deliver an excessively large and inefficient government bureaucracy (Niskanen 1971), perhaps on account of an additional asymmetric information problem between the politicians and the civil servants, or perhaps because politicians derive prestige from the size of their departments; either way, the result is that an unnecessarily high level of distortionary taxation is required to fund the X-inefficient public sector.

10.6 The Stability Agenda

The final high level objective of fiscal policy is stability—that is, to reduce the volatility of aggregate income. Macroeconomists will instinctively interpret that remit in the context of the business cycle, with finance ministers using the levers of fiscal policy to lean against cyclical deviations of activity and employment—and that is our focus here—but the financial crisis has reminded economists that low probability, high impact shocks can have a far more significant impact on welfare than the typical business cycle. Forward-looking policymakers will use the levers at their disposal to try and protect the economy from these shocks too. The policy response to the threats posed by climate change are an obvious example (de Mooij et al. 2012), whether taxes on pollution or investments in flood defences. Interestingly, finance ministers may not be alone in this—the macroprudential authority in the UK (the FPC) has staked out a position in this debate, using the tools at its disposal to pursue economic stability.

There is a clear micro dimension to the stability agenda. There are two distinguishing features of the wage profile of the representative agent over the course of her lifetime that may concern the social planner: first, earnings are uncertain, and in particular at any moment in time there is a risk of the loss of labour income due to unemployment or ill health; and second, that wages vary predictably with age, typically peaking in middle age, and falling to zero in retirement. Given diminishing returns from consumption in any particular period, the representative agent will likely want to purchase insurance against the risk of an unexpected loss of earnings during her working life, and save to manage the predictable loss of earnings in retirement. As noted above, where the provision of these services in the market is imperfect or absent altogether, there is a case for intervention, whether through the provision of social insurance or public pension schemes.

Turning to the role played by fiscal policy in stabilising the macroeconomy at a business cycle frequency we need to revisit the distinction between the automatic stabilisers and discretionary changes in the fiscal stance discussed earlier. As their name implies, the automatic stabilisers will naturally lean against cyclical swings in demand without finance ministers having to lift a finger. Indeed, in many respects the automatic stabilisers can be thought of as a near unintended consequence of the pursuit of conventional fiscal objectives. Governments do not pay benefits to the unemployed and raise revenue via taxes on income primarily because they wish to hard-wire a counter-cyclical policy response into the structure of the economy; it just so happens that these measures happen to shift the government budget into surplus in a boom and into deficit in a bust.

The debate about the appropriate role of fiscal policy in stabilising the economy over the business cycle focuses on discretionary policy where finance ministers take a conscious decision to enact transitory changes in the taxation or expenditure, with the prime objective of influencing the level of demand. There was a time where those changes in taxation or expenditure would play a major role in the counter-cyclical policy response; however, in recent decades a new consensus has emerged, with monetary policy expected to do the heavy lifting in smoothing out the variation in output and employment over the business cycle. That consensus is based on a couple of arguments (Taylor 2000):

First, *implementation lags*: it is believed that central bankers are more nimble on their feet than finance ministers. Monetary policymakers meet around once every six weeks, and if there is an emergency they have the option to meet at short notice. The decisions that the MPC take can be implemented immediately and will very quickly pass-through into asset prices. It might take a couple of years before the change in the stance of policy has its peak impact on demand and inflation but that reflects the rigidities in the economy. In contrast, changes in the stance of fiscal policy tend to involve much longer implementation lags. Changes in the levers of fiscal policy will typically happen only twice each year, and are then typically subject to parliamentary approval before being implemented. Indeed, Cimadomo (2012) arrives at the depressing conclusion that whilst the intention may be for fiscal policy to be counter-cyclical, the lags in decision-making and implementation when coupled with errors in estimating the true state of the economy in real time can all too easily result in the opposite: fiscal policy turns out to be pro-cyclical.

Second, *reversibility*: it seems likely that central bankers would be *less* concerned about the potential reputational damage involved in reversing course if the economy evolves in an unexpected direction such that the initial policy response no longer appears necessary and needs to undone (which is not the same thing as saying that they are completely unconcerned). That lack of flexibility could lead to discretionary fiscal policy contributing to, rather than suppressing, cyclical swings in activity. However, it must be said that a stylised fact in the monetary policy literature is that there are surprisingly few reversals, particularly if one assumes that the shocks which hit the economy are white noise (Sack 2000).

Third, *policy coordination*: if central bankers are given primary responsibility for counter-cyclical demand management then they need to be able to forecast the evolution of the economy, and that in turn requires an accurate forecast of the fiscal stance. In other words, the more predictable fiscal policy is—in terms of its impact on demand—the easier it is for central bankers to achieve their objectives. An unexpected discretionary loosening in fiscal policy starts to look like just another shock that central bankers have to contend with.

Of course, the consensus that finance ministers should take the back seat to central bankers when it comes to stabilising the economy hinges on the assumption that central banks are ready, willing and able to act. As we will go on to discuss later in this book that assumption may not be valid in certain circumstances: not for countries in a currency union and perhaps not when interest rates hit the zero bound.

10.7 If Not Stimulus Then What...Structural Reforms

The debate among economists about the conduct of fiscal policy has been preoccupied with calibrating the optimal pace of fiscal consolidation, to the detriment of meaningful discussion of the appropriate pursuit of the conventional fiscal goals of equity and efficiency. In the view of the author, the profession might have made a more positive contribution to the public good and given a better impression of the value added in macroeconomics if we had spent a little more time discussing the fiscal mix *within a given budget envelope* and concentrated on what could be done to ensure that the consolidation effort did minimal damage to the supply side of the economy and the standard of living of those at the bottom of the income distribution.

To be fair, this book is guilty of the same sin. In my defence, true fiscal policy—that is, the set of government policies that can potentially deliver on the fiscal authority's equity, efficiency and stability agenda—is more micro than macro, and therefore beyond the scope of this book. Credible answers to the key policy questions that confronted government ministers during this period—the case for HS2, or subsidising university tuition, or for nuclear power or even for the UK's membership of the European Union—cannot be found within the macroeconomist's toolkit alone. However, to atone for this sin of omission we can broaden our perspective if only for a moment to discuss the broad sweep of fiscal policy. Rather than serve up a smörgåsbord of structural policies we shall soon turn to sketch out the aspect of the fiscal agenda that interests macroeconomists the most (supply-side reforms) and then discuss a specific and critical example (reform of the tax code). But before we do that, we shall offer some brief thoughts on why progress on implementing structural measures tends to be slow.

10.7.1 Why Reform Is Difficult to Deliver

We have already discussed one reason why governments will find it difficult to drive through potentially Pareto-improving reforms which are expected to raise the level of potential supply and hence the standard of living of the representative household. Most reforms will make some people significantly worse off in the process of making many others a little better off. We might reasonably expect that the losers will be better informed about how much they stand to lose from the reforms and to be willing to spend resources ('lobby') to prevent them being implemented than those who gain. After all, the losers cannot be certain that they will be adequately compensated for their loss. As economists we should expect the opponents of reform to be more vocal and better resourced than its cheerleaders. Political pressure may prevent potentially Pareto-improving reforms being implemented.

In some cases, legal restrictions designed to protect the rights of the minority may prevent reforms which would benefit the majority. The debate around how to increase airport capacity in the South East is a case in point. In its final report, the Airports Commission made a 'clear and unanimous' recommendation: to increase capacity at Heathrow. However, there were a number of caveats around managing noise pollution and compensating the local community but most importantly of all, the clear and unanimous recommendation to expand Heathrow was conditional on there being no detrimental impact on air quality (Airports Commission 2015):

> Additional operations at an expanded Heathrow must be contingent on acceptable performance on air quality. New capacity should only be released when it is clear that air quality at sites around the airport will not delay compliance with EU limits.

Even if the social planner was ready, willing and able to financially compensate the residents of London for breathing polluted air, the law might prevent her from striking this deal. At the time of writing, it was unclear whether the Heathrow proposal could ever pass this test. In late 2015, the House of Commons Environmental Audit Committee urged the government not to formally approve expansion at Heathrow until the airport had demonstrated that it could satisfy the environmental preconditions and within a couple of weeks the government had announced that it was postponing taking a final decision until it had conducted further work on the environmental impact of increasing capacity at Heathrow.

Alongside the political and legal impediments to reform there is also an important economic constraint on the reform agenda. Well-designed structural reforms may enhance the supply side of the economy and therefore raise the level of demand in the long run but there is no guarantee that reforms will raise the level of demand in the short run. This result will tend to emerge in the rational expectations models that currently dominate the academic literature: supply-side reforms imply higher permanent income which unlocks higher current consumption as far as forward-looking representative agents are concerned. However, government ministers are unlikely to take much comfort from those theoretical results: they will fear short-run pain before long-run gain (which may arrive long after the date of the next general election).

The fact that the reform process tends to create losers as well as winners has implications for the near-term prospects for demand (for a given monetary policy stance). There are reasons to believe that the former (the losers) are more likely to cut back spending in response to their loss than the latter (the winners) are willing or able to spend their gains. In some cases, the drag on demand follows from the fact that the positive impact of reforms goes unnoticed. Those on the wrong end of the reform process may stand to lose a lot. When the government sweeps away the customs and practices that generate economic rents in a particular sector of the economy, the shareholders and employees of the companies that used to enjoy monopoly power in that sector will receive lower dividends and wages in the future. As we argued above, the losers are likely to be far better informed about the looming loss to their standard of living and adjust their spending patterns accordingly. Inattentive consumers may take some time to appreciate that they are better off—that their weekly pay packet stretches a little bit further—thanks to the decline in the cost of consumption given the elimination of monopoly power in one sector of the economy (Reis 2006). Structural reforms may to a rise in savings not spending in the short run.

In some cases the beneficiaries of reforms may be unable to spend the improvement in their permanent income even if they perceive it. Consider reforms which score highly on both equity and efficiency grounds—those which benefit outsiders in the labour market at the expense of insiders (Lindbeck and Snower 1986). If the government can improve the search effectiveness of the long-term unemployed and economically inactive or eradicate labour market institutions (two-tier contracts, last in first out lay off rules etc.) which work in the interests of those who have jobs rather than those who have lost them then it may be able to raise the future earnings potential of those on the margins of the labour force. However, these individuals are likely to face credit constraints and therefore it is hard to believe that they will be able to bring forward that consumption by borrowing against future expected incomes.

In many cases, there is likely to be considerable uncertainty about the final design of a package of reforms—let alone its ultimate impact across the distribution of households and companies—as the legislative process unfolds. That uncertainty is likely to depress spending. Both incumbents and potential entrants are likely to delay investing in new capacity in an industry which is the subject of reforms (the uncertainty over the UK's future trading relations with the European Union—at least at the time of writing—might have a similar impact on investment across a much wider range of industries). Likewise, Giavazzi and McMahon (2012) find evidence of a significant increase in household saving in Germany in the run up to 1998 general election, whose outcome was too close to call and which had the potential to lead to a material change in the direction of government policy.

Finally, we should also expect to find a 'pain puzzle' with structural policies. Bad outcomes will often tend to follow hot on the heels of policy interventions which can give the misleading impression that these structural policies are fundamentally misguided. But, as with the 'price puzzle' in monetary policy (where inflation often rises soon after a decision to tighten policy) and the 'credit puzzle' in macroprudential policy (where lending often contracts soon after a decision to ease policy), we need to control for the circumstances in which these measures are launched before we leap to conclusions about their impact. Politicians may be more willing or more able to pass politically contentious structural reforms when the economic outlook is bleak and it is clear that 'something needs to be done', so it would not be surprising if the implementation of reforms was correlated with periods of poor macroeconomic performance. Under this interpretation it would be more accurate to say that forecasts of a weak economy cause reforms to be implemented rather than the other way round (that the implementation of reforms causes a weak economy).

10.8 Supply-Side Structural Reforms

Supply-side improvements unlock increases in the standard of living of the population that can be sustained—what can be produced today and tomorrow and for the indefinite future can be consumed indefinitely too. As Nobel Laureate Robert Lucas observed in the context of the varied pace of development of the emerging economics, once one starts to think about the policy choices over the course of decades that might explain that variation in performance, it is hard to think about anything else (Lucas 1988).

The crisis gave fresh impetus to the calls for supply-side reforms: the dismal performance of productivity in the post-crisis era focused minds on the needs for doing whatever was possible to boost supply. For example, whilst acknowledging that 'it cannot be for a central bank to design a programme of such supply initiatives' the Governor of the BoE argued in early 2013 that 'in economic terms there has never been a better time for supply-side reform' (King 2013).

There are a whole host of much discussed measures which could potentially improve the supply side of the economy, either by increasing the quality or quantity of factors of production that are combined to produce output, improving the efficiency with which those factors are combined, or eliminating frictions in the market economy that lead to a suboptimal level of activity. Some of the more frequently discussed measures include:

- *Anti-trust legislation*: Measures which reduce the extent and influence of monopoly power in product or labour markets can drive the economy towards the efficient perfectly competitive benchmark, raising the sustainable level of output in the process.
- *Reducing distortionary taxation*: Real-world taxes change the price signals that are vital to the efficient allocation of resources in a market economy, distorting behaviour—for example, discouraging labour supply.
- *Active Labour Market Policies (ALMP)*: The collective name for measures designed to reintegrate the long-term unemployed and economically inactive individuals back into the labour force, expanding the effective supply of labour to UK companies;
- *Net migration*: Increasing the size of the working-age population will tend to raise the output of the economy (although there may be little gain in terms of output per capita); where the country can attract individuals with particular skills and experience, migration may facilitate the transfer of knowledge to UK companies, improving the efficiency of production.
- *Investments in labour quality*: Subsidising the accumulation of human capital —from raising attainment in primary school, to subsidising academic research, to investing in life-long learning—could increase the productivity of the workforce and therefore potential supply (although care needs to be taken to differentiate between the private and social benefits from investments in human capital as we shall discuss below).
- *Investments in core infrastructure*: The health of the public sector capital stock (broadly defined), from the networks which provide core utilities to the transport system, can influence the productivity of the private sector.

- *Patent policy*: Extending patent protection on new inventions will increase the return on those new ideas (at the cost of extending the shelf-life of monopoly power or excludability in the use of the idea), potentially raising future productivity by stimulating R&D spending.
- *Access to finance*: The terms on which entrepreneurs and existing small, medium and even large companies can get access to finance will influence whether they invest in the marginal project, and hence at the macro level, access to finance can influence the evolution of the supply side.

An important conceptual distinction needs to be made here between measures that are likely to improve the **level** of potential supply and those which have the potential to raise the 'trend' rate of **growth** of potential supply. In practice, the impact of those measures which raise the level of potential supply is likely to gradually emerge so empirically we are better off distinguishing between those reforms which are likely to temporarily raise trend growth and those which are likely to have a more persistent impact on trend growth. The latter are the Holy Grail of the structural reform agenda since they have the potential to have the greatest impact on the permanent income of the population. Reforms which raise trend growth also happen to be one way in which the lower bound problem in the monetary policy arena can be managed without having to raise the inflation target (raising the rate of trend growth is likely to raise the equilibrium real interest rate and will therefore tend to drive the neutral policy rate further away from the lower bound). Unfortunately, the quest for this Holy Grail is as challenging as its namesake: it is hard to think of measures which are likely to have a significant impact on trend growth.

The key question for economists in this, as in all debates about economic policy, is finding the friction. The case for government intervention should hinge on the robust identification of market failures or government failures which lead to a suboptimal outcome. For example, in the debate over tuition fees it is often assumed that there are significant positive externalities in the consumption of a university education (new information and ideas will percolate more rapidly through the economy, and the workforce may adjust more rapidly to technology induced shifts in labour demand, the more educated that workforce is). However, one could equally make the case that a university degree is merely a useful signal which allows graduates to flag to potential employers that they are innately more productive than other members of the population (Spence 1973; Murnane et al. 2000). From a private perspective it is rational for productive individuals to attend university even though they learn nothing from the experience (obtaining the signal will raise their pay), but from a social perspective higher education scores badly on both efficiency and equity grounds: productive individuals devote three years of their working lives to a socially pointless activity which then allows them to raise their wages at the expense of their less productive peers.

Perhaps the most important set of supply-side reforms and those which illustrate the importance of 'finding the friction' are measures which encourage the production of new ideas. Until the arrival of endogenous growth theory (Aghion and Howitt 1997), the fundamental driver of growth on the supply side was determined outside the model: macroeconomists tended to assume that growth in TFP was exogenously given. We now think of the production of the ideas—the new invention of new products and processes—like any other activity as one that depends on the inputs that are consumed in that process, and in particular spending on R&D. As noted above, patents on the output of that process will allow innovating companies to earn a significant private return on R&D (Griliches 1992). However, innovating companies will not be able to completely capture the benefits that other companies enjoy from the knowledge spillovers which their successful investments generate (Romer 1986). Indeed, Jones and Williams (1998) argue that conservative estimates point to a socially optimal level of R&D investment that is 'two to four times' the actual level of investment. That divergence between the social and private rate of return from private investments in R&D creates a case for a public subsidy for this activity, whether through: direct funding or subsidies of R&D; investment in human capital formation; and extending and improving patent protection (Griffith 2000). Of course, what matters is whether those tools are effective.

To take but one example, Bloom et al. (2002) present evidence that R&D tax credits do work. They examine R&D spending in nine OECD countries spread over the best part of two decades, and they find that tax incentives do raise R&D intensity (the ratio of investment to output): in particular a 10 % reduction in the cost of R&D can raise the level of R&D by around 1 % in the short run and close to 10 % in the long run. Their results are encouraging because the evidence on the efficacy of tax incentives encouraging more traditional investment in physical capital is less encouraging. Goolsbee (1998) argues that changes in the US tax code do boost investment demand but that predominantly leads to higher prices of capital goods, rather than a surge in the volume of investment, and this result might explain why the producers of capital goods are among those who lobby most vociferously for subsidising investment.

10.9 Tax by Design

A near constant theme in the debate over fiscal policy is the need to reform the tax code. The problem with the tax code is not just that it is overly complex— there is a widespread belief that it fails on our fundamental fiscal criteria too:

it is inefficient and unfair too. Johnson (2013) argues that there are three substantial challenges to improving the conduct of fiscal policy:

- *Tactical tinkering rather than strategic thinking*: Tax policy is made twice each year in the Budget and the Autumn Statement, with a tendency for decisions to be taken on the basis of a narrow analysis of the cost benefit of the marginal change rather than based on top down assessment of how the system as a whole is performing.
- *Lack of challenge*: There is too little challenge from the legislature and particularly within the executive, with experts in specific areas having too little influence on the design of policy
- *Ineffective and even unhelpful political and public debate*: The standard of the debate is not conducive to good decision-making; as Johnson observes: '[W]e have not arrived at our current balance between…income tax, VAT and National Insurance as a result of any kind of rational debate.'

Like many of its predecessors the incoming Coalition government was committed to address this problem. An Office for Tax Simplification (OTS) was established in summer 2010 as an independent office of HM Treasury (HMT), and its title suggests, its purpose is to advise the Chancellor of the day on how best to simplify the UK tax code, and in particular, reduce the burden of compliance on households and companies; its formal objectives are to:

- provide the government with independent advice on where there are areas of complexity in the UK tax system that could be simplified; and
- conduct inquiries into complex areas of the tax system, to collect evidence and advise the government on options for reform.

As of March 2015, the OTS had completed nine simplification reviews (on tax reliefs, small business tax, employee share schemes, pensioner taxation, partnership taxation, employee benefits and expenses, UK competitiveness, tax penalties and employment status), published 31 reports and papers and made 402 recommendations, of which 60 were deemed 'big picture'. Out of those 60 big picture recommendations, 16 had been accepted, 9 had been partly accepted, 22 were under review and 13 had received no response or had been rejected. An independent review of the work of the OTS (conducted for the Institute for Fiscal Studies' (IFS) Tax Law Review Committee [TLRC]) concluded that the OTS had a good track record, given the limited resources at its disposal, and that whilst there was still 'much left to do', the positive changes that had taken place would almost certainly not have occurred without the OTS (Bowler 2014).

In contrast to the sterile debate over the merits of fiscal stimulus, the profession has made a much more positive contribution in this area. A commission of experts ('the Mirrlees Review') recently offered a comprehensive answer to the question: what would an optimal tax system for a modern economy like the UK look like? There is not space here to do justice to the final report, *Tax by Design* (Mirrlees et al. 2011), but we shall summarise some of the key insights from the report. Three high level principles are emphasised:

- *(pragmatically) Progressive*: Reflecting the inevitable tension between equity and efficiency, the system should be designed to minimise the inefficiency generated in the pursuit of a desired level of progressivity, which as far as possible should be defined on the basis of lifetime outcomes.
- *Neutral*: The tax code should avoid inefficiently distorting decisions or unfairly discriminating between people or behaviours as far as possible. The obvious exception here is in the treatment of non-pecuniary externalities, but the Review concludes that the number of cases in which there is a solid case for departing from neutrality is 'far narrower than the exceptions we observe in practice'.
- *Designed to work as a system*: The tax code should be designed from a top-down perspective to meet the government's spending needs and evaluated as such. There is no need for each individual element of the system to satisfy every objective: in particular, there is no need for every tax to be progressive, so long as the system is.

The proposals in the Mirrlees Review extend far beyond the taxation of income, but we shall focus here on that key issue to give a flavour of what a progressive, neutral tax code that is designed to work as a system looks like. The authors argue for a single tax on income, with a simple rate schedule (i.e., a relatively small number of rates, calibrated on the basis of evidence on labour supply responses of different groups) and a single benefit to support those in need. In particular, they stress the importance of taxing all sources of income according to the same rate schedule. Business income would be taxed before it left the premises (i.e., via corporation tax) but the personal tax rates on income derived from companies (dividends and capital gains on shares) should be reduced accordingly to reflect the corporation tax that has already been paid, so that the *combined* rates of corporate and shareholder taxation would equal the tax rates on labour income. In the interests of neutrality, the authors recommend a deduction to account for the costs of generating income, whether that be the costs of production or critically the costs of financial investment. In the case of the latter, the Review suggests either treating cash that is saved as a one-off deductible expense or providing deductions each year for the opportunity cost of the capital that was saved up front; both approaches should lead to the 'excess return' being taxed, but the 'normal return' being exempt. There are exceptions to the rule of 'one tax schedule to rule them all': taxes to correct externalities are one example; taxes on pure economic rents (where they can be identified) are another, with the authors making the case for land value tax (subject to the authorities being able to produce reliable valuations).

Part of the problem with a 'from first principles' approach to defining a coherent tax system is that elements of the system can seem counterintuitive and to some eyes even manifestly unfair. A classic case in point is Mirrlees' (1971) own result that the optimal marginal tax rate on *exceedingly* high incomes might be zero. Consider the income of the highest earner in the country facing a positive marginal rate of taxation on earnings above that level; a zero tax rate would not cost the Exchequer a penny and would avoid the inefficient distortion to that individual's labour supply decision (see Mankiw et al. (2009) for a discussion of the theoretical and practical implications of this result). To take an actual example, the Review proposes a uniform rate of VAT—that is, doing away with the zero and lower rates on politically sensitive items such as food, on the grounds that the meagre gains from such a crude method of redistributing income do not justify the inefficient distortion to household behaviour created by changing the relative price of different goods. In isolation this proposal may seem regressive (and therefore unacceptable) but that can be compensated for elsewhere in the tax code—an illustration of the 'must work as a system' principle in action.

The Mirrlees Review has been widely acclaimed as a major contribution to our understanding of fiscal policy, but (predictably) there remain bones of contention. Atkinson (2012) identifies three concerns: first, the review is too rooted in the perfectly competitive benchmark; second, the analysis has failed to keep pace with societal change; and third, the report is too rooted in utilitarianism. Atkinson illustrates the first problem by highlighting how the proposal to remove the zero rating on food may not be robust to the reality that the distribution sector does not measure up the perfectly competitive benchmark; in an oligopolistic setting, the impact of the tax change is harder to predict. In terms of the second concern, Atkinson calls for more research into the variable geography of taxation, with a greater emphasis on taxation at the regional and supranational level alongside the more conventional national focus, and analysis of inequality that extends beyond the labour market towards wealth inequality and in particular a treatment of inheritance. Atkinson's third concern takes us back into the debate over 'nudges' and whether the social planner should exploit individuals' flawed understanding of the various ways through which governments raise money when designing tax policy ('if distraction means that the goose does not notice the feathers being plucked, should we use this device to reduce this hissing?') or should the government seek to make the system more transparent and reduce those misperceptions.

The key battleground in the debate over the tax code remains the cumulative impact of the tax and benefit system on labour supply for those at the margins of the labour force. Labour economists and policymakers alike have long been concerned about the delicate trade-off between protecting the standard of living of those at the bottom of the income distribution (the equity objective) and the potential for a complex tax and benefit system to actively discourage individuals in specific circumstances from seeking work (the efficiency objective).

Economists explain labour supply decisions in terms of a choice over consumption of goods (made possible through paid work) and leisure (made possible through not working) in terms of the usual apparatus of the point of tangency between a budget constraint (which traces out the feasible combinations of consumption and leisure that an individual can achieve depending on how many hours they work given the post-tax hourly wage that is on offer), and an indifference curve (which traces out the combinations of consumption and leisure over which the individual is indifferent). This picture starts to change when we allow for the fact that: there are some goods and services which can be both produced in the home or purchased in the market; that individuals will receive some residual level of benefit if they work no hours; those benefits may be withdrawn one for one with earned income or even lost entirely when an individual starts work, compounding the impact of taxes on labour income; and the individual may have to pay fixed and variable cost if they choose to work, such as the cost of commuting and childcare respectively.

The end result of the interaction of the incentives provided by the market and government policy could be a highly irregular budget constraint, with kinks and discontinuities that will distort labour supply decisions. In particular, we can identify two stylised problems:

- *Non-employment traps*: Work does not pay, in that optimal labour supply decision is not to work at all. Thanks to the presence of fixed costs of work and/or the withdrawal of benefits, some individuals face high replacement ratios (RRs: the ratio of net income when out of work versus when in work) and high participation tax rates (PTRs: the fraction of total earnings lost through tax and withdrawal of benefits).

- *Poverty trap*: Working more does not pay, in that the optimal labour supply decision is to not work above a certain number of hours. Thanks to changes in the rate at which benefits are withdrawn above a certain level of earnings or working hours and/or the introduction or increase in rate of taxation of labour income individuals face high effective marginal tax rates (EMTRs).

Adam and Browne (2010) document how the scale of these two problems has changed over the course of three decades given a sequence of reforms to the tax and benefit system which have had intended (and likely unintended) consequences for labour supply incentives. They found that although around half of working age adults face PTRS in a narrow range from 40 % to 60 % (which implies that their earnings buy them around half of what it cost to employ them) around 30 % of those out of work have PTRs in excess of 70 % (as opposed to only 10 % of those in work). Interestingly, Adam and Browne found that the incentives to be in work at all in 2009–10 were little changed on three decades earlier, although there had been significant changes through the period: incentives had weakened between 1978 and 1981, strengthened during the mid to late 1980s, and then weakened after 2003, although the incentives for lone parents bucked the trend, strengthening since 1979. Turning to EMTRs, Adam and Brown noted that for the vast majority of workers in 2008/09 an extra pound paid by their employer would translate into between 40 and 60 pence of goods and services, but there was a significant minority of workers who would only keep between 17 and 27 pence, thanks to the steep withdrawal of tax credits or housing benefit if they increased their earnings. They found that labour supply incentives weakened between 1978 and 2009, particularly for those with children.

References

Adam, S., & Browne, J. (2010). *Redistribution, work incentives and thirty years of UK tax and benefit reform*. IFS Working Paper 10/24.

Adler, M. (2006). Stardom and talent. In D. Throsby & V. Ginsburgh (Eds.), *Handbook of the economics of art and culture*. Amsterdam: North-Holland.

Aghion, P., & Howitt, P. (1997). *Endogenous growth theory*. Cambridge, MA: MIT Press.

Airports Commission. (2015, July). Airports Commission: Final report.

Alesina, A., & Rodrik, D. (1994). Distributive politics and economic growth. *Quarterly Journal of Economics, 109*(2), 465–490.

Alvaredo, F., Atkinson, A., Piketty, T., & Saez, E. (2013). The top 1% in international and historical perspective. *Journal of Economic Perspectives, 27*(3), 3–20.

Arrow, K. (1951). *Social choice and individual values*. New York: Wiley.

Atkinson, A. (2012). The Mirrlees Review and the state of public economics. *Journal of Economic Literature, 50*(3), 770–780.

Autor, D., Levy, F., & Murnane, R. (2003) The skill content of recent technological change: An empirical exploration. *Quarterly Journal of Economics, 118*(4), 1279–1334.

Barr, N. (1992). Economic theory and the welfare state. *Journal of Economic Literature, 30*, 741–803.

Barwell, R. (2013). *Macroprudential policy: Taming the wild gyrations of credit flows, debt stocks and asset prices*. New York: Palgrave.

Belfield, C., Cribb, J., Hood, A., & Joyce, R. (2014). *Living standards, poverty and inequality*; 2014, IFS.

Berg, A., & Ostry, J. (2011). *Inequality and unsustainable growth*. IMF Staff Discussion Note 11/08.

Besley, T., & Case, A. (1995). Does electoral accountability affect economic policy? *Quarterly Journal of Economics, 110*(3), 769–798.

Besley, T., & Preston, I. (2007). Electoral bias and policy change. *Quarterly Journal of Economics, 122*(4), 1473–1510.

Black, D. (1948). On the rationale of group decision making. *Journal of Political Economy, 56*(1), 23–34.

Bloom, N., Griffith, R., & Van Reenen, J. (2002). Do R&D tax credits work? *Journal of Public Economics, 85*, 1–31.

Blundell, R., Brewer, M., & Shephard, A. (2005). *Evaluating the labour market impact of Working Families Tax Credit using differences in differences*. HMRC Working Paper 4.

Bowler, T. (2014). *The Office of Tax Simplification*. IFS Tax Law Review Committee Discussion Paper 11.

Brewer, M., Sibieta, L., & Wren-Lewis, L. (2008). *Racing away? Income inequality and the evolution of high incomes*. IFS Briefing Note 76.

Brewer, M., & O'Dea, C (2012). Measuring living standards with income and consumption: evidence from the UK. ISER Working Paper 2012–05.

Card, D., & DiNardo, J. (2002). Skill-based technological change and rising wage inequality: Some problems and puzzles. *Journal of Labor Economics, 20*(4), 733–783.

Chattopadhyay, R., & Duflo, E. (2004). Women as policy makers: Evidence from a randomized policy experiment in India. *Econometrica, 72*(5), 1409–1443.

Chetty, R. (2015). Behavioral economics and public policy. *American Economic Review, 105*(5), 1–33.

Cimadomo, J. (2012). Fiscal policy in real time. *Scandinavian Journal of Economics, 114*(2), 440–465.

Coase, R. (1960). The problem of a social cost. *Journal of Law and Economics, 3*, 1–44.

Cowell, F. (1995). *Measuring inequality*. Oxford: Oxford University Press.

Dasgupta, P., & Maskin, E. (2004). The fairest vote of all. *Scientific American, March*, 92–97.

Dasgupta, P., & Maskin, E. (2008). On the robustness of majority rule. *Journal of the Economic Association, 6*(5), 949–973.

de Mooij, R., Keen, M., & Parry, I. (2012). *Fiscal policy to mitigate climate change: A guide for policymakers*. Washington, D.C.: IMF.

Dickens, R., & Manning, A. (2004). Has the national minimum wage reduced wage inequality? *Journal of the Royal Statistical Society, Series A, 167*, 623–626.

Downs, A. (1957). An economic theory of political action in democracy. *Journal of Political Economy, 65*(2), 135–150.

Feldstein, M. (2005). Rethinking social insurance. *American Economic Review, 95*(1), 1–24.

Forbes, K. (2000). A reassessment of the relationship between inequality and growth. *American Economic Review, 90*(4), 869–887.

Giavazzi, F., & McMahon, M. (2012). Policy uncertainty and household savings. *Review of Economics and Statistics, 94*(2), 517–531.

Goolsbee, A. (1998). Investment tax incentives, prices and the supply of capital goods. *Quarterly Journal of Economics, 113*(1), 121–148.

Goos, M., & Manning, A. (2007). Lousy and lovely jobs. *Review of Economics and Statistics, 89*(1), 118–133.

Gordon, R., & Dew-Becker, I. (2008). *Controversies about the rise of American inequality*. NBER Working Paper 13982.

Griffith, R. (2000). *How important is business RD for economic growth and should the government subsidize it?* IFS Briefing Note 12.

Griliches, Z. (1992). The search for R&D spillovers. *Scandinavian Journal of Economics, 94*, 29–47.

Guvenen, F., Kuruscu, B., & Ozkan, S. (2009). Taxation of human capital and wage inequality: A cross-country analysis. NBER Working Paper 15526.

Helfand, G., Berck, P., & Maull, T. (2003). The theory of pollution policy. In K.-G. Mäler & J. Vincent (Eds.), *Handbook of environmental economics*. Amsterdam: Elsevier North Holland.

Johnson, P. (2013). *Better budgets*. IFS Briefing Note BN137.

Jones, C., & Williams, J. (1998). Measuring the social return to R&D. *Quarterly Journal of Economics, 113*(4), 1119–1135.

Katz, L., & Autor, D. (1999). Changes in the wage structure and earnings inequality. In O. Ashenfelter & D. Card (Eds.), *Handbook of labour economics*. Amsterdam: North-Holland.

Katz, L., Loveman, G., & Blanchflower, D. (1995). A comparison of changes in the structure of wages in four OECD countries. In R. Freeman & L. Katz (Eds.), *Differences and changes in wage structures*. Chicago: University of Chicago.

King, M. (2013, January 22). Speech.

Krueger, A. (1974). The political economy of the rent-seeking society. *American Economic Review, 64*, 291–303.

Kumhof, M., Ranciere, R., & Winant, P. (2015). Inequality, leverage and crises. *American Economic Review, 105*(3), 1217–1245.

Lindbeck, A., & Snower, D. (1986). Wage setting, unemployment, and insider-outsider relations. *American Economic Review, 76*(2), 235–239.

Lipsey, R., & Lancaster, K. (1956). The general theory of the second best. *Review of Economic Studies, 24*(1), 11–32.

Lucas, R. (1988). On the mechanics of economic development. *Journal of Monetary Economics, 22*, 3–42.

Machin, S. (2011). Changes in UK wage inequality over the last forty years. In P. Gregg & J. Wadsworth (Eds.), *The labour market in winter*. Oxford: Oxford University Press.

Mankiw, N., Weinzierl, M., & Yagan, D. (2009). Optimal taxation in theory and practice. *Journal of Economic Perspectives, 23*(4), 147–174.

Mirrlees, J. (1971). An exploration in the theory of optimal income taxation. *Review of Economic Studies, 38*, 175–208.

Mirrlees, J., Adam, S., Besley, T., Blundell, R., Bond, S., Chote, R., Gammie, M., Johnson, P., Myles, G., & Poterba, J. (2011). *Tax by design*. Oxford: Oxford University Press.

Murnane, R., Willett, J., & Tyler, J. (2000). Who benefits from a GED? Evidence from high school and beyond. *Review of Economics and Statistics, 82*, 23–37.

Murphy, K. (1999). Executive compensation. In O. Ashenfelter & D. Card (Eds.), *Handbook of labor economics*. Amsterdam: North-Holland.

Murphy, K., Shleifer, A., & Vishny, R. (1991). The allocation of talent: Implications for growth. *Quarterly Journal of Economics, 106*, 503–530.

Niskanen, W. (1971). *Bureaucracy and representative government*. Chicago: Aldine-Atherton.

Nordhaus, W. (1994). *Managing the global commons: The economics of change*. Cambridge, MA: MIT Press.

Okun, A. (1975). *Equality and efficiency: The big trade-off*. Washington, D.C.: Brookings Institution.

Ostry, J., & Berg, A. (2014). Measure to measure. *IMF Finance and Development, 51*(3), 35–38.

Ostry, J., Berg, A., & Tsangarides, C. (2014). *Redistribution, inequality and growth*. IMF Staff Discussion Note 14/02.

Rawls, J. (1999). *A theory of justice*. Cambridge, MA: Harvard University Press.

Rebonato, R. (2012). *Taking liberties: A critical examination of libertarian paternalism*. Houndmills/New York: Palgrave.

Reis, R. (2006). Inattentive consumers. *Journal of Monetary Economics, 53*(8), 1761–1800.

Roantree, B., & Shaw, J. (2014). *The case for taking a life-cycle perspective*. IFS Report R92.

Romer, P. (1986). Increasing returns and long-run growth. *Journal of Political Economy, 94*(5), 1002–1037.

Rosen, S. (1981). The economics of superstars. *American Economic Review, 71*(5), 845–858.

Sack, B. (2000). Does the Fed act gradually? *Journal of Monetary Economics, 46*(1), 229–256.

Samuelson, P. (1954). The pure theory of public expenditure. *Review of Economics and Statistics, 36*(4), 387–389.

Sen, A. (2014). Arrow and the impossibility theorem. In E. Maskin & A. Sen (Eds.), *The arrow impossibility theorem*. New York: Columbia University Press.

Spence, M. (1973). Job market signalling. *Quarterly Journal of Economics, 87*, 355–374.

Stewart, M. (2012). Wage inequality, minimum wage effects and spillovers. *Oxford Economic Papers, 64*, 616–634.

Stiglitz, J. (1991). *The invisible hand and modern welfare economics*. NBER Working Paper 3641.

Taylor, J. (2000). Reassessing discretionary fiscal policy. *Journal of Economic Perspectives, 14*(3), 21–36.

Thaler, R., & Sunstein, C. (2008). *Nudge: Improving decisions about health, wealth, and happiness*. New Haven: Yale University Press.

Tullock, G. (1967). The welfare costs of tariffs, monopolies and theft. *Western Economic Journal, 5*(3), 224–232.

Welch, F. (1999). In defense of inequality. *American Economic Review, 89*(2), 1–17.

11

The Fiscal Multiplier

One of the central questions that this section of the book tries to answer is whether the decision by many of the world's finance ministries to embrace austerity in the aftermath of the financial crash was wise or not. In order to answer that question we need to think about the likely impact of fiscal consolidation on aggregate demand and employment. This chapter reviews theory and evidence on the likely impact of changes in the fiscal stance in normal times. The following chapter will discuss whether the conventional wisdom in normal times applies in abnormal times too.

11.1 Preliminaries: Why Fiscal Policy Works

It seems self-evident to the economic ingénue that an increase in government spending must surely boost aggregate demand, and cuts in spending will achieve the exact opposite. After all, an income tax cut or an increase in government spending should both mechanically boost disposable income and therefore boost consumption. In the simple student model, taxes on income and government spending feature in the appropriate place (with the appropriate sign) in the IS curve, which describes the locus of output and interest rate combinations that clear the goods market, suggesting that fiscal policy has the power to boost demand (and by extension employment).

© The Editor(s) (if applicable) and The Author(s) 2016   **329**
R. Barwell, *Macroeconomic Policy after the Crash*,
DOI 10.1057/978-1-137-51592-6_11

Nothing encapsulates that belief in the power of fiscal stimulus to support the economy more than the miracle of the balanced budget multiplier, which most students encounter early on in their exposure to macroeconomics, when our explanation of the level of output is still entirely demand driven. In this stylised setting an increase in spending which is financed through increased taxation can boost demand and output. The balanced budget stimulus 'works' because private sector agents save a fraction of their income. The first round effect of the fiscal stimulus therefore raises demand and from that point on we are left with the equal and offsetting response of private sector spending to the loss of income (from higher taxes) and the increase in income (the initial counterpart to higher spending). The something for nothing magic of the balanced budget multiplier invites the budding economist to conclude that fiscal policy must have an important role to play in the conduct of macroeconomic policy but even in the halcyon days of post war demand management it was well understood that fiscal stimulus would be less effective at boosting output if government spending leaked out of the economy via the consumption of imports (Baumol and Peston 1955) and would be ineffective if there were no idle resources in the economy (Wallich 1944).

Another powerful argument for fiscal stimulus can be found in the work of Paul Samuleson although in truth the argument applies to any effective form of stimulus: the so-called accelerator effect (Samuelson 1939). Imagine for the sake of argument that investment spending depends on the actual or expected state of aggregate demand. Fiscal stimulus will now have a much more powerful impact on demand, because the first round effect is amplified by the response of investment. This basic idea can be resurrected in a more sophisticated treatment of investment spending, which allows for uncertainty about the future, and in particular fear of what the future may hold, to influence behaviour. Most investment projects share three common features: they offer uncertain returns; they are partially irreversible (there are sunk costs which cannot be recouped if the project turns out to be unprofitable); and the decision to invest can be delayed. Under these circumstances, we can model the opportunity to invest like a call option in financial markets, whose value will depend on the extent to which the uncertainty about the potential profitability of the project is likely to dissipate over time (Dixit 1992; Pindyck 1991). For a company to be willing to make an irreversible investment it should expect that project to deliver sufficiently healthy returns to not only cover the costs of financing the project but also to justify giving up the option (to wait). It is certainly possible that the option value of waiting could vary over the cycle, and in particular it may rise in a recession as companies attach a higher probability to bad macro outcomes in which investments would yield extremely poor returns (Bernanke 1983). In this setting, any policy response which could manage down those fears of the future would lower the option value of waiting (or put another way the hurdle rate) and unlock increased investment. It is in this sense that Nobel laureate Paul Krugman has talked of fiscal stimulus crowding in investment spending during the crisis.

The final argument for fiscal stimulus is a simple but seemingly effective argument against monetary stimulus. Monetary policy works by exploiting nominal rigidities in the economy to lower real interest rates given control over short-term risk-free nominal interest rates. Lower real interest rates imply a shift in the relative price of spending today versus tomorrow. In effect, looser monetary policy encourages people to bring forward consumption from the future: to spend more today or save less. Some commentators claim that if the outlook is bad enough or if the private sector is carrying too much debt then monetary stimulus will prove ineffective: in what Richard Koo has labelled a 'balance sheet recession' (Koo 2003), the private sector will politely decline the invitation to spend more today *and less tomorrow*. Fiscal policy—or at least, certain forms of fiscal policy—appears to go one better by taking choice out of the equation: the government brings forward that spending by doing the spending itself and forces the private sector to spend less tomorrow in the process (because the private sector's future tax liability increases to finance the stimulus). The potential problem with this argument as we shall go on to discuss is that it treats private sector behaviour as fixed, and that assumption looks particularly problematic if we just argued that the private sector cannot be enticed to save less no matter how low real interests go.

11.2 Crowding Out

The budding economist's faith in fiscal stimulus is soon tested through exposure to the concept of crowding out—the idea that the positive impact of increased government spending on aggregate demand is partially or even entirely neutralised by offsetting movements in private-sector spending. In truth crowding out can occur through a number of mechanisms and it is helpful to distinguish between them.

First comes direct crowding out, where there is an immediate behavioural adjustment in private sector demand because the government is providing a service which might otherwise be purchased in the market. The provision of free school lunches or even healthcare might fall into the category: an increase in public provision leads to an offsetting reduction in the private consumption of these activities.

Next comes real crowding out where the design of macroeconomic policy is forced to confront the fundamental raison d'être of economics: scarcity of resources. We believe that the level of output is constrained on the supply side of the economy—by the quantity and quality of factors of production available to potential employers and the efficiency with which they can combine them to produce output (sometimes called total or multi factor productivity, TFP or MFP). In this more realistic setting, the government competes with the private sector for a scarce resource in factor and product markets, so an increase in government spending will reduce the capacity of the private sector to produce output. For a closed economy operating close to normal capacity levels, increased government spending can change the mix of demand, but it cannot permanently raise the absolute level of output. For a small open economy operating in a large global economy there is the possibility that cross border trade in inputs and outputs might ease these domestic supply-side constraints which lead to real crowding out. The increased demand for goods and services may be sourced from producers overseas (although at the cost of financial crowding out through the exchange rate—see below) and foreign labour may be encouraged to relocate, boosting the supply capacity of the domestic economy. Indeed, in the limit, a reduction in the costs of migration over recent years might have significantly increased the elasticity of labour supply to domestic companies, mitigating these real crowding out effects (Barwell 2007).

Then comes financial crowding out when the government is competing with the private sector for resources in financial markets rather than the real economy. Fiscal stimulus precipitates a change in asset prices which in turn triggers an offsetting adjustment in private sector spending. When it comes to the impact of government spending on asset prices the traditional focus is on interest rates where two distinct (if somewhat old fashioned) mechanisms have been highlighted.

The simple mechanism hinges on the transactional demand for money: the stimulus boosts income and therefore households will choose to hold more cash to facilitate greater spending. For a fixed supply of money, equilibrium requires an offsetting move in the speculative demand for money via a higher interest rate on bonds, which in turn will choke off interest-sensitive spending.

If we introduce equities into the framework as an additional asset class alongside money and bonds the outcome is ambiguous: the impact of the fiscal stimulus on asset prices will hinge on the extent to which households view bonds as a closer substitute for cash or for equities (Friedman 1978). If equities are seen as a close substitute for bonds then private sector investors will demand a higher return on equities in order for their portfolio to be in equilibrium with these similar assets (bonds and equities) accounting for a higher share, and that 'portfolio effect' will crowd out interest-sensitive spending. Conversely, if bonds and cash are close substitutes then the return on equity will need to fall in equilibrium (with investors being comfortable holding a smaller share of their portfolio in equity, and a higher share in the more similar cash and bonds) and the portfolio effect (lower yields) now crowds in interest-sensitive spending.

The discussion above has a closed economy feel to it, with the public and private sector competing for the domestic pool of savings, and debt-financed fiscal expansions bidding up domestic real interest rates, crowding out private-sector expenditure. In reality, the government (and for that matter private sector agents too) can tap the large pool of global savings; indeed, the conventional wisdom is that the barriers to cross-border capital flows are virtually non-existent, at least as far as developed countries are concerned. Capital should flow across borders to where it is most productive, with the global interest rate determined by the balance between desired savings and investment at the global level: the domestic imbalance is neither here nor there. In theory then, domestic investment can decouple from domestic savings and government spending does not crowd out investment. However, in practice, there is evidence that government spending can crowd out investment even in an open economy: domestic investment and savings appear highly correlated across countries—the so-called Feldstein Horioka paradox (Feldstein and Horioka 1980). Rather than conclude that capital is less mobile across borders than previously thought, Frankel (1985) observes that for savings and investment to completely decouple requires integration of goods as well as capital markets, and for uncovered interest parity to hold in capital markets (see later). In practice, global investors have no reason to arbitrage away a wedge between the rates of return that can be earned in different countries when those returns are expressed in the price of domestic output. In other words, fiscal stimulus can still crowd out domestic investment in an open economy when capital is mobile across borders.

In any case, even if domestic investment is resilient to a debt-financed increased in government expenditure, other elements of private-sector spending may not be. The inflow of foreign funds will likely lead to an appreciation in the currency, making imports more competitive and UK exports less so. In other words, crowding out can occur through net exports rather than investment. Indeed, there does appear to be a systematic relationship between the size of the state (in particular, the share of government consumption in GDP) and the real exchange rate (Ricci et al. 2008). Monacelli and Perotti (2008) demonstrate that fiscal expansions tend to lead to a decline in the relative price of goods (versus services) and the relative price of imports (i.e., the terms of trade appreciate). Hence Broadbent (2011) argues that the anticipation of a significant fiscal consolidation in the UK could explain part of the sharp depreciation of sterling at the start of the crisis as markets expected a necessary relative price adjustment that could crowd (back) in the production of traded goods (see later).

11.3 Forward Looking Households and Endogenous Savings

Fiscal stimulus is all about shifting the profile of taxation and expenditure through time with the objective of influencing the current level of aggregate demand. However, to this point our analysis of the private sector response to fiscal stimulus has had a decidedly static feel to it: we have simply queried whether an increase in public spending crowds out private sector spending today. Unless, we are willing to assume that private sector agents are myopic or easily misled then we need to allow for the fact that the consequences of higher government spending today (higher taxes tomorrow) might weigh on private sector spending today independent of the crowding out mechanism outlined above. In order to do that we need to say something about preferences over the timing of consumption and the constraints under which households operate.

When it comes to preferences over the timing of consumption the convention is to assume that people prefer consumption today to consumption tomorrow but only up to a point—on the basis that diminishing marginal returns from an additional unit of consumption in any given period are assumed to kick in. As a result, people will prefer a steady flow of consumption through time to the volatility of feast one year and famine the next—an insight which is captured in the familiar life cycle model of consumption, in which people smooth consumption in the face of an irregular but predictable flow of income over the course of their lifetime (savings during peak earnings years of middle age and dis-saving in retirement).

Turning to the constraints, the public and private sectors are subject to the same fundamental intertemporal constraint that the sum of discounted expenditures cannot exceed the discounted flow of resources and any initial endowment. In other words, the present value of consumption is constrained by the present value of post-tax income plus any endowment for households whilst the present value of government spending (broadly defined) plus the current value of net debt cannot exceed the present value of tax receipts for the government. The only difference is that we would normally think about the government having a much longer planning horizon than the household (outside the public choice literature at least): the government will be around to collect taxes on future generations long after the current cohort of workers is pushing up daisies.

Diamond's (1965) overlapping generations model illustrates how fiscal stimulus 'works' in this setting by creating intergenerational transfers. Consider an economy populated by countless cohorts of finitely lived households, who work for a period of time, building up savings, which they then run down in retirement before death. If the government cuts taxes in this model by issuing debt which it will redeem in the far future by raising taxes then it will raise the disposable income and consumption of the current generation of workers. However, those workers would typically only save a fraction of the boost to disposable income so those funds will not be sufficient to absorb all of the fresh debt that the government needs to issue to finance the tax cut. The demand for savings outstrips supply, putting upwards pressure on the interest rate, crowding out investment in physical capital in the process.

Now consider an extreme benchmark in which households are assumed to live forever and there are no capital market imperfections so that households can borrow money on the same terms as the government. Fiscal stimulus is a non-starter in this world. Households understand that they will be the ones who will ultimately pay for a tax cut today with higher taxes in the future. The profile of post-tax income may be more volatile—households will have more resources today and less tomorrow—but in present discounted value terms, these two effects offset leaving the household intertemporal budget constraint unchanged, and therefore lifetime consumption unchanged too. But households prefer to smooth consumption in the face of volatility in their resources over time so they will save the tax cut today in order to protect consumption tomorrow when the tax hike bites. In effect, private savings is simply the mirror image of public savings behaviour—as the government's increased demand for loanable funds brings forth its own supply—rendering the stimulus impotent.

Of course, it is reasonable to ask how much attention we should attach to analysis which is based on the assumption that households live forever. However, Barro (1974) argues that the result may still hold even if we relax this assumption. So long as people care about future generations and the fiscal legacy that they bequeath them then the countless cohorts in Diamond's model could still act as if they were an infinitely lived household or 'dynastic family'. All that is required is that the current generation is able to compensate future generations for the higher tax bill that they will incur. That compensation would most obviously occur in the form of an increased bequest (with current generations spending a lower fraction of their lifetime earnings) but it could arise in other ways—for example, the payment of college tuition fees or the provision of interest free loans—or even via reduced reverse bequests, with children providing less financial support to their parents in old age (see Kotlikoff 1988). These intergenerational bequests weave together the generations, creating a single decision making unit with the same infinite horizon as the government. The consumption of the dynastic family is determined by permanent income, and expectations of future taxes that will eventually be paid by future generations influence current spending. So government spending will have an equivalent impact on private spending, whether it is financed by current taxes or future taxes (debt today).

11.4 A Retreat from Ricardian Equivalence

Ironically, this fiscal impotence result is known as Ricardean equivalence: ironically, because David Ricardo did not believe that this extreme result would hold on account of 'public debt illusion' and tax evasion (Buiter and Tobin 1979). In point of fact, very few economists believe that Ricardean equivalence holds exactly; its purpose (like the Modigliani Miller theorems we will encounter later in the companion volume to this book) is to help identify the reasons why fiscal stimulus might work.

The obvious way to overturn the Ricardian equivalence result is to unpick Barro's assumption that the current generation is altruistic and willing to compensate future generations for the shift in the generational burden of taxation. There is a temptation to point out that some people do not have children and will not have such an obvious interest in their 'fiscal legacy'. Bernheim and Bagwell (1988) offer a more compelling critique, with what amounts to a proof by contradiction. They point out that rather than comprising a single dynastic family, with multiple generations of representative individuals, society is far better described as a complex network, with numerous individuals in each generation who marry forming linkages between dynasties. As a result, individuals who are not in the same micro family unit will share a common ancestor and if the mechanism that Barro describes holds then these linkages within generations should lead to much more pervasive and frankly implausible neutrality results. For example, another staple of fiscal policy—taxing the rich to finance transfer payments to the poor—should also prove ineffective, because the rich and poor are part of one big happy family, and are already ready, willing and able to reallocate funds between them.

In practice, the current generation will tend to be on the hook for the majority of any future tax burden that follows from a fiscal stimulus today. The pragmatic critique of the Classical orthodoxy on fiscal stimulus—that it is largely ineffective—has less to do with the assumption of altruistic individuals that allows Barro to resurrect the infinitely lived household and more to do with the assumptions about the way that infinitely lived household behaves and the environment in which that household operates in the Classical benchmark.

Even in a world of forward-looking optimising immortals a critical assumption is required to deliver the fiscal impotence result: that households can lend and borrow on the same terms as the government. If it was not clear before the crisis, then it is certainly clear now: capital markets are far from perfect. Although a small number of very large companies may be able to borrow money on similar terms to sovereigns, the vast majority of companies and households cannot: most will have to pay more to borrow money and are rationed in the amount that they can borrow, whilst those judged to be significant credit risks (i.e., the lender believes that there is a significant chance that the debtor may default on the loan) may be locked out of credit markets altogether. As a result of these constraints, households may be unable to achieve their optimal consumption plan: in particular they may not be able to borrow to support consumption today given either a transitory shock to income or expectation of stronger income tomorrow. Allowing for the presence of these capital market imperfections, changes our perspective on fiscal stimulus: a debt-financed tax cut can now be justified as a way to relax these credit constraints. Consider the example of a credit-constrained household: current consumption is too low so they will not save more today if the government cuts taxes today with the promise of increased taxes in the future. In effect, the tax cut allows these individuals to borrow on the same terms as the government, and the government is acting as a benevolent financial intermediary—with the tax cut as a loan, and future tax receipts as debt-servicing costs. Of course, the government must be able to collect those taxes in the future from these credit-constrained individuals, but the government is likely in a lot stronger position than a conventional bank in this regard. Now only the unconstrained households increase savings in response to the change in fiscal policy, leading to partial crowding out through the usual channels.

In theory, we speak about the future tax liability of the representative individual based on the fact that the government's intertemporal budget constraint must hold. In practice, even if individuals can calculate the tax schedule that will prevail in the future (i.e., the thresholds at which various tax rates kick in) their particular tax liability will be hard to calculate because their particular position in the pre-tax wage distribution in the future is highly uncertain today. Moreover, there is an interesting feature that an individual knows that she will pay no tax in states of the world where she is unemployed and her resources are very low and the marginal utility of consumption is high, and conversely, she will only pay a high tax bill when she is awash with resource and the marginal utility of an additional unit of consumption would be low. Barsky et al. (1986) conclude that a shift in the time profile of taxes (lower today, higher tomorrow) can therefore reduce precautionary savings and boost current consumption.

Beyond these problems of access to capital markets or the uncertainty about your own future tax liability there are more fundamental concerns about the sophistication that the theory demands of individuals. In practice, it is not realistic to think that households are constantly recomputing their lifetime earnings and what that implies for their optimal consumption plan. Inattention is a more plausible model of household behaviour. For example, Reis (2006) presents a model in which households optimise on an irregular basis—with a frequency which depends on the real interest rate (which determines the implications for wealth of 'mistaken' changes in savings when income changes) and their degree of risk aversion (the sensitivity of utility to those mistakes)—responding to all news on permanent income since the previous assessment and putting spending or savings on autopilot between times.

Even Reis' inattentive households optimise—they just do it less frequently than the agents in the textbook model—and that may still ask too much of individuals. Information may be costly to collect and costly to use in the process of optimisation. It seems more reasonable to assume that individuals are boundedly rational, taking decisions that perform reasonably well on the basis of simple calculations or rules of thumb (see Barwell (2013) for a review). Kotlikoff et al. (1988) provide a graphical illustration of this point in the closest thing economists get to a laboratory experiment. They surveyed a sample of supposedly sophisticated individuals (Boston University undergraduate and MBA students) and asked them to specify consumption choices given a hypothetical and relatively straightforward situation where current assets, future income and the date of retirement and death are all known. They find widespread evidence of inconsistent responses to identical circumstances, and a significant minority of people overdiscounted future resources.

In short, we have learned that the Classical benchmark of optimising, forward-looking individuals with perfect access to capital markets may not be appropriate for at least a fraction of the household sector. Gali et al. (2007) incorporate this insight into an otherwise conventional macro model by assuming that a fraction of the household sector are rule-of-thumb individuals (on account of 'a combination of myopia, lack of access to financial markets, or (continuously) binding borrowing constraints') who live hand to mouth and consume current income. The presence of these rule-of-thumb households make aggregate consumptions less sensitive to the negative wealth effects from higher future taxes (thanks to higher future taxes) and more sensitive to current disposable income. However, by themselves these rule of thumb households are not sufficient to prevent consumption falling in response to fiscal stimulus; we need to introduce nominal rigidity into the mix. Sticky prices prevent real wages falling too far when rising employment depresses the marginal product of labour. Disposable income rises and so too does consumption. If we further introduce an imperfectly competitive labour market into the model, with wages set by a trade union and then hours are set by the firm, then there is further scope for fiscal stimulus to boost consumption and employment.

One related strand of the macroeconomics literature which has grown in recent years is the adaptive learning literature. Research in this area explores whether the equilibria implied by models with bounded rational agents acting under imperfect information can converge upon the rational expectations benchmark. Evans et al. (2009) examine the impact of anticipated fiscal policy in this environment of adaptive learning. The focus on anticipated policy makes a good deal of sense given the time lags involved in implementing policy—between initial discussions, the legislative process and policy actually coming into law. Their model allows that policy announcements might lead to an immediate reaction by adaptively learning agents, prior to the implementation of policy. Critically, in the Evans, Honkapohja and Mitra model, agents 'learn' about interest rates using past data, revising their expectations in response to forecast errors. That is, households are not capable of immediately calculating the path that interest rates must follow in order for the household sector to be willing to consume what remains of output following an increase in government consumption in a world of balanced government budgets. However, the agents in these models are not totally unsophisticated: for example, they still understand the intertemporal consequences of fiscal stimulus.

Consider the impact of a balanced budget expansion (in taxes and spending). In the rational expectations benchmark, the interest rate drops in the period before the tax increase is phased in (and consumption falls), to ensure parity between the relative price and marginal rate of substitution between consumption today and tomorrow, and once the policy takes effect, the interest rate bounces back. A quite different path emerges for interest rates and their expectations under learning. On announcement of the policy change, agents compute their higher expected tax burden which other things equal depresses their optimal consumption path. Interest rate expectations are pre-determined so there is no offset in terms of discounting future post-tax income less heavily. As a result, interest rates have to fall to clear the goods market and stimulate consumption. Interest rates turning out lower than expected leads agents to revise down their expectations for the following period, helping to stimulate consumption, allowing actual interest rates to start to recover. When policy is eventually implemented, agents are no longer anticipating (and reacting to) a future reduction in income, and with low interest rate expectations, interest rates have to rise to choke off consumption. The authors also examine the impact of an increase in government spending financed by debt today and taxes at some point in the future. The somewhat surprising result is that the economy behaves in a near-Ricardian fashion. The logic here is that it does not really matter what agents think will happen to interest rates. Ricardian equivalence requires that agents understand the government's intertemporal budget constraint holds: different expected interest rate paths (discount factors) will imply different expected paths for taxes, but the discounted value of the stream of future taxes which influences current consumption will be the same.

11.5 The Supply-Side Multiplier

Although governments would prefer to raise money via lump-sum taxes which do not distort behaviour, finance ministers do not have that luxury in practice. A full accounting of the macroeconomic impact of fiscal policy must therefore address the consequences of changes in the scope and timing of distortionary taxes that will be required tomorrow to finance fiscal stimulus today.

Theory suggests that relaxing the lump-sum assumption could have significant implications. Indeed, Barro (1996) argues that the presence of distortionary taxes is the most important reason why a change in the timing of taxes would have second-order effects on the economy. Those who baulk at the rigorous straightjacket of modern dynamic general equilibrium theory may take the results with a pinch of salt, but the literature certainly provides interesting supply side parables which complement the more traditional demand side focus of fiscal stimulus.

Judd (1987) argues that a temporary cut in income taxes financed through debt today and higher taxes tomorrow will depress current consumption thanks to the distortionary impact of those taxes. First, there is an income effect. The capital stock today is fixed; the capital stock tomorrow is not. Shifting the burden of taxation from today into tomorrow therefore increases the excess burden of distortionary taxation, reducing permanent income and the current consumption of households. Second, there is a substitution effect thanks to changes in the timing of taxes which works in the same direction: current taxes on interest income falls, reducing the relative price of consumption tomorrow, encouraging savings today.

Baxter and King (1993) compare and contrast the impact of a permanent increase in government spending under lump-sum and distortionary taxes. With lump-sum taxes we can treat the increase in lump-sum taxes as a negative wealth effect, which leads households to reduce both consumption and leisure. In other words, labour supply increases to cushion the blow. That is not the end of the story: that increase in labour supply leads to a decline in real wages and an increase in the marginal product of capital. Investment increases, until the capital stock 'catches up' with the increase in labour supply (at the pre-shock capital–labour ratio), and that, of course, mitigates somewhat the initial hit to wealth. The end result is a long-run multiplier in excess of one. If instead the increase in government spending is financed through distortionary taxes, fiscal policy is contractionary. A supply-side multiplier emerges, as government policy blunts the incentive to work or invest, which in turn reduces the tax base, requiring a further increase in tax rates. The more elastic labour supply is, the more the tax base shrinks and the greater that required increase in taxes.

A comprehensive assessment of the impact of fiscal stimulus therefore requires a consideration of the magnitude of this supply-side multiplier. In the remainer of this subsection we will focus on a key determinant of that multiplier—the elasticity of labour supply. The usual starting point in this discussion is the Hicksian and Marshallian elasticities of labour supply: both are static concepts, capturing the response of labour supply to changes in wages, with the former capturing the pure substitution effect, and the latter incorporating the income effect too (which is negative if leisure is a normal good). The elasticity that most macroeconomists (at least those that use models with forward-looking households optimising consumption and leisure over their lifetime) refer to is the Frisch elasticity, which evaluates the impact of a change in the wage on labour supply holding the marginal utility of wealth constant. The Frisch elasticity measures how labour supply evolves over an individual's lifetime given their wage profile, tracing out the anticipated changes in hours worked as wages change over the working life. Of course, if news arrives on that wage profile—for example, thanks to a reform of the tax or benefit system—individuals will revise their lifetime consumption and leisure plans (and the marginal utility of wealth will likely change too), and labour supply shifts.

Taking these stylised concepts to the data is not straightforward. The competing demands on an individual's time are more complex than a simple choice between work and leisure. Although macroeconomists typically think in terms of labour input in terms of the total number of hours worked in the economy for the individual there are really two decisions—whether to participate in the labour market (to seek employment), and if successful, how many hours to work. Moreover, many if not most individuals will have to devote some time to work in the home producing services that could be purchased in the market (looking after children, or doing the household chores), and where individuals live in a larger household unit, specialisation in different tasks may occur (work in the market and work in the home) particularly when there are young children in the household. At certain points in their life, individuals may devote considerable time to developing their human capital outside the labour market, and that can create path dependence in labour supply (by raising the potential returns from supplying labour in the future).

Likewise, rather than a single wage offer confronting any job seeker, each individual faces a range of potential job offers. However, individuals do not have complete discretion over the number of hours they work at a particular wage rate in any particular vacancy. Nor can individuals instantaneously or costlessly search through the entire stock of vacancies to find their optimal combination of wage per hours and working hours—so compromises might have to be made.

The picture is further complicated by the interaction of the fixed costs of work, the phasing out of some welfare benefits with earned income, tax credits which require recipients to work a minimum number of hours and a discontinuous progressive tax schedule. The result is a kinked budget constraint, with strong incentives for certain individuals to refuse certain job offers altogether.

As a result of all these factors making sweeping generalisations about how labour supply responds to a change in taxes is not a sensible way to proceed. The response of hours worked to a change in the post-tax wage is likely to vary systematically across individuals, according to their circumstances, the prevailing tax and benefit system and the state of the labour market.

The first two chapters of the original volume of the *Handbook of Labor Economics* review the micro evidence on male and female labour supply elasticities respectively (Pencavel 1987; Killingsworth and Heckman 1987), with Blundell and MaCurdy (1999) providing an update in the third volume of the Handbook. These surveys present a consensus at least among most labour economists that the Frisch elasticity is low—very low (near zero) for prime-age men, and somewhat higher for women depending on their circumstances (Blundell et al. 1993)—and certainly lower than the benchmark figure typically calibrated into macro-models. For example, Rotemberg and Woodford (1997) use a Frisch elasticity of 9.5 which they note is 'certainly higher than the estimates obtained from microeconomic studies'.

11.6 It's Not What You Spend, It's How You Spend It

Although the profession has devoted a huge amount of time and effort into modelling and quantifying how the economy responds to shocks to government spending, relatively little attention has been devoted to thinking about how the government spends that money, and whether it matters. There are honourable exceptions, and this subsection briefly reviews some of the noteworthy contributions. The implicit or explicit default assumption in the literature is that government spending is on goods and services produced by the private sector to fund the provision of public services—or what economists label government consumption procurement. However, we can identify three other types of spending: compensation of the public sector workforce, transfer payments and investment in the public sector capital stock.

11.6.1 Compensation

The public sector is a major employer of labour. In the final quarter of 2014 the public sector employed around 5.4 million people, with around 2.9 million people working in central government, 2.3 million in local government and a little under 200,000 people working for UK public corporations. The public sector workforce has been shrinking as a by-product of austerity and is projected to continue doing so, with the share of the workforce accounted for by general government expected to fall from a peak close to 20 % in 2010 to around 15 % in 2018–19 (Cribb et al. 2014a). Pay is higher in the public sector than the private sector, but that can largely be accounted for by measurable differences between the two workforces; in other words, on a like for like basis the public sector pay premium is pretty small (Cribb et al. 2014a). At the start of the financial crisis public sector pay rose faster than in the private sector, but the implied increase in the public sector pay gap has been more or less unwound by several years of pay restraint in the public sector since then (Cribb et al. 2014b).

The missing piece of the jigsaw here is the supply-side implications of government spending on labour. Whatever value that people attach to the public services that the government provides—and it is likely considerable—we should also acknowledge that in the production of those services the government is employing a considerable fraction of the economy's stock of factors of production that might otherwise have been at the private sector's disposal. That is, given the structural factors that determine the equilibrium rate of employment in the economy, an increase in the size of the government's workforce inevitably starves the private sector of resources—a classic case of real crowding out.

The academic literature certainly suggests that distinguishing between procurement and compensation within government consumption is critical to understanding the impact of fiscal policy. Using a real business cycle framework, Finn (1998) illustrates how shocks to the procurement and compensation have opposite implications for private sector output, employment and investment. In contrast, a rise in government employment is met partially through the rise in labour supply and partially through a fall in private sector employment, lowering private capital's future profitability, depressing investment. Monacelli and Perotti (2008) also highlight the importance of splitting out the government's employment of labour from other components of spending. They report data which suggests no obvious difference between the goods–services mix of private sector spending and government procurement. It is only when we include government compensation that public sector spending has a detectable bias towards the services (non-traded) sector.

11.6.2 Transfer Payments

By any estimate, welfare spending accounts for a significant share of government spending. However, exactly what you define as welfare spending and therefore exactly how large you estimate the welfare budget to be is contentious (Hood and Johnson 2014). For example, should pension payments to people who used to work for the public sector and financial support for the disabled be included as part of the welfare bill?

To get a clearer picture of the state of welfare spending in the UK we need to look at more granular detail on spending on individual measures. Hood and Oakley (2014) provide an exhaustive decomposition of the £205 billion that was spent on social security benefits in Great Britain in 2013–14; we shall highlight here only those items which account for at least 1 % of the total spend:

- *Basic state pension*: £63.4 billion, or 30.9 % of the total social security spend
- *Housing benefit:* £23.9 billion, or 11.7 % of the total social security spend
- *Child tax credits:* £23.0 billion, or 11.2 % of the total social security spend
- *Additional state pension:* £19.5 billion, or 9.5 % of the total social security spend
- *Disability living allowance:* £13.7 billion, or 6.7 % of the total social security spend
- *Child benefit:* £ 11.2 billion, or 5.5 % of the total social security spend
- *Employment and support allowance:* £10.4 billion or 5.1 % of the total social security spend
- *Pension credit:* £ 7.1 billion, or 3.5 % of the total social security spend
- *Working tax credit:* £6.3 billion or 3.1 % of the total social security spend
- *Attendance allowance:* £5.4 billion, or 2.6 % of the total social security spend
- *Income-based JSA:* £3.9 billion or 1.9 % of the total social security spend
- *Income support:* £3.6 billion, or 1.8 % of the total social security spend
- *Statutory maternity pay:* £2.3 billion or 1.1 % of the total social security spend
- *Winter fuel payments:* £2.2 billion, or 1.1 % of the total social security spend
- *Carer's allowance:* £2.1 billion or 1.0 % of the total social security spend

As discussed earlier, and as the above list makes clear, the primary purpose of transfer payments is not to stabilise aggregate demand. However, it is worth considering the potential macroeconomic consequences of a large-scale change in transfer payments.

Romer and Romer (2014) exploit the frequent changes in Social Security benefits in the USA across several decades to examine the macroeconomic impact of changes in transfer payments. They find a large, immediate, and statistically significant impact of permanent increases in benefits on consumption. However, that response fades pretty fast—in contrast to the estimated impact of relatively exogenous tax changes. Romer and Romer argue that the explanation may lie with monetary policy, finding statistical and narrative evidence of a contractionary monetary policy response to permanent benefit increases that is not present for tax changes.

Turning to the theoretical literature, Oh and Reis (2012) step outside the standard representative agent complete markets set-up to illustrate how lump-sum transfers between different groups in the population can have a macroeconomic impact, boosting output and employment, in a world where individuals face idiosyncratic and uninsurable risk. Oh and Reis identify two distinct channels that emerge in this unconventional set-up: a 'neo-classical channel', where those who fund the transfer payments increase labour supply, and a 'Keynesian channel', where those who receive the transfer payments tend to have a higher marginal propensity to consume resulting in a boost to aggregate demand. Indeed, as discussed earlier, if the recipients of transfer payments are credit constrained then the impact on spending at the micro level could be significant.

Of course, to reach a definitive conclusion about the impact of transfer payments on aggregate outcomes we need to be mindful of the Lucas critique: that is, for policy interventions to change behaviour. In this case, we need to worry about the extent to which the presence of a social safety net, which will support consumption in future bad states of nature, changes the behaviour of households today. For example, we might expect to find lower precautionary savings in an economy with a more generous safety net, since individuals do not need to self-insure (Floden 2001). Nonetheless, there is good empirical and theoretical evidence to suggest that transfer payments could be an effective means of stimulating demand, particularly when monetary policy is impaired (McKay and Reis 2014).

11.6.3 Government Investment

Another implicit assumption in the macro literature is that government spending is intrinsically worthless—it corresponds to Keynes' (1936) lowest common denominator of digging holes in the ground:

> If the Treasury were to fill old bottles with banknotes, bury them at suitable depths in disused coalmines which are then filled up to the surface with town rubbish, and leave it to private enterprise on well-tried principles of laissez-faire to dig the notes up again (the right to do so being obtained, of course, by tendering for leases of the note-bearing territory), there need be no more unemployment and, with the help of the repercussions, the real income of the community, and its capital wealth also, would probably become a good deal greater than it actually is. It would, indeed, be more sensible to build houses and the like; but if there are political and practical difficulties in the way of this, the above would be better than nothing.

That assumption is obviously wrong, but as with much of macroeconomics, it might also be innocuous where much of government consumption procurement is concerned. However, one area in which this assumption is not innocuous is in spending on the public sector capital stock: government investment. Aschauer (1989) suggests that there might be an important link between private-sector productivity and the government's stock of physical capital, and that the anaemic rate of growth in the public capital stock might have played some role in the US productivity slowdown in the 1970s and 1980s. Aschauer emphasises in particular the importance of investment in public infrastructure, a finding which chimes with the folk wisdom that the health of core infrastructure such as the transportation network and public utilities grid serves an important function in enabling economic growth.

The idea that government investment is important and must be protected has impeccable theoretical credentials. For example, in the final section of their seminal paper discussed above, Baxter and King (1993) consider the possibility that the accumulated stock of government investment could raise private-sector productivity. Using an upper bound from the literature on the impact of public-sector capital on private-sector productivity (based on Aschauer's work), they find that the direct effect on output is eight times the size of the impulse to government investment, and the long-run multiplier could reach as high as thirteen! Government spending is able to elicit an expansion in labour supply and additional investment in the private-sector capital stock, shifting the economy to a new steady state with higher investment and consumption.

In practice, government investment has borne the brunt of fiscal retrenchment—gross public investment fell as a share of GDP almost continuously between the mid-1970s and the turn of the millennium—perhaps in part for reasons of political expediency, in the sense that cuts in investment are less visible and painful to the electorate in the short run (Clark et al. 2001). Indeed, it is precisely this concern that motivated the design of fiscal rules which differentiate between current spending and capital expenditure (see later). Nonetheless, government investment soon felt the pinch when the process of fiscal repair began: as with tax increases, the role of cuts in government investment in the consolidation programme was front-loaded. Tetlow (2013) estimated that by the end of that financial year, 'virtually all of the planned tax increases (95%) and cuts to investment spending (90%) are planned to have been implemented, while only 58% of the total cuts to benefit spending and under one-third (31%) of the overall cuts to other current (i.e. non-investment) spending will have been achieved.'

11.7 Macroeconometric Evidence on the Multiplier

So much for the theory on the macro impact of fiscal policy, what about the evidence? In this subsection, we will focus on the macro evidence on the fiscal multiplier, before turning to micro evidence on how individuals respond to fiscal interventions in the following subsection.

One obvious place to look for evidence on the impact of fiscal policy is in the time-series data on macroeconomic aggregates and headline measures of fiscal policy (government spending and tax receipts or rates) using structural vector autoregressions (or SVARs). That technique uses the basic VAR approach of modelling the time series properties of a small set of variables using the lagged values of those variables, but with restrictions imposed on the system suggested by the theory in order to identify the impact of genuine shocks (Blanchard and Quah 1989). The standard reference in the fiscal literature is Blanchard and Perotti (2002), who find that positive spending shocks and negative tax shocks boost activity, with multipliers that are small, and often close to one, and that government spending tends to depress investment and net trade but support consumption.

To help unpack these results we will focus here on Perotti's (2005) update of that paper. Perotti begins by estimating a five variable system: government spending, taxation, output, inflation and the long interest rate, from which he obtains the standard reduced form residuals: that which cannot be explained by the lagged variables in the system. He then argues that the residuals for the fiscal variables can be viewed as linear combinations of two components: the automatic response of tax receipts or expenditures to innovations in the economy and the random discretionary response, which should be uncorrelated with the other structural shocks (Perotti argues that a systematic discretionary response, which would involve a change in a policy instrument, could not be implemented fast enough to influence outcomes within the quarter). Perotti purges the former from the fiscal residuals (using estimates from the literature on the elasticity of taxes and spending to output, inflation and the long interest rate) to leave behind residuals from which structural tax and spend shocks and the usual impulse response functions can be constructed. Perotti finds that the impact of structural fiscal policy shocks on output is small, and interestingly has diminished over time—a result which he argues is most likely to reflect a change in the conduct of monetary policy. He also finds evidence of a decline in the variance of these fiscal shocks which has played a non-trivial role in the corresponding decline in the variance of output.

There is some scepticism in the profession about our ability to estimate the macroeconomic impact of fiscal policy 'shocks' from the macro data given the existence of 'fiscal foresight'. Changes in policy are often discussed well in advance of their official announcement; there is then a legislative lag between their announcement and their entry onto the statute book; and then a further lag before they become effective. Households and companies may have anticipated and responded to a shock to effective tax rates long before it materialises in the econometrician's dataset. Indeed, other research in the literature relies on this foresight. For example, Johnson et al. (2006) use the fact that the Bush tax cut which came into effect in Autumn 2001 was passed by Congress in the spring and publicised in George W Bush's election campaign the previous fall. The econometrician would conclude that there had been a 'shock' to tax receipts in Q3; US households would beg to differ. Leeper et al. (2008) present a pretty downbeat assessment of our ability to uncover the true impact of fiscal policy in the presence of fiscal foresight (they focus on tax, but the arguments apply to government spending too). In essence, the econometrician is conditioning on a subset of the state variables, so that the VAR innovations reflect the errors in estimating the state variables as well as the underlying shocks. Their conclusions are worth quoting at length:

> The challenge posed by taxes is unique because few economic phenomena provide economic agents with such clear signals about how important margins will change in the future…Misalignment of agents' and econometrician's information sets has disturbing implications for the econometric analyses that macroeconomists typically conduct. Impulse response functions and variance decompositions can be profoundly wrong…failure to address fiscal foresight can seriously distort many of the inferences that macroeconomists draw from empirical work.

Ramey and Shapiro (1998) advocate a narrative approach for identifying fiscal shocks—that is, the search in the historical record for evidence of when agents were actually surprised by news on the fiscal stance. In particular, they use changes in Business Week's forecasts of defence spending to isolate genuine 'shocks': unanticipated changes in spending. In particular their original analysis isolated three key events: the Korean War, the Vietnam War and the US response to the Soviet Union's invasion of Afghanistan, to which Ramey (2009) has subsequently added a fourth (9/11). It turns out that the shocks uncovered from the narrative approach Granger-cause the VAR shocks, but the VAR shocks do not Granger-cause the narrative shocks: evidence consistent with the fiscal foresight critique. In effect, the SVAR approach uncovers positive spending shocks several quarters after the journalists of Business Week have already identified them and communicated them to the general public. Ramey (2009) notes that the point extends beyond defence spending: a surge in the fertility rate like the Baby Boom has inevitable consequences for future spending on education. Under this alternative narrative identification scheme, government spending has a more marked impact on output: consumption falls and labour supply increases, stimulating investment. But if alternative dates are used—1951 Q3 as opposed to 1950 Q3 for the Korean

War and so on—then Blanchard and Perotti's results emerge with fiscal shocks stimulating consumption. Romer and Romer (2010) use a similar approach, based on Presidential speeches and Congressional reports, and find evidence that taxes have a significant (contractionary) macro impact: an exogenous tax increase of 1 % of GDP lowers real GDP by almost 3%.

Barro and Redlick (2009, 2011) offer an alternative take on the impact of government spending and taxation. They argue that focusing on variation in defence spending around World War II (and to a lesser extent World War I and the Korean War) represents the best chance of uncovering the true government spending multiplier, because changes in non-defence spending are likely to be far more vulnerable to problems of endogeneity. They argue that World War II was a genuine exogenous shock so defence spending should have largely been independent of the current state of the business cycle. Moreover, the changes in defence spending over this period were large in absolute size and the US labour market was moving from a state of considerable slack to full employment allowing analysis of the variation in the multiplier with the state of the economy. In the more recent version of the paper, Barro and Redlick (2011) use Ramey's (2009) proxy to identify persistent changes in defence spending, which might be expected to have a larger impact on GDP. Finally, Barro and Redlick note that in contrast to the countries of continental Europe, the war had little impact on the supply capacity of the US economy (or at least the capital stock). On the tax side, Barro and Redlick use lagged data on marginal income tax rates on the grounds that it ought to be exogenous with respect to activity—in other words, that changes in views about the prospects for activity do not influence current period taxes—and they also use information from Romer and Romer's (2010) analysis of Congressional reports to identify planned changes in the tax system—again lagged to avoid endogeneity concerns. Their basic strategy is to run regressions of the growth in real per capita GDP on the contribution of government spending to growth, changes in tax rates and some controls (specifically lagged indicators of the business cycle), and they also incorporate an interaction term, between their government spending variable and the lagged unemployment rate, to investigate how the spending multiplier might vary according to the degree of slack in the economy.

Barro and Redlick find an economically and statistically significant defence spending multiplier, with a contemporaneous multiplier of 0.4–0.5 that rises to 0.6–0.7 over two years, and if the increase in spending is persistent then the multiplier is found to 0.1–0.2 higher. With a multiplier less than one, some crowding out is occurring: Barro and Redlick find that private investment is most sensitive to increased defence spending, with a lesser impact on the other

elements of government spending and net exports, but no statistically significant impact on (non-durables) consumption. In contrast, persistent increases
in defence spending primarily crowd out other aspects of government spending. On the tax multiplier, they find a one percentage point increase in the
marginal tax rate reduces per capita GDP growth by 0.6 %. In the earlier
vesion of their paper, Barro and Redlick (2009) find evidence that the multiplier is sensitive to the degree of slack in the economy: in particular, at the
median unemployment rate in their sample (5.6 %), they arrive at a multiplier of 0.67, but that rises by 0.05 for every percentage point increase in the
unemployment rate. However, in Barro and Redlick (2011) they report that
the interaction term which captures the sensitivity of the multiplier to slack is
no longer statistically significant when they include the Ramey defence news
variable (perhaps because both variables are large on the eve of the United
States's entry into World War II).

11.8 Microeconometric Evidence on Behaviour

If the modern treatment of household behaviour is valid—that is, if households do optimise consumption over their lifetime given all available
information—then predictable and transitory changes in income ought to
have little impact on expenditure when they materialise. Forward-looking and
forewarned rational households should just smooth right through the changes
in disposable income that finance ministers engineer unless credit constraints
have driven those households off their optimal spending plans. One way to
ascertain whether this defeatist view of the impact of fiscal policy is reasonable is therefore to examine whether at the micro level, households behave in
the way that the theory suggests. As the following brief review suggests, the
evidence in favour of the life-cycle benchmark is hardly compelling.

Shapiro and Slemrod (1995) investigate the impact of the fiscal stimulus
enacted by President Bush (senior) in 1992. The standard rate at which income
tax was withheld in paychecks was reduced, boosting take-home pay for low-
to middle-income workers by about $28.80 a month for married workers and
half that for single workers. The policy had the effect of simply delaying the
timing of tax payments: that is, rather than being deducted immediately, taxes
would simply be paid later (the following spring). The authors inserted an
additional series of questions in the University of Michigan telephone survey
of consumers in April 1992 to discover how households planned to respond
to this change in the tax regime. Standard theory suggests that such a mere
shift in the timing of tax payments should not lead households to revise their

consumption plans, unless they are credit constrained. Shapiro and Slemrod's results suggest something different: 43 % of those who responded reported that they planned to spend most of the increase in take-home pay, and they could find no link between proxies for the incidence of credit constraints and households' responses.

Souleles (1999) examines the impact of income tax refunds on household spending. Critically, those refunds depend on income in the previous year, and are therefore predictable and should therefore not come as news to the household. Most US taxpayers receive a refund, with an average refund of close to $1000 at that time of the research, and refunds are typically mailed out in the spring, leading Souleles to focus on the behaviour of consumption between the first and second quarter. Total consumption is estimated to increase by 18 cents for every dollar of refund received (a result significant at the 5 % level). When Souleles corrects for the fact that some of the refund is received at the tail end of Q1, these estimates rise to between 35 and 60 cents. Beyond that headline result, he finds a varying response to the tax rebate—from a small and insignificant response of expenditure on food, to a statistically significant impact on a measure of non-durables which excludes items like clothing; but the largest impact is on durables. Souleles finds that non-durables consumption is more sensitive for those individuals who are likely to be credit constrained (at the bottom end of the earnings-normalised distribution of liquid wealth). However, durables consumption seems highly responsive for unconstrained individuals—which is difficult to reconcile with standard theory.

Parker (1999) focuses on two sources of the variation in the payment of US Social Security taxes to study the response of household spending: the cross-individual variation in the coverage of pre-announced tax increases in the 1980s, and the within year cross-time variation in taxes as individuals reach the known calendar year cap on contributions (Parker estimates that a typical taxpayer in 1986 would have enjoyed a $330 increase in post-tax income for the last three months of that year on account of hitting the tax cap of $55,424). Parker finds a statistically significant impact of these predictable changes in tax on consumption—a 10 % increase in post-tax income in a three-month period raises non-durable consumption in that period by approximately 5.4 %. Parker uses two proxies for the likelihood that credit constraints are driving these results: the age of a household and its ratio of liquid assets to its flow of non-durable consumption. Neither can explain away the response of consumption to predictable changes in income. Finally, Parker finds some evidence to support the hypothesis that some form of near rationality is at work: people bring forward consumption where the timing of consumption has little impact on utility—that is, spending on clothing is more sensitive to the shift in disposable income than spending on food.

Finally, Johnson et al. (2006) explore the response of consumption to the 2001 Bush (junior) tax cut. The Economic Growth and Tax Relief Reconciliation Act reduced the rate of income tax in the lowest bracket from 15 % to 10 %. The change was applied retrospectively to income earned in 2001 leading to rebates of between $300 and $600 being sent to US households. The rebates were predictable: the tax cut had been a key part of George W Bush's platform, Congress had passed the Act in May 2001 and the Treasury had written to taxpayers informing them of the upcoming rebate. The rebates were distributed on a random basis according to a digit of the individual's Social Security number. The authors find that expenditure increased by 11 % on food and by 37 % on non-durables (with the latter being statistically significant) during the three-month period that the rebate was received, with some evidence of higher spending in the following couple of quarters. Roughly two thirds of the rebate was spent in the quarter of receipt and the quarter that followed it. Finally they report variation in the consumption response according to pre-tax family income and the stock of liquid assets, consistent with credit constraints playing a role. For example, low income households spent 63 percentage points more of their rebate on non-durable goods and there is some tentative (i.e., not statistically significant) evidence that these households spent this money straight away.

References

Aschauer, D. (1989). Is public expenditure productive? *Journal of Monetary Economics, 23*(2), 177–200.

Barro, R. (1974). Are government bonds net wealth. *Journal of Political Economy, 82*, 1095–1117.

Barro, R. (1996). *Reflections on Ricardian equivalence*. NBER Working Paper 5502.

Barro, R., & Redlick, C. (2009). Macroeconomic effects from government purchases and taxes, NBER Working Paper 15369.

Barro, R., & Redlick, C. (2011). Macroeconomic effects from government purchases and taxes. *Quarterly Journal of Economics, 126*(1), 51–102.

Barsky, R., Mankiw, N., & Zeldes, S. (1986). Ricardian consumers with Keynesian propensities. *American Economic Review, 76*(4), 676–691.

Barwell, R. (2007). The macroeconomic impact of international migration. *Bank of England Quarterly Bulletin, Q1*, 48–59.

Barwell, R. (2013). *Macroprudential policy: Taming the wild gyrations of credit flows, debt stocks and asset prices*. New York: Palgrave.

Baumol, W., & Peston, M. (1955). More on the multiplier effects of a balanced budget. *American Economic Review, 45*(1), 140–148.

Baxter, M., & King, R. (1993). Fiscal policy in general equilibrium. *American Economic Review, 83*(3), 315–334.

Bernanke, B. (1983). Irreversibility, uncertainty, and cyclical investment. *Quarterly Journal of Economics, 98*(1), 85–106.

Bernheim, B., & Bagwell, K. (1988). Is everything neutral? *Journal of Political Economy, 5*, 75–122.

Blanchard, O., & Quah, D. (1989). The dynamic effects of aggregate demand and supply disturbances. *The American Economic Review, 79*(4), 655–673.

Blanchard, O., & Perotti, R. (2002). An empirical characterization of the dynamic effects of changes in government spending and taxes on output. *Quarterly Journal of Economics, 117*, 1329–1368.

Blundell, R., & MaCurdy, T. (1999). Labor supply: A review of alternative approaches. In O. Ashenfelter & D. Card (Eds.), *Handbook of labor economics* (Vol. 3, pp. 1559–1695). Amsterdam: North-Holland.

Blundell, R., Meghir, C., & Neves, P. (1993). Labor supply and intertemporal substitution. *Journal of Econometrics, 59*(2), 137–160.

Broadbent, B. (2011, September 26). *Rebalancing and the real exchange rate.* Speech.

Buiter, W., & Tobin, J. (1979). Debt neutrality: A brief review of doctrine and evidence. In G. Furstenberg (Ed.), *Social security versus private saving.* Cambridge, MA: Ballinger Pub. Co.

Clark, T., Elsby, M., & Love, S. (2001). *Twenty-five years of falling investment.* IFS Briefing Note 20.

Cribb, J., Disney, R., & Sibieta, L. (2014a). *The public sector workforce.* IFS Briefing Note 145.

Cribb, J., Emmerson, C., & Sibieta, L. (2014b). *Public sector pay in the UK.* IFS Report R97.

Diamond, P. (1965). National debt in a neoclassical growth model. *American Economic Review, 55*(5), 1126–1150.

Dixit, A. (1992). Investment and hysteresis. *Journal of Economic Perspectives, 6*, 107–132.

Evans, G., Honkapohja, S., & Mitra, K. (2009). Anticipated fiscal policy and adaptive learning. *Journal of Monetary Economics, 56*, 930–953.

Feldstein, M., & Horioka, C. (1980). Domestic savings and international capital flows. *Economic Journal, 90*, 314–329.

Finn, M. (1998). Cyclical effects of governments' employment and good purchases. *International Economic Review, 39*(3), 635–657.

Floden, M. (2001). The effectiveness of government debt and transfers as insurance. *Journal of Monetary Economics, 48*, 81–108.

Frankel, J. (1985). International capital mobility and crowding out in the U.S. economy: Imperfect integration of financial markets or of goods markets? NBER Working Paper 1773.

Friedman, B. (1978). Crowding out or crowding in? Economic consequences of financing government deficits. *Brookings Papers on Economic Activity, 3*, 593–641.

Gali, J., López-Salido, D., & Vallés, J. (2007). Understanding the effects of government spending on consumption. *Journal of the European Economic Association, 5*(1), 227–270.

Hood, A., & Johnson, P. (2014, November 4). *What is welfare spending?* IFS Observations.

Hood, A., & Oakley, L. (2014). *A survey of the GB benefit system.* IFS Briefing Note BN13.

Johnson, D., Parker, J., & Souleles, N. (2006). Household expenditure and the Income Tax Rebates of 2001. *American Economic Review, 96*(5), 1589–1610.

Judd, K. (1987). Debt and distortionary taxation in a simple perfect foresight model. *Journal of Monetary Economics, 20*(1), 51–72.

Keynes, J. (1936). *The general theory of employment, interest and money.* London: Palgrave.

Killingsworth, M., & Heckman, J. (1987). Female labor supply: A survey. In O. Ashenfelter & R. Layard (Eds.), *Handbook of labor economics* (Vol. 1, pp. 103–204). Amsterdam: Elsevier.

Koo, R. (2003). *Balance sheet recession: Japan's struggle with uncharted economics and its global implications.* Singapore: Wiley.

Kotlikoff, L. (1988). Intergenerational transfers and savings. *Journal of Economic Perspectives, 2*(2), 41–58.

Kotlikoff, L., Samuelson, W., & Johnson, S. (1988). Consumption, computation mistakes, and fiscal policy? *American Economic Review, 78*(2), 408–412.

Leeper, E., Walker, T., & Yang, S.-C. (2008). *Fiscal foresight: Analytics and econometrics.* NBER Working Paper 14028.

McKay, A., & Reis, R. (2014). *The role of automatic stabilizers in the U.S. business cycle.* mimeo.

Monacelli, T., & Perotti, R. (2008). Openness and the sectoral effects of fiscal policy. *Journal of the European Economics Association, 6*(2–3), 395–403.

Oh, H., & Reis, R. (2012). Targeted transfers and the fiscal response to the great recession. *Journal of Monetary Economics, 59*, S50–S64.

Parker, J. (1999). The reaction of household consumption to predictable changes in social security taxes. *American Economic Review, 89*(4), 959–973.

Pencavel, J. (1987). Labor supply of men: A survey. In O. Ashenfelter & R. Layard (Eds.), *Handbook of labor economics* (Vol. 1, pp. 3–102). Amsterdam: North-Holland.

Perotti, R. (2005). *Estimating the effects of fiscal policy in OECD countries.* Conference Proceedings of Federal Reserve Bank of San Francisco.

Pindyck, R. (1991). Irreversibility, uncertainty, and investment. *Journal of Economic Literature, 29*, 1110–1148.

Ramey, V. (2009). *Identifying government spending shocks: It's all in the timing.* mimeo.

Ramey, V., & Shapiro, M. (1998). Costly capital reallocation and the effects of government spending. *Carnegie-Rochester Conference Series on Public Policy, 48,* 145–194.

Reis, R. (2006). Inattentive consumers. *Journal of Monetary Economics, 53*(8), 1761–1800.

Ricci, L., Milesi-Ferretti, G., & Lee, L. (2008). *Real exchange rates and fundamentals: A cross-country perspective.* IMF Working Paper 08/13.

Romer, C., & Romer, D. (2010). The macroeconomic effects of tax changes. *American Economic Review, 100,* 763–801.

Romer, C., & Romer, D. (2014). *Transfer payments and the macroeconomy.* mimeo.

Rotemberg, J., & Woodford, M. (1997). An optimization-based econometric framework for the evaluation of monetary policy. *NBER Macroeconomics Annual, 12,* 297–361.

Samuelson, P. (1939). Interactions between the multiplier analysis and the principle of acceleration. *Review of Economics and Statistics, 21*(2), 75–78.

Shapiro, M., & Slemrod, J. (1995). Consumer response to the timing of income: Evidence from a change in tax withholding. *American Economic Review, 85*(1), 274–283.

Souleles, N. (1999). The response of household consumption to income tax refunds. *American Economic Review, 89*(4), 947–958.

Tetlow, G. (2013, May 8). *Cutting the deficit.* IFS Observations.

Wallich, H. (1944). Income-generating effects of a balanced budget. *Quarterly Journal of Economics, 59*(1), 78–91.

12

Monetary Dominance

Our discussion of the macroeconomic impact of changes in the fiscal stance has taken place in a monetary vacuum. Any assessment of the likely impact of changes in the fiscal stance which does not take account of the monetary policy reaction function is almost certainly flawed. As we will go on to discuss there is a concern in some academic quarters that in extreme circumstances central banks might lose control of the inflation outlook given a chronic failure of fiscal policy—so-called *fiscal dominance*. For the time being, our working hypothesis should instead be *monetary dominance*: that central banks have the capacity to achieve their price stability mandates, and will adjust the stance of monetary policy to prevent a persistent imbalance between aggregate demand and supply in order to do so. In this section we rectify this sin of omission and explain the implications for the fiscal multiplier: actual or counterfactual changes in the stance of monetary policy should neutralise the macroeconomic impact of changes in the stance of fiscal policy, We will then go on to discuss possible exceptions to the rule—the circumstances under which fiscal consolidation could still depress demand when we switch monetary policy on—and whether the post-crash UK economy qualifies as one of those exceptions.

12.1 The Dual-Control Economy

In the previous chapter we have encountered numerous fiscal levers and discussed theory and evidence on the potential for fiscal policy to influence the level of activity. In a world in which finance ministers retained prime responsibility

© The Editor(s) (if applicable) and The Author(s) 2016
R. Barwell, *Macroeconomic Policy after the Crash*,
DOI 10.1057/978-1-137-51592-6_12

for demand management, that material could guide an assessment of the likely transmission mechanism of those different fiscal levers and hence the appropriate response to a given shock or the likely implications of a change in the fiscal stance. Much of the discussion of fiscal stimulus in the popular debate proceeds on this basis. However, that is not the world we live in.

We have long since placed our trust in monetary policy as the principal tool of demand management, albeit aided and abetted by the automatic fiscal stabilisers, and responsibility for the conduct of monetary policy (so-called 'operational independence') has been passed from finance ministers to central bankers. That reality has profound implications for the debate around the capacity for discretionary fiscal stimulus to boost activity and employment.

Many people who learn to drive will be familiar with the concept of dual controls: they learn to drive in a car where the instructor also has a brake pedal so that she can control the car in an emergency. Monetary policy and fiscal policy work in the same way, with the central bank as the instructor able to apply the monetary brake if the finance minister puts her foot down on the accelerator. The point is that the monetary instructor (the central bank) is in control of the speed of the economy.

If central bankers are to deliver their price stability mandates, then they will tend to adjust official interest rates and influence expectations of their expected future path until the level of aggregate demand in the economy is sufficiently close to the level of aggregate supply, and is expected to remain so. That does not imply that central banks will necessarily fine tune the level of aggregate demand, constantly adjusting the stance of monetary policy to close the output gap in response to demand shocks; not least on account of the lags in the transmission mechanism. Moreover, when the economy is hit by cost shocks, central banks may be forced to tolerate a transitory deviation of demand from supply in order to counterbalance the direct impact on inflation of the cost shock. Nonetheless, a persistent and significant deviation of demand from supply would likely lead to a significant deviation of inflation from the target, and perhaps slippage in inflation expectations if allowed to go unchecked.

Central banks will therefore instinctively lean against shifts in aggregate demand around supply, no matter what their source—even if they originate in the finance ministry. As a result, fiscal policy should not have any significant impact on the level of demand and employment because the central bank cannot allow fiscal policy to have a significant impact on the economy. At this point a thought experiment is in order to fix ideas.

Let us assume for a second that households do not behave like a single dynastic family and a fiscal stimulus can boost aggregate demand. Further assume that the economy is in balance: the output gap is closed, inflation is in line with the target and both are expected to remain so. If we forget for a moment that the driving instructor (the central bank) is in control of the speed of the car (the economy) then if the government launches a sizeable and sustained fiscal stimulus we should expect activity and employment to increase. A positive output gap will emerge: companies will be working their factors of production above normal levels to meet strong demand and will experience a shortage of labour when trying to fill vacancies. Wages will tend to rise ahead of productivity and prices may rise ahead of costs, and inflation will rise above the target.

These developments will be fairly predictable from the moment that the stimulus package is announced. If the central bank wishes to stabilise the output gap and inflation, then it will need to tighten monetary policy, to bear down on demand. Indeed, given the lags involved between the announcement of at least certain fiscal measures, their legislative passage and their taking effect, the central bank has the option to try and nullify the impact of those fiscal measures on aggregate demand and inflation given the *relatively* rapid implementation of monetary policy. Of course, central banks are still left with the formidable task of calibrating the adjustment in the monetary stance that is required to neutralise the impact of the change in the fiscal stance. The point here is simply one of theory rather than execution: that the central bank can nullify the macroeconomic impact of fiscal policy.

In short, to a first order approximation, we should not expect to see a major impact of fiscal stimulus on the level of aggregate demand or inflation. Instead, we should expect to see a countervailing adjustment in the level of interest rates. Looser (less tight) fiscal policy leads to less loose (tighter) monetary policy. Fiscal policy can influence the mix of demand: finance ministers certainly can increase the share of government consumption and investment in the level of GDP. Likewise, the government can support the consumption of low-income households via a more generous welfare system. Central banks therefore do not impede the government's pursuit of its efficiency or equity agendas. It is just that central banks cannot allow finance ministers to have a material influence on the level of aggregate demand: they must adjust interest rates to bear down on the other components of demand to ensure that aggregate demand does not exceed aggregate supply.

Before we move on, a health warning is in order. Monetary policymakers may be able to offset a pre-announced adjustment in the stance of fiscal policy but it does not follow that monetary policy can perfectly insulate the economy from any shock. The lags in the transmission mechanism of monetary policy may be shorter than those for fiscal policy but they are still long and variable so the reader should not be lulled into a false sense of security. Central banks cannot perfectly fine tune the economy to ensure that the output gap is always close to zero.

12.2 The Mechanics of Monetary Dominance

The sceptical reader may raise an eyebrow at the claim that monetary policy systematically nullifies the macroeconomic impact of fiscal policy. The idea that unelected officials would consciously override the decisions of elected officials seems almost undemocratic and is rarely discussed and yet it is familiar to anyone who has worked in a central bank and a logical conclusion of the division of policy responsibilities. Given the central importance of this result to the discussion that follows, it is worth spending a little time justifying this result.

The first point to note is that when central bankers set official interest rates they will not calibrate the stance on a shock by shock basis—that is, working out the implied deviation from the neutral stance warranted by each disturbance that policymakers have identified. Instead, the aggregate stance will be calibrated based on the state of the aggregate economy and communicated accordingly. In other words, even if a change in the fiscal stance does have macroeconomic implications we should not expect to hear central bankers describe how far the monetary stance has been adjusted in response. More broadly we might expect central bankers to be relatively circumspect in communicating the fact that they are required to systematically lean against the potential macroeconomic impact of measures announced by elected politicians. Nonetheless, we would expect central bank communication to *reference* developments in fiscal policy; so for example, the May 2005 Inflation Report observed:

> Inflation reflects the balance between the demand for private sector output and the resources available to produce it. So the public sector can contribute to inflationary pressure by using resources that would otherwise be employed in satisfying private sector demand. Given the Government's nominal spending plans, its demand for resources is likely to grow quite quickly during the next few years.

In any case, large and sustained discretionary changes in the fiscal stance are relatively rare and therefore examples of this monetary offset will be hard to come by. That likely reflects a number of factors. First, the fact that finance ministers tend not to make major adjustments to the fiscal stance on a regular basis, with a significant change happening at most once per parliament. Second, that the period preceding the financial crisis was one of remarkable macroeconomic tranquillity, so there was no pressing need for a major fiscal intervention (whether there was a case for additional fiscal measures to tackle, say, inequality is a different question altogether). But third, it also surely reflects the fact that finance ministers understand the rules of the game that their predecessors designed: they are no longer responsible for demand management and monetary policy will nullify any macroeconomic stimulus.

The situation described above—an economy in balance, with aggregate demand in line with supply and inflation at target—is certainly not the kind of circumstance in which we would expect to see a discretionary fiscal stimulus. As the early phase of the financial crisis demonstrated, it is only when the economy is weak and a large gap is opening up between the level of aggregate demand and supply that we would expect to see a change in fiscal policy designed to boost demand. The sceptical reader would be right to question whether central banks would nullify the impact of fiscal policy in these circumstances. Indeed, in a deep recession we would typically expect to see monetary and fiscal policy working in tandem, with cuts in official interest rates alongside a discretionary fiscal stimulus. That observation might appear to contradict our basic result but it does not, and to understand why we need to think again about the counterfactual.

An assessment of the impact of any policy intervention should always be made relative to an *estimate* of what would happened in the absence of that intervention (or what economists refer to as the counterfactual). The question we therefore have to ask is what would have happened in the absence of a discretionary fiscal stimulus in a recession, and the answer is clear: a larger monetary stimulus. The central bank will have a view on the optimal trajectory for output and inflation under the circumstances—circumstances that include the stance of fiscal policy—and the stance of monetary policy will be adjusted to deliver that outcome. The looser the fiscal stance the less loose monetary policy needs to be. In other words, our result still holds: fiscal policy does not influence aggregate demand even in a deep recession, because the central bank dials back on monetary stimulus. To go back to our original analogy of dual controls, the more pressure the learner driver applies to her brake pedal the less need there is for the instructor to slam on the brakes.

We have made this argument in the context of a discretionary fiscal stimulus in a recession—looser fiscal leads to less loose monetary policy—but as a matter of record we could have made the same argument in the context of the automatic stabilisers. If we consider two otherwise identical economies except in respect of the size of the automatic stabilisers then we might expect to see a corresponding difference in the amplitude of the typical interest rate cycle in those two economies. Simply put, the more effective the automatic stabilisers are in supporting demand in the face of a transitory shock, the less the need there is for an aggressive monetary policy response.

The problem with arguments based on counterfactuals and hypotheticals is that they are based on a thought experiment rather than hard evidence. Fortunately, the Minutes of the MPC provide an insight into the thought experiments of those who set monetary policy during a period in which there was a significant fiscal stimulus. Consider the following excerpt from the Minutes of the November 2008 policy meeting, at a moment in time when the economy was in free fall (BoE 2008):

> The projections in the Inflation Report implied that a very significant reduction in Bank Rate – possibly in excess of 200 basis points – might be required in order to meet the inflation target in the medium term. However, a number of arguments were discussed for not moving Bank Rate by the full extent implied by those projections.
>
> First, the projections had used the normal convention that they were based on the Government's most recent published tax and spending plans. The Government had already announced its intention to bring forward some planned spending commitments. Moreover, the changing composition of output would lead to a fall in effective tax rates from those assumed in the projections. Consequently, it would make sense for the Committee to reassess the required scale of monetary easing after the Chancellor's Pre-Budget Report.'

Fast forward to the conclusion and we find that the Committee did indeed choose to reduce Bank Rate by less than the Bank's own projections implied:

> On balance, the Committee judged that an immediate reduction in Bank Rate of 1.5 percentage points to 3% was necessary to meet the 2% target for inflation in the medium term. At future meetings, the Committee would be able to reassess the developments in the economy taking into account the potential impact of any fiscal announcement, as well as the reaction of the exchange rate and financial markets more generally to the November interest rate decision and to the publication of the November Inflation Report.
>
> The Governor invited the Committee to vote on the proposition that Bank Rate should be reduced by 1.5 percentage points to 3.0%. The Committee voted unanimously in favour of the proposition.

The November 2008 policy meeting therefore provides a classic illustration of this hypothetical interaction between monetary policy and fiscal policy in a deep downturn: the MPC cut rates by less than the Committee's projections suggested was required in part because the Committee anticipated that the Chancellor would unveil a significant easing in fiscal policy within a matter of days. Sadly, we shall never know whether the members of the Committee speculated about what would happen if they announced a far larger cut in interest rates: would much looser monetary policy have led to the Chancellor scaling back the size of the fiscal stimulus that he was about to announce or would he have carried on regardless, potentially forcing the Committee to dial back the monetary stimulus at a later meeting?

The monetary dominance hypothesis advanced above—that changes in the stance of monetary policy will systematically nullify the best efforts of finance ministers to use fiscal levers to influence the level of demand and employment—does not apply always and everywhere. In the next three subsections, we shall focus on three challenges to this hypothesis.

12.3 Geographical Mismatch: Local Fiscal Dominance

One obvious way to break the monetary dominance hypothesis is to look for a geographical mismatch between the conduct of fiscal and monetary policy. Whether we look at fiscal policy conducted at the regional level within a country, or at the national level within a currency union we can no longer conclude that monetary policy will nullify changes in the fiscal stance. Of course, in neither case can the central bank be utterly indifferent to the launch of a stimulus package in a specific region because there will still be some impact on the level of aggregate demand, and that will have to be offset. However, two points should be noted. First, the adjustment in the monetary stance will depend on the economic significance of the region: the smaller the region, the smaller the impact of the stimulus on demand at the aggregate level and hence the smaller the policy response. Second, the monetary policy response will be felt in all regions: so the central bank will try to depress demand across all regions given a surge in demand in one. Just as we argued above that fiscal policy can influence the mix of the demand but not necessarily the level, in this context, local fiscal policy can influence the regional mix of aggregate demand if not the aggregate level.

The crisis has provided a painful illustration of this phenomenon. When a small country in a large currency union like Greece embarks on a sharp and sustained fiscal consolidation, then we should not expect much in the way of a monetary policy response, cushioning the blow. Indeed, to the extent that the ECB did loosen policy in response to the mechanical impact of much weaker Greek GDP and inflation on the Eurozone aggregates that easier monetary stance would have been felt across the entire currency union, boosting activity in Germany as well as Greece. As a matter of fact, to the extent that the transmission mechanism was impaired in the parts of the Eurozone periphery that were under acute stress, it is likely that the benefits of monetary stimulus were felt more in Germany than Greece. Had the tables been turned and it was Germany driving through fiscal consolidation the monetary response would have been more significant—but not because the ECB cares more about the fate of the average German citizen, but simply because the German economy accounts for a much larger share of the Eurozone economy and German austerity would have had a much bigger impact on price stability at the aggregate level. To be clear, the ECB did not just rely on conventional easing to support Greece in this particular example; our point here is simply to illustrate a classic case of the failure of the monetary dominance argument whenever there is a geographical mismatch between the conduct of fiscal and monetary policy.

The fact that a local fiscal stimulus can have a material impact on the level of demand and employment in that region suggests that the analysis of changes in government spending within a particular region might be a productive line of enquiry for measuring the fiscal multiplier in the absence of the countervailing monetary policy response that we should expect when fiscal measures are announced at the national level (or supranational level with a currency union). This is precisely what two recent influential contributions to the literature have done.

Nakamura and Steinsson (2014) exploit the fact that some US states, like California, benefit more from military spending than others, like Illinois. It is hard enough to believe that major wars, and the significant increase in military procurement that they trigger, are driven by the state of the business cycle rather than geo-political events; it is even harder to believe that the decision to go to war is driven by the relative health of those states which benefit disproportionately from military spending. Why does that matter? Because when studying the impact of increased military spending, we can treat it as an exogenous shock, rather than an endogenous policy response. Moreover, by focusing on regional data, Nakamura and Steinsson can control for aggregate shocks which should affect all US states. They retrieve a multiplier of 1.5: that is, if relative per capita government purchases increase by 1 % of regional output, then relative per capita output increases by 1.5 % in that region. One point should be highlighted about their research question: the regions which benefit the most from increased military spending do not pay a disproportionate share of the additional taxes required to pay for that procurement. California is getting something for nothing. The Nakamura and Steinsson results are not a test of the balanced budget multiplier, nor even the usual thought experiment of a debt-financed stimulus. How this influences the outcome is unclear: remember, the modern literature emphasises the importance of the supply-side multiplier with a something for something stimulus, with higher taxes leading to a negative wealth effect, which leads to an increase in labour supply, and increased investment in the capital stock.

Acconcia et al. (2014) focus on a peculiar feature of the Italian legal system to isolate the impact of government spending at the local level. The central government has the power to remove elected officials on a city council given evidence that organised crime is exerting influence over political decisions and replace them with external administrators appointed by central government. Typically, the decision to remove local officials leads in short order to the suspension of financing for local public works and investment programmes, which are only restarted when the original investigation into political corruption on the council has run its course. In short, Acconcia, Corsetti and Simonelli have a dataset in which there are large shocks to government spending at the level, which are exogenous to the state of the local economy. Controlling for the stance of policy at the national level and the tax burden of local residents, they estimate that the output multiplier of spending cuts at the regional level is 1.5, and even higher (1.9) if we are willing to assume that lagged spending is exogenous to current output.

12.4 Political Pressure and the Fear of Losing Operational Independence

Another obvious way to overturn the monetary dominance hypothesis is to argue that elected politicians will assert their democratic mandate and instruct their central bankers to accommodate the macroeconomic consequences of any change in fiscal policy. At face value this argument is not that compelling, at least in those economies where the central bank enjoys some measure of independence.

In the UK, the BoE has operational independence for the conduct of monetary policy, but it does not have goal independence. In other words, the politicians are still in control of the objectives, but responsibility for achieving those objectives and control over the levers of monetary policy has been passed to the Bank. The politicians cannot easily set policy by proxy, firing policymakers who refuse to do their bidding: the internal and external members of the MPC serve terms of several years, and so long as those individuals are more concerned with their reputations than their prospects of being reappointed then there is limited scope for finance ministers to engineer an immediate change in policy. In theory, these institutional arrangements, and others like them in other countries, should insulate central bankers from these political pressures, but in practice it is not quite so clear cut.

Economists agree on very little, but there is pretty broad and deep consensus in favour of central bank independence. It is therefore not such a surprise that economists have quickly become accustomed to the idea that independent central banks are a permanent fixture of the policy architecture. However, it is unlikely that central bankers are quite so sanguine on this score. Even the central banking leviathan, the Fed, is coming under increased pressure from mainstream politicians in the USA, who wish to audit the conduct of monetary policy. As Richard Fisher, President of the Federal Reserve Bank of Dallas observes (Fisher 2015):

> 'Audit the Fed' is nothing more than an attempt to override purely economic judgments and bend monetary policy to the will of politicians. It is misguided. I pray we don't go there. I can think of nothing that would do more damage to our nation's prosperity.

Fear of failure is a key consideration here—and in particular, asymmetric fear of failure, where far too little output and inflation is viewed as more dangerous than far too much at least at the current juncture (one might speculate that the asymmetry varies across countries depending on experiences; the asymmetry may operate in the opposite direction in countries which have experienced hyperinflation in living memory). Central bankers may conclude that a repeat performance of 1937 where a premature tightening in monetary policy is thought to have contributed to a downturn in demand that extended the pain of the Great Depression era (Romer 2009) might do for operational independence: politicians might have the opportunity and public support to take back the levers of monetary policy. It is at least possible that central bankers could be influenced by those concerns to keep monetary policy looser for longer in the recovery from this crisis to avoid making that mistake. This strategy could be justified internally as short-run pain (a suboptimal path for output and inflation) to preserve the long-run gain (from operational independence). There is after all recent precedent of what can happen to policy institutions which are deemed to have failed. As we shall go on to discuss in the companion volume to this book, the perceived failures of the pre-crisis regime for the supervision of the banks led to major institutional change—for example, in the UK, the Financial Services Authority (FSA) was dissolved, with responsibility for prudential supervision and regulation passing back to the BoE (see later).

This is not quite the end of the story. Beyond the political pressure and the asymmetric fear of failure there is another channel through which politicians can influence monetary policy. If politicians were sufficiently concerned that the central bank was pursuing an excessively tight strategy they can rewrite the objectives that the central bank is tasked with delivering. Indeed, one might argue it is far more efficient for a finance minister to simply rewrite the mandate of monetary policy to engineer a macroeconomic stimulus than to launch a fiscal stimulus and then try to pressurise the central bank to look the other way. There is a sliding scale here, between tweaking the instructions to the central bank over the relative importance of deviations of output and inflation from their respective targets or the time horizon over which inflation must be brought back to the target and the more extreme change in the nominal anchor (the inflation target). Of course, there is a downside here: the more that politicians are seen to interfere in the conduct of monetary policy and tinker with the mandate, the greater the threat to the credibility of the regime and the nominal anchor.

12.5 Fiscal Stimulus at the Zero Lower Bound (ZLB)

Many governments responded to the collapse in output during the acute phase of the financial crisis and unsurprisingly that sparked a renewed interest in research into the macroeconomics of fiscal policy, and in particular whether the monetary dominance hypothesis still holds when official interest rates hit the lower bound, which as we have discussed is not necessarily at zero but is often referred to as the ZLB all the same.

A handful of high profile papers—Christiano et al. (2011), Eggertsson (2011) and DeLong and Summers (2012)—which illustrated why the fiscal multiplier might be high (i.e., much larger than one) under these circumstances attracted a huge amount of attention, to the point where that headline result now defines the consensus. However, those papers are more nuanced than the headlines suggest, and are worthy of further discussion

Christiano et al.'s (2011) key result is that the government spending multiplier can be much larger than one at the lower bound and is increasing in the share of government spending whilst the economy is marooned at the lower bound. Their result is more compelling because it is derived using a model in which fiscal policy is relatively ineffective (the multiplier is less than one). To be precise, they obtain a hump-shaped profile for the multiplier given a three-year shock to government spending: on impact the multiplier is 1.6 and peaks at 2.3 five quarters into the stimulus package.

The mechanism that drives the result is relatively straightforward. Imagine for the sake of argument that there is a shift in household savings behaviour, such that households wish to defer consumption. In a flex-price economy we should expect to see a fall in the real interest rate to discourage savings so as to clear the goods market, But in our sticky price economy the central bank will respond by cutting nominal interest rates, and that depresses real interest rates so goods markets still clear with only a relatively modest fall in activity. However, if the central bank cannot cut nominal interest rates then real interest rates are left at the mercy of inflation expectations. The decline in activity puts immediate downward pressure on costs and agents will expect that disinflationary pressure to gradually feed through into prices. However, there is no offsetting adjustment in nominal interest rates so the real interest rate will rise and that will tend to discourage consumption and other interest sensitive expenditure (like business investment). A much steeper decline in activity is now required to clear goods markets such that the desire to smooth consumption over time is then sufficient to overcome the original desired increase in savings and the counterproductive rise in the real interest rate.

An increase in government spending can help counteract this downward spiral. The stimulus to demand will put upwards pressure on costs and that will moderate expectations of deflation and the corresponding surge in real interest rates. The timing of that stimulus package matters too. Christiano, Eichenbaum and Rebelo provide theoretical support for the demand for 'shovel ready' stimulus: government spending is far more effective if it comes on stream when the economy is still at the lower bound. They estimate that the peak multiplier falls from 2.3 to just over 1 when the fraction of a stimulus package that occurs at the lower bound falls from 100 % to 50 %.

Eggertsson (2011) explores how the presence of the ZLB can potentially overturn the conventional wisdom over the relative merits of different fiscal tools. He argues that the instinctive preference for supply-side measures no longer applies when monetary policy is no longer able to accommodate any expansion in the productive capacity of the economy. Theorists expect a cut in payroll taxes to lead in short order to an expansion in labour supply and a corresponding fall in marginal costs to which the inflation targeting central bank will respond. The end result is a modest positive multiplier from the payroll tax cut. At the ZLB, the multiplier flips sign, as the disinflationary impact of increased labour supply amplifies the counterproductive move in real interest rates. Eggertsson refers to this anomaly as the 'paradox of toil': if everyone wants to work more there will be less work to do. A more conventional 'paradox of thrift' will arise in response to a cut in capital taxes: the tax cut encourages people to save, which is precisely the opposite of what central banks would be trying to achieve if monetary policy was not out of action. Instead, Eggerstsson advocates fiscal measures which are likely to boost aggregate demand, such as a cut in sales taxes.

DeLong and Summers (2012) present an interesting cost benefit analysis of the case for fiscal stimulus at the lower bound. They focus in particular on the risk of hysteresis in a depressed economy: if the cyclical weakness in activity is allowed to morph into a structural weakness in activity then the cost of inaction rises significantly. Indeed, they illustrate that 'even a small shadow cast on future potential output'—that is, the scar from a depression is relatively shallow—tilts the cost benefit analysis in favour of fiscal activism. A simple numerical calculation in the introduction of their paper illustrates the point perfectly.

Imagine that the fiscal multiplier is 1.5 and that the real rate of interest is 1 % and is invariant to changes in the stance of fiscal policy. Further assume that for every $1 increase in GDP, tax receipts (net of transfers) improve by $0.33, and that for every $1 reduction in activity, potential output falls by $0.01. Given these assumptions a $100 stimulus package will raise GDP by $150, and that in turn will improve tax receipts by $0.50, partially funding the initial stimulus, so that government debt must rise by $50. The cost of servicing that increase in the debt is $0.50. However, a $150 increase in GDP implies that a $1.5 hysteresis scar on output is avoided, and that in turn implies a $0.50 deterioration in tax receipts is avoided. In other words, the fiscal stimulus is self-financing.

Before moving on, we should note the importance of the interest rate assumption in DeLong and Summers' work. As they highlight: 'only when a government must pay a substantial premium over the social rate of time discount in order to borrow is the economy unlikely to benefit from expansionary fiscal policy at the zero bound.' As we shall go on to discuss, whilst it might be safe to assume that the interest rate that the US government pays on its debt may prove largely insensitive to the size of that burden, it is not clear that it is prudent for all governments to make the same assumption.

One key feature of the analysis of the merits of fiscal policy in these unusual circumstances is the duration of the economy's staycation at the lower bound. This was a key critique of Cogan et al. (2010): that it was inappropriate to assume that official interest rates would be invariant to the fiscal stance, highlighting the long-standing concern in modern macroeconomics that nominal interest rate pegs give rise to instability. Carlstrom et al. (2014) revisit this question and illustrate how sensitive the multiplier is to the exit strategy. With a guaranteed exit from the lower bound after T periods, the multiplier is found to be small, but given that the size of the multiplier is convex in the duration of the stay at the lower bound then uncertainty over the point of departure can give rise to much larger multipliers (even a very low probability attached to a very long stay at the lower bound can have a significant impact on the multiplier).

12.6 The Conventional Wisdom Strikes Back with Unconventional Interventions at the ZLB

A critical assumption in this literature is that monetary policy is constrained at the lower bound. However, central banks were anything but inactive when official interest rates hit the lower bound at the start of the crisis. As we have already discussed, central banks expanded their balance sheets, in many cases printing money to purchase assets. If those in charge of monetary policy believed that these unconventional interventions had the potential to influence aggregate demand then we should still expect the logic of monetary dominance to apply within central banks: the announcement of a large fiscal stimulus ought to lead central banks to scale back asset purchases, whilst an acceleration of fiscal consolidation should lead to an expansion of the scale of asset purchases. Even in a world where unconventional monetary interventions are thought to be relatively ineffective—a large purchase programme has only a modest impact on aggregate demand—monetary dominance should still hold: it should still be the case that central banks have the capacity to off-set the macroeconomic impact of changes in fiscal policy, so long as the central bank is willing to use that instrument in sufficient scale. It is only where unconventional instruments are completely ineffective, or there is some upper bound on the use of these tools that we are back in a world where monetary policy is constrained.

Unsurprisingly, the papers discussed above recognise this reality, and therefore the defence of fiscal stimulus at the lower bound that it is claimed that they provide is rather more nuanced than some would have you believe. For example, Christiano et al. (2011) note that forward guidance is a viable alternative to fiscal stimulus at the lower bound:

> [A]n alternative way to escape the negative consequences of a shock that makes the zero bound binding is for the central bank to commit to future inflation. We abstract from this possibility in this paper. We do so for a number of reasons. First, this theoretical possibility is well understood. Second, we do not think that it is easy in practice for the central bank to credibly commit to future high

inflation. Third, the optimal trade-off between higher government purchases and anticipated inflation depends sensitively on how agents value government purchases and the costs of anticipated inflation. Studying this issue is an important topic for future research.

DeLong and Summers (2012) acknowledge that the central bank has room to maneouvre at the lower bound and highlight the risk of monetary dominance—that the central bank may use these unconventional tools less aggressively and that ultimately the central bank remains in control of the cruising speed in a dual control economy:

> [O]ur analysis has taken it as given that at the zero bound, monetary policy does not change when fiscal policy is altered. Central banks, however, do have room for maneuver, both in their ability to operate directly on a wider range of financial instruments than they use in normal times, and in their ability to precommit policy. As a matter of logic, it is possible that increased fiscal actions will call forth a contractionary monetary policy response by causing central banks to use these tools less expansively. Perhaps, then, as Gregory Mankiw and Matthew Weinzierl (2011) assert, arguments for fiscal expansion in a depressed economy are even better arguments for monetary expansion.

The argument for fiscal stimulus at the lower bound is then made either in terms of the constraints on unconventional monetary policy:

> With interest rates at the zero bound, the central bank may lack the power to manage aggregate demand by itself without pushing nonstandard monetary policy beyond the limits it regards as plausible. And even if the central bank believes that it has the power, it may lack the will—and may well lack the formal legal authority—to undertake nonstandard policy measures that might be better classified as quasi-fiscal policies. If, in a depressed economy, a central bank possesses both the power and the will to target real aggregate demand and offset any effects of fiscal expansion, then the policy-relevant multiplier…will be sufficiently small that expansionary fiscal policy fails to pass its benefit-cost test. But if the central bank lacks either the power or the will to do so, our argument applies.

In the end, DeLong and Summers simply argue that monetary policy cannot bear all the burden by itself, and that fiscal policy should be part of the mix. But as we have argued, with the cyclically adjusted budget in deficit and projected to remain so in many countries that is exactly what has happened. In short, the academic case for a much more aggressive fiscal stimulus at the lower bound than was actually put in place is not all it is cracked up to be.

Indeed, the paper that DeLong and Summers cite (Mankiw and Weinzierl 2011) concludes that conventional fiscal policy is the 'demand management tool of last resort', to be used when first unconventional monetary tools and second unconventional fiscal tools (which mimic the impact of monetary policy on the allocation of resources) have been exhausted.

12.7   The Final Nail in the Fiscal Stimulus Coffin: Fiscal Stimulus and Rate Hikes

Not everyone will be swayed by the argument presented above. QE sceptics will continue to believe that if finance ministers do more at the lower bound and central banks do less unconventional policy in response then the two will not cancel. However, we doubt anyone would be willing to make the same argument about rate hikes: few economists would dispute that an increase in official interest rates would weigh on demand. In other words, if finance ministers had announced a fiscal stimulus which was so powerful that central banks concluded that not only were asset purchases no longer warranted but that an increase in official interest rates was also required to achieve price stability then we would be back in our conventional world of monetary dominance. The monetary instructor would put her foot on the brake as the fiscal learner puts his foot on the accelerator: looser fiscal policy leads to tighter monetary policy.

That possibility may seem extremely unlikely given the depressed state of the developed economies in the post-crash era but in theory the MPC might have been forced to take just that decision in early 2011. In retrospect it might seem implausible that the Committee could have raised rates back in early 2011 but the inflation outlook was such a concern at that point that the Committee was seriously considering the case for a rate hike, as the Minutes reveal:

> The Committee considered the case for an increase in Bank Rate at this meeting. The domestic and global recovery had proceeded at least as well as expected. And the most likely prospect was for continued growth, despite the downside risks that remained. For most members, the balance of risks to medium-term inflation relative to the target had moved upwards over the past few months, reflecting the recent and prospective buoyancy of import prices and the possible impact of higher near-term inflation on public inflation expectations. That would suggest that a lower level of demand might be consistent with hitting the inflation target in the medium term, and so might argue for a withdrawal of some of the current monetary stimulus. Moreover, an increase in Bank Rate at the current juncture might lessen the risk that a larger increase became necessary

at a later stage if inflation persisted above the target. Members noted that a small increase in Bank Rate at this meeting would still leave monetary policy highly accommodative, and would not preclude the Committee from increasing the policy stimulus in future if that became necessary.

Indeed, two members of the Committee were already voting for an increase in Bank Rate at this meeting. We now know that others were close to joining them (Sentance 2011) but they were likely worried that an unexpected decision to raise interest rates might surprise the market and lead to an unintended sharp shift in market interest rates. It seems those individuals preferred to signal to the market that a rate hike was possible (if not probable) at the next meeting (by disclosing how finely balanced the decision was in the January meeting) and then if a decision was taken to raise interest rates to use the opportunity of the February 2011 Inflation Report to communicate the reasons for the decision and thereby minimise the risk of that undesirable shift in market interest rates—back to the Minutes:

> Some members also noted that an increase in Bank Rate at this meeting might be misinterpreted as a signal that the Committee would attempt to bring inflation back to the target excessively rapidly, which could cause expectations of a relatively sharp tightening of monetary policy that could have a detrimental impact on confidence and activity. There was a spectrum of views among Committee members about how much weight to place on the arguments for and against a change in the policy stance. For most members, recent developments implied that the risks to inflation in the medium term had probably shifted upwards. For some of those members, the decision this month was finely balanced. The analysis that fed into the forthcoming February Inflation Report projections would provide an opportunity to assess fully the developments since the previous Report, and to evaluate more thoroughly the risks to inflation in the medium term. The publication of the Report would also give the Committee the opportunity to explain fully its assessment of the outlook and its policy decisions.

Of course in the event the Committee did not raise interest rates at the February 2011 meeting, and the Committee would soon be voting to expand its asset purchase programme. The point of revisiting this period is because that finely balanced decision followed soon after the incoming government's decision to accelerate the pace of fiscal consolidation. If instead the government had announced an alternative strategy in which fiscal policy would have provided significantly more support to aggregate demand then it is not too hard to imagine that the incremental news on demand and inflation would have been sufficient to tip the Committee over the edge.

Another way to put the same point is that it was the inflation outlook and implicitly the supply side of the economy which appeared to constrain the amount of stimulus injected into the UK economy and therefore the prospects for recovery during much of the post-crash period, not fiscal policy.

12.8 Endnote: The Flip Side of the Monetary (and Financial) Dominance Coin

We have argued that given its mandate for price stability, the central bank is obliged to adjust the stance of monetary policy to lean against shocks to aggregate demand, including those which originate in the finance ministry and can therefore insulate the economy from the impact of fiscal consolidation, even potentially at the lower bound. There is a corollary to this result: finance ministers cannot rely on economic growth to bail out poor public finances.

The level of government borrowing certainly depends on the state of the business cycle—in a bust (boom) tax receipts are low (high) whilst welfare spending is high (low)—so other things equal, finance ministers are likely to prefer a boom to a bust (even if we ignore the fact that the electoral prospects of a government are also likely to vary with the business cycle). However, any hope that a debt burden can be reduced by engineering an extended economic boom founder on the monetary dominance hypothesis: the central bank cannot allow an extended economic boom because that would lead to an extended inflation overshoot that would not be consistent with their mandate.

This illustrates why finance ministers focus on the structural budget—that is, the state of the public finances once we strip out the impact of the business cycle. Finance ministers should expect the central bank to close the output gap and should therefore expect the headline budget to gravitate towards the structural position. Any plans to balance the books which depend on a path for demand which is inconsistent with the closure of the output gap (and more broadly the pursuit of price stability), or equivalently on a sustained, persistent and positive gap between the headline and structural budget, are likely doomed to fail on account of monetary dominance.

Indeed, with the advent of macro-prudential policy (see later) one could make exactly the same point about the financial cycle. There is now a policymaker who *may* be given responsibility for smoothing out that financial cycle, so any plans to balance the books on the basis of the strong tax receipts that the government receives in the upswing of a financial cycle (from sources such as capital gains tax and stamp duty) are also likely to fail on account of *financial dominance*.

In short, the only credible internally consistent plans are those which are based on the assumption that other policymakers successfully achieve their mandates, and therefore the business and financial cycles should be expected to have relatively little impact on the state of the public finances.

Before we move on, the flip side of this monetary dominance argument should be highlighted. We have argued that in most circumstances fiscal consolidation should not have a material impact on output and employment indeed *even at the lower bound*. It follows that it remains the responsibility of central banks and not finance ministers to lean against the business cycle even in those unusual circumstances and therefore any blame attached to fiscal policy for failing to support the recovery (leaving to one side the size of the structural deficit during this period) should be redirected to the doors of central banks (leaving to one side the path of inflation during this period).

References

Acconcia, A., Corsetti, G., & Simonelli, S. (2014). Mafia and public spending: Evidence on the fiscal multiplier from a quasi-experiment. *American Economic Review, 104*, 2185–2209.

BoE. (2008). Minutes of the November 2008 meeting of the Monetary Policy Committee.

Carlstrom, C., Fuerst, T., & Paustian, M. (2014). Fiscal multipliers under an interest rate peg of deterministic versus stochastic duration. *Journal of Money, Credit and Banking, 46*(6), 1293–1312.

Christiano, L., Eichenbaum, M., & Rebelo, S. (2011). When is the government spending multiplier large? *Journal of Political Economy, 119*(1), 78–121.

Cogan, J., Cwik, T., Taylor, J., & Wieland, V. (2010). New Keynesian versus old Keynesian government spending multipliers. *Journal of Economic Dynamics and Control, 34*, 281–295.

DeLong, B., & Summers, L. (2012). Fiscal policy in a depressed economy. *Brookings Paper on Economic Activity, Spring.*

Eggertsson, G. (2011). What fiscal policy is effective at zero interest rates? *NBER Macroeconomics Annual, 25*, 59–112.

Fisher, R. (2015, February 11). *Suggestions after a decade at the Fed.* Speech.

Mankiw, N., & Weinzierl, M. (2011). An exploration of optimal stabilization policy. *Brookings Paper on Economic Activity, Spring*, 209–272.

Nakamura, E., & Steinsson, J. (2014). Fiscal stimulus in a monetary union: Evidence from US regions. *American Economic Review, 104*(3), 753–792.

Romer, C. (2009, June 18). The Lessons of 1937. *The Economist.*

Sentance, A (2011, November 6). *Time to reform the MPC*, Blog.

13

When Bond Markets Attack

This section is about what happens when the public finances deteriorate to the point that market participants or even the general public reach the conclusion that debt may be on an unsustainable path and something needs to be done—whether that be fiscal consolidation, financial repression, inflating away debt or a formal restructuring. There is little agreement on where this point lies for an advanced economy like the UK, or how policymakers should respond if the public finances approach that danger zone, and in what follows we shall review the key issues.

13.1 Debt Sustainability and the 'No Ponzi' Condition

We have already encountered a simple expression for the primary budget balance required to stabilise the debt burden. However, there is a fundamental difference between stability and sustainability (see Chalk and Hemming 2000). The latter is fundamentally a forward-looking concept. The debt burden does not have to be stable today in order to be sustainable: debt may rise relative to GDP for a sustained period of time without causing undue alarm so long as there is an anticipation that the debtor will have the capacity to manage that larger debt burden in the future, perhaps even the far future. Likewise, debt may not be sustainable—in the sense that potential creditors are unwilling to roll over debt—even if the ratio of debt to GDP has been stable if those creditors become sufficiently concerned about the long-run trajectory of debt.

© The Editor(s) (if applicable) and The Author(s) 2016
R. Barwell, *Macroeconomic Policy after the Crash*,
DOI 10.1057/978-1-137-51592-6_13

The typical description of the circumstances in which a debt burden becomes unsustainable is a Ponzi game, after the Italian-American 'entrepreneur' Charles Ponzi, where a debtor does not have the resources to service outstanding debt from current income and therefore has to borrow ever more money each period to make ends meet, leading the debt stock to explode. Economists rule out these situations by assumption when solving an optimisation problem by imposing a transversality condition (a.k.a. 'no Ponzi' condition), ensuring that the optimal path pinned down by first-order conditions linking one period to the next is not an explosive path. But as the eponymous villain of this story proved, Ponzi schemes can flourish in the real world, at least for a time and therefore great care should be taken when imposing the no Ponzi condition by assumption in analysis of financial stability (Barwell 2013). Indeed, Cochrane (2011a) argues that these no Ponzi conditions have also been inappropriately applied in the analysis of monetary stability to rule out explosive nominal paths (hyperinflation).

The transversality condition that applies to the sustainability of government debt emerges when we try to use the simple framework outlined earlier to project forward the path of the ratio of debt to GDP into the far future. Essentially we can think of the discounted sum of the sequence of primary surpluses or deficits that the government will run in future periods linking the debt burden today and the present discounted value of the debt burden in some period in the far future. For debt to be considered sustainable today— or put another way, to rule out overaccumulation of debt tomorrow—this second term must converge to zero in the limit when T tends to infinity (although Bohn (1995) notes we should be cautious in our choice of all-important discount rate when calculating that present value in the uncertain real world). Our transversality condition therefore requires that a debt burden today must be matched by the sum of expected discounted future primary surpluses and privatisation proceeds tomorrow and into the infinite future.

13.2 Introducing Sovereign Credit Risk

We have already seen how the wedge between the cost of servicing debt and the trend rate of economic growth is a key ingredient in an assessment of debt stability and sustainability. Up to this point we have assumed that these terms are exogenously given, and in most circumstances that it is a reasonable simplifying assumption but in a sovereign crisis it is manifestly not. To see why not we need to begin with an explanation of what determines the level of the interest rate that drives the cost of servicing debt.

When the bank lends you money it will charge you a higher interest rate than it pays to borrow the money, in part because the bank needs to protect itself in advance against the risk that you might default on the loan. Essentially, those debtors who honour their obligations pay more for the loan in order to cover the cost of those who do not. Unsurprisingly, the bank will tend to charge more for loans where there is a greater probability of default (PD) or where the bank expects to get less money back in the event of default (i.e., there is a greater loss given default [LGD]), which is why the interest rate on your mortgage is a lot lower than the interest rate on an unsecured personal loan of similar size (if the banks were willing to lend unsecured on such a scale).

The same principles apply when financial institutions lend governments money by purchasing bonds. There is a diverse set of financial institutions active on the demand side of the sovereign bond market, from commercial banks to sovereign wealth funds, from pension funds to hedge funds, and their precise purpose for making investments in these securities may vary accordingly. However, none of those financial institutions can afford to be indifferent to the return on their investments. Those investors should therefore treat the government just like any other potential debtor and demand compensation for the risk of default in the return that they receive from their investment, and the size of that interest premium should depend on the perceived PD and LGD on the government debt. If the market receives bad news about fundamentals—it could be bad news on the cyclical state of the economy, which will temporarily lead to larger deficits and persistently higher debt burden; it could be bad news on the structural public finances, which imply a lower effective tax rate; or it could be concerns about the political situation, and the perceived capacity and commitment of politicians to deliver the primary budget position to stabilise the debt burden—then that interest premium should increase.

In the years leading up to the financial crisis the level of public debt was sufficiently low such that the perceived probability of any advanced economy government defaulting on its obligations was sufficiently remote such that the market demanded *relatively* little in the way of compensation for credit risk, although precisely how little is a matter of empirical debate. Ardagna et al. (2004) use several decades of data for 16 OECD countries to identify a significant impact of the public finances on the cost of servicing debt. They argue that a one percentage point increase in the primary deficit (expressed as a share of GDP) raises long-term interest rates by a mere 10 basis points; however, in a dynamic model this shock can eventually add 150 basis points to the rate after a decade. They also uncover a non-linear relationship between the cost of servicing debt and shocks to the stock of debt: only in countries where the debt burden is already significant does an increase in the debt stock lead to an increase in the interest rate. Laubach (2009) focuses on US data, and in particular the impact of the long-term projections of the Congressional Budget Office and the Office of Management and Budget (OMB) on long-term interest rates. He finds that a one percentage point increase in the projected deficit to GDP ratio raises long-term interest rates by 25 basis points. Finally, Engen and Hubbard (2004) conclude that a one per cent increase in the ratio of debt to GDP would raise long-term real interest rates by a mere three basis points, whilst noting that some estimates are not statistically significantly different from zero. However, they conclude with a warning:

> Our findings should not be construed as implying that 'deficits don't matter.' Substantially larger, persistent, and unsustainable levels of government debt can eventually put increasing strains on the available domestic and foreign sources of loanable funds, and can represent a large transfer of wealth to finance current generations' consumption from future generations which must eventually pay down federal debt to a sustainable level.

One could argue that in the pre-crisis era the market paid too little attention and therefore demanded too little in terms of additional compensation for the debt burden that did exist, and certainly too little to incentivise governments to improve the position (Manganelli and Wolswijk 2009). However, as events would demonstrate, the tranquillity of sovereign bond markets and the indifference of investors to debt could not be taken for granted. Laubach (2011) documents the instability of estimates of the sensitivity of Eurozone sovereign bond yields to fundamentals as we move between the two periods: increasing dramatically as we enter the financial crisis.

13.3 Introducing Positive Feedback

We have explained why the cost of servicing debt might vary systematically across sovereign issuers at a given point in time, and for a particular sovereign through time, according to their perceived credit worthiness. By extension we should expect to see the cost of servicing debt to rise when the public finances are seen to deteriorate. Our interest here is what happens when there is a significant slippage in the state of the public finances: the endogenous response of the cost of servicing debt can trigger a chain of events which can cause what looked like a relatively stable situation to quickly spiral out of control.

Systems which exhibit this feature are said to display positive feedback, which is the cause of much confusion. The defining feature of these systems is that the initial impact of a shock is amplified with the passage of time—driving the system further from the original (not so) steady state—irrespective of the direction of travel. Just because bad news can drive the system towards a bad place these dynamics should not be confused with negative feedback (where the system is self-stabilising). To fix ideas, vicious and virtuous circles are both examples of positive feedback.

To explain how this positive feedback mechanism can arise—how we can arrive at a situation where the bond market appears to attack a sovereign issuer, potentially driving the government into default—we will begin by outlining the basic mechanism and then introduce various bells and whistles in the following subsections until we arrive at a description of a potentially unstable system.

Consider an economy on the cusp of that threshold, where the burden of debt is already high but the primary budget balance is currently set at a level which stabilises that substantial debt burden. Now imagine that the market receives bad news on debt sustainability, which should lead the market to demand additional compensation against default risk and that means that the government will have to offer investors a higher return when it issues new debt. If that shock to the interest rate persists then it will gradually feed through into the average cost of servicing debt, and other things equal the initial primary budget balance will no longer be sufficient to stabilise debt (because the gap between the cost of servicing debt and rate of economic growth has shifted in an unfavourable direction). At some point the government will have to arrest the situation (otherwise, the debt burden is set on an explosive path) and that implies a bout of fiscal consolidation, improving the primary budget balance so that the debt burden is once again stable given the new higher cost of servicing debt. There is a temptation to argue that this shift in the stance of fiscal policy will automatically weigh on aggregate demand, leading to a further cyclical deterioration in the debt stock. However, for a country like the UK we should expect an adjustment in the monetary stance to offset the impact of consolidation on demand. In this instance, there is no great damage done.

Now let us repeat this thought experiment and instead assume a much larger shock to debt sustainability—for example, the outbreak of a financial crisis which leads to a significant accumulation of debt (via increased borrowing during the recession that follows and debt financed interventions to support the banking sector)—and then compound the problem by assuming that monetary policy is in some sense constrained, either at the lower bound or because the economy concerned is a small member of a currency union.

Now the initial increase in the cost of servicing debt and the implied correction in the primary budget balance is far larger. Without a one-for-one offset from looser monetary policy, that fiscal correction is likely to further depress demand, leading to further cyclical borrowing and accumulation of debt. Moreover, the scale of the required fiscal correction may exceed what politicians are willing and able to execute in a short space of time. The result may be an extended period over which the primary budget position is insufficient to stabilise the ratio of debt to GDP in the long run and in the meantime the cyclical weakness in demand further aggravates the debt accumulation problem. In these circumstances investors may be forced to revisit their assessment of the appropriate compensation for default risk because the transmission of the original shock has led to a further erosion in debt sustainability. That second round increase in the cost of servicing debt piles further pressure on the public finances, demanding further fiscal consolidation to stabilise the debt burden, and that in turn could lead to further fiscal-induced weakness in demand, and so on.

13.4 Economic and Political Amplification

Having outlined the basic feature of the positive feedback mechanism—creditors should demand a higher interest rate to compensate for the PD in response to bad news on debt sustainability but that higher interest rate puts further pressure on the public finances—we can now supplement our basic recipe with a couple of additional destabilising ingredients where the initial shock or its transmission further erodes potential investors confidence in the capacity of a government to service debt, leading to further increases in the interest rate. We begin with the obvious economic and political channels.

In the scenario described above there is a transitory period of weak aggregate demand which translates into a transitory increase in borrowing and a persistent increase in the debt burden, but eventually the output gap closes with the level of demand rising to meet the level of aggregate supply and in the process tax receipts will naturally rise to eliminate the cyclical borrowing problem. However, if instead the period of depressed demand leads to significant permanent damage to the supply side through hysteresis effects then further fiscal consolidation will be required to plug the gap left in the public finances by the implied permanent hit to tax receipts (the news on the level of aggregate supply multiplied by the effective tax rate). Worse still, if the depression damages the likely growth of potential supply (so-called super hysteresis) then the cumulative erosion of the public finances implies far greater fiscal pain in our debt stability expression.

Another lesson that the crisis has taught us is that public support for austerity is not infinite. The democratic process will not always deliver politicians who are committed to a timely improvement in the public finances and the more painful consolidation proves and the longer it lasts, the more likely it is that anti-austerity politicians are elected. News that a government plans to repair the public finances over a more extended time horizon—borrowing more in the interim, accumulating further debt—may raise questions in the minds of investors about the commitment to service debt, and that in turn will likely lead to investors demanding increased compensation for default risk. Indeed, those commentators who speculate about the merits of restructuring debt, that in normal times are typically found on the fringes of the political debate, may start to gather support among the general public in a crisis and that could really spook investors.

In short, a large shock to debt sustainability can be amplified through an erosion in the capacity (economic) or willingness (political) to service debt, with the corresponding increase in debt-servicing costs aggravating the need for fiscal consolidation which in turn leads to further economic pain and in extreme circumstances persistent damage to a sovereign's credit worthiness, which can then feedback via further increases in debt-servicing costs.

13.5   Bad News and Forced Sales

To understand a classic market-driven source of feedback we need to begin with a brief discussion of the government's creditors: who they are, and why they invest in government bonds. Mainstream macroeconomics has by and large treated the institutional reality of financial markets as tedious and irrelevant detail, such that the demand for financial assets can be modelled as if the household sector (on whose behalf those institutions act) traded in those markets. We have to make simplifying assumptions in many places if we want our models to be tractable, and where questions of monetary stability are concerned this assumption that financial institutions are irrelevant may be perfectly reasonable; however, it is unlikely that this assumption is reasonable where questions of financial stability are concerned (see Barwell (2013) for a discussion of this point). Our particular area of interest here—when and why the bond market 'attacks' governments—is a case in point.

A diverse range of financial institutions invest in government bonds, and they do so over different time horizons and for different reasons. The key point to note is that almost without exception these institutions are not investing their own money; they are agents acting on behalf of a principal. Indeed, in many cases some institutions will be acting as an intermediary in a chain that channels money from the principal to the ultimate agent making the investment, and if we look inside these institutions there are additional agency problems between the management of the firm and the person taking the investment decision. Why does this matter? Because there is almost always a significant information asymmetry between principal and investor and that tends to give rise to constraints on the behaviour of the agent to protect the principal's interests, and under certain circumstances these constraints can create forced buyers out of much of that investor base, amplifying the positive feedback mechanism. In particular, we can isolate two key mechanisms which operate to different degrees on different segments of the investor base.

First, many institutional investors are subject to formal or informal mandates which circumscribe the set of securities that they can hold. In normal circumstances these mandates can create a captive market for sovereign issuers, with a subset of the investor base constrained to invest in a very limited universe of high quality—perhaps defined in terms of a minimum credit rating—long-duration assets, in which sovereign bonds dominate. However, if the credit rating of a sovereign is downgraded, and particularly if that downgrade crosses a key boundary (such as the investment grade threshold) and particularly if the downgrade is idiosyncratic, then that could trigger forced sales (if all sovereign issuers are downgraded then there may be safety in numbers as the *de facto* minimum ratings threshold used by institutional investors may be lowered accordingly). These mandates are not always expressed in terms of ratings: during the Eurozone sovereign debt crisis many investors will have 'chosen' to divest all exposure to the periphery from their portfolios.

Second, all investors have a finite capacity to absorb losses on any given investment. Agents will invest in assets which they believe are cheap: where the price is below what the agent believes to be fair value. In theory, if the price of the asset falls too much given bad news (i.e., by more than the revised estimate of fair value) then a good investment opportunity has become an excellent opportunity. But what if the agent's model of fair value is flawed and the asset is worth less than he thinks? In practice, investors will typically operate under constraints: they will have to mark their positions to market (i.e., work out what their investment is worth based on current prices, relative to what they paid for them) and beyond a certain point they will be forced to cut their losses. Unfortunately, if your valuation of an asset that you already hold is far above what other investors are willing to pay for it then at some point risk management controls may kick in and you may have to stop buying what looks cheap and start selling at a price far below the one you paid to acquire that asset. Bad news that leads to a fall in the price of government bonds could therefore lead to a flood of forced sales.

In short, it is possible that very bad news on debt sustainability could lead to forced selling across a significant fraction of the investor base. The question is whether that sudden increase in the number of investors selling bonds in response to that bad news will influence the price. Basic economics suggests that it should: the price of an asset should respond to any imbalance between demand and supply. If that intuition is valid—if bad news which leads to falling prices can trigger forced sales which causes a further fall in the price—then the market and prices are potentially far more fragile than we might have otherwise assumed.

13.6 An Aside on Pricing Government Bonds

The reader may be somewhat surprised to learn that the modern literature on asset pricing does not always allow for something so crude as the imbalance between the number of buying and selling assets in the market at any particular moment in time to influence the price. Instead, asset prices are pinned down by fundamentals (see Cochrane (2005) for the modern treatment of asset pricing). A brief detour into the pricing of a stylised government bond, which pays regular coupons and the principal when the bond matures years from now, is therefore in order.

Let us begin with a hypothetical security which offers the same sequence of payments with absolute certainty (i.e., there is zero probability of default, or PD). The basic economic building block of asset pricing is the expected future path of short-term interest rates. Essentially, you should compare the returns that you will receive from investing in that hypothetical security (and receiving coupons and principal over many years) versus rolling your money over in a sequence of zero-risk short-term investments (e.g., in Treasury bills).

If you hold that security to maturity, then the nominal return is known with certainty (as we shall go on to discuss, the investor is still exposed to the risk that prices rise faster than expected over the lifetime of the bond); if the coupons and principal are linked to the value of an inflation index, then the real return is known. However, the value of that hypothetical security can vary through time in response to news on the expected future path of interest rates and for real-world investors who do not necessarily expect to hold to maturity that is an issue. If you buy that asset today and interest rates rise tomorrow then the price of that hypothetical security will fall: given the fixed coupon and principal repayments on the bond, the price must fall in order to deliver the new higher interest rate that the market demands.

We therefore expect the uncertainty about the future path of interest rates to influence the demand for (and therefore the price of) this hypothetical long-term security. In fact, we can isolate two effects: a convexity effect and a term premium.

The convexity effect results from the non-linear relationship between the price and yield of a bond. More precisely, the relationship between a change in yields and the corresponding change in the price of a bond varies according to the absolute level of yields such that bond prices rise more for a given decline in yields than they fall for an equivalent increase in yields. That convexity effect implies that the average price of a bond across different yield levels will be strictly higher than the price implied by the average level of yields. Bond holders will derive some positive value from this convexity effect - which will therefore be reflected in the current price - and the more uncertainty there is over the future level of yields, the greater this convexity effect is.

The term premium arises because investors should care about *when* they are likely to make a capital gain or loss on the bond. Investors will probably pay a premium for an asset which delivers strong returns when the rest of the portfolio performs poorly and consumption is low and there is a significant potential welfare gain from marginally higher income. In this case, our investors would pay a higher price and tolerate a lower yield (negative term premium) for bonds which they believe will act as a consumption hedge by delivering a capital gain (because interest rates unexpectedly fall) when the rest of the portfolio is likely to perform badly. In passing we should probably decompose the term premium into a real term premium reflecting news on real yields and an inflation risk premium with the former embedded in the yield on index-linked bonds and both the former and the latter embedded in the yield on conventional government debt.

Unlike our hypothetical security, there is a probability that the issuer of a bond will default: that is, will not make the coupon and/or principal repayments in full or on time, or both. As discussed above, investors should demand compensation for that risk. In particular, we can think of a credit risk premium which the investor demands, both to cover the expected loss on the security (reflecting the PD and LGD) and, analogous to the discussion over the term premium, the covariance of default with returns on the rest of the investor's portfolio.

In passing what we can say is that the compensation for credit risk that the market does demand does not always seem tied to the fundamentals that we think drives the quantity of credit risk for a particular security. Longstaff et al. (2011) show that almost two thirds of the variation in sovereign credit spreads derived from the credit default swap (CDS) market for a panel of 26 advanced and emerging countries between 2000 and 2010 can be explained by a single common factor, and that fraction rises to three quarters during the crisis phase (2007–2010). That first principal component is highly (negatively) correlated with the US stock market and positively correlated with the VIX index (a standard proxy for implied volatility). The conclusion?—that a global factor appears more important than local information in driving the compensation that investors demand for sovereign credit risk, and by extension that global investors may play an important role in determining local asset prices (so that funding shocks to global financial investors may filter fast into a broad constellation of asset prices).

When the issuer is a member of a currency union, there is a related risk for which investors may demand additional compensation: the risk of redenomination. If a country leaves that currency union then it seems likely that the sovereign concerned would restructure the terms of the debt and start paying coupons and principal in the new domestic currency, and investors would clearly not be indifferent to that. At the very least the creditor is exposed to exchange rate risk on the value of their portfolio, and in the case of weak countries leaving currency unions there is likely to be a significant depreciation upon exit, which implies a substantial write-down on the value of the security.

We now have the basic building blocks of our explanation of the return that investors will demand for holding government bonds. We can immediately see that the credit risk premium should widen in response to bad news about debt sustainability. We can also imagine that in a dire situation a redenomination risk premium might emerge for sovereign issuers in a currency union.

In short, we should expect to see the price of the bonds fall in the secondary market (i.e., the market for bonds that have already been issued) and the price of bonds in the primary market (for new issues) should fall in sympathy. How much prices fall will depend both on the perceived change in the quantity of risk (how much worse the situation has got) and the price of risk (how much compensation investors demand for exposure to a unit of risk). Unfortunately, the price of risk may be cyclical—that is, when the situation takes a turn for the worse investors become more risk averse and demand more compensation for a given exposure to risk, and that can amplify the fall in the price of risky assets. However, we do not yet have a mechanism where forced sales are amplifying the downward spiral, and to motivate that we need to introduce the liquidity risk premium.

Investors should place some value on assets which can easily be converted into cash to meet unexpected demands for payment; how much they value those assets will depend on how uncertain the timing and size of those demands upon them are and how easy it is to borrow money in the market. Of course, you can almost always sell an asset quickly if you have to; the point is how much of a discount to fair value you will have to swallow if you need to sell in a hurry, and that is likely to vary systematically across assets. We can therefore think of a liquidity risk premium which will capture the ease with which investors believe they can sell a particular asset. There is also an important size dimension here: large institutional investors will want to know how easy it is to liquidate a substantial position.

Bonds issued by major sovereigns are traded in deep and liquid markets where large numbers of transactions take place every day across a broad investor base and it is relatively easy for a single investor to exit even a large position. Those bonds typically score highly in terms of liquidity relative to say assets which are held by a much smaller number of niche investors, and transactions are far less regular and predictable. However, that ample liquidity in the government bond market may not exist in all states of nature. If bad news leads to a wave of forced selling and deters potential buyers from making an investment then current investors might become much more concerned about the ease with which they will be able to exit their position (i.e., the discount they will have to accept). The torrent of transactions can slow to a trickle.

To make matters worse, the market-makers (the investment banks who service end investors by standing ready to buy and sell bonds) may become more cautious in an environment of deteriorating liquidity and falling prices—particularly if they too have suffered mark to market losses on their inventory (Beetsma et al. 2013). As the market-makers step back, charging a higher spread between the price at which they will buy and sell, market liquidity will decline further. In the limit, the secondary market can virtually shut down and it will become impossible to issue new debt in the primary market, because the dealers will have no confidence that they will be able to sell the debt they purchase from the government to other institutions.

We have argued that bad news can lead to a reappraisal of the fair value of government bonds: investors will raise their expectation of the risk of default and lower their expectation of the ease with which they can exit a position in that security and that can depress the price of the security. This much is uncontroversial. However, there is an additional channel which is typically folded into the credit and liquidity risk premium which is worth highlighting in its own right: fear of bad news.

The term premium we encountered above reflects the compensation that the investor may demand for the volatility in the value of their investment (ultimately their consumption possibilities in different states of the world) that is driven by the potential for news on interest rates: essentially, you do not want to hold assets where you expect to suffer capital losses when the rest of your portfolio performs badly. We can imagine a corresponding term which reflects the impact of news on the PD or the potential liquidity of the asset. In other words, it might make sense to differentiate between the standard credit and liquidity risk premia, which reflect the marginal investor's beliefs about the PD and potential liquidity of an asset in different states of the world, and the potential for those beliefs to change in response to news.

It is the extent to which those beliefs about default risk and potential liquidity vary through time that will drive this component of the spread implicit in bond prices. The less stable those beliefs are, the more sensitive they are to news, the more volatile the compensation for credit and liquidity risk will be through time, and ultimately the more volatile bond prices will be through time. For investors who can be turned into forced sellers that volatility is a problem. Where the sovereign bonds issued in advanced economies are concerned, the key issue is fear of a catastrophe: a sufficiently large shock to the public finances such that bonds which are usually considered virtually default free and easy to liquidate for cash are now considered risky assets, and the probability of an outright restructuring cannot be ignored. So investors should demand compensation for greater potential volatility driven by the marginal investor's fear of catastrophe, and it turns out that this might not be that predictable.

13.7 Herds, Sunspots and Runs

Although economists instinctively model financial markets as efficient, with sophisticated investors setting prices on the basis of a rich information set that is common to all which should ensure that prices are in line with fundamentals, the reality is sometimes very different. Where there is significant uncertainty about fundamentals—about the true state of the public finances—market prices could be more fragile than is typically assumed. We know that the complete information assumption is inappropriate but economists tend to consciously or subconsciously discount the prospect of fragile markets that emerges in this world by assuming that there exists a sufficient number of sophisticated well-informed and well-financed investors who can systematically make money by shepherding prices back towards fundamentals, as Shiller (2003) observes:

> For these theoretical models to have any relevance to the stock market it must somehow be the case that a smaller element of 'smart money' or the 'marginal trader' can offset the foolishness of many investors and make the markets efficient.

However, this assumption is not innocuous: the 'smart money' may be able to make money by trading in the same direction as the rest of the investor base, driving prices further away from fundamentals (DeLong et al. 1990a) and may be concerned that their principal will conclude that they are not so smart if they are buying assets when prices keep falling (Shleifer and Vishny 1997).

Rather than relying on the smart individuals investing other people's money to anchor market prices on fundamentals, it is probably more realistic to think of numerous investors, each acting on the basis of a combination of public and private information that is incomplete, which makes for a rather less stable environment. The process of price discovery is more complex in this environment, because each investor's strategy is sensitive to what their peers are doing for two reasons.

First, the decisions taken by an investor will reveal something about their private information and that will help their peers learn something about the optimal strategy in the simple, perfect information equilibrium. The socially optimal outcome would be for every investor to take decisions based on their private information because that would solve the information problem. Unfortunately, it may not be in the interests of each investor to act in this way, which brings us to the second feature of this set-up.

Second, the payoff to a given strategy will depend on the strategies pursued by others: even if your private information suggests that the public finances are sound you might still sell bonds if you believe that everyone else has very different private information to you. In effect, you care about what other investors believe, and in turn, what each of those other investors believes that everyone else believes and so on—or as economists put it: 'higher order' beliefs matter.

Herds are liable to form in these environments, and there is nothing which guarantees that these herds form around the right answer (i.e., fundamentals). Once a few agents have acted in the same direction, the cumulated private information implicit in that common strategy dominates the value added in the private information held by any individual investor and the rational strategy is to join the crowd even if your private information is telling you to do the exact opposite (see Bannerjee (1992) and the review in Barwell (2013)). Indeed 'sunspot equilibria' can emerge (Cass and Shell 1983)—where what looks like irrelevant information determines the selection of the equilibrium (the term is a tongue-in-cheek reference to Jevons' work on whether sunspots cause business cycles). I may know that the common strategy of the herd is not based on private information, but if I am convinced that other investors will act on the irrelevant information in a predictable fashion then I still have an incentive to follow their lead: I do not want to be the only one buying bonds if everyone else is selling. In theory, I should be able to acquire assets at a knock-down price if the herd is acting on the basis of irrelevant information.

In practice, the price might keep falling further away from fundamentals and I will be forced to sell later and lower (DeLong et al. 1990b). In short, rational investors may have very little incentive to stand in the way of an irrational market—or as Keynes put it: 'markets can remain irrational longer than you can remain solvent'.

In the limit, the downward spiral in prices can eventually lead to a restructuring at which point those still holding sovereign debt may suffer a large write-down on the face value of the bond, although how much that investor loses will depend on what price they bought at. Multiple equilibria can emerge once the public finances are strained beyond a certain point—that is, the sovereign is only solvent so long as investors believe it is, and not otherwise—as Calvo (1988) observes:

> The implications for policy could be staggering…postponing taxes (i.e., falling into debt) may generate the seeds of indeterminacy; it may, in other words, generate a situation in which the effects of policy are at the mercy of people's expectations – gone would be the hopes of leading the economy along an 'optimal' path.

This feature may remind the reader of the literature on bank runs: namely that even those creditors of a bank who believe that it is still solvent will join the queue to withdraw their funds once that queue forms, because the positive net worth of the bank will be destroyed in the process of liquidating assets to meet the demand for funds (Diamond and Dybvig 1983). The same fear of being left with a residual claim of uncertain value can lead investors to run on a sovereign.

13.8 The Sovereign–Bank Nexus And Other Sources of Amplification in the Real Economy

The positive feedback mechanism we introduced at the outset of this section through which an initial shock to the state of the public finances is amplified can operate through the real economy as well as financial markets. The claim that the health of the public finances depends on the health of the real economy seems uncontroversial: a strong economy tends to go hand in hand with strong tax receipts and lower welfare spending. We have already discussed the basic mechanism through which an attempt to repair the public finances in response to an increase in the cost of servicing debt can prove self-defeating. The well-intentioned fiscal consolidation depresses activity—in certain circumstances—which then leads to further accumulation of debt, potentially aggravating the initial concerns around debt sustainability. We will now introduce two stylised channels of amplification—one which hinges on forward-looking behaviour and the other on the cost of funds—before turning to the main event.

Cole and Kehoe (2000) highlight how once the public finances slip into a "crisis zone", forward-looking behaviour by private sector agents can precipitate a restructuring that would not otherwise have happened. Fear of (as opposed to certainty of) the impending sovereign crisis can lead agents to cut back on investment and that depresses activity which can ultimately trigger the crisis—a feature they argue was exhibited in the Mexican crisis of the mid-1990s. They conclude that it is far better for the fiscal authority to be proactive—to take steps to shift the economy out of the crisis zone—rather that reactive and respond to events in this environment.

One might assume that the terms on which any particular agent can raise funds should primarily depend on their particular circumstances. However, Corsetti et al. (2012) highlight how the terms on which the government can raise funds can effectively impose a 'sovereign ceiling' on the terms on which (almost all) domestic agents can do likewise in capital markets. They note that during the European sovereign debt crisis, daily movements in credit default swap (CDS) spreads for government debt and nonfinancial corporate debt were strongly positively correlated (0.71) in Belgium, Greece, Ireland, Italy, Portugal, and Spain. In theory, one can justify this cap on the basis that the government can always resort to windfall taxes on the resources of domestic agents to bolster its own position. The presence of this 'sovereign ceiling' creates an efficient channel for contagion through which sovereign stress can be immediately transmitted to the real economy. Indeed, investors may price private sector debt at a (yield) spread *over* sovereign paper, so any increase in the interest rate on government debt can feed through one-for-one into private debt markets, representing an immediate and significant *de facto* monetary tightening that will likely depress activity.

The principal source of amplification in the real economy appears to operate via the banking system; indeed, the so-called sovereign–bank nexus was widely seen as a critical source of amplification during the crisis. The fact that banks are systemically important institutions is now well understood. A significant contraction in the supply of bank credit can have a material impact on the economy: the increase in the cost of credit for those who can still get access and an increase in rationing will weigh on spending. What was perhaps less well understood was how tightly intertwined the fate of the domestic banks and the sovereign are.

Consider first the asset side of a bank's balance sheet. Banks will typically hold financial securities including government bonds—in part to manage liquidity risk. As we have seen, the value of those assets will tend to drop during moments of sovereign stress. But we have also seen how sovereign stress can weigh on activity in the real economy and that means that the value of the bank's large credit portfolios will also take a hit. For a leveraged institution like a bank which funds the majority of its assets through debt rather than equity, significant reductions in the value of its assets can have a material if not fatal impact on its capital position, and that brings us to the liability side of the balance sheet.

The Corsetti et al. (2012) mechanism will also apply to the debt that banks issue in wholesale markets: it will become more expensive for the bank to issue debt even had there been no damage done to the balance sheet of the bank. The hit to net worth just exacerbates the problem: in just the same way that the bank retreats from retail credit markets, lending less and charging more, the bank will find it harder to raise funds from its creditors. Finally, as the events of 2007/08 illustrated, governments are prepared to step in and support systemically important banks when they get into difficulty and that implicit support helps banks to raise funds on more attractive terms than they would otherwise be able to on a standalone basis. However, when the public finances start to deteriorate, the capacity of the government to back-stop its banks may be called into question and that could lead to a further increase in the cost of funding for the banks as this implicit support is pulled away.

In short, an acute phase of sovereign stress could damage the net worth of the banks and lead to a significant increase in the cost of funding for the banks. At the very least that cost of funds will tend to be passed through into the terms on which banks will supply funds to the real economy—another *de facto* monetary contraction for the vast majority of households and small- and medium-sized companies that depend on the banks for credit. Moreover, we might expect banks to tighten credit conditions further, charging more and lending less, in the hope of shrinking their balance sheets and organically growing capital (given the higher spread between interest receipts and payments). Likewise, the banks may come under pressure to sell financial securities, including government bonds, to contribute to the process of balance sheet shrinkage.

The cumulative response of the banking sector to the initial significant shock to the public finances—aggregating across all these transmission channels—is likely to feed back into the public finances: a weaker economy means further cyclical borrowing and accumulation of debt; a key investor in sovereign bonds, and hence support for prices, may now be on the sidelines and in the limit could be a forced seller; and last, but not least, the perceived likelihood of the state having to provide financial support to prop up the banks has increased and that too could weigh on market sentiment (investors will attach some probability to a sharp increase in issuance in the future to fund that financial support). Market participants may then demand further compensation against default risk, governments will be required to impose additional austerity to balance the books, and the vicious circle keeps spinning.

13.9 Theory in Action: The Sovereign Debt Crisis

We have developed a theoretical model of positive feedback in sovereign debt sustainability with a number of complementary mechanisms operating in both financial markets and the real economy through which, under certain circumstances, an initial shock to debt sustainability may be amplified leading to further erosion in the public finances, potentially leading to a downward spiral into a restructuring event.

The practical question for policymakers is whether this cautionary tale is a theoretical curiosity or a genuine threat to the stability of the public finances. We shall briefly review an example of this mechanism playing out in financial markets: the European sovereign debt crisis. However, before moving on, it is worth noting that we need to be careful extrapolating from events in the Eurozone between 2010 and 2012. As highlighted above the amplification of sovereign stress within a subset of countries inside a currency union is fundamentally different because the economic policy response is more nuanced, and, as we shall go on to discuss, the early phase of the crisis actually intensified the sovereign–bank nexus, storing up trouble for the future.

The shocking speed and scale of the European sovereign debt crisis can be summarised in two facts. First, within a six-month period Greece went from borrowing on similar terms to the German government to being effectively shut out of financial markets altogether (Ardagna and Caselli 2014). Second, the spread between the yield on Italian and Spanish ten-year government bonds (relative to Germany) increased by 200 and 250 basis points over the year to July 2012 despite the fact that both governments had actually driven through reforms which in theory should have reassured investors about the medium-term outlook for debt sustainability (Cœuré 2013).

This is not the place to review the root causes of the crisis: the build-up of imbalances, the failure to complete the institutional policy architecture of the monetary union, and then the damage done during the first phase of the financial crisis. What is clear is that investors did *not* immediately run on the debt issued by the sovereigns of the European periphery in the immediate aftermath of the collapse of Lehman Brothers. Even if what followed was inevitable, investors did not seem to appreciate that 'fact'.

Instead, the fuse for the crisis was lit almost exactly a year after the acute phase of the financial crisis in late 2008. In October 2009 the incoming Greek government published a deficit forecast for 2009 of 12.7 % (*double* the forecast of the previous government) and announced irregularities in the previously published data on the Greek public finances, revealing larger deficits over the past too (Lane 2012). The news on the parlous state of the public finances soon led the market to question whether the sizeable Greek debt burden (estimated to be 115 % of GDP at that point) was sustainable, and market participants were not alone. Fitch downgraded Greece from A– to BBB+ in December 2009—the first of what would turn out to be a cascade of downgrades in the months that followed (Ardagna and Caselli 2014). The yields on Greek government debt rose sharply, and by May 2010 Greece was effectively shut out of markets.

The virus would soon spread to other countries in the European periphery with first Ireland and then Portugal shut out of markets in November 2010 and April 2011 respectively. But these were merely the opening acts of a crisis which would reach its climax in the summer of 2012 when the yields on Spanish and Italian government debt (the fourth and third largest economies in the Eurozone) spiralled higher, with the spreads over German sovereign paper reaching 600 and 500 basis points respectively.

The fact that sovereign spreads blew out during the crisis is not in doubt; what is less clear is precisely why: was this a simple reflection of a shift in market perceptions of credit worthiness on a standalone basis, or were some of the amplification mechanisms described above at work? De Santis (2012) highlights three factors in his review of developments in sovereign bond yields between September 2008 and August 2011: country-specific ratings downgrades, which as we highlighted earlier can act as a trigger for forced sales; increased risk aversion leading to safe haven flows towards German sovereign paper (at the expense of the rest, including strong core sovereigns like the Netherlands); and finally, contagion. In terms of the final factor, De Santis highlights how Moody's decision to downgrade Portugal's long-term credit rating in July 2011 was justified in part on the basis that events in Greece had set a precedent which would shape the terms on which Portugal would receive support in the future that would not be in the interest of current debt holders.

Speaking of which, another key factor in driving spreads higher during the crisis was the decision to give credence to the idea that the end game of the crisis would have to involve a restructuring of the debt in private hands. We argued earlier that in a world of incomplete private information where higher-order beliefs matter, even seemingly trivial news can shunt the system to a new equilibrium. It is difficult not to conclude that the Franco-German 'Deauville Declaration' in October 2010 which appeared to give the official seal of approval to the prospect of private sector involvement in solving the debt crisis helped to propel yield spreads higher (Lane 2012; ECB 2014).

The sovereign–bank nexus certainly played a role in amplifying stress during the crisis. Data extracted from the CDS markets for Eurozone banks and sovereigns—which provide information on the probability that market participants attach to the likelihood of a default by the issuer—reveal a startlingly strong correlation between the two during the crisis, both increasing at an alarming rate as the crisis built to a crescendo, only to fall back after the policy response. Mody and Sandri (2011) note that after the nationalisation of Anglo-Irish bank in the Republic of Ireland, a new dynamic emerged in financial markets where a perceived deterioration in the state of the financial sector no longer preceded a rise in sovereign spreads; now the two moved contemporaneously: stress was being transmitted in both directions. In terms of the amplification through the banks into the real economy via bank lending, Neri (2013) demonstrates that if sovereign spreads had remained at their April 2010 levels, the interest rates on new mortgage lending and loans to non-financial corporations in the periphery would have been 60 and 130 basis points lower at the end of 2011.

From a policy perspective the question is *why* the sovereign–bank nexus became so powerful. Acharya and Steffen (2013) describe the behaviour of the Eurozone banks between 2007 and 2013 as the 'greatest carry trade ever': that is, the banks were borrowing short-term to fund investments in long-term government debt, gambling on the survival of their sovereign to resurrect their balance sheet on a 'heads we win, tails you lose' basis. If the sovereign manages to retrieve the situation then the banks will make significant mark to market gains on the securities they purchased during the moment of stress; and in the event of a restructuring the banks fail too, and someone else picks up the tab (Cooper and Nikolov 2013). However, it is possible that policymakers might have contributed to this carry trade behaviour: a loophole in the regulatory capital requirements allowed banks to fund these investments in sovereign debt entirely through debt; alternatively politicians might have put pressure on this key investor in the sovereign bond market to continue buying when other investors stepped back, leading to increased home bias in the portfolios of the banks.

13.10 Locating the Precipice

We have discussed the mechanisms of positive feedback in creating a vicious circle towards default but we have said very little about where this mechanism kicks in. In truth, there is no hard and fast rule which pins down the point at which markets start to question debt sustainability. One factor that is likely to play a key role is the perceived capacity of a particular sovereign to take corrective action, and that will likely vary both across countries at a given moment in time and for a particular country through time. Clearly, the decision whether to service or restructure debt should also reflect an assessment of the costs of restructuring debt through different means, and we will return to this issue later in this section.

The government's capacity to stabilise debt will depend on how much work needs to be done. Simply put, the larger the 'primary gap' (Blanchard 1990b)—that is, the percentage point gap between the current primary budget balance and the level required to stabilise the debt stock—the larger the required increase in taxes and/or cuts in spending, and by extension the larger the potential drag on aggregate demand—the stance of monetary policy notwithstanding—and the electoral support of the government.

The state of the macroeconomy could also help or hinder any effort at fiscal consolidation. If the economy is in rude health then the macroeconomic cost may be easier to bear. Indeed, even if domestic demand is weak, consolidation may still be relatively pain free if the global economy is strong and there is ample demand for domestic output overseas, particularly given a significant realignment in the relative price of domestic and overseas output (Hjelm 2004).

The missing piece of the jigsaw here is the stance of monetary policy: the capacity of the government to balance the books will hinge in large part on the extent to which monetary policy can offset the macroeconomic impact of consolidation. Central banks can insulate an economy from large and persistent shocks to demand—including those which originate in finance ministries—in their pursuit of price stability that might otherwise weigh on debt sustainability; indeed, we argued earlier that this mechanism still applies at the lower bound on official interest rates. Finance ministers in countries like the UK can commit to a policy of fiscal consolidation safe in the knowledge that the central bank will loosen monetary policy in response. Fiscal authorities at the regional level or at the national level in a currency union cannot make the same assumption, and that implies that fiscal consolidation is more painful in those circumstances. Moreover, it seems much more likely that the problem of self-fulfilling expectations of a debt crisis are likely to emerge earlier (i.e., when the fiscal metrics are less alarming) in these circumstances.

The decision to retain control of the printing press is also a decision to retain the nominal exchange rate as a potential shock absorber in the event of a crisis. It is certainly possible, if not probable, that this added source of flexibility may reduce the likelihood that the vicious circle of positive feedback kicks in. Imagine that investors raised the probability that they attached to a default by the UK government on its debt obligations in response to very bad news about the state of the UK economy. The currency would likely depreciate, with investors selling sterling-denominated assets, including government bonds, which are now perceived to be more risky (more precisely, the tail risk of extremely poor returns on those assets has increased). Eventually, the currency should find a floor where it has depreciated so far that investors now expect the currency to appreciate in the future, and the implied capital gain on sterling-denominated assets is sufficient to compensate for the increased risks on those assets (note that in the meantime, the existing overseas holders of sterling-denominated debt have taken a big hit on the domestic purchasing power of their investment). This argument should sound familiar: it is a variant of the standard 'UIP jump' whereby the exchange rate depreciates in response to news that expected domestic returns have fallen relative to those overseas to the point where investors expect a gradual appreciation in the future to compensate for that yield differential. In this context, we might instead say that the sterling FX risk premium spikes higher in response to bad news, with investors requiring additional compensation over and above the risk-free return in sterling-denominated assets in order to hold these assets (once again via an expected appreciation).

We need to be a little careful with this argument: whilst the currency is depreciating global investors are suffering losses twice over on sterling assets (the domestic price of those assets is falling, and the relative price of sterling to other currencies is falling too); we do not know for sure how long it will take for sterling to find the floor; and we cannot be sure that a currency crisis will not trigger further stress in the domestic economy. For example, if domestic agents (such as banks) are running a maturity mismatch over their balance sheets in foreign currency, with short-term deposits funding long-term illiquid assets. In short, even if the jump down in the currency eventually helps to stabilise the situation by tempting global investors back it seems likely that the government bond market could be set for a bumpy ride in the short-run. Moreover, whilst macroeconomists tend to sing the virtues of a significant deprecation in the currency as a means to boost the net trade contribution to GDP, finance ministers who are concerned about social welfare will be conscious of the fact that a significant depreciation will also lead in short order to a significant squeeze in living standards via rising sterling import prices. Finally, control of the printing press also allows the possibility—but not the inevitability—of 'print your way out' of a debt problem (as we will go on to discuss) although printing enough currency to solve the debt problem may bring other headaches.

Other things equal then, it is fair to say that retaining control of the printing press means that countries should be less likely—and probably *much* less likely—to get into trouble in the first place. However, other things are not necessarily equal. When countries enter a currency union they should be aware that are more exposed to the idiosyncratic shock problem (if they are hit by a shock which does not impact their partners, then they can expect little help from monetary policy, especially if they are small in size relative to the currency union) and that means that there is a compelling case for structural reforms which make the domestic economy more flexible and therefore better placed to adjust to shocks without large fluctuations in output and employment (Mundell 1961). Whether it is in the nature of currency unions that the national business cycles become more synchronised over time, through greater integration, or less synchronised, thanks to greater specialisation in areas of comparative advantage, and hence whether the idiosyncratic shock problem becomes less or more acute with time, is ultimately an empirical question (Frankel and Rose 1998). More generally, we might also hope that governments which are members of a currency union would take a more prudent approach to the conduct of fiscal policy—for example, running with a lower debt burden—in anticipation that positive feedback could kick in earlier.

The government's capacity to take corrective action will also depend on the current fiscal mix for any given primary budget position. If tax rates are not already high (and therefore likely causing significant distortions in behaviour), if tax evasion is widespread (Slemrod 2007) or if there are valuable assets on the public sector balance sheet that could easily be sold, then it should be relatively easy to raise additional revenues. Likewise, where government investment is inefficiently high (i.e., on low rate of return projects), government spending on inputs or the provision of output in public services is deemed excessive or when transfer payments are counterproductive (because they distort behaviour) or offer poor value for money (because they involve significant deadweight losses), it should be relatively easy to reduce spending. In short, the worse the initial starting position, the more low hanging fruit there are and the easier it is to improve the primary budget position.

Finally, the capacity of the government to balance the books will also depend on a wider set of political and economic fundamentals. Countries which consistently deliver strong and stable governments, where trust in government is high, where the average standard of living is high and absolute and relative levels of poverty are low are almost certainly better placed to take and absorb tough decisions on the fiscal front. Unsurprisingly, credit rating agencies like Moody's therefore incorporate an assessment of the strength of domestic policy institutions and susceptibility to political risk in their official credit ratings, which provide an assessment of the sovereign's ability to pay its debts on time and in full. We shall return to this issue later in this book.

For actual and potential creditors of the government its capacity to do what it takes to service debt may be hard to gauge in real time. It seems likely that creditors would put some weight on the government's track record. Countries which have defaulted on debt in the past may be less trusted in the future. That is not to say that governments which have defaulted on debt in the past will be unable to issue debt, or even that they will necessarily pay a penalty in terms of higher debt-servicing costs. But it does mean that the appetite for their debt may dry up sooner—that is, at a lower debt burden—than for countries which do not have a track record of default.

References

Acharya, V., & Steffen, S. (2013). *The "greatest" carry trade ever?*. NBER Working Paper 19039.

Ardagna, S., & Caselli, F. (2014). The political economy of the Greek debt crisis. *American Economic Journal: Macroeconomics, 6*(4), 291–323.

Ardagna, S., Caselli, F., & Lane, T. (2004). *Fiscal discipline and the cost of public debt service*. NBER Working Paper 10788.

Bannerjee, A. (1992). A simple model of herd behaviour. *Quarterly Journal of Economics, 67*(3), 797–817.

Barwell, R. (2013). *Macroprudential policy: Taming the wild gyrations of credit flows, debt stocks and asset prices*. New York: Palgrave.

Beetsma, R., Giuliodori, M., de Jong, F., & Widijanto, D. (2013). *Price effects of sovereign debt auctions in the Euro-zone*. ECB Working Paper 1595.

Blanchard, O. (1990b). *Suggestions for a new set of fiscal indicators*. OECD Working Paper 79.

Bohn, H. (1995). The sustainability of budget deficits in a stochastic economy. *Journal of Money, Credit and Banking, 27*(1), 257–271.

Calvo, G. (1988). Servicing the public debt. *American Economic Review, 78*(4), 647–661.

Cass, D., & Shell, K. (1983). Do sunspots matter? *Journal of Political Economy, 91*(21), 193–228.

Chalk, N., & Hemming, R. (2000). *Assessing fiscal sustainability in theory and practice*. IMF Working Paper 00/81.

Cochrane, J. (2005). *Asset pricing*. Princeton: Princeton University Press.

Cochrane, J. (2011a). Determinacy and identification with Taylor rules. *Journal of Political Economy, 119*(3), 565–615.

Cœuré, B. (2013, September 2). *Outright Monetary Transactions, one year on*. Speech.

Cole, H., & Kehoe, T. (2000). Self-fulfilling debt crises. *Review of Economic Studies, 67*(1), 91–116.

Cooper, R., & Nikolov, K. (2013). *Sovereign debt and banking fragility*. NBER Working Paper 19278.

Corsetti, G., Kuester, K., Meier, A., & Mueller, G. (2012). *Sovereign risk, fiscal policy and macroeconomic stability*. IMF Working Paper 12/33.

De Santis, R. (2012). *The euro area sovereign debt crisis.* ECB Working Paper 1419.

DeLong, J., Shleifer, A., Summers, L., & Waldmann, R. (1990a). Positive feedback investment strategies and destabilising rational speculation. *Journal of Finance, 45*(2), 379–395.

DeLong, J., Shleifer, A., Summers, L., & Waldmann, R. (1990b). Noise trader risk in financial markets. *Journal of Political Economy, 98*(4), 703–738.

Diamond, D., & Dybvig, P. (1983). Bank runs, deposit insurance and liquidity. *Journal of Political Economy, 91*(3), 401–419.

ECB. (2014). The determinants of euro area sovereign bond yield spreads during the crisis. *ECB Monthly Bulletin, May*, 67–83.

Engen, E., & Hubbard, G. (2004). *Federal government debts and interest rates.* NBER Working Paper 10681.

Frankel, J., & Rose, A. (1998). The endogeneity of optimal currency area criteria. *Economic Journal, 108*, 1009–1025.

Hjelm, G. (2004). *When are fiscal contractions successful? Lessons for countries within and outside the EMU.* National Institute of Economic Research Working Paper 92.

Lane, P. (2012). The European sovereign debt crisis. *Journal of Economic Perspectives, 26*(3), 49–68.

Laubach, T. (2009). New evidence on the interest rate effects of budget deficits and debt. *Journal of the European Economic Association, 7*(4), 858–885.

Laubach, T. (2011). Fiscal policy and interest rates. In R. Clarida & F. Giavazzi (Eds.), *NBER international seminar on macroeconomics.* Chicago: NBER.

Longstaff, F., Pan, J., Pedersen, L., & Singleton, K. (2011). How sovereign is sovereign credit risk? *American Economic Journal: Macroeconomics, 3*, 75–103.

Manganelli, S., & Wolswijk, G. (2009). What drives spreads in the euro-area government bond market? *Economic Policy, 24*, 191–240.

Mody, A., & Sandri, D. (2011). *The Eurozone crisis: How banks and sovereigns came to be joined at the hip.* IMF Working Paper 11/269.

Mundell, R. (1961). A theory of optimal currency area. *American Economic Review, 51*(4), 657–665.

Neri, S. (2013). The impact of the sovereign debt crisis on bank lending rates in the euro area. Bank of Italy Occasional Paper 170.

Shiller, R. (2003). From efficient markets theory to behavioural finance. *Journal of Economic Perspectives, 17*(1), 29–48.

Shleifer, A., & Vishny, R. (1997). The limits of arbitrage. *Journal of Finance, 52*(1), 35–55.

Slemrod, J. (2007). Cheating ourselves: The economics of tax evasion. *Journal of Economic Perspectives, 21*(1), 25–48.

14

Repair, Restructure, Repress or Reach for the Printing Press

We have explored how in extreme circumstances the seemingly secure position of sovereigns in financial markets can start to slip away: given a sufficiently large shock, positive feedback can propel the government away from a sustainable low-risk, low-yield equilibrium towards a far more fragile high-risk, high-yield equilibrium and ultimately the markets closing on the government when investors expect a restructuring. In this section we will discuss the policy responses and potential end games in a debt crisis.

14.1 Selective Amnesia

The problem of how to handle a heavy government debt burden is not something that policymakers have had to grapple with in most of the advanced economies for some time. But it would not be true to say that the ratio of government debt to GDP has never been as high as it is today. On the contrary, the United Kingdom's debt burden is estimated to have been in excess of 250 % of GDP in the aftermath of the Napoleonic Wars, and in excess of 200 % of GDP at the end of the Second World War, and therein lies a problem. There is a risk is that the route through which those past debt burdens were solved may have slipped from the memory of the current generation of policymakers and economists and all that is left behind is a false sense of security. The fact that the bond markets did not attack in the past and that the debt burden was eventually resolved may leave the impression that high government debt does not pose an existential threat to an advanced economy which has retained control over the printing press (like the UK), and there is no need for emergency measures.

© The Editor(s) (if applicable) and The Author(s) 2016
R. Barwell, *Macroeconomic Policy after the Crash*,
DOI 10.1057/978-1-137-51592-6_14

That conclusion sounds less compelling if previous debt burdens were resolved through emergency measures. For example, if the debts accumulated in the First World War were partially solved through restructuring and the debts accumulated in the Second were solved through financial repression then it might not be safe to assume that the sustainability of debt and the goodwill of the government's creditors can be relied upon if a government rules out these options to the current problems but is not willing to commit to an alternative credible strategy.

That is not the end of the selective amnesia problem. We also need to remember that the unconventional solutions to debt burdens are not pain free: someone still pays. The one thing that economists should bring to the table when it comes to a discussion of how to solve a debt burden is a coherent cost benefit analysis of different options which includes the indirect effect of financial repression or inflating away the debt on the welfare of the household population. With this thought in mind, let us turn to the options on the table. Reinhart and Rogoff (2013) identify five ways to reduce a large debt burden:

(i) Economic growth
(ii) Fiscal adjustment-austerity
(iii) Inflation surprise
(iv) A steady dose of financial repression accompanied by a steady dose of inflation
(v) Explicit (*de jure*) default or restructuring

The first solution is much more complicated than it sounds: this is not about engineering a transitory boom in demand (which in most cases the central bank will be honour-bound to lean against). Solution (i) is about raising the trend rate of growth of the economy, which erodes the debt burden through a couple of key channels. First, if the cost of debt does not rise one for one in sympathy with the increase in trend growth then the 'interest rate versus growth rate' differential will work in the government's favour, shifting the trajectory of the debt to GDP ratio in the right direction according to our simplistic formula. Second, it should also be easier for the government to save more or spend less when the economy is growing faster: essentially finance ministers have to show restraint and prevent government spending increasing to entirely exhaust the increase in tax revenues that stronger growth brings. We have discussed solution (ii) already and implicitly assumed that at some point, in certain circumstances, further fiscal retrenchment can prove self-defeating. But before we turn to the more extreme solutions that are the main focus of this chapter, we first need to discuss an extreme spin on the conventional solution to the debt problem.

14.2 Expansionary Fiscal Consolidations

The orthodox response to a deterioration in the public finances is for finance ministers to drive through a significant consolidation: at a bare minimum to improve the budget balance to the point where the debt burden is stable, and then ideally to further improve the position in order to reduce the debt burden. As we have discussed, the orthodox view in the literature is that a significant and sustained fiscal tightening will weigh on aggregate demand—certainly if we do not factor in a countervailing monetary response—and as we have explained that can exacerbate the stress on the public finances, potentially tipping the economy into a downward spiral. However, there is a heterodox literature which suggests that, even in the absence of monetary easing, large fiscal retrenchments may have a positive impact on private sector behaviour, breaking the positive feedback mechanism at source.

The basic intuition behind this expansionary fiscal contraction result is that private sector agents are not indifferent to the state of the public finances (because they will pick up the tab), and a credible announcement of a significant consolidation could reassure them that known problems are being dealt with and a disaster scenario has been averted, which might then lead to a change in their savings behaviour. This result was established long before the repercussions of the (latest) financial crisis led many governments to conclude that a major consolidation was necessary. Nonetheless, this result was the cause of much controversy and consternation within the macroeconomics community because it appeared to provide intellectual support for a less expansionary fiscal policy even at the lower bound. In short, it appeared that austerity was pain free.

From the outset we should be clear that this result is not universally applicable. We need to assume that: the public finances are in a sufficiently dire state that debt sustainability is a genuine concern; private sector agents understand the implications of unsustainable public finances for their future standard of living and have adjusted their current behaviour accordingly; and those agents must also believe that the announcement of a consolidation programme is credible—that is, it will be delivered and it is sufficient to correct the problem. These are not trivial assumptions.

Blanchard (1990a) provides a neat rationalisation of the expansionary fiscal contraction result rooted in the economics of uncertainty and in particular fear of tail risks that we have encountered elsewhere in this book. Imagine that households and companies understand that the public finances are deteriorating and they believe that at some point there will be a correction; the only thing that is unclear is when that correction will occur. When the government only has access to distortionary taxes, the more it puts off the day of fiscal reckoning, the more pain it stores up for the future. Fears about potentially penal taxation in an Armageddon scenario if the consolidation is delayed too long could influence behaviour today, with individuals postponing investments in human capital and companies postponing investments in physical capital and jobs. When the consolidation is announced those fears recede and the hurdle rate on investment drops and spending increases. This argument is usually expressed in terms of the decisions of domestic agents, but it is equally applicable to those outside a country planning to make an investment in it, whether that be a foreign company choosing to invest in plant or machinery or a potential migrant choosing where to seek work.

Bertola and Drazen (1993) present a more formal exposition of this mechanism. They model government spending as a share of output as a Brownian motion, with positive drift—or in plain English, a random process with a tendency to rise through time. The government's budget constraint holds and therefore implies a corresponding upward trend in the tax burden. Of course, that trend cannot continue indefinitely: eventually the economy's capacity to produce the resources that government consumes would be breached. Instead, the generalised trend of expansion in government spending as a share of GDP may *and then will* be arrested and rapidly reversed when it hits one of two thresholds, dropping back to some known base level of spending. In particular, when spending reaches an intermediate trigger, government may choose to rein in spending. The private sector expects a consolidation with some probability at this point; but if it does not occur this intermediate target is revealed to be irrelevant in the current spending cycle and the boom in government spending can continue for a little while longer. However, when government spending (as a share of output) reaches a higher known trigger there is a hard stop: consolidation happens with certainty.

The discontinuous nature of the government spending process generates rich non-monotone responses of consumption to changes in government spending (as a share of output). At low levels of government spending, increases in government spending imply a less than one-for-one decline in consumption because the probability of a consolidation (and hence large cut in the size of government and the implied tax burden) has increased. However, a small increase in government spending that results in a breach of the intermediate target without a stabilisation occurring can lead to a large, discrete cut in consumption: expectations of an imminent cut in the tax burden have been confounded. Finally, as government spending closes in on the binding ceiling, increases in government spending lead to increases in consumption as the expected present discounted value of the tax burden falls because the era of big government (and high taxes) has drawn to a close (for this spending cycle at least).

So much for the theory, what about the evidence for these expansionary fiscal contractions? The empirical work which ignited interest in the possibility of expansionary fiscal contractions was a couple of decades old by the time the idea came back into fashion with the return of austerity in the post-crash era. Before we review the empirical literature on expansionary fiscal contractions a health warning of sorts is in order: much of the work has a distinctly reduced form feel to it. Researchers have tended to look for empirical regularities which are shared by 'good' fiscal consolidations, rather than necessarily causal factors. Nor is it always clear that the analysis adequately controls for the endogeneity of severe fiscal consolidations. Simply put, countries are more than likely to be in a deep hole when they enact significant consolidations packages with the level of aggregate demand far below aggregate supply. At the risk of setting the cart before the horse, the output gap must close one way or the other, so if countries can escape without severe scarring of the level or future growth of potential supply, then aggregate demand must expand at above the historical trend rate for a sustained period. Similar points could be made about the composition of consolidation programmes: those countries where government consumption or transfer payments had clearly got 'out of control' might be more likely to make cuts on that front and the growth penalty for making those cuts might be relatively small. It is less clear that the experience of those countries provides a useful template for others planning to embark on a consolidation where government consumption and transfer payments start from a more sensible position. Alesina and Ardagna's (2009) refreshingly candid assessment of their own regression analysis captures the concern perfectly: '[C]ausality issues are all over the place here and we do not claim to have solved them. These regressions should be viewed as correlations.'

Giavazzi and Pagano's (1990) initial contribution was motivated by the experiences of 'two small European countries'—Denmark and Ireland—which both managed to simultaneously deliver a substantial improvement in their fiscal position and achieve robust economic growth during the 1980s. For example, over a four-year period, the Danish government managed a turnaround in the primary budget in excess of 15 %, largely through discretionary increases in taxes net of transfers. That research raised an interesting question: are these episodes mere historical curiosities—rare exceptions to the Keynesian rule that fiscal policy hurts—or the tip of a heterodox iceberg?

Giavazzi et al. (2005) search for evidence of non-monotone responses to changes in the stance of fiscal policy across the OECD countries between 1970 and 2003. As you might expect, most changes in the fiscal stance are small in absolute magnitude, but they also find 128 'large and persistent fiscal impulses'—defined as an episode in which the OECD's estimate of the 'full employment surplus', changes by at least 1½ percentage points of potential output, per year over a two-year period—of which 73 were contractions and 55 expansions. Government investment typically bears the brunt of these large contractions: net taxes rise and government consumptions falls, but government investment tends to fall by four percentage points of potential output. The norm is for national savings to rise during fiscal contractions, but that is not the universal experience: there are examples where national savings fell (expansionary fiscal contractions), and in some cases quite significantly. Indeed, Giavazzi, Japelli, Pagano and Benedetti find that in contrast to what we tend to observe in the data, changes in net taxes and government spending have no impact on national savings in these large and persistent contractions at standard significance levels.

Alesina and Ardagna (2009) conduct a broadly similar search (over a slightly longer dataset and with a slightly different methodology) and locate 107 significant fiscal consolidation events, of which between 17 and 26 were successful depending on whether the metric of success is a decline in the debt to GDP ratio or strong growth performance (relative to what is typically observed in a fiscal adjustment). Alesina and Ardagna argue that the expansionary episodes have a clear signature in terms of the design of the consolidation package. In expansionary episodes, primary spending tended to fall (by more than 2 % of GDP) whilst revenues largely stood still; whereas primary spending was cut by rather less and revenues increased by over 1 % of GDP in other episodes. They note in particular that spending on transfers tends to fall in expansionary fiscal contractions and otherwise rise and argue that this is a critical ingredient of a successful consolidation ('it is very difficult if not impossible to fix public finances when in trouble without solving the question of automatic increases in entitlements').

14.3 Inflate Away the Debt

It is often said that countries which have retained control of the printing press cannot fall victim to the positive feedback mechanism described in the previous chapter. However, this argument that the printing press is a fail-safe defence against debt catastrophes should be treated with caution. The argument is typically presented in the following form: if the government issues debt in the currency it issues then it can print as much of that money as it wants at effectively zero marginal cost, and can therefore always pay those debts, and would surely never need to default. To think more about this problem we need to revisit our simple debt stability expression, and now focus on the budget constraint for the consolidated public sector, that is when we fold in the central bank. Now there is an additional term in our expression reflecting the proceeds from 'seigniorage'—the change in the monetary base. In a world of fiat money, the marginal cost of creating more money is zero to all intents and purposes, but the value of that money is not. In theory, seigniorage offers government an alternative means to balance the books rather than endure the macroeconomic pain of fiscal consolidation: just print more money.

Unsurprisingly, there is a catch. The liabilities of the government are a real phenomenon and when it services those debts it must transfer resources to creditors, and that means that someone else pays. With conventional taxes this process is transparent; with seigniorage the process is not, but the mechanism is the same. Increasing the money supply will drive up prices and that will depress the real value of the money currently held by the private sector. In effect, the authorities are imposing an 'inflation tax' on the private sector (Friedman 1971). To be clear, it is typically assumed that this inflation tax on money is *anticipated* (Buiter 2007). In practice, when people speak about governments inflating their way out of a debt problem they typically have something more straightforward in mind—namely that the burden of debt is eroded by *unanticipated* inflation, because the denominator (nominal GDP) will rise with inflation, but typically the debt burden will not. If we focus on the flows rather than the stocks, we can see that an increase in the rate of inflation will naturally feed through into current and future tax receipts but not the fixed nominal payments on conventional government debt. Once again, there is a catch; in fact, there are several.

First of all, we should re-emphasise that inflating away the debt is not a pain-free solution. In this case, the government's creditors receive a lower real return on their investments in fixed income assets (which pay a fixed nominal return), thanks to surprise inflation. Be in no doubt: this is a soft restructuring of the debt. The reader may think that a solution in which financial institutions bear the burden of repairing the public finances is strictly preferable to conventional fiscal consolidation; however, we need to keep in mind that institutions like insurance companies and pension funds are investing on behalf of the household sector. Moreover, there are the additional conventional costs of higher and likely more volatile inflation which also need to be factored into the cost-benefit analysis of addressing the debt burden in this way.

Second, we have made a non-trivial assumption about the type of debt security that the government issues: namely that the debt is conventional and has a very long maturity. When the government issues debt where the value of the coupon and principal repayments are linked mechanically to price indices (as governments increasingly have, with the United Kingdom being something of a trend setter, issuing the first index-linked gilt being in 1981) then the benefits evaporate: the debt burden is uprated with inflation (a point to which we shall return shortly). Even where conventional debt is concerned, so long as the debt is short-term then there are practical limits to what can be done with 'inflation surprises.' Once investors realise what the government has done, they will demand a higher nominal return to hold government debt to compensate them for the higher rate of inflation, and in all likelihood they may demand additional compensation (a higher yield) for the risk of additional inflation surprises in the future. That higher interest rate in the secondary market (for existing bonds) will start to feed through into the cost of issuing new debt in the primary market. It is only when the debt has an extremely long maturity—so it takes an eternity for the higher interest rate in the secondary market to filter through into the primary market—that this soft restructuring pays real dividends because only then is there sufficient time for the government to inflate away the debt.

The fact that the incentive to inflate away debt is tied to the maturity structure of debt will not be lost on investors, and that suggests a natural tension between the current debt burden and the capacity of the government to issue long-term debt in equilibrium. If the debt burden is too high then investors will expect the government to renege on a promise of low inflation (Missale and Blanchard 1994). As it happens, the UK government is among the best placed to benefit from this strategy, given the relatively long maturity of the debt that has been issued, although the UK has also issued a relatively large proportion of index-linked debt too.

In practice, numerical analysis suggests that a short sharp shock of surprise inflation is insufficient: a permanent change in the inflation target is required to have a meaningful impact on the debt burden (Krause and Moyen 2013). For example, Krause and Moyen (2013) illustrate how a permanent four percentage point increase in the inflation target could lower the real debt burden in the USA by around 30 %. Moreover, we cannot take it for granted that it would necessarily be easy for a central bank to easily generate a controlled burst of inflation in a severely depressed economy (Akitoby et al. 2014).

Academics have spent a good deal of time worrying about the risk that unsustainable public finances could ultimately result in higher inflation—indeed, that the central bank could prove powerless to prevent the rise in inflation: a hypothesis is commonly referred to as *Fiscal Dominance*. The seminal reference here is the *Unpleasant Monetary Arithmetic* of Sargent and Wallace

(1981). Imagine that a government committed to run a primary deficit into perpetuity and issues index-linked debt to begin with to finance those deficits. The price level in this model is pinned down by the Quantity Theory—that is, clearing the money market, so that demand matches the supply of money injected by the central bank. There may be no limit to the government's deficits in this model, but there is a limit on the amount of debt that the private sector wishes to hold, and remember that by issuing index-linked debt the government needs to raise more resources to service that debt. At that 'fiscal limit' where the demand for debt has been satiated, the central bank loses control of inflation because (it is assumed that) the need for seigniorage income to plug the fiscal gap takes precedence over the need to stabilise inflation, which is now a function of the headline deficit (i.e., including interest payments) and therefore the debt stock at the 'fiscal limit' (Leeper and Walker 2011). Indeed, if money demand depends on expected future inflation then the central bank could start to lose control of inflation before the fiscal limit is reached: attempts to raise the price of money to keep inflation in check would simply exacerbate the fiscal black hole (raising the cost of servicing debt).

The modern take on this problem is labelled the Fiscal Theory of the Price Level (FTPL). Now we focus on a government issuing conventional (nominal) debt, which could be ultimately financed by real resources in the conventional manner (higher taxes, lower spending) or in the unconventional manner (i.e., seigniorage). The FTPL suggests an alternative outcome where the government cannot or will not raise the real resources to service debt through either route and forward-looking agents conclude that inflation is inevitable if the government is to remain solvent (Leeper and Walker 2011). Prices rise *now* and the central bank is powerless to resist. Cochrane (2005) famously illustrated the principle of FTPL by analogy to the valuation equation for a stock: government debt is a claim on future primary surpluses in just the same way that stocks are a claim on future corporate profits. Cochrane writes the price level as the ratio of the nominal value of government debt divided by the expected present value of future primary surpluses. If the nominal value of debt doubles and the government commits to an unchanged path for the primary surplus then the price level should double, in just the same way that if a company doubled the number of shares in the market without any change in earnings expectations we would expect the share price to halve.

The question is whether the FTPL is a genuine threat to monetary stability. Canzoneri et al. (2001) offer some reassuring evidence on this score: they argue that there is overwhelming evidence in post-war US data for what they call the Money Dominant regime. In particular, they find that the ratio of debt to

GDP tends to fall after positive news on the primary surplus—in other words, governments use part of that positive surprise surplus to pay down debt.

14.4 Financial Repression

Inflating away the debt is a soft form of restructuring: the long-term creditors of the government receive a lower real return on their investment than they had anticipated as inflation erodes the purchasing power of the coupon and principal repayments on long-term debt. Reinhart and Sbrancia (2011) describe an alternative even softer—that is, less transparent—form of restructuring: financial repression.

The concept of financial repression as a solution to a debt problem is not a new one. The term first appeared in the literature over four decades ago (McKinnon 1973; Shaw 1973), which is perhaps not such a surprise since most economists believe that financial repression is *the* explanation for the relatively pain-free reduction in the post-war debt burden. Having said that, many macroeconomists assumed that financial repression was something that happened somewhere else—specifically, in the emerging market economies (Giovannini and de Melo 1993)—and in many cases some time ago. Indeed, some development economists believe that in the process of weaning themselves off the apparatus of financial repression several decades ago these economies became more vulnerable to financial instability (Diaz-Alejandro 1985).

The basic principle of financial repression is that the government exploits its privileged position as the regulator of the financial system to reduce the cost of servicing and paying down debt by creating a captive market for the securities that the government issues, such that domestic institutions will still invest in government debt when those securities offer meagre returns let alone decent compensation for the risk of soft and hard restructuring through inflation and default.

Reinhart and Sbrancia (2011) highlight three pillars of financial repression through which the government intervenes to hold down the cost of servicing debt. First comes explicit or indirect caps or ceilings on interest rates, which might be implemented via regulations, ceilings on the rates at which banks lend to government or in the days before the operational independence of central banks, targets for official interest rates. Second comes measures which create and maintain a captive pool of domestic investors including: capital account restrictions and exchange controls; taxes on banks in the form of high reserve requirements; and prudential regulations requiring domestic financial institutions (such as pension funds) to hold government debt. Third comes a variety of arm's length measures through which the government can influence the institutional demand for government debt, such as direct ownership of the banking sector.

Reinhart and Sbrancia (2011) go on to document the role played by financial repression in reducing the post-war debt burden. They define 'liquidation years' as those in which the ex post pre-tax real interest rate (the weighted average of the return on debt deflated by the actual rate of inflation) was negative; note that this is a conservative threshold since we might expect that in the absence of repression, real interest rates should have been positive. It turns out that this measure of real interest rates was sub-zero in the UK for almost half of the period between 1948 and 1980; had we used a less conservative threshold the fraction of liquidation years would rise to almost three quarters (interest rate less than 1 %) and to close to one (less than 3 %). If we multiply the negative real interest rate by the stock of debt we can calculate a liquidation effect—the contribution of financial repression to reducing the debt burden. Reinhart and Sbrancia (2011) find that the annual liquidation of debt averages 3–4 % of GDP each year during this post-war period.

The other ingredient of financial repression as an instrument of debt reduction is *chronic* inflation. If the authorities can stop nominal interest rates rising in response to an increase in expected inflation then inflating away the debt becomes a more plausible proposition. In their analysis, Reinhart and Sbrancia find that a relatively small proportion of their 'liquidation years' coincide with 'inflation surprises' (when the rate of inflation is significantly higher than the recent trend). Instead, the post-war debt reduction is better characterised by repression and a sustained period of a little too much inflation, although it is true that in years where there was a dramatic reduction in debt, surprise inflation does play a role. Indeed, Hilscher et al. (2014) argue that a decade of a particular form of financial repression—in the limit, forcing financial institutions to roll over debt at zero interest rates—coupled with a dose of inflation could come closer to halving the US debt burden.

For those left with the impression that financial repression is the pain-free solution to the current debt problems a couple of health warnings should be flagged. First, it might be possible to artificially lower the return on government debt via financial repression without capital moving elsewhere in search of reasonable returns when capital controls are in place and many other countries are following a similar strategy (so real interest rates are very low everywhere). It is less clear that the current generation of policymakers have this option. Second, even if financial repression is a realistic proposition, we need to keep in mind that there is a counterpart to the artificially low rate of return on government debt; domestic creditors are receiving meagre returns.

In other words, the ultimate principal—domestic households end up paying the price. Third, we might also expect to see a misallocation of capital as a result of any chronic distortion of market prices, and that inefficiency should be factored into any welfare analysis of the relative merits of different routes to debt reduction. Fourth, as we shall discuss later in this book, the government has given up the levers of financial regulation to operationally independent institutions so it is harder for finance ministers to implement this strategy than it once was.

14.5 Restructuring

We have talked a lot about the risk of default and the compensation that investors demand for default. It is now time to talk about the actuality of default. As Reinhart and Rogoff (2009, 2013) document, sovereign 'credit events' are more common than you think they are, not least because some of the debt reduction strategies that fall under this category can be difficult to identify, and may appear to be voluntary. The term 'credit event' is deliberate and covers what is a large continuum between restructuring at one end of the spectrum and repudiation on the other (Friedman 2000). At the restructuring end of the spectrum we have any change in the timing or quantum of coupon or principal repayments on the bond, which could come in the form of a conversion of the current bond into a new security. We can see examples of both when it comes to the resolution of the debt burden that the UK accumulated during the course of World War 1, with the consolidation of debt into a 3.5 % perpetual issue (Reinhart and Rogoff 2013), and the UK's participation as both creditor (to many countries) and debtor (to the USA) in the mass restructuring of June 1934 (Reinhart and Trebesch 2014)—as one US newspaper put it 'All debtors to the US excepting Finland to default today' (New York Times 1934).

Our starting point is to recognise that governments choose to service or default on debt. As Buiter and Rahbari (2014) observe, 'the debtor has his fun up front' when he borrows additional resources. From that point on, the debt contract is pure grind, repaying the interest and principal on the loan, and when the net present discounted value of continuing to abide by the contract and service that debt turns negative it is hard to see why debtors would choose to continue to honour the contract. Indeed, we might well frame the question: why do countries with seemingly crippling debt burdens continue to service debt?

The standard explanation for why governments continue to service debt long after the point where it appears that the debt is unsustainable is the fear of 'cold turkey'. That is, governments may be concerned that having defaulted on existing obligations 'once bitten, twice shy' potential creditors will be unwilling to lend the government new funds. If governments are locked out of capital markets and unable to borrow to fund spending for an extended period after a restructuring then it may be optimal to continue servicing what looks like an unsustainable burden (Eaton and Gersovitz 1981). However, it is unclear how powerful this 'retain a reputation for repayment' mechanism is when governments can reinvest the funds that would otherwise be used to service debts (Bulow and Rogoff 1989). Nor is it clear that those governments which default are locked out of capital markets for too long (Lindert and Morton 1989).

Another conventional explanation for the reluctance to restructure is the additional macroeconomic pain that a default could cause in the domestic economy (Dooley 2000; Arellano 2008). De Paoli et al.'s (2006) review suggests that output losses following a sovereign default tend to be large and long lasting—with a median loss of output *per year* of 7 % in the crises that tend to follow a sovereign restructuring, which have an average median length of eight years; however, it is difficult to know what fraction of that output loss can be attributed to the *cause* of the restructuring and what fraction to the *consequences* of the restructuring. The domestic banking system plays a pivotal role here: the banks are a key investor in government bonds, so the losses that follow a restructuring can trigger a domestic banking crisis, which as recent events have illustrated can amplify the downturn in demand as the supply of core financial services dries up, and the larger the banking system the greater the potential deterrent against sovereign default (Gennaioli et al. 2014).

More generally, we should distinguish between those circumstances where debt is held domestically or by overseas creditors: in the case of the former, a sovereign debt restructuring looks a lot like a wealth tax, which will have predictable consequences both from an efficiency and equity perspective. Restructuring financial assets held by domestic agents will reduce their net worth and tend to exacerbate credit frictions—credit will become more expensive and more tightly rationed—and that will likely weigh on demand, over and above any wealth effect on consumption. There will be significant distributional costs too: the government's creditors take the hit in a restructuring, not those who might have benefited from fiscal largesse when the debt burden was being built up. When debt is held overseas, these domestic efficiency and distributional concerns do not apply.

An alternative explanation for the reluctance to restructure lies in politics. Alongside the fear of being shut out from international capital markets politicians may fear being isolated on the global political stage and the ramifications of a default on the decisions of other governments in areas such as foreign aid, trade or even defence (Sachs 1986). Diaz-Alejandro (1984) emphasises the domestic consequences of default:

> To a moderate leader the political consequences of default present a mixed picture. For a while, the leader may bask in nationalist glory, but the forces unleashed by default, especially an active one, may threaten constitutional order and could reopen the gates to populist-nationalist authoritarian generals-after all, the nation would be surrounded by enemies.

There are long-standing concerns about the structure of the sovereign debt market, and the extent to which it could be an impediment to the efficient and orderly resolution of problems of unsustainable debt prompting calls for reform.

There are two classic justifications for reform which result from the classic asymmetric information problem: to reduce deadweight losses and minimise moral hazard (Rogoff and Zettelmeyer 2002; Eichengreen 2003). First, uncertainty over the true state of the public finances and the capacity of the government to repair the situation can give rise to a protracted dispute as the creditors and debtor haggle over the terms of any restructuring during which time significant damage could be done to the domestic economy. Second, the fact that international organisations and other governments often come to the support of an ailing sovereign can often provide an opportunity for the initial private creditors to escape the costs of restructuring, and since the official sector creditors who take their place tend to be paid in full too, that leaves domestic taxpayers picking up the tab. This concern over 'moral hazard'—that the good intentions of the international official sector lets investors off the hook—gave rise to a determination to involve the private sector in the resolution of sovereign debt crises, albeit with mixed results (Eichengreen 1999).

Bolton and Jeanne (2007) argue that a kind of Gresham's law for sovereign debt may apply. Each investor has an incentive to protect herself from a selective default by the sovereign on a subset of the outstanding stock of debt. The government may respond to that concern by issuing debt that is hard to restructure in order to lower the cost of debt—for example, by inserting a unanimity requirement on restructuring the debt.

Lest the reader be left with the conclusion that post-crisis problem of unsustainable debts—particularly in the Eurozone periphery—is that the creditors have too much power and are preventing the inevitable resolution of the problem, it is worth pondering whether the opposite could be the case. Shleifer (2003) argues that the problem with the sovereign debt market is that creditors have too few rights, not too many. He argues that it is precisely when the recovery process in the event of restructuring is predictable and when recovery rates are high (using our earlier terminology, the LGD is low) that creditors will be more willing to lend, and more willing to lend on more attractive terms. Sovereign defaults can be a messy process; in the words of Bulow (2002): '[T]here is nothing remotely comparable to…corporate bankruptcy procedures in the world of sovereign debt.' Governments may default and pay back only a fraction of both what they borrowed and what they can afford to pay; legal disputes can run for years and there is very little scope for investors to seize assets (Shleifer 2003).

14.6   ……Or Get Help

Having considered the solutions to a debt crisis we will end with a brief discussion of a potential alternative: get help. Whether getting help is a viable alternative to the solutions described above depends on the diagnosis of the problem. If the government is the victim of a 'sunspot attack' in the bond markets—a belief that the public finances are unsustainable that is not justified by fundamentals but nonetheless proves self-fulfilling—then temporary assistance might be the answer. But if the debt burden is unsustainable then as noted above, temporary assistance can simply let private investors off the hook, allowing them to escape the pain of the inevitable restructuring. Help can come in two forms, as the European crisis has illustrated: from the official sector overseas (other governments and supranational institutions) and from the domestic central bank.

14.6.1 International Rescue: The IMF and the Conditionality Debate

In practice, when countries get into difficulty they tend to turn to the International Monetary Fund (IMF); other governments may lack the means to provide bilateral loans on the scale required or as we shall go on to discuss the expertise to act as lender of last resort. Indeed, lending to members states who are experiencing balance of payments problems (or are at risk) is one of three core responsibilities of the IMF (the other two being surveillance and the provision of technical assistance and training). It is standard practice for the country concerned to agree a package of measures with the IMF which is then presented to the Fund's Executive Board for approval. Conditionality is the watch word. Resources are then released in tranches upon successful execution of those reforms which are designed to resolve the underlying problem. A typical timeline under the IMF's workhorse lending instrument (the Stand-by Arrangements [SBA]) would be for funds to be released over the course of one to two years and then repaid within three to five years.

The Eurozone crisis has brought the Fund's role in international rescue to the attention of a wider set of macroeconomists. To begin with it was not obvious that the IMF would be involved. As problems began to mount in Greece, the then President of the Eurogroup (of Eurozone finance ministers) Jean-Claude Juncker remarked on 14 January 2010: 'We do not think that assistance from the IMF to Greece would be appropriate or welcome'. However, the IMF would go on to play a central role in the policy response to the Eurozone debt crisis alongside its partners—the ECB and the European Commission—in the so-called *Troika*, a confederation of interested parties who were collectively responsible for surveillance and negotiation (but not funding). The packages which were ultimately agreed were certainly atypical, both in size and duration, relative to the programmes that the Fund provided in Latin America and Asia (Pisani-Ferry et al. 2013) and the involvement of other governments in both providing funds (even to the extent of bilateral loans from Denmark, Sweden and the UK for the Irish bail-out) and the design of the programmes.

The Greek deal remains the principal bone of contention: the economy has been mired in a deep depression, the restructuring of private-sector claims on the Greek government failed to bring resolution and the intitial bail-out has had to be significantly extended and enlarged (Pisani-Ferry et al. 2013). Relative to that Greek tragedy, the programmes in Ireland, Spain and Portugal look an unqualified success, with all three managing to successfully exit. Going right back to the beginning, the IMF's original Greek SBA was certainly *unusual*: the package was very large (although the Fund only contributed 30 % of the package, the programme was the largest on record relative to the recipient's quota); it was the first (but not the last) programme for a member of the euro area; and most important of all, the debt burden was set to remain high over the lifetime of the programme. The last point was particularly problematic because it required a tweak in the Fund's criteria for providing emergency access: the IMF staff were unable to argue that there was a high probability that the debt was sustainable and therefore the programme had to be partially justified on the basis of the threat of contagion to other countries in the event of a Greek crisis (IMF 2013). With the benefit of hindsight those concerns certainly seem well justified, and many can justifiably claim to have been wise before the event (Eichengreen 2010).

There is not space here to do justice to the debate over the approach taken to crisis resolution in the European debt crisis. We shall focus here on just one key issue: the fact that support from international creditors came with strings attached. From the very beginning, with the 25 March statement by the Heads of State and Government of the Euro Area, there was a clear emphasis on conditionality:

> This mechanism, complementing International Monetary Fund financing, has to be considered ultima ratio, meaning in particular that market financing is insufficient. Any disbursement on the bilateral loans would be decided by the euro area member states by unanimity subject to strong conditionality.

There was nothing new in this emphasis on conditionality—it is fundamental to how the Fund operates as we have seen—or for that matter criticism of it. Indeed, there had been a clear increase in the Fund's use of conditionality from the 1970s to the late 1990s, although the IMF had started to respond to the critics in the years leading up to the financial crash by 'streamlining' the set of conditions down to those of direct macroeconomic relevance (Bird 2007). The Fund's whole approach had certainly come under sustained attack long before the Euro crisis, including from vocal and highly respected critics in the academic sphere (Stiglitz 2002; Sachs 1989, 2004), although the evidence appears to suggest that the IMF adjusts the scope of conditionality in light of local circumstances and domestic opposition, rather than extracting the maximum possible conditions from those most in need of help (Stone 2008). Much of the debate around conditionality focuses on specifics— claims that the IMF misdiagnosed the problems facing debtor nations and therefore imposed misguided policies on them—but the real problem with conditionality may be that the fundamental premise is flawed: if the debt burden is too heavy it may not be possible to design a programme where the debtor nation is better off receiving support under certain conditions and then paying its debt in full rather than doing without a programme and writing off part of the debt load (Sachs 1989).

If we want to make sense of this debate over conditionality we need to start from fist principles and understand the role played by institutions like the IMF. Khan and Sharma (2001) motivate the use of conditionality as a substitute for collateral in more traditional forms of finance; indeed, they note that the Articles of Agreement of the IMF explicitly acknowledge the trade-off between collateral and conditionality, in that countries which pledge collateral can obtain waivers on certain conditions. Khan and Sharma draw an analogy with the relationship between venture capitalists and collateral-short business start-ups, where it is not uncommon to find the contingent transfer of control rights, such that if the situation takes a turn for the worse venture capitalists can protect their investment by preventing the business gambling for resurrection.

Jeanne et al. (2008) characterise the conditional support that institutions like the IMF provide as a solution to the commitment problem inherent in a classic debt problem. When a country gets into trouble it needs immediate funding to solve its liquidity problem and it needs to implement reforms to solve its solvency problem. Without the IMF, creditors will worry about moral hazard—if they provide funding today to ease the liquidity crisis, the country will not deliver on the reform agenda tomorrow—and therefore will not provide the funding. With the conditional support of the IMF, creditors can have greater faith that countries will follow through on reforms. Jeanne, Ostry and Zettelmeyer argue that the key question for the IMF is therefore not whether a country is 'illiquid but solvent', but instead whether it is 'conditionally solvent'—that is, whether it will be able to meet its obligations if it drives through reforms. The question then is to how best to design the conditions: the 'optimal covenant' between the IMF and the country.

Khan and Sharma (2001) make two key points. First, the focus of conditionality should shift towards 'outcomes'—the achievement of tangible macroeconomic results—rather than implementation of measures which it is hoped might lead to good results in the future. Second, countries must 'own' their programmes—not least because of the standard asymmetric information problem: it will be down to the country to implement the reforms. Khan and Sharma cite the comments of the former Managing Director of the IMF, Per Jacobsen, who said the following when discussing a possible programme for Spain more than half a century ago, which whether they have been applied in practice or not, are worth repeating:

> [S]uch programs can only succeed if there is the will to succeed in the countries themselves…[the IMF] does not impose conditions on countries; they themselves have freely come to the conclusion that the measures they arrange to take – even when they are sometimes harsh – are in the best interests of their own countries.

More controversially, Ostry and Zettelmeyer (2005) advocate a greater role of ex ante conditionality: that is, rather than requiring countries take corrective action in return for support once they get into trouble, the IMF could instead insist that countries take preventative action if they want to be able to guarantee access to support should they get into trouble in the future. They suggest a practical way to implement this proposal: each country would be allocated a rating as part of the annual Article IV surveillance that the IMF conducts which would then determine the extent of IMF support that country could expect to receive in the event of a future crisis. The advantages of the proactive approach are clear, but hopefully so too is the key problem: economists will question whether this model is time consistent—would the IMF be able to stick to its guns and refuse support to systemically important countries which get into trouble that had received a low ranking in the past for failing to address mounting imbalances?

The reader may be forgiven for concluding that only the emerging economies and those nations trapped within a currency union would ever need to call on emergency support from the IMF. Those with longer memories know different. In September 1976 the UK government approached the IMF for a loan of $3.9 billion—at that time the largest request the Fund had ever received, and one which required the IMF to ask the US and German governments for additional funds in order to meet the request. The crisis appears to have been precipitated by the defeat of the then Prime Minister Wilson's Public Expenditure White Paper in March 1976 and was ultimately resolved through the loan and the government's acquiescence in sizeable cuts in the deficit, although there was considerable opposition within the government: Tony Benn, Secretary of State for Energy, proposed an alternative economic strategy of imposing import quotas, enforcing exchange controls, and introducing a Capital Investments Committee to direct capital expenditure to prioritised areas (Rodgers 2009). Interestingly, by the following year the fiscal position had improved, buoyed in part by revenues from North Sea oil, and the loan was not drawn in full.

14.6.2 The Central Bank to the Rescue

Where the national central bank has the capacity to save its sovereign it might seem a more natural port of call in a storm. After all, the central bank's balance sheet is an effective tool of crisis management (Barwell 2013), and finance ministers might expect that it could and should be put to work to protect the public finances in a crisis. From a pragmatic perspective, central bank purchases can act as a fire-break, preventing the escalation of contagion, and conveniently have the effect of lowering the cost of funding the consolidated balance sheet of the public sector.

We noted how a key feature of stress in financial markets was that a sharp decline in the price of government bonds can make forced sellers out of true believers: even those investors who believe that the public finances are sound may be forced to sell—and can certainly be prevented from increasing their position—because of the constraints under which agents who invest on behalf of a principal are forced to operate. A central bank does not play by the same rules. The central bank has the deepest of pockets given its capacity to issue outside money and is therefore not subject to the same constraints. Moreover, the belief that the central bank will intervene to put a floor underneath the price of government bonds can change the behaviour of private sector investors: now they believe that their losses from maintaining their position may be capped from below.

Central bank purchases of domestic government debt will also tend to reduce the cost of servicing the public sector's debt burden. If we take as our perspective the consolidated balance sheet of the public sector then we can see that by printing money to 'buy back' the debt that the government has issued, the central bank has effectively transformed the liabilities of that entity, away from long-term risky debt securities towards ultra-short-term risk-free central bank money. The interest rate spread between those two securities may run to several percentage points, which could represent a significant saving.

Given the potential power of central bank purchases, one might ask why this option does not feature more prominently in the list of solutions to a debt problem. The answer lies in the earlier discussion of fiscal dominance. If the central bank is understood to be buying sovereign debt with the objective of stabilising the market in response to the threat of a buyers' strike, then investors may conclude that the operational independence of the central bank has been compromised and the pursuit of price stability has been subordinated to the goals of fiscal policy. At this point the nominal anchor which stabilises the economy may start to slip as inflation expectations rise. Looking further ahead, investors may be concerned about the end game: if the central bank winds up as the principal creditor of the government then it will be driven into technical insolvency (a negative capital position) should the government default. As discussed earlier, this situation is not fatal, but it might well involve printing money on an industrial scale to recapitalise the balance sheet via seigniorage.

It is precisely for this reason that legal restrictions have been put in place to prevent Europe's central banks from engaging in quasi-fiscal operations. Article 123 of the Treaty on the Functioning of the European Union prohibits those central banks—including the BoE—from engaging in monetary financing. There is an explicit ban on purchasing government bonds in the primary market, but there is also a more general restriction on measures which would have the effect of allowing governments to avoid taking action to repair the public finances—which could encompass purchases of debt in the secondary market and voluntary participation in a debt restructuring. As ECB Chief

Economist Peter Praet observed, the purpose of that restriction is to safeguard monetary dominance (Praet 2015):

> [T]he independence that has been given to the ECB (and, in particular, the purpose of the monetary financing prohibition enshrined in Article 123 of the Treaty) is precisely to ensure that the central bank has full control over its balance sheet – that it cannot be forced by governments into monetising deficits or inflating away debts – and hence that monetary dominance is preserved.

The ECB created two purchase programmes during the course of the European debt crisis to help stabilise the situation. Paradoxically, the second programme which has yet to be used has proved more powerful than the first which was used extensively. First came the SMP, which involved sterilised bond purchases in the secondary market of debt issued by sovereigns that had come under pressure. The ECB did not announce quantitative targets for purchases, the likely duration of the scheme or yield or spread targets that would determine success criteria. Instead, the stated purpose of the scheme was defined as follows (ECB 2010):

> The objective of this programme is to address the malfunctioning of securities markets and restore an appropriate monetary policy transmission mechanism.

It would be wrong to say that the SMP failed. It does appear as though the announcement of the scheme had an economically significant effect on bond yields. Eser and Schwaab (2013) estimate that per €1 billion of SMP purchases had a 1–2 basis point on the five-year yield on Italian debt and up to 20 basis points on the corresponding Greek security, and find tentative evidence of longer-lasting effects of bond purchases, perhaps due to the reduced supply of bonds in private sector hands or a signalling effect on default risk.

The second programme, which as yet remains to be used, was the Outright Monetary Transactions (OMT). The OMT was unofficially launched by the President of the ECB, Mario Draghi, in a speech on 26 July 2012, when he sent markets a powerful message: 'Within our mandate, the ECB is ready to do whatever it takes to preserve the euro. And believe me, it will be enough'. The details of the OMT would come a couple of months later and differed from the SMP in a number of respects: the Governing Council made clear that there was no ex ante restriction on the scale of purchases; purchases were limited to the front-end of the curve (i.e., bonds with a residual maturity of three years or less); and would be conditional on governments entering into and adhering to a programme (which requires the government to deliver on fiscal consolidation and structural reforms) and maintaining full market access. The ECB attached considerable importance to the last constraint in justifying why the OMT did not contravene the prohibition on monetary financing (Cœuré 2013):

> OMTs do not eliminate the market as a disciplining device for governments. What OMTs do do is to complement the market, which in the current crisis has been abrupt and unreliable, by another incentive mechanism.

In the event, this conditional safety net underneath the sovereign bond market has not been tested. It is difficult to know whether it was the mood music (the 'whatever it takes' and potentially unlimited) that mattered rather than the modalities in changing investor sentiment, or whether it was the conditional nature of the scheme which convinced investors that the scheme was time consistent (the ECB would be able to buy in size precisely because they could now have greater confidence that politicians would not renege on their part of the deal). In any case, Altavilla et al. (2014) do find evidence of a significant movement in bond yields on the dates of the key announcements around the launch of the scheme.

In this section, a theoretical distinction has been made between central bank's purchases of government debt designed to restore price stability (that was discussed elsewhere in this book) and those designed to safeguard the public finances—between preserving monetary dominance and falling victim to fiscal dominance. In practice, that distinction may be hard to draw both in terms of cause and effect: the circumstances in which a central bank launches an asset purchase programme in order to restore price stability are likely to be precisely those in which the public finances will come under pressure, and large-scale bond buying should bring much needed relief to the debt management office, easing the path of future issuance and lowering the effective cost of servicing debt. Indeed, the first phase of the BoE's QE programme appears to have had precisely this effect, with CDS spreads spiking before and falling significantly after purchases began (Breedon et al. 2012). This, of course, is precisely why the ECB's QE programme is controversial in some quarters.

References

Akitoby, B., Komatsuzaki, T., & Binder, A. (2014). *Inflation and public debt reversals in the G7 countries*. IMF Working Paper 14/96.

Alesina, A., & Ardagna, S. (2009). *Large changes in fiscal policy: Taxes versus spending*. NBER Working Paper No. 15438.

Altavilla, C., Giannone, D., & Lenza, M. (2014). *The financial and macroeconomic effects of OMT announcements*. ECB Working Paper 1707.

Arellano, C. (2008). Default risk and income fluctuations in emerging economies. *American Economic Review, 98*(3), 690–712.

Barwell, R. (2013). *Macroprudential policy: Taming the wild gyrations of credit flows, debt stocks and asset prices*. New York: Palgrave.

Bertola, G., & Drazen, A. (1993). Trigger points and budget cuts: Explaining the effects of fiscal austerity. *American Economic Review, 83*(1), 11–26.

Bird, G. (2007). The IMF: A bird's eye view of its role and operations. *Journal of Economic Surveys, 21*(4), 683–745.

Blanchard, O. (1990a). Comment. *NBER Macroeconomics Annual*, 111–116.

Blanchard, O. (1990b). *Suggestions for a new set of fiscal indicators*. OECD Working Paper 79.

Bolton, P., & Jeanne, O. (2007). *Structuring and restructuring sovereign debt*. IMF Working Paper 07/192.

Breedon, F., Chadha, J., & Waters, A. (2012). The financial market impact of UK quantitative easing. *Oxford Review of Economic Policy, 28*(4), 702–728.

Buiter, W. (2007). Seigniorage. *Economics*, 2007–10.

Buiter, W., & Rahbari, E. (2014). Why governments default. In R. Lastra & L. Buchheit (Eds.), *Sovereign debt management*. Oxford: Oxford University Press.

Bulow, J. (2002). First world governments and third world debt. *Brookings Papers on Economic Activity, 1*, 229–255.

Bulow, J., & Rogoff, K. (1989). Sovereign debt. *American Economic Review, 79*(1), 43–50.

Canzoneri, M., Cumby, R., & Diba, B. (2001). Is the price level determined by the needs of fiscal solvency? *American Economic Review, 91*(5), 1221–1238.

Cochrane, J. (2005). Money as a stock. *Journal of Monetary Economics, 52*, 501–528.

Cœuré, B. (2013, September 2). *Outright Monetary Transactions, one year on*. Speech.

De Paoli, B., Hoggarth, G., & Saporta, V. (2006). *Costs of sovereign default*. Bank of England Financial Stability 1.

Diaz-Alejandro, C. (1984). Latin-American debt; I don't think we are in Kansas anymore. *Brookings Paper on Economic Activity, 2*, 335–403.

Diaz-Alejandro, C. (1985). Good-bye financial repression, hello financial crash. *Journal of Development Economics, 1–2*, 1–24.

Dooley, M. (2000). *Can output losses following international financial crises be avoided?* NBER Working Paper 7531.

Eaton, J., & Gersovitz, M. (1981). Debt with potential repudiation. *Review of Economic Studies, 48*(2), 289–309.

ECB. (2010, May 10). *ECB decides on measures to address severe tensions in financial markets*. Press Release.

Eichengreen, B. (1999). Is greater private sector burden sharing impossible? *IMF Finance and Development, 36*(3).

Eichengreen, B. (2003). Restructuring sovereign debt. *Journal of Economic Perspectives,* *17*(4), 75–98.

Eichengreen, B. (2010). *It is not too late for Europe.* VoxEu.

Eser, F., & Schwaab, B. (2013). *Assessing asset purchases within the ECB's Securities Markets Programme.* ECB Working Paper 1587.

Friedman, M. (1971). Government revenue from inflation. *Journal of Political Economy, 79*(4), 846–8656.

Friedman, B. (2000). How easy should debt restructuring be? In C. Adams, M. Pomerlano, & R. Litan (Eds.), *Managing financial and corporate distress.* Washington, D.C.: Brookings Institute.

Gennaioli, N., Martin, A., & Rossi, S. (2014). Sovereign default, domestic banks and financial institutions. *Journal of Finance, 69*(2), 819–866.

Giavazzi, F., & Pagano, M. (1990). Can severe fiscal contractions be expansionary? Tales of two small European countries? *NBER Macroeconomics Annual, 1990*(5), 75–122.

Giavazzi, F., Japelli, T., Pagano, M., & Benedetti, M. (2005). *Searching for non-monotonic effects of fiscal policy: New evidence.* NBER Working Paper 11593.

Giovannini, A., & de Melo, M. (1993). Government revenue from financial repression. *American Economic Review, 83*(4), 953–963.

Hilscher, J., Raviv, A., & Reis, R. (2014). *Inflating away the public debt.* mimeo.

IMF. (2013). *Greece: Ex post evaluation of exceptional access under the 2010 stand-By arrangement.* IMF Country Report 13/156.

Jeanne, O., Ostry, J., & Zettelmeyer, J. (2008). *A theory of international crisis lending.* IMF Working Paper 08/236.

Khan, M., & Sharma, S. (2001). *IMF conditionality and country ownership of programs.* IMF Working Paper 01/142.

Krause, M., & Moyen, S. (2013). *Public debt and changing inflation targets.* Deutsche Bundesbank Discussion Paper 06/2013.

Leeper, E., & Walker, T. (2011). *Perceptions and misperceptions of fiscal inflation.* BIS Working Paper 364.

Lindert, P., & Morton, P. (1989). How sovereign debt has worked. In J. Sachs (Ed.), *Developing country debt and economic performance.* Chicago: University of Chicago.

McKinnon, R. (1973). *Money and capital in economic development.* Washington, D.C.: Brookings Institute.

Missale, A., & Blanchard, O. (1994). The debt burden and debt maturity. *American Economic Review, 71*(3), 309–319.

New York Times. (1934, June 15). *All debtors to the US excepting Finland to default today.*

Ostry, J., & Zettelmeyer, J. (2005). *Strengthening IMF crisis prevention.* IMF Working Paper 05/206.

Pisani-Ferry, J., Sapir, A.,& Wolff, G. (2013). *EU-IMF assistance to euro-area countries.* Bruegel.

Praet, P. (2015, March 11). *Public sector security purchases and monetary dominance in a monetary union without a fiscal union.* Speech.

Reinhart, C., & Rogoff, K. (2009). *This time is different.* Princeton: Princeton University Press.

Reinhart, C., & Rogoff, K. (2013). *Financial and sovereign debt crises.* IMF Working Paper 13/266.

Reinhart, C., & Sbrancia, M. (2011). *The liquidation of government debt.* NBER Working Paper 16893.

Reinhart, C., & Trebesch, C. (2014). *A distant mirror of debt, default and relief.* NBER Working Paper 20577.

Rodgers, C. (2009). The politics of economic policy making in Britain: A reassessment of the 1976 IMF crisis. *Politics and Policy, 37*(5), 971–994.

Rogoff, K., & Zettelmeyer, J. (2002). Bankruptcy procedures for sovereigns: A history of ideas. *IMF Staff Papers, 49*(3), 470–503.

Sachs, J. (1986). Managing the LDC debt crisis. *Brookings Paper on Economic Activity, 2*, 397–440.

Sachs, J. (1989). Conditionality, debt relief and the developing country debt crisis. In J. Sachs (Ed.), *Developing country debt and economic performance.* Chicago: University of Chicago.

Sachs, J. (2004). How to run the international monetary fund. *Foreign Affairs*, July–August, 60–64.

Sargent, T., & Wallace, N. (1981). Some unpleasant monetary arithmetic. *Federal Reserve Bank of Minneapolis Quarterly Review, 5*, 1–17.

Shaw, E. (1973). *Financial deepening in economic development.* New York: Oxford University Press.

Shleifer, A. (2003). Will the sovereign debt market survive? *American Economic Review, 93*(2), 85–90.

Stiglitz, J. (2002). *Globalisation and its discontents.* New York: W.W. Norton.

Stone, R. (2008). The scope of IMF conditionality. *International Organization, 62*, 589–620.

15

The Institutions of Fiscal Policy

In this chapter, we turn to discuss the politics of fiscal policy—namely the reason why the democratic process might not deliver optimal outcomes—and the proposals that economists have made for how to address these deficiencies.

15.1 Political Business Cycles and Deficit Bias

In their search for explanations of the business cycle it did not take long for economists to identify politicians and their willingness to exploit fiscal levers to achieve reelection as a potential suspect. The textbook example here is the Nixon administration—indeed Rogoff (1988) labels Richard Nixon 'the all-time hero of political business cycles'. As Abrams (2006) describes, the Nixon administration was able to engineer an impressive pick-up in the pace of growth from 2.8 % in 1970 to a stunning 7.7 % in 1972 (which coincidentally was the year when Nixon was up for reelection). Indeed, Abrams uses the now infamous 'Nixon tapes' to document how the President was able to bring direct and indirect (via the Director of the OMB, George Shultz) pressure on the newly appointed chairman of the Fed, Arthur Burns to keep monetary policy as loose as possible—which with the benefit of hindsight helps to explain why the federal funds rate dropped by four percentage points between January 1970 and July 1972. A couple of excerpts from a conversation between Nixon and Shultz are worth repeating, one revealing Nixon's intentions, the other illustrating the veiled threat to Burns (that the President can appoint who he wants to the Fed Board):

© The Editor(s) (if applicable) and The Author(s) 2016
R. Barwell, *Macroeconomic Policy after the Crash*,
DOI 10.1057/978-1-137-51592-6_15

[Nixon to Shultz] 'Do you feel, as far as Arthur and the money supply, we got that about as far as we can turn it right now, have we? I mean as far as my influence on him, that's what I'm really asking.'
[Shultz to Nixon] 'I think it was good to have that discussion about the procedures for appointment [to the Board] so that he sees that he doesn't have complete control'.

In terms of the theory of the political business cycle, the classic reference is Nordhaus (1975) which imagines a wily politician exploiting a naïve electorate to time the boom and bust of the business cycle to fit the electoral timetable. That mechanism did not sit comfortably with the rational expectations revolution—policymakers should not be able to systematically fool rational agents—and so in time a new model of the political business cycle emerged. Rogoff (1990) proposes an equilibrium model of the political cycle which is rooted in the asymmetric information problem. Politicians differ: some are more competent than others at efficiently providing public goods. Rogoff's model argues that an incumbent has an incentive to act in ways which suggest that she might be competent as elections approach which could lead to otherwise inexplicable swings in government consumption. In any case, if we remain true to the hypothesis of monetary dominance, then politicians should only be able to influence the state of the macroeconomy—that is, the level of demand rather than the mix—if central bankers choose or are required to look the other way (Maloney et al. 2003), as Chairman Burns appears to have done.

Broadening our horizons somewhat the literature provides a number of explanations for the so-called deficit bias—that is, the tendency for governments to systematically borrow too much. Perhaps the simplest way to explain a deficit bias is through what could be called naïve or irrational behaviour on the part of policymakers and or voters. As Chote (2013) explains if people have overoptimistic expectations about the future rate of growth of the economy or the health of the public finances, or if they have hyperbolic preferences (in the sense that difficult choices are forever delayed until tomorrow, see Laibson (1997)), then we might expect to see governments systematically spending too much today. Our remaining explanations for the deficit bias are rooted in the political process in some way, shape or form.

The classic explanation for the deficit bias is that the current generation will systematically exploit the fact that future generations cannot cast a vote in elections today by electing politicians who will spend today at the expense of higher taxes in the far future (Musgrave 1988). Note that this is the antithesis of the Barro's Ricardian equivalence result that we encountered earlier, where it was assumed that the current generation would save more today in response to fiscal profligacy today in order to fund generous bequests which would unpick the apparent intergenerational transfer. In passing, identifying when fiscal policy is being skewed in favour of the current generation is a little harder than you might think: it is not as simple as distinguishing between investment and consumption—the huge expenditure involved in fighting the Second World War being a particular case in point (Robinson 1998).

Another standard explanation for the deficit bias is the externality that can arise in the presence of special interest groups (Velasco 2000). In a fragmented political system with a number of groups making competing demands for transfer payments there is a tendency for each group to ignore the impact of their demands on the level of general taxation: the so-called 'common pool' problem (von Hagen and Harden 1995; Krogstrup and Wyplosz 2006). The more heterogeneous the population, the more numerous the niche special interest groups which care about spending on a particular area, the greater the deficit bias.

The deficit bias may simply reflect the polarised nature of the political debate. Alesina and Tabellini (1990) illustrate how government debt can become a strategic variable which politicians use to influence the decisions their successors (opponents) take. In particular, the equilibrium level of government debt is higher than that which the social planner would choose and in particular the more polarised the electorate the greater the deficit bias and the level of debt. As President Reagan's budget director once observed to a US senator, running large deficits: 'gives you an argument for cutting back programs that really weren't desired and giving you an argument against establishing new programs you don't really want' (Anrig 2010).

Having explained how the political process can give rise to a systematic bias towards excessive deficits and the accumulation of debt, we shall briefly discuss whether it is within the means of the political process to rectify the situation and drive through the institutional reforms which we shall go on to discuss. It is often claimed that it takes a crisis to bring 'politicians to their senses'; for example, Rodrik (1996) notes:

> [I]f there is one single theme that runs through the length of the political economy literature it is the idea that crisis is the instigator of reform.

The 'it takes a crisis…' hypothesis seems plausible: politicians will need the general public to appreciate that there is a problem if they are to build a mandate to take painful decisions. In passing, the idea that it takes a crisis to force politicians to take tough decisions helps explain the resistance in certain quarters to the policies pursued by the ECB through the European debt crisis. Some commentators say that the strategy pursued by the ECB has been too successful in extinguishing the existential crisis that confronted Europe, removing the precondition for politicians driving through essential fiscal and structural reforms. The President of the ECB dismisses this critique, arguing that there is no link between the passage of reforms and the monetary stance (Draghi 2015):

> [W]hen we talk about structural reforms, we often talk about labor market reforms, judiciary, education, health care, change the political space of the electoral system. Do you think any of these five things are really linked to interest rates—that governments really think, well, maybe tomorrow I start changing my judiciary because the interest rates are too high? I think they have no relation.

An interesting suggestion in the literature is that it might require progressive politicians to drive through reforms, in just the same way that it took a right-wing hawk (Richard Nixon) to open diplomatic negotiations with communist China (Cukierman and Tommasi 1998). Precisely because these politicians are believed to be instinctively sceptical about the merits of 'market friendly' fiscal reforms it is easier for these politicians to make the case for those reforms.

Fabrizio and Mody (2008) review the evidence on the circumstances in which institutional reforms flourish in a panel of European countries between 1994 and 2004. They find that large deficits are not a catalyst for reform; on the contrary, they find that large deficits are likely consistent with strong claims on the budget process and a resistance to reform. In effect, there is a bifurcation in the sample between countries with small deficits and strong institutions and those with large deficits and weak institutions. Fabrizio and Mody do find that large shocks can trigger reforms although a united government appears to be a necessary ingredient—fragmented coalitions are less likely to grasp the nettle of reform. Finally, they also find evidence of the 'Nixon to China' hypothesis: left-leaning governments are more likely to drive through reforms than those on the right.

15.2 Writing Fiscal Rules

We have reviewed how the conduct of fiscal policy may be subject to political pressures which lead to suboptimal outcomes. Economists are familiar with this problem: left to their own devices, politicians would be sorely tempted to manipulate the levers of monetary policy to generate a 'surprise' burst of output and inflation, and sooner or later private sector agents would come to expect those surprises, and the result is an inefficiently high-level of inflation (Kydland and Prescott 1977). That observation prompted research into various institutional reforms which might solve this time inconsistency problem in the monetary sphere and there is a temptation to transplant those suggestions—including setting policy by a rule, to take all discretion out of the process—into the fiscal debate to solve a similar problem.

From the outset, we should be clear that we use the standard strict definition of fiscal rules (e.g., Kopits 2001)—namely, a *permanent* constraint on fiscal policy, expressed in terms of a summary indicator of the state of the public finances. In particular, this definition is intended to differentiate between a numerical constraint on the discretion of finance minister (rules) and the more fuzzy soft constraints imposed by fiscal councils (Wyplosz 2013), which we shall go on to discuss.

In practice, there are formidable hurdles which need to be overcome in order to set policy by a rule in the fiscal domain. The first fundamental problem is one of democratic legitimacy: fiscal policy is inherently more politically sensitive than monetary policy; intra- and intergenerational distribution of resources are at the core of fiscal policy. Rules which place politicians in a fiscal straightjacket are an implicit constraint on the electorate and are therefore not only contentious, but also fragile. No government can bind the hands of its successors, so there is always the possibility that a future government may rewrite, temporarily suspend or permanently remove the rule and politicians may try to do precisely that when the rules bind. Remember, fiscal rules would not be necessary if the electorate punished imprudent governments at the ballot box: on the contrary, politicians may find it politically rewarding to be ill disciplined (Wyplosz 2013).

The second fundamental problem is the sheer complexity of the task. A good fiscal rule needs to keep an eye on the past, present and future—referencing the legacy stock of debt that has been accumulated as a result of *past* decisions; the state of the public finances and the economy, and specifically the proximity of the monetary policy stance to any lower bound, in the *present* day; and the known pressures on the public finances that are likely to arise in the *future* on account of factors such as demographic change. Writing down a rule which can encompass that complexity and distil it into a plausible and implementable policy prescription is no mean feat.

Those who write fiscal rules have more modest ambitions than the academics in the monetary arena: rather that prescribing the optimal policy stance—as for example, the Taylor Rule does—fiscal rules simply try to prevent finance ministers from taking *very bad decisions* in order to safeguard debt sustainability. One way to do that is to 'rule out' even a transitory period of excessive borrowing, but the implied loss of flexibility might be seen to have significant economic costs (putting all the weight of counter-cyclical stabilisation onto monetary policy) and therefore politically infeasible (Wyplosz 2005). Even hard-wiring long-run debt sustainability into an implementable fiscal rule is easier said than done, being inherently dependent on fiscal projections far into the future. In practice, those writing the rules will almost always incorporate a generic 'exceptional circumstances' escape clause, given the difficulty of writing down a sufficiently sophisticated rule which can accommodate all possible circumstances (i.e., what should be done during and in the aftermath of man-made and natural disasters) which introduces an explicit element of discretion implicit in the rules (which is always implicitly there given the option of future governments to rewrite the rules).

Turning to the practicalities, Kopits and Symansky (1998) have come as close as anyone to articulating a set of ideal criteria for fiscal rules. They are as follows:

- *Well defined*: The calibration of the rule should be well defined in the sense that the variable which is constrained, the institutional coverage and the escape clauses are sufficiently well articulated to avoid unnecessary ambiguity.
- *Transparent*: The framework is sufficiently transparent to enable adequate independent monitoring in real time, for example, with respect to the government's capacity to comply with the rule via creative accounting or forecasting.
- *Adequate*: Simply put, the design of the rule should be adequate to achieve the desired objective (e.g., debt sustainability).
- *Consistent*: The framework should be both internally consistent (in the case of multiple fiscal rules) and consistent with the overarching macroeconomic framework.
- *Simple*: The rules should be sufficiently simple so that they are understood by the general public alike, in order to build support for constraining fiscal policy in order to safeguard debt sustainability, which in turn should reduce the risk of future governments diluting the framework.
- *Flexible*: The framework should be sufficiently flexible so that it can accommodate exogenous shocks to the public finances, such as natural or man-made disasters.
- *Enforceable*: Can the framework be enforced in practice, which will rely in part on the credibility of any sanctions for non-compliance?
- *Efficient*: Is the framework supported by the broader policy agenda, or would adherence to the rule require inelegant and likely inefficient adjustments in taxation and spending given a failure to address other weaknesses in the budget process (i.e., multi-year plans for spending, efficiency reviews etc.)?

15.3 Debt Ceilings

If we are going to start calibrating rules circumscribing the path of government debt then we ought to think hard about what the appropriate level of government debt is. However, it is hard to find a definitive statement about what the optimal debt burden is in the academic literature. Indeed, there is a school of thought that the whole idea of an optimal debt ceiling is defunct. Imagine that a government breached such a ceiling: it would be faced with a choice between significant short-term consolidation (higher taxes, lower spending) to get back below the ceiling, or living with a higher debt burden and tolerating slightly higher taxes or lower spending in perpetuity in order to fund the increased cost of servicing debt. Which of those options the government chooses should depend on the relative size of the real interest rate and the rate at which we discount the future. In theory then the 'optimal' debt ceiling could itself be a random walk, drifting up or down in response to shocks to the public finances (Schmitt-Grohe and Uribe 2004). In fact, the closest the literature comes to a clear prescription is the well-publicised work of Carmen Reinhart and Ken Rogoff that when the ratio of gross external debt to GDP closes in on 100 % there is a marked impact on the pace of economic growth, and that for emerging market economies that growth penalty kicks in at lower debt levels (Reinhart and Rogoff 2010).

A sensible, albeit extreme, starting point in this discussion is what Stiglitz (1988) labelled Say's law of government deficits. In a world in which the government can raise revenue through lump sum taxes without inefficiently distorting behaviour and there is no attempt to redistribute resources between households that can access capital markets on the same terms as the government then deficits are irrelevant. If the government finances a cut in lump sum taxes through increased borrowing then the demand for government debt will rise to meet the increase in supply as households save more in expectation of future tax increases. If we construct an infinitely lived household by knitting together infinite generations of mortal households with a concern for the welfare of those who follow then even attempts to transfer resources between the generations will prove fruitless. We can write down an intertemporal budget constraint for that immortal household which is the mirror image of the government's, and where the stock of government debt (an asset of that immortal household) is irrelevant too (Barro 1974).

Once we relax these extreme assumptions, a role for fiscal policy emerges and in the process the stock of government debt ceases to be an irrelevant accounting entry. For example, Buiter (1983) relaxes the assumption of perfect capital markets. Now the governments acts as a 'superior financial intermediary', exploiting the more attractive terms on which it can raise funds to smooth the disposable income and expenditure of otherwise credit-constrained private sector agents. Add sufficient rigidities to the model to allow for the possibility of a large and persistent shortfall in demand and a rationale emerges for running deficits and the accumulation of debt in the kind of environment that the developed economies have found themselves since the financial crash.

If instead we relax the assumption that the government is able to raise revenue through non-distortionary lump sum taxes we travel in a very different direction. Now the social planner seeks to build up a stock of assets, financed through taxes on capital in the short run so that in steady state government consumption is financed through the interest earned on those assets with distortionary taxes set to zero (Chamley 1985, 1986; Judd 1985).

Another charge that is typically levelled against active fiscal policy is that government borrowing crowds out investment in physical capital by driving up the real interest rate, and thereby reduces the productive capacity of the economy. Perverse as it may seem, there are circumstances in which that is no bad thing. Imagine an economy where the savings of each generation of workers (to support consumption during their retirement) finances the gross investment made by companies in the productive capital. Diamond (1965) demonstrated that a steady state can emerge in a competitive economy where the capital stock is too large—that is, each generation is saving too much, and consuming too little. This so-called dynamic inefficiency emerges when the return on capital is below the trend growth rate of the economy (effectively the sum of productivity growth and population growth). In theory, in this environment, the government can enhance welfare by issuing debt to absorb private sector savings and thereby avoiding overinvestment in capital. However, this result may have little practical relevance; Abel, Mankiw, Summers, and Zeckhauser (1989) argue that dynamic inefficiency may be little more than an academic curiosity of limited practical relevance.

Aiyagari and McGrattan (1998) present a framework which incorporates all of these features: welfare-enhancing role for government debt to loosen credit constraints and smooth consumption in the real economy and the potential costs through crowding out the formation of physical capital and the distortionary impact of taxes. The qualitative results are not surprising: the optimal stock of debt depends on the balance of these arguments. More interesting is their conclusion that the welfare function is very flat—that is, there is very little cost associated with deviations from the optimal stock of debt.

We have only scratched the surface here. As Buiter (1998) argues, the prudent or optimal debt burden today should reflect various structural features of the economy which bear on the future health of the public finances, such as anticipated trends in demography and productivity. Initial conditions matter too: a debt burden of 272 % may not be imprudent if you have just emerged from the

Second World War; likewise, it would not have to be optimal for Europe to try to immediately hit the 60 % debt target given the debts that have been accumulated during the financial crisis (and to a greater or lesser extent, the period before). Equally, if the public sector capital stock is in parlous state then there is a clear case for debt-financed investment to raise productivity. Finally, the optimal debt stock should also reflect an assessment of the risk of further catastrophes *in the future*, which would necessitate a rapid accumulation of debt—to the extent that governments are concerned about the risks posed by a large debt burden. The expected frequency and severity of those crises should be reflected in the stance of fiscal policy today—with the government taking out insurance by running with a low debt burden in 'peace time'. Indeed, Buiter concludes:

> A one-size-fits-all figure such as the 60% ceiling of the Maastricht Treaty makes no sense at all.

Nonetheless, we observe that debt ceilings are a common feature of fiscal rules. In practice, debt ceilings are combined with strictures on the required speed of convergence to the ceiling—which may or may not depend on current circumstances—so that countries which breach the ceiling are not expected to immediately get back under, but the 'crude' constraint of the ceiling remains.

The literature suggests more sophisticated alternatives to crude debt ceilings which still satisfy the desire to protect future generations. (Emmerson et al. 2013). The first best from a theoretical perspective would be to anchor the rule on the 'solvency criterion' where an assessment is made as to whether the government's intertemporal budget constraint is satisfied under current policy settings: that is, over the infinite future will the government raise sufficient tax revenue to fund spending and pay down debt. The rule could require the government to satisfy that constraint within some specified time period with some additional constraint on the speed of convergence defined in terms of the 'intertemporal budget gap': the scale of the *permanent* increase in taxes or cut in spending that would be required to satisfy the constraint. The second best alternative is a 'sustainable commitments' measure which would constrain the fraction of tax receipts that can be pre-committed to servicing debt. This measure is superior to the debt ceiling both in its treatment of off balance sheet liabilities that are not captured in PSND and because it takes account of the cost of servicing debt (*persistently* lower interest rates mean a higher debt load is easier to sustain). Both of these measures have the advantage over the crude ceiling of being more comprehensive in coverage of liabilities and to varying degrees closer to the theoretical benchmark of sustainability. However, the crude debt ceiling has one thing in its favour: simplicity—unlike model constructs, it's easy to assess whether the rule has been breached or not.

15.4   Fiscal Rules in Practice

Fiscal rules have become an increasingly common feature of the policy land-scape: in 1990 only five countries had rules in place that constrained central government, but by 2012 that figure had risen to 76 if we include rules which operate at the supranational level and typically those rules tend to constrain debt and the budget balance (Schaechter et al. 2012). In what follows, we shall review how fiscal rules were implemented in the UK and at the European level in the years before the crisis and the reforms that have taken place since then.

15.4.1 Golden Rules and Fiscal Mandates: The UK Experience of Fiscal Rules

In the 1998 Finance Act, the UK government formally adopted two fiscal rules as part of its 'Code for Fiscal Stability'. They were respectively:

- *The Golden Rule*: In the long run, the government would only borrow to pay for investment; over the course of the economic cycle, current spending would be financed through taxation and as a result, the current budget would be in balance or surplus.
- *The Sustainable Investment Rule*: The government must keep the level of PSND (i.e., net of short-term financial assets) at a 'stable and prudent' level, defined as less than 40 % of GDP.

These rules clearly restricted the government's *theoretical* room for manoeuvre on the fiscal front, although it is worth noting that had the UK decided to join the single currency, the Stability and Growth Pact (SGP) *ought to have* restricted the government's *actual* room for manoeuvre, since the government *should have been* subject to penalties for running excessive deficits (Emmerson et al. 2006), although as we will go on to discuss the SGP was all bark and no bite during this period.

The motivation for the Golden Rule is to safeguard intergenerational equity—to ensure that future generations do not have to pay for government spending from which they receive no benefit. However, the accounting distinction between capital expenditure and current spending is unlikely to perfectly delineate spending that future generations do and do not benefit from. We have already noted how future generations will benefit from 'current' spending on defence during a major conflict like World War II. Future generations will also benefit from investments in their human capital via 'current spending' on education; on the other hand, they will have to fund the pensions of those who are currently employed in the provision of public services enjoyed by current generations which will not show up in government spending for years to come (Chote et al. 2008). Likewise, the focus on PSND in the sustainable investment rule partially excluded investment undertaken by the private sector in capital that is effectively rented by the government. As of mid-2004 only a little more than half of the capital value of these so-called PFI deals was recorded on the public sector's balance sheet, and under reasonable assumptions inclusion of the totality of the spending under these PFI deals would have pushed the sustainable investment rule close to breaking point by the mid-noughties (Emmerson et al. 2006).

The Golden Rule could also legitimately be accused of having been too backward looking in design, and in the process created incentives for governments to make arbitrary adjustments to the fiscal stance (Emmerson et al. 2013). Imagine for the sake of argument that there is no uncertainty about the evolution of the business cycle and it is clear that economy is fast approaching the end of the current cycle and the government is on track to just hit the Golden Rule with a current budget that is in balance on average over the soon to end cycle. If the government then learns that tax receipts are likely to disappoint over what remains of the cycle then it will have to choose between breaching the rule or temporarily raising taxes or cutting spending in order to preserve the average value of the current budget balance *over the past*.

The chief criticism of the fiscal rules over this period is that there was too much flexibility in the framework. The Code did not put in place an independent arbiter to judge whether the government was abiding by its own rules, nor were there any penalties for failing to play by the rules, other than any electoral penalty paid at the ballot box (Chote et al. 2008). A key feature of the Golden Rule was the assessment of the rule over the course of an economic cycle, rather than every year (as was the case with the sustainable investment rule), in order that the government would not have to 'balance the books' in a recession which would mean unpicking the automatic stabilisers, putting more pressure on monetary policy to stabilise the economy. However, this meant that the delicate judgements on dating the business cycle took on huge practical significance because they determined whether the surpluses in good years could be used to average out the deficits in other years. Indeed, the decision to 'rewrite history' and redefine the economic cycles on which the Golden Rule was calculated (adding two years of budget surpluses to the cycle) when it appeared that failing to have done so might have led to the rule being breached led to accusations that the government was 'moving the goalposts' (Chote et al. 2008) and sapped confidence in the framework.

With the onset of the financial crisis, the government decided to exploit the flexibility in the Code for Fiscal Stability which allowed for the rules to be temporarily suspended in exceptional circumstances. A temporary operating rule was adopted in their place under which the government was obliged (HM Treasury 2008)

> to set policies to improve the cyclically-adjusted current budget each year, once the economy emerges from the downturn, so it reaches balance and debt is falling as a proportion of GDP once the global shocks have worked their way through the economy in full.

A year later the government announced that it intended to pass new legislation which would impose additional constraints on the future path of fiscal policy— in order to cement faith in the sustainability of the public finances. That Fiscal Responsibility Bill would require the government to: deliver incremental year-on-year reductions in PSNB as a share of national income between 2010–11 and 2015–16; ensure that PSNB as a share of national income in 2013–14 would be no more than half its level in 2009–10; and PSND falls as a share of national income between 2014–15 and 2015–16 (Chote et al. 2010). As can be seen, these constraints make no allowance for inconvenient events in the future which might once again blow the public finances off course; although as with the pre-crisis regime, it was not clear what penalty the government would impose upon itself in the event of a failure to meet these targets.

In the event a new government was elected in the 2010 election and that brought major changes to the institutions of fiscal policy. In particular, the incoming government introduced two fiscal targets:

- *The Fiscal Mandate*: The primary target—the projection for the CACB— must be in balance or surplus by the end of a five-year forecast horizon.
- *The Supplementary Target*: as the name suggests a secondary target— PSND—should be falling as a share of national income in 2015–16.

Both targets are forward-looking—a desirable property of any fiscal rule since debt sustainability is inherently a forward-looking concept. But coherence comes at a cost: it is impossible to be sure today whether these targets will be achieved in the future given the inherent uncertainty. Instead, an assessment must be made of the probability that the targets will be met under current policy settings based on inevitably imprecise forecasts. It should also be said that the time horizon over which both of these measures are evaluated is somewhat arbitrary. The (original) calibration of the fiscal mandate provides the Chancellor with considerable latitude, in that he or she was only required to 'balance the (cyclically adjusted current) books' over a five-year time horizon. Indeed, the design of the mandate does not exclude the possibility that consolidation is forever postponed. In theory, a Chancellor could forever fail to eliminate the deficit on the CACB but continually pledge to take (fresh) steps which would be forecast to achieve balance in the following five years. The Supplementary Target provides some comfort here in that unlike the mandate it was (originally) calibrated relative to a fixed point in time: if the government wanted PSND as a share of national income to be on a downward trend by 2015–16 then it would have to make progress on deficit reduction. The weakness of the Supplementary Target was that it had a limited shelf-life: it placed no restriction on the debt burden beyond 2015–16. Of course, the key feature of the new framework was not the calibration of the new rules but the watchdog put in place to guard them: responsibility for assessing whether these forward looking targets will be met has been contracted out to an independent authority: the OBR—of which more later.

In December 2014, the fiscal rules were revised to partially address these concerns: the Fiscal Mandate now required the CACB to be in balance by the end of the third year of the five-year forecast horizon; and, the revised Supplementary Target now required that net debt should fall between 2015–16 and 2016–17. The former removed some room to manoeuvre that existed in the original calibration of the Mandate; the latter largely reflects the fact that the government was unlikely to achieve the target (the government has been on track to miss the original Supplementary Target since the Autumn Statement of December 2012) and there remains no medium-term constraint on the debt burden, other than indirectly via control of the cyclically adjusted budget.

An additional rule was introduced earlier in 2014 which constrained spending in a particular area under a pre-determined ceiling: the 'welfare cap' (n.b., not to be confused with the 'benefits cap', which applies at the micro level to the amount an individual family is allowed to receive in benefits). The design of the welfare cap mirrors the forward-looking nature of the mandate, placing a cap on welfare spending 'in scope' (which includes all expenditure on benefits and tax credits excluding the state pension, jobseekers allowance and housing benefit for those on jobseekers allowance) over a rolling five-year forecast horizon, and subject to a small margin for (forecast) error, a government is obliged to seek parliamentary approval (to raise the cap) if its plans set it on course to breach the cap.

Following the general election in Spring 2015, the Chancellor unveiled a change in the medium-term fiscal framework. Specifically, the new mandate requires a surplus on public sector net borrowing by the end of 2019–20 and in each subsequent year, supplemented by a requirement that public sector net debt should fall as a percentage of GDP in each year to 2019–20, after which it would continue to do so if the mandate is met. His new charter encoded the principle that the government should run surpluses in 'normal times' in the fiscal mandate. Only if the UK economy was hit by a 'significant negative shock' would a future government have the latitude to run a deficit. The extent to which the rule will constrain future finance ministers depends on the definitions of 'normal times' and 'significant negative shock' and who gets to make the judgement call to suspend the requirement to run surpluses. The Charter defines a 'significant negative shock' as occurring when (real) GDP growth falls below 1 % on a rolling four-quarter-on-four-quarter basis, either in the most recent four-quarter period, during the time the assessment is being made, or growth is expected to fall below that threshold over the forecast horizon—and it is the OBR that is required to make that assessment (HMT 2015).

The implications of the OBR reaching the conclusion that the economy has been hit by a negative shock depend on the circumstances. If the economy was previously considered to be in 'normal times' and the requirement to deliver a surplus applied, then that requirement is then suspended and the government is obliged to set out a plan for how it is going to get the public finances back on an even keel (i.e., back into surplus)—a plan which should include fiscal targets that would be presented to Parliament and assessed by the OBR (HMT 2015). However, if the shock hits the economy when the requirement has already been suspended then the government is merely obliged to assess the appropriateness of the existing fiscal targets that were established when the surplus requirement was suspended.

The new mandate requires the government to deliver surpluses rather than obliging the government to simply set policy in such a way that it expects to deliver surpluses in the future. If the forecasts are evaluated on the basis of the median outlook then it follows that finance ministers can still be in compliance with a forward-looking rule even if there is little more than a 50:50 chance that the surplus will ever materialise. A finance minister that is evaluated on the basis of actual delivery is likely to set policy in such a way that there is a significantly higher probability of achieving a surplus than essentially 50:50, or put another way that there is a significant surplus on the median projection (IFS 2016). That in turn implies that fiscal policy will be structurally tighter. Whether that is a good or bad thing depends on your perspective: fiscal policy will tend to exert a larger drag on aggregate demand given a focus on delivery, which implies a slightly looser monetary stance to compensate, and hence the debt burden will tend to fall at a faster pace.

The other interesting feature of the new mandate is that it incorporates investment spending, whereas the previous rule focused on the current budget. It follows that the marginal investment project is now evaluated against the cost of raising funds through additional taxation, as opposed to through additional debt. Of course, there was already a soft constraint on debt-financed investment spending via the Supplementary Target (IFS 2016) but the new approach imposes a more binding constraint on investment irrespective of the cost of borrowing funds in capital markets to finance that investment.

As it happens, at the time of writing, the government's record was more hit than miss when it came to compliance with its own fiscal rules. The March 2016 Economic and fiscal outlook reports that the ratio of net debt to GDP was expected to rise between 2014 and 2015 (but fall thereafter) and that spending on welfare 'in scope' was expected to exceed the cap in every year of the forecast. Indeed, the pressure on the welfare budget has only grown since then, following the government's decision to reverse a planned cut in personal independence payments and to announce that there were no plans for further welfare savings over the lifetime of the Parliament in the immediate aftermath of the Budget.

15.4.2 The Stability and Growth Pact: Pre-crash Failure and Post-crash Reboot

It was clear from the outset that the creation of a monetary union would require constraints on fiscal policy at the national level, given concerns that loose fiscal policy could complicate the pursuit of price stability in the short run, weigh on economic growth in the long run, and that the usual market constraints on reckless behaviour (risk premia in fixed income and currency markets) may not arise inside a currency union (ECB 2008). A number of safeguards were put in place to encourage fiscal responsibility—in particular, the prohibition on monetary financing (discussed earlier) and 'bail-outs' of one member state by another, or the European Union itself—but this was not considered sufficient. Countries had been required to meet convergence criteria—including on the state of the public finances—in order to join the single currency, but once members those constraints no longer applied. The SGP would emerge to fill that vacuum, largely at the behest of German politicians (Heipertz and Verdun 2004), which is ironic given the part played by the German Chancellor Gerhard Schröder in 'reforming' the pact when faced with the prospect of struggling to live within the rules (Reiermann and Wiegrefe 2012). The SGP fleshed out the strictures that already existed within the Maastricht Treaty on avoiding excessive deficits. Indeed, in the words of the then Vice President of the Bundesbank (and future ECB Chief Economist) Jurgen Stark:

> the pact was, in fact, the answer to monetary union without a political union, just like a virtual European finance minister.

Unfortunately, the virtual finance minister would prove virtually powerless, as the first proper test of the framework demonstrated. The Pact famously has two arms—a preventative arm which required countries to put the public finances on an even keel, and a corrective arm which provided the incentives to correct excessive deficits (the excessive deficits procedure [EDP])—but at the core of the SGP were two rules which were inherited from the Maastricht convergence criteria:

- *Deficit Rule*: Member states were expected to target budget positions over the medium-term which were at least close to balance, which was originally understood to mean a position which would provide sufficient margin to avoid breaching the 3 % Maastricht limit under normal circumstances.
- *Debt Rule*: The ratio of government debt to national income must not exceed 60 % unless the ratio is sufficiently diminishing and approaching the target at a satisfactory pace, although breaches of the debt rule would not trigger an EDP until the Six Pack came into force (see below).

The problem with SGP was enforcement. Commission staff needed the support of the Commissioners to launch proceedings and then the Commission needed the support of a qualified majority of the national governments to take concrete action. The 'sinners' retained the right to vote and if they could win sufficient support—perhaps among those who expected to sin in the near future—then they could stymie the sanctions in the pact (Schuknecht et al. 2011).

The good fiscal work of the late 1990s started to unravel as the European economy slowed at the turn of the Millennium and countries started to run 'excessive deficits' which should have triggered consolidation or consequences under the SGP. Instead, the Pact suffered a near-death experience. The first sign of trouble was in early 2002 when the Council rejected the Commission recommendation to issue an early warning to Germany and Portugal, but the breaking point was the Council's refusal to endorse the Commission recommendation to issue 'notices' to France and Germany (the last step in the process before sanctions) and instead put the process in abeyance (Morris et al. 2006). The German Chancellor observed: 'We don't want to leave the stability pact, but we want to interpret it in an economically sensible way' and implied that the French and Italian governments felt the same way (Scally 2003). Even the Commission President railed against blind enforcement of the rules (Prodi 2002): 'enforcing the Pact inflexibly and dogmatically, regardless of changing circumstances. That is what I called – and still call – stupid'.

As a result of this painful episode the SGP underwent a series of reforms. In some respects the reforms were positive with greater specificity introduced into the framework, via country-specific 'medium-term objectives' (MTOs) built into the preventative arm. However, beyond that, the effect of the reforms was to weaken the SGP by diluting the strictness of the 3 % deficit limit and relaxing the time horizon over which countries would have to comply with the rules (Schuknecht et al. 2011). Moreover, problems remained on the implementation front: with the failure to follow through on the concerns raised by the ECB about both the state of the Greek public finances and the reliability of the data the most obvious example.

However, it would be a mistake to claim that the SGP was a complete failure. On the eve of the crisis progress was being made on the fiscal front, with almost all countries below the 3 % deficit ceiling and most countries had achieved their MTO or were close to doing so (ECB 2008). How much of the credit belongs to the SGP and how much to the macroeconomic backdrop is open to debate. Annett (2006) argues that the SGP did influence the stance of fiscal policy in a number of European countries if we are willing to shift our focus away from France, Germany and Italy. It may not be a coincidence that the SGP proved more effective beyond the high profile cases of the largest European countries; Annett argues that smaller countries may be more accustomed to (and therefore accepting of) external scrutiny and might have more to lose from non-compliance, and that countries which had experienced volatility in the past may see greater benefits in the stability that adhering to a credible external anchor can bring. Nonetheless, experiences in the crisis underscored the need for further reform to provide the necessary fiscal discipline in a monetary union, and so was born the European Semester, Six Pack, the Fiscal Compact and the Two Pack.

The European Semester, which was introduced in January 2011 (following recommendations from the Van Rompuy Task Force) articulates a formal timetable for the surveillance of economic policy. The European Semester covers three blocks of economic policy coordination: *fiscal policies*, in order to ensure sustainability of public finances and in particular compliance with the SGP; but also *structural reforms*, focusing on promoting growth and employment in line with the Europe 2020 strategy; and finally, prevention of excessive *macroeconomic imbalances*. The Semester starts in November of the previous year with the publication of the European Commission's *Annual Growth Survey*, which analyses progress and identifies key policy priorities, and the *Alert Mechanism Report*, which acts as an early warning indicator: identifying emerging trends and imbalances that could ultimately threaten individual countries or the entire currency union. In March, the Commission publishes an economic assessment for each country and in April the countries report back with specific policy proposals. The process draws to a close in the summer, with the Commission formulating country-specific recommendations in May, which are then discussed and ultimately endorsed by the Council in July.

The Six Pack, which came into force in December 2011, strengthened both the preventative and corrective arms of the SGP: it defines a significant deviation from the MTO and an adjustment towards it; it allows for the launch of an EDP given a failure to comply with the debt criteria; it codified the graduated system of penalties for non-compliance up to a limit of 0.5 % GDP for members of the single currency; and last and most important of all, the Six Pack introduced reverse qualified majority voting for decisions on the application of those sanctions for euro area countries, making it harder for sinners and soon-to-be sinners to block penalties (de Haan et al. 2013).

The Fiscal Compact came into effect as part of the Treaty on Stability, Coordination and Governance, which was signed by 25 of the member states of the European Union (but not the UK), and was only binding for members of the single currency. The Fiscal Compact required countries to write stringent fiscal rules into legislation at the national level (in a 'binding' and 'permanent' way) and those who failed to do so were potentially subject to fines (0.1 % GDP). Those rules would demand convergence towards the country-specific MTO, with a floor on the structural deficit of 0.5 % of GDP (and 1.0 % of GDP for those with a debt ratio significantly below 60 % of GDP). Critically, the Fiscal Compact required an automatic response to fiscal slippage (i.e., a deviation from the MTO or the adjustment path towards it) with escape clauses only for exceptional circumstances. Importantly, compliance with the rule should be monitored at the national level by independent institutions—another example of the increased importance attached to fiscal councils.

Finally, the Two Pack is a couple of regulations which were based on Commission proposals published in November 2011 which related to the annual budget process and surveillance. In terms of the regulation on the budget, the Two Pack seeks to establish a common timeline, with Eurozone countries publishing their medium-term plans and their draft budget by end-April and mid-October, respectively, and then passing the budget by end-December. The Commission has the power to request revised plans for countries deemed to be in 'particularly serious non-compliance' within weeks of submission, and has enhanced responsibilities for monitoring countries subject to an EDP, including requesting an independent audit of the general government accounts (ECB 2013). Turning to the second regulation, the Commission has the *option* to escalate the surveillance process where countries are experiencing, or are at risk of experiencing, financial instability which could have wider repercussions for other members of the single currency, and must escalate if a country is in receipt of financial assistance from the IMF or the European rescue funds (the European Financial Stability Facility or the European Stability Mechanism).

The European fiscal framework can be boiled down to a small number of (relatively) simple rules: budget deficits should be below 3 percent of GDP; gross public debt should be below 60 percent of GDP, and if it is not then 1/20 th of the gap should be closed each year; the structural budget balance should be greater than a country-specific medium-term objective (MTO), and if it is not then the structural balance should increase each year by 0.5 percent of GDP; and real government spending should not grow faster than trend growth in potential supply, and spending should grow at a slower rate than supply for countries where the structural balance does not satisfy the MTO (Claeys et al. 2016).

There is one small problem, those rules have threatened to constrain behaviour, often in depressed economies within the currency union where fiscal consolidation is perceived to be economically and politically costly. Exceptions and over-rides have been incorporated into the rules, with the Commission playing a pivotal role in assessing how much flexibility can be applied in interpreting the rules in any given situation. For example, countries may deviate from the required adjustment path towards their MTO if they embark on major structural reforms that should deliver long-term benefits on the public finances (ECB 2015). However, the guardians of Europe's fiscal rules still face formidable obstacles in enforcing prudence. Like many of their peers they face the challenge of trying to bolt the fiscal door long after the horse bolted. However, unlike their peers, they know that individual countries cannot count on monetary easing to counteract the contractionary impact of fiscal consolidation: sticking to the rules will hurt. Moreover, the constraints on policy are inherently more politically contentious because they are a supra-national construct that is monitored and enforced by 'alien' political institutions.

15.5 Fiscal Councils

As has already been alluded to above, the latest policy innovation in the fiscal realm has been the emergence of fiscal councils. In 1960, only one country (the Netherlands) had an active fiscal council and in the three decades that followed that number rose to five; however, after 2005, the number of fiscal councils rose sharply to 29 by early 2013 (IMF 2013) and there is considerable diversity in the size and scope of those institutions (Calmfors and Wren-Lewis 2011).

A number of academics had long advocated delegating some element of the budgetary process to an independent body (see among others, Wren-Lewis 1996; Calmfors 2003; Wyplosz 2005) as a partial solution to the problems outlined above. Delegation to independent experts is a familiar solution to evidence of a chronic failure of the political process to deliver good outcomes in a particular area. As Wyplosz (2008) notes, these examples—ranging from the judicial system to the regulation of banks to the determination of the national minimum wage—tend to share several common features: the institutions are given a precise mandate; some judgement is involved in the process; those taking decisions are experts in the field; decision-makers are granted operational independence; and typically, the decision-makers are accountable to elected officials.

The brief history of fiscal rules in the UK and the European Union illustrated the potential role for fiscal councils: to prevent finance ministers from marking their own homework, and systematically taking decisions about the stance of policy and compliance with the rules based on an overly optimistic assessment of the current state and future evolution of the economy and the public finances. Indeed, there are a large number of roles that fiscal councils can fulfil: ex ante evaluation of whether fiscal policy is likely to meet its targets; ex post evaluation of whether it has done so; analysis of long-run sustainability and optimality of policy; analysis of transparency in the conduct of policy; costings of various government proposals; macroeconomic forecasting; and even normative recommendations (Calmfors and Wren-Lewis 2011). Cutting to the chase, a useful high-level distinction can be drawn between two variants of fiscal council (Wyplosz 2005):

- *Soft fiscal councils*: In all but name, a lobby group for fiscal discipline—the soft fiscal council acts as an advisor, making public recommendations about the optimal path for the fiscal stance, but takes no decisions.
- *Hard fiscal councils*: A decision-making body which sets the overall fiscal stance. As per the constrained discretion that central banks enjoy, the hard fiscal council would have the latitude to adjust the aggregate fiscal stance in

response to shocks, rather than being compelled to deliver a particular outcome at a particular point in time—or what could be described as flexible fiscal discipline targeting.

The idea of an unelected hard fiscal council imposing a fiscal stance upon the elected representatives of the people may seem anathema but it is important to note that Wyplosz is not recommending that the hard council would take the line by line decisions on tax and spend which are inherently political. Instead, the hard council is setting the overall budget envelope to prevent intergenerational transfers and protect future generations who do not get to vote on the current fiscal stance.

In the monetary policy realm, delegation to an independent institution which enjoys 'constrained discretion' in the conduct of policy is widely believed to be superior to slavish devotion to a rule. In other words, delegation to an (operationally) independent institution is seen as a substitute for setting policy by a rule. In contrast, fiscal councils and fiscal rules are viewed more as complements than substitutes; neither rules nor institutions are necessary nor sufficient conditions for fiscal discipline, but both working in tandem, with institutions given the authority to apply legal rules, could prove powerful (Wyplosz 2013).

The key issue for fiscal councils is their independence. Fiscal rules are at least transparent: they can be relied upon to always give the same output given the same inputs and it should be relatively easy to detect whether the government has deviated from the rule. Sceptics may worry that a fiscal council could be 'lent on' by the government to massage its analysis and public recommendations. There are a number of ways in which the independence of fiscal councils can be enshrined in law (IMF 2013): banning public officials from giving instructions to the council; a transparent selection process for the membership of the council based on merit; long and non-renewable terms of office; and a clear dismissal process to avoid the Thomas Becket problem ('*will no-one rid me of this turbulent fiscal council?*'). Questions of independence naturally lead to the issue of who should serve on these councils. Calmfors and Wren-Lewis (2011) identify four generic members: academics; experts on the public finances drawn from within the civil service; professional economists; and former politicians (current politicians are obviously not ideal candidates for such a role).

A secondary issue is resourcing: governments might be able to stymie the best intentions of an independent fiscal council by starving the institution of resources. It will be difficult for the senior management of the council to piece together an accurate assessment of the state of the public finances and the appropriate fiscal stance without access to detailed information—and in particular raw data that has not been filtered by the government 'machine'—and analytical support (IMF 2013).

15.6 The Office for Budget Responsibility

The UK's fiscal council, the OBR, was initially established in interim form in May 2010. The key decision making body within the OBR is the Budget Responsibility Committee (BRC), which has executive responsibility for performing the core functions of the OBR, and in particular making the key judgements which drive the OBR forecasts. Sir Alan Budd served as midwife for the OBR—a chairman who miraculously managed to meet almost all of the Calmfors and Wren-Lewis' criteria for membership of a fiscal council (Budd was a former academic, Chief Economic Advisor to the Treasury, member of the MPC and Economic Advisor at a financial institution)—but would soon be succeeded by Robert Chote, a former director of the IFS.

The Budget Responsibility and National Audit Act 2011 put the OBR on a formal footing, identifying the key purpose of the now statutory body as 'to examine and report on the sustainability of the public finances'. As Chote (2013) explains the OBR has four key duties in pursuit of that overarching aim:

(i) *Holding the pen on the official forecasts*: The OBR is responsible for producing the official forecasts for the macroeconomic outlook and the public finances which the Chancellor is required to publish twice each year in the Budget and Autumn Statement.

(ii) *Judge and jury at the macro level*: The OBR is required to assess whether the Government is more likely than not to comply with its own rules.

(iii) *Line-by-line scrutiny at the micro level*: The OBR is asked to make a call on the fiscal implications of every tax and spending measure which is announced in the Budget or Autumn Statement: to accept or reject the Treasury's estimate of the cost (or savings) or announce that it did not have sufficient time or evidence to make an informed decision.

(iv) *Assess sustainability*: The OBR publishes analysis of the state of the public finances in the long run based on 50-year projections.

And given the evolution of the fiscal rules since the creation of the OBR, a fifth duty has emerged:

(v) *Welfare watchdog*: The OBR monitors the government's performance against the welfare cap, publishing analysis of the evolution of welfare spending in an annual *report*.

There is much to recommend this remit: ownership of the forecasts and assessment of the rules being contracted out to an independent authority; a probabilistic assessment of the outlook; a focus on the long run, which where fiscal policy is concerned is almost surely more important than the level of borrowing in the near term; and scrutiny of the merits of individual measures. However, there are legitimate questions to be asked about the wisdom of using a 'better than 50% chance' benchmark to assess compliance with the fiscal rules.

There are three standard measures of the central tendency of a distribution: the mode, the median and the mean. The mode is the single most likely outcome, the median is the middling outcome when those outcomes are ranked in order, and the mean is the average outcome. The problem with a median-based criteria of fiscal discipline is that it lacks the simplicity of a criteria based on the mode, in that to calculate the median you need to know all possible outcomes in order to rank them, and it lacks the sophistication of a mean-based criteria, in that the absolute values of all other possible outcomes (aside from the median) are irrelevant, other than to rank those different outcomes.

To fix ideas, imagine a set of forecasts which suggested that there was a 60 % probability that the structural current budget would be marginally in surplus three years from now, but there was a 40 % probability that there would be a very large deficit. The mode and the median of that skewed distribution for the CACB would both be a small surplus; the mean would show a deficit. Surely, two key lessons learned from the crisis in the economic policy sphere are that we cannot assume the distribution of possible outcomes is well behaved—that is, symmetric, in which case the mode, median and mean are all the same—and policymakers should at the very least think about adjusting the stance of policy today to take account of the consequences of low risk-high impact risks crystallising. The 'better than 50 % chance' benchmark does not encourage the Chancellor to do that. However, this weakness is compensated by the analysis which the OBR provides around its central case forecasts which describe outcomes and compliance with the rules in off-central case scenarios.

When it comes to the critical issue of the degree of independence that a fiscal council enjoys, the OBR has been granted complete discretion in the pursuit of its duties, so long as it does so objectively, transparently and impartially. Indeed, the Charter for Budget Responsibility makes clear that the OBR's independence stretches as far as discretion over: the methodology by which the OBR produces its forecasts, assessments and analyses; the judgments made in developing these forecasts; the content of OBR publications, which are completely at the discretion of the OBR (subject to fulfilling the minimum requirements contained within the Act and this Charter); and the OBR's work programme. However, the Charter also makes clear that 'the OBR should not provide normative commentary on the particular merits of Government policies'—that is, it should stick to the positive economics ('what is'), and avoid making value judgements ('what should be').

The OBR has a relatively small permanent staff (of around 20 people) comparable to a single division in one of the BoE's directorates, and that means that the BRC will always be dependent on the civil service for information and analysis in order to reach an informed assessment of the state of the public finances. The OBR's access to information is enshrined in the Act, the Charter and the Memorandum of Understanding between the OBR and the government departments on which it depends: HMT, HM Revenue and Customs (HMRC) and the Department for Work and Pensions (DWP). The OBR has a statutory right to full and timely access to all Government information relevant to its analysis, and can request any information—including macroeconomic models and forecasts as well as data—and assistance in understanding it from HMT, HMRC and DWP (with the exception of confidential information regarding taxpayers and benefit claimants). The current Chairman has made clear that he would make his concerns public if he felt that the OBR was being starved of necessary information and assistance (Chote 2013).

Finally, on the accountability front, the OBR places a huge amount of information into the public domain, from its flagship publications to more detailed analytical reports and working papers and briefing papers, and is typically called to give evidence to the Treasury Select Committee (TSC) around the time of the Budget and the Autumn Statement. Moreover, the TSC has a veto over the appointment of individuals to, and their removal from, the BRC.

Has the OBR made a difference? There is a temptation to try and answer this question with the only tangible metric we have at our disposal: the accuracy of the OBR's forecasts relative to its peers. But from the author's perspective at least, that would be a mistake given the uncertainty attached to any point forecast of the future. The value added is surely in the institutional safeguards against deficit bias, and the quality of the commentary around complex issues of fiscal risks and debt sustainability (Besley 2010), where the OBR has already made a positive contribution.

References

Abel, A., Mankiw, N., Summers, L., & Zeckhauser, R. (1989). Assessing dynamic efficiency: Theory and evidence. *Review of Economic Studies, 56*(1), 1–19.

Abrams, B. (2006). How Richard Nixon pressured Arthur Burns. *Journal of Economic Perspectives, 20*(4), 177–188.

Aiyagari, S., & McGrattan, E. (1998). The optimum quantity of debt. *Journal of Monetary Economics, 42*(3), 447–469.

Alesina, A., & Tabellini, G. (1990). A positive theory of fiscal deficits and government debt. *Review of Economic Studies, 57*(3), 403–414.

Annett, A. (2006). *Enforcement and the stability and growth pact*. IMF Working Paper 06/116.

Anrig, G. (2010, January 26). "Strategic deficit" redux. *Prospect*.

Barro, R. (1974). Are government bonds net wealth. *Journal of Political Economy, 82*, 1095–1117.

Besley, T. (2010, September 21). Evidence to the Treasury Select Committee.

Buiter, W. (1983). The theory of optimum deficits and debt. In *The Economics of Large Government Deficits*, Federal Reserve Bank of Boston, Conference Series 27, 4–69.

Buiter, W. (1998). *Notes on "A Code for Financial Stability"*. NBER Working Paper 6522.

Calmfors, L. (2003). Fiscal policy to stabilise the domestic economy in the EMU? *CESifo Economic Studies, 49*, 319–353.

Calmfors, L., & Wren-Lewis, S. (2011). What should fiscal councils do? *Economic Policy, 26*, 649–695.

Chamley, C. (1985). Efficient taxation in a stylised model of general equilibrium. *International Economic Review, 26*, 451–468.

Chamley, C. (1986). Optimal taxation of capital income in general equilibrium with infinite lives. *Econometrica, 54*(3), 607–622.

Chote, R. (2013, May 9). *Britain's fiscal watchdog*. Speech.

Chote, R., Emmerson, C., & Tetlow, G. (2008). *The fiscal rules and policy framework*. IFS Green Budget.

Chote, R., Emmerson, C., Sibieta, L., & Tetlow, G. (2010). *Reforming UK fiscal institutions*. IFS Green Budget.

Claeys, G., Zsolt, D., & Leandro, A. (2016). A proposal to revive the European Fiscal Framework, Bruegel Policy Contribution, 2016/07.

Cukierman, A., & Tommasi, M. (1998). When does it take a Nixon to go to China? *American Economic Review, 88*(1), 180–197.

de Haan, J., Gilbert, N., Hessel, J., & Verkaart, S. (2013). How to enforce fiscal discipline in EMU. *Swiss Journal of Economics and Statistics, 149*(2), 205–217.

Diamond, P. (1965). National debt in a neoclassical growth model. *American Economic Review, 55*(5), 1126–1150.

Draghi, M. (2015, December 4). Remarks made at the Economic Club of New York.

ECB. (2008, October). Ten years of the Stability and Growth Pact. *Monthly Bulletin*.

ECB. (2013). The "Two-Pack" regulations to strengthen economic governance in the euro area. *Monthly Bulletin, April*, 53–55.

ECB. (2015). Flexibility within the stability and growth pact. *Economic Bulletin, 1*, 33–35.

Emmerson, C., Frayne, C., & Love, S. (2006). *The government's fiscal rules*. IFS Briefing Note 16.

Emmerson, C., Keynes, S., & Tetlow, G. (2013). *The fiscal targets*. IFS Green Budget.

Fabrizio, S., & Mody, A. (2008). *Breaking the impediments to budgetary reforms*. IMF Working Paper 08/82.

Heipertz, M., & Verdun, A. (2004). The dog that would never bite? *Journal of European Public Policy, 11*(5), 765–780.

HMT. (2008). The Government's fiscal framework.

HMT. (2015). Charter for Budget Responsibility, Summer Budget 2015 update.

IFS. (2016). The IFS Green Budget.

IMF. (2013). *The functions and impact of fiscal councils.* Policy Paper.

Judd, K. (1985). Redistributive taxation in a simple perfect foresight model. *Journal of Public Economics, 28*, 59–83.

Kopits, G. (2001). 'Fiscal rules: Useful policy framework or unnecessary ornament. IMF Working Paper 01/145.

Kopits, G., & Symansky, G. (1998). *Fiscal policy rules.* IMF Occasional Paper 162.

Krogstrup, S., & Wyplosz, C. (2006). *A common pool theory of deficit bias correction.* CEPR Discussion Paper 5866.

Kydland, F., & Prescott, E. (1977). Rules rather than discretion: The inconsistency of optimal plans. *Journal of Political Economy, 85*(3), 473–491.

Laibson, D. (1997). Golden eggs and hyperbolic discounting. *Quarterly Journal of Economics, 112*(3), 443–447.

Maloney, J., Pickering, A., & Hadri, K. (2003). Political business cycles and central bank independence. *Economic Journal, 113*, C167–C181.

Morris, R., Ongena, H., & Schuknecht, L. (2006). *The reform and implementation of the stability and growth pact.* ECB Occasional Paper 47.

Musgrave, R. (1988). Public debt and intergenerational equity. In K. Arrow & M. Boskin (Eds.), *The economics of public debt.* London: Macmillan.

Nordhaus, W. (1975). The political business cycle. *Review of Economic Studies, 42*, 169–190.

Prodi, R. (2002, October 21). *A stronger, better stability and growth pact.* Speech.

Reiermann, C., & Wiegrefe, K. (2012, July 16). Chancellor Schröder's Legacy: Germany's leading role in weakening the euro. *Spiegel.*

Reinhart, C., & Rogoff, K. (2010). Growth in a time of debt. *American Economic Review: Papers and Proceedings, 100*, 573–578.

Robinson, M. (1998). Measuring compliance with the golden rule. *Fiscal Studies, 19*(4), 447–462.

Rodrik, D. (1996). Understanding economic policy reform. *Journal of Economic Literature, 34*, 9–41.

Rogoff, K. (1988). Comment. In S. Fischer (Ed.), *NBER Macroeconomics Annual.* Cambridge, MA: MIT Press.

Rogoff, K. (1990). Equilibrium political budget cycles. *American Economic Review, 80*, 21–36.

Scally, D. (2003, August 30). Germany's budget deficit to breach EU guidelines again. *The Irish Times.*

Schaechter, A., Kinda, T., Budina, N., & Weber, A. (2012). *Fiscal rules in response to the crisis.* IMF Working Paper 12/187.

Schmitt-Grohe, S., & Uribe, M. (2004). Optimal monetary and fiscal policy under sticky prices. *Journal of Economic Theory, 114*, 198–230.

Schuknecht, L., Moutot, P., Rother, P., & Stark, J. (2011). *The stability and growth pact*. ECB Occasional Paper 129.

Stiglitz, J. (1988). *On the relevance or irrelevance of public financial policy*. In *The economics of public debt*. Proceedings of the 1986 International Economic Association Meeting, MacMillan Press, 4–76.

Velasco, A. (2000). Debts and deficits with fragmented fiscal policymaking. *Journal of Public Economics, 76*(1), 105–125.

Von Hagen, J., & Harden, I. (1995). Budget processes and commitment to fiscal discipline. *European Economic Review, 39*(3), 771–779.

Wren-Lewis, S. (1996). Avoiding fiscal fudge. *New Economy, 3*, 128–132.

Wyplosz, C. (2005). Fiscal policy: Institutions versus rules. *National Institute Economic Review, 191*, 70–84.

Wyplosz, C. (2008). Fiscal policy councils: Unloveable or just unloved? *Swedish Economic Policy Review, 13*, 173–192.

Wyplosz, C. (2013). Fiscal rules. In A. Alesina & F. Giavazzi (Eds.), *Fiscal policy after the financial crisis*. Chicago: University of Chicago Press.

Afterword

This book was originally conceived as two quarters of a single volume on the conduct of economic policy in the UK in the aftermath of the financial crisis. Once writing began in earnest it soon became clear that the word limit of the publisher could not accommodate the lofty ambitions of the author given his inability to explain himself concisely. One book became two, and two almost became four. The separation of the material in the original manuscript between the familiar disciplines of monetary and fiscal policy in one volume and the less familiar world of regulatory policy on the other was the obvious choice to make. However, one downside of the divorce is that it is harder to draw together the threads of related arguments in debates that span policy arenas. This afterword is intended to compensate for that shortcoming, to highlight the key conjectures and conclusions from this crash course in post-crash economic policy.

The art of macroeconomic policy is often illustrated to budding economists through the analogy of an engineer optimising a mechanical system. Unfortunately, the student is left with the impression of an omnipotent policymaker who can insulate the economy from the simple shocks that supposedly destabilise the system with a deft calibration of the policy levers at her disposal. For example, in that perfect world we would observe variation in Bank Rate as the Monetary Policy Committee (MPC) responds to the classic business cycle shocks to demand but no variation whatsoever in inflation. The implicit lesson learned—that policymakers can solve all problems—is problematic.

There are limits to what even omniscient policymakers can do to stabilise the economy in the face of shocks with the levers at her disposal. Even with

© The Editor(s) (if applicable) and The Author(s) 2016
R. Barwell, *Macroeconomic Policy after the Crash*,
DOI 10.1057/978-1-137-51592-6

complete information about the underlying structure of the economy and its current state, our policymaker is still dealing with tools that influence the economy with a lag and there may be practical or legal constraints on the extent to which those tools can be deployed. In reality, policymakers have an incomplete understanding of the structure and state of the economy and that further complicates the calibration of the policy response. In particular, uncertainty about the impact of policy interventions will tend to temper the ambitions of the policymaker, driving us further from the idealised policy outcome. In short, it is unreasonable to expect policymakers to smooth out all the shocks in even a relatively stable macroeconomic environment. But of course, the post-crash environment was anything but stable.

The post-crash generation of policymakers found themselves operating in far more challenging circumstances than their predecessors. Policymakers had a smaller body of theory and evidence to fall back on to help them explain the current behaviour of the economy, to forecast its future evolution and to calibrate their use of unconventional tools (and the impact of unconventional tools used by others). Moreover, the scale of the problem was far greater than anything that most of their predecessors had been required to grapple with, and perhaps that only became clear with the passage of time and the failure of the initial treatment to achieve the desired results. To further complicate matters, it was far from clear that the default assumption that the economy was currently experiencing a standard (albeit seismic) cyclical deviation around a fixed steady state was still valid. The crisis appears to have done lasting damage to the level of, and perhaps even the growth rate of, productivity. The real interest rate(s) that clears the market(s) for loanable funds appears to have fallen. Through boom and bust, financial imbalances have built up in the public and private sectors, changing behaviour (e.g., reducing the sensitivity of spending to interest rates) in ways that are not easily captured in a traditional framework that linked flows (of income, output and expenditure) to prices.

In short, an objective assessment of the conduct of policy during this period must be based on realistic expectations of what policymakers could achieve under the circumstances. But that assessment must also reflect the objectives of those policymakers, and the extent to which they were compatible.

There was an inevitable and uncomfortable tension between the post-crash goals of the different policy regimes. Measures to repair strained balance sheets in the public and banking sectors are not conducive to kick-starting a rapid and robust recovery in demand. Whether those conflicting objectives ended up having an impact on the level of output or employment comes down to whether you believe that unconventional monetary policy (in particular, quantitative easing) is a crude substitute for conventional monetary easing at the lower bound. That is, the debate about the appropriate conduct of policy hinges on the question of whether central banks could still achieve their price stability mandates even if fiscal and prudential policymakers exacerbated the downturn in aggregate demand through the pursuit of a balance sheet repair agenda.

Much of the public debate around the appropriate conduct of post-crash macro-policy answers that critical question by assumption—monetary policy was impotent at the lower bound—although, sadly, it was not always explicit that this (strong) assumption was even being made, let alone justified. Moreover, even if this assumption was valid it is still far from clear what we should infer about the post-crash stance of policy for three reasons.

First, the policy prescription that is the logical conclusion of the *assumption* that monetary policy is somewhat ineffective at the lower bound is a *relative* one: that the fiscal stance should be looser than might otherwise be considered appropriate because fiscal stimulus is more potent once interest rates reach the lower bound. This (fragile) conclusion should not be confused with the absolute statement that fiscal policy should have been looser than it actually was. In order to make the latter statement we would first need to acknowledge that the fiscal authority was running a large structural deficit and second we would have to reflect on the behaviour of inflation during this period and the scope for additional macro-stimulus.

Second, the conclusion reflects a debate that is fixated on the conventional levers of macro-policy and the optimal fiscal—monetary mix to the exclusion of the consequences of changes in the stance of prudential policy which was also important from a macroeconomic perspective during this period. In theory, one could presumably argue (although the author would not) that it was prudential policy rather than fiscal policy that was 'too tight'—that it was the transition to the new regulatory state that was the policy straw that broke the monetary camel's back, exerting too great a drag on demand via the contraction in the supply of bank credit for monetary policy to handle. Under this (to my mind, flawed) argument, it would have been better to introduce reforms to increase the resilience of the banking sector at a more leisurely pace whilst pressing ahead with austerity, perhaps at an even faster rate than finance ministers were able to deliver.

Third, even if it was the case that with the benefit of hindsight central banks could not close the output gap at a satisfactory pace given the fiscal and prudential direction of travel it does not follow that the policy mix was flawed. The acid test of the policy mix is certainly not the modal forecast for the level of output or the output gap.

For a start, policymakers will care about the balance of risks around the outlook. Even if the near-term path of output was the only thing that the social planner cared about, it seems near certain that she would at the very least set policy on the basis of the mean rather the modal path of output given uncertainty about the economic system she is trying to optimise. She might even take a conservative approach and set policy such that even in the worst case scenario the level of output is not so bad. If finance ministers thought that there was a small risk of a very bad outcome in the future (e.g. a genuine fiscal crisis) if they spent more or taxed less, then it might make sense to submit to austerity even if they expected it would probably hurt.

Furthermore, the near-term profile of output is not the only thing that the social planner cares about. The fiscal authority cares about getting the debt burden down today in order to create greater space to support the economy in the (far) future with fiscal stimulus in the event of another crisis. The prudential authority cares about getting leverage down today in order to reduce the likelihood that the economy suffers another financial crisis in the future. Lower output today might be a perfectly acceptable price worth paying in order to manage these medium-term risks.

If macroeconomics and macroeconomists are for anything it is to provide serious answers to serious questions about the optimal policy mix which in turn demand serious analysis which recognises our uncertainty about the structure of the economy and the complex objectives of policymakers. Simple answers based on the assumptions that particular policy levers are totally ineffective, developments in certain policy arena are irrelevant, that all that matters is the near-term profile of gross domestic product (GDP) and that the structure of the economy is known with certainty is strictly for the birds.

This brings us to another key lesson learned: the importance of clearly articulating the objectives of the respective policy regimes. For example, part of the problem with the public debate about the conduct of fiscal policy during this period was the failure to evaluate decisions and outcomes according to the goals of a modern fiscal authority: stabilising the economy in response to business cycle shocks is a peripheral part of the fiscal agenda.

The task of articulating objectives falls first and foremost to the politicians and, above all, to finance ministers. They could make a start by putting their own house in order and providing greater clarity around the calculus that guides the conduct of fiscal policy. There are age-old debates about how finance ministers should weigh outcomes for different individuals in the population or navigate the trade-off between improving equity and efficiency. At present, actions scream louder than whispered words. The current fiscal mandate requires surpluses on headline borrowing in 'normal times' which seemingly subordinates the pursuit of efficiency to the intermediate objective of reducing the debt burden at least at the margin: the balance between current income and expenditure could override the long run cost-benefit analysis that should guide the decision to invest in infrastructure.

One might think that little more needs to be said about the objectives of monetary policy but there is still considerable ambiguity around the preferences that guide decision-making—for example, around the relative importance attached to deviations of aggregate demand and inflation around the level of aggregate supply and inflation, respectively, and how the implied loss varies according to the size and sign of the deviation. As the former deputy governor of the Sveriges Riksbank (the Swedish central bank) and academic expert Lars Svensson has long argued, central bankers should be more transparent about the (monetary policy) loss function.

The real concern about objectives lies in the prudential domain. There is a worrying lack of clarity about the remit of the micro- and macroprudential regimes which most central bankers would likely consider unacceptable in the monetary domain. If micro- and macroprudential policymakers do not know what they are trying to achieve, it is hard to see how they can be expected to deliver an outcome in the ballpark of optimal, or how they can be held to account for their decisions by elected officials. Telling the FPC to set macroprudential policy in order to avoid another systemic financial crisis is on a par with telling the MPC to set monetary policy in order to avoid hyperinflation.

None of the above should be confused with a defence of the particular mix of monetary, fiscal and prudential policy that was chosen by the coalition government in 2010. Rather I am making a case for an analysis that is rooted in a rational assessment of the objectives and constraints under which policymakers operate. For example, a coherent critique of post-crash fiscal policy might have relatively little to say about the pace of consolidation and would instead focus intently on the design of the consolidation strategy: Could the government have delivered the same pace of deficit reduction whilst doing less damage to the supply side and imposing a smaller burden on those least able to pay? Moreover, it is critically important that the policy debate is rooted in general equilibrium analysis. For example, it might be true that sovereign states which have retained control over the printing press do not need to formally default on debt and are therefore not at risk of a fiscal crisis but that does not mean that servicing debt by printing money is a fiscal-free lunch, a pain-free solution to a debt problem.

Another common thread running through these two volumes is the rapid pace of institutional reform in the economic policy arena. In particular, the Bank of England has accumulated significant new powers and responsibilities since the crash, with the governor established as the apex policymaker. Whether the current arrangements are optimal is unclear: the single-peaked solution may ease policy coordination but it also has its downsides. First, there is a heightened risk of groupthink: that is, a single view of the world dominates the conduct of economic policy, leaving the system more exposed to risks that are not captured by that view of the world. Second, there is a risk of overreach: it is debatable whether any one institution can master so many complex policy briefs. Third, there are risks to the central bank's reputation for competence if there is a major failure in any policy regime, and that could have serious consequences: a central bank shorn of its reputation for competence may find it harder to stabilise the system in a crisis. Fourth, there will likely be a temptation inside the central bank, and pressure from the outside, to blur the lines between these policy regimes—to use the instruments of multiple regimes in pursuit of the objective of one—a concern which is already being raised by some central bank governors within the Eurozone.

The institutional reforms have not been confined to the world of central banking. The fiscal crisis that has afflicted sovereigns to varying degrees since the crash has reinvigorated the debate over the role for institutional constraints on the conduct of fiscal policy. The pre-crisis regime was far from an unqualified success, and the post-crisis reforms show signs of promise. However, as this book went to press the OBR's latest EFO publication was reporting one hit and two misses on the government's fiscal targets. Questions remain around the value of rules that finance ministers do not have to abide by.

The lessons learned in the crisis have also raised serious questions about the interaction of the macroeconomic policy regimes.

There is a broad consensus that the equilibrium real interest rate has declined, that the world is less stable than we thought during the so-called Great Moderation and that unconventional monetary stimulus is not a perfect substitute for conventional rate cuts. It would appear that central banks will hit the lower bound more often in the future that we anticipated before the crash when the current inflation target was chosen. Many economists have therefore concluded that the inflation target needs to rise or the institutional constraints which prevent central banks cutting rates deep into negative territory need to be removed to manage this problem. However, a more demanding micro- and macroprudential regime ought to deliver a more resilient economic system, in which the large negative shocks which drive interest rates to the lower bound occur less often. A structurally tighter prudential regime may therefore reduce the need to move the nominal anchor and should reduce the precautionary motive of the fiscal authority to run with low levels of government debt in normal times to provide the capacity to deploy fiscal firepower in a future crisis.

Both options involve costs: higher inflation on the one hand, tighter credit conditions on the other. A rigorous cost benefit analysis is required to calibrate the new steady state.

Likewise, the calibration of the prudential regimes—the tolerance of the authorities to financial crises—should reflect the capacity of the fiscal and monetary authorities to mop up afterwards and the fundamental structure of the economy. If the inflation target is raised to create more scope to cut nominal interest rates in a crisis, if a credible fiscal regime delivers sound public finances with the capacity to increase spending in a crisis and, whilst we are at it, if structural reforms deliver a more flexible economy that can better cope with infrequent but severe shocks then perhaps it is safe to operate with a less draconian regulatory regime. Otherwise, the authorities may wish to re-examine whether the post-crisis reform agenda has achieved a sufficiently prudent level of resilience.

Perhaps the final lesson learned is hubris. The crisis has revealed how little we know about how the macroeconomy and financial system behave, particularly when subject to large shocks. The economic policy debate had become increasingly dominated by a particular view of how the system behaved which effectively relegated financial instability to the dustbin of economic history by assumption—ironically just as a spectacular episode of instability was about to flare up. Analysis of credit flows, debt stocks and asset price bubbles had become distinctly unfashionable. Our collective post-crash moment of clarity should have profound implications for the conduct of policy in fair weather as well as foul. One would imagine economists in policy institutions—and ideally in academia too—will spend a lot more time thinking about the more neglected areas of macroeconomics and finance. Future generations of policy-makers in the monetary and fiscal sphere are likely to spend a little more time focusing on a risk management approach, modelling macro outcomes whilst respecting heterogeneity and without assuming rationality, thinking about the likelihood and potential severity of tail risks on the horizon and how best to avoid and/or prepare for them, and a little less time on fine-tuning the central case outlook. That way we might avoid another crisis on the scale that prompted me to write this book.

References

Acharya, V., & Rajan, R. (2013). Sovereign debt, government myopia and the financial sector. *Review of Financial Studies, 26*(6), 1526–1560.

Adam, S., & Browne, J. (2013). *Do the UK Government's welfare reforms make work pay?*. IFS Working Paper 13/26.

Aghion, P., & Saint-Paul, G. (1993). *Uncovering some causal relationships between productivity growth and the structure of economic fluctuations: A tentative survey.* NBER Working Paper 4603.

Alesina, A., & Roubini, N. (1992). Political cycles in OECD countries. *Review of Economic Studies, 59*(4), 663–688.

Barr, N. (2010). *Paying for higher education*. Submission to the Independent Review of Higher Education Funding and Student Finance.

Barry, F., & Devereux, M. (2003). Expansionary fiscal contraction: A theoretical exploration. *Journal of Macroeconomics, 25*, 1–23.

Barwell, R., & Burrows, O. (2013). *Growing fragilities? Balance sheets in the great moderation*. Bank of England Financial Stability Paper 10.

Barwell, R., & Chadha, J. (2013a). Turning forward guidance into 20:20 vision. *Central Banking Journal*, September.

Bean, C. (2011, November 3). *The economic outlook*. Speech.

Belfield, C., Chandler, D., & Joyce, R. (2015). *Housing*. IFS Briefing Note 161.

Berglöf, E., & Gérard, R. (1997). Soft budget constraints and credit crunch in financial transition. *European Economic Review, 41*, 807–817.

Bernanke, B. (1999, January 9). *Japanese monetary policy: A case of self-induced paralysis*. Paper presented to the ASSA meeting.

Bernheim, B. (1989). A neoclassical perspective on budget deficits. *Journal of Economic Perspectives, 3*(2), 55–72.

Bertola, G., & Rogerson, R. (1997). Institutions and labor reallocation. *European Economic Review, 41*(6), 1147–1171.

Blanchard, O., & Giavazzi, F. (2003). Macroeconomic effects of regulation and deregulation in goods and labour markets. *Quarterly Journal of Economics, 118,* 879–907.

Blinder, A., & Solow, R. (1973). Does fiscal policy matter? *Journal of Public Economics, 2*(4), 319–337.

Bloom, N. (2014). Fluctuations in uncertainty. *Journal of Economic Perspectives, 28*(2), 153–176.

BoE. (2011). Minutes of the January 2011 meeting of the Monetary Policy Committee.

Brewer, M., Browne, J., & Wenchao, J. (2011). *Universal credit: A preliminary analysis.* IFS Briefing Note 116.

Browne, J., & Roantree, B. (2013). *Universal Credit in Northern Ireland.* IFS Report R77.

Brynjolfsson, E., & McAfee, A. (2013). *The second machine age: Work, progress and prosperity in a time of brilliant technologies.* New York: Norton.

Buiter, W. (1977). Crowding out and the effectiveness of fiscal policy. *Journal of Public Economics, 7,* 309–328.

Buiter, W. (1985). Guide to public sector debt and deficits. *Economic Policy: A European Forum, 1,* 13–79.

Buiter, W. (2007a). *Seigniorage.* NBER Working Paper 12919.

Caballero, R. (2010). *Understanding the global turmoil: It's the general equilibrium stupid.* VoxEU.

Caballero, R., & Simsek, A. (2009). *Fire sales in a model of complexity.* NBER Working Paper 15479.

Carroll, C., & Samwick, A. (1988). How important is precautionary saving. *Review of Economics and Statistics, 80*(3), 410–419.

Chandler, D., & Disney, R. (2014). *Housing market trends and recent policies.* IFS Green Budget.

Chote, R., Emmerson, C., & Tetlow, G. (2009). *The fiscal rules and policy framework.* IFS Green Budget.

Chutasripanich, N., & Yetman, J. (2015). *Foreign exchange intervention: Strategies and effectiveness.* BIS Working Paper 499.

Clarida, R., Gali, J., & Gertler, M. (2000). Monetary policy rules and macroeconomic stability: Evidence and some theory. *Quarterly Journal of Economics, 115,* 147–180.

Croushore, D. (1996). Ricardian equivalence with wage-rate uncertainty. *Journal of Money, Credit and Banking, 28*(3), 279–293.

Dale, S. (2012, December 12). *Sticky inflation.* Speech.

Davis, S., & Haltiwanger, J. (1990). Gross job creation and destruction: Microeconomic evidence and macroeconomic implications. *NBER Macroeconomics Annual.*

Debrun, X. (2011). *Democratic accountability, deficit bias, and independent fiscal agencies*. IMF Working Paper 11/173.

Debrun, X., & Kumar, M. (2007). *The discipline-enhancing role of fiscal institutions: Theory and evidence*. IMF Working Paper 07/171.

Drazen, A. (2001). The political business cycle after 25 years. In B. Bernanke & K. Rogoff (Eds.), *NBER Macroeconomics Annual*. Cambridge, MA: MIT Press.

ECB. (2012). Euro area labour markets and the crisis.

ECB. (2014). Real interest rates in the euro area: A longer-term perspective. *ECB Monthly Bulletin, July*, 30–33.

Federal Reserve Board. (2003, August 12). Minutes of the Federal Open Market Committee.

Feige, E., & Pearce, D. (1976). Economically rational expectations. *Journal of Political Economy, 84*, 499–522.

Fernández-Villaverde, J., Rubio-Ramírez, J., Sargent, T., & Watson, M. (2007). The ABCs (and Ds) of understanding VARs. *American Economic Review, 97*(3), 1021–1026.

Frankel, J. (1992). Measuring international capital mobility. *American Economic Review, 82*(2), 197–202.

Gomez-Salvador, R., Messina, J., & Vallanti, G. (2004). *Gross job flows and institutions in Europe*. ECB Working Paper 318.

Griffith, R., Redding, S., & Van Reenen, J. (2004). Mapping the two faces of R&D. *Review of Economics and Statistics, 86*(4), 883–895.

Hallerberg, M., Strauch, R., & von Hagen, J. (2004). *The design of fiscal rules and forms of governance in European Union countries*. ECB Working Paper 419.

Hausman, J. (1985). Taxes and labor supply. In A. Auerbach & M. Feldstein (Eds.), *Handbook of public economics* (Vol. 1, pp. 213–263). Amsterdam: North-Holland.

Heifetz, A., Shannon, C., & Spiegel, Y. (2007). What to maximise if you must. *Journal of Economic Theory, 133*(1), 31–57.

IMF. (2012, October). World Economic Outlook: Coping with high debt and sluggish growth.

IMF. (2014). UK Article IV consultation.

Johnson, P. (2015). *UK consumer price statistics: A review*. UK Statistics Authority.

Jones, C. (2005). Growth and ideas. In P. Aghion & S. Durlauf (Eds.), *Handbook of economic growth*. Amsterdam: North Holland.

Judd, K., & Hubbard, G. (1996). Reflections on Ricardian equivalence. *Brookings Paper on Economic Activity, 1*, 1–50.

Judd, J., & Rudebusch, G. (1998). Taylor's rule and the Fed: 1970–1997. *Federal Reserve Bank of San Francisco Economic Review, 1998*(3), 3–16.

Kahn, L. (2010). The long-term labor market consequences of graduating from college in a bad economy. *Labour Economics, 17*(2), 303–316.

Kell, M. (2001). *An assessment of fiscal rules in the United Kingdom*. IMF Working Paper 01/91.

King, M. (2002, November 19). *The inflation target ten years.* Speech.

Krugman, P. (1986). *Pricing to market when the exchange rate changes.* NBER Working Paper 1926.

Laubach, T. (2010). *Fiscla policy and interest rates.* In R. Clarida & F. Giavazzi (Eds.), *NBER international seminar on macroeconomics.* NBER.

Layard, R. (2006). Happiness and public policy: A challenge to the profession. *The Economic Journal, 116,* C24–C33.

Lucas, R., & Rapping, L. (1969). Real wages, employment, and inflation. *Journal of Political Economy, 77*(5), 721–754.

Monetary Policy Committee. (1999). *The transmission mechanism of monetary policy.* Report prepared by Bank of England staff under the guidance of the Monetary Policy Committee.

Moody's Investors Service. (2013, September). Rating methodology: Sovereign bond rating.

Moscarini, G., & Postel-Vinay, P. (2009). *Large employers are more cyclically sensitive.* NBER Working Paper 14740.

Neiss, K., & Nelson, E. (2003). The real interest rate gap as an inflation indicator. *Macroeconomic Dynamics, 7*(2), 239–262.

OBR. (2013, December). *Economic and fiscal outlook.* HMSO.

Pissarides, C. (1990). *Equilibrium unemployment theory.* Oxford: Blackwell.

Popov, A., & van Horen, N. (2013). *The impact of sovereign debt exposure on bank lending: Evidence from the European debt crisis.* DNB Working Paper 382.

Restuccia, D., & Rogerson, R. (2007). *Policy distortions and aggregate productivity with heterogeneous plants.* NBER Working Paper 13018.

Robinson, M. (1988). Measuring compliance with the Golden Rule. *Fiscal Studies, 19*(4), 447–462.

Rogoff, K. (1996). The purchasing power parity puzzle. *Journal of Economic Literature, 34*(2), 647–668.

Rogoff, K. (2014). Costs and benefits to phasing out paper currency. In J. Parker & M. Woodford (Eds.), *NBER Macroeconomics Annual.*

Romer, P. (1990). Endogenous technical change. *Journal of Political Economy, 98,* S71–S102.

Rotemberg, J., & Saloner, G. (1986). A supergame-theoretic model of price wars during booms. *American Economic Review, 76*(3), 390–407.

Simon, H. (1955). A behavioral model of rational choice. *Quarterly Journal of Economics, 69*(1), 99–118.

Sims, C. (1998). *Stickiness.* Paper presented at the Carneige-Rochester Conference on Public Policy.

Slemrod, J. (2007). Cheating ourselves: The economics of tax evasion. *Journal of Economic Perspectives, 21*(1), 25–48.

Stark, J. (2003, December 2). *Ten years of Maastricht – Currency union leading to political union?* Speech.

The Economist. (2015, August 28). The Bank of England will follow the Federal Reserve.

Tobin, J., & Buiter, W. (1979). Fiscal and monetary policies, capital formation and economic activity. In G. Furstenberg (Ed.), *Government and capital formation*. Cambridge, MA: Ballinger.

van Steenis, H., & Goodhart, C. (2013, September 15). Make Help to Buy a permanent private sector scheme. *Financial Times*.

Ventura, J. (2002). *Towards a theory of current accounts*. NBER Working Paper 9163.

Ziebarth, N. (2011). *Misallocation and productivity during the Great Depression*. mimeo.

Index